D1367507

CIRCLES OF HELL

CIRCLES OF HELL

The War in Italy
1943-1945

ERIC MORRIS

Crown Publishers, Inc.
New York

Published by Crown Publishers, Inc., 201 East 50th Street, New York, New York 10022. Member of the Crown Publishing Group.

Originally published in Great Britain by Random House UK Ltd. in 1993.

Random House, Inc. New York, Toronto, London, Sydney, Auckland

CROWN is a trademark of Crown Publishers, Inc.

Manufactured in Great Britain

Library of Congress Cataloging-in-Publication Data is available upon request

ISBN 0-517-57810-7
10 9 8 7 6 5 4 3 2 1

First American Edition

The Sons of General Clark
Stand up and sing the praise of General Clark,
Your hearts and voices raise for General Clark,
Red, white and blue unfurled upon the field,
Its message flaunts Clark's sons will never, never yield.
We'll fight, fight, fight with heart and hand,
As soldiers true embattled staunch will stand,
The Fifth's the best army in the land,
FIGHT, FIGHT, FIGHT.

The *Battle Hymn* of Headquarters Fifth Army. The author is anonymous although rumoured to have been Mark Clark himself.

"Damn fine road, men!"

Illustration by Bill Mauldin © United Feature Syndicate, Inc.

Contents

Preface

Circles of Hell is not an orthodox military history detailing the Italian campaign from the Sicily beaches to the Po Valley. It is a study of the inadequacy of Allied leadership at the top and the effect that had on the conduct of the campaign and the fate of ordinary soldiers.

Winston Churchill took an inordinate degree of interest in Italy, certainly up to the fall of Rome. He meddled, or inspired, depending upon your viewpoint and much of the responsibility for what went wrong was his alone. No war is fought in a political vacuum and the campaign in Italy suffered from more than its fair share of deals, compromises and expediencies.

Many of the generals too, mismanaged the campaign in virtually every department of military affairs. There were sins of commission: the narrow-minded pursuit of self-interest, the feeding of egos and the promotion of careers and advancement. There were sins of omission: lack of imagination, incompetence, selfish nationalism and prejudice. The result was a record which is frankly appalling, one made even more so given that the Allies in Ultra were reading German battle signals and therefore had a clear insight into enemy intentions. The top commanders in Italy had a seat at the enemy conference table and they still managed to get it wrong.

The plight of the fighting soldiers stands in stark contrast. They were pitted against a professionally competent enemy who possessed the additional advantages of weather and terrain, and who were better led. It is hardly surprising that the predominant concern of the front-line soldier was survival in conditions which more closely replicated the trenches of the First World War than any other campaign in Western Europe. Essentially the campaign was fought by infantry, gunners and engineers, an élite who held in universally low esteem those 'rear-area stallions' who lived off the fat of the land and had the first pick of everything. *Circles of*

Hell tells the story of the front-line soldiers – principally Americans, British, New Zealanders, Canadians, Indians and Poles. In the autumn of 1944, and depending on one's definition, there were 23 nationalities fighting with the Allies. But their nationality is of no consequence because their experience owed little to race, creed or colour.

Many features of the campaign are mirrored in the wars which are with us today. Air power proved a blunt instrument which never lived up to the promises of its apostles. Artillery and an overwhelming superiority in fire power always led the pundits to exaggerate their effects upon enemy casualties.

The war in Italy also brought about a terrible suffering for the civilian population. Out of hunger and want people plumbed the depths of human degradation, sold their souls and bartered their bodies for food. In the aftermath of war large cities, such as Naples, suffered the plagues of medieval Europe – typhus, cholera, dysentery – and venereal disease was endemic. Corruption and organized crime were the camp followers of the Allied armies in their progress through the Italian peninsula.

Circles of Hell is a catharsis and a personal pilgrimage for me. I first encountered the Italian campaign in 1968, when, as a young and inexperienced lecturer at Liverpool University, I was seconded to the Armed Forces to teach Military History to army officers studying to enter the Staff College. I was fortunate enough to meet General Sir Oliver Leese and other commanders who fought that campaign and to hear what they had to say. Subsequently I wrote about Italy and its numerous battles, and I interviewed General Mark Clark.

There were always unexplained gaps in the information and treatment of the Italian campaign, and these were only partly resolved by the revelations of Ultra. But I am also conscious that there have been various attempts to justify the Allied actions in Italy, in terms both of grand strategy and battle tactics. Italy has been 'justified' in a way in which the Western Front, North Africa and the Pacific have never been; the nearest equivalent is possibly the Burma campaign after Imphal and Kohima. But, like Burma, none of the so-called justifications ever rang true. There was another side too. The British were spiteful in their behaviour to the Italians, treatment that continued long after the war.

The Italian campaign is beset by controversy – the bombing of Monte Cassino, the slaughter at the Rapido river, Anzio, the fall of Rome, etc. These, and the biggest controversy of them all – why was the campaign fought in the first place – go to the very heart of *Circles of Hell*.

Eric Morris
Barry, 1993

Acknowledgements

My debt of gratitude extends to so many people who helped to produce this book. First, to the veterans on both sides of the Atlantic who told me their stories and shared their experiences with me. Others sent me their stories and their permission to include these accounts in the book.

While researching in the United States it was my great good fortune to meet Professor Sidney Matthews. Sidney is not only a distinguished scholar on the Italian campaign, but served with that band of American military historians who wrote the US Official History. Sidney gave me copies of his interviews with Generals Marshall and Mark Clark and with Earl Alexander, together with relevant pages from General Clark's personal diary which were made available at the time of the interview. For this treasure-trove of material, our discussions and subsequent letters of advice and encouragement, I am especially grateful.

Thereafter in the United States it was very much a case of researching at a distance and I would particularly like to acknowledge the tremendous assistance of Vincent Lockhart, Willis Jackson, Roy Livengood and Doc Waters who brought logistical ease, organization and hospitality to my undertaking. In Italy, General Enrico Boscardi and Dr Franco Magrini shared their knowledge and expertise on the Italian Army and were magnificent hosts in Rome. It was the Italian Embassy who first put me in touch with General Boscardi.

Ten years ago I wrote a book about Salerno. At the time I interviewed veterans from that campaign. I have been able to incorporate many of their experiences elsewhere in Italy in this book. Leah James, who is my daughter, and Nick Marsh were excellent research assistants who spent many hours trawling the files at the Public Records Office, the Libraries in War Studies at King's College and the Royal United Services Institute in London. The Librarian and staff of my local library in Barry have traced books and articles and given an excellent service.

The tapes were transcribed by Louise Figgins, Leah James and my wife, Pamela. Leah and Pamela transposed my handwriting onto word processors and produced an impeccably typed manuscript. Paul Sidey of Hutchinson, besides being a tower of strength and encouragement, edited the manuscript and improved the text immeasurably. The team at Random House, including Roger Walker for graphic design and Alex McIntosh, the copy-editor, have worked with skill and a deft touch.

Authors don't usually acknowledge their agents. But Michael Sissons loves Le Marche almost as much as the MCC; he has been a source of inspiration from concept to completion, as well as keeping a paternal eye on deadlines.

Dr Peter Savigear taught History and Politics at Leicester University until his tragic death in October 1992. Peter was a dear friend, always ready with good ideas and a sympathetic ear. Keith Simpson, now at the Cranfield Institute for Security Studies and a colleague from our days teaching War Studies at the Royal Military Academy Sandhurst, assisted on matters concerning the German Army. Drs Diane Keith and Christopher Morris, my son, both of whom have military experience, have prescribed on medical issues. David Steeds, at the University College of Wales Aberystwyth read the draft manuscript, corrected my many errors and furnished sound advice. Neil Jones and Sue Morgan at Roddam's Travel worked wonders in arranging flights and travel in the United States, as well as the logistics of my forays into the Italian countryside. Vera Williams gave me some of the photographs which appear at the end of the book and belonged to her late husband. My thanks also to Nardina Battye for the use of her photograph. All other photographs appear courtesy of the Imperial War Museum.

Last, and by no means least, is the debt to Pamela and my family, whose love and forbearance helped sustain me through the dark and lonely hours.

Abbreviations

AA	Anti-aircraft
AAI	Allied Armies in Italy
ACIGS	Assistant Chief of Imperial General Staff
AFHQ	Allied Force Headquarters
AFV	Armoured Fighting Vehicle
AMG	Allied Military Government
AOC	Air Officer Commanding (British)
AOK	Army Headquarters (German)
APC	Armoured Personnel Carrier
ARV	Armoured Recovery Vehicle
A/Tk	Anti-Tank
BGS	Brigadier General Staff (British)
CC	Combat Command (A or B) (US Army)
CCRA	Commander, Corps of Royal Artillery
CCRE	Commander, Corps of Royal Engineers
CCS	Combined Chiefs of Staff
CG	Commanding General
CGS	Chief of General Staff
CIGS	Chief of Imperial General Staff
CIL	Italian Corps of Liberation
CLNAI	Committee of National Liberation of Northern Italy
CMF	Central Mediterranean Forces
CO	Commanding Officer
COS	Chief of Staff
CP	Command Post
CRA	Commander Royal Artillery
D-day	The day and date designated by Commanders for a major operation and used as such for planning purposes. The use of the term D-day avoided naming that day and thus enhanced security.
Do	Dornier (German aircraft)
DUKW	Amphibious truck in which
	D Year of manufacture (1942)
	U Amphibious
	K All-wheel drive
	W Dual rear axles
E-Boat	German and Italian fast-attack torpedo boats
ENIGMA	The German military enciphering machine invented in the 1920s. Because the codes were changed daily and there were different models for the various branches of the Armed Forces, the Germans considered ENIGMA was totally secure. In fact, a combined effort by French Intelligence, Polish mathematicians and cryptanalysts resulted in the building of two ENIGMA encoders. The Poles gave one each to the British and French in 1939.

FCP	Forward Control Post
FEC	French Expeditionary Corps
FOO	Forward Observation Officer
Fw	Focke-Wulf (German aircraft)
GHQ	General Headquarters
GOC	General Officer Commanding (British – applied to division and above)
He	Heinkel (German aircraft)
HE	High Explosive
H-hour	The time designated on D-day for the start of an operation
IAF	Italian Air Force (Co-belligerent)
JIC	Joint Intelligence Committee
JPS	Joint Planning Staff
Ju	Junker (German Aircraft)
LCA	Landing Craft Assault
LCI(L)	Landing Craft Infantry (Large)
LCT	Landing Craft Tank
LCT(R)	Landing Craft Tank (Rocket)
LofC	Lines of Communication
LSI	Landing Ship Infantry
LST	Landing Ship Tank
MAAF	Mediterranean Allied Air Forces
MASAF	Mediterranean Allied Strategic Air Force
MATAF	Mediterranean Allied Tactical Air Force
Me	Messerschmitt (German aircraft)
MEF	Middle East Forces
MG	Machine gun
Mk	Mark (of equipment)
NAAFI	Navy, Army and Air Force Institute
OB	Commander in Chief (German)
OKW	Oberkommando der Wehrmacht functioned as Hitler's military staff under his direct command. It was the ground force headquarters and Kesselring as OB South was subordinate to this organization.
OKH	Oberkommando der Heeres was the German Army High Command. The Commander in Chief of the Army conducted the operations of the army in the field as instructed by OKW.
OSS	Office of Strategic Services (American forerunner of the CIA)
Pak	Anti-tank gun (German)
PG	Panzer Grenadier
PIAT	Projector Infantry Anti-Tank (American 'Bazooka', German 'Panzerfaust')
PR	Photographic Reconnaissance
PT	Patrol Torpedo Boat (US Navy)
Pz	Panzer Division or Corps
Pzkw	German tank Pzkw V Tiger Tank Pzkw VI Panther
RA	Royal Artillery
RCT	Regimental Combat Team (US Army)
RSMA	Central Security Department of the Third Reich
SAC	Supreme Allied Commander
SAS	Special Air Service
SBS	Special Boat Squadron (later changed to Service)
SHAEF	Supreme Headquarters Allied Expeditionary Force
SOE	Special Operations Executive
SP	Self-propelled
SS	Schutzstoffel: literally translated protection or guard detachment. Paramilitary formation of the Nazi Party
Ultra	Special Security Classification (ie Ultra Secret) given by the British to intelligence gained from breaking the code of the standard German military radio enciphering machine, the ENIGMA
USAAF	United States Army Air Forces
Waffen-SS	The permanent volunteer combat units of the SS
WT	Wireless Telegraphy

I

In the Name of Liberation

In May 1945 the Second World War in Europe was over. Allied armies
had fought their way up the length of the Italian peninsula, mile upon
blood-soaked mile, and finally grounded arms upon the Austro-Swiss
border.

Gunther Drossinger was a 20-year-old corporal in the Storm Battalion
of the 1st Parachute Division. He was also a survivor: the Storm Battalion
had begun the last battle before Bologna just 60 strong; they had fought
their way across the Lombardy Plain, swum the Po and were prepared to
make a stand before the Alpine passes at the time of the cease-fire. There
were six men left in the battalion, and yet they were still a disciplined
fighting force.

The German parachute divisions in Italy were acknowledged by friend
and foe alike as simply the best. The Division had been in at the outset,
thwarting Montgomery's own paratroopers on the plain before Catania in
July 1943 and thereafter fighting every step of the way northwards. The
paras turned and stood before Rome, and denied the Allies the
'Incomparable City' throughout the long, bitter months of 1943–44,
suffered the bombing of Cassino and then inflicted humiliation upon a
vastly superior enemy, before retreating once more. In May 1945, even
though the war was over, the paratroopers had not surrendered. Gunther
Drossinger and his comrades and men from other veteran formations
joined with American troops on patrol in the northern hills above Lake
Caldonazzo.

The Allies had fought their war and were none too keen to risk life and
limb intervening in the squalid political affairs of a people they held in
contempt. They had won the war and were not prepared to tempt Lady
Luck in keeping the peace. The young Germans, however, who knew only

the profession of arms, were quite prepared to soldier on for three square meals a day and all found; in any case it was infinitely preferable to prison camp. Their task was to protect the private estates and large farms from a common enemy, the Italian partisan.

'The Italians have been made drunk with lies for one hundred and fifty years,'[1] wrote Francesco Saverio Nitti in 1945 after he had returned to his native land from years in exile for his opposition to Fascism. Mussolini's regime was founded on a lie, an iron state in which all men had to pretend they were warriors and all women Roman matrons. The partisan movement, in the name of liberation, was also founded on a lie. The partisans of Italy would have us believe that theirs was a long and noble struggle against the evils of Fascism, occupation and repression in a bitter winter campaign of 1944–45, after the Allies' advance had stalled in the high Apennines just south of Bologna. There were some resistance groups who did perform a valiant service and many of their members paid the price. But the vast majority of partisans, some 200,000 or more, joined the ranks only after the cessation of hostilities. Indeed some sources claim that by June 1945, two months after the end of the war, about 700,000 partisan certificates had been distributed, in most cases on payment of a small fee.

Even those partisan groups which stuck it out through the last six months of the war had made little contribution to the war effort; instead they were riven by factionalism and political infighting. There were communists, socialists and Christian Democrats; there were royalists and republicans; but all of them were recruited from men fleeing forced labour in Germany. In the final days there were Fascists on the run and there were many more bandits and criminals who saw in a political slogan an opportunity for plunder.

In the spring and summer of 1945 there was confusion and turmoil the length and breadth of Italy, but especially in the northern part of the country. There were three governments in the land. There was the Allied Military Government (AMGOT) which ran the country at least as far north as Bologna and Pisa. But they were the occupiers, the ones whose behaviour had by this time earned them nothing but detestation and loathing. It seems to have been the fate of the Italian to suffer at the hands of bad rulers and in this regard AMGOT proved no exception.

Then there was an Italian government led by Ivanhoe Bonomi, which sat in Rome and did what the Allies told it to do. But then, Italy has always been a land of regions where government from Rome, whatever its complexion, is largely ignored, except as the target for an occasional sneer.

Then there was the north, the last part of the country to be liberated and the bastion of Fascism. Technically the northern provinces were under the direction of an ad hoc group of partisan leaders called the Committees of National Liberation of Northern Italy (CLNAI). For a few months in 1945 the CLNAI had free run over northern Italy and there was carnage. Not only did the partisan groups fight one another, they also plundered at will and slaughtered those who were suspected of being Fascists. Allied military patrols, and even joint patrols with German units, could do little to restore order until the blood lust was satiated. The Italian authorities today admit to 17,322 deaths but the true figure could be as high as 100,000 men, women and children. Some areas were worse than others, the most notorious being the so-called 'death triangle', the provinces of Bologna, Ferrara and Modena. In many cases whole families were butchered, including the youngest children; homes were ransacked and every item of furniture and clothing looted so that nothing remained. Women and young girls were raped, some so many times that death must have come as a merciful release.

It is almost impossible to present an accurate picture of what happened and why, because all the sources are biased. Thus, for example, the Christian Democrats together with those of the conservative and Catholic right wing believe that the vast majority of the atrocities were carried out by communists acting under orders from Moscow.

There is no foundation to this conspiracy theory. Besides the sheer physical problems of coordination and direction, the communist partisans were no more disciplined than the rest of the partisan groups. The so-called civilized world has watched aghast at the atrocities committed in what was once Yugoslavia: much the same thing happened in Italy 45 years earlier. People, under certain circumstances, are capable of despicable acts of cruelty on others. The Italians in the north emerged from the artificiality of Fascism hungry, discredited, the object of derision, 'cornuti e mazziati' – cuckolded and beaten up. Their property had been looted and their womenfolk violated. It is hardly surprising that there was a public outburst of anger and rage. It wasn't a case of Catholics killings Muslims but rather people who were slaughtered in the name of a label – Fascist, Collaborator – by mobs and by those who had ready access to arms, and who used the absence of law and order as an opportunity to rob, loot and kill.

There was a mass psychosis at work. The German occupation had paraded the impotence of the people; it was a time of deep humiliation and injured pride. The execution of Mussolini and his mistress, Claretta

3

Petacci, by members of the 52nd Garibaldi Brigade and the subsequent public display and mutilation of their bodies in one of Milan's main squares, set the tone. Liberation demanded a public purge. Much the same happened in France, albeit on a smaller scale. The interesting parallel is that in both cases the worst excesses occurred not in small rural communities of the sort guarded by Gunther Drossinger, but in the big cities.

Later in June, even though some semblance of order had been restored, authority's hold over the country was still tenuous. There was still a latent security threat from armed groups of communist partisans, part of an orchestrated campaign waged on both the political and military fronts to secure power. The Allied attitude, at least towards the prospect of a communist government, remained ambivalent and so long as their own forces or property were not involved, they adopted a 'hands-off' approach towards incidents of violence. Thus on 25 June, a group of well-armed partisans attacked the Carabinieri barracks in Minervino, a town in Puglia. They disarmed and interned 80 Carabinieri in their own barracks and released seven prisoners from custody. A battalion of Carabinieri, 500 strong, was sent the next day to rescue their comrades and a pitched battle ensued. The local bishop intervened and negotiated a cease-fire which resulted in the interned Carabinieri being released, and the partisans and the police battalion withdrawing from the area.

In the north of Italy, Fascist pockets of resistance continued to cause problems. In the hill country of the Val Travaglia region north of Milan, isolated groups of armed Fascists plundered houses and stole cattle. Allied intelligence had a report that one of the leaders was a German SS officer on the run.

The one thing the Allies failed achieve, although it had been one of the avowed aims of the Italian campaign, was the eradication of Fascism; arguably they were more successful in Germany than in Italy. The Allied occupation of Italy left a large number of former Fascist Party officials and members untouched. There was no choice, there were so many of them, especially in the civil service and local government, that the country could not have functioned without their cooperation. Even so, neo-fascism was not initially considered to constitute any organized threat to the internal security situation. By the autumn of 1945 however, Allied military intelligence was beginning to revise its assessment as more and more evidence came to hand which pointed to a bold and organized plan of action by extreme right-wing and neo-fascist elements.

In early November 1945 the Allies were aware of a clandestine organization called 'Squadre d'Azione Mussoliniane' (SAM) which comprised prominent members of the Fascist party and officers from the 'Tagliamento Legion' a Blackshirt paramilitary group. There are few secrets in Italy and it was not long before Allied counter-intelligence uncovered a widespread network of SAM groups, mostly in the larger industrial cities in the north, but with cells in Venezia and Tuscany. The homes of suspected members were raided and a sizeable quantity of arms, uniforms and propaganda literature was recovered. SAM also had links with neo-fascist elements in Rome and southern Italy, and the Allies learned of the 'Divisione Arditi d'Italia';[2] and other like-minded groups. There was a threat to internal stability but how serious was it? Was SAM an independent clandestine organization, or was it the organizing nucleus of a widespread neo-fascist movement? Nobody had the answer.

The Italians are capable at times of joining demented political mass movements. It was Fascism before the war and in the chaos that followed the ending of hostilities in 1945, large numbers flocked to the communists. The latter had, by this time, come out of the hills and onto the streets of the big northern cities, well-organized, disciplined, reputedly financed by the Soviet Union, and ready to proclaim the worker's paradise. They frightened the bulk of the Italians out of their wits, most of whom ran for cover and solace behind the cassocks of their priests. The latter, in response to the direction of the Vatican, encouraged their flock to support the Christian Democrats, but that support did not coalesce on a national scale until the Italians were recipients of American largesse in the form of Marshall Aid.

There is an old Italian proverb: '*Fidari e bene, non fidari e meglio*' (To trust is good, not to trust is better); perhaps this helps explain why the forces of extremism, both communist and neo-fascist, were to retain an influence and respectability on the Italian post-war political scene. In recent times the communists have lost ground, a reflection, of course, of the collapse of the Soviet Union and the discrediting of Marxism; but neo-fascism is arguably stronger now than at any time since 1945.

Italy lurched into the postwar world in a state of political turmoil and crisis and this was very largely the result of the Allied invasion and the manner of their occupation of the country. The one thing the Allies failed to do from the very outset was to secure the trust of the Italians.

Notes

1. Barzini, Luigi, *The Europeans*, Simon and Schuster, New York, 1983, p 169.
2. *Movimento Universitario Nazionale* (NUM) and the *Fronte dell'Uomo Qualunque*.

2

Why Sicily?

The Italian campaign began in Sicily. The decision to invade the island, code-named Operation Husky, was taken in January 1943 when the Anglo-American war leaders and their top military advisers met at Casablanca. The first plan proposed an immediate seizure of Sicily in March 1943, even before the North African campaign had been concluded. Such a bold stratagem had a great appeal to General Marshall and the Joint Chiefs in Washington. There were risks attached to such an enterprise but there was much to suggest that success was very possible. The plan contained the priceless advantage of surprise; it would have been the last thing the Axis could have anticipated. Enemy defences were known to be weak and the garrison, at least in terms of first-class fighting troops, minimal.

Eisenhower was not at all enthusiastic and attributed the proposal to the amateurism of war planners who had yet to experience the uncertainties of battle. But since it had been endorsed by Marshall, he had at least to go through the motions and so he directed his staff to look at the option more closely. At the end of April, he telegraphed Marshall that a surprise attack was out of the question; it was far too risky. Marshall accepted the judgement but commented that, 'orthodoxy had replaced the boldness which had won great victories for Nelson and Grant and Lee.'[1] Thereafter everyone settled into a more conservative mould where, from the outset, Operation Husky in both its planning and execution was to expose the raw nerve of deep divisions between senior commanders; such schisms did not necessarily parallel nationality.

The campaign, in concept and planning, did neatly encapsulated the different approaches to war adopted by Britain and the United States. Britain had a long history of fighting big continental powers but had tried to do so by attacking them in the flanks, preferably even via the back door, but always seeking to weaken them at the extremities. Thus the land war against Napoleon was waged in Spain and Portugal while a preferred option against Imperial Germany had been a thrust at the Dardanelles.

The Americans, on the other hand, were a continental power who saw such actions as an unnecessary diversion away from the main effort. Better to confront the enemy early on, fight the big battle as the decisive engagement which leads to an early end to war. A shorter war would invariably result in fewer casualties and lower costs than those incurred in long-drawn-out struggles. The US Civil War was littered with well-meaning but ineffectual attempts to fight the 'decisive battle'.

The British, of course, had a horror of such encounters. The generals in 1943 had been young officers in the First World War who had endured the incompetence of *their* generals and, now in a position to influence and to command, were determined not to inflict such casualties upon their troops; yet at Cassino they were to replicate the trenches of the Western Front more faithfully than in any other campaign they fought.

The Americans wanted to fight the decisive engagement against the Germans; this, they believed, had to be in France. At first they wanted that battle in 1942 but had been persuaded by the British to undertake the landings in North Africa. At the time the Americans had little to contribute, and this made argument with the British difficult. In conferences they could only talk of a potential force for they had no experienced divisions, and very little war materiel to demonstrate what they could do. In the summer of 1942 the United States was primarily concerned with the situation on the Eastern Front where the Russians were engaging the bulk of the German Army. If the Russians were defeated, the Americans expected the Germans and the Japanese to push on and join forces in the East. This in turn did not spell defeat for the Americans, at least in the view of the Combined Chiefs of Staff, for they were optimists, but would require the creation of 200 divisions or more, when they were already having serious trouble with manpower in building to the planned 90, and would result in a prolongation of the war.

So desperately was the situation viewed at the time, that, at the first meeting in London of the Combined Chiefs in June 1942, Marshall proposed a landing on the coast of northern France to divert German strength away from the Russians, even if there was a prospect of the Allied force being destroyed. Not unnaturally the British Chiefs and Churchill opposed the plan. They argued that the Allies were not ready to carry it out successfully and that it would result in inordinately high casualties.

The next morning, after the meeting, Marshall had breakfast in his room; he was convinced that something had to be done. Pushing aside the breakfast tray he began to draft the paper that gave the US approach to Operation Torch; and so the Americans came, reluctantly, to the Mediterranean. In this paper Marshall intentionally included a clause that was to be a constant cause of friction and sometimes trouble. He put in the Pacific allotments for the benefit of 'holding a stick' over the British. General Marshall expected to use the threat of sending war materiel to the Pacific 'as a club' against the British whenever they wanted to carry out some operation that didn't fit in with the US strategy for Europe.

By the time of the Casablanca summit six months later the Russian position had improved, but they were still in desperate straits. The Americans again wanted the landings in France, a Second Front, as the operation was already called, to be undertaken once the North African campaign had been concluded. From this they were once again dissuaded by the British.

Admiral Pound, the First Sea Lord, first introduced the Sicilian option to General Marshall and his staff. He pointed out that with Sicily as a base and fortress the Allies could eliminate a long sea voyage around Africa from British ports to Alexandria and thereby make a saving of 252 merchant ships. But it was the powerful case mounted by Sir Alan Brooke which won the day. Brooke argued as follows:[2] the Germans, with 44 divisions in France, could deal with any threat the Allies could bring against them from the United Kingdom without withdrawing any forces from Russia. Instead, therefore, the United Nations should force Italy out of the war, which would compel Germany not only to occupy the Italian peninsula but to replace the Italian forces in the Balkans as well. Thus preparations to attack Sicily would have the effect of forcing the Germans to disperse their military forces to defend not only Sicily, but Sardinia, Greece and the Dodecanese, which, combined with the need to provide protection from the air for their sea lanes, would result in a far greater diversion of resources from the Russian Front than any that could be provided by a cross-Channel operation. But, warned Brooke, the Combined Chiefs of Staff should be very careful about extending Allied operations into Italy itself. 'We should be very careful of accepting any invitation to support an anti-Fascist insurrection. To do so might only immobilize a considerable force to no useful purpose.' Those words must have come to haunt Brooke time after time in the months and years that lay ahead.

It seems, therefore, that while everybody agreed on the desirability of knocking Italy out of the war, nobody was prepared to put forward any kind of concrete plan for bringing about this happy event. It was not perhaps to be expected that the Combined Chiefs would look beyond the invasion of Sicily to an attack on the Italian mainland; but one might have expected some plan to have been made for intensifying air warfare and stepping up propaganda. Instead the British, at least, continued to pursue the will-o-the-wisp of bringing Turkey into the war as a belligerent.

The Allies established a planning team in the Ecole Militaire in Algiers to draw up various recommendations for the invasion of Sicily and to look at alternatives such as Sardinia. A new army – the Fifth Army – was created and Major General Mark Clark, Eisenhower's deputy, was given command. He was allowed a headquarters staff and tasked to plan operations such as Sardinia and Corsica. But these were seen as remote contingencies, for at least in so far as General Marshall was concerned, the prime objective was to open up the Mediterranean, and Sicily would achieve this end. The Americans saw Sicily therefore as the culmination of the North African campaign not as the start of something new. Sardinia was not taken seriously since that was simply a threat to Italy and nobody at that time anticipated a campaign in Italy.

Even so, the Italians did figure in the planning. At Casablanca the Allies had agreed the formula of unconditional surrender. This was an alliance war aim which resided in the realms of high strategy and had some bearing upon generals in the field planning campaigns to achieve their objectives. In March 1943 General Eisenhower asked for a directive on political warfare, as part of his preparations for Husky, both before and after the invasion. Eisenhower asked whether the use of threats or promises or both against the Italians was in line with the policy of the United States and British governments, and which was likely to obtain the best results. Accordingly signals were despatched to London and to both the Joint Staff Mission and the US Chiefs in Washington, and the result was a confusion over aims and objectives.

The British Chiefs of Staff replied that Eisenhower should follow the lines of the agreed Anglo-US government policy as a preliminary to the operation and that he would be informed of post-operational policy as soon as this had been settled. The Joint Staff Mission in Washington answered that neither they nor the US Chiefs of Staff knew of any such policy and asked that the question be addressed to the State Department.

In fact Anthony Eden, the British Foreign Secretary, and his American counterpart, Cordell Hull, had already started to correspond on this question and some recommendations had been placed before Churchill who, in turn, cabled Harold Macmillan, the Resident Minister in Algiers, for his thoughts. Eventually the Allies agreed that there should be a hard and later a soft approach to propaganda aimed at the Italians. Eisenhower was instructed to take a firm line and base propaganda until the assault upon the following principles:

> To impress upon the Italian people the hopelessness of their position in the war.
>
> We should carry on the war in Italy with all possible forces and upon all occasion by attacking by land, air and sea.
>
> To encourage in our propaganda and by all other means passive resistance and sabotage of the Italian war effort.
>
> To avoid ridiculing the Italian armed forces or the Italian people, or inciting them to premature revolt.[3]

Eisenhower was instructed to modify the propaganda line when the time came to invade according to a formula devised by Cordell Hull, namely:

> We should hold out to the Italian people, without making any specific political or territorial commitments, the hope that Italy, as a nation, will survive after the defeat of the Fascist Government and that neither we nor our Allies have territorial ambitions with respect to that territory which is, and has always been, essentially Italian.

In April 1943 a strong difference of opinion arose over the exact timing of the switch from hard to soft propaganda. Eisenhower urged that the change should be made at once and for purely military reasons: the Italian forces were expected to offer determined resistance in Sicily and, in consequence, the cost of the operation might depend very largely on the extent to which it was possible to undermine their morale beforehand. He did not feel that Cordell Hull's formula went far enough to reassure the Italians and if this statement were withheld until D-day it might be entirely lost in the heat of the battle.

Instead Eisenhower proposed a new set of principles for immediate use in the propaganda campaign:

> That the choice between a continuation and a cessation of hostilities rests with them.

That a cessation of hostilities on their part will be accepted by the Allies as evidence of good judgement, entitling them eventually to a 'Peace with Honour.'

That the policy of the Allied Governments pledges full nationhood for Italy after the defeat of the Axis and the removal of the Fascist Government and assures full benefits as provided in the Atlantic Charter.

That in consequence Italy has every interest in ceasing hostilities and that the only obstacle to honourable peace is the policy of the Fascist Government.

Eisenhower's military bosses on both sides of the Atlantic signalled their agreement but the politicians, wedded to the principle of unconditional surrender, had different ideas. Churchill at the time was attending the 'Trident' conference in Washington.

Anthony Eden took up the challenge.

I have [he wrote] informed the Prime Minister in Washington of certain doubts I feel. I fear that if the Prime Minister and the President make such a declaration now, so long a time before the event, its effect will wear off in the interval. We might then be asked, in the interests of the Husky operation, to produce some further set of promises to the Italians. There are no further promises that we can safely make. I should therefore prefer to adhere to the original timing.[4]

Roosevelt and Churchill got their heads together and on 20 May 1943 the following telegram was despatched to Eisenhower in Algiers.

Reference your telegram of 17 May on the subject, the President has expressed the following views on Psychological Warfare for HUSKY.

The Prime Minister concurs:

Most certainly we cannot tell the Italians that if they cease hostilities they will have peace with honour. We cannot get away from unconditional surrender. All we can tell them is that they will be treated by the US and the British with humanity and with the intention that the Italian people be constituted into a Nation in accordance with the principles of self determination. This latter would, of course, not include any form of Fascism or dictatorship.

Thus the die was cast and little further thought was given to the Italian people.

Notes

1. Matthews papers.
2. CAB 101/144.
3. CAB/104.
4. Ibid.

3

Condemned to Succeed

In retrospect it seemed the British and Americans were condemned to succeed, but at times their differences and difficulties in agreeing a common strategy in the Mediterranean appeared to be wellnigh impossible. Indeed, it can be argued that no other campaign in the Second World War produced such acrimony and deep division. Some have argued that this was because the Americans believed the British, from the outset, harboured a secret agenda to invade Italy, but this is not the case. Before the fall of Mussolini neither London nor Washington saw the Italian peninsula as the route to Germany; indeed previous staff studies had already concluded that it was too long and too easily defended.

General Sir Harold Rupert Leofric George Alexander, late of the Irish Guards, the third son of the fourth Earl of Caledon, fitted exactly the American concept of a modern British general. Indeed in the late autumn of 1943 the *New York Times* columnist Frank L. Kluchohn provided this excellent pen portrait:

Although he is 52, Alexander, with his athlete's figure and Grecian profile, bears a striking resemblance to the late John Barrymore in his prime. The general's close cropped moustache – it tended to be bushy in earlier days – goes well with his regular features. In his favourite field uniform of breeches, high boots, jacket with red facings and cap with red band, this Irishman reminds one of a deadly poised rapier. His outstanding feature, cold blue eyes, capable of freezing under stress, point to the steel in his character.

He has a fine smile, but when those hard eyes turn really cold his subordinates feel the inherent authority he possesses. His voice is soft and melodious until he wants to emphasize a point, then it becomes clipped and brittle. A champion athlete who has always kept in tip-top shape, he moves

14

with a light rhythm and balance that point to another facet of his character. Alexander never allows himself to be upset.

He does not have that extraordinary power to inspire the troops possessed by Montgomery and Patton, but he knows men, how to pick and handle them. He knows what they are capable of doing. This is the mark of all successful commanders. Once he has picked a man for a job, he backs him to the limit.[1]

Again prophetic words in the last sentence when one takes into account Alexander's role in the sacking of American corps commanders, Dawley at Salerno and Lucas at Anzio.

The American diplomat and Roosevelt's representative in the theatre, Robert Murphy, considered Alexander to be 'the ablest of the British generals in the Mediterranean theatre of war'.

Maybe the Americans would have taken a more measured view of Alexander had they been aware of his opinions of them. In February 1943, when he first had had a chance to see the Americans in battle, Alexander had concluded that the American materiel, human and otherwise, was magnificent. He felt that the American troops were inexperienced and were at the time of little value in battle, but that with experience they would develop and become as good troops as any. To give the American combat leaders the benefit of British experience, Alexander formed battle schools behind the front in Tunisia. He mixed platoon leaders at the school from US and British forces in Tunisia so that this would be accomplished, and for prestige purposes mainly, had a mixed team of instructors, British, Americans and some French.

By the end of the Tunisian campaign and under the inspired leadership of Patton and Bradley, Alexander was among the first to concede that there had been a tremendous improvement in the morale and fighting qualities of the American forces; they were not, however, in his opinion, up to the standard of British troops.

As far as the British were concerned, even amongst themselves, there were distinctions to be made. The Eighth Army under Montgomery was the elite fighting force in North Africa whereas divisions from the First Army were regarded as mediocre and second-rate. Indeed such discrimination was to plague the Italian campaign, certainly for as long as Montgomery was in the theatre, and probably even longer.

From the very outset the Americans had not rated either Montgomery or the Eighth Army highly. Marshall fully expected the Eighth Army to have lost again in the desert, even after El Alamein. In his view the British had committed almost every mistake in the book. It was no model campaign, while Montgomery, in Marshall's words, left something to be desired as a field commander.

So at ease was Montgomery with his own abilities that he fully expected to be given overall command of the Allied armies in Sicily. But Eisenhower was opposed to Montgomery because he was abrasive, tactless and arrogant when it came to dealing with allies. In this view he was supported by Churchill. There was in Montgomery an urge to dominate, a desire to impose his will over others which made it next to impossible to coordinate military operations with another army commander. In North Africa Churchill was happy to have Alexander above Montgomery to compensate for such weakness in temperament, but the arrangement had not worked. Montgomery walked all over Alexander and either got his own way or deliberately ignored his directives; this, of course, was made all the more easy because of Alexander's style of leadership as an Army Group commander. He believed[2] that generals of armies had to be treated more delicately than corps or division commanders. They were top-level people, first-rate men each of whom had certain characteristics which had to be taken into account in his dealings with them. Some army commanders had to be pushed with a little ginger, like Leese, who was deliberate in attack and methodical (he had been trained in the Montgomery school). Some, on the other hand, like Patton and Clark were 'pushers' who frequently had to be restrained.

Alexander would try to win his army commanders over to any plan he had for an operation, saying in effect 'this is the situation' and asking their opinion. If they had good reasons which seemed logical to him and worthwhile, he would modify the plan. If not, he would tell them that was his order. Rather than encourage a coordination in strategies between the two armies, it was a recipe for individualism and military particularism. Alexander never exerted his authority over what was meant to be his command, an army group; and indeed for as long as Montgomery was in the theatre he acted as his apologist and patron.

General Eisenhower, though Supreme Commander in the Mediterranean theatre, was little better. He never interfered with the tactical direction of operations after Alexander took over command in Tunisia. He let Alexander run the battle and behaved more like an absentee chairman of the board. When it came to planning for Sicily, Alexander had, of course, to get Eisenhower's approval. Ike would also take those decisions which affected other branches of the services such as the air and naval forces simply because they were under his overall command. Thus Eisenhower assumed a more direct role in the planning for landing in Italy simply because Alexander was then involved in the conduct of the Sicilian campaign.

Alexander saw his job as directing operations but to keep Ike, as the overall commander, fully informed of all he was doing. It appears to have been an easy and comfortable arrangement but this changed after Wilson became Supreme Commander when Eisenhower returned to England to assume responsibility for the Second Front.

Once he had been passed over for higher command Montgomery lost interest in planning for Sicily; he relegated liaison to a junior team and concentrated on overcoming the last remnants of Axis resistance in North Africa. Immediately after the cease-fire had sounded and the photo-opportunities of the Axis surrender in North Africa had been exhausted, Montgomery went home to Britain on leave.

In England he was feted as a national hero. He stayed at the Grosvenor Hotel in Park Lane and was mobbed wherever he went; the War Office drafted in ADCs to cope with the fan mail and gifts that were showered upon the hero of Alamein. The War Cabinet went along with, and indeed actively encouraged, this display of national sentiment, for Britain was into the fourth year of war and there had been precious few successful generals to cheer. But those who knew Montgomery best believed that he was affected by such fame and public adoration. Freddie de Guingand, his brilliant and long-suffering Chief of Staff wrote: 'He lost a little of his simplicity and realised that he was a power in the land and that there were few who would not heed his advice. In fact he realised that he could afford to be really tough to get his own way.'

Montgomery returned to North Africa in June and walked straight into a flaming row over the operational proposals for Sicily. The planners had been hard at it since Casablanca and at first their task had proved wellnigh impossible. Staff had been diverted from the conduct of current operations to plan for something which some believed was impossible; the invasion of an enemy shore. The last time this had been attempted was Gallipoli in 1916. In North Africa the Vichy French were supposedly neutral and the only other experience had been the debacle at Dieppe. It was a widely held wisdom that amphibious operations were so difficult that only veteran troops could be used as a spearhead and these divisions were at the time still in battle. So the planners could only guess at their condition after the North African campaign, when indeed it would be over, and how much time should be allowed for rest, re-equipment and retraining.

The island of Sicily, its geography and the known military dispositions also placed heavy constraints on the planners. At this stage in the war, and in the state of evolution of those special skills in amphibious operations, it was generally accepted that it was essential to capture a port as quickly as possible. Then there were the island's airfields, concentrated in two groups to the south and south-west of Mt Etna. These had to be neutralized, then captured and finally made operational as quickly as possible.

HQ Force 141, the central planning and operational headquarters for the invasion of Sicily, was established in the Ecole Normale at Bonzarea near Algiers on 12 February 1943. Major General C.H. Gairdner, CGS Force 141, directed the preliminary planning and consulted Alexander, who was still involved in fighting the Tunisian campaign, only on the most pressing matters. The planners used as their base line an appreciation and outline plan prepared by the Joint Planning Staff (JPS) in London for the Casablanca Conference. The main features of the JPS plan were two distinct assaults, one by a British task force in the east of the island and the other by an American task force in the west. In a bold and imaginative move airborne troops were to be landed on the toe of Italy to raid and interdict enemy reinforcement routes. Patton and Montgomery had already been designated by the Combined Chiefs of Staff as commanders of the Western and Eastern Task Forces respectively (WTF and ETF).

In March, Force 141 planners recommended a change to the plan. Their attention was drawn to what they saw as the great tactical importance of the south-east corner of the island. They proposed that both task forces should assault that portion of the island; this was seen as the easiest route to Messina and the enemy lines of communication. This plan was rejected however, on the grounds that a force of ten divisions, which was agreed to be necessary to compete with the anticipated garrison of eleven Italian and two German divisions, could not be maintained through the ports on the south-eastern seaboard. The early capture of Palermo, as well as Catania and Syracuse, was deemed essential for the maintenance of the force. The planners thus returned to the original draft with one or two modifications, the most notable of which was a decision to use the airborne troops to neutralize the beach defences, instead of raiding supply routes in Calabria.

The plan was presented to General Eisenhower and his principal commanders, Alexander, Cunningham and Tedder in Algiers on 13 March and received their approval. The next stage was to discuss the operation in detail with the Task Force commanders. Montgomery and Patton had already been summoned to Algiers for a meeting on 18 March.

On 15 March Major General Gairdner received a telegram from General Montgomery. At that time Eighth Army was deeply embroiled in a frontal assault on the Mareth Line where even the Italians were giving them a hard time. Montgomery stated that the plan for Sicily broke every commonsense rule of practical warfare, was completely theoretical, had no hope of success and should be completely recast. It was back to the drawing boards once again. Montgomery despatched General Dempsey to represent his views on Sicily at the conference on 18 March. Once it was known that Montgomery was not going to turn up, Alexander and Patton both sent deputies.

Montgomery's opposition centred around the need to capture the ports of Syracuse, Augusta and Catania as soon as possible after the landings; for this he needed at least one more division of infantry. The problem was that there weren't the landing craft available, so one of the landings of the Western Task Force would have to be sacrificed. At this stage the beaches at Gela were the objective of a single division, but to sacrifice this force would leave important airfields around Ponte Olivo excluded from operational objectives. Neither Admiral Ramsay nor Air Chief Marshal Tedder could think of abandoning this assault, and the latter insisted that the only way to achieve air supremacy was to capture the airfields.

The conflicting requirements of the air force and the army could not be reconciled, and so General Gairdner was despatched to Alexander for his arbitration. Alexander backed Montgomery and Tedder, but at the expense of the Americans. He therefore proposed to abandon the American assault on Sciacca, the objective of which was to secure the airfields at Sciacca and Castelvetrano from where fighter cover could be provided to support the attack on Palermo on D + 2. Alexander also decided to transfer one American division to the ETF for the assault on Gela with the airfields at Ponte Olivo as their objective and to hold the remainder of Patton's Western Task Force in reserve until a suitable opportunity arose to use it to capture Palermo. He justified his decision, which in essence relegated the Americans to the substitutes' bench, on the grounds that the south-eastern ports were sufficient for Allied needs and Palermo could wait. The decision was passed on to Eisenhower who questioned it all very carefully but gave it his support. His proviso was that the airfields at Ponte Olivo could eventually be used to support the attack on Palermo.

Patton's reaction at being moved out of the order of battle in favour of Montgomery can be imagined, but even before his anger had subsided it was a case of back to the drawing board once more. The plan had been forwarded to London and Washington. On 25 March the British Chiefs of Staff cabled the Combined Chiefs of Staff their objections. They were strongly opposed to the cancellation of the American landings since in their opinion it was vital that Palermo should be in Allied hands by D + 2, at the very latest. They suggested that Eisenhower should come up with the additional divisions and the landing craft necessary to meet Montgomery's requirements. Within a week the problem had been resolved. An additional British division was to be mounted from Malta so as to reduce to a minimum the distance over which it had to be transported, and slotted in to the invasion plan for D + 1.

This solution enabled Force 141 to produce a plan which satisfied the needs of Montgomery and the air forces. The plan restored the assaults of the WTF in the western part of Sicily as originally planned. It gave the EFT an additional division to meet the objection that the Avola assault lacked weight. And it provided for the capture of the south-eastern airfields regarded as essential by the air force and navy. Everybody was happy and agreement was quickly secured. On 5 April Gairdner took the plan to Alexander in Tunisia. The following day Alexander and Gairdner visited Montgomery and the plan was agreed. It was presented to General Eisenhower on 6 April who approved it at once; he then sought the agreement of the Combined Chiefs in Washington who soon fell into line. The planners at Force 141 breathed a sigh of relief and prepared to settle down to the tactical phase of the detailed plans and operations for the assault landings.

Notes

1. Quoted in Adleman, Robert and Walton, George (Col), *Rome Fell Today*, Little, Brown and Company, Boston, 1968, p 101.
2. Matthews interview with Alexander.

4

Rumour, Rancour and Acrimony

The jubilation among the staff at Force 141 was premature. Indeed they were about to enter a most difficult and trying time, caught between opposing points of view which were, in turn, exacerbated by the bruised egos of two prima donnas. In the ensuing weeks nobody emerged with very much credit, not even Eisenhower. The divisions were not on national lines since some of the most bitter argument was between Montgomery on the one hand and Cunningham and Tedder on the other. Alexander throughout appears weak and vacillating, incapable of taking a firm decision in the face of Montgomery's opposition.

In part the problem was that none of the senior commanders had any faith or confidence in the plans and the various alternatives on offer, and there was bitter debate as a result. These differences were never fully reconciled. The unforgiving Admiral Cunningham, for example, forbade his staff to mention Montgomery's name in his presence. Anglo-American resentments were allowed to fester and colour the strategic direction of the war in the Mediterranean, to the detriment of the Allied cause and to the benefit of the Germans.

Throughout the planning phase to date, success had been anticipated upon a universally accepted premise: that the German forces in Sicily would not exceed two divisions. In his telegram of 28 March, despatched after General Montgomery's objections to the London plan had surfaced, Eisenhower warned the Combined Chiefs of Staff that if the Germans were to concentrate substantial forces in Sicily, the project should be abandoned. The Combined Chiefs responded immediately and expressed their complete disagreement, but Eisenhower was adamant. He was joined by Alexander and Admiral Cunningham and a further telegram was despatched to Washington which spelled out their reasons:

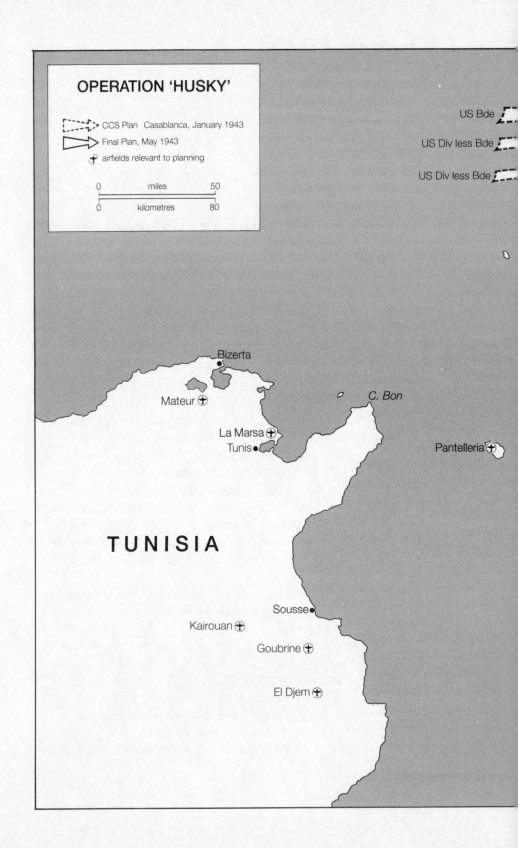

OPERATION 'HUSKY'

CCS Plan Casablanca, January 1943
Final Plan, May 1943
✈ airfields relevant to planning

| 0 | miles | 50 |
| 0 | kilometres | 80 |

US Bde
US Div less Bde
US Div less Bde

Bizerta
Mateur ✈
La Marsa ✈
Tunis ●
C. Bon
Pantelleria ✈

TUNISIA

Sousse ●
Kairouan ✈
Goubrine ✈
El Djem ✈

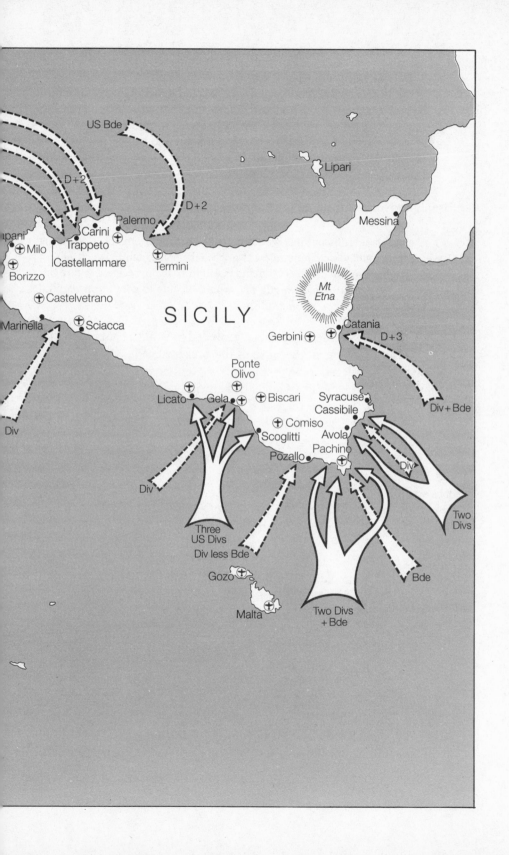

a) Loss of strategic and tactical surprise was inevitable.
b) If German troops preponderated (*sic*), the land forces in the region would be under German command, with a consequent stronger will and capacity to resist than might be the case under Italian command.
c) It was probable that German formations would be retained as a mobile reserve for counterattack when it was known where our forces were landing.[1]

Eisenhower went further and elaborated his concern after D-day.

> The most dangerous periods would be between D-day and D + 2 during which time immediate counterattacks might take place, and between D + 3 and D + 6 when the enemy commander would have appreciated where our landings were, and their strength, and would be able to commit his central reserves to a deliberate counterattack.

When Churchill saw the telegram he exploded in wrath. That Operation Husky could be cancelled because of the presence of just two German divisions he considered to be preposterous. Neither was Eisenhower left in doubt that the Combined Chiefs had any intention of abandoning the Sicily operation, but nevertheless the seeds of doubt had been sown and the rift had by no means healed when Montgomery once again joined the fray.

On 23 April, Eighth Army ceased to play the leading role in Tunisia and Montgomery was free to turn his attention to Operation Husky. Two days earlier he had summoned Oliver Leese, then commanding XXX Corps, and had told him that an invasion of Sicily was planned for 10 July 1943. He gave his copy of the draft plan to Leese and instructed him to go through it with de Guingand in Cairo and to be ready to discuss it when he arrived in Cairo. On studying the plan it was immediately apparent to both Leese and de Guingand that the British and American armies were far too dispersed. There were 20 different landing points on a front of more than 100 miles, and this they felt was asking for trouble.

Montgomery, when he arrived, agreed with them and immediately telegraphed Alexander as follows: 'Planning so far has been based on the assumption that the opposition will be slight and that Sicily will be captured relatively easily. Never was there a greater error. The Germans and also the Italians are fighting desperately now in Tunisia and will do in Sicily.'[2] Montgomery proposed a modified plan and once again the great and the good acceded to his request for a fresh conference at which he could present his objections to the existing plans and his new proposals.

The conference was arranged for 27 April in Algiers but Montgomery cried off at the last minute with a bad chill. De Guingand was deputized to attend, but his aircraft crashed on takeoff and he had a bad concussion; thus Leese set off for Algiers.

Leese presented Montgomery's proposals to Alexander, Cunningham and Tedder; Patton was there too. In a nutshell it involved concentrating the Eighth Army landings around Avola and the Pachino peninsula even though this would mean that the south-eastern airfields (13 in number) would be uncovered in the critical stages.

Admiral Cunningham did not approve. He favoured dispersed landings to reduce the target concentration and insisted that the enemy airfields had to be neutralized or captured, otherwise the time that ships could be offshore was very limited. In this he was supported by Tedder; unless the army could capture the airfields, he was altogether opposed to the operation. The air force lobby was one of brutal statistics: if the enemy were permitted to use the airfields, enemy aircraft would operate over the beaches for 45 minutes every hour. The carriers would be required to counter any threat from the Italian Navy and could not contribute to the land battle.

Alexander sided with Eighth Army but Cunningham and Tedder were implacably opposed. The ensuing deadlock had by this time become personal; the relationship between Montgomery on the one hand and Tedder and Cunningham on the other had by now assumed all the intensity of a blood feud. Leese was sent back to Montgomery with instructions to find a compromise, perhaps yet another division in the Eighth Army assault plan would be acceptable?

The next day Alexander flew to Cairo, taking Gairdner with him. Montgomery made his case even more forcibly and there was unanimous agreement. Alexander drafted a telegram to Eisenhower in which he recommended the new plan. Montgomery showed the telegram to Admiral Ramsay (who was in command of the naval side of the Eastern Task Force) first, and he advised against sending it since its contents might 'make other people suspicious'. Montgomery, in what was an unusual display of tact on his part, agreed with Ramsay, so instead he telegraphed Alexander to say it was 'much better to have everything in open court', and suggested calling another full-scale conference in Algiers on 2 May.

The big guns were wheeled out on this occasion. Eisenhower, Cunningham, Tedder, Montgomery, Patton and Bedell Smith (Eisenhower's Chief of Staff) and Gairdner attended. Patton arrived on the second afternoon and missed the critical session. General Alexander and Air Marshal Coningham (AOC Eighteen Army Group) were unable to attend because low cloud prevented their aircraft from leaving their headquarters. Leese came with Montgomery and was intrigued to watch the army commander buttonhole Bedell Smith in the urinals of the Ecole Normale shortly before the conference began and, in the time that it took them to empty their bladders, sell him the whole plan.[3]

Montgomery spoke to a prepared script. It began as follows:

> I know well that I am regarded by many people as being a tiresome person. I think this is very probably true. I try hard not to be tiresome; but I have seen so many mistakes made in this war, and so many disasters happen, that I am desperately anxious to try and see that we have no more; and this often means being very tiresome. If we have a disaster in HUSKY, it would be dreadful.[4]

In essence Montgomery advocated a concentrated Anglo-American landing. He proposed that Eighth Army should land astride the Pachino peninsula and advance on Syracuse and Augusta; the Americans were to land on his left flank and guard against an enemy counterattack.

Montgomery might be capable of clear and decisive thinking, and an exponent of action, but this did not necessarily make him right. In fairness however, Admiral Ramsay, who was generally acknowledged as the expert in amphibious warfare, favoured Montgomery's proposals although he was the first to acknowledge that the latter's bearing and behaviour could be counter-productive.

> Monty has thrown a spanner of considerable size into the works and in doing so he caused almost complete disruption of work besides increasing, if possible, his unpopularity. It is really most unfortunate that he should do so many things that make him unpopular and so far to the contrary. . . . The trouble is that he adopts the attitude that he is now omnipotent.[5]

Montgomery reverted to the suggestion that the only solution was to throw the entire American effort into the south-eastern assault on the left flank of the Eighth Army, a subsidiary and supporting role.

Cunningham and Tedder were both outspoken in their criticisms but Eisenhower accepted Montgomery's thesis and gave his approval even before he had consulted Patton. The latter behaved with extraordinary good grace during the time he was at the conference, successfully masking his true feelings that Eisenhower had sacrificed American forces on 'the altar of Allied solidarity'. Eisenhower, for his part, must have been aware that Patton was less than happy with a subordinate role. He therefore recommended to Marshall that he should have equal status with Montgomery. Marshall, aware of the rancour and ill-feeling that had been generated, gave immediate approval for Patton's I Armoured Corps becoming the Seventh (US) Army on D-day.

Marshall was back in the Mediterranean in June 1943 with Winston Churchill. On this occasion he and General Eisenhower were left to handle the British Chiefs alone. At that time there was plenty of evidence that Italy was about to collapse.[6] Marshall urged that Rome should be bombed into submission. The British, however, were vehemently opposed, especially Anthony Eden, who protested that the cultural importance of Rome and its treasures should be kept quite separate to the war.

Marshall gave short shrift to what he saw as platitudes by the British Foreign Secretary. 'I consider the blood of the present to completely outweigh the desire to preserve the historical treasures of antiquity.' He was convinced that a powerful demonstration of Allied air strength would bring about the collapse of Italy, but there were none to support him in council; even Eisenhower seemed dubious. Nevertheless the apparent choice between Italian antiquities and Allied lives was to reappear over Cassino just months later.

Montgomery was now calling the shots over the planning for Sicily. There was a leadership vacuum. Eisenhower preferred to play the chairman of the board and chose not to become directly involved. Alexander lacked the resolution, determination and intellect and so it was made that much easier for Montgomery to fill the void.

Notes

1. CAB/106/363. The Planning of the Invasion of Sicily (Draft).
2. Ibid.
3. Ryder, Rowland, *Oliver Leese*, Hamish Hamilton, 1987.
4. See Annex 1. Source: The Dwight D. Eisenhower Library, Abilene, Kansas.
5. Ramsay Paper, letter to his wife dated 21 April 1943. Quoted in Barnett, Corelli, *Engage the Enemy More Closely*, Hodder and Stoughton, 1991.
6. Matthews interview with Marshall.

5

Intelligence and Deception

Military intelligence had little influence on the decision to land in Sicily. This was a political decision taken at the highest levels by war leaders who did not take into account any considerations such as enemy strengths, deployments or terrain, etc. They simply directed that the operations should take place, but thereafter their subordinates devoted far more time, effort and resources to the detailed planning of Operation Husky than they did for any subsequent landings in the Mediterranean. Irrespective of any calculations or assessments about the dubious fighting qualities of the Italian troops, Sicily was, the commanders still believed, fraught with risk.

There were two prime areas of concern. The first was that after the victory in North Africa, a landing in Sicily was blindingly obvious. The enemy were very aware of the island's military importance and the opportunities presented to the Allies by its capture. The second concern was a fear that the enemy might get wind of Allied intentions and the awful consequences that would inevitably follow. Again there was little concern for what the Italians might do, with the possible exception of the battle fleet; but the Germans were another matter. The result was that Operation Husky was subjected to a comprehensive and very elaborate set of interlocking deception plans at both the strategic and tactical levels. Deception, like propaganda, tends to be more effective if one can reinforce enemy preferences and prejudices rather than attempt to create an entirely new idea.

Sicily proved to be no exception. The Allies reinforced German (ie Hitler's) prejudices by planting the thought that neither Sicily nor Italy was being contemplated because the Italians were a spent force and thus not worth the trouble. Instead Sicily and Italy were to be neutralized from the air and bombed into submission while the Allies tried for bigger game.

Allied strategy involved two major campaigns and a number of diversionary operations. The main deception plan centred on a mythical Twelfth British Army in Egypt. The ostensible intention, ironically very close to Winston Churchill's hopes and ambitions, was to exploit the opportunities in the Balkans. The word was to be put about that the Twelfth Army was to invade Greece in the summer and thereby persuade the Turks to join the Allies. Thereafter a substantial force was to be deployed through Turkey to open a second front against Bulgaria and link up with the Russians. The second imaginary thrust was to be made by Alexander's Army Group. The Eighth Army was to invade the South of France and a new French Army which had been formed in North Africa was to exploit an advance up the Rhone Valley towards Lyons. At the same time Patton's Seventh Army was to attack Sardinia and Corsica.

It was the task of tactical deception to reinforce these plans by planting pieces of evidence to help the enemy to construct their own jigsaw which would lead them to the desired conclusion. In the teeming cities of North Africa and the Levant there were the nests of 'controlled' agents and informers who could be relied upon to carry the word. The landing in North Africa had also brought to the Allies' table the mixed blessings of French intelligence and in particular the formidable resources of the infamous Deuxième Bureau. The problem was that many of the French operatives were feared to be double agents (in favour of the enemy) and therefore definitely not to be trusted.

Of course the Allies did enjoy one major advantage and that was that, by and large, the enemy were strategically blind. The Allies had complete command of the air over North Africa and dominated much of the Mediterranean airspace as well. Except for the occasional sneak attack there was little the Luftwaffe or their Italian Air Force colleagues could do to bring back information on what was happening over the horizon. If the airspace was therefore so devoid of the enemy it does make one wonder why so much time and effort was devoted to the construction of dummy landing craft, trucks and guns, etc for the Twelfth Army because they certainly didn't fool the people on the ground.

More successful was the use of bogus radio traffic and communications. Squadrons of Royal Signal Corps operators were kept hard at work transmitting from 'HQ Twelfth Army in Cairo' and even more men in the fabrication and encoding of these false messages. At the same time great care was exercised in keeping the radio traffic from the headquarters planning Husky, in Malta and Algiers, to a bare minimum. It is in this context that Operation Mincemeat made its contribution to the deception plan. In September 1942 a transport aircraft carrying staff officers crashed into the sea off Spain while en route to Gibraltar. There were no survivors and some of the dead were washed ashore on Spanish beaches and later buried in a proper ceremony by the local authorities. Fortunately none of these officers carried any important or incriminating documents.

In April 1943 the British repeated the exercise, but this time as part of a deception plan. A man who had died of natural causes in London was given the identity of a Major Martin, Royal Marines who served on the staff of Vice Admiral Lord Louis Mountbatten, then Chief of Combined Operations. A War Office briefcase was chained to 'Martin's' wrist. This briefcase contained three documents: the proofs of a manual on Combined Operations produced by Mountbatten's headquarters to which Eisenhower had agreed to write a foreword (this was a bulky document and explained the use of a briefcase); a letter of introduction from Mountbatten to Admiral Sir Andrew Cunningham; and the 'incriminating document', a personal letter dated 23 April written by Lieutenant General Sir Archibald Nye, Vice Chief of the Imperial General Staff, to General Alexander, discussing the proposed landings in Greece.

'Major Martin' was in fact transported in the submarine *Seraph* and floated ashore off Huelva, together with a capsized rubber dingy, in the early hours of 30 April. Huelva was chosen because the currents were favourable and the Germans were known to have an enthusiastic and energetic Vice Consul. The body was discovered by local fishermen later that morning and the authorities informed. The British naval attaché in Madrid, who had been brought in on the act, made immediate representations, on cue, but the Spaniards, true to form, opened the briefcase, photographed the documents, handed a set to the Abwehr, put the originals back and belatedly handed 'Major Martin' over to the British diplomatic mission, who arranged a decent Christian burial. The documents, in the meantime, were despatched to Abwehr Headquarters in Berlin where their subsequent influence was monitored by London through Sigint, or Signal intelligence, itself a codeword or cover for Ultra.

General Nye's letter reinforced German preferences. Hitler had long since lost patience with the Italians and had been concerned for some time about the Balkans and the Aegean. The document was therefore seen as proof to support his prejudice rather than as a piece of intelligence to be assessed and evaluated as to its authenticity.

Did the deception plans work? Were the Axis made to believe that the blindingly obvious Sicily was not to be the next target for an Allied offensive? Many historians have written that the plans, and especially 'Mincemeat', were brilliantly successful[1] and cite three pieces of evidence to support their case. In May 1st Panzer Division, then refitting in Brittany, was redeployed to Greece; the movement orders were identified and deciphered by Ultra. The second piece of evidence was the absence or paucity of German divisions (there were just two) in Sicily at the time of the invasion. Lastly the Abwehr and German military intelligence were apparently convinced of the authenticity of 'Mincemeat'.

The result was that on 12 May a general warning was despatched by the Wehrmacht-Fuhrungsstab (Military Intelligence) to all commands in the Mediterranean to prepare their defences against possible enemy landings with priority accorded to Sardinia and the Peloponnese. Further proof could be drawn from the fact that between March and July 1943 the number of German divisions in the Balkans was increased from eight to 18, with seven going to Greece. During the same period one division was despatched to Corsica and another to Sardinia.

The Italians were convinced that Sicily was the main Allied objective, but the Germans had long since ceased listening to them. General Von Senger und Etterlin,[2] who was appointed as a liaison officer with the Italian Sixth Army in Sicily, claims that the invasion did not come as a surprise. But his view is countered by Field Marshal Richthofen, C-in-C Luftflotte 2 which covered the southern Mediterranean, who was convinced that Sardinia rather than Sicily was the target and redeployed his squadrons accordingly. Richthofen did not get on with Field Marshal Albert Kesselring, the German C-in-C in southern Italy and in any case the Luftwaffe, like the Royal Air Force, was a law unto itself when it came to grand strategy.

So what the German military high command anticipated was a limited offensive in the Mediterranean – Crete perhaps or the Peloponnese. They did not take the possibility of an Allied landing in the South of France at all seriously and Sicily was also discredited.

The prime reason for not reinforcing Sicily appears, however, not to have been because of the deception plan. Hitler believed the Italians were on the verge of capitulation. Contingency plans were already in place which would allow for the German armed forces in Italy to seize control over key installations considered necessary to ensure an orderly withdrawal. Hitler was therefore loth to risk deploying more divisions into Italy where they could easily have become engulfed in the chaos of an

Italian collapse, and this would have applied even more so in the vulnerable island of Sicily. Operation Mincemeat therefore was a brilliantly conceived and executed intelligence operation. But it would be wrong to accord it all the accolades for the absence of a significant number of German divisions in Sicily; that was the result of a political decision taken by Hitler who probably would have been of the same mind had 'Mincemeat' never been mounted.

When it came to the invasion, British intelligence did have a remarkably accurate picture of Italian military deployments and this despite the fact that the usual means were not available. There was, for example, a paucity of information from Sigint, both Ultra and other radio interception. This was because Sicily and Italy had a very good telephone network which was both more efficient and certainly more secure than radio transmissions. Secondly, of course, because Sicily was an island there was no battlefield intelligence through reconnaissance, patrols or captured enemy soldiers.

So how did they do it? By this stage of the war there were literally hundreds of thousands of Italian prisoners of war. The majority of them were in North Africa and Palestine, but there were sizeable contingents in the United Kingdom, Canada, East and South Africa and more still in India, but all their mail passed through Cairo. There was a huge volume of such mail, much of it from relatives and friends who were serving in the Italian armed forces. These letters had supposedly been through their own censorship, but in the cheerfully inefficient way in which the Italians approached all matters military, they proved to be a goldmine of information. Many envelopes had the sender's name and service address on the outside; others in the letter itself would mention where they were serving. Checking the military correspondence to Italian POWs proved to be a full-time occupation for dozens of linguists in the Intelligence Corps but the payoff was enormous.

It was also essential that the planners chose the right sort of beaches for the invasion forces and this sort of work was very new. Of particular concern were the gradients of the beaches, the presence of sand bars, the nature and composition of the sand or the shingle and a dozen other requirements. Many of the answers to those questions were found by an organization called COPP or Combined Operations Pilotage Parties. These were canoeists who would paddle ashore from a submarine and conduct a reconnaissance under very hazardous conditions. Air photography and its interpretation had very much come into its own by 1943 and these new skills were also applied to the selection of beaches.

There was one other aspect of military intelligence which is worthy of mention if only because of the terrible blunder in its commission, and the truly horrendous consequences which have been experienced ever since. The one major American contribution to the intelligence effort supposedly led to the renaissance of the Mafia, but the dividing line between fact and fiction, truth and legend remains frustratingly obscure.

The old truism about Mussolini is that he had three notable achievements before his grandiose military ambitions got the better of him: he drained the Pontine Marshes, made the trains run on time and stamped out the Mafia in Sicily. When the latter were suppressed the leaders were either imprisoned or fled to the United States. Mussolini's methods were certainly draconian. His 'Iron Prefect', Cesare Mori, was given a free hand. Thousands were flung into prison, hundreds, guilty or innocent, tortured into making confessions, property was confiscated and families forced into poverty. Nevertheless the organization survived, albeit in a more shadowy form. Those who fled to the United States arrived in time for Prohibition and the opportunities that were thus presented to start afresh.

In the rural interior of Sicily it was a different story. To this day there are few isolated farm houses. Those who work on the land live in villages for safety. The rural Mafia were also the guardians of the feudal system and wielded considerable power. This is also bandit country. A formidable mountain terrain, honeycombed with caves and deep canyons, allowed banditry to flourish for centuries. Even in 1943 some 30 bands roamed these mountains, a pool of desperate men who worked for the highest bidder, be he mafioso or feudal owner.

It is at this point that legend intrudes. Lucky Luciano was a Mafia 'capo' serving a 30-year prison sentence for racketeering, in Dannemosa prison in the United States, at the outset of the Second World War. He was supposedly approached by the US government who offered him his freedom in return for helping to establish an effective resistance movement in Sicily immediately prior to the invasion of the island. The head of the Mafia in Sicily, the '*capo di tutti capi*', was of little use. Don Vito Cascio Ferro was dying in an Italian prison, but a successor had already been chosen.

Stories abound as to how Luciano made contact with the incoming '*capo di tutti capi*', Don Calogero Vizzini, in his hometown of Villalba. But legend has it that Vizzini was persuaded to throw in his lot with the Allies and bring his organization with him. In alliance with Genco Russo of Mussomeli, another Mafia leader of note, he was able to deliver the whole of western Sicily to the American forces and thereby facilitated Patton's lightning advance to Palermo. There is no substantive evidence[3] to prove or refute these stories. There have even been Senate Committees of Investigation[4] which have drawn a blank, which only encourages the conspiracy theorists to suggest that this simply points to the power of the Mafia. The fact that Lucky Luciano was released on parole in 1946 for his 'extensive and valuable aid to the Navy in the war' and deported to Italy, seemingly endorses the case of those who believe the United States did a deal with the Mafia.

The answer is probably more straightforward. There were undoubtedly many American GIs who, when they landed in Sicily, were returning to the land of their forefathers. Similarly, in the absence of a clearly defined policy with regard to the civilian population and in the chaos which reigned before the Allied Military Government (AMGOT) got its feet under the table, this was a time for opportunities. Many Mafiosi who were released from prison when their towns were liberated were able to present themselves as anti-Fascists, political prisoners. The Fascist administrators were booted out and their places were taken by known Mafia members. The Americans, for example, installed Vizzini as mayor of Villalba and even made him an honorary colonel! Colonel Charlie Poletti, appointed by the Americans as their Military Governor in Italy, was described by Lucky Luciano as 'one of our friends'. Mafia members were foisted onto a naive American and British officer corps by people whom they trusted, such as priests. Others trusted their interpreters and there were many. Some Allied officers in rear-area appointments allowed themselves to be corrupted.[5]

The result is not in doubt. Within days of the Allied landings the Mafia had re-established its network and was quickly in a position to command and control a flourishing black market, initially in local wines and military supplies. The rest is history.

Notes

1. For many years Sheppard, David, *The Italian Campaign 1943 – 45* (Morrison and Gibb, 1968) was considered the authoritative tract. More recently Strawson, John, *The Italian Campaign* (Secker and Warburg, 1987) and Hunt, Sir David, *A Don at War* (Frank Cass, 1990) make the case that the deception was successful.
2. Von Senger und Etterlin, General, *Neither Fear Nor Hope*, MacDonald, 1963, p 133.

3. For a more detailed account see: Villari, Luigi, *The Liberation of Italy*, C.C. Nelson Publishing Company, Appleton, Wisconsin, 1959) and Sterling, Claire, *The Mafia*, Hamish Hamilton, 1990.
4. Senator Estes Kefauver.
5. The classic case was Vito Genovese, a leading Mafia capo and multiple killer in New York, who had fled to Sicily before the war to avoid a murder charge. Taken on as an interpreter he became senior interpreter at HQ Fifteenth Army Group at Caserta near Naples before he was recognized by US Military Intelligence and sent back to the United States under arrest.

6

Know Your Enemy

The problem which the Italian as a fighting man presents to his enemies and to his generals is that he is unpredictable; no-one can be sure how he will fight on the day – or indeed whether he will fight at all. The result is that the Italian does not enjoy a high military reputation. Much of this is largely undeserved, for history is littered with examples of the Italian soldier confounding his enemy who had every reason for expectation of victory. In the First World War, for example, after suffering a humiliating defeat at the hands of the Austrians at Caporetto in October 1917, raw Italian infantry, against all the odds, held the invaders at the Piave river, thereby saving Venice. Having stabilized the front, the Italians then beat the Austrians to the punch and launched an offensive which sent the enemy into a headlong flight and back across his own borders.

Comparisons between the Italian Army and the Wehrmacht never make for comfortable reading, but since they were the enemy it has a purpose in the context of this account. The Germans had a long and proud military tradition based on Prussian prowess and laced with periods of outstanding success. The Italians, in contrast, had no such history or tradition. The unification of Italy came about by foreign intervention not the Piedmontese army, which was frequently seen off the field of battle by the Austrians. The Italians embarked upon the Second World War with a vastly inflated opinion of their own military capabilities and one, indeed, which was at first accepted by the British and the French. The navy was good, possessing fast, modern and well-designed warships which, had Mussolini given his admirals their heads rather than prefer a fleet-in-being, might have given a good account of itself against the Royal Navy. The air force, modelled on the teachings of Guilio Douchet, an apostle of strategic air power, had some good bombers but lacked modern fighters.

The army was poorly equipped, horse-drawn and lacked modern armour. The artillery wasn't bad, even by German standards, but the veteran divisions and professional soldiers had become corrupted by years of Empire and ruthless occupation. Although the Fascist Blackshirt battalions looked the part, they were soon to learn that political fervour is no substitute for sound military training.

When compared to their German, American and British counterparts, Italian senior officers were an average of ten years older; thus in May 1943 all Italian army commanders and the Chief of the General Staff were well into their sixties. Promotion in the Italian Army was slow and cumbersome and the quality of junior officers, even judged by their superiors, was regarded as mediocre – though not in bravery:

> As long as it is a question of risking one's skin they are admirable; when instead they have to open their eyes, think, decide in cold blood, they are hopeless. In terms of reconnaissance, security, movement to contact preparatory to fire, coordinated movement and so on, they are practically illiterate.[1]

Even so, the Italians confounded the British on more than one occasion in the Second World War. One division stood its ground in the trenches at El Alamein and was destroyed and others fought the Anglo-Americans to the bitter end in North Africa two years later. Montgomery, for one, expected the Italians to fight stubbornly for their own soil.

Montgomery and his generals were overcautious. The Italians had had the stuffing knocked out of them in North Africa. Italy lost the war on what Italian merchant seamen called the 'route to death', the convoy route which plied between Italian ports and Tripoli, Benghazi and Tunis. In three years the Italians lost at sea a million tonnes of shipping and huge quantities of materiel as well as thousands of their soldiers and sailors.

For the Italian military all vestiges of partnership had by now been dissipated. There were one or two exceptions among the senior officers. Kesselring still believed in the Italians as worthy allies, but most of the German hierarchy sided with Rommel who regarded them as worthless. Liaison officers frequently spoke of an Italian inferiority complex, *Minderwertkeisgefühl*, with regard to the German military; and racist overtones were widespread in the attitude of many German soldiers towards the Italians, soldier or civilian.

Rommel recommended to Hitler that once the Allies made their next move in the Mediterranean, the Third Reich should conduct an orderly retreat through the Italian peninsula, abandon Sicily and Sardinia and hold a line along the River Arno between Pisa and Rimini. The Field Marshal proposed that the troops who were released by this stratagem could be despatched to the Eastern Front, there to stem the real threat. Rommel also advocated a similar course of action in Greece and that, maybe, was his mistake, for Hitler, who would not countenance any voluntary surrender of territory, promptly despatched 13 divisions to the Balkans.

On the question of Italy Hitler vacillated for much of the early summer. His inclination was to side with Kesselring. The surrender of southern Italy would give the Allies airfields for their bombers. The strategic bomber offensive was getting into its stride, the Americans by day and the British by night. Not only were the German defences concentrated in the north to counter the threat from Britain, but a number of key German industries were in the process of being relocated to the southern Reich, out of harm's way. These would be vulnerable to an offensive launched from Italy's airfields. It was a compelling argument and one which Kesselring, as a Luftwaffe officer, could put across with the utmost credibility. He, like Montgomery, believed that the Italian would fight for his homeland, and all the more so with German arms and Wehrmacht divisions to stiffen resolve.

Hitler was confronted by conflicting advice from two senior officers. Uncharacteristically, the Führer shrank from reaching any positive decision with regard to Italy. Instead, a number of contingency plans were prepared. The most important, code-named Asche, catered for a 'worst-case scenario' of an Italian surrender. There were no Italian units left in Russia but there were some 600,000 troops outside Italy, most on garrison and lines-of-communication duties in the Balkans, Crete and Southern France.

The German political leadership were especially worried about Mussolini whom they still saw as the guarantor of the Axis. As Goebbels expressed in a diary entry from 3 March 1943: 'The Duce is really our only completely dependable support in Italy. As long as he is in control we need have no fear.'[2] The problem was that Mussolini's Fascist regime had never assumed total control in Italy and could not stand comparison with that of Nazi Germany when it came to a police state with all its associated instruments of repression. Although opposition parties were disenfranchised, political leaders lived in comfortable retirement; the Italian aristocracy clustered around their King, an odious little man who had compromised every last principle to maintain the fiction of the Royal House of Piedmont on the throne.

King Victor Emmanuel II was no alternative to Mussolini. He lacked the backbone and the political courage. The fact that in May 1943, after the debacle in Tunis, he confided to General Puntoni, his military ADC, 'I am afraid that at any moment the British government or the King of England may approach me direct in order to negotiate a separate peace'[3] simply illustrated how far he was removed from the real world. The Germans knew this but were not disconcerted by the comings and goings at the Royal Palace and had a fair idea of what was being discussed; after all there were no secrets in Rome.

The problem was that Mussolini had no personal bodyguard along the lines of *Liebstandarte* or SS formations. When it came to a crisis and the army sided with the rebels, Mussolini had no alternative power base. Himmler had persuaded Mussolini of the need for such a force and indeed SS officers had been seconded to create and train a bodyguard unit, but it was not ready in time. So the Germans prepared for the worse. The various contingencies within Plan Asche included the disarming of Italian formations outside Italy and the seizure of those installations in the country necessary to ensure an orderly withdrawal for German formations.

Ominously, Rommel was placed in command of a new Army Group B with its headquarters in Munich. His orders were clear and unequivocal. In the event of Plan Asche being activated, he was to seize northern Italy, south to the Pisa–Rimini Line, disarm the Italians and assume command over all German troops in the country. In these circumstances Army Group B had three missions. It was to be an army of occupation, a force to intimidate the Italians and, if required, a strategic reserve which could be despatched south to hold Rome. If the third mission became the primary objective, then we can assume that Rommel would have displaced Kesselring in command. Thus, even though Hitler did appear to vacillate, it made little difference to the Italians, for Mussolini was no longer master in his own house. A negotiated peace with the Allies might once have been an option, but no longer. The door had been slammed firmly shut in Casablanca with the declaration of unconditional surrender. There were those in the government in Rome who were convinced that their country was about to be invaded. Mussolini would probably have risked all and taken whatever German units Hitler could have spared, except that he was, by this time, very aware that large numbers of German troops could easily have been interpreted as an army of occupation which would undermine his already weakened power base. Until June 1943 there were about four German divisions in Italy; all were in the process of being reconstituted after being destroyed in previous encounters. The 90th Light Division, veterans of the Afrika Korps and destroyed at Tunis, was in Sardinia. The 15th Panzers, the other stalwart of Rommel's original desert command, was being rebuilt in Sicily. The 16th Panzer Division was destroyed at Stalingrad and in March 1943 a second division was reformed in France before moving to Taranto in southern Italy. Lastly there was the (1st) Parachute Panzer Division 'Herman Goering'. The designation as a parachute division was honorary only. The unit was still being formed in 1943 when elements were despatched to Tunisia and destroyed when Army Group Afrika collapsed in May. Meanwhile the rest of the division was assembled in Italy for shipment to Africa, but was committed to the defence of Sicily instead.

In June the Allies captured Pantelleria. This island lay 150 miles north-west of Malta and had a tremendous reputation as Italy's Rock of Gibraltar.[4] There was simply no way the Allies could verify the truth of the island's strength, so military wisdom dictated that the worst-case opinion prevailed. In the belief that it concealed a nest of deadly E-boats and squadrons of Stukas lurking in bomb-proof shelters waiting for the opportunity to fall on any invading force, the island was to be captured. The task of reducing the island's defences was given over to the air forces. In ideal weather conditions a bombing offensive was launched in what were almost controlled laboratory conditions; in fact it was code-named Operation Workshop. The main target of Pantelleria occupied eight square miles on which 6,400 tons of bombs were dropped between 1 and 11 June in 5,218 heavy, medium and fighter-bomber sorties.[5] In the meantime a landing force, 3rd Infantry Brigade Group, embarked and arrived offshore at the appointed hour. But there was no fighting and the Italian commander surrendered his garrison of 4,600 Italian troops and 78 Germans to a landing party from the Coldstream Guards. The Italian general claimed that the island's water supplies had been polluted by the bombing.

No matter, the apostles of air power loudly trumpeted their victory and Pantelleria was used to further their case for yet more resources to be dedicated to the air offensive against Germany. The unpalatable truth was later presented by an Operational Research Team whose evidence was brushed aside. It was found that of the 130 guns on the island only 16 were destroyed or damaged, the underground hangars were intact and fewer than 200 of the garrison had been killed. The small town and port on the island had, however, been flattened.

The Allied bombers and warships then turned on neighbouring

Lampedusa whose commander was made of sterner stuff. He held out for 24 hours before surrendering his 4,600 troops to the pilot of a Fleet Air Arm Rescue Swordfish who had earlier made a forced landing on the airstrip.

After Pantelleria the Germans did send further reinforcements to Italy. The 29th Panzer Grenadiers, the Falcon Division as it was nicknamed, was an outstanding unit which was destroyed at Stalingrad. A second 29th was formed in the spring of 1943 in south-western France and thence deployed to Italy in the first week of July. The second division was destined to spend the remainder of the war in Italy and lived up to its reputation as one of the finest in the Wehrmacht. Similarly the 26th Panzers had been all but decimated on the Russian front in 1942 before being sent to Brittany to reform. Originally recruited from the Potsdam area this fine formation was destined to fight out the war in Italy and was to prove another formidable opponent.

So, if one of the purposes or objectives of the Sicily campaign was to draw off German forces from the Eastern Front and thereby reduce the pressure in Russia, then, even before the landings occurred, the Allies had gone some way towards achieving their aims. Reconstituted German divisions were despatched to Italy. Had the Allies closed down the Mediterranean, which was Marshall's preferred option, these divisions might well have found themselves marching westwards once they were back up to strength. Their cadres comprised veterans returning to the colours, either after recovering from wounds or having completed extended training courses. The Hermann Goering was the only green division in the theatre, something which became painfully obvious once the Allies landed.

Field Marshall Kesselring despatched General Fredo Von Senger und Etterlin, an outstanding officer and a devout Catholic, to be his liaison officer with the Italian Sixth Army in Sicily. Von Senger arrived in June, but before leaving Germany he was briefed personally by Hitler who 'was already reckoning with the early defection of Italy'. They discussed the prospects of German troops in Sicily having to fight alone without the Italians in the event of an invasion.[6] Further meetings with General Warlimont and Field Marshal Keitel[7] were equally pessimistic in their judgement of the proposals for success.

The commanding General of the last army of any significance in the history of Italy was Generale d'Armata Alfredo Guzzoni. He was a fat, pompous little man who sported a dyed wig. Guzzoni had previously been Deputy Chief of the General Staff and then commanded a corps in

Albania in 1939. It did not help matters either that Guzzoni kept a Hungarian Jewess as a mistress who was well known in Rome for her defeatist chatter, and so he had been retired. Now, at 66, Mussolini brought him back into active service to command the Sixth Army in Sicily, an island which he had never visited.

All army commanders rely heavily on their Chiefs of Staff. Colonel Emilio Faldfella was a good, young and very capable officer, but he had never served with Guzzoni before, which was contrary to Italian practice; he too had never served in Sicily.

The Italian way of command was at odds with accepted military practice or procedure at that time. An army commander, for example, did not exercise rigid control but rather sought coordination from his corps and divisional generals. This method was in part a product of the freemasonry which was an important feature of the Italian senior officer corps. Seen in its context, freemasonry among the military was a secret society in a police state, a progressive liberal anticlerical tradition in a clerical society. And thus it was outlawed by Mussolini. So an Italian army commander was a *'primus inter pares'*, a system which can work well when the days are good and there is absolute trust and confidence; but in a tight defensive situation subordinates need more than mere recommendations.

The Italian garrison in Sicily numbered about 200,000 men and the quality varied from very poor to barely adequate. Most were rear echelon and supply troops. In the fighting forces there were the six so-called coastal divisions which were regarded even by the Italians as very low-grade troops. These were largely locally recruited Sicilians who were too old or infirm for active service. Their officers were equally pitiful and their equipment mirrored their status.

The southern coastline was guarded by the 206th and 207th Divisions and the 18th Brigade. Their coastal artillery was antiquated, much of it pre-First-World-War and of British manufacture and there was about one anti-tank gun for every five miles of beach. These were static divisions in every sense of the word; they had very few motor vehicles. There were 48,000 men in four Italian mobile divisions. Two, the Aosta and the Napoli, were largely composed of Sicilians, poorly trained, indifferently led and with a morale that generally reflected the island's attitude to the war, Mussolini and all things Roman. They formed XII Corps and were stationed in the west of the island to defend Palermo.

The Assieta was a little better, but was well below strength, lacked mobility and supporting field artillery. Lastly there was the Livorno, the only division to have seen active service, and though at full strength and reasonably mobile it lacked radios and was very short of ammunition. With headquarters at Piazza Armerina, they formed the XVI Corps and guarded the east.

Guzzoni, who was a more capable officer than his appearance suggested, was never very sanguine about his chances from the outset. Before the landings he assessed a German division in terms of firepower as the equivalent of half an Allied division while his best, the Livorno, he rated as worth a quarter. There was no chance that he could build up his war stocks, in fact the very reverse, for there was a shortfall in their daily requirements. The primitive nature of the Sicilian roads, coupled to a mountainous terrain, would also prevent the rapid movement of reinforcements from a central reserve to a threatened front.

So Guzzoni deployed small tactical groups, mobile where possible, relatively close to the beaches. He also recognized that when the Allies came, the main target would be the airfields. So he concentrated all his efforts on their defence. Static formations of infantry and artillery were dug in behind minefields and barbed wire; at least that is what the situation maps displayed in army headquarters. The reality was disturbingly different.

There was little in the way of genuine liaison or indeed communication between the Italians and the Germans. General Von Senger maintained the outward appearance of conformity and observed the niceties of diplomatic protocol, but in reality he exercised full and independent command in the field over the German troops. In this task he answered to Kesselring at his headquarters in Rome who remained ever the optimist, as he had throughout the whole of the North African campaign.

The problem was where to deploy the two German divisions. The better of the two was the 15th Panzer Grenadiers, but even this lacked the mobility and punch of the Panzer Grenadiers of old. The Hermann Goering Division was much weaker; it had only three battalions of infantry. Between them the two divisions could deploy only 160 tanks and 140 field artillery pieces.

The arguments which bedevilled German generals in Normandy first surfaced for the defence of Sicily. What is the most suitable or appropriate deployment for armoured formations to resist an amphibious landing? There were those who favoured deployments very close to the shoreline so that counterattacks could be launched before a beachhead could be established by the invader. Others believed in holding back the armour until the axis of the main threat became apparent. The argument was never resolved because there was no clear-cut military solution; the optimum was dependent upon questions of air cover, terrain and communications.

In Sicily Guzzoni and Von Senger believed that the Allies would strike in the south-east. Kesselring, who throughout the Italian campaign always managed to overestimate Allied maritime strength and amphibious capabilities, expected a simultaneous attack aimed at Palermo. Kesselring prevailed, and the German divisions were deployed in a series of battlegroups. Von Senger makes the point that the decision to assign the Herman Goering division the crucial task of defending the eastern part of the island was a mistake, the magnitude of which only became apparent in the first and second days of the landings. The imbalance caused by its lack of infantry was exacerbated by the poor fighting quality of the troops and shortcomings in leadership of many of its officers. However, the Axis had one thing in their favour, and this, in its own way, was to figure prominently in the battle for the island. They had interior lines of communication. At its narrowest, the straits of Messina were just two miles wide and thereafter there were road and rail networks which stretched northwards through Italy into Germany. Reinforcements and supplies could be pumped along this artery more quickly than the Allies could respond by sea.

And the one thing Guzzoni and Von Senger got right was to convince their masters in Rome and Berlin that, despite all the intelligence to the contrary, Sicily was the intended target.

Notes

1. General Claudio Trezzani to Marshal Pietro Badoglio, Chief of General Staff, 1940 quoted in Steinberg, Jonathan, *All or Nothing*, Routledge, 1990, p 207.
2. Lochner, Louis P. (ed.), *The Goebbels Diaries 1941–43*, Garden City, NY, 1948.
3. Deakin, F.W., *The Brutal Friendship, Mussolini, Hitler and the Fall of Italian Fascism*, Penguin, 1966.
4. It has a smaller sister called Lampedusa.
5. Forty-five Allied aircraft were lost.
6. Von Senger, *Neither Fear Nor Hope*, p 126.
7. Lieutenant General Walter Warlimont was one of the key staff officers in the German High Command. Field Marshal Wilhelm Keitel was Chief of the High Command of the Armed Forces (OKW).

7

The Invaders

What made the expedition so famous was not only its astonishing daring and the brilliant show that it made, but also its great preponderance of strength over those against whom it set out.

Thucydides

Sicily has been the target for invasion on numerous occasions in its history. Thucydides describes one invasion in the year 413 BC when Athens, then at its peak as a Mediterranean maritime power, sent the best of its fleet and its army against Syracuse. It ended in the near-total annihilation of the invaders and the execution of the Athenian generals in command.

Operation Husky was the biggest D-Day of the Second World War. It was bigger than Normandy and bigger than any of the invasions in the Pacific. Two thousand five hundred ships and landing craft carried or escorted 80 battalions of infantry and 400 battle tanks along with 14,000 vehicles and 1,800 guns. The troops were in seven infantry divisions (three British, one Canadian and three American), an American armoured division along with two British and one Canadian armoured brigades, three British Commandos and a battalion of US Rangers. There were other special forces included. Elements from two airborne divisions, one British and the other American, were to drop in ahead of the main assault to seize some vital features. The initial objective of this mighty force was to secure a beachhead along 100 miles of coast, 90 miles of which was defended by the luckless 206 Coastal Division whose 7,500 reluctant part-timers in uniform disposed 56 pieces of artillery, 34 mortars and 700 machine guns. But just in case the Axis defences proved

45

to be formidable, there were a further two British and one American division held in reserve.

And yet, despite this vast preponderance of force, Montgomery and many of his senior commanders were not at all optimistic about the invasion. Oliver Leese, in command of XXX Corps, confided in a letter to his wife written on 9 June:[1] 'The chances of bringing this off are none too good. I'd like to shoot the **** who chose this plan – and send his head on a pitcher back to Mountbatten and his useless racket.' This lack of faith is all the more remarkable given that Allied Intelligence assessed enemy strengths with pinpoint accuracy.

On 19 May, Force 141 issued Operation Instruction No 1 and on May 21 issued Operation Instruction No 2. These operational instructions set forth the final plan.

Before the campaign in Sicily began, Alexander gave the Eighth Army the mission on the east coast because he felt that this would require the hardest fighting to take Syracuse, the airfields there, and Catania. For this job he felt that the Eighth Army, from the start, should have the more difficult role. While American troops had improved greatly during the Tunisian campaign, Alexander still did not have the same confidence in them as in the British. So, in the initial phase of the operation, the American Seventh Army was to land, create a bridgehead, take airfields and form a line covering the Eighth Army's flank.

At the time of the Kasserine Pass, General Alexander had spoken patronizingly of American troops. The mistake he made was to sustain this attitude long after the situation had radically changed, even when American troops in Italy had to bear the brunt of the fighting because of the exhaustion of British divisions. At the Yalta conference, Alexander remarked to General Marshall, 'Of course American troops are *basically* trained' to which Marshall responded, 'Yes, American troops start out and make every possible mistake. But after the first time, they do not repeat these mistakes. The British troops start out in the same way and continue making the same mistakes over and over for a year.'

In one sense it is unfair to saddle Alexander with all the blame, for this negative attitude towards American troops was widespread in British circles. On one occasion after the Normandy landings, King George VI started to tell Marshall how fine it was have Eisenhower in nominal supreme command with Montgomery in real command, at his side. 'That's very interesting, Your Majesty,' responded Marshall, and went on his way.[2]

Before the attack began on Sicily, Alexander did not draw up any detailed plans for the exploitation phase. He felt that it would depend on what the Germans did and how they used their reserves. Alexander believed that the key to the defence of the island was the network of road centres and roads emanating from the Enna area, and that the logical thing for the Germans to do was to use those roads to reinforce threatened areas. It was Alexander's concern for this road network that led him to adopt a step-by-step approach to the campaign. The Operation Instructions did not make any reference to a wider strategic picture of where Sicily was to fit into a master plan, because there wasn't one. The intention was simply to force the enemy to evacuate the island for its own value, not to use Sicily as a killing ground into which Axis forces could be enticed, trapped and destroyed. There are parallels for the United States and Britain with Operation Granby in 1991 in the Gulf. The generals were ordered to expel the Iraqis from Kuwait with minimum casualties to their forces; there were no instructions to destroy the invading army, to prevent their escape, nor indeed to bring about the downfall of Saddam Hussein. In Kuwait, as in Sicily nearly 40 years before, the Anglo-American forces operated a strategy with very limited objectives. Nobody wanted to become embroiled in a war in Iraq and similarly, there was no intention to invade Italy.

In 1991 the Anglo-Americans harboured the expectation that military operations would bring about the downfall of their enemy, Saddam Hussein. Mussolini fell from power because of the Allied invasion of Sicily. In both campaigns the Anglo-Americans had to live with the consequences. At the time of writing Saddam Hussein is still in charge in Baghdad and it is George Bush who has fallen from power. In 1943 the Allies allowed the Germans to make good their escape from Sicily, and the Anglo-Americans were sucked into the mainland in a campaign which was to cause bitter acrimony as well as misery and pain in equal measure for the soldiers and the Italian civilians. And for no great purpose.

In 1943 the Anglo-Americans were a mixture of veterans and new boys. On the British side the First Army had been disbanded after the North Africa campaign and so they were all now part of the glorious and victorious Eighth Army; but the enmity and tensions still remained. Montgomery wisely mixed old and new in the assault formations which were to land, shoulder to shoulder, astride the Pachino peninsula.

British and American infantry divisions were far more mobile than their German and Italian counterparts, but that was not always an advantage. In a country like Italy where the roads were poor, traffic congestion was a major problem. An infantry division typically had over 4,000 vehicles. On a single road the division could tail back over 50 miles.

The British assault divisions were to land in a concentrated force astride the Pachino peninsula and thence more quickly take Syracuse, Augusta and Catania, east-coast ports vital to Allied success. The 50th Tyne and Tees Division comprised Territorial veterans from the Western Desert who at this time had their roots in Northumberland, Durham and Yorkshire; they took their inspiration and strength from a fierce regimental loyalty. Battalions of the Duke of Wellington's Regiment, the Durham Light Infantry, Northumberland Fusiliers were miners, shipbuilders and steel workers in civilian life. Sicily was destined to be their last campaign in the Mediterranean.

XXX Corps, another name to conjure with from the Western Desert, was a similar mix of old and new. There had always been a mystique attached to the 51st Highlanders, with the result that the division's reputation had frequently been out of step with its performance. A fierce divisional, as opposed to regimental, identity and loyalty were the hallmarks of this Territorial division composed of Highland battalions.

Canada's army originated in the militia formed by the French in the seventeenth century, continued and supplemented by units formed in British Canada. The militia fought the United States Army twice (the War of Independence and the War of 1812), sent contingents to the Boer War and a corps to France in the First World War. By the summer of 1943 the Canadian Army numbered more than a quarter of a million. There were three infantry and two armoured divisions and two tank brigades in Britain. Two brigades of 2nd Canadian Division had yet to see action, though some had been overseas for three years.

Canada's Chief of the General Staff, Major General A.G.L. McNaughton was an elderly, disagreeable and, amongst senior British officers, unpopular officer. McNaughton was determined none of the Canadian forces should be employed separately. It was impossible, however, to employ the entire force in the Mediterranean and so they had had to sit out the war to date in the defence of the United Kingdom though they had paid a terrible price when elements of the 2nd Canadian Division were sacrificed on the altar of British incompetence at Dieppe: three-quarters of their number were casualties. Sicily was to prove an uncomfortable baptism of fire, both for the Canadians and their young divisional commander, Guy Simmonds.

The British army also contained in its order of battle a number of independent Guards and infantry brigade groups. They formed part of the field force and were included with a division, or more usually a corps, as the need arose.

The Seventh Army was led by Patton. Alexander was very fond of 'Georgie', excitable, temperamental; 'a horse that you had to keep a rein on – a dashing steed that always wanted watching'. Alexander always considered that Patton was a commander who would make a tactical plan irrespective of administrative difficulties and then had a tendency to say that supply would follow tactics, rather than tactics follow supply. Patton's command was grouped in two sub-task forces for the landings. The assault was to be carried out by II (US) Corps which, like the British, comprised a mixture of old and new.

The Americans had a holding role: they were to cover the left flank of the Eighth Army until the latter had secured a good line and their beachhead. The line ran roughly along the area Canicatti–Caltanissetta, or a little beyond it to include Gerbini airfield. To such a cautious man as Alexander, it was of paramount importance to prevent any attempt by the enemy to drive a wedge between the two armies.

The II US Corps was commanded by Omar Bradley. Alexander considered him to be the best American field commander, an excellent tactician who thought problems through, and well-balanced, not impetuous or temperamental like Patton. Bradley had two Regimental Combat Teams from the 'Big Red One', the 1st US Infantry Division, as his veteran force, although such expressions are relative when applied to the Americans. The 1st (US) Infantry was a regular division which nevertheless had a proud tradition to maintain from the First World War. The division had landed in North Africa and had fought throughout that campaign. Alongside was the 45th Infantry Division which was about to experience its baptism of fire. The division was a National Guard formation with its infantry regiments recruited originally in Oklahoma, Colorado and Arizona. It was called the Thunderbirds after an Indian insignia it wore as a shoulder patch. This was because the division had large numbers of the Great Plains Indians among its ranks, Sioux and Cherokee from Oklahoma and Colorado, Apache from Arizona and even Seminole from the Florida Everglades. The division was combat loaded in the United States for a ship-to-shore operation. Each assault battalion was loaded on its own ship, usually an attack transport, and thence sailed in convoy for the Mediterranean.

The second task force comprised Lucian Truscott's 3rd (US) Infantry Division. Truscott was a shy, handsome man who, at 49, was lucky to have combat command. But then Truscott, like so many of his contemporaries, had experienced meteoric promotion. In 1940, for example, he was still a major. But Truscott was a fine combat commander who inspired confidence in his troops and in his senior commanders.

Truscott had helped to create the Rangers, the US Army's equivalent of the British Commandos; he had witnessed the slaughter at Dieppe and had served as Eisenhower's field deputy in the North African campaign before taking over command of the 3rd Infantry. Truscott and Bradley had shared concern over the American military performance in North Africa and were determined to remedy the faults before they closed with the enemy again in Europe. He found the air of complacency which accompanied the end of what he regarded as, at best, a mediocre campaign, to be quite dangerous. American troops were unwilling both to close and to maintain contact with the enemy, while their reconnaissance skills were poor.

When he took command of the 3rd Infantry he found not only a division which was still under-strength, but one which was flabby and unfit, operating a peacetime regime. Truscott immediately introduced Commando standards. Normally infantry marched at two and a half miles per hour. He had the 3rd Division speed-marching at five miles an hour. He introduced route marches where the pace was set at 4 mph for 20 miles and 3.5 mph for up to 30 miles. The men called it the Truscott Trot.

Early in June, the 3rd Division was still more than 1,000 men under-strength. Even at this stage in the war, replacements were proving to be a problem. Finally headquarters decided that the 34th Infantry Division, which was not destined to take part in Husky, should provide replacements to bring the assault divisions up to strength.

At the end of the Tunisian campaign, a rumour began among the American troops, nobody knew how or when, but it spread like wildfire. The story was that the war was over for the 1st and 34th Infantry Divisions which had fought in North Africa; other divisions were to take their place. Despite every attempt to refute the story the rumour persisted and gathered strength. But finally it emerged that instead of going home they were destined for a fresh campaign, either as an assault division or as reinforcement to another that was.

Truscott in his biography[3] stated that 'there was an intense reaction among them that required stringent measures of control'. There was in fact a near-mutiny in some units where the line officers and senior NCOs had lost all semblance of control. The 3rd Infantry Division absorbed 1,000 replacements, more than half of whom had no wish to join; all of them wanted to go home. Within days the inevitable happened. There were incidents of self-maiming when soldiers 'accidentally' shot themselves while cleaning their weapons; of course there were no witnesses.

Truscott decided on a Draconian solution to the problem. He told his subordinate commanders that the next man would be court-martialled, found guilty and sentenced to a long term in prison. An incident occurred that same night. Charges were preferred and a court convened immediately. The prisoner, who had shot himself in the hand, was tried without delay, found guilty and sentenced to 50 years in prison. The prisoner, now in a state of much greater shock than that inflicted by his wound, exercised his right of appeal to his commanding general, who was, of course, Truscott. The sentence was confirmed and read out to every soldier in the division that same day. There were no more incidents of self-inflicted wounds in the 3rd Infantry Division. Truscott had his way on another matter too: 'Never was any division more fit for combat and more in readiness to close with the enemy than the 3rd Infantry Division, when we embarked for the invasion of Sicily.'[4]

Notes

1. Ryder, *Oliver Leese*, p 136.
2. Matthews interview with Marshall.
3. Truscott, Lucien, *Command Missions*, Arno Press, New York, 1979, p 205.
4. Ibid., p 207.

8

H-Hour

The Italian sailors apparently confined their small craft to harbour and themselves to bed.

Cunningham's Official Despatch

The date and time for assault had been fixed for 10 July at 0245 hours. It was all to do with clever calculations on moonlight; it would be light enough for the airborne forces and dark enough to conceal the approach of the landing craft. It was the last time the Allies were to attempt a major amphibious operation in the middle of the night.

The convoys contained a mixture of ships. There were transports which had been custom-built for the task in hand, whilst others were converted cross-channel ferries and the like. Both, however, were involved in ship-to-shore operations which meant that they would rendezvous with landing craft at the beachheads to transport the troops ashore. In some instances the assault transports had their own landing craft, but these were few in number, and the operation was to prove a shambles. Landing craft found it next to impossible to effect a rendezvous with the motherships and there had been little time to practise disembarking techniques.

The bulk of the troops, however, were combat loaded for a shore-to-shore operation. Larger assault ships, LCTs, LSIs and LCTs loaded the troops in North Africa and Malta for delivery directly to the beachhead. This was a new technique which had its baptism at Sicily. The landing ships, large and small, were manned by hastily trained emergency commissioned officers and seamen who were still learning the job and were definitely not to be trusted out on their own. Manoeuvring in close formation was a hit-and-miss affair; enthusiastic they were, skilled they were not. One problem they encountered was that the LSTs and LCIs were both designed for beaches with much steeper gradients than that of the Sicily shoreline. This meant that they had to beach a long way out, which had tragic consequences for their heavily laden troops. Sicily was also a first for the ubiquitous DUKW.[1] This remarkable vehicle, a self-propelled lighter at sea and a medium-sized tactical truck ashore, made it possible to support a landing over open beaches without a port.

The convoys converged on Sicily from all points of the compass. Some had sailed from the United States and Great Britain, making great detours in the process to avoid the U-boat packs, for in 1943 the Battle of the Atlantic was still far from over. There were losses, not in the Atlantic, but in the Mediterranean where the Germans still had about 17 U-boats operating.[2] Three ships carrying men and supplies from the Canadian division were sunk. There were also 45 Italian submarines and even though they hadn't sunk an Allied ship in over a year, nobody was about to take any chances. Admiral Cunningham was also concerned about the Italian battle fleet. Morale, the Allies knew, was bad; the ships were short of fuel and spent all their days tied up alongside, but on paper they presented a major potential threat. There were six battleships, seven cruisers, 50 destroyers and 150 Italian and German E-boats.

Cunningham deployed his battle squadrons and accompanying carriers to protect the assault convoys for, as he states in his naval order for Husky, 'if the Italian Navy is ever going to fight, it must fight now in defence of its country.'[3]

Once the convoys were at sea officers broke open their sealed orders and briefed the troops under their command. The intelligence information they had to share was patchy and frequently wrong. Sicily was an island where maps would have been hard to come by – it did not attract many foreign visitors in the years before the war – and Italian maps, in any case, were old and inaccurate. Aerial photography was also poor and this had less to do with technology and more to do with inter-service cooperation, or in this instance its absence. Throughout the planning and preparation for Sicily at the divisional level, the naval and army staffs had worked together exceptionally well, but with the air forces it was another story and this transcended nationalities. So when the convoys sailed, divisional commanders and below had no information as to what, if any, air support they could expect on D-day.

What the divisions did possess was a list of targets in their area which the air forces would attack. But once ashore the commanders had no idea what sort of fighter cover would be provided. After D-day, divisional commanders were invited to submit requests for air support to a Target Committee, located in North Africa; such requests, no doubt submitted in triplicate, could not possibly by entertained on less than twelve hours' notice.

In contrast, there was an abundance of good, accurate intelligence on the beaches themselves and this was a result of the daring and dangerous missions conducted by beach reconnaissance teams of naval, army and Royal Marine officers (though with a large preponderance of Royal Engineers) whose task was to reconnoitre a beach, its shoreline and the immediate hinterland. Ramming 1,000 tons and more of assault ship onto a beach was a hazardous business and could be undertaken only with the help of the latest, most complete, and most detailed information. Most charts of coastal waters contained only scant information to the low-water mark, while the ordnance survey maps of the land were devoid of contours below the high-water mark. The task of COPP was to fill in the gaps. They operated in two-man teams, usually in a canoe launched from a submarine, though some were also trained as frogmen.

At this time, when amphibious operations were still in their infancy, the equipment used by a COPP team was rudimentary. Their canoes, a kind of two-man kayak, carried survey equipment, containers for soil samples, simple survey tools and a car battery. The latter was used to power a signal light if the team was acting as a beacon for a raiding party. There were also the crew's personal weapons, usually Sten submachine guns. The waterproof flashlight was an ordinary small pencil torch, encased in a condom. A couple of enamel mugs for bailing completed the stores. With so much equipment and two men to carry, the canoes were low in the water, and buoyancy 'sausages' were attached to give a little more stability. However, these could not be fastened and inflated until the canoes had been manoeuvred out of the 30-inch-wide forward torpedo hatch on the submarine. Even then, the worst moment was still to come. It was no easy thing to launch the canoe and then scramble on board from the wet and slippery saddle tank of the submarine. The whole business had to be undertaken in darkness and with a minimum of time and fuss, for no submarine captain relished being surfaced in shallow water close to an enemy shore.

For Operation Husky the COPP teams had done their work well, though most of the information was more directly relevant to the planning teams than the assault troops. Their clandestine nocturnal activities also went unnoticed, which is more than could be said for the convoys now at sea.

54

Although enemy air activity had by this time become but a shadow of its former glory, it was still not inconsiderable. The impression is frequently given that the Allies had complete command of the skies. In 1943 with the combat flying time of a Spitfire being about 30 minutes, and even less for those which were carrier-borne, there was still ample opportunity for Axis reconnaissance aircraft to carry out their missions. The airfields in Sicily had been heavily bombed and badly damaged, but fighters don't need long runways and Allied air forces' claims in Sicily, as everywhere else, were inflated by wild and unsubstantiated claims.

According to Von Senger the landings did not come as surprise. The following is an extract from the war diary of Von Senger's liaison team with Italian Sixth Army.

9 July
6.20 pm: Radio message from 2nd Fliegerkorps indicates the presence of six convoys totalling 150 to 200 vessels in the waters north of Malta and Gozo.
8.05 pm Radio for C in C Sentli: 150 landing craft at 4.30 pm in a position north of Malta, steering north.
11.15 pm Chief of Staff Italian Sixth Army to General Senger: We anticipate an attack at dawn against Catania and Gela.[4]

The Sixth Army headquarters at Enna may have been alert to the impending danger but their concern was not shared by the divisional and sector commanders. This was partly because of the method of Italian command; Guzzoni advised and coordinated rather than ordered and directed.

The other factor was the weather, for on the afternoon of 9 July there was a fierce Mediterranean storm. A north-westerly wind gusting to Gale Force 7 struck the armada when it was about twelve hours' sailing from the enemy coast. Landing craft and high-sided assault transports rolled viciously even in a gentle swell. An LCT was 200 feet long and fully loaded weighed over 800 tons. In these conditions a flat-bottomed broad-nosed landing ship had all the sea-keeping qualities of a floating grand piano. It carried a full load of five Sherman tanks, the crews of which found what shelter they could from the storm. The conditions in the packed transports and LCIs were almost indescribable. As the weather deteriorated the decks ran with vomit; the troops gave up trying to retrieve weapons and equipment from this squalid mess. Some were too ill to care and lay in their own filth; none was untouched for the fetid atmosphere in the cramped accommodation spaces induced sickness in even the strongest stomachs. Officers and men alike succumbed to this most terrible malady. One British soldier died from seasickness, his stomach ruptured from hours of racking convulsions.

General Truscott sailed with Vice Admiral Connolly USN, the naval commander of his task force, in the command ship USS *Biscayne*. The latter, a small 3,000-ton seaplane tender converted to a combined operations role was uncomfortable enough and when night fell and the storm reached a new intensity, the convoy was reduced to 2.5 knots to ease some of the suffering. It made little difference; around them were the landing craft loaded with seasick, sea-weary and thoroughly drenched soldiers who asked no more than a beach on which to land.

An hour before midnight the storm subsided as quickly as it had arisen. Admiral Cunningham was in overall charge of the naval forces, exercising command from the subterranean headquarters on Malta. The tunnels there were plagued by sand flies after two years of siege warfare, and conditions were almost as miserable as those at sea. Cunningham had received warning earlier that morning of an impending storm, but took the decision not to cancel the operation. Eisenhower was to face a similar dilemma for Normandy and he gambled, successfully as it turned out, that the weather would moderate as his forecasters predicted. Cunningham was an old seadog – he had 45 years of naval service, much of it in the Mediterranean – and he knew that such storms were of short duration. As the sea abated the armada closed to within radar range of the Sicilian coast, but the Italian operators, convinced that an invasion was impossible in such conditions, did not believe what their screens were telling them.

At dusk, Royal Navy ships sounded 'Action Stations' and the Americans went to 'General Quarters'. Seven submarines surfaced offshore to serve as beacon markers for their appointed beach sectors. Anti-clockwise, from east round to north, were HMS *Safari*, *Shakespeare*, *Seraph*, *Unrivalled*, *Unison*, *Unseen* and *Unruffled*.

Montgomery and Patton had units of amphibious shock troops at their disposal. The airborne divisions, Commandos and Rangers were invaluable in isolating beachheads and securing flanks when used properly. The Commandos and Rangers did well against paltry opposition, but the airborne operation was a shambles and, in the event, a shocking waste of skilled manpower. It was the biggest such operation since Mercury, the German assault on Crete in April 1941, and the honour of spearheading the invasion of Sicily and thereby the opening of the Second Front went to the Red Devils.

At dusk 100 American Dakotas and 30 twin-engined British

Albemarles[5] left their airfields in Tunisia as tugs pulling 147 gliders. On board were men of the 1st Battalion, The Border Regiment, 2nd Battalion, The South Staffordshire Regiment and the 9th Field Company Royal Engineers. Together they comprised 1,500 men of the 1st Airborne Landing Brigade of the 1st British Airborne Division. The gliders, American steel and fabric Wacos and the larger British all-wood Horsas, were flown by pilots of the superb Glider Pilot Regiment. The target was the vitally important Ponte Grande bridge, a bottleneck which guarded the road to Syracuse.

Two hours later, a further 230 Dakotas from the 52nd Troop Carrier Wing left adjacent fields with 3,400 paratroopers from the 81st (US) Airborne Division's 505th Regimental Combat Team (RCT); their commander was Colonel James Gavin. Their task was to seize the Piano Lupo, the high ground behind the Gela beaches which were to be assaulted by 1st (US) Infantry Division, and the airfields further inland at Ponte Olivo.

The airborne forces were poorly briefed for the operations even though Ultra intercepts had correctly identified the German divisions and their deployment. Gavin, for example, had no idea that his dropping zones were perilously close to a panzer division. The airborne operations were a calamity, brought about by a combination of circumstances. The problem with special forces is that they are expensive to raise and to train, and once in existence are under constant pressure to prove their worth, especially to a sceptical military establishment which would be just as happy if there were no so-called private armies.

In the British case, whereas the 1st Airborne Division had proved its value in the later stages of the North African campaign (it was after all the Germans who dubbed them the Red Devils because of their ferocity in battle), the concept of glider-airborne operations was untried. The divisional commander was Major General G.F. Hopkinson, a keen amateur pilot and glider enthusiast, who was convinced that glider-borne operations could be as effective as those by parachutists. Montgomery had a problem. The capture of the Ponte Grande bridge was vital to his plans and could not be left to infantry advancing out of the beachhead. He had contemplated giving the job to the commandos but Hopkinson convinced him that it was a task tailor-made for his new Air Landing Brigade. The plan was for the South Staffs to take the bridge by means of a *coup de main* while the Borders captured and held Syracuse. The plan was bold, imaginative and foolhardy for it did not take into account the capabilities of the troops. In fairness, Montgomery had his doubts about the feasibility of a glider-borne operation at night, but Hopkinson pleaded his case with skill and persistence. The planners were very surprised to learn that the normally ultra-cautious Montgomery had given approval for the operation.

In truth, Hopkinson had let his enthusiasm override his common sense. He was a classic example of a commanding officer who posed a greater threat to his men than did the enemy; there is no place in the modern battlefield for the overgrown boy scout, but the Second World War is littered with men of his ilk. Glider pilots had barely mastered their clumsy and dangerous machines in daylight – they were called flying coffins. None had flown at night. Photographs in and around the proposed landing zones revealed a rock-strewn terrain of small fields and high dry-stone walls.

On the night, both air armadas encountered 35 mph winds which buffeted them off course. Heavy Italian AA gunfire greeted their arrival and the flight formations disintegrated. Montgomery, in his memoirs, blames the tug pilots, which is also unfair. In many cases towlines were released prematurely over the sea – in some instances by the tugs, whose crews panicked and in others by glider pilots who had misjudged the distance to the shore and their landing zones. Sixty-nine gliders crashed into the sea and 252 soldiers were drowned. Of the remainder a further 59 crash-landed somewhere in southern Sicily, ten were forced back to North Africa and only twelve landed close enough to the target to affect the issue. One glider landed intact and the troops moved out to attack, only to find they were on the airfield at Malta and blocking the main runway. Another came down near the old Mareth Line in Tunisia.

The Ponte Grande bridge was assaulted and captured by just 73 Red Devils.

The Americans fared a little better. The aircrews were very inexperienced; only the lead aircraft in each squadron, for example, carried a trained navigator. The high winds and poor navigation resulted in the aircraft being disastrously off course by the time the leading echelons made a landfall over Sicily. Anti-aircraft fire broke up formations, although it accounted for only eight aircraft. The head winds and Dakotas which flew twice as fast as they were supposed to over the dropping zones liberally dispersed paratroopers over Sicily. Only one battalion landed intact – 25 miles from the target. The paratroopers did not suffer anything like the casualties of their British counterparts, but some who were captured were tortured and killed, mostly by Italian soldiers.

The commandos and Rangers had a much easier time of things. Their mission was to spearhead the seaborne assault and to seize specific targets – pillboxes, strongpoints and defensive features – ahead of the main force.

H-hour was 0245 hours on the morning of the 10 July. Captain Anthony Wilkinson was a 23-year-old troop commander in 41 Royal Marine Commando. Sicily was his first battle and he landed soaking wet and on the wrong beach, but that didn't matter. Anything was better than being seasick on the landing craft.

The voyage out hadn't been too bad. They had sailed from England in the *Durban Castle*, a Royal Mail steamship from the prewar South African run, converted into a trooper and big enough to carry the whole marine commando and a battalion of Canadians as well. They had weathered the storm in reasonable comfort, but the fun and games began when it was time to debark. The method first used on the *Durban Castle* was that the men climbed into the landing craft, which were then lowered, fully loaded, by davits, into the sea. In the heavy swell that was still running, two boats were dashed against the side of the liner; they shattered and tipped the marines into the sea. Luckily they were all wearing lifejackets and so they climbed up the scrambling nets and calmly waited their turn once more.

It was about eight miles to the shore and within minutes every one of the 30 marines in the landing craft, including Wilkinson, was as sick as a dog. Luckily the coxswain had his wits about him and found the marker to the beach, a sonic buoy placed by a COPP party earlier that evening. Unfortunately the storm had caused the buoy to drag its anchor, hence the wrong beach. By this time, however, Wilkinson couldn't care less; he had never felt so awful in all his life. 'God,' he thought, 'I can't do anything, leave alone fight.' The landing craft bottomed on a sand bank about 200 yards from the shore. The ramps came crashing down and Wilkinson, without any hesitation yelled, 'Right men, follow me,' and jumped straight into the sea. Not one gave his seasickness a second thought.

The water got deeper rather than shallower, and all the 60-man troop had to swim for the beach. They wore lifejackets but were cluttered with weapons and impedimenta of all shapes and sizes. The marines, besides extra ammunition, carried two gallons of fresh water. Officers were loaded down with large bottles of mepacrine tablets, to counter malarial mosquitoes. They also carried large bottles of Vitamin C tablets, which considering that Sicily was chock full of fruit and vegetables, made little sense.

In the eight-mile run into the shore the spearhead forces had been accompanied by a naval bombardment of awe-inspiring proportions. The battleships *Nelson*, *Rodney*, *Warspite* and *Valiant* made up for their disappointment at the non-appearance of the Italian fleet and poured broadside after broadside into the designated beachheads. Cruisers and destroyers moved closer inshore and joined in as well. The Americans had questioned the need for such a massive support, but the British, after Dieppe, were under no such illusions.

It was the ingenious British who introduced yet another new weapon at Sicily; it was called the LCT(R). These were ordinary tank landing craft with superimposed decks on which were stacked rows of rockets. Each craft carried about 1,000 five-inch rockets. These were electrically fired in salvoes by the commanding officer, usually a sublieutenant RNVR, who sheltered in a little steel cupola above the wheelhouse. Every other member of the crew jammed cotton wool in his ears and sought sanctuary below decks to avoid the sheet of flame that the rockets threw out.

The contribution of the landing craft rockets to Operation Husky lasted about four minutes, but it was devastating. The effect of the fire of 1,000 rockets in a confined area is roughly the equivalent of 30 regiments of field artillery or 30 cruisers, each with a broadside of twelve six-inch guns. The sight of these monsters in action beggars description. There is a whistling roar of a dozen express trains and trails of arching fire as salvoes hit their targets. Subsequent salvoes hit further inshore as the ship moves at three knots until all its pods are empty. The deafening thunder of hundreds of simultaneous explosions as the projectiles detonate the minefields and obliterate the defences blocks out all other sound. The Italians who manned the beach positions must have thought the Day of Judgment was upon them. It was but a foretaste of the retribution for Mussolini's rashness in declaring war three years before.

Notes

1. DUKW was a maker's code
   D – year of manufacture (1942)
   U – Amphibious
   K – All-wheel drive
   W – Dual rear axles.
2. Barnett, *Engage the Enemy More Closely*, p 636.
3. Ibid., p 636.
4. Von Senger, *Neither Fear Nor Hope*.
5. The Armstrong Whitworth Albemarles was designed as a light reconnaissance bomber but lacked the performance and armament so was pressed into service as a tug/tactical transport.

9

D-Day: The Allies Ashore

The storm of the previous day had abated, but a heavy swell remained and there was a pounding surf on a sandbar to greet the landing craft as they made the final run to the shore. The surf was more than enough to test the skills of even the most accomplished seamen, with the inevitable result that many of the smaller landing craft were swamped and some capsized. Even the coxswains of the LCTs were caught unawares. They broached and slammed into the beach broadside on. By the end of the first morning some two hundred landing craft were casualties and lay like so many whales stranded upon the shore.

One of the LCIs was carrying $2 million, which was the responsibility of Lt Colonel Ross Routh, Paymaster of the 45th (US) Infantry Division. The money, packed in six metal safes, was brought ashore with the leading echelons because in Routh's opinion, 'There are three things that if the troops can get, their morale will improve; if they get their mail, if they get good food, and if they get paid they feel like turning the work in, even if they can't spend it.'' Routh must have doubted the wisdom of those words when he came ashore that morning because the money was missing, and he had signed for it. Eventually he traced the coxswain of an LCI which carried the money; he explained that he couldn't make it through the surf so he dumped the six safes in shallow water beyond the surf. After a frantic search Routh located the boxes and salvaged the contents; the money was soaked through and close to pulp. Undaunted and highly relieved, Routh moved inland and commandeered the nearest suitable building with a large flat roof; it happened to be the local Fascist headquarters. Routh's paymaster team rigged some clothes lines on the roof and with the use of paper clips hung the dollar bills out to dry. He had the divisional police post a guard on the building; he was not going to tempt fate a second time.

There was very little enemy resistance on the first day. This was a result of the poor quality of the enemy coastal defence forces, the element of surprise and the impact of the naval bombardment. Indeed, the planners must have breathed an enormous sigh of relief at the failure of the enemy to resist, and in this sense Husky set a precedent for subsequent amphibious operations, but with unforeseen repercussions. With every amphibious landing throughout the Italian campaign the Allies failed to assess enemy intentions correctly and thereby themselves were wrong-footed. Thus Montgomery's crossing of the Straits of Messina was in anticipation of a vigorous defence when in the event the Eighth Army punched empty air. Mark Clark's landing at Salerno was a 'calculated risk' which counted on a rapid exploitation, but instead was caught in an enemy counterattack. The landings at Anzio were based upon a near-certain expectation of an immediate enemy riposte, when instead it was the Germans who were wrong-footed and so while the Allied troops dug mighty big holes and fortified the beachhead, the road to Rome lay wide open!

Anthony Wilkinson, our marine troop commander, was ashore and quickly appreciated that he was on the wrong beach. He had made a detailed study of the photographs and in the grey half light of dawn the silhouettes were all wrong. Reference to a map showed that he needed to move his troop about half a mile to the east to reach the beach on the Pachino peninsula. Wilkinson ran up the exposed beach treading rusting wire under his rubber-soled boots; he gave no more than a fleeting thought to mines – it was more important to find some cover and then regroup.

All the six troop commanders had a different instrument to rally their men; Wilkinson had a hunting horn to the sound of which B Troop came running. Their target was a gun emplacement and pillbox on the airfield at Pachino. There was not much fight in the Italians who soon signalled their desire to surrender once Wilkinson and his marines had laced their position with machine-gun and small-arms fire. The Italians filed out with their hands held high, but one concealed a small grenade which he threw at one of the Marines, a corporal. The grenade burst in his face, blew his eye out and the whole side of his face. The Marines were enraged; the corporal was a popular man in the troop and before Wilkinson could intervene every Italian in the gun position was shot dead. They made the corporal as comfortable as circumstances allowed, and a medic injected morphine to ease the pain, but he died shortly after.

B Troop moved on across the airfield and the Italians offered only token resistance from their bunkers. This took the form of small-arms fire at long range, but once the attacking troops closed in they quickly surrendered. Inevitably the Marines took casualties, with further incidents of the type quoted above. Lance Corporal Alf Branscombe was shot through the shoulder by an officer who used his own men (they were in the act of surrendering) as a shield. On this occasion the Royal Marines were more discriminating, the officer was singled out and summarily executed. This happened on the perimeter of the airfield where the grass was long. Branscombe's mates laid him down in the grass and bandaged the wound as best they could. They took his rifle with the bayonet in, pushed it into the ground and tied a scrap of shell dressing on the trigger guard and then moved on to the next objective. Branscombe lost track of the time. By now it was daylight. He heard foreign voices and he thought, 'This must be the end for me.' Then he heard someone say in English, 'Over there.'

Branscombe looked up and saw a couple of 'Royals' who were escorting a group of Italian prisoners. Two of the latter crossed hands to form a seat and carried him back to the beach and a casualty clearing station. Within hours he was on board a hospital ship lying offshore, lying between crisp white sheets en route for North Africa.

By early afternoon Oliver Leese's XXX (Br) Corps were firmly ashore and the Canadians had taken over from the Royal Marines on Pachino airfield. Even though the Italians had ploughed up the landing strip, Royal Engineers set to work and by late afternoon the field was ready to receive the first aircraft. The Highlanders in the meantime captured the town of Pachino and linked up with the leading elements of 231st Independent Brigade in the village of Noto. More than 1,000 Italians had surrendered. The majority were pressed into beach parties, unloading landing craft and carrying stretcher cases into the boats for the return journey.

General Dempsey's XIII Corps had landed on the east coast beyond Cape Passero where their progress was much slower because of some determined and accurate enemy shell fire. During the morning infantry from 50th (Br) Infantry Division captured Avola and linked up with XIII Corps in Noto. In the meantime the lead battalions from 5th (Br) Infantry Division moved first to occupy the high ground inland along which the road and railway led northwards to Syracuse.

The heaviest fighting of the day in the British sector was at the Ponte Grande bridge. By dawn a number of stragglers from the airborne disaster had found their way to the bridge. The Italian garrison had long since taken to their heels and the new owners set about defending their prize. The Italian garrison from Syracuse mounted a furious counter-attack. The bridge and its defences were raked by heavy machine-gun and mortar fire while Italian infantry supported by armoured cars made a number of determined attacks. The Red Devils, equipped only with small arms, put up a determined resistance but casualties mounted. By mid-afternoon there were 15 survivors and they had run out of ammunition. They threw their weapons in the river and surrendered. The Italians were once again in possession of the Ponte Grande, but theirs was but a fleeting moment of glory. The paratroopers who had survived were marched off in the direction of Syracuse, but their captors were ambushed by a patrol from the 2nd Battalion Northamptonshire Regiment and in turn became the captives. Half an hour later Ponte Grande was stormed by Bren-gun carriers from the 2nd Battalion Royal Scots Fusiliers, and the bridge was once again in British hands.

The battle for Ponte Grande had been a notable achievement and General Montgomery was later to give fulsome praise to the Red Devils, claiming that the possession of the bridge had saved the Eighth Army at least a week in battle.

The Americans had a much tougher time. Many of the difficulties were caused by encountering enemy defences which were still largely intact, for they had not been subjected to the same volume of naval gunfire which the British had used. Also, the German panzers were deployed very much nearer to the American beachhead. Patton, despite his idiosyncrasies, was a very orthodox officer who believed passionately in the value of tactical surprise, so much so that it was worth taking considerable risks. There was no heavy preliminary bombardment in the American sector; the warships opened fire only when the landing craft were making their final run into the beach. Mark Clark was to follow a similar path at Salerno, but against a more formidable opponent his assault battalions were to take heavy casualties.

Patton was fortunate in Sicily for the Italians offered, at best, a lacklustre defence. Even so there was more than one anxious moment. Immediately before H-hour the headquarters ship USS *Biscayne*, sailing about 7,000 yards offshore, was caught in the beams of four searchlights deployed on Monte Sole. The ship was held in the beams for about 20 minutes and, in the words of General Truscott, 'it was light enough to read a book.' But there was no other enemy reaction, and then, quite inexplicably, the lights went out; perhaps the position had been secured by the Mafia. From an Allied viewpoint the incident in itself speaks much for naval discipline; not a gun in the fleet opened fire even though the flagship was locked solid in the beams from the searchlights.

The 82nd Airborne Division was less than a year old and had barely completed its battle training. The paratroopers had been widely dispersed over southern Sicily but, undaunted, the men gathered together in small groups and proceeded to wreak havoc among the Italian coastal defence units. Pillboxes were destroyed, vehicles ambushed, telegraph wires cut and the Italians were frightened out of their wits. In the meantime about 200 paratroopers had captured the high ground at Piano Lupo which overlooked the beaches.

General Lucien Truscott had about 50,000 men under his command. Not only was there by this time his superbly trained 3rd Infantry Division, but also a regiment's worth of tanks from the 2nd (US) Armoured Division and a battalion of Rangers. Truscott's command on the left flank of the American operation had the easiest day. There were problems, nevertheless, over launching the landing craft in the dark and with the LCIs getting their gangways down; the first troops were not on shore until an hour after the official H-hour. In the event it mattered little. Resistance proved desultory and by midday Truscott was informed that all the objectives, including the small fishing port at Licata, had been secured and casualties were less than 100 men.

The 1st (US) Infantry Division had the reputation for being a cocky outfit which thought a good deal of itself and treated everybody else with contempt. There had been incidents of indiscipline in North Africa where the division had celebrated the liberation of a town in a manner which had not pleased the citizenry or their own military hierarchy. The result was that there were those in the military establishment who would not have been too displeased if the Big Red One learned a little humility in Sicily. Neither did it help that Bradley had scant respect for Terry Allen, the divisional commander, and even less for his deputy, Kermit Roosevelt, son of President Teddy Roosevelt. But the men of the Big Red One had confidence in themselves and in their leaders, which was just as well because they landed in the face of determined resistance. Behind the Italian 18th Coastal Brigade lay the Livorno Division at Caltagirone, and a panzer battlegroup from the Herman Goering Division.

Despite opposition, the Americans made progress. Elements from the 16th Regimental Combat Team linked up with the paratroopers on the Piano Lupo, but there were no heavy weapons or artillery ashore. The 26th Regimental Combat Team in the meantime captured the airstrip at Gela-Farello.

Colonel Darby commanded X Force, which comprised two battalions of his Rangers and another of Engineers. John Hummer was a 19-year-old technical sergeant in Company C 1st Ranger Battalion. He carried a 2.36-inch rocket launcher. The plan was for him to be one of the first off the boat and to be in position ready to demolish any pillbox that gave them trouble. They encountered mortar fire on the run into the beach; Company E lost a boat and everybody on it to a direct hit. Hummer's boat grounded and even before the ramp was down he had leapt over the side and up to his neck in water. The rocket launcher was battery-operated; soaking wet it was not worth a damn. It is at moments like these that you find out who your friends are; Company C lost interest in Hummer now that he was no use to them. The target was Gela. The port and its installations had been blasted by the navy immediately prior to the landing; the pier was demolished and much of the town was on fire. Civilians fled in panic through the burning streets and there were many casualties as the Italians experienced the full horror of total war. By 0800 hours, Gela was in the hands of X Force, and Darby put the 200 captured Italian coast gunners to work to quench the flames.

Before Sicily the 45th (US) Infantry had the reputation of being the best-trained division in the American Army. The one area where it was weak, however, was amphibious warfare training. The division had practised off Cape Cod, Massachusetts, the previous summer and autumn, but nothing since. It had also sailed directly from the United States. Equipment and baggage which had been loaded in the holds of the ships in New England remained that way until they could be off-loaded later in Sicily. There was no second chance to repack or make adjustments. While two regimental combat teams landed in reasonable order, a third, the 157th RCT encountered considerable confusion on the beaches; units were mixed up and the beachmasters had little chance to exert any control while it remained dark.

In war, operations almost never go to plan, and it is on occasions such as this that the responsibility for creating order out of chaos rests heavily on the shoulders of the junior leaders, young officers and sergeants. But the very men who should have been taking charge were running around like headless chickens. Once daylight came the magnitude of the problem became apparent; units of the 180th RCT, for example, came ashore eight miles north to six miles south of their designated beaches. Discipline was reasserted and the units gradually sorted themselves out. In one sector, order was restored sufficiently for one company to head inland and reach the paras on the Ponte Dirrillo, but they were the exception. It was just as well the Italians had left them in peace, for if there had been a determined defence the Thunderbirds would have suffered heavy casualties. The beachhead perimeter was thinly held by lightly armed paratroopers who could have done little to prevent a determined counterattack by tanks and infantry. The Americans were exceedingly fortunate.

By about nine o'clock in the morning the lead elements of the 45th (US) Infantry Division began to move off the beaches and inland, north and westwards to their objectives, the most important of which was a large airfield at Comiso.

Notes

1. Interview with author.

10

D-Day and Beyond: The Enemy Strikes Back

Saturday 10 July broke fine and warm; there was no wind. Admiral Bertram Ramsay was on the bridge of the headquarters ship *Antwerp*, a cross-channel packet converted to a Fighter Direction Ship. He later wrote to his wife:

> It was almost unreal to find oneself off Sicily with Etna looking down on the scene of the landings. Hundreds, literally, of ships of the largest size down to the smallest and one had to pinch oneself to make sure one was not in a dream. ... The coast looked too sleepy and peaceful. ... The opposition was surprisingly poor, but there was just sufficient to make it clear that we were really undertaking a warlike operation.[1]

The British had had a much the easier time of things. After the fall of Syracuse the evening before, Augusta was handed to them on a plate, by an act of treachery. The Italian port commander, Admiral Leonardi, radioed Sixth Army that Augusta was under direct attack from land and sea. The garrison did have the decency to tarry long enough to spike their coastal artillery and put a torch to the magazines before taking off in rapid time for Catania.

Admiral Ramsay would not have been so sanguine in his remarks had he been in Admiral Connolly's shoes and responsible for the Americans in the Western Task Force; for the enemy here – both Italian and German – were made of sterner stuff.

General Guzzoni must have despaired at some of the reports that were reaching his headquarters, especially from the German liaison officers who told of large numbers of Italian soldiers wandering about the countryside. Many members of the coastal divisions simply changed into civilian clothes and took off for their villages, others surrendered by the battalion.

Nowhere that day was Guzzoni able to respond in an organized or coordinated way to the invasion. His staff were inundated with calls from the coastal divisions and even units further inland, who were targets of the spoiling attacks from marauding bands of American and British paratroopers. The Germans, in any case, were bent on fighting their own war so the best Guzzoni could do was to order counterattacks against the more threatening developments in the vicinity of his mobile units. This meant attacking the Americans.

One Italian general had already obtained a first-hand account of events. General Truscott recounts[2] an incident where, unbeknown to him, Michael Chinigo, an accredited war correspondent, hitched a ride with the 7th Infantry and landed with the leading echelons. In the early hours of the invasion Chinigo was with a group which had reached a railway station about a mile inland, and the telephone was ringing. Chinigo, who was of Italian stock, picked up the receiver and answered: '*Pronto.*' It was the local Italian divisional commander who had been awakened by the sound of gunfire and needed reassurance that the Americans had not landed. Chinigo was able to reassure the general, who presumably returned to his bed. Elsewhere there were different reactions. It was about five o'clock that morning when the first reports of enemy parachutists in the region of Comiso and San Pietro were received at Von Senger's headquarters. Later, word arrived that gliders had landed at Augusta.

The first confirmation that landings had occurred was received just after seven. Gela was immediately identified as a danger spot and without more ado the Herman Goering Division was ordered to counterattack. General Guzzoni ordered Mobile Group E, a battle group from the Livorno Division, to advance southwards from Niscemi to Gela. The Axis counterattack was not coordinated, neither was any attempt made to synchronize the attacks and thereby reduce the effectiveness of the American defenders.

The Herman Goering Division was not ready for battle. Many of its officers, including its commander Conrath, were ex-policemen selected and given accelerated promotion because of their political loyalty, but quite unschooled in military tactics. Most of the panzer crews had only recently taken delivery of their tanks and were, in any case, experiencing problems with the brand-new Panzer V. The Tigers were mechanically

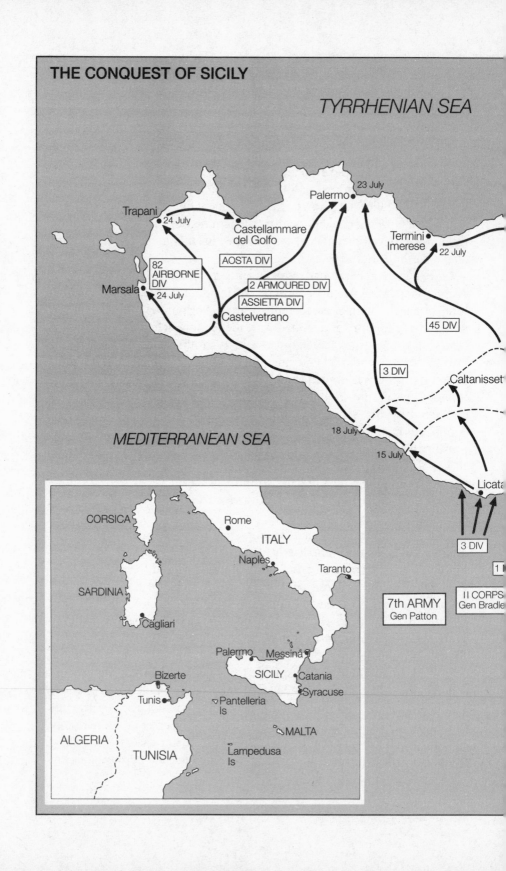

THE CONQUEST OF SICILY

TYRRHENIAN SEA

Trapani
24 July

Castellammare
del Golfo

Palermo
23 July

AOSTA DIV

Termini
Imerese
22 July

82
AIRBORNE
DIV

2 ARMOURED DIV

ASSIETTA DIV

Marsala
24 July

Castelvetrano

45 DIV

3 DIV

MEDITERRANEAN SEA

Caltanissett

18 July

15 July

Licata

3 DIV

CORSICA

Rome

ITALY

Naples

Taranto

SARDINIA

Cagliari

Palermo

Messina

SICILY

Catania

Bizerte

Pantelleria
Is

Syracuse

Tunis

MALTA

ALGERIA

TUNISIA

Lampedusa
Is

7th ARMY
Gen Patton

II CORPS
Gen Bradle

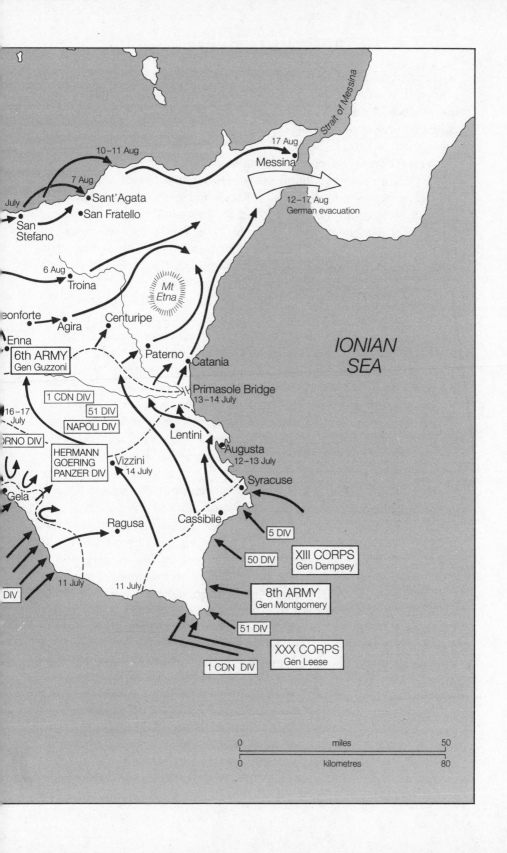

10–11 Aug

17 Aug

Strait of Messina

Messina

7 Aug

July

Sant'Agata

San Fratello

12–17 Aug
German evacuation

San
Stefano

6 Aug

Troina

Mt
Etna

eonforte

Centuripe

Agira

IONIAN
SEA

Enna

Paterno

Catania

6th ARMY
Gen Guzzoni

1 CDN DIV

Primasole Bridge
13–14 July

16–17
July

51 DIV

NAPOLI DIV

Lentini

ORNO DIV

HERMANN
GOERING
PANZER DIV

Vizzini
14 July

Augusta
12–13 July

Gela

Syracuse

5 DIV

Ragusa

Cassibile

50 DIV

XIII CORPS
Gen Dempsey

11 July

11 July

8th ARMY
Gen Montgomery

DIV

51 DIV

XXX CORPS
Gen Leese

1 CDN DIV

0   miles   50

0   kilometres   80

unreliable and prone to overheating. Conrath was a brave and resolute officer, if somewhat slow-witted. Though he planned to attack before nine o'clock, it was not until late afternoon that the attack got underway. Allied tactical strike aircraft repeatedly shot up the division's assembly areas south of Biscari. Somehow Conrath had also managed to separate his panzers from his panzer grenadiers. Unsupported tanks are very vulnerable, as Conrath found out when his columns of armour were constantly harassed in the narrow lanes by bands of American para-troopers. The result was that it fell to the Livorno Division to strike the first blow against the invaders. Their first attempt was badly disrupted on the Piano Lupo by the paras. But the Italians did not give up, and, much to American chagrin, worked their way round to outflank the defenders on Piano Lupo, and threaten the town of Gela itself.

It had been a disconsolate John Hummer who had taken part in the conquest of Gela, but now came his chance. Italian tanks and armoured cars were approaching the town and, except for some 4.2-inch mortars belonging to the Chemical Company of the Engineers, Darby's people had no fire support. The latter should have been provided by 1st (US) Infantry Division, but they were nowhere to be seen. The Rangers came across a battery of French 75-mm field guns that had been emplaced as coastal guns. Hummer was pressed into action as a gunner. He helped turn the guns round to point along the coastal road where the Italians were already in view. There were ample stocks of ammunition to hand, but the guns lacked both breechblocks and sights. A Ranger found an ordnance store nearby and the breechblocks inside, but the sights were nowhere to be seen. They fitted the breechblocks, guessed the elevation and range, and opened fire on the Italians. Darby in the meantime had found an Italian heavy machine gun which he mounted on the roof of his CP and joined the battle. Some of the Italian tanks made it into the narrow rubble-strewn streets of Gela, but, without infantry to support them, found themselves in serious trouble. Darby's Rangers engaged them with grenades, bazookas and blocks of TNT which were thrown from the rooftops. The Italians pressed on. Darby took on one tank single-handed.[3] When he found that his machine gun was of little value, he hurried down to the beach, found a 37-mm gun just unloaded, split the box of ammunition with an axe and hurried back up the hill. When he opened fire, the first round bounced off, but the second round penetrated and the tank stopped just 100 yards away. Darby then ran forward, placed a thermite grenade on the top of the tank, and roasted the crew out. Eventually the Italians fell back. There was scarcely a survivor who was unwounded.

A second attack began almost as the first died away. A battalion of infantry from the Livorno Division descended upon Gela from the north-west. Presumably the attacks were meant to be simultaneous, but the infantry were late. The latter advanced in a formal, even parade-ground manner, with no heed to the finer points of fire and movement, and paid the price. The combined fire power of X Force was now free to turn all its attention upon the luckless foe. The Italian formation was torn apart and the survivors fled in disarray.

Together with a small staff and escort Patton had left the HQ ship *Monrovia* in the Admiral's barge at about nine that morning and landed at Gela half an hour later. A scout car was provided and the General set off to visit the headquarters of 1st (US) Division about three miles to the south-east on the coast road. He stopped at Darby's CP on the way through Gela, which was fortunate, for had he continued he would have run straight into the main Italian attack.

From before dawn the beachhead and the ships offshore were subjected to frequent enemy air attacks. Allied air cover was at best patchy and depended largely on combat air patrols (CAPs) from airfields on Malta; there were bound to be gaps, and then the Stukas attacked with a vengeance.

In dawn's early light the *Benson* class destroyer USS *Maddox*, on patrol off Gela, was an early casualty to a Stuka dive bomber. A bomb must have penetrated the magazine for the destroyer exploded in flames and sank in less than two minutes. There were just 39 survivors out of the wartime complement of 250 men. Minutes after, the minesweeper USS *Sentinel* suffered a similar fate. Later in the afternoon the Liberty ship, *Robert Rowan*, loaded with a cargo of ammunition, took a direct hit. The ship was wreathed in smoke for half an hour and then suddenly it exploded in an enormous fireball that roared thousands of feet into the sky.

As far as the American and Royal Navies were concerned, it was the Luftwaffe that posed the greatest threat throughout the campaign. Besides the *Robert Rowan* and the *Sentinel* two American LCTs were sunk on D-day and that night the hospital ship *Talamba*, brilliantly lit in accordance with the Geneva convention, fell victim to air attack.

The panzers of Conrath's Herman Goering Division eventually lumbered into battle at 1400 hours. The tanks manoeuvred ineptly onto the Piano Lupo where Darby's artillery, the paratroopers and a timely reinforcement of Sherman tanks and field artillery from 1st (US) Infantry Division were sufficient to see them off. Conrath regrouped and tried again, but with insufficient infantry, the panzers were understandably fearful of the bazookas and anti-tank guns.

A third and potentially more dangerous attack was launched by panzer grenadiers who were supported by a company of the brand-new Tiger tanks. The German commanders were untried and inexperienced, with the result that the infantry and armour attacked separately. Their orders were to assault the Piano Lupo from the east. The defender of this sector was 1st Battalion 180th Infantry under Colonel William Schaefer, part of the 45th Infantry Division. The terrain in Sicily favoured the defence and made no distinction as to nationality. The Tigers found it next to impossible to manoeuvre among the terraces of olive groves and the Americans repulsed the first attack. A furious Conrath sent his divisional Chief of Staff to sort out the problem and under his goading a second attack, this time with two battalions of panzer grenadiers and the Tigers working together, proved too much for the defenders. Colonel Schaefer and his battalion were overrun and the majority were taken prisoner. More ominously the route to the beachhead now lay open to the Germans.

The 45th (US) Infantry rose to the occasion. A second battalion of infantry, this time with artillery in support, mounted an immediate counterattack. It was more than enough for the Herman Goering panzer grenadiers in their first engagement; they turned tail and fled, all the way back to Biscari. It is impossible to escape the conclusion that it was the Italians rather than the Germans who posed the greatest challenge to the Allies on D-day.

Patton met up with General Allen about two miles south of Gela and so missed the action in the afternoon, but he did return to Gela towards dusk. While on the beach awaiting a boat to take him back to *Monrovia*, he recorded in his diary[4] one of the most stupid things he had ever seen soldiers do. There were about three hundred 500-pound bombs and several tons of 20-mm ammunition piled on the sand and in between the bombs and the boxes some soldiers were digging foxholes. Patton told them, in his forthright manner, that if they wanted to save the Graves Registration Unit burial duties that was a fine thing to do, but otherwise they'd be better advised to dig elsewhere. At that moment two Me 109s came over and strafed the beach; the soldiers jumped right back into the same holes they had dug. Patton didn't say a word. He continued to walk up and down and soon shamed them into climbing out.

The Allies extended their toehold in Sicily. Truscott had the port of Licata working and throughout the night brought his tanks ashore. On the right flank the advance elements of the 45th Infantry moved further inland, linking up and sometimes taking over from paratroopers in the occupation of towns such as Vittoria and Santa Croce Camerina. One battalion captured Ragusa where they were supposed to link up with the Canadians. But there was no sign of them. One dividend in Ragusa proved to be the capture of the main telephone exchange. Italian-speaking Americans took over and were most helpful in the information they gave to worried Italian officers who telephoned unwittingly for the latest situation.

It was in the centre, Allen's 1st (US) Infantry Division, that the Americans were weak. The Piano Lupo was still only thinly held by paratroopers and infantry. The beaches had been subjected throughout the day to air strikes and long-range shellfire which had impeded the unloading of the landing craft. The result was that there were still too few tanks ashore. While the Allies tried to consolidate their hold on the beachhead, General Conrath regrouped his division and sacked his senior commanders. Bright he wasn't, but none could doubt his courage and determination as he prepared to return to the attack the next morning.

General Guzzoni conferred with Von Senger. They agreed that the Allies had completed their landings for the time being and, now that the extent of the beachhead had become apparent, it made sense to deploy all the forces at their disposal. Von Senger ordered the 15th Panzer Grenadiers to withdraw from the west, where it was deployed to counter a threat to Palermo. Kesselring in Rome objected when he was informed of the decision and advised that at least part of the division should remain to cover the beaches in the west of the island. Von Senger argued his corner and Kesselring conceded.

New orders were received in Guzzoni's headquarters at Enna. Von Senger was instructed by OKW and Kesselring that German divisions, together with those forces that the Italians could muster, should concentrate against the Americans at Gela. The intention thereafter was to advance against the Allied left flank and hit Eighth Army. Guzzoni could not agree. In his opinion the two German divisions were not strong enough to advance against two Allied armies along a front of 100 miles or more. He favoured an immediate withdrawal to new defensive positions in the forbidding country around Etna. There, he believed, it would be possible to delay the Allies long enough to arrange for the evacuation of the bulk of the forces and equipment. It was a sound plan, far more astute than Hitler's vainglorious insistence on immediate counterattacks, but he too conceded under pressure and issued orders to the Livorno Division for a maximum effort the next day.

In the German armed forces, orders to commanders in the field were obeyed to the letter. The Herman Goering Division was still in a position to attack and so Von Senger instructed Conrath to try once more at first light, again towards Gela. It would take some time before the 15th Panzer Grenadiers could be brought into the fight, but it was vital to keep the Allies off balance. On Sunday 11 July, D + 1, Conrath led his panzers against Terry Allen's 1st Division. He planned a three-pronged attack. One battalion of Panzer IVs was to drive down Highway 117 from Ponte Olivo; a second assault was to be along the road from Niscemi into Piano Lupo; the remaining Tigers with infantry in support were to attack from Biscari to the Ponte Dirillo and thence all three were to link up on the plain at Gela. Guzzoni ordered the Livorno Division to attack Gela itself from the west and, after its capture, to link up with the panzers of the Herman Goering Division for an advance on the beachhead.

The battle began at 0615 hours, shortly after daybreak, and it was to last until the afternoon. Terry Allen had prepared as best he could, moving Darby's Rangers, less two companies, onto the Piano Lupo, and a couple of battalions from 26th RCT had dug in along Route 117 between Gela and the airfield at Ponte Olivo, which was still in enemy hands. The Axis had command of the air throughout the day. Despite all the promises of the Royal Air Force, the first sortie in support of the embattled 1st (US) Infantry Division did not appear until late in the afternoon. American infantry, dug in on Route 117, held firm and the Livorno Division's attack on Gela also stalled. The main threat developed on the Piano Lupo where Conrath personally directed the battle.

Now Gavin and his paratroopers took a hand. Gavin had spent much of D-day gathering together his forces and marching across Sicily 'to the sound of the guns'; en route he collected a couple of howitzers and remnants of the 45th Infantry. Gavin struck Route 115, the Vittoria–Gela road, and took up a position on a ridge called Biazza ridge, which was tactically the western equivalent of the Piano Lupo. Gavin's ad hoc unit resisted a series of assaults by an enemy force infinitely superior in fire power and numbers, but correspondingly inferior in resolve and the quality of leadership.[5] In the meantime the Livorno Division, finding a gap in the defence, began to move on Gela. The town was defended by Captain Lyle and two companies of Rangers. Lyle called in the cruiser USS *Savannah* for fire support and devastatingly accurate 6-inch salvoes decimated the Italian formations. The Livorno Division was finished as a fighting unit.

Patton was ashore and in the thick of things at Gela, dressed as he had been the day before in polished black leather boots and burnished helmet, and wearing his two ivory-handled revolvers. He stayed with Lyle for a time before moving on to Terry Allen's CP, but on leaving instructed the young officer who was then coordinating the *Savannah*'s guns to, 'Kill every one of the bastards.'

Conrath's armour continued to probe along the Piano Lupo and some tanks got within 2,000 yards of the sea and opened fire on the beachhead. DUKWs in the anchorage loaded 105-mm howitzers from freighters in the anchorage and headed for the beach; the guns were brought into action as soon as they reached the shore. Conrath radioed Enna that the 1st (US) Infantry Division was reembarking to escape his counterattack. This is a bizarre affair which nevertheless has a ring of truth. In 1956 Guzzoni's Chief of Staff (by then General Emilio Faldella) published an account in which he stated that Sixth Army had intercepted a signal sent by Patton at 1130 hours that morning which read:

Bring the equipment on the beaches and be ready to reembark. Patton.[6]

All the American commanders have subsequently denied that Patton ever issued such an order, although the entry does appear in the Sixth Army War Diary.[7] Did Terry Allen give the order from his embattled CP? Or could it have come from a senior member of his divisional staff? Somebody on the beach sent a message to that effect on the day, and used Patton's name to give it the necessary force, even though such an order was quite unrealistic and, in the event, impossible to execute. There is no reference to the instruction in any of the American War Diaries.

It was the sheer volume of firepower plus the added metal from the *Savannah*'s sister *Boise* which saw off Conrath's panzers. The Germans were nervous before the battle and to be pulverized by a fire power against which there is no answer, namely cruisers five miles offshore, is enough to destroy the morale of the toughest troops. So while the allied air forces were conspicuous by their absence, it was naval gunfire which saved the army's bacon in the beachhead; this was to happen again and again in the Italian campaign.

As night fell on D + 2 another pattern was also established in the Italian campaign. The Allies had achieved a brilliant strategic surprise – a large-scale landing on a hostile and defended shore – only to be followed, not by a rapid exploitation inland, but by stalemate.

Notes

1. Barnett, *Engage the Enemy*, pp 644–5.
2. Truscott, *Command Missions*, p 217.
3. Three days later Patton awarded Darby the Distinguished Service Cross (DSC), the United States' second-highest award. Patton offered Darby promotion and command of a regiment in the 45th Infantry Division but he refused on the grounds that he wanted to stay with his Rangers.
4. Patton, George S., Jr, *War as I Knew It*, Bantam Books, 1947, p 55.
5. Besides 700 men of the 1st Panzer Grenadier Regiment there was a battalion of SP artillery and a company of Tiger tanks.
6. *Lo Sbarco e la Difesa della Sicila*, Rome, 1956.
7. The author also talked with senior officers of the Italian Army's Historical Office who confirmed the account.

II

Consolidation and Pursuit: After a Fashion

There was another tragedy to be played out before the passing of D + 2. Patton was sufficiently concerned about the situation in Terry Allen's sector to order in immediate reinforcements. Reuben Tucker's 504th Parachute Regiment Combat Team were selected for this honour. It was to be a night drop into DZs marked out on the Gela plain below the Piano Lupo. At dusk the lead flights from a total force of 147 Dakotas took off from their airfields in Tunisia; on board were 2,300 paratroopers. Tucker had voiced his concerns about the feasibility of a night drop and the obvious risk of the aircraft being fired upon by their own forces. His fears were brushed aside by superiors and instructions were issued for orders to be transmitted around the assembled ships and batteries on shore to expect friendly aircraft. General Matthew Ridgway, the 82nd Airborne commander was on the beachhead. He had a premonition and so visited a number of gunsites; none had received any orders. Patton independently also had second thoughts. He tried to cancel the operation but he was too late.

The packed anchorage had been on the receiving end of a German air attack just half an hour before the lead Dakotas appeared in the night sky; the gun crews were still closed up at action stations. What happened was inevitable; a single gun on one ship opened fire. As its tracer arched into the sky every anti-aircraft gun on every ship and ashore fired indiscriminately into the closely packed formations overhead; the pilots had just throttled back to begin the run into the DZ. There was carnage. Six Dakotas were shot down with their paras still on board. Some paratroopers managed to bail out, only to drown at sea. A further 37 planes, badly damaged, dropped out of formation and limped back to North Africa, carrying their dead and wounded. Some crash-landed in Sicily.

Seventeen Dakotas, having dropped their paratroopers, were shot down as they flew south over the anchorage. Sixty pilots plus air crew and 97 paratroopers were killed. Twenty-three aircraft were lost and 37 others severely damaged. Tucker survived, as did about 500 of his men, to drop reasonably close to where they intended. A further 1,200 jumped and were scattered over the length and breadth of southern Sicily.

In the recriminations that followed, everybody blamed everybody else. But the navy came in for the heaviest censure whilst the more traditional souls in the military establishment, looking at the airborne record to date in the Sicily campaign, questioned the validity of the concept itself. Too little thought was given to the prevailing battle conditions. The American anchorage had been subjected to frequent enemy air attack over the previous 48 hours and precious little had been glimpsed of a friendly aircraft. So far as the gunners were concerned, the skies were hostile. The American naval historian[1] also makes a telling point: what would have happened if the Dakotas had appeared over the beachhead in the middle of an air raid?

Kesselring flew to Sicily early the next morning to meet with Guzzoni and Von Senger at Sixth Army headquarters in Enna. Once apprised of the situation he confirmed all the decisions which had been taken and then raised the question of whether further German divisions should not be sent to Sicily. Ever the optimist, he hankered after another Dieppe. Guzzoni and Von Senger tried hard to dissuade him. Von Senger indeed emphasised that success in the campaign should now be measured by a delaying action and evacuation from the island. He expected the Allies to launch another amphibious operation, probably in the vicinity of Catania, which would give them a major port and effectively cut the road to Messina. There was also a risk that the Allies would mount a large amphibious operation into Calabria which would effectively seal the Sicilian garrison into the island; that is what Von Senger would have done had the roles been reversed.

The Italian commander was nothing if not a realist. The destruction of the Livorno Division meant that the Sixth Army had shot its bolt, at least in so far as mounting counterattacks. At best the remnants could be relied upon for field artillery, something at which the Italians had traditionally excelled, and maybe static defence if stiffened with Germans. So, eventually, a plan of action was agreed. The Axis forces were to undertake a slow and systematic withdrawal to a defence position anchored on Mount Etna and known as the San Stefano Line. The ultimate objective was evacuation, but only when the Allies had been delayed for as long as was possible.

These suggestions were despatched to Hitler who was also fully briefed on the fighting condition of the Italian Sixth Army. The decision-making process and chain of command sidelined Mussolini. The German High Command took over the running of the campaign in Sicily and Von Senger's role vis-à-vis Guzzoni changed accordingly. Unusually for Hitler at this stage of the war, his instructions made sound common sense. There was to be no last stand; Stalingrad and Tunisia had deprived the Wehrmacht of such options. But neither did OKW have any regard for Allied boldness or derring-do. Montgomery was already categorized as a 'plodder who took no risks' and the Americans were rashly dismissed as crude and shallow with no relish for a fight. So, in a calculated risk that the Allies would not land in Calabria, German reinforcements were despatched to Sicily in numbers adequate to fight the delaying actions but without jeopardizing the opportunities for evacuation.

The Germans had the measure of Montgomery. After the fall of Augusta, Eighth Army's advance was painfully slow. There were extenuating circumstances which have been quoted at length by British apologists, and these include such considerations as that the route into the Catania plain was through countryside which favoured the defence. The smoking Mount Etna was a frightening obstacle which towered above the battlefield and left the soldiers with the itchy feeling that their every move was being observed, which indeed it was. There were few opportunities for Montgomery to bring his superiority in tanks and artillery into play. Some of the airfields which had been captured were, by 15 July, beginning to deploy fighter aircraft, but by and large the Luftwaffe was still more of a threat to the Allies than the Royal Air Force was to the enemy. And finally, the bulk of the German defences were concentrated against Eighth Army because the shortest route to Messina lay up the east coast highway by way of Catania.

But it was also the case that the British and Canadian infantry battalions didn't like Sicily and found it very difficult to adjust their fighting methods. Eighth Army veterans, for example, were singularly unused to walking and without the luxury of transport found that they had to return to basics when it came to choosing what to carry and what to leave behind. There were civilians around too, more than in Tunisia, and they were proving to be a distraction in more ways than one. Even taking all of these considerations into account one cannot escape the conclusion that by D + 5 at the latest the initiative was swinging heavily in favour of the Germans. Thereafter they controlled the pace and the momentum of the battle. Their powers of recovery had been remarkable, but in this they were assisted in no small measure by British lethargy.

The Americans, in contrast, were champing at the bit. Patton had never been happy with the subordinate role foisted on him by Alexander, which he had accepted at Eisenhower's insistence for the sake of Allied fraternity. Even when some minion on Alexander's staff in an attempt to make the pill more palatable dreamed up expressions such as Patton's 'shield' to Montgomery's 'sword', it made no difference, but, 'an order was an order and he would do his goddamdest to carry it out.'

Something else was beginning to rankle with the Americans. Montgomery and the British were getting all the praise and glory. Broadcasts from BBC Overseas Services Forces Radio were full of bulletins about the exploits of the Eighth Army; there was precious little mention of the Americans.

Alexander did not have a clear idea of what to do next. Montgomery was making slow progress, but there was no pressure of time, or sense of urgency because there was no decision about what the objective would be after Sicily. Neither was Montgomery about to risk his future career and take risks in Sicily; no decisions had yet been made about the senior command appointments for North West Europe. There were plenty of rumours, however, and in sergeants' messes of the Highland Division, forever the fountainhead of credibility when it came to questions of 'what next', the word was out: after Sicily the division was off home to prepare for the real Second Front.

Latrine rumours were in full spate beyond the Sicilian shores. Corporal Alf Branscombe had been taken by hospital ship first to a field hospital in Bizerte. He then leap-frogged down the coast of North Africa to Algiers and ended up in HMS *San Angelo*, which was a Royal Navy hospital. By this time his wound had begun to heal. One day the ward sister came to him.

'Well, you should really go back to England. Unfortunately transport isn't that easy, so we suggest you rejoin your unit.'

'That's in Sicily,' replied Branscombe.

'Fine,' said the sister. 'I will arrange your discharge papers. Draw a 24-hour ration and a blanket and go down to the docks. You'll probably get a lift.'

With his arm in a sling, but still in battledress, with a blanket and rations, Alf thumbed a lift down to the docks. There was not much around so he bunked down in a warehouse which was being used by an RASC dock party – stevedores in uniform – for the night. On the second day he bumped into a Royal Marine sergeant and explained his problem. The marine was part of a gun crew[2] on a Royal Navy cruiser which was due to sail as escort for a convoy bound for Sicily. A passage was arranged and later that evening Alf joined the ship. He was given a hammock and a space in the Royal Marines' mess deck.

The convoy sailed after dark. Alf climbed into his hammock and settled down; he remembered looking up at the gleaming white ceiling before the lights went out. Hours later he woke to the call for action stations. The alarms sounded and the lights flashed. He looked up and ceiling was black. Suddenly the cruiser heeled over and increased speed and the black ceiling moved; there was a frantic scurrying and he was showered by hundreds of falling cockroaches. He made his way up on deck. Two merchant ships had been torpedoed and the cruiser stopped to pick up survivors. Later that morning the Marine sergeant sought Alf out.

'I'm sorry, but we're having to change course now. We are not going to Syracuse. We're off to India via the Suez Canal.'

Alf's face must have been a picture. 'Don't worry,' said the sergeant, 'we are stopping off at Valetta to disembark the survivors, you can leave the ship there.'

Alf left the cruiser at Valetta where life was more ordered than Algiers. He was accommodated in the Royal Marine barracks on the hill above the harbour and there he waited for a passage to Sicily. He had time to relax and enjoy Malta in midsummer. He also got his battledress cleaned up a little, but there were no replacement uniforms to be had. Malta, after all, was only just emerging from a period of prolonged siege. After three days, passage was found in an LCT bound for Sicily; on board he was joined by half-a-dozen other men from a mixture of units who were trying to rejoin their parent outfits. In those days in the Mediterranean soldiers convalescing after being wounded dreaded the prospect of being sent to the Replacement Depots. Chances of going back to their old units and their mates were slim and these camps enjoyed a notorious reputation for petty discipline and bull; the Americans had a similar arrangement.

The LCT docked in the middle of the night, and they were bundled off. There was a Bedford utility truck waiting. Branscombe, who was the senior rank, was greeted by the driver with the words, 'I am not sure how far the German line is, but I think I know where the transit camp is,' and off they went. It was a very dark night and from away over to the left came the sights and sounds of battle. The sky was lit up by the occasional bursting shell or flare, accompanied by the stutter of a machine gun and the rattle of small arms. Within minutes they had left the tiny fishing village behind and the truck bumped and swayed along a rough dirt track which wound its way into the hills. They drove without lights and Alf sat alongside the driver and peered out into the night. It was about half an hour later when the driver suddenly stopped and said, 'I think I've gone too far.' They hadn't seen a soul since the harbour and there are no night sounds in Sicily. The silence was deafening and the men were scared. It didn't help that except for the driver's Sten gun they didn't have a weapon among them.

It wasn't easy, but they managed to turn the truck round on the narrow track and headed back the way they had come. There was a fork in the track and a military directional sign was tacked to a tree. 'I know where the transit camp is, it's just over the hill,' said the driver and everybody relaxed.

The driver dropped them off at the transit camp; it seemed to be just a collection of tents. There was no guard and as far as Alf could make out there was no gate either. The others decided to bed down where they were but Alf's blood was up. It had been a long day and he had been badly scared. It was time to find someone in authority. He stumbled over a guy rope in the dark and a man came out of the tent.

'Have you got a mosquito net?' the figure asked.

'No I haven't got a mosquito net,' replied Alf. 'All I've frigging well got is a frigging blanket and what I'm standing up in.'

'Well you'd better come into my tent, it has a mosquito net.'

Alf crawled inside and laid his blanket out on the ground. 'This is a right transit camp,' he complained. 'Nobody here to see you in, no cup of tea, no frigging welcome.'

'Well, some are like that,' the man replied.

'Whoever runs this camp wants hauling over the coals,' was Alf's parting shot.

Alf slept late and when he awoke he was taken to see the Camp Commandant. It was the man with the mosquito net. Alf saluted and said, 'I've done it all wrong haven't I?'

'Not really. Not to worry, you'll be on your way in an hour.'

The quest to find 41 Royal Marine Commando wasn't over yet. Branscombe travelled across Sicily, stopped at a couple of transit camps for the night and set out the following morning with vague instructions as to where to find his unit, invariably inaccurate. One morning he was trudging down a main road on the outskirts of Catania when a vehicle passed; somebody gave a shout and the truck stopped. They were marines from his troop. Alf Branscombe was home.

Notes

1. Morison, Samuel (ed.), *Sicily–Salerno–Anzio*, Little, Brown and Company, Boston, 1975, p 120.
2. On cruisers and bigger ships the Royal Marine complement manned one of the turrets.

12

A Foretaste of Things to Come

Alf Branscombe had been away from his unit for two weeks and in that time, at least as far as the Eighth Army were concerned, waging war in Sicily had been an awful experience. Eighth Army had split their advance. Montgomery sent XXX Corps, under Oliver Leese, with the Canadians as spearhead, along Highway 124 towards Enna, an important road junction, and Sixth Army Headquarters. XIII Corps under Kirkham, in the meantime attacked along the coast road to Catania; their main opposition was battle groups from the Herman Goering Division which after D + 2 had got into its stride and was putting up a stout defence.

The infantry divisions had left the bulk of their first- and second-line transports back in North Africa, a decision soon regretted. The infantry had to march everywhere and carry most of their needs on their backs. It was hardly surprising that whatever zest there might have been for battle was quickly dissipated. Then there was the weather. It was the hottest time of the year, and in a war of infantry where everything had to be manhandled, and uphill, the temperature took its toll. Severe sunburn, blistered faces and gippy tummy from eating the local grapes to slake the men's thirst, caused acute discomfort.

The main problem was the Germans; they were simply better at defence in that terrain and climate than the Eighth Army was in attack. A foretaste of what was to come was experienced on the night of 13–14 July when yet another airborne operation was attempted. At this stage Montgomery was still confident of an early capture of Catania. The Primasole bridge which spanned the Simeto river was the vital gateway and carried the road that led from the hills into the plain of Catania. On the night in question, 1,900 men from 1st Parachute Brigade of the 1st British Airborne Division led by Brigadier Gerald Lathbury were to land in Sicily. The 2nd Battalion Parachute Regiment was commanded by Lt Colonel John Frost who recalled an inspection of his battalion by Montgomery in early July.

Afterwards, in his usual fashion, he gave them all a pep talk in which he warned that: 'There are some who think the Italians are very nasty people. My Eighth Army has killed quite a lot of them – they are easy to kill.'[1] At dusk 126 Dakotas and 19 Albermarle tugs set out from Kairouan in Tunisia to capture the bridge by parachute and glider. Montgomery told one of his ADCs about the para drop and confided, 'I shall be in Catania tomorrow morning.' After the previous tragedies every effort was made to ensure that itchy-fingered gunners in ships and on shore were fully briefed and would not open fire. What the Red Devils did not know was that the Germans had despatched the first of their own reinforcements to Sicily. Twenty-four hours earlier, in a textbook operation, 1,400 men of the 1st Parachute Regiment of the 1st Parachute Division had flown from their base in Avignon, France, to a DZ not 300 metres from that chosen by the British.

The Luftwaffe He IIIs troop carriers had flown the whole way unescorted. The lead elements of this air armada were indeed intercepted over the Straits of Messina by a squadron of American P-38 Lightnings. A massacre was avoided when the Lightnings, low on fuel, were forced to break off contact in order to reach their airfields in North Africa, and their sighting of the enemy troop transports was not reported.

Catania had been under heavy air attack from the Royal Air Force all afternoon, the skies thick with medium bombers and Spitfires hovering in close attendance. A disaster was averted because of the German timing. The drop was due to begin at a quarter past six, when the Germans knew the skies would be empty of the Royal Air Force; the latter, true to form, were always back at their airbases tucking into high tea.

The German 1st Parachute Regiment made a copybook jump and more reinforcements were to follow the next day, with supporting units being flown into Catania.

At ten o'clock on the night of 14 July the Dakotas were in sight of Sicily. The first guns to open fire were from Allied ships off the coast of Malta (presumably nobody had thought to tell them) and thereafter it was the same old story. Gunners on some of the ships moored off the Sicily beaches opened fire as did the German flak batteries. Twenty-six aircraft turned back, fully laden, for North Africa. Fourteen aircraft were shot down and the remainder so dispersed that paras and gliders landed as much as 20 miles away from their intended DZ.[2] Fewer than 200 men with three anti-tank guns reached the bridge. They were able to overpower the Italian guards and remove demolition charges which had been placed in readiness by Italian engineers. Thereafter the two paratroop forces were locked in combat. The British held out throughout the first day, the original group reinforced by stragglers who eventually found their way there. At 1730, their ammunition all but exhausted, the survivors withdrew to a ridge south of the river, from where they were able to prevent equally determined German engineers from resetting demolition charges. An hour later the situation had deteriorated even further. The German paras received the support of an 88-mm gun and there was nothing for it but to pull back to a line of hills 1,000 yards to the south. The Germans then took control of the bridge.

Relief for the Red Devils in the form of a brigade of Durhams from 50th British Infantry Division was making very slow progress. They were constantly harried and blocked by a skilful rearguard action mounted by the Herman Goering Division, who had successfully frustrated the British ever since the fall of Syracuse. The footsore Durhams eventually put in an appearance, but after marching 20 miles that day in 95-degree temperatures they were in no fit state to mount an immediate attack. One company went to help. Sherman tanks from 44 Royal Tank Regiment also turned up. These were in radio contact with the cruiser HMS *Newfoundland* which was able to put down withering broadsides which kept the Germans at bay.

When the Durhams took over from the paras the siege of Catania began. It was to take the three battalions of the brigade and their armoured support three attempts and 48 hours to clear the 1st Parachute Regiment from the Primasole bridge. It cost the brigade 500 men to clear 1,000 yards of ground. Although horrifying at the time, such casualty statistics were not out of place in subsequent battles on the Italian mainland.

On 16 July Hitler gave orders for further reinforcements to move into Sicily and a well-oiled contingency plan swung into action. The German defence of the island was in the hands of Headquarters XIV Corps which had been deployed into Calabria back in June, ready to cover Sicily should the Allies invade. Its commander, the one-armed[3] Prussian General der Panzertruppen Hans Valentin Hube assumed control. (Von Senger continued to coordinate affairs with Sixth Army.) Hube had been a panzer commander on the Eastern Front and was one of the best exponents of tank warfare in the Wehrmacht.

Further reinforcements were provided. The remainder of the 1st Parachute Division arrived from Avignon; the 29th Panzer Grenadiers crossed from Calabria. The arrival of German battalions without their own means of transport resulted in a number of serious clashes with Italian units. The German battalion commanders had been ordered to motorize themselves by taking over the vehicles of those Italian troops that were no longer fighting. This led to some shooting and casualties on both sides. Kesselring ordered the numerous Luftwaffe flak batteries which defended the airfields into action as field artillery. Smiling Albert, as ever optimistic, had briefed Hube that with all those forces at his disposal he should be able to counterattack and drive the Allies into the sea.

All Hube could do was to consolidate his defence around Catania, and anchor the Etna line to allow a progressive withdrawal from inland before an eventual evacuation. Hube was no diplomat and made it abundantly clear to Guzzoni in one of their very few meetings that all the command decisions to be taken in Sicily would be German. There was nothing that Guzzoni could do. The strategic direction now became the responsibility of Kesselring as C-in-C South rather than Commando Supremo in Rome, and the tactical battle was in Hube's hands. There were still substantial numbers of Italians, mostly in coastal units, but the Italian Sixth Army Command henceforth played only a token role. It still issued administrative instructions and received reports, but these were more concerned with ration returns than the battle.

Montgomery pressed XIII Corps to continue the attack. Catania, with its airfields and deep-water port was essential. But movement on a large scale could be observed from the slopes of Mt Etna, and Hube by this time had sufficient forces for his needs. Attacks by both 5th and 50th Infantry Divisions were blunted by the paras and the now improved Herman Goering Division. Thwarted, Montgomery made the classic blunder of dividing his forces. Instead of bringing XXX Corps into the line and hitting the Germans with an overwhelming superiority of fire power, he sent Leese off around the west of Mount Etna with the intention of delivering a long left hook behind the defences at Catania.

After a week of constant action, battle-weariness had set in. The 78th British Infantry, the Battleaxe Division, held in reserve in North Africa, was deployed to Sicily and joined Leese. Eighth Army now had five divisions and brigade groups against elements of four German divisions and those Italians who cared to join the party. These were hardly overwhelming odds.

Alexander was having his problems too. The Royal Navy lost his signal section when they moved the Army Group headquarters from Malta to its new location in Cassibile. The signals section was landed, by mistake, at

Gela. When Alexander found out what had happened, he was hopping mad, and sent an abrupt signal to Admiral Cunningham demanding action.[4] Cunningham came to see Alexander in person and said: 'General, I received your telegram. Do you know what I do with telegrams like that? I throw them in the bloody waste basket. There was some piffling little mistake about signals, but I don't have to take that sort of message from you.'

Alexander looked at Cunningham and said, 'Well Admiral, we're going to have a big scrap if you don't get back my signals to me here.'

Patton also gave Alexander a hard time. The Americans had seized all their objectives and their commander was restless. He disliked the idea of playing second fiddle to Montgomery while the latter gathered all the laurels. Palermo drew Patton like a lodestar.

It was 100 miles to Palermo, partly through mountains. What Patton had in mind was to break through the mountains with his infantry whereupon he would then commit the 2nd (US) Armoured Division in a spectacular sweep to capture Palermo. This would be touted as the first great exploit of American armour.[5] Truscott was brought into the plot and immediately recognized two things. Firstly that the slog through the mountains would fall to his infantry and secondly the armour would thereafter encounter little but demolitions.

Patton had his staff present the plan to Fifteenth Army Group. On the first occasion, which was on 16 July, Alexander's decision was that Patton should continue his secondary role until the Eighth Army had secured a firm line. Alexander was afraid that if Patton pushed out prematurely all over the western end of the island the Germans might then step between the two and drive in on Eighth Army's flank.

Patton, never a man to take no for an answer, especially second-hand, went to see Alexander in person: 'General, I do hope that I am not going to have to stay in this defensive role, am I? I want to get on with it and push out.' Alexander explained his thinking. Patton listened, drew himself up and with a look like thunder on his face said, 'Yes, General,' saluted, spun on the balls of his highly polished boots and abruptly left the room.

A number of factors conspired to force Alexander to reassess the situation. It was clear that he would be unable to keep a rein on Patton. If he waited too long to give the order, he must have feared that old blood and guts would say, 'to hell with this,' and push out anyway.[6]

Another problem was that by 16 July the Eighth Army advance had slowed to a crawl and Montgomery's decision to do a left hook around Etna had left the important town of Enna exposed. Relations between the

British and Americans had also been soured by squabbles over ownership of roads. There might be merit in allowing 'Georgie' to push on and cut the island in two at San Stefano di Camastra, thereby isolating the enemy in the western part of the island. Then Patton could drive on Palermo and clear up in the west. The capture of Palermo would give the Seventh Army a port, thus improving its logistical situation. Currently it was still reliant on the British port at Syracuse and this had led to other unfortunate incidents over unloading schedules.

Lastly, once the island had been cut, Alexander reasoned that there was every advantage to be gained by striking along the north coast road and the inland road, Troina–Randazzo, to drive the enemy back to Messina. This drive by Seventh Army would help take the pressure off Eighth Army in the siege of Catania. However, one look at the map shows that a concentrated thrust through the middle of the island via Enna to Troina and Randazzo would isolate the western part in any case, making an armoured thrust on Palermo unnecessary. But Georgie had to be placated, so Alexander gave him a directive which required a drive up the centre of the island along the axis outlined above, and the opportunity to exploit to the west. In a typical British compromise it was not made clear which mission had priority.

Truscott was under no illusions. He was convinced that Patton's obsession with Palermo was not merely to emulate Rommel's reputation as a leader of armour, but to exceed it and rub Montgomery's nose in the dirt at the same time.

Patton quickly swung into action. He had already brought the remainder of the 2nd (US) Armoured Division ashore and had it reunited with Combat Command B. He formed a Provisional Corps under General Geoffrey Keyes with the 3rd (US) infantry and elements of the Rangers to blast the route through the mountains. In the meantime 45th (US) Infantry and 1st (US) Infantry in Bradley's II Corps were despatched up the spine towards Enna.

Truscott could see little virtue in an operation which was to take American troops away from the main centre of enemy resistance, but he also determined, in such an exercise in futility, to beat the armour into Palermo. The advance began on 19 July; the fitness training and route-marching which the 3rd had undertaken in North Africa now paid dividends. In blistering heat and stifling dust, the battalions marched at a rate which exceeded that of a Roman Legion. On the second day even the Rangers had fallen behind, complaining of exhaustion.

There were an estimated 16,000 Italian soldiers in this part of Sicily and there was some resistance and demolition, but the speed and momentum of the advance caused confusion even amongst those Italians who were determined to put up a fight. The vast majority, however, were weary of war, hated the Germans, and surrendered in such numbers that it was embarrassing.

Truscott wrote to his wife:

> This is a most interesting island – and in ways unexpected to me. I have never seen so much poverty and filth. Natives are obviously but a jump ahead of starvation. Seeing this, I can understand the growth of our slum districts in cities like Chicago and New York. The country seems to be predominantly agricultural, but at least 95% of the population lives in the towns and villages. These towns nearly all date from medieval days, houses are usually of stone, close packed between narrow streets and filled with unwashed women, children and men living and playing in the filth of the barnyards which are the streets.[7]

On the morning of 22 July advance elements of the 3rd (US) Infantry looked from the high ground onto Palermo. There was no resistance but explosions could be seen in the city which meant that Germans were destroying installations.

Truscott radioed Seventh Army repeatedly throughout the afternoon for permission to enter the city. Permission was refused. Patton was still some way behind with his beloved armour and to him alone was to fall the honour of leading American troops into the first European city to fall. Later in the afternoon a delegation from the city came and offered to surrender the city. They implored the Americans to come and prevent the Germans from destroying the port and looting the city of its treasures.

Truscott tried another ploy. He radioed General Keyes, a more reasonable man, and explained the situation. Keyes instructed Truscott to send in small reconnaissance parties to the city to protect the port. And Truscott wisely decided to bivouac outside the city limits. At 2230 that night Patton drove into the city of Palermo at the head of an armoured column. He encountered two battalions' worth of 3rd (US) Infantry patrolling the streets.

The next morning Truscott was ordered to report to Patton, in his quickly established headquarters in the Royal Palace. The greeting was gruff and yet good-humoured: 'Well, the Truscott Trot sure got us here in a damn hurry.'

Notes

1. War Diary PRO (WO/169/10344).
2. Frost had been a consistent critic of what he regarded as the very poor use made of airborne troops. He has always maintained that the correct solution would have been to drop the whole division on the plain before Catania at H-hour of D-day; the port and its airfield would have been in Allied hands from the outset.
3. He had been badly wounded at the Battle of the Marne in 1914.
4. Matthews interview with Alexander.
5. Truscott, *Command Missions*, p 227.
6. Although in the Matthews interview Alexander states: 'George Patton was too loyal to have disobeyed my order.'
7. Truscott, *Command Missions*, p 227.

13

A Crooked Deal

For the Allies, force projection in the Mediterranean was warfare at a distance. The long exterior lines of communication stretched all the way back to Britain and North America. In July 1943 to sustain that war effort required some 900 merchant ships and countless escorts to convoy them through waters threatened by U-boats. The Americans, with their eyes set firmly on North West Europe and with the competing needs of the Pacific very much in mind, were more aware of the effect that this supposedly secondary theatre of operations was having on the main priorities.

Even so, as the Sicilian campaign spluttered to its inevitable conclusion, much hot air had been expended in deciding where next to attack. One option that was given serious consideration was the invasion of Sardinia. This was certainly favoured by Eisenhower and Cunningham and was considered a strong enough candidate for Mark Clark's Fifth Army to be tasked with the preparation of detailed plans. Confusing the issues were the top-heavy and politically tortuous command structure in the Mediterranean Theatre and the presence of powerful personalities and prima-donna generals alongside weaker men in other responsible positions.

But where next? This was the dilemma that filled the agendas of innumerable conferences and strategy meetings that spanned two summits – Washington in May and Quebec in August 1943. At whatever level the discussion was engaged in, the British and Americans could not agree. Churchill, whose influence in the Mediterranean had always been significant, was now becoming more intrusive and, much to the chagrin of the Americans, found the Balkans particularly attractive. A campaign there would, in his judgement, deny the Germans vital raw materials, menace Axis lines of communication to the Russian front, demoralize Hitler's eastern satellites and encourage insurrection in Greece as well as in Yugoslavia and even bring Turkey into the war.

Washington was not impressed, but they did not have anything to recommend in its place. Marshall and his team, however, were convinced of one thing: no new campaign should erode the resources already earmarked for the Second Front – North West Europe – nor undermine a vigorous pursuit of the war in the Far East. The Americans were anxious to close down the northern shores of the Mediterranean as an active theatre of operations. Some saw it as a military cul-de-sac. Marshall viewed the Mediterranean as a leech sucking up American manpower and resources. The figures spoke for themselves; by July 1943 the United States had a third of a million troops in the theatre and less than 60,000 in England. In the ledger of grand strategy the liabilities far outweighed the assets.

On 24 July and after a particularly heavy Allied air raid on Rome, a majority on the Fascist Grand Council passed what was in effect a vote of no confidence in Mussolini. Ousted from power, all of Il Duce's authority and functions reverted to the Crown. The Fascist Grand Council, overawed by the gravity of their action, left the meeting in silence. None slept at home that night.

Meanwhile, the arrest of Mussolini was being quietly arranged. The Duke of Acquarone, the Court Minister, sent instructions to General Vittorio Ambrosio, Head of Commando Supremo, whose deputies and trusted agents in the police and the Carabinieri acted forthwith. The key telephone exchanges, the police headquarters and the offices of the Minister of the Interior were quietly and unobtrusively taken over. A small force of military police was posted out of sight near the Royal Villa.

Mussolini spent the morning of Sunday 25 July in his office and visited some areas in Rome which had suffered in the recent bombing. He asked to see the King and was granted an audience at five o'clock. Mussolini had no real grasp of the seriousness of his position:

I thought the King would withdraw his delegation of authority of 10 June 1940 concerning the command of the armed forces, a command which I had for some time past been thinking of relinquishing. I entered the villa therefore with a mind completely free from any foreboding, in a state which, looking back on it, might really be called unsuspecting.[1]

On reaching the royal abode, he noticed that there were everywhere reinforcements of Carabinieri. The King, in marshal's uniform, stood in the doorway. The two men entered the drawing room. The King said:

> My dear Duce, it's no longer any good. Italy has gone to pieces. Army morale is at rock bottom. The soldiers don't want to fight any more.... At this moment you are the most hated man in Italy. You can no longer count on more than one friend. You have one friend left, and I am he. That is why I tell you that you need have no fears for your personal safety, for which I will ensure protection.

Mussolini replied:

> You are taking an extremely grave decision. A crisis at this moment would mean making the people think that peace was in sight, once the man who declared war had been dismissed.

The King accompanied Mussolini to the door. 'His face,' says Mussolini, 'was livid and he looked smaller than ever, almost dwarfish. He shook my hands and went in again.'

Mussolini descended the few steps and walked towards his car. Suddenly a captain of Carabinieri stopped him and said, 'His Majesty has charged me with the protection of your person.' The officer led Mussolini towards an ambulance standing nearby. He got in and was joined by his secretary. A number of Carabinieri and plain-clothes police squeezed in; two sat next to the rear doors. They were carrying submachine guns.

The elderly Marshal Pietro Badoglio, an opponent of Mussolini, was invited by the King to form a new administration. Badoglio was 72 years old and had enjoyed a long and distinguished military career. He was Chief of the General Staff at the end of the First World War, was governor of Libya and had led Italian troops in the war against Ethiopia. Never a fan of the Fascists, he opposed Italy's entry into the Second World War and resigned from active duty.

Two days after his appointment, Badoglio disposed of Mussolini. Il Duce was taken to be interned on the island of Ponza, some 30 miles off the Gulf of Gaeta on the west coast. The new government, which did not include a single prominent Fascist, authorized Badoglio to open secret negotiations with the Allies. The Anglo-Americans, by entering into that dialogue, immediately surrendered the initiative to their opponents.

The Allies were, however, one jump ahead of the would-be conspirators. Ever since the victory in North Africa, the British Foreign Office and American State Department had been collaborating on the drafting of a surrender document. The project was not going well and there were major differences, with the British demanding much harsher conditions than the Americans considered necessary. News of Mussolini's fall was received in London on 26 July and the Prime Minister lost no time in wiring Roosevelt on the possible opportunities it presented:

> Changes announced in Italy probably portend peace proposals. Let us consult together so as to take joint action. The present stage may only be transition. But anyhow Hitler will feel very lonely when Mussolini is down and out. No one can be quite sure this may not go further.[2]

Roosevelt had already heard the news and penned his own thoughts. Their telegrams crossed:

> the news from Rome came, but this time it seems to be true. If any overtures come we must be certain of the use of all Italian territory and transportation against the Germans in the north and against the whole Balkan Peninsula, as well as the use of airfields of all kinds. . . . It is my thought that we should come as close as possible to unconditional surrender followed by good treatment of the Italian populace. But I think also that the Head Devil should be surrendered together with his chief partners in crime. In no event should our officers in the field fix on any general terms without your approval and mine. Let me have your thoughts.[3]

Even while the two leaders were exchanging thoughts Eisenhower acted. On 27 July he made a broadcast to the Italian people which had been vetted by Murphy and Harold Macmillan, his political advisers.

> We commend the Italian people on ridding themselves of Mussolini, the man who involved them in war as the tool of Hitler and brought them to the verge of disaster. The greatest obstacle which divided the Italian people from the United Nations has been removed by the Italians themselves. The only remaining obstacle on the road to honourable peace is the German aggressor who is still on Italian soil. You want peace. You can have it immediately. We are coming to you as Liberators. Your part is to cease immediately any assistance to the German Military Forces in your country. If you do this we will rid you of the Germans and deliver you from the horrors of war. As you have already seen in Sicily our occupation will be mild and beneficent. Your men will return to their normal life and to their productive avocations and, provided all British and Allied prisoners now in your hands are restored safely

to us and not taken away to Germany, the hundreds of thousands of Italian prisoners captured by us in Tunisia and Sicily will return to the countless Italian homes who long for them. The ancient liberties and traditions of your country will be restored.[4]

Whose responsibility would it be to handle any negotiations with the Italians? Eisenhower must have regretted the invention of the telegraph. In the days of sail his political masters would have had no chance other than to allow him free reign to strike what deal he could with a beaten foe. But now he had to communicate with London and Washington, and they with one another before an answer was forthcoming.

Marshall and the American Chiefs of Staff backed Eisenhower when he complained of the delay. Lord Halifax (the British Ambassador) reported from Washington that Marshall's view was that Eisenhower must be able to take advantage of an offer of surrender to make immediate military dispositions. He might for instance want to send several divisions into Rome at once, and even a nominal continuation of hostilities might prevent this.

The Allied leaders indulged in much wild speculation – the Italians would allow the Germans to leave, or would prevent them from leaving or indeed the Germans would choose to leave. Churchill got tetchy with Eisenhower for assuming that an overture would come to him, for the Italians might just as easily make an approach via the Vatican, Switzerland or Portugal. Anthony Eden got upset with Cordell Hull at the State Department and Churchill became angry with Eden for being too finicky over the legality of an Italian armistice. All of this occurred before the Italians had even made an approach.

Amid all of this only one man gave any thought to what the Germans might have in mind – George Marshall: 'In this very connection it must be remembered that in North Africa a relatively small German garrison had produced a serious factor of delay to our operations. A German decision to support Italy might make intended operations extremely difficult and time-consuming.'[5] It is quite astonishing, but in all the official documents and papers which are now available, as well as the memoirs and biographies of the notables, there is no other reference at this time to any consideration of the fighting qualities of the Germans.

Flights into the realms of fantasy continued until 4 August when Churchill left on the *Queen Mary* for the Quadrant Conference at Quebec. The Italian surrender seduced the British into producing strong arguments to support a limited operation on the Italian mainland and the Americans succumbed to British pressure.

Meanwhile Badoglio was assuring the Germans that nothing had changed. Thus on the day he was appointed he made the following proclamation to the Italian people:

Italians! By order of His Majesty the King Emperor, I today assume the military government of the country with full powers. The war goes on. Italy, hit hard in her invaded provinces, in her destroyed cities, maintains her given word, a jealous guardian of her thousand-year tradition. Let the ranks be serried around His Majesty the King Emperor, a living image of the Fatherland, an example for all. The order I have received is clear and precise and it will be carried out scrupulously and whoever cherishes illusions of being able to disrupt normal development or trying to disturb public order, will be inexorably punished.

Long live Italy, Long live the King.

Signed, Marshal of Italy Pietro Badoglio
Rome: July 25th, 1943[6]

The announcement, which was published in numerous London newspapers and armed forces newspapers in the Mediterranean, was also accompanied by columns of speculation about when the Allies would invade mainland Italy. So what happened subsequently could hardly have come as a surprise to the Germans.

The Italian people and the Germans were united in their response to Badoglio's proclamation. No-one believed a word of it. The German High Command had been refining a contingency plan *Fall Achse* (Axis Project) which had been in place since about May 1943 and had two scenarios. The first assumed an Allied invasion while Italy was still an ally of Berlin, which would create enormous problems and entail some sacrifice of German manpower. A second scenario worked on the premise that the Allies would invade after the Italian capitulation at which point Germans in the south would retire rapidly on Rome.

At about the same time that Badoglio made his announcement Kesselring convinced Hitler that there was every reason to attempt a defence of Italy south of Rome. Even though the latter grumbled that: 'That fellow Kesselring is too honest for those born traitors (the Italian politicians) down there.'[7]

Hitler acceded to Kesselring on two counts. The first was the sheer impracticality of evacuating territory south of Rome without abandoning large numbers of German troops and significant quantities of war materiel. Secondly he recognized the importance of the airfield complex around Foggia. Accordingly the German General Staff issued a further amendment to Fall Achse. The decision to hold and defend south of Rome was implemented in terms of the tactical planning and preparations; thus the first steps were taken which were to result in the terrible winter battles for the Rapido, the Liri Valley, Cassino and Anzio.

The Germans and the Anglo-Americans had something else in common – a concern that King Victor Emmanuel and his new Prime Minister were consummate conspirators and opportunists whose primary concern was not the well-being of the Italian people but the survival of the Royal House of Savoy. There can be little doubt that this odious pair duped Kesselring into believing that he could rely on the full support of the new administration, the armed forces and the people, come the day when the Allies invaded.

The Italian surrender must go down as one of the most bizarre and mismanaged episodes in the history of modern war. The Italians wanted to have their cake and eat it; they wanted to surrender, swap sides and become a co-belligerent with the Allies. The secret negotiations began with emissaries sent to neutral Lisbon, and later to Allied-occupied Sicily. The latter required that Italian aircraft should be granted safe conduct so that they could land on an Allied airfield without the gunners opening fire, and that was no mean achievement.

The Italians believed they had proved their worth simply by ditching Mussolini. But what the emissaries at the time (and Italians subsequently, who blame the Allies for their lack of trust) failed to appreciate was the sheer loathing in which their nation was held, especially by the British. The Americans were perhaps a little more ambivalent; there was, after all, a substantial Italian electorate at home which would doubtless welcome the emergence of Italy as an ally rather than as an enemy. But the overriding consideration was that the Allies could not have stomached an immediate embrace of an old adversary; and it was dangerously naive for the Italians to have imagined otherwise.

The Italian game plan was simple. They asked the Anglo-Americans to invade, giving Rome good reason to surrender. The Germans, seeing the Italian dilemma, would accept the status quo and not exact revenge for such treachery. In a sense the Italians were trying for a repeat of the Vichy French capitulation in North Africa, but from the outset were hopelessly optimistic both in their assessment of the forces the Allies would commit for their protection and the degree to which they would share their intentions.

If there was such unease and indeed revulsion at dealing with turncoats, why did the Allies bother? Because Italian capitulation could be orchestrated to fit into Allied plans. There were, after all, some 61 Italian divisions in the field; many were on static guard, line-of-communications and garrison duties in the Balkans and France. They would have to be replaced with German manpower. A British assessment which was widely accepted was that the Germans would be forced to deploy some 24 divisions into the Mediterranean region, drawing some from the Eastern Front.

It was Eisenhower who reconciled the differing Anglo-American views. He recommended to his masters in London and Washington a limited Italian front. The purpose would be to deploy strategic bombers to the airfields at Foggia and thereby to launch a new air offensive on Germany from the south. But fleets of bombers needed considerable resources to sustain their effort, so a major port would be required to supply them and the divisions needed to defend them. Naples was the obvious choice. The operation was code-named Avalanche.

Plans which Fifth Army had worked on were refined to risk nine divisions to hold Italy while the air forces were deployed. On 14 August Churchill and Roosevelt, together with their military staffs and advisers, met at Quebec for what became known as the Quadrant Conference. There was, as always, plenty of wheeling and dealing, but the Americans were better organized for handling the tricky British this time and Roosevelt and Marshall triumphed. The conference reaffirmed 1 May 1944 as the date for the invasion of Normandy, and all other operations in Europe were subordinated to that aim. Eisenhower was instructed to accept the unconditional surrender of the Italians, to capture Sardinia and Corsica and to keep the pressure on the Germans. On 17 August, D-day for Avalanche was confirmed as 9 September and the landing would be in the Bay of Salerno, some 40 miles south of Naples.

There was one area of general agreement. Not even the British contemplated the invasion of the very tip of southern Italy as a prelude to the capture of the whole country; but they must have left Washington at least mildly satisfied that a continued military presence in Italy kept open the Balkan options. A limited sortie into Italy was also a recognition of the resources available in what remained of the campaign season before the onset of winter prevented amphibious operations.

Marshall was prepared to risk nine divisions to hold southern Italy while getting the Allied forces deployed. All the Americans wanted in Italy was a safe position to cover the airbases at Foggia and to tie down some German strength. It was a strategy of limited liability but, as President

Johnson was to find in the case of Vietnam 30 years later, what happens when these limits are reached? Long after the invasion of Italy had occurred, Marshall received a letter from his old professor, Matthew Hull, warning him that neither Napoleon nor Lee would have gone into Italy from the south.[8] This was the only time during the war that Marshall bothered to explain American strategy to a member of the general public, and this was because Hull was his old professor. In his reply Marshall listed the troops, supplies and installations that had to be taken into Italy and ended by writing that: 'Napoleon never had to do that, neither did Lee, nor Grant for that matter.'

Notes

1. CAB 101/144.
2. Ibid.
3. Ibid.
4. Ibid., pp 65–6.
5. Howard, Michael, *Grand Strategy*, Vol IV, Weidenfeld and Nicolson, 1968.
6. The *Star*, London, 26 July 1943.
7. Adleman and Walton, *Rome Fell Today*, p 77.
8. Matthews/Marshall interview.

14

The End of the Beginning

Constraining military options was the American insistence that nothing
should be undertaken in Italy which would put at risk the mounting of
Operation Overlord on 1 May 1944.[1] This in turn meant that divisions
which were earmarked to spearhead the Normandy invasion by virtue of
their combat experience in the Mediterranean would need to move back
to England by a deadline set at mid-October. More importantly, they
could not be risked in battle after the Sicilian campaign was over. Of equal
concern were all the other military assets, not least the landing craft which
would have to make the long voyage home before the onset of the winter
gales. Marshall stuck resolutely to his decision that nine divisions and no
more would be spared for an Italian adventure.

Operation Pointblank was the code-name given for the Anglo-
American bomber offensive launched from England:

> to accomplish the progressive destruction and dislocation of the German
> military, industrial and economic system and the undermining of the morale
> of the German people to a point where the capacity for armed resistance is
> fatally weakened . . . so as to permit initiation of the final combined operations
> on the continent.[2]

At the Quebec Summit Pointblank was specifically declared to be the
primary pre-invasion effort against Germany.

The most immediate influence of the Quebec Summit on the
Mediterranean was the withdrawal or transfer of six heavy bomber groups
for England. Eisenhower fought hard to retain them. He clashed with
General Ira Eaker, who commanded US Eighth Air Force, and even took
issue with Marshall, but to no avail. Eisenhower believed that bombers

had a vital role to play in supporting amphibious operations. The longer-range bombers kept options open for landings as far north as the Gulf of Genoa; their loss constrained the choice to objectives nearer to Sicily and North Africa such as Salerno and Taranto.

First of all, however, the war had to be won in Sicily. The German defences around Mount Etna have been likened to the lines of Torres Vedras. For close on three weeks Montgomery battered in vain against them. It would have been different had the Allies despatched a division or so into the mountains of southern Calabria to disrupt the German lines of communication. Airborne troops, Commandos and Rangers, most of whom were unemployed at this time, were tailor-made for such a role. A secure Calabria was essential for the Germans as the base from which they could mount the evacuation of Sicily.

The Germans could not understand why the Allies did not seize the opportunity. Generaloberst Heinrich von Vietinghoff, about to command the newly formed German Tenth Army in Southern Italy, maintained it was:

> a costly mistake not to have attempted an invasion of Calabria prior to the end of the Sicily Campaign. From the German standpoint it is incomprehensible that the Allies did not seize the Straits of Messina, either at the same time as the invasion or in the course of the initial actions, just as soon as the Germans troops were contained. On both sides of the Straits – not only in the north-east corner of the island but in southern Calabria as well – this would have been possible without any special difficulty.[3]

In many respects too, the Eighth Army's gradual fall from grace during the Sicilian campaign was a reflection of the shifting balance in Anglo-American relations. The campaign had begun with Eighth Army in the driving seat and very much the senior partner. After Montgomery failed to take Catania as promised, Alexander placed the Seventh Army on an equal footing and allowed Patton to drive for Palermo. Thereafter the race for Messina was on, and although Patton did not cover himself with the glory his apologists would have us believe, the American Seventh Army was the first there. It was a moral victory and pointed to an American superiority over the British. Messina fell on 17 August and, from that day onwards, it was the Americans who were in the driving seat and Britain the junior partner. What is less understandable is how the Germans were able to evacuate not only most of their own forces – some had to be sacrificed in the final rearguard – but also the bulk of those Italians who were interested in crossing over to the mainland.

The evacuation came as no surprise to the Allies. On 31 July a unit of the Eighth Army shot a German officer who had in his possession a briefcase full of marked maps and detailed instructions on the final defence of Sicily and the subsequent evacuation. The briefcase was in Montgomery's hands that same evening. Alexander came to the former's Command Post and warnings were despatched to Tedder and Cunningham. The Germans escaped from Sicily with nearly all their military impedimenta, heavy artillery, first- and second-line transport and much else besides.[4] No German soldier was allowed to board an evacuation ferry without his personal weapons. If the British had tried that on the beaches at Dunkirk, the navy could have gone home early.

In the face of overwhelming odds the Germans made a brilliantly designed and executed withdrawal. It was something they were to do time and again in the Italian campaign, until the very last retreat of all, when they were to suffer a defeat as complete as any inflicted. But by that time it didn't matter for the war was well and truly lost.

The Allies allowed the Germans to escape. This was not the fault of the armies who had striven valiantly to prise the Germans loose. The failure lay with the navy and the air forces to interdict the Straits of Messina and the hinterland. The waters were shallow and mined, and the shores were lined with batteries of anti-aircraft guns, but there was, even so, a fundamental failure on the Allied part.

Tedder wrote to Portal at the Air Staffs in London assuring him that his air forces would make a supreme effort to prevent the German evacuation, yet in the event it was, at best, half-hearted.

So what went wrong? It was a combination of factors which, when taken in tandem with tired and dispirited Allied armies, resulted in a lethargic and ill-coordinated inter-service response. Even though Eighth Army Intelligence reported back to Army Group Intelligence that an evacuation was underway, the air forces, still very much a law unto themselves, were slow to respond.

The Allied High Command were convinced that the Germans were evacuating most of their forces at night. Consequently the Wellington bombers of No 205 Group RAF carried out nightly attacks. Known as the 'Milk Run to Messina', they inflicted heavy casualties. But these raids did cause the Germans delay and not a little grief to the extent that von Liebenstein,[5] the German naval officer who masterminded the evacuation, shifted the onus to daytime operations. His masters agreed to this more because of the absence of Allied air activity over the Straits during the hours of daylight. The ferries, both civilian and military, carried barrage balloons which proved to be an effective deterrent to individual aircraft attacks. But the main factor was the utter predictability of what the Germans called 'Anglo-Saxon habits'. The Germans could set their watches by the timing of air attacks, day and night, and this allowed them to plan their short sea crossing accordingly.

With the possible exception of sorties by British MTBs and MGBs based on Augusta, the Royal Navy's role in the evacuation was that of a bystander. The small craft did attempt to interfere at night, but were beaten back by shore batteries and search lights. The larger ships never attempted a passage of the Straits. Memories of the disaster which befell Royal Navy battleships when they attempted to force the passage of the Dardanelles in 1915 clearly had an influence. Cunningham had served on a destroyer in those days and saw it all. Now an admiral, with a richly deserved reputation for aggressive action throughout the Mediterranean campaign, Cunningham became faint-hearted and irresolute. Yet the Royal Navy had ample intelligence on the few shore batteries which supposedly protected the Straits; they were known to be obsolescent, mounted in open unprotected batteries and with crude fire-control mechanisms. Other coastal defence fortifications had had their guns removed in 1915.

The German Army delayed their retreat successively along three lines of defence.[6] In this stratagem they were assisted once again by geography. Sicily tapers towards Messina and so, as troops departed and reduced front-line strengths, they were able to withdraw to a shorter line.

Sicily was bitterly contested right up until the last day. But in the so-called 'race to Messina' neither Patton nor Montgomery covered himself with glory. The Germans stood their ground when it suited their purpose and made the Allies pay dearly for every yard of advance. Patton tried some imaginative amphibious hooks which he entitled 'end runs' (from the baseball term), but none succeeded in stampeding the Germans. The distance from Palermo to Messina along the coast road was roughly similar to the distance the Seventh Army had covered from the Gela beachhead to Palermo. The latter took three days; it was to take them 17 days to reach Messina which was captured by Truscott's 3rd Infantry Division. It was an advance across terrain so mountainous that the division replaced its first-echelon transport by 400 mules and 100 pack horses.

Inland, along Route 120, there were some bruising encounters. Terry Allen miscalculated the degree of enemy resistance at Troina, Sicily's highest city. Expecting only a rearguard action, he allocated just a single regiment to the attack. But the whole of the 15th Panzer Grenadiers held Troina in strength. The battle for the city was a bitter, six-day street-by-street encounter in which both sides suffered heavily. Allen reinforced the attack; more and more of the 1st (US) Infantry were sucked into the battle. The Germans launched 24 counterattacks in the six days and the 15th Panzer Grenadiers suffered 40% of their strength as casualties. The Americans were exhausted, and Bradley moved the 9th (US) Infantry into the line, relieving Allen of command at the very height of the battle.

Montgomery finished the campaign having managed to offend just about everyone in sight. Lt General A.G.L. McNaughton, GOC Canadian Army Overseas, who was based in England, flew out to the Mediterranean with the express purpose of visiting the Canadian troops in the field. Montgomery not only forbade him to come but threatened to place him under close arrest if he ever landed in Sicily. McNaughton, not surprisingly, complained. While stiff diplomatic notes winged their way back and forth across the Atlantic, Alexander backed up Montgomery. McNaughton appealed to Eisenhower, who replied that he could not interfere in a family affair of Commonwealth countries.[7] Montgomery even managed to upset the establishment. Behind the fighting units came members of the Allied Military Government (AMGOT), officers who assumed the reins of government over conquered territories. The fighting soldiers regarded such 'civilians in uniform' usually with ill-disguised contempt, often not without justification.

Earlier in the campaign, Montgomery had written formally to Major General Lord Rennell of Rodd, in charge of Civil Affairs Administration in Italy and the Middle East, complaining of AMGOT's slowness and inefficiency. Rennell came in person and got short shrift from Montgomery who barely spared him the time of day. The noble lord wrote to his good friend Sir James Grigg, the Cabinet Secretary, who in turn dropped a note to Montgomery; the latter replied thus: 'Rennell resented my criticism of his show. In my opinion they have a very poor lot of chaps in AMGOT; old school ties, the peerage, diseased guardsmen etc.'[8]

Patton's clash with authority was more spectacular and damaging. He might have reached the pinnacle of his military career, and could regard Sicily as his triumph rather than Montgomery's, but Patton's fall from grace was swift and near-fatal. The so-called 'face-slapping episode' was in fact two separate incidents, when Patton physically abused soldiers suffering from combat fatigue. In the second incident Patton threatened a young soldier with a pistol and punched him heavily to the head. News of the incidents spread quickly, so it was inevitable that war correspondents should find out and investigate further. Instead of filing a story, a delegation went directly to see Eisenhower in Algiers. Eisenhower was already aware of the incident; doctors at the hospital who had witnessed the attack had filed a report through medical channels. Eisenhower sent a letter of censure by hand of a senior officer to Patton, upbraiding him for 'brutality and abuse of the sick'. The letter was delivered by Major General John Lucas, who was Eisenhower's personal deputy at the time. Lucas advised Patton to make a very public act of contrition; he was to apologize personally to the men involved and thence to every division in the Seventh Army. It was not until November, however, that the incident became public knowledge in the United States. With Congress calling for his head, Marshall and Eisenhower barely hung on to Patton.

Patton's eventual departure from Italy was not viewed with any great regret by many of the men who had served under his command. Contrary to myth, Patton was not at all popular. He was a martinet when it came to instilling discipline even to those troops who were resting after a period of battle. The press called him 'blood and guts'. The GI response was direct and irreverent: 'Yeah – our blood and his guts'.

Some 60,000 German soldiers fought in Sicily. Half became casualties. And when the last one left, he closed the door firmly behind him. More than 500,000 Allied servicemen served in Sicily of whom approximately 450,000 were members of either the Seventh or Eighth Armies. Allied casualties numbered 31,158 men.

Communiqués by the commanders to their political masters at home in which they claimed a resounding defeat of the enemy were reflected in the newspaper headlines and on the radio. The truth was known by the fighting men, who were the first to admit that the Germans had given them one hell of a time. None relished the thought of what might lie ahead.

Notes

1. It was estimated that Overlord would require nine divisions for the assault and a further 20 divisions to follow up.
2. Casablanca Memorandum quoted in the *Encyclopedia of World War Two*, Secker and Warburg, 1978, p 501.
3. *Overall Situation in the Mediterranean up to the Landing on the Italian Mainland*; an appreciation written by Von Vietinghoff, held in the US Army's Military History Institute and quoted in D'Este, Carlo, *Bitter Victory: The Battle for Sicily 1943*, Collins, 1988, p 527.

Of all the accounts and biographies written by and on the senior commanders in the theatre only Eisenhower had the grace to acknowledge that the Allies had blundered.

4. The evacuation which was completed by 17 August totalled:

	German	Italian
Troops	39,569	70,000
Vehicles	9,605	256
Guns	94	75
Tanks	47	12

   1,000 tons of ammunition
   970 tons of fuel
   15,700 tons of supplies

5. Fregattenkapitän Baron Gustav von Liebenstein; his correct title was Sea Transport Leader, Messina Strait. He was responsible for the movement of all military traffic across the Straits throughout that summer.

6. San Stefano Line, San Fratello Line, Tortorici Line.

7. In fairness to Montgomery there has always been a story that Montgomery acted this way because Guy Simmonds, commanding 1st (Canadian) Infantry Division, begged him to keep McNaughton away.

8. As quoted in Lamb, Richard, *Montgomery in Europe*, Buchan and Enright, 1987, p 30.

15

Dialogue Between the Deaf

A lost opportunity or the best that could be salvaged from a messy business? To this day verdicts on the complicated Italian armistice negotiations reflect national perceptions. The Italians are convinced that if only the Allies had trusted them and offered the necessary military support, the Germans in occupation would have been ousted, Italy made safe and thousands of lives saved.

Senior American and British commanders rued the day the Italians appeared at the tent door waving a white flag; their tortuous negotiations distorted Allied grand strategy. 'Maintenance of the Aim' is one of the widely acknowledged principles of war. The Allies took their eyes off the ball and paid a high price in consequence.

The Germans had a fair idea of what was afoot. Senior Allied commanders also knew that the Germans knew. Ultra intercepts on this, as on all others aspects of the conduct of the war, gave the Allies an invaluable insight into German intentions, plans and deployments. One such signal will suffice to illustrate the point: it was the transcription of a naval signal despatched on 27 July:

Instructions issued by Admiral Commanding Aegean Ops 1730/26/7:[1]

Italy situation not cleared up. Possibility of defection must be reckoned with. On arrival in port get in touch immediately with German Admiral. In case of hostilities on the part of Italians resort ruthlessly to arms.

Churchill was right. The Italians first established contact in Lisbon. A meeting was arranged in Lisbon between General Guiseppe Castellano, an aide to General Vittorio Ambrosio, Head of the Commando Supremo, Major General Walter Bedell Smith of the United States and Brigadier

Ken Strong who headed Eisenhower's intelligence staff and represented Britain.

In Lisbon Castellano was given copies of a comprehensive surrender document (the 'Long Terms') and an executive summary of the Military Armistice (the 'Short Terms'). These were themselves the result of tortuous and tetchy exchanges between the British Foreign Office and the US State Department and were still in draft form. The United Nations had yet to be informed of what was being done in their name. The Commonwealth had to be put fully in the picture, and Russia had to be brought up to date on the negotiations; Stalin later made a spirited attempt to delay matters by proposing three-power talks.

Castellano was due to depart on 22 August. He was given a deadline of midnight 30–31 August for the Italian government to signal its acceptance of a military armistice over a special radio link.

The Italians in the meantime had become alarmed at Castellano's apparent procrastination and despatched a second and more senior delegation to Lisbon. Brigadier Giacomo Zanussi was Principal Staff Officer to General Marco Roatta, Chief of the General Staff. He flew to Lisbon with Lanza di Trabia, an interpreter, and General Carton de Wiart VC, a one-eyed British general who had been captured in 1941, as proof of their good intentions. It is not clear whether the two Italian delegations met and compared notes in Lisbon, but we must assume they did, at least in the privacy of their own embassy. Castellano left and returned to Rome with the Short Terms.[2]

On 27 August the British Ambassador in Lisbon handed General Zanussi the final text of the Long Terms, the comprehensive surrender document. Zanussi immediately expressed alarm that the Italians were required to make a public surrender. This condition and others requiring immediate cessation of hostilities would leave Italy at the mercy of the Germans, who had about 15 divisions in Italy, though not all were up to strength. Zanussi asked for more time for his government to consider the terms of the comprehensive document. He was flown first to Gibraltar en route for Sicily and Rome.

Eisenhower and his people were not at all pleased that the Comprehensive Document was en route to Roatta. This general was known to have strong pro-German sympathies,[3] and Castellano had informed Strong that Roatta had not been taken into confidence by the Badoglio government. Would the whole affair now be compromised? The aircraft taking Zanussi from Gibraltar was diverted to Algiers. There he was placed under house arrest and interviewed by Macmillan and Murphy.

The comprehensive document was taken from him. His companion, Lanza di Trabia, was then allowed to continue the journey, carrying a letter from Zanussi addressed to General Ambrosio urging the Italians both to accept the armistice terms and to send Castellano to Sicily to coordinate timings.

Italian military support, given the mounting evidence of German military strength, was now considered essential. Indeed an armistice concluded and announced before Operation Avalanche was regarded as essential to its success. Eisenhower was keen to have Italian assistance before and during the critical period of the actual landing. There is, however, no evidence to suggest how these concerns were passed on to Mark Clark and his planners at Fifth Army.

30 August was a day filled with suspense in Allied Headquarters. The time limit agreed with General Castellano expired at midnight. Later that evening word came through that Castellano would come to Sicily the next day. Murphy, Macmillan and General Zanussi flew from Algiers to Syracuse and met Castellano.

Castellano explained that circumstances had changed. Given the influx of German troops into Italy the government was no longer master in its own house. This meant it would be impossible for the armistice to be announced ahead of the main Allied landings, and indeed the Italians would need to be convinced that the Allies intended to put sufficient troops ashore to guarantee the safety of the King and his government in Rome. At this point Castellano had the brass neck to request details of the Allied plans.

This had now become a dialogue between the deaf. The Italians assumed that the Allies were prepared to treat them, if not as equals, at least as partners; they also wanted the Allies to guarantee to protect them from the consequences of their sin. Castellano envisaged that the Allies were about to land with 15 divisions near to Rome, at Anzio. The Allies dared not reveal their plans for fear of betrayal and because their inadequacy would send the Italians scuttling for cover, ie back to the German fold. Castellano stated that he would have to return to Rome. General Bedell Smith made it clear that there could be no amendment to the terms, but the deadline could be extended to midnight 1–2 September, at which point there must be a firm acceptance or a refusal.

Irrespective of the German response, the Allies intended to carry the war onto the mainland and drive the Germans out, whatever suffering this might cause the Italian people. There was nothing the Italian government could do to prevent the country becoming a battleground, but by giving the Allies their full support and cooperation, the scale of suffering would be reduced. Castellano carried this message back to Rome, and he was allowed to take Zanussi with him. That evening the negotiating team (Bedell Smith, Strong, Macmillan and Murphy) met with Alexander in his trailer at the Army Group's advanced headquarters at Cassibile. Clearly the Italians needed to be stiffened, and so it was decided to recommend to Eisenhower that the 82nd Airborne should land at Rome and support the four Italian divisions stationed there to protect the government. This offer should be communicated to the Italians over the radio link. The next day Eisenhower telegraphed his approval of the plan and confirmed that a message had been transmitted to Badoglio.

The only problem was that the 82nd Airborne was at that time the key to Mark Clark's battle plan at Salerno. He intended the division should be dropped to seize the bridges over the Volturno river and thereby prevent the Germans from sending reinforcements south. Clark's master plan had the Fifth Army in Naples on D + 5 and this depended on the 82nd holding the Volturno line. They would, by that time, be in desperate need of support and reinforcement themselves. By his own account[4] Clark had experienced considerable difficulty in convincing Ridgeway, the 82nd Airborne's divisional commander, that his plan was feasible. The two were close friends and contemporaries (they had been classmates at West Point), and Clark eventually won the day. But when the 82nd Airborne was redeployed for Rome nobody thought to tell Mark Clark.

Meanwhile at 2200 on the night of 1 September news came from Rome that 'the answer is in the affirmative'. The next morning Castellano and his delegation arrived at Cassibile. Alexander received a copy of a telegram sent from Badoglio to Eisenhower stating that Castellano was coming with full powers to sign. A tented area was prepared in an olive grove near Alexander's headquarters, although at this stage the intention was to leave everything in the hands of the negotiating team. However, when Castellano was asked if Italy was now ready to sign the armistice, he replied, much to the Allies' annoyance, that they had no authority to do so. But the Badoglio government had accepted the plan for the airborne division and wanted to discuss the military plans in greater detail. Murphy and Macmillan popped across the grove to Alexander's headquarters and asked for his assistance. So the scene was set for a piece of 'opéra bouffe'.[5]

Putting on his best uniform and assuming his grandest manner, Alexander took his Humber staff car with the Army Group commander's flag flying and motor cycle outriders. They roared into the grove where

Castellano and Montonoro, his interpreter, were standing talking with Macmillan and Murphy, they having legged it back across country.

Alexander didn't beat about the bush: 'Good morning,' he said to Macmillan and Murphy. 'I have come to be introduced to the General. I understand he has signed the instrument of surrender.'

Macmillan replied as had been agreed: 'I am sorry to say, sir, but General Castellano has not signed the instrument and says that he hasn't the authority from his government to sign such a document.'

On cue Alexander flew into a rage. 'Why, there must be some mistake!! Only this morning I have seen the telegram from Marshal Badoglio stating that he was to sign the armistice agreement! In that case this man must be a spy. We must arrest him!'

Alexander paused for effect and then continued: 'The only way out of this is for the General to send a telegram confirming that Badoglio has given the authority to sign.'

The performance was a success. The Italian delegation drafted a message from Castellano to Marshall Badoglio:

Part I   The Commander-in-Chief, Allied Forces, will not discuss any military matters whatever unless a document of acceptance of the Armistice conditions is signed. As operations against the Peninsula will begin very shortly with landings, this signature is extremely urgent.

Part II   The Allied Commander-in-Chief would accept the signature of General Castellano if authorized by the Italian government. Please send this authorization within the day by this means and give urgently to Minister Osborne[6] a declaration that I have been so authorized.

Part III The Commander-in-Chief will operate with the arrangements already explained by me and with sufficient forces to ensure the degree of safety that we desire. I am personally convinced that the operative instructions of the Allies are such as to ensure the needs which we discussed in the conference of the morning of 2nd September.[7]

The following morning a telegram was received from Badoglio acknowledging Castellano's message of the night before and stating that: 'the affirmative reply given on 1st September contained implicit acceptance of the armistice terms,' but made no reference to the British Minister at the Vatican. This telegram was then cancelled from Rome without explanation.

It was not until 4 pm that a revised reply came which said: 'General

British Beaches in Sicily. An LSI responds to the Beachmaster's call while an LCT waits its turn. Unloading was easy enough but it proved more difficult for these vessels to leave the beaches in the near tideless Mediterranean.

Food for Thought. The Good Soldier's guide to Sicily, but written by those who had never been there.

Sicily, July 1943. Montgomery in classic pose. But for whose benefit?

The Truscott Trot.

Canadian and Highlanders in a photocall before a Mussolini Mural. Sicily. July 1943.

When in Rome. In Sicily a siesta was an accepted part of the working day, mission of mercy or not.

So pleased you could make it. Mark Clark greets Montgomery at Salerno. There is more to this than meets the eye – see page 194.

The Anglo American Alliance. British soldiers are introduced to the bazooka, but their American teachers appear less than impressed.

Sleight of hand. Soldiers learn the techniques of clearing a minefield by feel: a very clever but simple simulation.

Naples at last.

The British cross the Volturno. Courtesy of the Americans.

Artillery at Anzio.

French Colonial Horse Cavalry. Fine in the Atlas Mountains but there was little opportunity to exploit such talents on a crowded and confined Italian battlefield.

The empties after the Million Dollar Mountain.

The Monastery takes a pasting.
Cassino, February 1944.

The only way to supply the forward
units on Castle Hill, May 1944.

German paras captured
after the Third Battle of
Cassino. March 1944.

The Texans at San Pietro. Probably a posed shot for a documentary made by John Huston.

German prisoners after Operation Diadem. May 1944.

Castellano is authorized by the Italian government to sign acceptance of the armistice conditions. The declaration which you asked for[8] will be delivered today.'

After receipt of this message the formalities were quickly concluded. At 4.30 pm the military armistice was signed by General Bedell Smith for General Eisenhower and by General Castellano for Marshal Badoglio in the presence of Signor Montanari, Brigadier Strong, Commodore Sick, Robert Murphy and Harold Macmillan. Thereafter the full surrender terms were transmitted to General Castellano.

Alexander believed that securing the armistice was an important achievement. Although the Italians had not fought particularly hard in Sicily, Alexander feared that without the armistice the Italians might put up more of a struggle on their own soil. He remembered that one particular division had fought ferociously at El Alamein, had stayed in trenches until killed or captured, but had not retreated an inch. Alexander felt that surrender would also be a body blow to the Germans and would be a crucial factor in disorganizing German resistance and defence in Italy. The Allies appeared to have everything to gain and nothing to lose.

Information Service specialists were flown from Algiers to join General Alexander and the Italians. It was agreed that the armistice should be broadcast simultaneously by General Eisenhower and Marshal Badoglio at 6.30 pm local time on the day of the airborne landing. This day, to be called X-day, would be notified to the Italians by a special broadcast on the BBC Italian Service. It would take the form of two short talks on the subject of Nazi activities in the Argentine at a specified time.

There remained only five days in which to coordinate military plans. One of the most important was the projected landing of the 82nd Airborne in Rome, code-named Giant II. Success depended upon designated airfields being secured by the Italian Army and for transport to move the Americans into the city.

Airfields at Guidonis, Littario, Cerniteri and Forbara were to be made available by the Italians. The plan was to fly in one RCT on the night of Avalanche D - 1. The remainder would join on subsequent nights as the situation allowed. The plan also included the bizarre suggestion that additional ammunition, supplies and heavy weapons could be sent in landing craft up the Tiber. Quite what the Germans would be doing all this time was not addressed. A senior officer from the 82nd Airborne was to go to Rome to coordinate arrangements. The Italians also undertook to open the ports of Taranto and Brindisi to the Allies. The 1st (Br) Airborne was ordered to land at Taranto with light weapon scales by cruiser and destroyer.

That morning Clark received an urgent instruction to fly across to Sicily to meet Eisenhower. They shared a house in Algiers, so it seemed a little strange to be summoned to Sicily. There Eisenhower gave Mark Clark all the details of the Italian surrender. 'When you hit the beach, the Italians drop out of the war.'

This was the first Mark Clark had heard about the Italian armistice. German generals were better informed.

'We've got to drop an airborne division in the vicinity of Rome,' added Eisenhower.

'Whose silly idea is that?' asked Clark.

'Both the British and the American governments, the Joint Chiefs of Staff, the Italians; it is the price to pay.'

'Well, it won't do any good up there dropping it in the midst of six or seven German divisions,' replied Clark. 'And my whole scheme of manoeuvres is based on the 82nd Division,' he continued. 'Where are you going to get your airborne division?' asked Clark with more than a hint of anxiety.

'The 82nd, of course,' replied Eisenhower.

'You can't have that, that's mine. My whole plan of manoeuvres is based upon them.'

'Wayne, this has been decided by the government. Besides I know it will please you, when it drops it passes to your command.'

'Thanks Ike, that's like having a half interest in a wife. Do you need me any more?'

'No,' replied Eisenhower.

It is hard to imagine that Eisenhower could not have been aware of the significance of the 82nd Airborne for the Salerno landings. And yet an extract from a situation report despatched by Eisenhower to London and Washington on 3 September reads as follows:

AVALANCHE. There are now no Airborne Troops employed. A certain strengthening of seaborne lift has been made possible by diversion of additional landing craft from the later stages of Baytown. The reinforced RCT of 82nd Airborne Division which formed part of floating reserve has been withdrawn for task outlined below (i.e. Rome) and has been replaced by a 2nd RCT of 45th Division.[9]

This would suggest that as far as Eisenhower was aware, only a part of the 82nd Airborne was to be used at Salerno and even then in the secondary role as a floating reserve. Or was he deliberately playing down the role of the 82nd Airborne so as to minimize the apparent price of its redeployment?

It was too late for Mark Clark to change his plans. Ports along the North Africa coast were full of ships loaded with Fifth Army. The first convoys were due to sail in 24 hours. He would have to go with what he had got and hope that the Italian capitulation would make the difference. Clark's decision to risk everything on surprise, however, now seemed more important than ever.

Notes

1. CX/MSS/C.158.
2. The Italian delegation had apparently expected to travel on to London to negotiate further, hence General Carton de Wiart's presence. The General offered to return to Rome and captivity, but Zanussi released him from his terms of parole and any other obligations. General Carton de Wiart travelled on to London and subsequently was appointed by Churchill as his personal representative to Chiang Kai Shek.
3. Roatta was tried as a war criminal in 1946 and found guilty, but he escaped before sentence was passed.
4. Author's interview with Clark.
5. This account is taken from the Matthews/Alexander interview, p 2.
6. British Minister at the Holy See.
7. CAB 101/144.
8. Ie to the British Minister at the Holy See.
9. CAB 101/144, p 135.

16

Start at the Bottom

Why should we crawl up the leg like a harvest-bug from the ankle upwards? Let us rather strike at the knees.

Winston Churchill, August 1943[1]

Even though the armistice had been signed it had no meaning until it could be made public. In the intervening period the Allies continued to kill Italians. Three days after the signing of the armistice, one of the heaviest air raids of the war to date was launched against Frascati. Situated about 20 miles south-east of Rome, Frascati was a legitimate military target by virtue of numerous German military headquarters and staffs. But the Allied bombers, with their usual degree of imprecision, managed to cause slight damage to one such installation and kill hundreds of women and children in the process.

In the meantime, Montgomery had deigned to cross the Straits of Messina. Despite the fact that Eighth Army intelligence estimated no more than three German battalions in south Calabria[2] and did not expect any German response before the Gioia Plain, 30 miles north of Reggio, Montgomery laid on an artillery barrage which would have impressed those at Passchendaele or the Somme. It can only be described as a self-indulgent extravaganza. At 0345 hours in the morning of Tuesday 3 September and four years to the day since the declaration of war, 600 guns from Eighth Army signalled the return of the Allies to mainland Europe by the unloading of 400 tons of ammunition onto the Italian shore. Nor was that all. The battleships HMS *Nelson*, *Warspite*, *Rodney* and *Valiant*, the monitor HMS *Erebus*, destroyers and gunboats joined in for good measure, as did a goodly proportion of American artillery on Sicily as well.

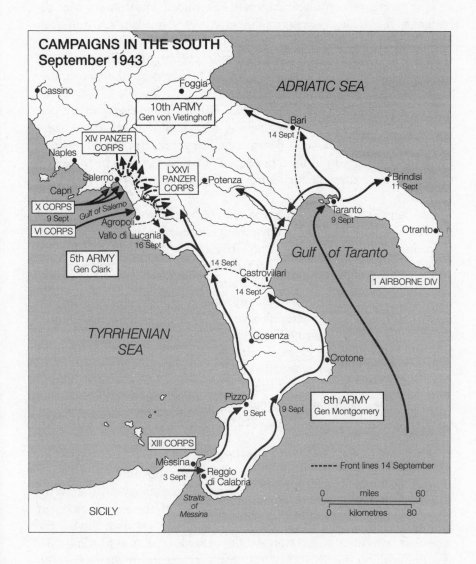

CAMPAIGNS IN THE SOUTH
September 1943

ADRIATIC SEA

Cassino

Foggia

10th ARMY
Gen von Vietinghoff

Bari
14 Sept

XIV PANZER
CORPS

Naples

LXXVI
PANZER
CORPS

Potenza

Brindisi
11 Sept

Salerno

Capri

Gulf of Salerno

X CORPS
9 Sept

Taranto
9 Sept

Otranto

Agropoli

VI CORPS

Vallo di Lucania
16 Sept

Gulf of Taranto

5th ARMY
Gen Clark

14 Sept

Castrovillari

1 AIRBORNE DIV

14 Sept

TYRRHENIAN
SEA

Cosenza

Crotone

Pizzo
9 Sept

9 Sept

8th ARMY
Gen Montgomery

XIII CORPS

------ Front lines 14 September

Mèssina
3 Sept

Reggio
di Calabria

miles   60

SICILY

Straits
of
Messina

kilometres   80

119

There were no identifiable targets to be reduced. Far from resisting the landings, the Italian garrison soldiers emerged unscathed from their bunkers, and offered to help in the unloading of the boats. If just a fraction of this effort had been concentrated on preventing the Germans from evacuating their forces across the Straits of Messina, the war in Italy might well have been a very different affair.

Why was all of this effort expended? To satisfy one man's vanity.

For the invasion of Italy the chain of command remained the same – Eisenhower, Alexander, Tedder and Cunningham. But the direction of the land battle cried out for an overlord, a coordinator, to be in tactical control; Montgomery lobbied hard to achieve this end – for himself, of course.

As originally conceived there was to have been a two-corps invasion of the 'foot' of Italy. Operation Baytown was the code-name for an attack immediately after the conquest of Sicily across the Straits of Messina. This was to be followed by X (Br) Corps landing at Gioia on the north-east coast of the 'toe', code-named Buttress. Since both operations were exclusively Eighth Army, Montgomery wasn't too displeased with the turn of events; that is until 17 August when his little world fell apart. On that day the Joint Chiefs confirmed Operation Avalanche as a two-corps attack by Fifth Army on Salerno, but Fifth Army then comprised just VI (US) Corps. So Buttress was cancelled and X (Br) Corps under Horrocks moved from Eighth Army to Fifth Army and American command. And because of the additional landing craft needed to support Avalanche, Operation Baytown was down-graded to a landing by a reinforced brigade of just four battalions.

Montgomery protested in the most forceful of terms. He conjured up the demons of massive German counterattacks and the prospects of a landing that would be defeated. He belaboured Alexander until he got his own way. Herein lay the inherent weakness of the Allied chain of command. Eisenhower as the Theatre Commander continued to behave rather as a remote Chairman of the Board, with his headquarters geographically remote across the Mediterranean in Algiers. With Alexander, as the Managing Director, the Army Group Commander was 'a man weakly of will and dim of brain',[3] who, in any case, never could stand up to Montgomery. Alexander allowed Montgomery to upgrade Baytown to an assault by XIII Corps which comprised 5th (Br) Infantry, 1st (Cdn) Infantry Divisions and 231 Independent Brigade, supported of course by every piece of artillery in Eighth Army.

It was absolutely essential that there be a coordinated strategy between

Avalanche and Baytown. Landing craft and assault shipping were in very short supply and given enemy resistance (at this stage neither Montgomery nor Clark was party to the details of the Italians negotiations), there would be a narrow margin of superiority over the enemy. Reinforcements for the Salerno beachhead were in North Africa or Sicily; this meant that the Germans and the Italians had more immediate access to reserves than would Mark Clark. That is why the 82nd Airborne had such a critical role in the battle plan. As far as reinforcements were concerned, from the outset those most immediately to hand were seen as Eighth Army advancing up from the south.

Moon and tide dictated the date for Salerno in the mindset of the planners, so flexibility could only be with Eighth Army. Given the risks involved at Salerno, it was vital that Eighth Army should be sufficiently far up the coast to exert an influence on the battle very shortly after the landings. To this end Eisenhower directed that Operation Baytown should be launched on 30/31 August. But Montgomery refused, claiming that he could not possibly be ready before the night of 4/5 September. As justification for the delay, he insisted that the naval support could not be ready and quoted Cunningham to that effect. Cunningham was furious at having his name taken in vain. But then Montgomery revealed, not for the first or last time, a facility to lie instantly and effortlessly when it suited his purpose.

Finally, Operation Baytown was agreed for the night of 3/4 September. It is 270 miles along coastal Highway Route 8 from Reggio to the southern extremities of Salerno Bay, a journey which these days can be undertaken in a matter of hours by autostrada. In 1943, when the roads were poorly surfaced and easy to block, it would take a very vigorous advance to sustain a fast enough pace to reach Salerno in reasonable time. The 3rd (US) Infantry at the Truscott Trot might have managed it, but Montgomery did not like to take chances and, with his eye firmly fixed on the command appointments for Overlord, was not about to tarnish his record. And the fact that Avalanche, which was a bigger operation than Baytown, had been given to an untried American general caused him deep offence and injured his pride. In his view the roles should have been reversed and Salerno tasked to the vastly more experienced Eighth Army.

Lt General Mark Wayne Clark was a graduate of West Point, whose previous combat experience was spread over a few short weeks in the First World War. Like most of his contemporaries Clark's career progressed slowly through the inter-war years and then, after 1940, his promotion was meteoric – Lt Colonel to Lt General in under three years. Tall and rangy, likened by many to the film star, Gary Cooper, Mark Clark at 46 was convinced that this was a young man's war. He attempted to build around him a staff and subordinate command of like-minded men. Fifth Army Chief of Staff was Alfred Greunther, at 43 the youngest major general in the US Army and already known as the brains of the army for his dazzling performance in Staff and War Colleges. Greunther fulfilled his potential, for after the war he followed in Eisenhower's footsteps as Supreme Allied Commander Europe (SACEUR) in the North Atlantic Alliance.

Clark's problem was that on the American side his corps and divisional commanders were his seniors in years and military service. The VI (US) Corps was commanded by Major General Sawley, far senior or the Army list. Fred Walker and Troy Middleton of the 45th Infantry had been his instructors at War College. Walker commanded the 36 (US) Infantry Division, a National Guard formation drawn from Texas (it was known as the T Patchers because of the Texas T) which had been in training for three years but had yet to see battle. In Italy the 36th acquired a reputation, largely undeserved, for being an unlucky division. It is hard to understand why Mark Clark allowed the Texans to lead at Salerno when there was an opportunity for a more gradual, secondary introduction. Walker, however, had argued long and hard for the privilege and perhaps Mark Clark felt he owed his mentor the opportunity.

The British also had their share of problems. Lt General Sir Brian Horrocks, the ebullient and experienced corps commander, had been sent to command X Corps by Montgomery. Unlike the Texans, both British Territorial divisions had seen action before. Neither, however, could be said to have had a happy war to date, and for their own different reasons were anxious to put the experiences of North Africa behind them.

The 56th (City of London Division) was known as the Black Cats, after its Dick Whittington shoulder patch. The division left the United Kingdom in 1942, spent some time in India, thence to Persia and Iraq. The Black Cats arrived in Tunisia in time to make a frontal attack up a hill called Enfidaville where it was badly mauled. Afterwards the 201st Guards Brigade replaced one of the Territorial brigades as a stiffener.

The battalions that composed the other division originally came from the north-west Midlands and the West Riding of Yorkshire. The 46th Infantry, a Territorial division, whose shoulder flash was the oak tree of Sherwood Forest, had been at war since the early days. It had fought with the BEF in France in 1940 and three years later experienced the campaign in Tunisia.

The British suffered casualties even before the assault ships left North

Africa for Salerno. Despite supposed Allied air superiority, the Luftwaffe carried out night bombing raids against the invasion shipping in the North African ports. One evening Horrocks was dining with the senior staff and commanders of the 46th Infantry Division in an officers' mess at Bizerta. There was an air raid and when the General and his party went outside to watch the fireworks, Horrocks was struck by a large piece of falling shrapnel from an AA shell and was badly wounded.

Mark Clark was told of the incident by his ADC, Lieutenant Warren Thrasher. The message was brought to Clark's villa by General Greunther; Clark at the time was having a swim in the sea. 'Swim out to General Clark and tell him that General Horrocks has been critically injured in an air raid. He will not be able to continue in command of X Corps and we need to discuss the question of a successor,' ordered Greunther. Thrasher stripped down to his underclothes and dutifully swam out, to find himself being swamped by the waves as he trod water and tried to talk. Clark was obliged to hold Thrasher under his ears until he delivered the message.

Alexander's choice was Lt General Richard McCreery, a supposed tank expert. Opinions differed on 'Dreary' McCreery. Auchinleck had sacked him because he refused to implement radical changes in the structure of armoured and infantry formations. These changes had in turn been recommended by Auchinleck's own Chief of Staff, the brilliant but temperamental Major General Smith-Dorman. Shortly after, Churchill sacked Auchinleck and replaced him with Alexander. Alexander sacked Smith-Dorman and chose McCreery to be his Chief of Staff. When Fifteenth Army Group was created as an Anglo-American command it was deemed sensible for Alexander to have an American as his Chief of Staff. McCreery was nudged aside. He returned to England and joined the planning staff for Overlord. In August 1943 McCreery was flown back to North Africa.

The 46th Infantry was led by Major General Freeman-Attwood, at the time one of the youngest division commanders in the British Army. While the division was in a sealed camp waiting to board its assault craft, the General wrote home to his wife saying that he hoped shortly to be in those parts where they had spent their honeymoon. The letter was picked out in a random security and censor's check. Freeman-Attwood lost his command and his career.

So within days the British were looking for new corps and division commanders. The loss of Freeman-Attwood had a serious effect on the division as a fighting force – not so much on the ordinary soldiers, most of whom regarded generals as distant and lofty figures to be avoided at all costs, but on the senior staff and fighting commanders, for together they made a team dependent upon mutual confidence and trust. The new divisional commander, Major General Hawesworth, was a man proven in battle. He had commanded the splendid 4th Indian Division in the desert campaign. However, he knew little of the overall battle plan, the role that was expected of his division, nor indeed the strengths and weaknesses of his own officers and their commands.

There were very few who considered the Bay of Salerno to be an ideal choice for an amphibious landing. There were better beaches north of Naples in the Gulf of Gaeta, but they were out of range of Spitfires flying from airfields on Sicily; indeed the planes could barely make it to Salerno and at Montecorvino there was an airfield whose early capture was vital.

The Bay of Salerno, which extends from Sorrento to Agropoli in the south, is shaped like a Roman amphitheatre. Behind the gently shelving beaches, there is a narrow coastal plain, dissected by a number of rivers of which the Sele, almost at midpoint, is the biggest. Just a few miles inland across a coastal plain lush with market gardens, vineyards and olive groves, are the foothills of the southern Apennines, sufficiently high to command the beaches. There are over 20 miles of beaches at Salerno, but there are few exits and the routes through the hills to Naples, 40 miles to the north, are by way of narrow passes or defiles.

Even though he had lost the services of his airborne division, Mark Clark had a bold and imaginative plan, one that would doubtless have won plaudits at a War College.

The lessons of Husky had re-emphasized the importance of capturing a major port within days of the landing. Mark Clark planned to be taking the surrender of Naples by D + 5 and saw surprise as the key to success. There was to be no preliminary bombardment of the beaches.

The Sele river formed both a corps and international boundary in the Fifth Army battle plan. The beaches to the south belonged to the Americans. They were to guard the British right flank, where they were to join hands some nine miles inland at Ponte Sele, take the high ground and link up with the Eighth Army coming up from the south. If the Fifth Army were going to be in Naples five days after coming ashore, then the passes or defiles which controlled that road had to be taken quickly. If the Germans got there first it would be a case of them putting the cork in the bottle and penning the Allies on the beaches where they could be systematically destroyed by artillery.

Mark Clark assigned the defiles to be captured and held by special forces. Three battalions of Darby's US Rangers were to land at Maiori on the scenic Amalfi coast, on the far left flank of X Corps, then secure the coast road and deploy inland over the mountains above Salerno to the Nocera Pass, which guarded the route onto the plain of Naples.

Less than six miles to the right of the Rangers lay the fishing village of Vietri. Its shingle beach was the landing site for No 2 Army and 41 Royal Marine Commandos who were to secure the route out through the hills above Salerno and a narrow valley called the La Molina defile. If all went according to plan, these crack, but lightly armed special forces, would be relieved in turn by the 46th Infantry who would hold the shoulders open for 22nd Armoured Brigade, part of the 7th (Br) Armoured, who were scheduled to land on D + 1, to break through and drive hard for Naples.

Avalanche was a bold plan. Everything hinged on the speed of the enemy reactions.

Fifth Army had done its sums[4] in estimating the strength of the opposition. They expected to encounter one German armoured division in the beachhead area together with two or three para battalions. Thereafter by D + 5, when Mark Clark planned to be in Naples, they expected the armoured division to be reinforced by a further division and a half of under-strength armour, a para division and one and a half panzer grenadier divisions. The build-up of Fifth Army by that time gave cause for concern in London when the Chiefs of Staff came to study the plan at the end of August; for it was clear from Ultra that the Germans might even outmatch Allied strength.[5] The only thing that could swing the balance back in the Allies' favour would be the early arrival of Eighth Army at the beachhead. But that was a remote possibility.

Mark Clark can be censured for his poor use of intelligence and for being dismissive of the problems he might encounter in establishing and defending his beachhead. In his timetable to capture Naples he was hopelessly optimistic.

Why didn't Clark wait for a few extra days? The German divisions in the area were not meant to stay, and, under gentle prodding from Montgomery, were retreating northwards. Three weeks before the landing, Ultra reported Hitler's decision to pull out of south and central Italy. If Clark had waited, they would have cleared the area and Fifth Army could have enjoyed a virtually unopposed landing. But Salerno and Messina were a case of bilateral vanities. Both Clark and Montgomery had to have their own shows.

Salerno was botched – flawed in concept and defective in planning and execution. For different reasons, Montgomery regarded Avalanche as hair-brained, and feared that the Germans would mount powerful counterattacks against his own forces. He planned and fought the Eighth Army campaign in Calabria in order to be quite separate to that of the Fifth Army at Salerno. Meanwhile the Canadians advanced at a leisurely pace up the east coast to reach Catanzaro Lido by 9 September, sustaining no battle casualties at all. More critical to the fate of the Fifth Army was the advance of 5th (Br) Infantry which proceeded cautiously up the west coast to reach Gioia Tauro on 6 September, by which time most of Mark Clark's forces were at sea.

Earlier, on 5 September, Montgomery met with Alexander on the airfield at Reggio. There the Army Group Commander brought him up to date on the latest developments; this not only included a detailed briefing of Avalanche, but the Italian surrender and Operation Slapstick, the aptly named plan to send the British airborne division into Taranto. Montgomery was aghast. He warned that while the Italians would not fight (a complete volte-face from his earlier predictions), the Germans were in great strength and would concentrate on Avalanche, while the Allies were too weak and too widely dispersed. Alexander impressed upon Montgomery the need to advance quickly through Calabria so as to influence Salerno at the earliest opportunity.

On the eve of Avalanche, 231 Brigade, bolstered with two full Commandos used up precious assault craft and landed at Santa Venere, more than 150 miles south of Agropoli. There was a short, sharp engagement with a rearguard from the 29th Panzer Grenadiers but by evening the brigade had pushed on a further 20 miles.

As the British and American infantry hit the beaches at Salerno, Montgomery ordered 5th Infantry to close up to Nicastro, some 100 miles from Agropoli where it would be allowed to rest for three days. Eighth Army had suffered precious few casualties, had ample transport at their disposal and hundreds of obliging Italian POWs to do much of the heavy lifting and carrying. Some even formed work gangs and helped clear the annoying road blocks caused by German demolitions, while the soldiers enjoyed the hospitality of the local inhabitants from the towns and villages they had liberated.

Notes

1. Churchill, Winston S., *The Second World War: The Hinge of Fate*, Vol IV, Cassell, 1951.
2. There was only one.
3. Barnett, *Engage the Enemy*, p 628.
4. WO/106/3990, para 12.
5. Clark planned to have his three assaulting divisions 56 (Br), 46 (Br) and 36 (US) ashore with light scales, one RCT 45 Division on assault scales, part of 22 Armoured Brigade and just three battalions of tanks (the plan at that stage also included 82nd Airborne). There were not the landing craft and transports available to carry more.

17

False Dawn

On 8 September, the day scheduled for the airborne landing in Rome, the Italians suddenly developed cold feet. A message was received from Marshal Badoglio over the radio link:

> Owing to changes in the situation which has seriously deteriorated and the presence of German forces in the Rome area, the announcement of the armistice is no longer possible since the capital would be occupied and the Italian Government taken over forcibly by the Germans. The operation [concerning the airborne division] no longer possible as I lack the forces to guarantee the airfields.[1]

The truth of the matter was that after the surrender instrument had been signed the Italian High Command had done nothing. Some might maintain that there was no way the Italian armed forces could have stood up to the Germans in occupation, but some units did resist, and more strongly than the record has hitherto suggested. If the Rome garrison had acted as a united force, and the people of Rome had taken to the streets, the German High Command would have been hard pressed to restore control. Given the uncertainty in Berlin, there is reason to suppose that the Germans might have cut their losses and retreated north.

If the Italians did not know all the Allied intentions, they did at least have detailed access to Operation Giant II, the American landing on Rome. This indicated that they were not to be rescued by the Allies, but to be assisted in defending themselves.

Reports from Luftwaffe and Italian aircraft who were shadowing Mark Clark's convoys showed as early as 6/7 September that the Allies were probably heading for Naples. That very morning the Chief of Staff of the Italian XIX Corps, which had its headquarters in Naples, ordered the local Coastal Division headquarters in Salerno that: 'From 2330 hours 7th September this zone is declared to be in coastal alarm following the departure of enemy convoy from Sicily heading for Salerno.'[2] On the evening of 7 September Brigadier General Matthew Taylor and Colonel Gardiner arrived in the Holy City. They assumed their mission was to coordinate the airborne operation, indeed they met with General Carboni who said:

> If the Italians declare an Armistice the Germans will occupy Rome and the Italians can do little to prevent it. The simultaneous arrival of the US airborne troops would only provoke the Germans to more drastic action. Furthermore the Italians would be unable to secure the airfields, cover the assembly and provide the desired logistical aid to the airborne troops. If it must be assumed that an Allied seaborne landing is impossible north of Rome, then the only hope of saving the capital is to avoid overt acts against the Germans and await the effects of Allied attacks in the south.[3]

Carboni stated that he knew the Allied landings would be at Salerno which was too far away to aid directly in the defence of Rome.

Taylor, however, was shocked by the Italian position and demanded an interview with Badoglio. They met about midnight.[4] Badoglio reiterated the position and asked Taylor to signal Eisenhower to postpone the armistice and cancel the airborne landing. Taylor refused, and Badoglio signalled Eisenhower himself.

Maxwell Taylor did however draft a message of his own for Eisenhower.

> In view of the statement of Marshal Badoglio as to inability to declare armistice and to guarantee fields GIANT TWO is impossible. Reasons given for change are irreplaceable lack of gasoline and munitions and new German dispositions. The summary of the situation as stated by the Italian authorities is that the Germans have 12,000 troops in the Tiber area and the Panzer Grenadier Division increased by attachments to 24,000. The Germans have stopped supplies of gasoline and munitions so that the Italian divisions are virtually immobilized and have munitions only for a few hours of combat.
>
> Shortages make impossible success of the full defence of Rome and the provision of logistical aid promised to the airborne troops. The latter are not wanted at present as their arrival would bring an immediate attack on Rome.
>
> Badoglio requests Taylor return to present government views. Taylor and Gardiner await instructions. Acknowledge.[5]

At 0800 the following day, 8 September, AFHQ acknowledged receipt of Badoglio's message. The Italian volte-face came as a shock to the Allied commander, to be followed almost immediately by a sense of disgust and anger. Eisenhower was in Bizerta meeting with his senior commanders, so Algiers relayed the message to him and simultaneously to Washington.

Eisenhower was the first to react and cabled the Combined Chiefs of Staff: 'I have just completed a conference with the principal commanders and have determined not to accept the Italian change of attitude.'[6]

Now was the time for cool heads. The immediate concern ought to have been the implications for Avalanche. At this late stage there was no chance to cancel the operation although it must have been deeply disconcerting to discover that Badoglio knew all about Salerno. Nevertheless, a logical appraisal must have reached the conclusion that a broadcast to which the Italians would not respond would only serve to alert the Germans. The Italians had asked for the broadcast to be delayed, and it was undoubtedly to Mark Clark's advantage to meet Italian rather than German defenders at Salerno.

Eisenhower replied to Badoglio:

Part I. I intend to broadcast the existence of an armistice at the hour originally planned. If you, or any part of your armed forces, fail to cooperate as previously agreed, I will publish to the world a full record of this affair. Today is X-Day and I expect you to do your part.

Part II. I do not accept your message of this morning postponing the armistice. Your accredited representative has signed an agreement with me, and the sole hope of Italy is bound up in your adherence to that agreement. On your earnest representation the airborne operations are temporarily suspended.

Part III. You have sufficient troops near Rome to secure the temporary safety of the city, but I require full information on which to plan earliest the airborne operations. Send General Taylor at once to Bizerta by aeroplane. Notify in advance time of arrival.

Part IV. Plans have been made on the assumption that you were acting in good faith and we have been prepared to carry out future operations on that basis. Failure on your part to carry out the full obligations of the signed agreement will have the most serious consequences for your country. No future action of yours could then restore any confidence whatever in your good faith and consequently the disillusionment of your government and nation will ensue.[7]

At 5 pm the same evening a Washington telegram was received at AFHQ in Algiers:

It is the view of the President and the Prime Minister that the agreement having been signed you should make such public announcement regarding it as would facilitate your military operations.

To Eisenhower or Smith personal attention. No consideration, repeat no consideration need be given to the embarrassment it might cause the Italian government.[8]

Other organizations also insisted on getting in on the act. A signal was decoded that afternoon from the Joint Intelligence Committee. Marked 'Most immediate', it read: 'We suggest that if airborne division is sent to Rome every effort should be made to capture all Japanese officers and officials including Ambassador and diplomatic and consular staff.'[9] It was just the sort of helpful suggestion that Eisenhower and his seniors needed at this stage in the proceedings! In the meantime General Taylor was left to kick his heels in Rome. Badoglio ignored Eisenhower's request to have him flown to Bizerta, even supposing that safe passage could have been arranged.

So, fearing that his message had not been received, and aware that the first wave of airborne troops was scheduled to take off at 6.30 the same evening, Taylor sent the further signal: 'Situation innocuous.' This was the agreed code for the cancellation of Giant Two. It was as well that Taylor did this, since aircraft of the first wave were already loaded and awaiting the order for take-off. The failure to have cancelled the operation much earlier can only be explained by the obsession of Eisenhower and his principal commanders with Italian duplicity, and the confusion this must have generated in Allied Forces Headquarters. If Taylor had not sent the second signal there would have been mayhem, and another airborne operation disaster.

Eventually Eisenhower went ahead as planned, and at 6.30 pm broadcast the news of the armistice. Reuters put out a flash a quarter of an hour later followed by a repeat of the Eisenhower broadcast by the BBC News Service at 7.20 pm that same evening. The Italian government was caught absolutely by surprise and, in a panic, some members rushed to the Royal Palace. Raffaele Guariglia, one-time Ambassador to the Holy See and now Foreign Minister, met Badoglio in the antechamber of the King's reception room and asked him for the true situation. 'We're fucked,' replied the Marshal. Since nothing had been picked up from Rome radio, a declaration in Italian was also broadcast by Algiers radio, following the text given to General Castellano by Marshal Badoglio as the declaration he intended to make.

It still remained to be seen if the Marshal would at some later time speak himself. No provision had been made for a radio broadcast but Badoglio rushed to the studios of Rome Radio. It was a considerable relief to AFHQ when they learned that the declaration had been made and in exactly the terms agreed upon.

> The Italian Government having recognized the impossibility of continuing the unequal struggle against overwhelming enemy power, with the object of sparing the nation any further and grave disasters, has asked General Eisenhower, Supreme Commander of the Allied Anglo-American Forces, for an armistice; the request has been granted. Consequently, all acts of hostility against the Anglo-American Forces on the part of the Italian Forces shall cease.[10]

Immediately German forces began the encirclement of Rome. Badoglio and the Royal Family installed themselves in a state of siege in the main building of the Ministry of War, while scattered fighting was already taking place at the gates of Rome. Discussions in the Ministry of War took place in an atmosphere of mounting tension and panic. Then, in the small hours, a convoy of five vehicles passed through the Eastern gates of Rome and took the road for Pescara on the Adriatic coast. Later that night two corvettes took on board a party which consisted of the Royal Family, together with Marshal Badoglio, his government and officials. The only person to protest was Crown Prince Umberto, but his was a lone voice. The corvettes slipped their moorings and sailed south for the port of Brindisi which they reached safely on the morning of 10 September. Italians have debated the propriety of this decision ever since, but this is only to confuse the issue. Their flight left the capital leaderless at a time of national crisis, and it sealed the fate of the House of Savoy.

Earlier, and on the opposite coast, when the Italian surrender had been announced, the van of the Avalanche invasion fleet was in sight of Capri. Lieutenant Richard Leeke, a platoon commander in 1st Company, 6th Battalion Grenadier Guards, first spotted the island in late afternoon. He pointed it out to the LST's first lieutenant who in turn brought out a chart and took a bearing. He confirmed it to be Capri, to the north of Salerno Bay, and added that the convoy had strayed a little too far to the east, that is near to the mainland. Leeke was appalled.

Almost everybody packed into the transports and assault ships heard one or other of the English-language broadcasts. From horizon to horizon these ships and their escorts echoed to thunderous cheers. Leeke's Guardsmen sang as if the war was already over. At a stroke Eisenhower had blunted the finely honed fighting edge of Mark Clark's troops. Raw young Americans jumped for joy. 'Vino and signorinas from the beachhead to Naples.' Other men in the 36th Division thought that the landings would be another dry run, yet another exercise after three years of nothing but exercises. The great cry had been they were to be the first American troops to land in Europe in this war. Now the fire went out of their bellies.

Amongst the more experienced in the British divisions there was just as much jubilation. Salerno was the first occasion in the Second World War on which British troops en masse were issued with condoms. Resourceful soldiers about to go into battle put these packets of rubber to all sorts of uses other than that for which they were intended. Partially inflated, the officers found they were ideal repositories for candles, matches and chinagraph pencils to mark maps and the like. Soldiers, expecting a wet landing, used the condoms to waterproof the spout of their rifles and Sten guns. Some optimists, upon hearing the news of the Italian surrender, attempted to salvage the condoms and repackage them.

There were other soldiers, the Special Forces, some Americans and a lot more British, who, after years of war, had learned that in the art of survival one of the prime rules was not to believe anything you could not see with your own eyes. These men went about the business, quietly, of preparing for battle, but the majority, despite the efforts of their officers and NCOs, were lulled into false hopes and expectations.

They would have been less sanguine had they known that units of the 16th Panzer Division were even then assuming control of the excellent defensive opportunities that Salerno had to offer. Major General Rudolph Sieckenius, the divisional commander, divided his force into four battle groups to cover the front of the Gulf of Salerno. Each battle group was named after its commander.

Salerno Bay and its environs had been the responsibility of the locally recruited Italian 222nd Coastal Division. Their commander had tried to stand on his honour when the panzers arrived on the scene. He was quietly taken to one side and shot. His men were only too pleased to hand over their weapons to the Germans, vacate their trenches and gun emplacements and scuttle off to their homes and civilian life. It so happened that the panzer defences were at the strongest sector of Salerno Bay which had been allotted to the raw American 36th Division. Along the shoreline strongpoints, each garrisoned by a platoon of troops, bristled with light and heavy machine guns. These were interspersed with a number of quadruple 20-mm anti-aircraft guns, their barrels depressed in readiness for their anti-infantry role. The concentrated firepower of high explosive shells would be devastating against thin-skinned landing craft and unprotected troops. In the sand dunes, 75-mm and the dreaded 88-mm anti-tank guns were dug into emplacements. Further inland, platoons of tanks and panzer grenadiers in armoured half-tracks were poised for local counterattacks. In the foothills batteries of mobile and self-propelled artillery looked down on the beaches.

Strangely, Mark Clark remained convinced that surprise was still possible. The British, under McCreery, chose studiously to ignore instructions to that effect: but at least for the Americans there was to be no preliminary bombardment. When the Americans hit the beaches the defences would be ready and intact.

Notes

1. CAB 101/144, p 136.
2. Morris, Eric, *Salerno*, Hutchinson, 1983.
3. CAB 101/144.
4. Previous accounts have claimed that Badoglio kept Taylor waiting until late on 8 September, but this was not the case.
5. CAB 101/144.
6. Ibid.
7. Ibid.
8. Ibid.
9. WO/106/3993.
10. WO 214/23.

18

Operation Achse (Axis)

Italy was the only country in the Second World War to surrender twice. The first, in theory, was to the Allies, the second was for real and to the Germans. In the north was the intolerant Rommel, in command of Army Group B, which comprised three corps of eight divisions including some 200 tanks. With these considerable forces at his disposal he moved quickly and seized the main population and communication centres. He promptly disarmed his Italians and then herded them towards the Alps and forced labour in Germany.

While attention may tend to focus on the jealousies that surfaced on the Allied side, it is easy to overlook similar tensions amongst the German High Command in Italy. Kesselring may well have pressed the Führer to delay the retreat northwards because it meant more troops would come under command of Rommel in Army Group B. There was certainly no love lost between the two men, and their animosity can be traced back to Afrika Korps days. They also adopted quite different approaches to the Italian capitulation. Rommel, as we have seen, rounded up every Italian soldier he could lay his hands on and had them shipped back to Germany as forced labour. Their presence in the factories and on the farms would release German men for military service. Kesselring adopted a more liberal attitude and, with one or two exceptions, allowed the Italian soldiery in his area to pile arms and go home. Rommel was most displeased, as a signal subsequently decoded by Ultra shows.

To C-in-C South, signed Rommel on 11/9:
Ref your letter No 8019

In accordance with the Führer's order all disarmed soldiers are not to be released, as otherwise, they will in a short time, be rearmed and reequipped, fight against us on the side of the enemy. They are rather to be retained as POWs and to be removed to Germany at once. The POW collecting point must take away their small arms and ammunition, clothing, equipment, bicycles, horses, vehicles with rations etc for transport back [word or so smudged].

By order of the Führer I have taken over executive powers in Italy. Please refrain from appeals.[1]

Hitler had given Rommel responsibility for executing Operation Achse while Kesselring concentrated on countering the Allied invasion; he was, however, premature in claiming that he had overall command in Italy.

President Roosevelt and Winston Churchill tried to exhort Badoglio to act decisively. A telegram, jointly signed, read as follows.

Marshal, it has fallen to you in the hour of your country's agony to take the first decisive steps to win peace and freedom for the Italian people and to win back for Italy an honourable place in the civilization of Europe.

You have already freed your country from Fascist servitude. There remains the even more important task of cleansing the Italian soil from the German invaders. Hitler, through his accomplice Mussolini, has brought Italy to the verge of ruin. He has driven the Italians into disastrous campaigns in the sands of Egypt and the snows of Russia. The Germans have always deserted the Italian troops on the battlefield, sacrificing them contemptuously in order to cover their own retreats. Now Hitler threatens to subject you all to the cruelties he is perpetrating in so many lands.

People of Italy, now is the time for every Italian to strike his blow. The liberating armies of the Western world are coming to your rescue. We have very strong forces and are entering at many points. The German terror in Italy will not last long. They will be extirpated from your land and you, by helping in this great surge of liberation, will place yourselves once more among the true and long-proved friends of your country from whom you have been so wrongfully estranged.

Take every chance you can. Strike hard and strike home. Have faith in your future. All will come well. March forward with your American and British friends in the great world movement towards Freedom, Justice and Peace.[2]

This ringing piece of Churchillian prose fell on deaf ears. The truth was that the Italians, devoid of leadership and example, had no spirit for the fight.

The Germans waged a short, sharp war on the Italians abroad and there were some bloody encounters. The Aegean island of Kephalonia was garrisoned by the Acqui division under General Antonio Gandini. The garrison resisted the Germans for a week and, when the survivors eventually surrendered, they were shot on the spot. In contrast, the commanding general and the entire staff of the recently constituted Italian Army Group East were seized in Tirana by a handful of paratroopers and a quarter of a million men were immobilized.

There were probably about 12,000 German troops in Rome at this time, many dressed in civilian clothes, but they all had orders and knew what to do. Five minutes after Badoglio's broadcast, General Jodl, at the Führer's headquarters, signalled regional commanders in France, Italy and the Balkans to implement Operation Axis. The Germans knew that the Italian Army could not function without orders. The answer was therefore to seize headquarters and paralyse the command structure:

> [The Germans] put their Fifth Columnists, most of them German-Italians from the Tyrol, to work inside the city. The agents moved fast. They went to all the Italian Army bureaus, where, at the point of a pistol, they disarmed the commandants, took over their offices and despatched orders disbanding whatever troops were under their jurisdiction. They cut telephone wires at vital points in the city, seized radio stations and broadcast misinformation. They posed as Italian officers and openhandedly distributed furloughs among the enlisted men.[3]

The Italians, for their part, had a contingency plan of sorts. Marshal Ambrosio had issued orders to his commanders under the code-name OP44, which stipulated that Italian military units were to react against the Germans 'with a decisive dimension' – but what did this mean?

Badoglio had charged General Carboni, the Rome Area Commandant, with the defence of the city, and had then departed for southern Italy. When Carboni saw his chief getting out of town, he decided to skip too. Other members of the senior staff followed. This wanderlust spread all through the officer corps to the other ranks. Thousands of key personnel left their posts; some made for the hills and the partisans, others just went home.

A group of paratroopers, men from the II Battalion Paratroop Regiment 6 under Colonel Walter Gericke, were despatched to capture the General Headquarters at Monterotondo, north-east of Rome. The paratroopers were based at an airfield near Foggia and even though they were aware of the Italian surrender, Gericke had received no instruction to attack. Patrols were sent out and they found that long stretches of telephone cable had been cut by the local population. By the time that communications had been restored it was past midnight. Finally the word came, and the paratroopers prepared to mount a dawn attack. Gericke had managed to carry out a reconnaissance of the area and had identified a number of suitable DZs for his companies. The lumbering J52s were greeted by Italian anti-aircraft fire and a number of paratroopers were hit as they jumped from the planes.

The fight for Monterotondo was bitter. The Italian garrison contested the town street by street and there were casualties on both sides. Each house had to be cleared, and it was late in the afternoon before Gericke's men could mount an assault on the army headquarters itself, which was housed in the Castello. Using captured artillery the paratroopers subjected the Castello to a heavy bombardment and in time-honoured fashion concentrated their fire to create a breach in the massive walls. Once that had happened the Italians raised a white flag from the tower and surrendered.

After the departure of the fugitives, the veteran Marshal Caviglio took it upon himself to negotiate the capitulation of the Rome area garrison, while Foreign Minister Guariglia, who had also remained behind, tried to maintain some semblance of government. But with no orders or instructions from Badoglio there was little he could do. The Germans quickly overcame the isolated pockets of resistance. Some regular units of the army and ad hoc bands of Roman citizens defended key points in the city and paid the price for their resistance.

There were an estimated 65,000 Allied prisoners of war in Italy, most of them in camps well to the north of Rome. Very few were able to make good their escape when news reached them of the surrender. Each camp had a Senior British Officer (SBO) and their view was that the most sensible thing to do was to sit tight and await the arrival of the Allied armies. Most took the view that the Germans would retreat northwards and that rescue was only a matter of days away. Others considered that, since the situation was so muddled and nobody knew what the Germans would do, thousands of Allied prisoners on the run would only add to the confusion and also delay an orderly repatriation. Some ordered all ranks to be confined to camp.

This decision to stay put was soon discredited when the bulk of the Italian guards, for once showing more initiative than their captives, decided to head for home before the Germans arrived. Operation Achse contained contingencies for the Allied POWs and, within a very few days, large numbers of POWs were once again under lock and key awaiting transport northwards to the Third Reich. Some made use of the period of confusion to escape and the lucky ones were hidden in the hills by families who took the most enormous risks to protect these men from enemy searches. These people were extremely brave; the penalty for being caught with Allied soldiers was often death for the menfolk and the destruction of their property.

In many remote hill communities the arrival of Allied POWs was regarded quite pragmatically as another pair of hands to do essential farm work. There would be women too, whom the war had made widows, or whose menfolk were simply missing, while there were young and single women living in communities where eligible men, or indeed any men, were in very short supply. Where a warm welcome was offered some soldiers found little inducement to return to the war. Many others worked their way southwards and crossed to the Allied lines. They included General Dick O'Connor, the first desert commander, until he was captured by Rommel in 1941. O'Connor later commanded a corps in Normandy.

Ever since the coup Mussolini had been interned, first on the island of Ponza and later at La Maddelena, off the coast of Sardinia. There was however a sizeable German garrison on Sardinia and the island was a potential Allied target; so fearing a *coup de main*, Badoglio moved Mussolini for a third time at the end of August.

The relationship between Mussolini and Hitler was an odd business. There were obvious political and propaganda advantages for the Fascist cause in liberating Il Duce, but there were other issues involved. In the very early days, when Hitler moved to annex Austria, Mussolini chose not just to stand aside rather than intervene, but to encourage Hitler in the venture. Perhaps the Führer now felt that it was time to repay the debt. There was also a genuine friendship between the two men. One of the first to visit Hitler after the abortive 20 July bomb plot in 1944 was Mussolini. Hitler also referred to Mussolini when he was ousted as the 'valuable object'. So whatever the real reasons, Hitler entrusted the task of rescuing Mussolini to Standartenführer (Colonel) Otto Skorzeny from the Reichssichershauptamt (RHSA) or State Security Office, where he worked in the department concerned with espionage. The mission was code-named Operation Oak.

Il Duce was traced to San Grasso, a small mountain resort high in the Abruzzi in Central Italy. On the morning of Sunday 12 September 90 German paratroopers landed by glider on the slopes in front of the hotel where Mussolini was confined. He was rescued without any casualties to either side and flown by Skorzeny in a light aircraft off the mountain and eventually to a meeting with Hitler. Hitler had proposed moving the elite 1st SS Panzer Corps – composed of the Liebstandarte Adolf Hitler and the Das Reich Waffen-SS Divisions – from Army Group South in Russia to Italy. He believed that the politically motivated SS divisions would form a nucleus around which the Fascist elements in the Italian Army could rally.

The meeting at Rastenburg quickly convinced Hitler that Mussolini had little stomach for reviving his Fascist state or even exacting revenge on those who had betrayed him. He was persuaded to create a new Fascist Republic Party and ensconced as the puppet ruler of the Salo Republic, an Italian rump Fascist state centred at Rocca delle Caminate near Garganao on the shores of Lake Garda.

The loss of two key divisions from a vulnerable sector of the Russian front was not a good idea and Hitler was prevailed upon to change his mind. So instead the SS Panzer Group Headquarters under Sepp Dietrich and the Liebstandarte (minus its tanks and heavy equipment) were transferred to Italy to act as Mussolini's minders.

Sepp Dietrich's first duty on reaching warmer climes was to travel to Rome and escort Clara Petacci, Mussolini's mistress, back to Il Duce's bedchamber. The Liebstandarte found the Italian sojourn a pleasant interlude and a time to re-equip. The regiments were deployed throughout the major cities of the north – Bologna, Milan, Florence etc – as a very visible deterrent to the local population.

A skeleton administration of uncertain allegiance sat in the capital, now open to the movements of the German Army. At Salerno the King and Badoglio were eventually to set up a limited government under the eyes of an Allied Commission and with no effective external authority. The Italians were now engaged in a civil war. The country was, in any case, a patchwork quilt of conflicting loyalties. Members of families and communities, divided in their loyalties, fought and killed one another in a separate conflict which made few gestures to the humanitarian norms of battle. But it was the Germans who came off best from this whole messy affair. A policy of damage limitation kept their military options open south of Rome while the Salo Republic would both relieve the Germans from having to administer the territory and help secure their lines of communication.

The Allies gained just one advantage from this sorry mess. In the early hours of Friday 10 September the British battle squadron stood off the coast of Sardinia. At 0825 there hove into sight a large fleet – the Italian battle fleet. This had left its base ports of Genoa and Spezia after dark on the night of the 8th, in accordance with Allied instructions, and was bound for Malta. Ever since first light it had been harried and hounded by the Luftwaffe. Dornier DO217K–2 aircraft, operating from airbases, caused havoc. The flagship *Roma*, brand new, was hit and blew up with heavy loss of life, including the C-in-C, Admiral Bergamini. The battleship *Italia* was also heavily damaged.

On the morning of 11 September Admiral Cunningham cabled the Admiralty: 'Be pleased to inform their Lordships that the Italian Battlefleet is now anchored under the fortress guns of Malta.' In this pompous manner, which was intended to smack of the Nelson touch, he effectively described the only tangible thing that the Allies had got out of the Italian surrender.

Notes

1. CX/MSS/C.182.
2. CAB 101/144, pp 143–4.
3. Letter from Rome, Daniel Lang, 7 July 1944. *New Yorker War Pieces*, Bloomsbury Publishing Ltd, 1989, p 341.

19

Avalanche: D-Day at Salerno

The beaches at Salerno were defended not by compliant Italians, but by German panzers. By 0330 hours on 9 September, as the Fifth Army's assault waves headed inshore, the 16th Panzer Division completed its takeover of the Italian positions and was ready to repel the invaders. The panzers were not caught by surprise. Lieutenant Rocholl[1] commanded a unit of three armoured cars in the reconnaissance regiment of the 16th Panzers. Ever since they had moved into southern Italy the unit had been pestered by the frequent alarms about an Allied landing. At 1400 hours on 8 September, division headquarters had broadcast 'Attention Operation Feuerbruist'. This was the first warning; however, the troops continued with their afternoon rest. Suddenly, at about 1630 hours the regiment came on the air again with 'Attention Operation Orkan'. This was to signal that the invasion convoy was actually in sight. The siesta was over.

Rocholl and his squad were to cover Salerno; other reconnaissance patrols were deployed to watch Castellammare and Vietri. The armoured cars, SdKfz, the standard light armoured reconnaissance vehicle of the Wehrmacht, were fuelled, armed and ready to go. Rocholl went over to company headquarters for his battle instructions and radio ciphers. He also learned of the Italian surrender. It came as no surprise.

Rocholl was ready to leave. He saluted, in Wehrmacht fashion, and shook hands with his company commander before stepping out to brief the crews of his armoured cars; the big eight-cylinder water-cooled Horch engines purred in the background. Briefings over, the crews clambered into their vehicles. Rocholl fixed the map case into place on the armoured mantel in front of him and checked that his Schmeisser machine-pistol was within easy reach. At high speed the young officer led his column down the main road from Battipaglia to Salerno. Everywhere Italians were standing in groups, deep in excited discussions about their country's capitulation.

Rocholl had chosen an observation post on top of the mountain ridge near the sea and to the south-east of Salerno. From this commanding position he had a clear view north-west towards Salerno and Vietri and south-east along the entire coast as far as the Plain of Faiano. A section of troops from his own 3rd Company, with a heavy machine gun, were dug in nearby. Beneath them was an Italian position, now abandoned, which comprised a coastal battery and some machine guns.

Darkness descended; Rocholl ordered his men to prepare an evening meal. There were potatoes to be fried on the Esbit cooker, the Wehrmacht's equivalent of a small field stove, and as many tomatoes and olives as the soldiers could eat; these were the staple crops of the farms in the plain of Salerno and it was harvest time. Just about to clear up after the meal they were startled by a terrific explosion. Frying pans and eating irons were hurled aside as the soldiers rushed to man their positions. Rocholl ran to the edge of the hill to witness a terrifying yet beautiful spectacle. The mole in the harbour at Salerno had been blown up by their engineers. Explosion followed explosion and soon warehouses and numerous small ships in the harbour were ablaze. The warehouses appeared to Rocholl to be empty, for they burned to the ground in no time. But a larger coastal steamer burned the whole night through.

The night passed slowly for the Germans. Rocholl ordered his men to rest in relays. Most had only recently completed their training and, new to battle, were too keyed up to sleep at first. Gradually they did manage to settle down and catnap. Towards midnight there was the sound of aircraft overhead. The soldiers shrugged their shoulders deep into the shell scrapes they had dug besides their vehicles, but Rocholl realized that this was the Luftwaffe, not the British night bombers that had plagued their lives since the panzers had set foot in Italy. The irregular beats of the unsynchronized engines faded as the planes headed out to sea. The moon shone as a weak crescent very low on the horizon. Rocholl had his night-vision binoculars to his eyes, but he could see nothing. Suddenly, on the horizon, a formidable anti-aircraft barrage tore skyward. The broad curtain of gunfire showed up clearly the full length of a convoy. The invasion had begun.

D-day was to prove bloody and inconclusive. First ashore, the Special Forces encountered little or no opposition. The American Colonel Darby left one battalion of Rangers on the coast road and headed inland with his

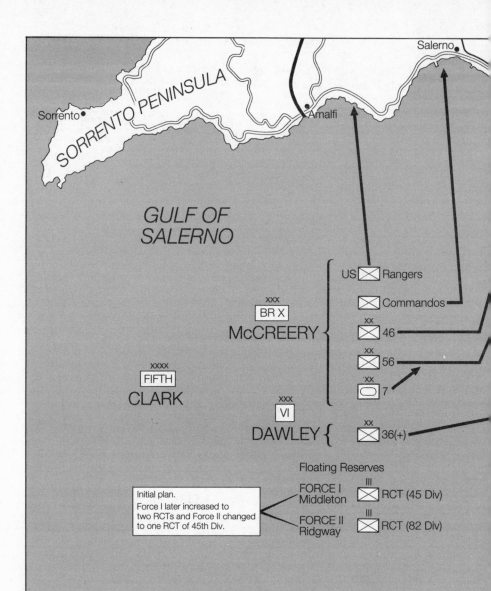

Sorrento •

SORRENTO PENINSULA

Amalfi •

Salerno •

GULF OF SALERNO

US ⊠ Rangers

⊠ Commandos

```
  xxx
 BR X
```
McCREERY {

```
  xx
```
⊠ 46

```
  xx
```
⊠ 56

```
  xx
```
▢ 7

```
xxxx
FIFTH
```
CLARK

```
 xxx
 VI
```
DAWLEY {

```
  xx
```
⊠ 36(+)

Floating Reserves

FORCE I
Middleton

```
 III
```
⊠ RCT (45 Div)

FORCE II
Ridgway

```
 III
```
⊠ RCT (82 Div)

Initial plan.
Force I later increased to
two RCTs and Force II changed
to one RCT of 45th Div.

SALERNO CAMPAIGN
September 9, 1943

```
0            miles            10
0          kilometres         15
```

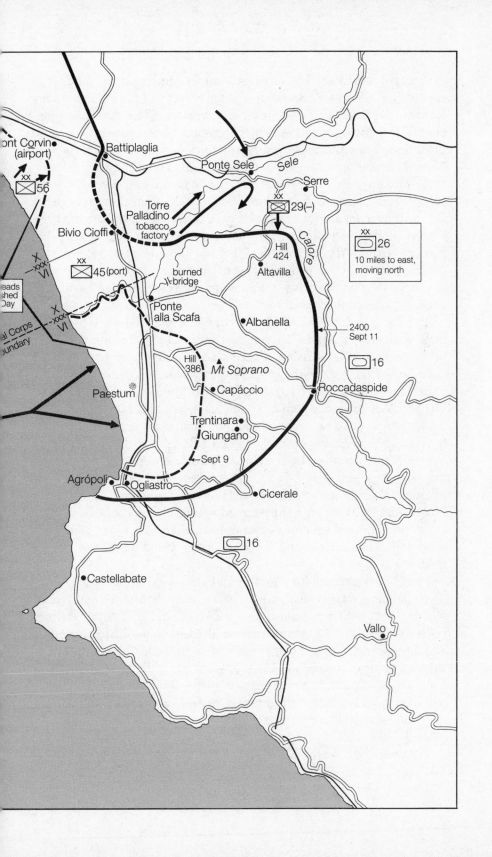

ont Corvin
(airport)

Battiplaglia

Ponte Sele

Sele

Serre

xx
56

xx
29(–)

Torre
Palladino
tobacco
factory

Bivio Cioffi

Calore

Hill
424

xx
26

10 miles to east,
moving north

xx
45(port)

Altavilla

burned
bridge

X
xxx
VI

eads
shed
Day

Ponte
alla Scafa

Albanella

2400
Sept 11

al Corps
oundary

X
xxx
VI

Hill
386

Mt Soprano

16

Paestum

Capáccio

Roccadaspide

Trentinara
Giungano

Sept 9

Agrópoli

Ogliastro

Cicerale

16

Castellabate

Vallo

1st and 3rd Battalions. The main force moved straight up the rough track towards the Chiunzi Pass, which is at the very top of the mountain spine forming the interior of the Sorrento peninsula. On either flank other companies spread out to sweep the ground. Progress here was more difficult over mountainous country with thick woods and deep ravines. So it was a cautious advance, and the ground had to be searched carefully to make sure no enemy were left behind to raid communication lines. It was six miles, all uphill, to the Chiunzi Pass. But the Rangers were superbly fit, and the reconnaissance elements were in the pass by just after sunrise. Darby and the main force arrived later and looked down on the sprawling plain of Naples. About a mile to their front and 1,000 feet below lay the Nocera defile with the main road clearly visible as it cut its way between the rocks. Beyond, Vesuvius, ominous and dark clouds streaming from its cone, dominated the plain.

The Rangers dug in where they were and Darby, for the first time since he landed, radioed Mark Clark on the command ship *Ancon* and told him of the success of his mission. There are two things to note. Nationality came top of the list. Darby by-passed the chain of command. He was under the operational control of the British X Corps' commander General McCreery to whom he should have reported. He was not where he was supposed to be. German reinforcements for counterattack would not travel to Salerno by way of the Chiunzi Pass but by the Nocera defile. Where Darby deployed he remained a passive observer of the German units that counterattacked from Naples. Even if he had been in the right place he did not have the heavy weapons or artillery to dominate the Nocera defile. Whether lightly armed special forces could have withstood a determined armoured assault is another matter, but Darby had not fulfilled his mission and the Fifth Army would pay dearly for this failure.

The British commandos – marine and army – did not do much better. Their landing was harder and the subsequent hours decidedly more bloody. The two Commandos, No 2 (Army) and 45 (Royal Marine), collectively known as Layforce, were embarked on the LSI *Prince Albert* and three British LCIs. Their commanders, in the lull before the storm, shared a bottle of vintage port in the officers' bar of the *Prince Albert*. Both Commandos landed at the marina at Vietri, some seven miles east of Salerno. Vietri is a little fishing village tucked between the hills and the sea. Immediately above Vietri was the little village of Cava and the La Molina defile.

The principal objective was to secure their defile. First, they had to take and hold the high ground on both sides of the valley. With their training and expertise in mountain warfare they were ideally suited for such a role. Second, they had to prevent the enemy either from carrying out demolitions to block the pass, or indeed retaking it. But the commandos were elite light infantry and lacked the heavy weapons and support to fight a sustained defensive engagement. Their main task was to defend the road bridge that spanned a gorge on the edge of Cava. If the enemy destroyed the bridge or held the defile they could pop the cork in the bottle, seal the Allies into their beachhead, isolate the Rangers at Nocera and mop up at their leisure.

The commandos were diverted from their main task by the enemy resistance in Vietri, and by the time the village had been secured there was stiffening resistance the further they moved inland. When they did reach La Molina, they found the Germans were dug into well-defended positions which could be reinforced and resupplied because the Rangers were not at Nocera where they should have been. The 46th (British) Infantry had the fire power and armour to prise the Germans out of the defile, but their landing below Salerno had not fared well. Enemy demolitions and skilfully sited rearguards delayed the capture of Salerno itself which had to be cleared street by street. In the scorching heat it was an action replay of Sicily except that now the men had to contend with choking dust clouds of falling masonry. The parched and inadequately equipped young infanteers who had landed with very different expectations spent a wretched first day on the mainland of Europe. It was only a foretaste of what was to come. It was late afternoon by the time that an advance element of infantry had linked up with the commandos. By that time Mark Clark's carefully constructed War College solution was already looking decidedly tattered round the edges.

German resistance along the beaches that day was patchy. With only one division to watch 30 miles of waterfront it could hardly have been otherwise, but for ground which mattered 16th Panzers fought tenaciously and successfully. A brigade of Royal Hampshires failed to secure Montecorvino airfield, their day constantly disrupted by a series of counterattacks which ended with neither side in possession. But since the airfield was vital to the Allies, the Germans could claim the victory. With no air support ashore, everything had to come up from Sicily.

Battipaglia is an important road and rail junction. The town was captured early in the day by the 9th Battalion Royal Fusiliers who were then fatally exposed because the only support armour were their own Bren-gun carriers. British Shermans were still being unloaded onto the beach.

By the end of the first day the X (British) Corps were ashore with 23,000 troops, 80 tanks, 325 guns and more than 2,000 vehicles of all shapes and sizes. The Corps, landing on a seven-mile section of the beach, had been given the objective of securing a beachhead that embraced the town of Salerno, the airfield at Montecorvino, the passes out of the plain, Battipaglia and an important road junction at Eboli. The Corps failed to meet almost all of these objectives despite some ferocious fighting, some of it at close quarters.

The Americans to the south had the worst time of all. After the Luftwaffe had attacked the armada out at sea, it was clear that any hope of surprise had been compromised. McCreery ordered a naval bombardment as the assault craft headed inshore. Clark, nevertheless, hung on to his original strategy, and, even though there were the warships available, refused a naval bombardment. It was a major blunder.

The greenhorn Texans approached their beaches in silence. As the first wave of their landing craft grated on the dark sand and their ramps ground into the gentle surf, a strident voice came over a loudspeaker. 'Come on in and give up. We have you covered.' German or American? Nobody ever knew. Flares suddenly flooded the foreshore with brilliant white light. Machine guns and mortars raked the landing craft, which simply disintegrated, their wooden frames overwhelmed by a hailstorm of fire from the front and on the flanks. Other boats, caught a little way out, drifted helplessly, sailors and infantry obliterated by air bursts. Beyond the surf, landing craft milled around in confusion. Young coxswains, many new to battle, were reluctant to run the gauntlet and deliver their precious cargo of soldiers to the shore. Their failure threw all the unloading schedules into disarray. There were more problems further out to sea. The minesweeping operations in the American sector had gone badly wrong. The naval officer in charge, overwhelmed by the responsibilities of command, had a nervous breakdown, retired to his cabin and locked the door on the world.

General Walker, the division commander, stepped ashore with his staff a little after 0800 hours that morning. It had taken their landing boat more than five hours to make the twelve miles from ship to shore; during that time he was totally out of touch with events. Delays, uncertainties, inexperience and congestion in the sea lanes all helped to prolong what should have been a relatively short sea journey.

Despite the ferocity of enemy fire, the momentum created by successive waves of landing craft and the discipline instilled in soldiers by a relentless training cycle, took the Texans gradually up the beach and into cover in the scrub and irrigation ditches beyond the dune line. Infantry moved forward in small groups towards the railway, which was about one and half miles inland. The Germans had about two companies' worth of panzer grenadiers to cover the four beaches in the American sector. Once the Texans began to probe inland the defenders on foot had no alternative but to fall back across the coastal plain to the foothills beyond. From there the Germans were able to smother the beaches and inshore waters with artillery fire.

The British monitor HMS *Abercrombie* returned fire with her massive 15-inch guns, later to be joined by the cruiser USS *Savannah* which brought her six-inch batteries into a devastatingly effective anti-tank role. But German counterattacks increased in intensity throughout the day, and the absence of tanks and artillery ashore until the afternoon meant that the enemy armour had to be fought by infantry. Unusually for the Germans, their attacks lacked both substance and coordination; had they been up to scratch the American beachhead would have been in severe trouble.

By evening, the Americans were more or less ashore, despite the fact that only two (Red and Green) of the four beaches were open and able to receive landing craft. But control and discipline were bringing order to the earlier confusion, and the Anglo-Americans settled down to their first night on the European mainland. Though exhausted and drained by the experiences of the day there was little chance of sleep. The Germans kept up their bombardment, and mosquitos and flies descended to feast off the battlefield. The repellent cream the troops had smeared on their arms and faces proved to be useless. And human faeces attracted huge swarms (the troops, who had gorged themselves on fruit all day had, by evening, succumbed to stomach cramps and violent attacks of diarrhoea) as did the dead bodies that still lay awaiting burial.

Mark Clark studied the situation in the Operations Room in *Ancon*. At Salerno the battle plan had called for the Anglo-Americans to join hands at the Sele bridge. Instead the gap between them ran the length of that river to the sea, and in places was over ten miles wide. This meant that from the outset the Allies fought two quite separate battles at Salerno. Mark Clark also failed to appreciate the significance of the Sele Corridor, and was drawn to the high ground which gave the Germans the advantages.

The Fifth Army battle plan which envisaged the swift capture of Naples was already meaningless. The men who landed at Salerno on Thursday 9 September were destined to take three weeks to reach Naples and to suffer 12,000 casualties in the process.

Elsewhere the Allies were demonstrating maritime supremacy and helping to make the beachhead at Salerno secure. There were very few German troops garrisoned at Taranto, and the Italians suggested that the Allies seize the port and use the magnificent naval base for their own needs. Alexander and Cunningham planned to carry elements of the 1st (British) Airborne Division from Bizerta to Taranto. It was to be called Operation Slapstick. It was hoped the landings would promote confusion and uncertainty and help things at Salerno. Later it was intended to feed into the port two of Montgomery's divisions and the headquarters of V Corps to exploit an advance inland to take airfields at Foggia, 80 miles away over the mountains.

Slapstick lived up to its codename. Like so much of the Italian campaign, the idea was sound, but it lost the edge in practice. The four cruisers of the 12th Cruiser Squadron, together with the fast minelayer HMS *Abdiel* and the US cruiser *Boise* carried the airborne troops. Loading a landing craft was difficult enough, but the cruisers presented almost insurmountable problems to the harassed staff officers, who had little idea of the amount of space available or the clearance between decks to store equipment.

The force landed at Taranto unopposed. The only casualties came from the tragic loss of *Abdiel*, which hit a mine when swinging at anchor, and sank with heavy loss of life. Once ashore the Red Berets lost no time in moving quickly inland. The paratroopers had not been able to bring first-line transportation with them, so they were largely immobile. Lacking heavy weapons, they could do little but probe forward gently. At first the enemy were nowhere to be seen, and by 11 September the paratroopers had secured two other valuable ports on the Adriatic coast, Bari and Brindisi. Some tanks and armoured cars would have made all the difference, for it was good open country and the Germans had few tanks of their own in the area. Instead the Germans moved in battalions from their own parachute division and effectively sealed the British into their beachhead.

And what of Montgomery? That evening he signalled Alexander: 'My divisions are now strung out and the infantry . . . must be rested. Am halting main bodies of divisions on the line Catanzaro to Nicastro. Divisions will then wind up their tails and have two days rest.'[2]

Notes

1. Morris, *Salerno*, p 157.
2. Ibid.

20

Consolidation – After a Fashion

It is of the utmost importance that you maintain pressure upon the Germans so that
they cannot remove forces from your front and concentrate against Avalanche.[1]

Alexander to Montgomery,
10 September 1943

From Von Vietinghoff's headquarters at Caserta to Kesselring in Rome
and Hitler with his top generals in their bunker in East Prussia, the Allies'
positions and deployments in the south of Italy were closely analysed.
There were British paratroopers without any vehicles at Taranto and
other troops in Brindisi, courtesy of the Italian Navy, but the main threat
was at Salerno where Mark Clark clung to a narrow beachhead. His
nearest support, apart from the troops still waiting to come ashore, lay
with Montgomery whose divisions were some 200 miles to the south at
Nicastro, making a very leisurely advance. The Germans had no intention
of holding on to Southern Italy and were in two minds about Rome. But
Kesselring considered that Salerno presented a heaven-sent opportunity
to deal the Allied cause a heavy blow.

In the first 24 hours the 16th Panzers had identified not Eighth Army
veterans but a green American division plus two British divisions that
were held in low esteem, all commanded by a general experiencing his
first taste of command in the field. As well as the gap along the Sele
Corridor and the confusion between the British divisions, Kesselring
appreciated that the Allied beachhead lacked depth, so, even if reinforcements were waiting out to sea, there was no room for them to deploy.

Kesselring was convinced that Montgomery was temperamentally
incapable of trying any startling new moves. He ordered Von Vietinghoff

to leave the minimum forces necessary to screen the Eighth Army in Calabria and concentrate everything to hand on Salerno. It was a race between the two opposing armies. The Fifth needed to rush reinforcements and build up their fire power so they could break out of the vice-like grip of the enemy in those encircling hills. The critical factor was the landing craft – their seatime, the time to unload, and above all, their capacity.

Mark Clark had gone into battle knowing that there were not enough landing craft to furnish his needs at Salerno. Clark had wanted to land with two divisions in the US VI Corps; he had enough craft for one and one-third divisions. The absence of port facilities aggravated the problem; everything the Allies needed had to be manhandled ashore over open beaches. All Mark Clark could do was pray for fine weather. Even the slightest change for the worse would whip up the waves and create a swell. In such conditions cargoes could not easily be transferred from freighter to landing craft and no skipper likes to beach his LCT through a surf.

The Germans had the advantage of interior lines and a shorter distance over which to move their forces. To reinforce the hard-pressed 16th Panzers, Von Vietinghoff had elements of four divisions, all of which were in striking distance of the beachhead.

After the experience in Sicily, Von Vietinghoff decided not to contest the beaches but to build up his forces and then attack from high ground. The XIV Panzer Corps would look after the northern battle involving the Special Forces and the British divisions in X Corps. The LXXVI Panzer Corps were to handle the Americans south of the Sele river. The Luftwaffe Parachute Panzer Division Herman Goering was still recovering from Sicily in Naples; only 30 tanks and 21 assault guns were operational and it was still short of infantry. But it was the closest available force, so Von Vietinghoff reinforced it with two battalions from the 1st Parachute Division, then stationed in Apulia.

The 15th Panzer Grenadier Division was deployed further north on the Gulf at Gaeta, even though it was also critically short of armour, with just seven tanks and 18 assault guns. Both divisions received their marching orders before last light on 9 September, but deployment to the battlefield was fraught with delays and problems. Long columns of trucks and armoured vehicles encountered hostile Italians. Bitter crowds in the teeming streets of Naples slowed the pace to a crawl and there were many angry scenes. The 15th Panzer Grenadiers had a similar experience in Baronissa, where units became isolated and separated.

The German divisions from the south had further to travel and so took longer to reach Salerno. The 29th Panzer Grenadiers remained immobilized for two days near the Gulf of Policastro in Calabria waiting for fuel. This was a self-inflicted wound. On 8 September a German naval officer at the port of Sapri, convinced the Allies were about to land in overwhelming strength, panicked and scuttled a tanker-load of fuel. This encouraged an equally ardent Wehrmacht quartermaster to put the local army fuel dump to the torch.

The 26th Panzers, which had been providing the rearguard against the Canadians in Calabria, had left its tank battalions in Rome. Their current operation was considered unsuited to tanks and their place was taken by 1st and 4th Battalions of the Parachute Division. It took the tank battalion a week to reach the battle front.

Despite Alexander's explicit instructions, Montgomery and the Eighth Army presented no threat to the redeployments. But all of the German divisions suffered from the attentions of the Allied air forces as they moved on Salerno. Road and rail communications were hammered by medium bombers. At the same time the Mitchells and Flying Fortresses of the Strategic Air Force bombed the two main crossings over the Volturno river at Cancello and Capua. Destruction of the bridges would present Mark Clark with a river crossing later in the year. Had these bridges been defended by the 82nd Airborne, would they have survived intact as well as proving a more effective method of denying a passage to the enemy? Or, as with Arnhem, would it have proved a bridge too far and resulted in the sacrifice of the airborne division?

American Liberators of the Middle East Air Command pounded the airfields at Foggia and denied their use to the Luftwaffe, who were unable to influence the land battle in any significant fashion. Clear weather at high altitudes permitted incoming German aircraft to be spotted quickly, and the Lightnings and Spitfires kept the enemy at bay. Much of the time, however, there was a haze at low altitudes and over the sea and the beaches. This enabled Focke-Wulf-190s equipped with under-wing bomb racks to launch hit-and-run attacks.

The Royal Air Force contributed two wings, each of five squadrons of Spitfires, to the air battle. The fighters operated from adjoining landing strips bulldozed out of the vineyards near Falcone in Sicily. From there the beachhead at Salerno was at maximum operating range. The planes were equipped with 90-gallon overload or drop tanks which actually doubled the amount of fuel. The wings had come in with the North African landings in November 1942 and by this time ought to have been a seasoned force. However, some of the senior pilots had exceeded their operational tours and were assigned to other duties for a rest. And many of the best pilots had been killed during ground strafing in Sicily.

Ground strafing was responsible for the loss of more aces in both the British and American air forces than any other form of air combat. Low-level onslaughts were often against obsolete aircraft or occasional road convoys, and were never worth the loss of a skilled pilot. The pilots themselves dreaded such missions where, instead of pitting their skills against another in the sky, they were offering themselves as targets to every ground gunner within range.

Air cover at first and last light over the beachhead was provided by the carrier-based Fleet Air Arm Seafires. The RAF wings were not able to fly at night from their primitive airstrips. But the Fleet Air Arm became less effective as the battle progressed. The Seafires, flying off converted escort carriers which had a top speed of 20 knots, needed a ten-knot wind to get airborne. Most days there was hardly a breath of air, while deck landing accidents quickly reduced their numbers and fighting efficiency.

The Strategic Air Force deployed nine squadrons of Lightnings. These excellent fighters provided the high altitude cover, but were hampered by the absence of radar over the beachhead.

In the American sectors the second day ashore was devoted to consolidation and expansion. The Texans had spent a long and frightening night anticipating a determined panzer attack in the morning. Instead the Germans broke off contact and seemingly melted away. It came as a very welcome surprise. Nevertheless, the beaches were still badly congested. The army had failed to provide sufficient troops to clear stores and unload waiting landing craft. One beachmaster refused to accept any landing craft that were not accompanied by work parties.

The 179th Regimental Combat Team from the 45th (US) Infantry Division landed on Blue Beach in the American sector. Their landing left just battalions of the 157th RCT and some additional artillery as the total float reserve to Fifth Army.

Mark Clark toured the beachhead. He was anxious to establish his own army headquarters on land as soon as possible, but he had to curb his impatience. The first priority had been to have Dawley and his corps headquarters fully ashore and operational but this was taking longer than anticipated. Clark brought his signals staff with him to look for a suitable location for the Fifth Army command post. They decided on a house – Baronissa villa – which the locals called *Villa Rossa*, for the exterior walls were painted in a deep red. It was large, imposing and relatively undamaged. The villa was located close to the estuary of the Sele river and on the seaward side of the railway and main highway. It was conveniently close to the British corps headquarters but more importantly was in the American sector and close to Dawley. Mark Clark had strong reservations about Dawley and believed he would need support if all did not go according to plan.

But that Friday morning the mood was one of optimism, after the trials and tribulations of the previous day. Clark met with his two divisional commanders, Walker and Middleton, and reviewed the situation. They were tremendously encouraged by the lack of German resistance. Clark ordered his divisional commanders to push inland, and dislodge the Germans from the high ground. Indeed the situation looked so good that, before he went to see McCreery and the British, he sent a message to General Alexander saying he would soon be ready to break out of the beachhead and advance on Naples. The visit to Dick McCreery disabused Mark Clark of such dreams. Clark had driven along the shoreline and its immediate hinterland to reach the British corps sector for the first time; he became very concerned by the considerable gap that existed between the two corps.

The two generals were to strike up a reasonable relationship although it was not until later in the campaign that they would become good friends. This first morning on the mainland of Europe Clark was not particularly looking forward to his meeting. One problem was that he didn't know much about the British troops under his command. On more than one occasion in the preparation for the landings Clark had complained to Eisenhower about the bi-nationality of his army. The complications of command were incredible, and logistical problems compromised the flexibility of his forces. Though Clark never said as much to Eisenhower, he believed that Salerno had been made an Anglo-American affair because if these, the first landings on mainland Europe had failed, then the two countries would have shared the blame.

McCreery had all the reserve and mannerisms of a typical British cavalry officer, except that he chose to be scruffy, eccentrically so. He was as tall and thin as Clark, and always sported what the American dubbed 'high water breeches', khaki pants that were about five inches short in the leg. McCreery was also possessed of a stammer. When excited he became almost incoherent. At this moment, however, dress was the last thing on either man's mind. The British were having a bad time of it against mounting opposition. Earlier that day the Germans had counterattacked at Battipaglia, where a feature called the Tobacco Factory had become the focus of attention. The 9th Battalion Royal Fusiliers had been cut off and left without support. German artillery knocked out the six-pounder anti-tank guns of the Fusiliers; elements of the 26th Panzers, Mark IV tanks and paratroopers, mounted a series of penetrating assaults. Large number of the Fusiliers surrendered at the first opportunity.

A counterattack launched by 3rd Battalion Grenadier Guards with a squadron of Shermans from the Scots Greys in support was ill-coordinated and beaten back with heavy losses. This failure sealed the fate of the Fusiliers: barely a company's worth were able to break out of the encirclement.

McCreery was convinced that the battle for the beachhead was about to begin. He doubted the ability of his hard-pressed troops to link up with the Americans at Ponte Sele, let alone reach Naples in four days. The British Corps commander was also worried about Darby's Rangers, and shared Mark Clark's concern over the gap on the right flank and the low flat country between Battipaglia and the Sele river. The two generals discussed the problems in considerable detail before Clark returned to the American sector. He determined to reorganize and redeploy VI Corps as quickly as possible across the river and also onto the high ground.

General Dawley protested strongly when Clark outlined his orders. He had ended up with a longer front to defend with insufficient troops. Mark Clark ordered a battalion task force to move to Maiori by sea as soon as possible to support the Rangers. This would bring them under British command. The 1st Battalion of the 143rd Infantry was at the time the 36th Division reserve infantry and bivouacked at Vannulo. The battalion of commander Lt Colonel Fred Walker Jr, son of the commanding general, prepared to move, and was joined by a company each of medium tanks, tank destroyers, a battery of field artillery and combat engineers. It took the task force three days before its advance guard landed at Red Beach.

Clark also decided to shift the VI (US) Corps boundary across the Sele river to link up with the British and to use the two-battalion 157th RCT to plug the gap. When he reached the *Ancon*'s Operations Room he was told that the 157th RCT had already landed, but on the south side of the river. Clark was furious. Admiral Hewitt explained that he had been ordered by Allied Headquarters in Algiers to return the landing ships immediately; they were required to begin their countdown for sailing to the United Kingdom. All that Hewitt could do in the absence of Clark was to dump the troops and their stores on the nearest convenient beach.

The 36th Divisional Combat Engineers were already hard at work replacing the bridge across the Sele and this allowed the 157th RCT to cross over into the British sector at dawn the next morning.

Clark had made some necessary redeployments but was still not convinced that the Germans were about to launch a major counterattack. He though McCreery was being unduly pessimistic. He ordered Fred Walker to get his Texans into the surrounding hills, where they became sucked into a vicious firefight for a hill village called Altavilla. The real significance of the Sele Corridor still eluded him.

Notes

1. Morris, *Salerno*, p 158.

21

Quiet Warnings

I am not satisfied with the situation at Avalanche. The buildup is slow and they are pinned down to a bridgehead which has not enough depth.[1]

Throughout the weekend the Germans increased the pressure against the Allied bridgehead. Once again the British sector bore the brunt of the action. Elites battled it out on the hills above Maiori and Vietri as German paratroopers attacked Rangers and commandos. All the while the enemy artillery bombardment increased in intensity, and a sense of foreboding gripped the divisional and corps staff as every attempt failed to break through this ring of steel.

The Scots Guards attacked another key position also called the Tobacco Factory. It was a botched affair. Three companies put in a copybook night attack across open ground, but there were no tanks in support and the Guards were decimated. This was the last attempt to break out of the beachhead. First the British and later the Americans went on the defensive and surrendered the initiative to the enemy.

The tactics employed by the Germans during the four days of counterattack (Saturday to Tuesday, 11–14 September) made full use of their advantage. Tanks and assault guns, closely supported by infantry in half-tracks, concentrated at exposed parts of the line and made quick probing stabs. If a particular attack did not invite further exploitation, the enemy withdrew to his original position, reformed and moved off to strike elsewhere. These were the classic tactics of a mobile defence at which the Wehrmacht had become skilled practitioners.

The Americans suffered heavily that weekend because they fought an encounter battle. Clark had expressly ordered Dawley to break out of the beachhead. The result was that columns of American infantry had advanced beyond a notional perimeter defence which amounted to little more than a gunline when they were struck head-on by German armoured infantry. The corps plan devised by Dawley's overworked staff[2] was sound enough. He had three columns on the move. On the left flank the two battalions of 157th RCT had crossed the Sele river into the British sector and moved inland to attack Eboli, a small town about three miles from the Sele river. If the Americans could take Eboli, the German positions in and around Battipaglia would be outflanked. The British, in turn, could threaten the German grip on the airfield at Montecorvino. Once the field was secured air support could be immediately on tap.

On the right flank Walker dispatched his Texans to the hills. They had captured Altavilla with deceptive ease, and redeployed in preparation to move onto the ridge line that ran above and behind the town northwards to overlook the ground above the Ponte Sele.

In the centre, the main force of the 179th RCT was ordered to continue its advance up the Sele Corridor to Ponte Sele, where they could cut Route 19 and the main German supply lines.

The vital ground in VI Corps sector was the flood plain between the Sele and Calore rivers. The plain forms a corridor of low ground starting at Serre, a village twelve miles inland that nestles at the foot of the hills. The corridor descends gently to the junction of the two rivers, just five miles from the sea. This was the obvious line of advance for any defender in launching a counterattack against a beachhead, yet its significance did not become apparent until the first American troops actually deployed there. Mark Clark and his Fifth Army staff had not appreciated the importance of Persano as the key point in any defence against an armoured thrust through the corridor. Persano was a hamlet squatting on top of a low hill in the Sele Corridor. It had a commanding view of the plain, particularly the crossing point over the Sele river. The original D-day objective, the Ponte Sele, remained the objective, the point where the two corps would link to complete the beachhead perimeter, the Americans coming through the high ground to the right from Altavilla and the British completing the pincer movement by way of Battipaglia and Eboli.

There is little doubt that the American command structure was fractured and uncoordinated. Mark Clark may not have liked Dick McCreery, but he was aware of his competence and left him to fight the X Corps battle without interference. In the American sector there were four headquarters crammed, cheek by jowl, into a shallow perimeter, in some instances within walking distance. But the absence of communication was alarming. At Walker's 36th Division Headquarters,[3] some of the senior staff officers were manifestly incompetent. Information and data on the situation maps were out of date at the Division CP. As a consequence Corps and Army headquarters were poorly served. Middleton and the more experienced 45th (US) Division were less of a liability.

Rather than confront the problem head-on, Clark's solution was to glean the intelligence he needed by making regular personal visits to the front line. His accelerated promotion over men such as Walker, Middleton and Dawley perhaps made them reluctant to cooperate. And, of course, this was Clark's first experience of command in battle. When it was over Mark Clark did succeed in stamping his authority on Fifth Army and there were some wholesale sackings, but too many ordinary soldiers were to pay the price for weakness and vacillation in the high command.

The 45th (US) Infantry had fought through the Sicilian campaign and considered themselves to be a veteran formation, which they were, compared with the T Patchers from Texas. The 179th RCT advanced with the infantry at the front. Their armour, tank-destroying artillery, was strung out to the rear. They should have known better. Above Persano the 29th Panzer Grenadiers sprang an ambush from front and flank. The infantry were cut off from their heavy support and surrounded. The Thunderbirds, in keeping with their western roots, 'circled their wagons' at last light and waited for the panzer grenadiers to do their worst. Although they had suffered heavy casualties, the Thunderbirds must have offered a more spirited resistance than they realised, for when dawn broke the enemy had gone. They were able to make good their escape back down the corridor, link up with their support and return to the comparative safety of the beachhead perimeter.

At about the same time the 157th RCT, advancing on the left with tanks in support, bumped into the main line of German resistance at another tobacco factory which lay just off Highway 18 to Eboli. The factory occupied a piece of rising ground which covered a crossing point over the Sele river and the main highway beyond.

Meanwhile, offshore, the Luftwaffe launched a massive effort against Allied warships. Mindful of the lesson learned at Sicily, Von Vietinghoff knew that the tremendous asset offered by naval gunfire had to be neutralized before he could instigate the main counterattack ashore. In the first three days of the invasion, the Luftwaffe recorded more than 450 missions by fighters and fighter-bombers against the mass of shipping in the bay. They sank four transports and seven landing ships, and damaged many more. The only major warship casualty was the Royal Navy monitor *Erebus* which had been disabled by a mine on D-day.

The cruisers, destroyers and a second monitor, HMS *Roberts*, had performed a valiant service for the troops onshore. The effects of a naval salvo landing on a concentration of tanks and half-track was enhanced by the total frustration of the enemy. It was impossible to fight back against such a fire. Hitler decided to intervene and ordered the squadron that had savaged the Italian battle fleet just a few days previously to attack the warships in Salerno Bay with their radio-controlled bombs.

The Luftwaffe had two models of the radio-controlled anti-ship missiles, a forerunner of the Chinese Silkworms. Both had fins and rocket boosters to allow corrections to the flight path. They were armour-piercing and of similar weight in warheads. One was faster but had a shorter range. To all intents and purposes these weapons, called the HS293 glide bomb or *Fritz X* by the Germans, were invulnerable. After their successful debut in the Mediterranean, Allied scientists, desperate to find an antidote, advanced the theory that since the weapons were radio-controlled, electronic pulses, such as those emitted by an electric razor, might be able to knock them off course. The open flagdecks and bridges of cruisers and destroyers were quickly equipped with extra powerpoints and officers stood by, razors pointed skywards! The electric-razor defence was a farce. And conventional anti-aircraft guns could not keep track of a small weapon flying at close to the speed of sound.

The Dornier 217 was a twin-engined bomber which was nearing retirement. Like the venerable B52s of today, however, a stand-off capability gave the aged plane a new lease of life, for it allowed them to unload some distance from the target and its defences. The bomb itself gave off a thin trail of smoke which allowed the bomb aimer to steer by a primitive form of radio control (via tail-mounted spoilers).

The Marseille-based 11/KG100 squadron made their first attack on Saturday 11 September. The cruiser USS *Philadelphia* took a near miss when a Fritz X hit the sea just a few feet off her starboard bow. The explosion close-tested every seam in the 12,000-ton cruiser and caused considerable damage, though she remained operational.

An equally important target for the Luftwaffe was the command ship *Ancon* (AGC4).[4] Her size, bulk and forest of aerials made her extremely conspicuous.[5] The Luftwaffe's tactic was to send in a flight of FW-190s at masthead height to distract the air defences while the Dorniers circled high overhead. Some 500 yards off the *Ancon*'s stern the cruiser USS

Savannah was threading her way through the crowded anchorage at 15 knots to take up station to bombard the shore. Those on the bridge of *Ancon* were watching the *Savannah*, a magnificent sight in the midday sun, when they saw a smoking bomb directly above topple over and dive at terrific speed into the cruiser. A direct hit was scored on the top of No 3 turret. Designed to penetrate five and a half inches of armour, the two inches of armour plate, which was the standard of the *Brooklyn* class cruisers, offered little resistance. The warhead penetrated all the way to the handling room in the bowels of the ship. When the bomb detonated, a large hole was blown in the ship's bottom and opened a seam in her side. Sea water flooded in and extinguished several boilers. The bows gradually settled until the foredeck was nearly awash and the stern rose clear of the water. One hundred men or more were killed outright.

Discipline and seamanship saved the *Savannah*. While expert repair crews were found from the salvage tugs that clustered around the stricken cruiser, her own men were able to correct the list by pumping from the fore to the aft bunkers. At the end of a very busy day the *Savannah*, under her own steam and escorted by a clutch of destroyers, left for Malta where more thorough repairs could be completed. As she limped clear of the anchorage the ordeal was just beginning for four members of her crew. They were the operators who manned the small auxiliary radio room, a compartment located deep in the bowels of the ship and some decks below where the bomb exploded.

The compartments above, beneath and around the radio room were flooded and the water was shoulder-deep in the radio shack. The men there could not swim out because the door was blocked by wreckage. There could be no hope of rescue until the cruiser could be dry-docked and her flooded compartments themselves pumped dry. The plight of the trapped men was known because a single voice pipe, two and a half inches in diameter thick and connected to the bridge, had survived the impact.

The men were to remain entombed for the four days it took the *Savannah* to reach Malta. The voice pipe was used to pump fresh air into the compartment; drinking water and some liquid food were also passed down to the trapped men.

It was hardly surprising the 11/KG100 were under orders to attack the cruisers. On Sunday alone the USS *Philadelphia* fired almost 1,000 rounds of six-inch shells on tank and troop concentrations, main road junctions and suspected ammunition dumps. In the process she came under attack on two further occasions from 11/KG100 but the 'nimble

Philly' dodged the missiles. In the British sector three light cruisers, a monitor and numerous destroyers performed an equally valuable service.

What is less easy to understand is why the Luftwaffe also turned their attention to the hospital ships. Though fully illuminated, properly marked with large red crosses on their white-painted hulls and superstructures and standing well out to sea as decreed by the Geneva Convention, three came under attack at various times during the battle. The *Leinster* suffered superficial damage as did the *Somerset*, but the *Newfoundland* was hit and set on fire; she was scuttled.

The situation onshore was deteriorating and Mark Clark became increasingly concerned. Try as they might neither the British nor the Americans could find a way off the beachhead which, in any case, was beginning to appear perilously shallow as the sequence of German counterattacks gathered momentum.

By this stage in the proceedings the fighting men at Salerno knew they were in serious trouble, but the true nature of their predicament only became apparent when they listened to the Overseas Service of the BBC. The daily bulletins described a desperate battle for the beachhead with the Germans trying to drive the Allies back into the sea. The broadcasts were not only strongly slanted in favour of the British but spoke repeatedly of Montgomery's Eighth Army brushing aside enemy resistance and dashing to their rescue. The bias infuriated the Americans, especially the already publicity-conscious Mark Clark. Anglo-American relations took a severe knock at Salerno.

The broadcasts were not entirely accurate. Montgomery dawdled in Calabria. He ordered 231 Infantry Brigade, which reached the Amato river on 10 September, to rest for three days. Recce patrols from 5th Infantry Division entered Amantea on 12 September and the next day probed as far as Cosenza, an important regional centre some 140 miles from Salerno, without sight or sound of the Germans. The general situation was so peaceful that one reconnaissance patrol even took the train into Cosenza.

These were halcyon days for the Eighth Army. The weather was glorious, the fruit abundant and the local inhabitants suitably grateful with their gifts of wine and poultry and much else besides. After the travails of North Africa and Sicily the British and Canadians – officers and men alike – were not about to pass up such a wonderful opportunity to play the liberator. Alexander had urged haste, but Montgomery replied with imperious despatches which spoke of advancing 100 miles in seven days and infantry which were exhausted from the march. Alexander knew that

Eighth Army had ample transport. Some 5,000 trucks had crossed the Straits of Messina in the last weeks alone, so why the procrastination?

Montgomery knew that he could get away with this insubordination; when push came to shove he knew better than most that Alexander was weak-willed. Montgomery also had a healthy respect for the enemy. The mighty Eighth Army was in name only in Calabria; in reality it numbered less than three divisions. If the Germans turned, Montgomery believed they would easily better the forces he had under his command.

Lastly, Montgomery regarded Avalanche as hare-brained and reckless. He had studied the Ultra intercepts and concluded that the Fifth Army would have to contend with some tough tank and panzer grenadier divisions who were in easy reach of Salerno. In his view the very best outcome that could be expected at Salerno was a Pyrrhic victory. There was little point in putting his command at risk too.

Montgomery's judgement was almost to be a self-fulfilling prophecy for the momentum of German counterattacks climaxed on Monday 13 September and nearly spelt disaster in the beachhead.

Notes

1. Alexander to War Office, 12 September. Morris, *Salerno*, p 203.
2. Amazingly Dawley had yet to establish a proper corps headquarters with a full staff deployed. He had rushed ashore prematurely on D-day with a skeleton team and hadn't recovered properly since.
3. Interview, author with Warren Thresher, then ADC to General Mark Clark.
4. *Ancon* was a former transport and before that had been a Panama Railroad Liner: besides Salerno she served at Sicily, Normandy and Okinawa.
5. Only the Fifth Army Command Post was ashore at this time.

22

Counterattack: Crisis in the Beachhead

Throughout the whole Italian campaign, there were only three occasions when the Germans launched major counterattacks – in response to the amphibious landings in Sicily, Salerno and at Anzio. At Salerno the Germans came the closest to success, despite the fact that their counterattacks lacked coordination, weight and impetus. The worst days covered the Sunday, Monday and Tuesday. The brunt of the attacks were concentrated against the Americans, although many of the British troops in the hills or trying to keep the Germans away from the airfield at Montecorvino would contest such a statement. In true Clausewitzian style, however, General Von Vietinghoff had identified the American Corps as offering the best chance for success because of the strategic importance of the Sele Corridor, pointing like a dagger into the very heart of the beachhead. The Texans were also targeted as green troops most likely to break under fire.

While none can question Clark's courage or commitment – he toured the American front line continuously and was frequently in the thick of things – some of his orders reflected inexperience in battle and others were simply wrong.

Salerno was never the neat battle beloved of military historians who look for lines and arrows on a map to describe the situation. Salerno was typical of modern conventional war – a messy affair of small-unit engagements spread across an often ill-defined and constantly changing front. But amidst all the confusion and noise of battle Mark Clark increasingly behaved as his own corps commander. Dawley was sidelined, eventually into oblivion. And he was just one among a number of senior commanders and staff officers who were found wanting and, having failed the test of war, were relieved and sent home.

Late on the Sunday afternoon, Clark visited Dawley at the Corps CP which had been established amidst the ruins of a Greek temple at Paestum close to the beach in the southern part of the American sector. Clark had spent the greater part of the day touring the front; Warren Thresher, his young ADC, was with him. Though Thresher was a comparative newcomer to war he was immediately struck by the difference between the message of the situation maps in the CP and the true state of affairs on the ground.

Clark was concerned about two areas in particular. The first was the gap which still existed between the British right flank, which petered out at St Lucia, and the American left which extended no further than a hamlet some three kilometres to the south at Biffo Cioffo. Clark now saw the struggle for Persano as clear evidence of the enemy's intentions. He was still not fully aware of the significance of the Sele Corridor and the threat it posed to the integrity of the beachhead. However, so long as the Americans held Persano, which guarded the entrance to the corridor, their position was relatively secure. Currently the village was held by a depleted and badly mauled 1st Battalion of 179th RCT. Altavilla and the surrounding hills seemed of minor significance.

It irritated Clark that Dawley looked at the battle in a traditional, even orthodox sense – and his attention focused on the high ground. In times past, possession of the high ground was considered to be the key to battle. So the corps commander rated Altavilla as that key. When the Germans counterattacked and caught the Texans unawares, the town was abandoned. Dawley ordered General Walker to retake it as soon as possible. Clark should have countermanded the order to attack Altavilla, but he did not. Perhaps his own inexperience of combat and the oft-quoted fog of war were in part to blame. At this stage of the battle, things were happening thick and fast, demanding instant decisions.

Clark failed to make his position clear to Dawley on Altavilla. Instead, he ordered his corps commander to redeploy all available units of the 45th (US) Infantry north of the Sele river to extend the American line beyond Biffo Cioffo to St Lucia. Secondly he ordered that Persano and the gateway to the corridor should be adequately defended. Dawley was equally determined to continue the battle for Altavilla and this policy he felt free to pursue, since the army commander had only disagreed, not forbidden. The two American divisions, with barely sufficient troops to defend the ground they were already holding, were thus about to assume responsibility for even more terrain and to move off in three directions to fulfil the orders. They marched full tilt into a German counterattack.

Given Clark's loss of confidence in Dawley, he should have relieved him and assumed direct command of the American sector until the crisis had passed and a suitable replacement could be found. But Clark demurred. Subsequently he defended his inaction by maintaining that with a crisis pending it was the wrong moment to intervene, but there are ample precedents in military history to condemn this lack of resolve.

Clark's instructions and Dawley's persistence placed an enormous strain on an already overstretched 36th Division and Walker protested this to his corps commander. In Walker's judgement, his Texans could barely cope with the task in hand and were in no shape to assume additional responsibilities or to mount another attack into the hills. Dawley assured Walker that one battalion would suffice to hold Persano, neglecting to advise him that the equivalent of five battalions from the 45th with full support elements had been defeated in the Sele Corridor in the previous 24 hours. Dawley later explained his action by claiming that if the Texans had taken Altavilla, then Persano and the corridor would be covered in any case. He also insisted that Troy Middleton had not informed him of the battle which the 179th RCT had just fought and lost in the corridor.

Walker was an experienced professional commander who knew that he had been given instructions beyond the capabilities of his command; he did not push the issue, however, and the instructions were not reconsidered. A similar set of circumstances was to occur months later in the Liri Valley and the disaster of the Rapido river was the result.

At about the time the Americans began their redeployment, visitors arrived in their sector, travelling overland from the south. They were the first arrivals from Montgomery's Eighth Army. Unfortunately, they were two carloads of war correspondents, not fighting soldiers. Alan Moorehead and his colleagues, frustrated at the slow progress in Calabria and anxious to be where the action and the news were to be found, had taken off into the hills alone and unarmed.[1] The distance between Nicastro, which was the main base for Eighth Army, and Paestum was about 120 miles. It took the party two days to make the journey, avoiding the occasional enemy patrol and spending the night in a convent en route. For unarmed war correspondents to make the link-up ought to have been deeply shaming for Montgomery, but by now he considered himself to be beyond the reach of such criticism.

Von Vietinghoff, in contrast, scented victory. That Sunday evening he had become aware of the gap between the American and British corps, and, since no general in his right mind would allow a gap in his lines, assumed it had a purpose. The conclusions reached by his staff and endorsed by Kesselring was that Fifth Army had, of its own volition, formed itself into two pockets as the first step towards complete evacuation of the beachhead! Over the next couple of days, the army commander interpreted every event as further evidence to support this argument. Hence, when reports arrived that another convoy had arrived in Salerno Bay, it was assumed to be the additional ships necessary to withdraw the troops.

To allow the Allies simply to withdraw was not enough. This was the opportunity to inflict a humiliating defeat. If Von Vietinghoff could destroy the Fifth Army on the beaches and prevent it from escaping, such a lesson might further postpone what Berlin feared most, a major invasion across the English Channel.

Walker despatched the 2nd Battalion 143rd Infantry to Persano. The battalion had no heavy fire support, no tanks or self-propelled artillery, just those batteries in the divisional gunline which had also been tasked to support the attack on Altavilla. Early on the Monday afternoon the battalion was overrun. It had occupied a position some one and a half miles north of Persano, in accordance with the instructions Dawley had issued to Walker. Little had been done by the battalion to strengthen its position other than to deploy its anti-tank guns and hastily lay a few mines to the front. Not that it would have made much difference. A German battlegroup spearheaded by a dozen Panzer Mark IVs and assault pioneers in half-tracks hit the Americans head-on and with little warning. Elements of the support company, crews manning the .50-calibre machine guns and the four 57-mm anti-tank guns panicked, fled to the rear and left the rifle companies to their own devices. The Germans swarmed forward and Lt Colonel Jones, the battalion CO, in desperation ordered his men the duck down low in their foxholes while he called for friendly artillery to be directed onto the position. The guns, however, were fully occupied in providing covering fire for those troops who were falling back after another failure at Altavilla, two and a half miles to the right. In the absence even of small-arms fire, the Germans walked onto the position.[2]

The attack at Altavilla was also in deep trouble. The 3rd Battalion 143rd Infantry had captured the town earlier that day after taking heavy casualties in the process. The Americans however, took too long to prepare for the next stage which was the capture of high ground, Hill 424, behind the town. Before they could move out the Germans struck, with a ferocious concentration of mortar and artillery fire. Caught in the open the Americans were forced to give ground, leaving some men trapped in the town.

Technical Sergeant Kelly won the Medal of Honour that evening. He was trapped with a small group on the third floor of a building that looked out onto the main square. He fired his BAR until the barrel got so hot the shells wouldn't go through it. Then he found a .30-calibre machine gun which he used to good effect. All that remained was a supply of 60-mm mortar shells, though quite what they were doing on the third floor of a building in the middle of town has never been fully explained. Kelly took up a high explosive shell, and pulled the first safety pin. In normal use the second pin is released when the shell strikes the bottom of the mortar barrel before being projected out of the tube. Kelly didn't have a mortar barrel, so he rammed the base of the shell hard on the stone floor until the pin popped out, then lobbed the shells out of the window onto the Germans below. Kelly later made good his own escape and returned to the American lines.[3]

A last attempt was made to retrieve the situation at Altavilla. The 1st Battalion 142nd Infantry, already battle-weary and depleted in numbers, was ordered to take the town. With unerring accuracy salvoes of friendly fire rained down on the battalion as it advanced in column of march through a shallow gulley below Altavilla. The column disintegrated, and the Americans fled into the surrounding countryside in search of cover. Panic spread as the infanteers tried to outpace the bursting shells and each other, shedding arms and equipment as they ran. All thought of capturing Altavilla was banished. General Walker was the first to appreciate the extent of that potential disaster and took it upon himself to redeploy his forces and shorten the line.

With no reserves available (as luck would have it the battalion earmarked for the Rangers was already at sea) he also ordered an immediate retreat to a new line. La Cosa creek, little more than a small stream which paralleled the coast in the divisional sector for some eight miles, now became the front line. Walker then went immediately to Dawley and explained the situation. The corps commander readily concurred with Walker's decision and ordered an immediate withdrawal to the new line. There the Americans would make their last stand. Walker divided the division's front into three sectors and placed a brigadier general in command of each sector. The brigadiers were Willie Wilbur, who had won the Medal of Honour in North Africa and was the beachmaster at Salerno, along with 'Iron Mike' O'Daniel, the division's chief artillery officer and Otto Lange, the deputy divisional commander.

By any stretch of the imagination this was an unusual step since they superseded the three colonels in command of the division's regimental combat teams – Martin, Forsythe and Werner – who became the sector's second-in-commands. Walker had little faith in this triumvirate of colonels, all of whom were showing signs of wear, and this after only five days of combat.

Dawley sealed his fate shortly after his meeting with Walker. He telephoned Clark and reported that the Germans had broken through the Persano front.

'What are you going to do about it?' Clark asked. 'What can you do?'

'Nothing,' responded Dawley. 'I've got no reserves. All I have got is prayer.'

Clark called Thresher to make ready his jeep and escort. Together they left the CP, not to meet with Dawley, but to check the line where the Calore and Sele rivers joined. This is where the nearest troops to Persano were deployed.

As the light began to fade, the German spearhead which had wiped out the defenders at Persano continued their advance, albeit with great caution because they couldn't believe the ineptitude of the American deployments. When they came within tank gun range of the junction of the two rivers, the tanks fanned out along the north bank of the Calore and opened fire on the rear areas and supply parks. There was panic. The panzers were just two miles from the sea.

Through his binoculars Clark could clearly see the German tanks. He had no doubt that if the enemy were able to mass their troops in sufficient numbers to force a crossing of the Sele, he had nothing to stop them from reaching the sea.[4] The only troops who stood between the Germans and the sea were some supporting artillery of the 45th (US) Infantry Division. These guns saved the day in the American sector and quite possibly the battle. Had the German advance continued through to the beaches, there would have been mayhem. The American line could have been attacked, rolled up from the worst of all places – the crowded areas of B Echelon, amid the piles of supplies that lined the beaches and shore area. For though the enemy would have been exposed to the massed gunfire of the ships offshore, the battle on land would have been fought at such close range that naval broadsides would have caused as much damage to the Allies as to the Germans.

The panzers were confronted by the massed guns of the 189th Field Artillery under Lt Colonel Hal Muldow and the 158th Field Regiment under Lt Colonel Russel Funk. Both battalions had their batteries deployed about 1,000 yards back from the junction of the Sele and the Calore. There were ten yards between the artillery pieces which had been stripped to the minimum five-man crews. The additional men, armed with 1903 Springfields and .30-calibre machine guns, were sent forward to a gentle slope just south of a burned bridge to dig in and hold the line.

The Bellini Palace had been commandeered by the Fifth Army for its administrative and main headquarters. It was just a couple of hundred yards behind the gun line, across a main road and a railway line. On Clark's orders indignant clerks, typists, stenographers and mess orderlies with clean fingernails and uniforms were rousted out, given a shovel, a rifle and 50 rounds of ammunition and packed off into the line. A few key members of staff remained behind to prepare to evacuate the head-quarters at ten minutes' notice. The army commander was taking no chances. He ordered that a PT boat stand by. If needed, it was to take him and his immediate staff to the British corps where he intended to continue the battle. There was little sympathy for the plight of Fifth Army headquarters' staff among the fighting units. They had no business being so close to the front, but the rumour was they were there because it was the most spacious and comfortable villa in the area. 'In their enthusiasm for comfort, they overlooked the tactical situation.'[5]

While the clerks were drafted in as infantry some of the staff officers decamped back to ships in the bay. Walker was also tasked with the protection of Fifth Army and Corps headquarters. He was ordered to despatch a tank destroyer company and a battalion of infantry for their protection. The general considered there was no necessity for this, but an order was an order. He deployed a couple of platoons' worth of TDs and one of his infantry battalions that had suffered heavy losses to ride shotgun. They would still be available as a division reserve. In the meantime, Clark and Thresher drove up and down the highway collecting odd units and despatching them to the point of maximum danger. They found a self-propelled gun which was crawling back in search of a base workshop with clutch trouble. Thresher climbed on board and acquainted the commander with the facts of life. The SP lurched around and struggled into firing position.

Further down the highway they found a company of tank destroyers. Armed with the 90-mm or three-inch calibre high-velocity gun in an open turret, the tank destroyer is a formidable weapon. The company was quickly deployed into position and soon made its presence felt.

The artillery had already opened fire on the German tanks. The 155-

mm howitzer is not intended for the anti-tank role, and, at a range of about 1,000 yards, the 95-pound projectiles made a nasty mess.

By jettisoning the rule book, which was more concerned with the avoidance of accidents during peacetime, and skipping basic procedures like not pulling the lanyard before the crew was the regulation distance from the guns, the rate of fire could be increased. The gunners fired a round every 20 seconds and maintained that rate of fire until darkness fell and the panzers retired to Persano.

Later that night the skies reverberated with the roar of aircraft. Flight upon flight of Dakotas banked overhead and followed the shoreline to drop elements of the 82nd Airborne as an immediate reinforcement. On the ground the DZ was clearly marked by two lines of flaming beacons forming the letter T. For the first time that campaign every Allied anti-aircraft gun remained silent.

Notes

1. Moorehead's own excellent account of his adventures can be found in Moorehead, Alan, *Eclipse*, Hamish Hamilton, 1947.
2. The majority of the battalion, including Lt Colonel Jones were captured. Only nine officers and 325 enlisted men made good their escape.
3. Kelly's claim to this unorthodox method of firing a mortar shell was carefully authenticated before the award was confirmed. The press dubbed him 'Commando Kelly, the one-man army'.
4. Interview with author, Atlanta, August 1990.
5. Walker, Fred L., *From Texas to Rome*, Taylor Publishing Company, Dallas, 1969, p 249.

23

Reinforcements, Contingencies and Controversies

On 14 September General Alexander received a signal from Winston Churchill:

1. I hope you are watching above all the Battle of Avalanche which dominates everything. None of the commanders engaged has fought a large scale battle before. The Battle of Suvla Bay was lost because Ian Hamilton was advised by his CGS to remain at a remote control point where he would know everything. Had he been on the spot he could have saved the show. At this distance and with time-lags I cannot pretend to judge, but I feel it is my duty to set before you this experience of mine from the past.
2. Nothing should be denied which will nourish the decisive battle for Naples.
3. Ask for anything you want, and I will make allocation of necessary supplies with the highest priority irrespective of every consideration.[1]

The Army Group commander took his leader's message to heart, but he had also put in place a number of contingencies. He too had been aware of the lack of progress in the beachhead, but the first hint that Fifth Army was in trouble had only come the previous day. McCreery had contacted him direct, ignoring the proper chain of command through Fifth Army, wanting infantry reinforcements as a matter of priority. Alexander had immediately endorsed the request and passed it through channels, marked urgent, for action to be taken in the reinforcements depots of North Africa.

Alexander finally also pulled rank on the independently minded Montgomery.

The advance guard of the Eighth Army had taken Crotone, a port on the Adriatic coast just south of the Gulf of Taranto. Montgomery then designated Castrovillari, 70 miles up the peninsula, as his next objective, which he planned to reach on 15 September. It was still another 75 miles to Paestum.

This wasn't good enough. Alexander ordered Montgomery to intervene at Salerno, regardless of logistical risks. 'The situation on Fifth Army's front,' he said, 'is not favourable. The earlier you can threaten the forces opposite Fifth Army the better. The next few days are critical.'[2] Alexander then made arrangements to board a destroyer for passage to Salerno and informed Mark Clark that he planned to be in the beachhead on 15 September.

For Mark Clark there were reinforcements more immediately to hand. Ever since he had been informed that the 82nd (US) Airborne were once again available, he had given much thought as to how best to deploy the unit. Various ideas were discussed and discarded, including remounting the original operation to seize the bridges over the Volturno.

A second contingency was planned in sufficient detail to allow for a warning order to be sent to Ridgway and his division in Sicily. Clark had earlier discussed with McCreery the possibility of using the airborne troops to clear what had become known as the Sorrento Barrier. After all, the Rangers were not in the right place, German supplies and reinforcements were pouring through the Nocera defile, and Clark needed to open up the route to Naples as soon as possible. Clark asked for Ridgway to prepare operations to land a combat team on the beaches near Torre Annunziata and Castellammare, on the northern edge of the peninsula, and in the heavily defended Bay of Naples. In response to these requests the 325th Glider Infantry began to embark on LSTs immediately, where they stayed until the ships eventually sailed on 15 September for Maiori. Another contingency called for a single battalion drop on Avellino, at that stage an important German communications centre. The paratroopers were to interdict enemy supply routes and shoot up convoys.

The use and abuse of airborne formations was a vexed question for both Allies and Axis. An airborne division is an expensive way of waging war. It is composed of elite formations, hand-picked volunteers that are costly to recruit, train and maintain. It seemed absurd to leave such a superb breed of fighting men on the sidelines during a battle, even if there did not appear to be a suitable role for them. The result was that more often than not their precious talents were wasted on hasty or ill-conceived enterprises.

On that bleak Monday morning Clark needed the 82nd to reinforce his beachhead. In this he read the battle precisely and anticipated German intentions, for he called upon Ridgway before the German's main offensive later that day. But the manner in which he made his request was unusual, if not bizarre. There was no coded message, yet Fifth Army was in radio contact with Army Group Headquarters. Instead Clark chose to write a personal letter and have this hand-delivered to Ridgway. Was this because he feared a possible breach of radio security? Or did he fear interference of another sort from Alexander's headquarters?

Dear Matt, [Clark wrote]

I know it takes you 30 days to make up your mind where you'll drop that precious 82nd Division of yours, but I'm in trouble and I want you, I'm relying upon you to carry these instructions out exactly as follows. I want first a combat team to drop tonight in this drop zone on this map which is as close to the beach as we can get for protection. I guarantee that nobody will shoot up your planes like they did in Sicily. I will have officers briefed at every AA site and on every ship. I will guarantee that even if they come and bomb the hell out of us nothing will answer. I want the next Combat Team to the DZ on the following night and I want you to come with it and the next night I want the third. I know you can do this.

Wayne[3]

By this time a US army squadron which was used for the direction and observation of artillery fire had a few planes operating during daylight hours from the rough dirt strip close to Paestum. The squadron flew British Spitfires, albeit with American markings. Warren Thresher brought Captain Jacob R. Hamilton, a pilot, to the General's command post.

'Son, you know where General Ridgway is?' Clark asked.

'Yes sir,' Hamilton replied. 'His headquarters is on a dirt strip at Licata in Sicily.'

Clark gave him the folded message and said, 'General Ridgway. Personal. His eyes only. Get this to him, son.'

When Hamilton approached Licata he called up the control tower and told them he had a message for Ridgway. The tower replied that the General had just taken off in a Dakota, so the young pilot opened his throttle and gave chase. Hamilton caught up with the C-47 and flew alongside, flapping his wings to draw the pilot's attention. The Dakota turned back and both planes landed at Licata, where Hamilton handed the note to General Ridgway.

The General read the note, took out his pad and wrote: 'Dear Wayne, Message received. Can do. Matt.' In the interwar years they had served together in the 15th Infantry Regiment of the 3rd Division. 'Can do' was the regimental motto.

Hamilton flew back to Paestum and delivered the reply to General Clark. Fifth Army staff and liaison officers were despatched to ensure that every AA gunsite would be silent from 2100 hours that evening, whatever the provocation. A similar message was passed from ship to ship in the bay. Just before midnight Colonel Reuben Tucker of the 504th Parachute Infantry jumped from the lead plane of the 30 Dakotas that brought the first wave of his troopers to the beachhead. There were no incidents and it was a perfectly executed operation. A second flight of 41 aircraft arrived an hour later, and one company landed behind enemy lines.

Earlier that evening, while waiting for the airborne forces, Clark called his senior commanders to the CP for a crisis conference. It was a little after 1930 hours when Generals Dawley, Middleton, Walker and Gruenther (the Fifth Army Chief of Staff) gathered to discuss the situation.

Clark was clearly concerned that Salerno could become another Gallipoli or Dunkirk. As army commander he believed that he had to plan for every contingency. Clark may have been inexperienced in the higher direction of war, but he was keenly aware what was involved in the career stakes. An army commander who is taken by surprise is an immediate candidate for replacement. Contingency planning therefore had to embrace the unpalatable and that meant the possibility of evacuation. There was a stunned silence when that awful word was uttered. Some around that table must have thought of the disaster that befell American forces on their evacuation of the Philippine peninsula of Bataan in April 1942, the single biggest defeat in the military history of the United States.

Clark expounded his thoughts. There were all sorts of factors to take into account, not least the many hundreds of tons of war materiel in dumps in the beachhead. In the case of a retreat they could not be destroyed simply by putting a match to them. The army commander decided to follow War College procedures, and presented his subordinate commanders with a *fait accompli*. He had already issued orders to Fifth Army staff to prepare two contingency plans.[4] These were code-named Sealion[5] and Seatrain, and each was based on the premise of one corps acting as host for the other to withdraw into. Despite the urgency of battle and a deep sense of foreboding, the irony of the situation could not have been lost on those present; Middleton and Walker had been instructors at the War College when Clark was the star student.

The field commanders were totally opposed to the plan and made their views known. Dawley protested formally, but was ignored by Clark. At first Middleton didn't say anything. He just turned his head and spat on the ground. Warren Thresher watched the incident; he couldn't decide whether Middleton was just getting rid of something in his mouth or indicating that he didn't agree. Thresher looked at Clark. There was no mistaking his response. Thin-lipped, he stared hard at Middleton and waited for the generals to have their say.

Walker pointed to the strength of the La Cosa Line. He was sure that any German attack anywhere along his front, which would have to cross open ground, would take a severe beating. In fact, if the Germans continued their practice of attacking with tanks in small groups, they would offer little threat. Walker was so confident that when Clark offered him the paratroopers as reinforcements he accepted them as Divisional Reserve.

Middleton was equally sure of his ground, insisting that the 45th's positions north of the Sele were rock-solid. Clark listened to their arguments, undeterred. The contingency planning went ahead, albeit in great secrecy. Clark was wrong, and this decision pursued him for the remainder of his military career. In any case, the divisional commanders ignored the order. When he returned to his CP, Middleton issued an order which would have made evacuation impossible. It was simple and to the point: 'Put food and water behind the 45th,' he said. 'We are going to stay here.'

Fighting words, but a naive move. Until that time, the fighting soldiers hadn't even considered the idea that the whole corps might be forced to withdraw. Nevertheless the exhortation had the desired effect. It became the battle cry of the Thunderbirds in Salerno.

Incredibly, no-one saw fit to inform General McCreery. There were liaison officers from the British Corps at Fifth Army headquarters and, in theory, they must have been involved in the planning. But the reality was that the only contingency on which any work was undertaken was Sealion, the withdrawal of the Americans into the British Corps area. In the urgency of the moment, all thought of inter-Allied relations and the chain of command was brushed aside. After the meeting Gruenther approached Admiral Hewitt to discuss Mark Clark's plans. Hewitt also protested, at the same time pointing out an obvious practical problem: beaching a loaded landing craft and withdrawing it empty is quite different from beaching an empty landing craft and then withdrawing it when full, especially in the nearly tideless Mediterranean Sea.

Hewitt, nevertheless, interpreted Clark's contingency plans as an instruction, and proceeded to mobilize his naval forces to undertake an evacuation if one part of the beachhead came under fire. The command ship USS *Ancon*, then in Algiers, was ordered to sail immediately, load six-inch shells at Palermo, and return to the beachhead at full speed. In the meantime, all unloading was stopped over the American beaches.

The Admiral called Commodore Oliver, who was Senior Naval Officer to the X Corps beaches, to a conference on board the flagship USS *Biscayne*. Hewitt also asked that HMS *Hilary*, the command ship, be made ready to embark General Clark and his staff should the need arise before the *Ancon* could reach the beachhead. The Commodore protested but was told to get on with things. Oliver then asked if General McCreery had been consulted or even informed. No one on *Biscayne* knew the answer, but it was generally assumed that he had been.

McCreery hadn't. His immediate reaction to Oliver's news was to jump in a jeep, drive south to army headquarters and confront Clark face to face. In the event other matters intruded, and there is no documentary evidence to confirm that such a 'discussion' did take place. Within an hour of his meeting with McCreery, Oliver sent a despatch to Malta and his commander-in-chief, Admiral Cunningham, to enlist his support in thwarting what he was convinced was a foolhardy exercise.

Cunningham had also received a despatch from Hewitt, requesting big gun support:

> The Germans have created a salient dangerously near the beach. Military situation continuing unsatisfactory. Am planning to use all available vessels to transfer troops from southern beaches or the reverse if necessary. Unloading of merchant vessels in the southern beaches has been stopped. We need heavy aerial and naval bombardment behind the enemy positions using battleships or other heavy naval vessels. Are such vessels available?[6]

The following evening Hewitt's flagship decoded the reply from Admiral Cunningham:

> Count on me for all assistance you want and I will try to help you all I can. *Valiant* and *Warspite* are on their way to join you. *Nelson* and *Rodney* are available for your use.[7]

Before leaving for the beachhead Alexander contacted Patton who was still with Seventh Army in Sicily. His divisions were being prepared for passage back to the United Kingdom. The General's future still remained uncertain, so it was hardly surprising that when Alexander asked for reinforcements he was the soul of cooperation. Patton detailed Truscott and his 3rd (US) Division, still the best unit in his depleted command, for deployment to Salerno. The division was brought up to strength with drafts from 1st and 9th Infantry Divisions. The latter were ready for transportation to England and were none too pleased to be moving back into combat so soon. Truscott ordered his troops to stand-by areas and then boarded a warship for Salerno to confer with Mark Clark on how best to employ the division. There were protests from some in the 1st (US) Infantry Division, but Truscott's reputation preceded him and there were no incidents. The same could not be said for the British infantry reinforcements that Alexander had instructed should be sent to Salerno.

Even as the advance party of reinforcements supplied by the 82nd Airborne dropped into the beachhead that Monday evening, the momentum generated by British military bureaucracy was in full spate. There was, however, one strange oversight or discrepancy that has never been explained. The message for reinforcements had been sent from Alexander's advance headquarters in Syracuse to Philippeville in Algeria. It was from ports in French North Africa that the British divisions had sailed for Salerno; it was where they had their bases, and reinforcement camps. Nevertheless, at 1700 hours on 14 September, Company Sergeant Major (CSM) Green of the infantry reinforcement section, No 155 Transit Camp, which was located at Tripoli some 450 miles from Philippeville, received a couple of signals ordering him to provide 1,500 men without delay.

Tripoli was the rear area, serving Eighth Army. Transit camps were not pleasant places for a soldier to spend his days. The transit camps in the British Army served a variety of needs, but the most important was to provide reinforcements to front-line units. Consequently, both new groups of troops and men who had recovered from wounds, were sent to the camps until vacancies were found. The camps were large, sprawling affairs with a shifting, restless population. The regime was harsh, the intention being to encourage men to seek employment rather than become long-term residents. An infantry soldier spent two weeks on a battle-fitness course and then moved across to the reinforcement area to await a draft. It was the policy of the transit camp commandant, wherever possible, to return men to their parent units which helped foster the regimental tradition on which the British Army prided itself.

At the subsequent courts martial, CSM Green was an important witness. He testified that in the instructions for the Avalanche Draft, reinforcements for the 51st Highland and 50th Tyne and Tees Division were specifically mentioned. It was men from those divisions, many of them still convalescing from wounds received in Sicily, who volunteered for the draft as word spread that their comrades were in trouble at Salerno. The scene was now set for what later became the Salerno mutiny.

Late on Monday night Mark Clark called Warren Thresher over to his trailer. Clark asked him to read a letter which he had dictated. It was addressed to Eisenhower and related the incidents at VIth Corps CP and subsequent conversations with Dawley. Clark asked Thresher to read it carefully and to tell him if there was anything that was not correct or not the truth. The letter recommended that Dawley be relieved.

Notes

1. Gilbert, Martin, *Road to Victory 1941–45*, Guild Publishing, 1986, p 503.
2. Jackson, Nigel, *Alex*, Weidenfeld and Nicolson, 1973, p 217.
3. Morris, *Salerno*, p 242.
4. Gruenther, of course, as Army Chief of Staff would have been involved.
5. Sealion or Seelowe was the code-name given to Führer Directive No 16, the preparations for the invasion of England in July 1940.
6. Morris, *Salerno*, p 252.
7. Ibid.

24

The Reckoning

The first German assault of the day was launched against Middleton's 179th RCT to the north of the Sele river. At about 0800 hours ten tanks spearheaded a battalion of infantry but the enemy attacked without the benefit of thorough reconnaissance. At a range of less than 100 yards the combined fire from two American battalions of infantry, with artillery, tanks and tank destroyers in support, decimated the enemy. The infantry kept probing for a weakness but could find no holes in the American perimeter and withdrew. Further attempts were made against positions occupied by the 157th Infantry, but this time the intervention of the cruiser USS *Boise* with her six-inch broadsides in support of the field artillery proved overwhelming.

The Germans made one last attempt against the Thunderbirds. The tactics they used indicates their own sense of frustration. Men appeared carrying white sheets. They got within a couple of hundred yards of the American line before the ruse was spotted. The men dropped the sheets, which were a screen for more soldiers behind and tried to rush the trenches. They were cut down before they could close down the distance.

The much-heralded German drive to the sea along the La Cosa creek did not occur until after midday on the Tuesday. The artillery bombardment of the defenders, supported by naval gunfire offshore, kept the enemy at arm's length and the panzers eventually fell back with heavy casualties.

The relationship between Mark Clark and his subordinate commanders continued to deteriorate. Later that afternoon Clark went to Walker's CP, and, without any preliminary discussion of the tactical situation, demanded,

'What has gone wrong with the 36th Division?'[1]

'Nothing has gone wrong with the 36th Division. Everything is all right,' Walker retorted.

The latter dismissed the attack on Altavilla as a reconnaissance in force and blamed the disaster at Persano on Dawley's failure to brief him fully. Clark left shortly after, but there was now a distance and a mistrust between the one-time master and his pupil.

The Germans attacked along the La Cosa creek on two further occasions that afternoon but the Texans had the situation under control. What irritated Walker was the frequency of messages from both corps and army headquarters directing, 'Not one foot of ground is to be given up', 'There must be no retreat', etc, all of which gave him the impression that Clark and Dawley were needlessly worried about the Texans' ability to repel a German attack.

General McCreery made no contingency plans for a withdrawal, having dismissed Clark's proposals as unworkable and, in so far as the British were concerned, unnecessary. There were a couple of anxious moments, but the line held firm.

That evening the second wave of reinforcements from the 82nd Airborne arrived in Salerno. One hundred and twenty Dakotas dropped 2,100 men of the 505th Parachute Infantry into the DZ south of Paestum. The AA gunners at sea demonstrated that they had at last become house-trained. The paratroopers were moved into reserve at Agropoli. Clark had no need of their services at present, but he knew that, when it came, the breakout would have to be spearheaded by fresh troops. There was a more foolhardy mission to drop the 2nd Battalion 509th Parachute Infantry behind the German lines. Clark had resurrected the old ideas about raiders, and had selected Avellino as the target.

Everything went wrong. The 46 planes that carried the 600 men were scattered, and so were the paratroopers, over 15 square miles of countryside. General Clark always maintained that, even so, paratroopers operating in small groups raided German supply convoys and successfully disrupted their lines of communication. Amazingly, 400 men made it back to Allied lines, but there is no evidence to suggest that so small and dispersed a force made the slightest impact.

Even before the first paratroopers reached their supposed drop zone, Kesselring's course was clear. Hitler ordered a gradual withdrawal north, towards Rome, and a scorched-earth policy to be put into effect. Kesselring conferred with Von Vietinghoff. The latter, for the first time, was aware of the proximity, in relative terms, of the Eighth Army. To disengage would be a difficult manoeuvre, for his left flank would have to fall back north and east to close off the entire peninsula. Brindisi, Bari and Taranto were already in Allied hands, and there was always the risk that the Allies might try another amphibious hook further up either coast.

Kesselring instructed Von Vietinghoff to make one last attack against the British, which would keep the more dangerous of the Allied forces occupied, while the troops opposite the Americans prepared for a phased withdrawal. Kesselring's staff had already identified four delaying positions south of Rome. The first would be from Salerno through Potenza to Barletta on the Adriatic coast.

That Tuesday evening, as the battle gradually died down on the ground, the skies filled to the roar of engines as Wellingtons, Mitchells and Bostons took over from the daylight raids. Tedder was as good as his word and there was indeed a maximum effort. The bombers blasted the main roads from Salerno to Naples and Castellammare, and destroyed more of the rail network which fed Battipaglia.

The effect of the air raids, both day and night, is best summed up in the 29th Panzer Grenadiers' Divisional History:

> Even though we already knew from Sicily what Allied air superiority meant, the strafing we underwent at this time and particularly on 14 September, put all our previous experience in the shade. It was an achievement if one small vehicle made one short journey darting from cover to cover, and completely unscathed.[2]

On the Allied side the time of reckoning for the mistakes made in Operation Avalanche began on Wednesday 15 September. The first casualty was Brigadier Otto Lange, the Assistant Commander of 36th Infantry Division. Early that morning Walker had set out on a tour of inspection of the Cosa creek defences. En route he came upon General Lange and his party in bivouac and just getting up. Lange admitted that he had not completed Walker's instructions because he was tired. Walker sacked him on the spot. Clark confirmed the order and appointed Brigadier Wilbur as Assistant Divisional Commander. This was done without consulting Walker, who saw Wilbur as Clark's spy in the camp and a further reflection of Clark's lack of trust in the division and its commander. In this assessment Walker was to be proved wrong. Wilbur was outspoken and tough-minded; he had won the Congressional Medal of Honour in the Torch landings and took the 36th to his heart. Subsequently he was to pay a high price for such loyalty.

On the morning of 15 September the destroyer HMS *Offa* delivered Alexander to the beachhead. He was accompanied by his American Chief of Staff, General Lemnitzer, and Air Marshal Coningham, who commanded the air support for the beachhead. The Army Group commander wasted no time in responding to his Prime Minister's message.

General Alexander (Salerno) to Prime Minister (at sea) 15 September 1943.
I feel sure you will be glad to know that I have already anticipated your wise advice and am now here with Fifth Army. Many thanks for your offer of help. Everything possible has been done to make Avalanche a success.
Its fate will be decided in the next few days.[3]

Alexander's biographers overstate the contribution he made at Salerno. To state in his message to Churchill that (Salerno's) 'fate will be decided in the next few days' was a gross distortion of the truth and an insult to the British and Americans who had fought the battle to date. Ultra intercepts on 14 September showed that Tenth Army had already used up all its reserves.

Reinforcements were now pouring ashore. The leading elements of both Truscott's 3rd (US) Infantry and the British 7th Armoured Division had now arrived on what was rapidly becoming a very crowded beachhead. By the following morning Clark's Fifth Army at Salerno numbered 170,000 men. Such a force was the equivalent of seven divisions and far outnumbered the depleted and dispirited German Tenth Army. Von Vietinghoff, by scraping the bottom of the barrel, found perhaps 20 tanks to lead a final counterattack, while Clark had more than 200 British and American Shermans at his disposal.

So what was Alexander's contribution at this stage of the battle? He joined Admiral Hewitt on board the flagship USS *Biscayne* where he was fully briefed on the contingency plan to withdraw the American corps. Alexander immediately countermanded Clark's instructions.

The letter which Clark had written to Eisenhower recommending Dawley's relief was never sent. Instead Clark asked Alexander to visit Corps headquarters without him. This was a very unusual step, since military etiquette alone would have required that Clark should be in attendance. In these circumstances no army commander would welcome an unescorted visit by his superior to his subordinates! This begs the question of whether Clark was seeking to evade the responsibility for firing his senior subordinate general and moreover, one who was his senior on the Army List.

General Dawley welcomed his distinguished visitors to the corps command post and conducted them into a small tent that served as the map room. It was stiflingly hot despite the relatively early hour. Alexander asked Dawley what his future plans were for the corps. The response was embarrassing for all who witnessed the scene of a man under great strain who, with shaking hands and voice, outlined in uncertain terms the future for his command. On the return journey to Fifth Army headquarters both Alexander and Lemnitzer agreed that the most disturbing feature they had observed was a corps staff who had lost confidence in the decisions and leadership of their commander.

Alexander and Lemnitzer joined Clark at his command post.

'You've got a broken reed on your hands, Wayne,' Alexander said.

'I know it,' replied Clark.

As Army Group commander, Alexander had the authority to relieve Dawley on the spot. But then so did Clark. In the event both men ducked the issue. Alexander took refuge for his indecision behind international diplomacy. It was all a matter of inter-Allied harmony and he preferred that Eisenhower should shoulder the responsibility.

Alexander decided to stay at the beachhead overnight and accommodation was arranged at the Fifth Army's command post. That evening Alexander cabled Eisenhower that he was favourably impressed by Clark's calmness under such pressure, but was less favourably impressed by Dawley. He advised that Eisenhower should visit the beachhead at the earliest opportunity.

Eisenhower arrived on Saturday 18 September. It must had been something of a relief at last to see the situation on the ground for himself. Throughout the critical moments of the German counterattack, Eisenhower had paced the office in Tunis, monitoring the reports and rumours from the beachhead. It was he who had been required to make the command decisions about the landings at Salerno Bay despite the planners' qualms over the shortage of landing craft. He knew very well what had been agreed at the Quebec Conference and the plans for Overlord, a landing on the French coast in the spring of 1944. If Salerno ended in disaster he would be out of the running for the top command.[4]

The rumours had come thick and fast. There were garbled reports that Clark had withdrawn Fifth Army headquarters from the beachhead, had re-embarked his command ship, and that he had decided to evacuate VI Corps. German Ultra intercepts, especially those from Luftflotte II, spoke of the US 36th Division 'in headlong flight', describing Salerno as a second Dunkirk. Eisenhower had found himself negotiating with Marshall and the Combined Chiefs in Washington for the redeployment of ships and troops earmarked for Overlord, as well as the recall of air units which had already left the theatre. It was an uncomfortable experience and one he did not wish to repeat.

Mistakes had been made, and Eisenhower was determined that there should be a reckoning. There were three possible candidates; Clark as the army commander carried ultimate responsibility; Dawley as the Corps Commander in whose area the problems had occurred; and Walker whose division had suffered the critical setbacks.

General Lemnitzer went out in a patrol boat to meet Eisenhower who travelled in the cruiser HMS *Charybdis*; he used this opportunity to brief Eisenhower on the Dawley problem. Eisenhower listened for a while and then burst out angrily. 'Why doesn't Wayne relieve Dawley?'

Mark Clark greeted Eisenhower when he stepped ashore and asked him, like Alexander, to visit Dawley unaccompanied. Lemnitzer took Eisenhower, together with Admiral Hewitt, to be briefed by the corps commander, who appeared even more nervous than the day before. Later that afternoon the full command party, Eisenhower, Mark Clark, Hewitt, Dawley, Ridgway and Lemnitzer visited 36th Division's command post. Walker was asked to give a full account of the division's activities throughout the period of the counterattack.

At one stage Eisenhower rounded furiously on Dawley. 'How did you ever get your troops into such a mess?' he demanded. Dawley stumbled through an explanation of sorts, but it was obvious to Walker that he had no grasp of the tactical detail. He was about to intercede when Eisenhower changed the subject. Walker assumed that Eisenhower wanted to hold Dawley responsible for a mess that in his opinion didn't exist. But he kept quiet; it could so easily have been his neck on the block.[5]

The party left 36th Division to drive north across the Sele to visit Middleton at his command post; later the party would go on to the British corps. Eisenhower shared a jeep with Clark and they discussed Dawley.

'Wayne, you had better take him out,' Eisenhower said.

'Well, Ike, I've come to that conclusion and I want to put Ridgway in command.'

Clark had already made Ridgway Assistant Corps Commander and had informed Dawley of the appointment.

'It's your baby, Wayne,' Eisenhower said. 'We'll hear what Washington has to say.'

Three commanders had reached the same conclusion about a subordinate, yet not one would grasp the nettle.

Dawley did little to promote his cause, though he must have been aware that his future was in doubt. Later that afternoon, while returning from a reconnaissance, Walker, who travelled with Clark and Dawley, was witness to an argument between the two men.[6] Dawley criticized some of Eisenhower's and Clark's decisions, particularly in the planning for Salerno, and even referred to them as boy scouts. Clark, not unnaturally, took offence at such remarks and ignored Dawley for the remainder of the day. In the light of these events it is exceedingly difficult to find a charitable explanation for the letter which Clark sent to Dawley that evening.[7]

Headquarters Fifth Army

Dear General Dawley

As your Army Commander, I want to congratulate every officer and enlisted man in the Fifth Army on the accomplishment of their mission on landing on the western coast of Italy. All the more splendid is your achievement when it is realized that it was accomplished against determined German resistance at the beaches. Every foot of your advance has been contested.

We have arrived at our critical objective; our beachhead is secure. Additional troops are landing every day, and we are here to stay. Not one foot of ground will be given up.

General Montgomery's battle proven Eighth English Army, our partner in the task of clearing German forces out of Italy, is advancing from the south and in a matter of hours its presence will be felt by the enemy. Side by side with this Eighth Army the Fifth Army will advance to occupy Naples, Rome and other cities to the north and to free Italy from German domination.

I am highly gratified by the efficient manner in which the US VI Corps and the British X Corps have worked side by side in mutual support, each being proud to serve by the side of the other. Their performance has justified the confidence placed in them by the people of the United Nations. They know that we shall drive on relentlessly until our job is done.

I desire that the contents of this letter be communicated to all ranks of your command.

Sincerely yours
Mark W Clark
Lieutenant General USA
Commanding

Dawley penned a note and despatched Clark's letter to his three divisional commanders, Walker, Middleton and Ridgway; it read:

Ist Ind.
Headquarters, VI Corps

To: Commanders, all units and organizations.

The receipt of this letter is a matter of intense satisfaction to me. To you who have made such a commendation possible belongs the credit. Carry on. We are on the way.

E J Dawley
Major General US Army
Commanding

Later that same evening Eisenhower sent a cable to General Marshall in Washington:

Dawley is a splendid character, earnest, faithful and well informed; but he cannot exercise high battle command when the going is rough. He grows extremely nervous and indecisive.[8]

Such perfidy one would associate with a medieval church court rather than a twentieth-century army on the battlefield; nevertheless, the request to relieve Dawley caused Marshall serious misgivings.[9] Dawley had been his assistant in the First World War. Subsequently Marshall had regarded Dawley highly as a training commander in the States. General McNair, the all-powerful head of the Army Ground Forces, had also picked out Dawley as a future battle leader (he had also identified Clark and Eisenhower). No wonder Clark and Eisenhower balked at relieving such a powerful protégé, without reference to Washington. But Mark Clark did not get his way as regards Ridgway. Major General John Lucas, Eisenhower's eyes and ears in Sicily and subsequently II US Corps Commander, was appointed to VI Corps instead. Clark was not best pleased. Failure for the army commander to secure his preferred choice could be interpreted as a slight, as well as an implied criticism that he was not without blame for the near disaster at Salerno.

Walker was not delighted either. He was the senior divisional commander and would not have refused promotion. Before they sailed for Salerno, Clark had given an undertaking to Walker that if anything happened to Dawley he would assume command. By this time, however, Walker had lost respect for his commanding officer and did not attempt to hide his feelings. Even if the 36th Infantry had performed well, he could have had little expectation of advancement.

As well as Otto Lange, the Divisional Artillery Commander and the Chief Engineer were relieved. And Colonel Forsythe, who had commanded the 142nd Infantry, was posted to army headquarters at Clark's insistence, because he considered him too old for the job. Walker was furious, and regarded the replacement as another Clark implant and an

188

unwarranted interference on the part of the army commander. On the staff, the G2, G3 and G4 ended the battle in hospital, either sick or suffering a nervous breakdown. None returned.

The attrition rate among the nine battalion commanders was even more startling. Two were captured, and five were relieved of their commands. Fred Walker Junior was reassigned by his father from commanding his battalion to be G3 of the division. Though Walker defended the decision on the grounds that Fred Junior, as a graduate of the Command and General Staff School at Fort Leavenworth, was the best-qualified officer for the appointment, there were inevitable cries of nepotism. For a division which had just been through such a baptism of fire it was an unwise decision and, in the event, did little to further Fred Junior's career as a regular army officer.

Later, after his return to the United States for reassignment, now reduced to his substantive rank of colonel, Dawley went to see Marshall to explain what had happened. He was very bitter and showed Marshall the letter written by Clark, saying, 'I can't understand how Clark could relieve me one day and say this about me to my troops the next day.' Marshall felt sorry for Dawley, but, as he was going out through the door the General added that, after listening to the whole story, he didn't entirely agree with what Clark had done.

'He should have relieved you sooner,' Marshall said.

Notes

1. Walker, Fred L., *From Texas to Rome*, Taylor Publishing Company, Dallas, 1969, p 245.
2. Morris, *Salerno*.
3. Churchill, Winston S., *The Second World War: The Closing Ring*, Vol V, Cassell, 1952, pp 127–80.
4. Butcher, H.C., *Three Years with Eisenhower*, Heinemann, 1944, p 369.
5. These anxieties are reflected in Walker, *From Texas to Rome*, see pp 255–8.
6. Walker, *From Texas to Rome*, p 258.
7. Morris, *Salerno*, p 301.
8. Ibid.
9. Matthews interview with Marshall, p 8.

25

Naples: At Long Last

The Germans may claim with some justification to have won, if not a victory at least an important success over us.

Alexander's entry
War Diary of Fifteenth Army Group
25 September 1943[1]

The battle-wise troops in the front line did not have to be told that the crisis was over. Shells began to fall farther and farther inland. There were new faces and fresh uniforms as reinforcements flooded in to take up the advance for the breakout. Trucks and tanks stood nose to tail blocking all exits out of the beachhead.

On 18 September Fifth Army intelligence confirmed a general withdrawal by the Germans. Reconnaissance patrols from 179th Infantry moved right through the corridor and at day's end came to rest at Ponte Sele. A patrol from the 36th Infantry came down from the hills above Altavilla, and were joined by a troop of armoured cars from the British 56th Infantry Division. The Fifth Army had at last secured their D-day objectives, albeit ten days behind schedule.

Earlier the previous afternoon, Lieutenant Quail, a liaison officer with General Bucknell's 5th British Infantry Division, arrived at Walker's headquarters to agree the coordination for a rendezvous. Eighth Army was marching up Highway 19 and was then at Montesano, some 25 miles south of the command post. Montgomery signalled Mark Clark saying that he was glad his forces had joined up with Fifth Army. Clark flashed back. 'Received your message. I have felt nothing.' The meaning was crystal clear: the junction of the two armies had had no effect on the battle.

In the British sector above the Sele river, there was another drama about to be acted out. The Avalanche Draft of 1,500 men had been rushed across the Mediterranean in three fast cruisers only to be dumped in the X Corps transit camp, little more than a field behind some sand dunes. They were left to fend for themselves for a few days during which time rumours spread and anger mounted. The truth was soon out. They were not to reinforce their old divisions but rather the 46th and 56th Infantry Divisions. Neither was there a crisis at the beachhead.

The whole situation was grossly mishandled. In the absence of firm leadership and discipline, resentment grew. In their defence, the men were deeply loyal to their own regiments or in the case of the Scots, to the Highland Division. They feared that if they joined unfamiliar regiments from the Midlands, Home Counties and Hampshire, not only would they be separated from their mates, but they would never get back to their parent units.

Despite much grumbling, the vast majority made the best of things and joined their new battalions. A hard core of 300 men held firm and demanded the right to rejoin their old units. McCreery made an unprecedented address. He told them an error had been made, and gave his personal undertaking that they would be given every opportunity to return to the units of their choice once the corps objectives had been secured.[2] In the circumstances this was about as fair an offer as anyone could expect and some recognized it as such. The majority, however, 192 men, still stood firm.

A staff officer stood in front of the assembled ranks. 'Parade! Fall out on the road and pick up your kit and move off to the 46th Division area,' he ordered. The 192 men remained rigidly to attention. Some were convinced that, since justice was on their side, the worst that could happen would be a charge of disobeying a lawful order in the field. Most stood firm because they were confused or because their mates remained.

Another officer appeared. He read out passages from King's Regulations and the Mutiny Act. The men were stunned. Every soldier knows that the penalty for mutiny is death by shooting.

Squads of military police descended. The men were disarmed and marched off to a compound next to the German POW cage. The Germans jeered and called them cowards and deserters. The disgrace of the veterans was complete. Degraded and humiliated, they were eventually shipped back to North Africa and court-martialled. All were found guilty. Three sergeants were sentenced to be shot, and the remainder to long terms of penal servitude, ten years for corporals and seven years for the others. Some had medals for gallantry, won in the Western Desert, which were stripped from them. This shameful affair, from which no-one emerged with any credit, ended with the sentences immediately being suspended, on the condition the men agreed to return to the fight – albeit in new units.[3]

The Germans have always regarded Salerno as a victory. Von Vietinghoff praised his troops, and reported to Berlin that Tenth Army had taken 5,000 prisoners as well as inflicting massive casualties. In reality, given the confined battlefield and the sustained ferocity of the fighting, casualties were remarkably light.[4]

At the time, press and radio made great play of the intervention by Eighth Army which had arrived like the 7th Cavalry in the nick of time. General de Guingand, Montgomery's Chief of Staff, wrote: 'Some would like to think, I did at the time, that we helped, if not saved, the situation at Salerno. But now I doubt whether we influenced matters to any great extent. General Clark had everything under control before Eighth Army appeared on the scene.'[5]

To what extent such considerations influenced the attitudes of ordinary soldiers is unclear, but it undoubtedly influenced the attitude and outlook of the more senior commanders. Montgomery, in his supercilious fashion, considered himself to be the saviour of the hour, and Mark Clark was deeply resentful at being cast in a subordinate role. Later, when he succeeded Alexander as Army Group commander, his approach changed. But, for as long as he led Fifth Army, Mark Clark unabashedly promoted his own self-image. Fifth Army became Mark Clark's Fifth Army and its commander remained deeply suspicious and highly critical of the British troops that served under him.

None of the three divisions that were fully deployed, 46th and 56th British and 36th US, performed particularly well, and they were not acknowledged as top-line units, least of all by the Germans. In later operations the two British divisions were regarded by Fifth Army command as barely adequate, while the Texans acquired the unfortunate tag of being an unlucky outfit, not just for themselves, but for others with whom they came into contact. Soldiers in the field are superstitious, like sailors at sea. The 36th had a reputation of turning a battle sour. Nobody wanted to be associated with them.

So what saved the day at Salerno in the face of such a lacklustre performance? Von Vietinghoff was to claim that it was the concentrated and accurate fire from the Allied warships that frustrated his armoured counterattacks on 13 and 14 September, the two critical days.

It could, of course, be argued that it was in the German interests to attribute their failure to that element over which they had no control. The Royal Navy also claimed that the battleships saved the day for the Americans. The cruisers, destroyers, monitors and gunboats of various shapes and sizes had lent tremendous support. But *Warspite* and *Valiant* did not arrive until 15 September, by which time the worst was over. Twenty-four hours later *Warspite* was smothered by German radio-controlled bombs; she took two direct hits and a number of damaging near-misses and was towed away to Malta for repairs.

Salerno showed that a resolute defence comprising infantry dug in and supported by ample artillery can outwit an attacker, especially if the attacker makes unforced errors. General Von Vietinghoff's handling of his divisions in the counterattack phase is open to criticism. At various times he had elements of seven German divisions[6] but persisted in making small unrelated, even opportunistic forays, involving battalion-sized combat groups. Had Von Vietinghoff waited and made a concerted attack en masse against the 36th Division via the Sele Corridor, despite Allied air superiority, the Germans might well have overwhelmed the defenders. Subsequently, it was to be the Germans in the defence who were to frustrate the Allies and control the pace of the battle. And the Allies would be the ones who made the mistakes when attacking positions that were known to be heavily defended.

In Walker's judgement, Dawley handled his job as well as, or better than Clark handled his.[7] But Clark's position was never under serious threat. Short of a major reverse, his dismissal would have been exceedingly damaging to inter-Allied relations and morale. American command had proved wanting in North Africa and there had been a major shake up. After Sicily, Patton was under a cloud. Salerno was the first American-commanded operation on the European mainland. Politically Clark was untouchable. The public on both sides of the Atlantic had high expectations. The Allies were on the offensive and the days of sacking army commanders, common enough in the dark times, was over.

Montgomery arrived by destroyer at the Salerno beachhead on 21 September. Clark was still seething at the Englishman's behaviour. Warren Thresher was with Clark when the destroyer dropped anchor some distance offshore near to Agripoli. The ADC was despatched to commandeer a DUKW to escort the Eighth Army commander ashore. Thresher called a passing DUKW over and scrambled aboard. He looked in the cargo hold. There was a 500-lb bomb slopping around inside, although the crew didn't seem too disconcerted. There were a number of war correspondents standing with Clark, so Thresher scrambled out and whispered to his chief, 'Sir, there's a 500-pound bomb in there.'

The biggest smile Thresher had seen in a week or more spread across Clark's face.

'Go ahead, son,' he replied.

Thresher climbed back aboard the DUKW and the driver headed back down the beach into the water and out to the destroyer. The DUKW manoeuvred alongside and Montgomery clambered down the Jacob's ladder. Only when he was safely aboard did he look down to see what was slopping about in the hold. Thresher remembers his face was a picture.

Pictures were taken, plenty of them. Not of Montgomery riding into Salerno in a DUKW with a bomb, but of him reaching down to shake Clark by the hand. Thresher could just imagine the captions that the British Eighth Army propaganda machine would write to accompany the photographs. Clark was obviously thinking along the same lines and Thresher saw him give a hard but almost imperceptible tug. It was enough to unbalance Montgomery who could only save himself by jumping off the DUKW. More photographs were taken, but Clark now towered above Montgomery who looked positively diminutive beside him. The two men retired to Clark's caravan for a quiet chat. Clark began by saying that the Fifth Army was just a young army trying hard to get along, while the Eighth Army was a battle-trained veteran, and that Monty had far more experience in battle than he and that he would appreciate his advice. Monty 'ate this crap up'[8] and indicated that he thought Clark would do all right. Clark was enjoying sending the old man up. Then, before he left, Monty said,

'By the way, do you know Alex?'

'Why, I've met him,' replied Clark.

'Well, I say there, he may order you to carry out some crazy plan. If he does, just tell him to go to hell.'

Clark replied, 'I'll tell you about it if he does and you can tell him to go to hell.'

Monty said he would.

There were still some weeks of bitter fighting before the Allies broke free of their shallow beachhead. There were some desperate battles, with the Cava defile for the British and Altavilla for the Americans figuring prominently in the after-action reports and battle diaries. The Tenth Army was determined that their own withdrawal was to be an orderly affair in which they were to inflict maximum casualties upon the Allies at minimum cost for themselves.

Mark Clark had moved substantial reinforcements, including elements of the 82nd Airborne and tanks from the Royal Scots Greys to the Chiunzi pass to bolster the Rangers. Eventually, Fifth Army did break free. American paratroopers and Rangers rode British cavalry Shermans down into the plain at Nocera and thence into a ruined city.

Naples fell on 5 October and Mark Clark entered the city in triumph. It was his wife's birthday. Fifth Army had suffered 12,000 casualties in the process but the first major city on the European mainland had been captured by an American-led army, and that is what mattered.

Notes

1. Morris, *Salerno*, p 306.
2. In the event, McCreery was as good as his word. After the fall of Naples, the survivors of the Avalanche Draft were paraded in their units and offered the opportunity to return to their parent battalions: very few did so.
3. Their problems did not end with a reprieve because their records went with them to the new units. There have been a number of attempts recently to secure a Royal Pardon; but the truth is that in law the men were guilty of mutiny. There can be no extenuating circumstances for mutiny on the battlefield, and to acknowledge that soldiers have the right of free choice is to set a very dangerous precedent.
4. The official histories give the following figures for Salerno to 18 September:

	British	Germans	Americans
Wounded	2734	2002	835
Killed	725	840	225
Missing	1800	630	589
Total	5259	3472	1649

5. De Guingand, Sir Francis, *Operation Victory*, Hodder and Stoughton, 1947, p 312.
6. The German divisions, all of part of which fought at Salerno, besides the 16th Panzers, included Herman Goering, 15 Panzer Grenadiers, 29th Panzer Grenadiers, 26th Panzers, 1st Parachute Division.
7. Walker, *From Texas to Rome*, p 258.
8. Matthews interview with Mark Clark, p 73.

26

A Strategy of Unlimited Liability

Beyond the narrow plains on the east and west coasts, the terrain was enormously difficult, even in the southern reaches of peninsular Italy. Narrow valleys were broken by intensely cultivated plots. Rugged mountains towered to elevations of 5,000 feet and higher. Single-track roads traced their way over the mountains by way of narrow defiles, across numerous stone bridges and viaducts, and clung precariously to ledges carved out of precipitous cliffs.

And these were the main roads! Secondary roads leading to tiny mountain villages took the form of unmade tracks or mule paths. The Italian peasants who scraped a living in such a bleak landscape had no interest in the high ridges and mountain tops, but these commanding heights were vital in war. In such circumstances, pack mules became the mode of transport, but there were places even they could not reach; supplies were then carried on the backs of soldiers. In the mountains, pack mules became the normal first-line transport for infantry and artillery units. One feature of the enemy's scorched-earth policy was the slaughter of those draught animals (which they could not use), rather than allow them to fall into Allied hands.

In this terrain it was relatively easy for the Germans to impede the advance by means of demolitions. Along the coastal highways, a popular German tactic was to fell lines of big trees to interlock across a road, usually in places where there was no alternative route. The obstacle would be booby-trapped, mined and targeted by artillery or mortars. It would take time, man-hours and a steady drip of casualties to clear the obstacle. And there would be dozens of them.

In the mountain towns, apart from blowing bridges and culverts, a favourite trick was to blow in the fronts of old stone buildings thereby filling streets with rubble. The rubble could neither be by-passed nor removed, and invariably it was booby-trapped. Once the traps had been cleared the only way forward was to build a road over the rubble, often at the level of the first floors of the gaping buildings.

The pace of the advance beyond Naples northwards to the line of the River Volturno and the next significant natural obstacle depended on the combat and field engineers. Such men were in constant employment, building bridges and roads, constructing by-passes, clearing minefields and, when the need arose, grabbing side-arms and fighting as infantry. There was no weapon more valuable, or more in demand, and no target which had a higher priority for German mortars and artillery than the engineers' bulldozers.

As if the terrain wasn't bad enough, winter came early that year and the miseries of the Allied soldiers multiplied. Rain fell incessantly and heavily, day after day. Small streams became raging torrents with sufficient kinetic energy to sweep away a fully laden three-ton truck or swamp a two-storey-two-bent trestle bridge. The rain was more of an obstacle to the Allied advance than either the enemy or the terrain.

The Fifth Army were about as well prepared for such weather as the Wehrmacht had been in the first winter before Moscow. The Germans froze and the Allies drowned. Camps and supply dumps located in the coastal plains were flooded. Field hospitals became seas of mud and gale-force winds ripped away the tents of operating theatres and wards. Surgical sterility and cleanliness had no meaning and dedicated medics slaved to avoid secondary infections.

The Americans were marginally better off because of the superior quality of their kit. For the British fighting soldier, in leaking boots and gaiters and shoddy battledress, life was abject misery. Any thought of combat took second place to the need for warmth, shelter and, above all, somewhere dry. The worst thing about mud, beside impeding the advance, is that it causes trench foot. As October gave way to November and the temperature dropped, the advance northwards slowed to a crawl. It was impossible to keep feet dry and front-line soldiers frequently found themselves in water-filled foxholes and trenches for days and later, at Cassino, weeks at a time. Often boots could only be cut off and feet swelled like balloons. There were many instances of amputation.

In these atrocious conditions the contrast between the relative comfort of the rear-area formations and the fighting units was very marked indeed, and transcended nationality. Front-line soldiers, whether Fifth or Eighth Army, held their rear-area brethren in contempt. Such feeling found expression in the cartoons drawn by Bill Mauldin, an American GI, who had started the war with the 45th (US) Infantry Division. His cartoon characters 'Willie' and 'Joe' became household names in Italy. But their irreverent cynicism served as a useful safety valve and boosted morale. The rear-area stallions complained bitterly and some senior officers sought Mauldin's hide, but Mark Clark protected him and recognized his value. In the same way that the British general, Bill Slim, was to stand the description of the 'Forgotten Army' on its head and, in a perverse fashion, to foster his Fourteenth Army's morale in Burma, so in Italy front-line soldiers of all nationalities (and I suspect Germans too) were proud to identify with Willie and Joe.

Another feature which drove a wedge between the front line and rear-area stallions was corruption. Supply units always got the pick of the supplies even though their needs were less. Such is the way of war, but in Italy wholesale military corruption spread into the civilian population and thence organized crime. The origins were in Sicily where, by October 1943, occupation of the island had descended into decadence. Drunkenness was widespread among British and American troops as was venereal disease – one soldier in four being infected among the white troops, three in four among American Negro units, in spite of the many condom distribution stations which were established.[1]

Some base-area troops had moved to the mainland, so expectations were high by the time Naples was captured. But the rot set in; within a week of occupation the black market was ruling the roost.

Naples had suffered considerably from Allied bombing attacks, and, in the final days before their evacuation, the Germans carried out wholesale destruction of port installations, communications and public utilities. When the Wehrmacht rearguard finally began to evacuate the city there was even an uprising of sorts, though nothing on the scale of popular myth and legend. There was some skirmishing over four days which resulted in 50 dead Italians and less than a dozen Germans.[2] Nevertheless, the city felt that by this gesture it had purged itself of past sins and had earned the respect of the Allies. This was not forthcoming, especially from the British who continued to treat the Italians with contempt.

Lance Corporal Frank Battye was a 24-year-old Yorkshireman who served in No 863 Company Royal Engineers. This was a unit attached to Eighth Army largely made up of specialists who were trained to handle anything from bulldozers to dockside cranes. The sappers had landed at Syracuse in July 1943. In Italy Frank Battye drove a bulldozer from Syracuse to the Po river. In October 1943 he found himself part of a ten-man squad, driving a steam crane on Bari docks, unloading Liberty ships bringing in supplies for the Eighth Army. For the most part it was munitions, bombs and shells. Sometimes they would unload a ship full of American PX goodies and then they hit the jackpot. Thieving at Bari docks was a highly organized affair, organized by the Military Police who had been drafted in as Docks Police.

Each morning a truck would take the squad to the docks. The Military Police met them at the gates.

'Now then lads, what ship are you working on?'

'No stealing, no pinching,' was the instruction. 'Tell us what you want and it will be delivered to your billet.' And it was. Warm winter clothes, sugar, rum, whatever was on the shopping list, would find its way to the sappers.

In Naples, where the port was operated by the Americans who used Italian labour, nothing was sacred, and the front lines suffered as a consequence. The wonder drug penicillin, for example, so important in countering secondary infections, was also a cure for gonorrhoea. It had a very high black-market value and sometimes was used as a form of currency. Prostitution was rampant and venereal disease spread like wildfire.

Italian cities welcomed the Allies, if only because their arrival meant an end to the suffering, the bombing and the shelling. The welcome soon turned sour after the local people suffered the indignities of systematic looting, invariably by the second echelon and rear formations (fewer opportunities were afforded to the fighting men). There was precious little sympathy from the military authorities, who treated the Italians more as a conquered people and in the absence of sanctions, pillage and abuse were a common enough experience.

Another consequence of liberation was an increase in the price of consumer goods, especially food. In Naples, no less than in Sicily, the impact of the Allied occupation was intensely inflationary and attempts to hold prices at existing levels broke down completely. The Allied Military Government found itself quite unable to enforce its own regulations. The quality of life deteriorated as other goods and public services, gas and electricity, became in short supply. Petty officialdom masquerading in uniform imposed on the Italian people a mass of restrictions, rules and regulations which won the Allies few friends and were designed to keep the population docile and subservient. The people did what they had to do in order to survive; but the experience has left a scar which will take the passing of more than one generation to eradicate from the national memory.

Neither did the Allies advance their cause when they foisted the King and his court of camp followers along with the biggest sycophant of them all, Badoglio, upon the Italian people.

On 29 September Badoglio had proceeded to Malta. He was accompanied by Generals Ambrosio and Roatta, and by Admiral De Courtea, who spoke for the navy and General Sandalli of the air force. They were received with full military honours by General Eisenhower on the spacious quarterdeck of the battleship HMS *Nelson*. The time had come for some arm-twisting, for the Italians to join the Allies as 'co-belligerents' – a term specially invented for the occasion since at the time it had no meaning in international law, neither could it be found in the Oxford Dictionary. Earlier, in August, the Italians, during the armistice negotiations, had been presented with the 'Long Terms' which contained 39 clauses. Suitably revised, and finally agreed to, it was eventually signed as the Instrument of Surrender aboard HMS *Nelson*.[3]

The Italian delegation complained that the Instrument implied an unconditional surrender, but the intention of the Allies was unequivocal. The terms of the surrender were to be executed by an Italian government under the direction of an Armistice Commission. There was no military government except for operational purposes. Italy had been a full and co-equal partner of the Axis alongside Germany and Japan. Where both Germany and Japan suffered the full indignities of military occupation and government, the Italians got off remarkably lightly. Some Italian writers[4] maintain that the Instrument of Surrender did not restore sovereign power to Italy in any meaningful sense; in this judgement they are quite correct. Italy could hardly have expected anything better. The United States and Great Britain were totally committed to the defeat of the Third Reich, and Italy, once an enemy, was now required to play its part.

In the Allied view 'co-belligerency' was a way for the Italians to work their passage back to respectability. The Instrument of Surrender did promise better times ahead. The temporary nature of the conditions was emphasized by a commitment to 'democracy' – full and free general elections and a free choice of government once the Germans had been expelled. Given that the House of Savoy and the Italian General Staff had been so closely associated with Mussolini, the Allied position was perfectly logical.

Conditions for the Italians could improve in time according to their commitment and contribution to the war effort. However, with the Germans still in physical possession of four-fifths of the Italian landmass and nine-tenths of the population, Badoglio's reluctance to accede was understandable. Neither can the Italians have been impressed by the time taken and difficulties encountered by the Allies in securing their chunk of Italy. A simple calculation would have shown that, on current performance, it would take another three years to clear the Germans out, and this made no allowance for winter. In the meantime, the wrath that the Germans could visit upon the Italian people in response to such a step was not hard to imagine. Indeed the decision by a government to declare war upon another power in virtual occupation of its territory could be interpreted both as foolhardy and irrelevant, unless accompanied by a general call to arms. Badoglio had no intention of proceeding down that path.

For the Allies, co-belligerence did have a political importance. Hitler had already ensconced Mussolini as Head of the Salo Republic of Italy with his capital at Gargagno on Lake Garda. Technically Mussolini's cabinet did exercise authority over non-military matters, but the Salo Republic was a sham. The Germans were in full military occupation and control. Nevertheless the Salo did have to be challenged with an alternative fountainhead for Italian loyalty and commitment.

Badoglio signed the Instrument of Surrender but balked at co-belligerence. He sought a compromise whereby Italian troops could fight alongside the Allies. General Alexander, however, rejected the offer of two Italian divisions then in Corsica and the 184th Parachute Division 'Nembo' which was in Sardinia at the time of the armistice. Neither did he express any interest in the offer of Italian prisoners of war. For the British at this stage the thought of fighting alongside Free Italians was a very disturbing prospect, but that position began to change within a very short period of time.

The King held out for a little while but finally the Court succumbed and from 3.00 pm on 11 October Italy considered it was at war with Germany. There could be no formal presentation of ultimata through diplomatic channels. Instead, Badoglio telegraphed the Marquis Paolucci de' Calboli, the one-time Ambassador to Madrid, an ardent Fascist who had joined the other side at the armistice, to tell his German colleague in Madrid that Italy was at war with Germany, and would he please inform Berlin.

Why did the Allies bother with such a charade? After all, the original objectives given to the Fifteen Army Group, namely the capture of the airbase complex at Foggia and the port of Naples, had been accomplished.

Yet on 2 October Alexander had prescribed future operations of the

Eighth and Fifth Armies. They were to be conducted in two phases. The first was to be an advance to seize a line from Termoli on the Adriatic coast through Isernia and Venafro to Sessa near the Mediterranean. The second phase was to be an advance to a line well to the north of Rome. Clark's instructions were to seize a bridgehead across the Volturno and then strike out for the Liri Valley and northwards to Rome. Montgomery was tasked to continue the advance by way of Termoli and Pescara from whence ran the most southerly non-mountainous lateral road to the capital. Alexander and Montgomery privately believed that this was the most direct route.

Mark Clark still had the X (Br) Corps under command. He had earlier questioned this because of the logistical problems created by a bi-national army. Alexander had explained it was easier administratively to leave things the way they were and the problem of transferring the corps across the Apennines was not worth the candle. Mark Clark did not believe a word of it. So far as he was concerned the continued presence of X (Br) Corps was the British hedging their bets. Whichever Army got to Rome first, there would be a British input and therefore a British PR victory.

But why had the Allies changed their objectives?

A tremendous euphoria pervaded the Allied High Command, not just in the Mediterranean but in Washington and London. Based on their success at Salerno, the Joint Intelligence Committee reflected their masters' optimism and declared that the Germans would now retreat northwards beyond the Plain of Lombardy, their main objective being to conserve manpower. On 21 September Alexander issued a broad strategic directive which envisaged the capture of Rimini and Florence by Christmas! Churchill read the paper and signalled Alexander that he would meet him in Rome before the end of the month! No wonder Alexander spurned the Italian offer of troops. According to his calculations, it appeared to be all over bar the shouting! The euphoria lasted barely a fortnight, but it was long enough for the orders to be promulgated from Army Group down to army and thence to corps and divisional level.

Ultra compelled the Allies to revise their plans. On 8 October, a signal intercepted and decoded from LXXVI Panzer Corps gave details of three successive defence lines south of Rome, the last of which was referred to as the 'final winter line'. There was sufficient information and topographical detail to show that the line was also called the 'Bernhardt Line'.[3] A few days later the Allies received information about a major, even more formidable defence line which was to be built coast-to-coast in the

Apennines north of Florence. There were details on German troop deployments in Italy which showed that first-rate fighting divisions from the strategic reserve (ie Army Group B) were to be deployed south of Rome.

It is hardly any wonder that Alexander drew the immediate conclusion that Rome would not be taken before some heavy fighting around the mountains of Cassino: 'Here,' he wrote in his memoirs, 'was the true moment of the birth of the Italian Campaign.'[4]

Churchill and Eisenhower were to express similar sentiments. But there was no reassessment of strategies and objectives. Would it have been possible to return to the original strategy of limited objectives and liabilities to match? Could the orders have been unscrambled to allow a period of reflection while the generals went back to the drawing board? That was not possible; the battlefield dictated that the advance should continue, at least in theory. By early October the rains and mud had become a real problem. At the same time, some top-rate divisions were already being withdrawn ready for their return to England and Overlord.

All that Marshall and the American Joint Chiefs wanted in Italy was a safe position to cover the airbases at Foggia and to tie down German strength. But Marshall had not expected the Germans to make such a hard fight of it. According to Marshall[5] it was the British, especially Churchill, who were pressing the Americans to get more involved with the Italian campaign. This was against Marshall's better judgement, but he felt he didn't have a strong hand to play. American divisions in Africa and Sicily had done fairly well, but several commanders had been relieved. Thus, in discussions with the British, the Americans had promises rather than substantial accomplishments to bring as bargaining chips to the negotiating table.

The German decision to hang on to southern Italy was in Marshall's judgement a strategic blunder. But a reduction in Allied fighting units swung the military balance in favour of the Germans and perversely provided a *raison d'être* for continuing the campaign. The Allied generals could now make the case that economy of force, a traditional principle of war, now applied in Italy. A small number of Allied divisions were tying down greater numbers of the enemy. Alexander showed that in September the Allies had 13 divisions in the theatre compared to the enemy's 18. And every German division in Italy was one less fighting the Russians in the east or threatening the Allies next year in the west. If the formula was expanded to embrace the whole Mediterranean region, ie by virtue of an Allied presence in Italy, the enemy would have to defend the coastline of France, the Balkans and Greece; then the balance was even better.

There were two weaknesses to this argument. The first, in modern parlance, can be described as 'creative accounting'. To use divisions as a yardstick for measuring the military balance was, even in 1943, highly misleading. German divisions were already much smaller than their Allied equivalents and taking into account heavy weapons, ammunition and ready availability of reserves, the disparity was even greater.

The second weakness was that the arguments for containment also worked in reverse. Every Allied division fighting in Italy was one less available for Normandy or elsewhere. Indeed, alarmed at the apparent disparities, Eisenhower went before the Combined Chiefs to argue for reinforcements. Using Alexander's calculations, he was able to show that by mid-October the Allies would be down to eleven divisions, while the Germans would have 25 in Italy.

There were sufficient grounds for anxiety and more divisions had to be found. The Polish Corps was in the theatre and the excellent New Zealanders were back after their period of leave following victory in North Africa. There were also some Free French divisions available in North Africa, along with British divisions which had almost completed refit and retraining. In the United States some of the new GI divisions were formed and about ready; and Alexander was forced to look again at the Italians.

The transition to a strategy of unlimited liability was virtually complete.

Notes

1. Gayne, G.R., *Italy in Transition*, 1946, p 213.
2. More Italians died when a German delayed action bomb exploded at the city's main post office some days after the liberation.
3. Montgomery ought to have been flattered – it was named after him.
4. Quoted in Bennet, Ralph, *Ultra and Mediterranean Strategy*, Hamish Hamilton, 1989, p 253.
5. Matthews interview with Marshall, p 9.

27

Across the Volturno – Not Without Acrimony

In the European War I was always concerned with four factors: casualties, duration, expense and the Pacific. The Pacific could not be left waiting indefinitely. We had to go ahead brutally fast in Europe. We could not indulge in a Seven Years War. A king can perhaps do that, but you cannot have such a protracted struggle in a democracy in the face of mounting casualties. I thought that the only place to achieve a positive and rapid military decision was in the lowlands of North Western Europe. Speed was essential.[1]

General George Marshall

In Marshall's judgement Hitler made the same mistake in Italy as he had in Northern France; had he drawn back rapidly to the Rhine, as his staff advised, this would have created problems. The Allied commanders were convinced that Hitler had made a terrible blunder in forcing his generals to stand and fight south of the Po.

Was this simply a device to make the best of a bad job? Once the troops were committed to battle, especially in a country like Italy, it was very difficult to pull them out. Marshall remained highly suspicious of Churchill's motives, and was concerned that Roosevelt might be persuaded to support the British Prime Minister in his ambitions for a Balkan campaign. He worried, whenever those two men spent time together, that Roosevelt might commit the United States by loose talk. 'When President Roosevelt began waving his cigarette holder you never knew where you were going.'[2]

In conferences the British always spoke in terms of policy. With their parliamentary traditions and experiences with the Cabinet, they were accustomed to speaking with one voice to an agreed policy. Churchill largely controlled what the British said. It infuriated the Americans when the British did not give their own individual views. The Americans could never come to terms with the fact that it was only the top leaders who spoke. There were conferences when Field Marshall Sir John Dill, as head of the British Joint Staff Mission to the United States, never said a word if Churchill or Sir Alan Brooke attended.

The Americans doubted British sincerity. Thus London's support for landings in the South of France as a second phase to Overlord was interpreted by the Americans as a device to keep troops in the theatre.

This lack of trust and communication at the highest levels was reflected by the armies in the field. Relations between Montgomery and Clark remained distinctly cool. Alexander tried to head off trouble by ordering Montgomery to despatch one of his best senior officers to Fifth Army to be Deputy Chief of Staff with the prime task of liaison. Montgomery sent Charles Richardson, his excellent brigadier general staff, and the latter quickly established a good working relationship with Al Gruenther. But it defied the good offices of both men to effect a rapprochement between the two army commanders. Montgomery didn't like competition in the press and public relations campaign and Mark Clark's vanity would not allow him to assume the role of the subordinate.

Much of the blame lay with Montgomery. There was one incident, not long after the link-up at Salerno, when Clark visited Eighth Army's tactical headquarters. Montgomery pretended to be out, even though Clark knew that he wasn't. On another occasion, late in October, Montgomery invited Clark to Eighth Army. He sent Noel Chavasse, an ADC, to make arrangements. Two days later he signalled Clark: 'Chevasse has told me your plans therefore there is no need for you to come.'[3]

Despite the appalling weather, difficult terrain and resolute German resistance, the Allied armies closed up to the German defences along the Volturno and Biferno rivers. Montgomery did not find campaigning in Italy to his taste but he did catch the Germans by surprise when a commando force outflanked Termoli at the mouth of the Biferno river. It was the last success he was to enjoy in Italy.

The forward brigades of the 78th Infantry Division were the nearest British troops and they were eight miles south of Termoli when 1,000 men from the Commando Brigade, troops from 40 Royal Marine and No 3 Army Commando together with the Special Raiding Squadron,[4] captured Termoli. The commandos were joined by elements of the 56th

Reconnaissance Regiment, the 8th Argyll and Sutherland Highlanders and the Kensingtons (London), the division's support battalion, when heavy rains washed away an engineers' bridge across the Bifurno. The Germans launched a series of counterattacks spearheaded by the 16th Panzers and over a 48-hour period there was some very bitter fighting.

The British forces also came under fire from members of the local population. The commandos suffered casualties from grenade and sniper attacks and this was only stopped when Lt Colonel John Dunford Slater called the male population together and threatened mass execution in retaliation. He later wrote that this 'sent them home in a more cooperative frame of mind'.[5] So much for the Allies being welcomed as liberators.

Reinforcements were rushed in by sea. Two American LSIs carried a battalion of Royal Irish Fusiliers into Termoli harbour under fire. The landing ships offered little protection to the men packed below decks and the American crews had locked the hatches; the last thing they wanted was a load of panicking soldiers on deck. For a short while, as the ships made their final approach to harbour, they came under small-arms fire and there was chaos below decks. The conditions on those crowded troop decks defies imagination. Under fire, in the pitch dark and confined in a thin steel box which offered no protection, all vestiges of discipline broke down as men fought with one another to get out, and the wounded were trampled underfoot.

Once ashore, the Royal Irish Fusiliers were rushed into battle and it was touch and go for another day before the engineers had erected a new bridge across the Biferno and relief came in the form of the 38th (Irish) Brigade.

Hitler, furious at the failure of 16th Panzers, sacked Major General Rudolf Sieckenius, their commanding general.

On the left flank the Fifth Army was also learning the hard way how to attack river lines. By that stage General Lucas had three veteran infantry divisions in his VI Corps. There was Truscott's 3rd Infantry, Middleton's 45th Infantry, now very much in need of a rest, and Ryder's 34th Infantry which had arrived in the line from Sicily towards the end of September.

The Fifth Army closed up to the Volturno on 3 October and prepared to make its first major river crossing of the campaign. In normal times the Volturno is a gently flowing river with numerous fords and crossing points. Heavy rains had turned it into a raging torrent 2–300 feet wide, six feet and more in depth and with steep, mud-slicked banks as much as ten feet high.

It might have been possible to outflank the river line altogether with a major amphibious operation, but the landing ships were simply not available. Less than 300 LSTs were in existence in October 1943, almost all built in the United States. Of these, 139 were in the Mediterranean, 67 of them manned by the Royal Navy under Lend-Lease, and a small contingent earmarked for Overlord. This meant a long, slow voyage home (they had a top speed of twelve knots) through the Mediterranean and across the Bay of Biscay in winter which was not a pleasant prospect. There were a further 62 new production LSTs promised for Overlord. Everything else was allocated to the war in the Pacific.

There was no alternative to a river crossing. Heavy rains, poor roads and devastatingly accurate German artillery caused further delay to the Fifth Army preparations. Speed was essential. Clark already had his eye, not on the Volturno but on what intelligence assessments were calling the Winter Line, some 40 miles through mountainous terrain to the north. The longer it took Fifth Army to reach the Garigliano, the more formidable were the enemy defences.

Clark ordered a two-corps attack for the night of 12 October. The British on the coastal sector had a 20-mile river front through relatively flat farmlands. The Americans on their right had 35 miles of front which ran into rocky uplands and deep gorges.

Von Vietinghoff considered the 'very cleverly planned and forcefully executed attack' of the 3rd Infantry Division as the key action at the Volturno. Truscott had planned the operation with meticulous care and was able to conceal his intentions from the enemy until the moment of assault. He kept one of his regiments and half his artillery well out of the sight and range of the enemy. His quartermaster staff begged, borrowed and stole every item of equipment, from waterproofing materials and ex-Italian Navy lifejackets to improvised bridging materials.

The enemy, battalions of the Herman Goering Division, offered stout resistance. But the 7th Infantry Regiment which led the assault had five battalions and some armour across by late afternoon. More important, they secured Mount Caruso, which dominated the area. Under fire, the engineers got two bridges across and this allowed jeeps and trucks with heavy weapons and supplies into the bridgehead. By 14 October a bridge capable of taking tanks spanned the Volturno and the division had secured a bridgehead four miles deep – too large to be crushed. Surprise and aggressive tactics had secured success at the cost of 400 casualties.

The 34th Infantry also gained a bridgehead across the river, but its assault battalions took a further 24 hours before they had succeeded in forcing the enemy back from the river and securing their crossing points. The Americans were across but the British X Corps did not do at all well.

Although they were on the flat coastal plain, the approach to the river was across flat open fields which provided the Germans with an excellent killing ground. The river banks, 25 feet high in places, and flood levees were formidable obstacles in their own right.

McCreery had objected to Clark's orders for a night attack so Clark visited his CP. McCreery thought that crossing the Volturno was the most difficult job he had faced and told Clark so. 'We accept your order, of course,' McCreery continued, 'But I have to say that I am embarrassed when a young American commander gives British troops orders that we don't like.'[6]

The British failed to get reconnaissance patrols across the Volturno, so when they came to attack they did so without any precise knowledge of how wide the river was, its depth, or enemy dispositions on the opposite bank. Compared to the American effort the British were to pay the price for such inadequate preparation. The amphibious assault was a shambles. Behind a massive corps artillery bombardment augmented by the Royal Navy, the tanks landed safely ashore only to bog down in the marshland. Mines and anti-tank guns accounted for those tanks which tried to deploy forward.

The two infantry brigades had a rough time and both bridgeheads were nearly overrun before they were finally able to establish a precarious toehold by the end of the first day. Dogged resistance and massed artillery proved decisive thereafter. The brigades progressively expanded their bridgehead and moved inland.

The 7th Armoured Division secured a small bridgehead and did its job of attracting enemy fire and diverting attention. The 56th Infantry got nowhere and gave up trying. The main assault was made near a destroyed railway bridge, an obvious point which the Germans had well-covered. The assault troops soon pulled back and the division commander, judging that further attacks were impractical, made no further attempt.

When Clark heard about this on 14 October, he gave the 56th Division one of Truscott's hard-won bridges and the Black Cats crossed the river. Clark drew some very unfavourable comparisons between the performance of the two divisions. How come Truscott's 3rd Infantry had crossed and built three bridges yet the Black Cats on their left had failed to secure even a small beachhead? Perhaps the answer lay in the fact that two days before the crossing Major General Graham, the division commander, had been seriously injured in a road accident. Brigadier Lyne of 169 Brigade had assumed temporary command of the division.

The division was also at the end of its tether. At Salerno it had twice borne the brunt of violent Germans counterattacks and without a break had continued as part of the advance to the Volturno. Clark never made reference to the division's condition, nor did he acknowledge the critical influence that the loss of a commander just before a battle can have upon a unit's cohesion and morale.

Clark had yet to appreciate that the British and the American armies had different philosophies. The Americans wanted the attack to be fast and aggressive, feeling that the faster they got stuck in, the fewer casualties would be suffered. The British used artillery, of which they believed there was never too much, and they pulled back if the opposition was tough, and used the artillery again.

In Clark's eyes the British were to blame. 'McCreery did not want to get across the river,'[7] he said.

In the case of VI Corps, the attack was launched by two divisions which had not been at Salerno, while the 45th (US) Infantry were given a minor role. Clark did have legitimate grounds for complaint, however, on another aspect of the operations, when the BBC announced that a large British force had crossed the Volturno with only a small American detachment.

Major General Gerald Templer,[8] the fiery commander of the 1st British Infantry Division, which had just about re-equipped and retrained after the North African campaign and was still in Algeria, was ordered to assume command of the 56th Infantry Division. He arrived at the Volturno on 15 October, hardly an auspicious time to assume command.

There were other command changes in the wind. Montgomery was not reticent in opening his own promotional campaign aimed to get him out of the Italian mess and into the top job for Overlord. On 4 October he had signalled Churchill direct, without bothering with proper channels of communication, military etiquette or plain good manners:

> We have advanced a long way and very quickly. It had to be done in order to help 5 Army, but it has been a great strain on my administration which had to be switched from the Toe to the Heel during operations and which is now stretched to the limit. . . . When I have got control of Termoli Campobasso I will halt for a short period. After the halt I will advance with my whole strength on Pescara and Ancona. I shall look forward to meeting you in Rome.[9]

Not content with this travesty of the truth he opened up a direct correspondence with Sir Alan Brooke, Chief of the General Staff. The objective was to stake his claim for an Army Group command in Overlord.

> I fear the Fifth Army is absolutely whacked. So long as you fight an army in combat teams and if the idea is that everyone should combat someone all the time you do not get very far. My own observation leads me to the conclusion that Clark would only be too delighted to be given quiet advice as to how to fight his Army. I think he is a very decent chap and most cooperative; if he received good and clear advice he would do very well.[10]

Notes

1. Matthews interview with Marshall, p 22.
2. Matthews interview, p 30.
3. Lamb, Richard, *Montgomery in Europe*, p 53.
4. The designation of 2nd SAS for operations in the Mediterranean.
5. Ladd, James, *Commandos and Rangers of World War II*, MacDonald and Jane's Ltd, 1978, p 147.
6. Blumenson, Martin, *Mark Clark*, Jonathan Cape, 1985, p 149.
7. Matthews interview with Mark Clark, Part II, p 55.
8. Later to gain fame as Governor General in Malaya during the period of the Emergency.
9. WO 169/8497.
10. Lamb, *Montgomery in Europe*, p 56.

28

New Faces

Fifteenth Army Group had lost seven divisions to Overlord and with the onset of winter had to share, and sometimes take second place with, its ports and lines of communications to meet the needs of the strategic air forces operating out of Foggia. Within three weeks of taking control, the Allies had opened up ten airfields, all eventually equipped with steel-clad runways on which were deployed some 35,000 personnel to fly and maintain 800 aircraft. To sustain this effort the Allied air forces were allocated 300,000 tons of shipping.

This was just the start. In North West Europe the American Eighth Air Force was taking a terrible beating in its daylight offensive. On 14 October some 60 B17s were lost and a further 138 heavily damaged in the infamous raid on the ball-bearing plants at Schweinfurt. Air superiority over Germany had been lost and the opportunity to attack from the south, from Italy, became a matter of urgency.

Progressively through the winter Allied air strength was built up. By the turn of the year in Italy, Sardinia and Corsica more than 45 airfields had been constructed, many equipped with paved or steel plank runways, some over a mile long. A special supply base was opened at the port of Bari which serviced the needs of 100,000 US Air Force personnel. Oil pipelines were laid, one from Manfredonia to Foggia being capable of supplying 100,000 gallons of 100-octane fuel a week.

On 1 November General Jimmy Doolittle took command of the newly created Fifteenth Air Force, which was primarily dedicated to the combined bomber offensive against Germany. The Fifteenth Air Force comprised heavy and medium groups of bombers with long-range fighters as escort. Upon formation it numbered about 500 aircraft and by Christmas this figure had risen to 800 plus. When Rome fell in June 1944 the Fifteenth Air Force had an operational strength of 1,200 heavy bombers alone. The combined bomber offensive against Germany, code-named Operation Pointblank, had first call upon their service but they could be detailed for air operations in support of the land campaign in Italy. Throughout much of the winter period, however, weather conditions prevented such assistance on a regular basis.

There was also the Tactical Air Force in the Mediterranean theatre. This consisted of the XII Air Force and the Desert Air Force, largely composed of medium and fighter bombers and fighter aircraft. This support of the land battle frequently resulted in a higher casualty rate than that experienced by the ground forces. The Allies might have had air superiority, but a combination of weather, terrain and enemy flak took a heavy toll. Thus at the time of the Volturno crossing, air force casualties averaged 7.69 per 1,000 per month compared to 6.33 for Fifth and Eighth Armies.

It was also the case that the Allied commanders had an entirely misplaced faith in the ability of their air forces, strategic and tactical, to produce a swift decision. Eisenhower was persuaded by his air commanders that air power alone could stifle the German lines of communication southwards across the Po Basin to the battlefront. For once Clark and Montgomery were at one in their assessment of the poor value of bombing. But there was little they could do about all the new arrivals that had to be fed, clothed and armed. By the end of November there were over a quarter of million men and 7,000 operational aircraft in the Allied air forces in the Mediterranean theatre.

To service their needs Bari was filled to capacity with freighters. The port frequently had 30 or more Liberty ships and freighters tied up alongside or waiting in the harbour roads for a berth. This in turn meant that it became a favoured target throughout the winter for night attacks by the Luftwaffe.

On 2 December the port experienced an attack which resulted in the highest number of Allied casualties from a raid on a port since Pearl Harbor. Unbeknown to the British harbour authorities, the US Liberty ship *John Harvey*, which had tied up at the quay that afternoon, carried a cargo of two thousand 100-pound mustard bombs. President Roosevelt had ordered that these weapons were to be held in Italy and used, but only in retaliation to a German first use of chemical weapons.

The *John Harvey* blew up as a result of a direct hit which killed the crew, the only people who knew of the ship's lethal cargo. After the raid the local military hospitals admitted 800 military casualties (the number of civilians is unknown) and within hours 600 were showing symptoms of mustard gas poisoning. But at first the doctors had no reason to suppose that the blistered and discoloured skin, blindness and swollen genitals were caused by mustard gas. When the authorities did become aware, an immediate 'cover-up' was ordered. The injured men were quickly dispersed to hospitals throughout the theatre and in some instances back to the United States. How many men eventually died from cancer is not known. The secret has been well-kept.

There were now more new faces amongst the ground forces. Doubtful of the quality of their training and combat status, the Allied High Command had refused to allow the Free French to participate in the Sicily campaign. In the event, a *groupement* of *goumiers* fought alongside the Americans in the central massif and did sterling service. The goumiers came from Morocco; a goum was the equivalent of a company. Three goums formed a *tabor* or battalion and three tabors formed a groupement or brigade.

The First French Army was formed in North Africa in 1943 by drawing upon colonial divisions of the Vichy French, three in Algeria, and two in Morocco, and the Free French Division which had fought with such success alongside Eighth Army in the Western Desert.

It was hard enough integrating the Europeans in the Free French and Vichy contingents, while the colonial troops had their own national sensitivities which had to be preserved. A Moroccan proverb says that a 'Moroccan man is a lion, an Algerian man is a man and a Tunisian man is a woman'.[1] It was important to keep these formations apart.

At the end of September, at the insistence of their Chief, General Giraud, and with no Allied assistance, a small French force liberated the island of Corsica in a three-week campaign. The fighting component was drawn from the 4th Division Marocaine de Montagne, trained in mountain warfare, with ski troops and mountain specialists with pack mules.

The Allied High Command's initial reluctance to deploy a fighting Free French Force changed after the decision to fight on past the Volturno. The Americans agreed to fund the venture, to feed arm, equip and pay for the French divisions. Eventually the French were to deploy more than five large divisions to the Corps Expeditionnaire Français (CEF). The command was down-graded from an army to a corps because the French were to be subordinate to Mark Clark's Fifth Army.

The first two divisions began to arrive in November 1943. These were the 2ᵉ Division d'Infanterie Marocaine (DIM) and the 3ᵉ Division d'Infanterie Algérienne (DIA). At first they confirmed all the Allies' worst fears. They were inadequately equipped and clothed for the winter campaign, poorly trained and spent as much time as they were able taking it out on the Italian civilians. However, their fighting qualities gradually improved, and in General Alphonse Juin they had an inspired commander. But rape and pillage remained a problem for the whole time they served in Italy.

The Fifth Army was destined to receive two more units to swell its ranks before Christmas. The 1st (US) Armoured Division fought the North African campaign from the Torch landing until the enemy surrender. Thereafter Hell on Wheels as it was popularly known, was withdrawn for a lengthy period of retraining and re-equipping. Elements did participate at Salerno, but the division as a unit did not arrive in Italy until mid-November when it assembled at Capua.

Lastly there was the First Special Service Force. Known as the North Americans, this was a mixed Canadian/US force of five battalions equipped to light infantry scales. They were commanded by Lt Colonel Robert T. Frederick, a quiet daredevil with the good looks of a Hollywood film star, who was worshipped by his men. After their encounter in battle the Germans dubbed Frederick's men the Black Devils. They invariably attacked at night, had blacked-out faces and gave no quarter. The unit was originally recruited from Canadian and American woodsmen, lumberjacks and explorers. They were trained as special forces skilled in parachuting, raiding and sabotage in winter warfare conditions. The North Americans were first used in an amphibious spearhead against the Japanese-held island of Kioka, in the Aleutians, but the Japanese had already left. For the North Americans it was a case of finding a war to fit their talents. Italy beckoned and, with disbandment the most likely alternative, it was Hobson's choice.

Churchill arranged for Eighth Army to receive about 100,000 men to compensate for those who had been withdrawn to England. The II Polish Corps had a tortuous history even before it reached the Middle East. When Russia invaded the eastern provinces of Poland in September 1939 about 1,700,000 Polish men, women and children were deported to the Soviet Union. Some Poles escaped the Russo-German pincers and made their way via Romania and France to England. A Government-in-Exile was established in London headed by President Wladyslaw Rackiewicz and Prime Minister Wladyslaw Sikorski. After the German invasion of Russia in July 1941 the Free Poles were more or less obliged to follow Britain's lead and reach an understanding with Stalin. The fact that much of Eastern Poland had been occupied did little to foster good relations. Nevertheless it was agreed in August 1941 that Poles detained in Russia would be recruited into a new army and the nucleus of two infantry divisions was established at Orenburg in the Soviet Union. Major General Wladislaw Anders, himself an ex-prisoner, was appointed to command the new army.

The Russians were less than forthcoming over equipment, training, weapons and even food for the new force. The men were reduced literally to the point of starvation. However, in December 1941, the Russians agreed to raise the force to six divisions and to allow 25,000 men to leave for the West. Another contingent left Russia in the summer of 1942.

In the Middle East the Poles came under British command. They were completely re-equipped, organized, and trained to British standards and organizational procedures. In North Africa they met up with the Independent Carpathian Rifle Brigade, a Free Polish unit which had served in the Western Desert. The Poles were integrated into the II Polish Corps which comprised 3rd Carpathian Rifle Division and the 5th Kresowa Infantry Division. Shortage of manpower, however, meant that each division comprised two rather than the usual three infantry brigades. Reinforcements always remained a problem for the Poles, especially as their casualties were invariably greater than those of other Allied formations. Perhaps, like the Free French, they had something more to fight for than either the British or the Americans. The French were fighting for the liberation of France and the restoration of their military honour and self-respect. The Poles believed they had nothing to prove when it came to honour but needed to convince the Western Allies of their military worth so that a free and independent Poland would be enshrined in the Anglo-American war aims. Uniting both the Free French and the Poles was a detestation of the Germans and an impatience to return to their homelands. As a way of resolving their manpower shortage, once in Italy the Poles resorted to the unorthodox solution of recruiting Polish prisoners of war (men from the territory annexed by Germany, forcibly recruited into the Wehrmacht, and subsequently captured by the Allies).

In December 1943 the 3rd Carpathian Rifle Division disembarked at Taranto and joined the Eighth Army. The 5th Kresowa Division arrived later and the corps was fully deployed by the following spring.

Two other formations joined Eighth Army before the year was out. The 2nd New Zealand Division moved into the line in November. After North Africa the division had moved back to Egypt for a long rest and leave. There had been considerable dissatisfaction expressed in the forthright manner associated with the New Zealanders about the lack of British armoured support throughout the desert campaign. Their 4th Infantry Brigade was converted to armour and so it was as a mixed division of two infantry brigades and an armoured brigade that the New Zealanders arrived in Italy.

The 4th Indian Division was another veteran force. It had fought the Italians in the Western Desert in December 1941 and thence taken part in the East African campaign. As a division it fought from El Alamein through to Cape Bon. After such a long campaign it was in need of a long rest and re-equipping. The division arrived in Italy in December.

Lastly there were the Italians. At the behest of the Allies a force was scrambled together from those units that were immediately available. The General Staff of the Italian Army put together an ad hoc formation called 1° Raggruppamento Motorizzato (1st (Italian) Motorized Group). It comprised three infantry battalions of which the best was the 51st Bersaglieri, an officer training unit. Early in November the group was deployed to Avellino where it came under Fifth Army command and a month later moved into battle.

The Italian baptism of fire was at Monte Lungo in December. It proved to be a disastrous experience, of which more later. Later that month Eisenhower chaired a conference at Army Group Headquarters to address the whole question of a future Italian Army.[2] The Allies had reached their decision before the conference convened. The Italian delegation led by Marshals Badoglio and Messe were not at all impressed when they learned what was in store. The Italian generals insisted that if they were to fight, their troops must be at least as well-equipped as the Allies, but the poor showing at Monte Lungo did not help their cause.

A new Italian Army was not an immediate priority for Fifteenth Army Group. There wasn't the sea transport available to repatriate troops from POW cages in North Africa, nor the resources to service Italian military needs and in any case the Allies felt that their first commitment was to feed and clothe the Italian civilian population. As for arms and weapons, nothing could be made available until the equipping of eleven French divisions in North Africa was completed. In addition the Allies decreed that the Italians could not use their own arms and ammunition, since these were required for the partisans in Yugoslavia to engage the maximum number of German divisions.

The message was clear, the Italian Army was a second-class force which could function provided that it did not get in the way of the players in the big league.

Notes

1. Rosignoli, Guido, *The Allied Forces in Italy 1943–45*, David and Charles, 1981.
2. WO 178/66. It was a very high-powered meeting. Eisenhower and Alexander with their respective Chiefs of Staff, the President of the Allied Control Commission and General Robertson (who commanded the AFHQ Advanced Admin Echelon) met with Marshals Badoglio and Messe.

29

Breaching the Winter Line

We will hit the Germans a colossal crack.[1]
Montgomery to Eighth Army, November 1943

On the western side of the Apennines there were two highways that divided just north of Capua and led to the Eternal City. Route 7 was the more straightforward coastal road that crossed the Pontine Marshes and then turned right through the Alban Hills into Rome. Highway 6 ran in a north-westerly direction carving a route through mountain ranges into the Liri Valley and under the shadow of Cassino, before winding through more mountains which led to Frosinone and thence to Rome.

Early in November 1943 the Allies had a fair idea of what lay between them and Rome. Rommel had been despatched to France to prepare the defences of the Western Wall. Ultra told the Allied commanders this and much more. The classic teachings of war stipulate that an enemy should be attacked at his weakest point, not his strongest. The Allies had a fair idea of what made up the German in-depth defences along what was described as the Winter Line. That was where the enemy was at his strongest, but, as we shall see, the Allied High Command had now got themselves into a position where there was no alternative.

First to be tackled was a series of outposts code-named the Barbara Line: behind that was the more heavily fortified Bernhardt Line, anchored on the hills around Cassino and making the fullest use of the Garigliano and Rapido rivers.

The Winter Line was a series of defences in depth which spanned the Italian waist, the narrowest point of the peninsula south of Rome. Such was the lie of the land, the loss of any single position could not endanger the entire system. The axis of any advance northwards invariably lay

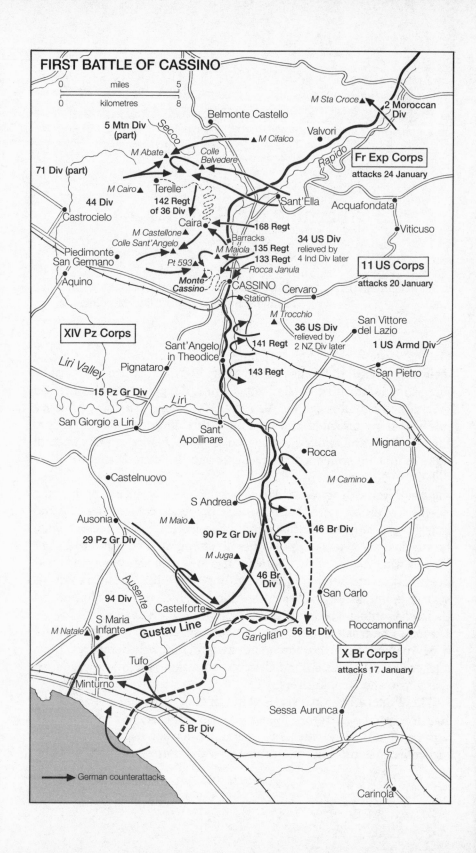

FIRST BATTLE OF CASSINO

miles 0 — 5
kilometres 0 — 8

5 Mtn Div (part)

Belmonte Castello

M Sta Croce ▲

2 Moroccan Div

▲ M Cifalco

Colle Belvedere

Valvori

Secco

M Abate ▲

Fr Exp Corps

attacks 24 January

Rapido

71 Div (part)

M Cairo ▲

Terelle

Sant'Ella

Acquafondata

44 Div

142 Regt of 36 Div

Caira

Viticuso

Castrocielo

M Castellone ▲
Colle Sant'Angelo

168 Regt

Barracks

34 US Div
relieved by
4 Ind Div later

11 US Corps

attacks 20 January

Piedimonte
San Germano

M Maiola

135 Regt

133 Regt

Pt 593 ▲

Rocca Janula

Aquino

Monte Cassino

CASSINO

Cervaro

Station

M Trocchio ▲

San Vittore
del Lazio

XIV Pz Corps

36 US Div
relieved by
2 NZ Div later

1 US Armd Div

Sant'Angelo
in Theodice

141 Regt

San Pietro

Liri Valley

Pignataro

143 Regt

Liri

15 Pz Gr Div

San Giorgio a Liri

Sant'
Apollinare

Rocca

Mignano

Castelnuovo

M Camino ▲

S Andrea

Ausonia

M Maio ▲

29 Pz Gr Div

90 Pz Gr Div

46 Br Div

M Juga ▲

Ausente

46 Br Div

San Carlo

94 Div

Castelforte

Roccamonfina

M Natale ▲

S Maria
Infante

Gustav Line

Gariglian

56 Br Div

X Br Corps

attacks 17 January

Tufo

Minturno

5 Br Div

Sessa Aurunca

German counterattacks

Carinola

across the natural obstacles of rivers and mountains. There was no opportunity for the Allies to deploy their superiority in armour, and, once the winter had started, they lost their advantage of air power. It was to be a close encounter of infantry, engineers and artillery; a bitter attritional struggle for every yard of ground. German demolitions were so effective that a small rearguard could always put up a fierce struggle while the main body fell back to garrison the next position.

Opposing the Fifth Army was the XIV Panzer Corps which, since October, had been commanded by General Von Senger und Etterlin, who had returned to the mainland after liaison duties with the Italian C-in-C in Sardinia. Both Von Senger and his predecessor, General Hube, regarded the Bernhardt Line as better than the Gustav. The latter ran across the plain following the river lines but did not include the great blocks of Monte Cassino and Monte Samuccro, which commanded the approaches to Cassino.

Von Senger had four divisions to defend the Bernhardt Line. The flatlands and coastal plain of his right flank were guarded by the 94th Infantry Division. Inland was the 15th Panzer Grenadiers whose commander, General Gräser, was a typical Prussian. Having been seriously wounded on several occasions he walked with the aid of sticks, but his infirmity never prevented him from appearing in the front line. The division had one weakness. It contained a large contingent of *Volksdeutsche*, men who came from the occupied zone in Poland, from whose ranks large numbers went missing in battle.

The left flank, which rested high in the Central Apennines, was garrisoned by the 305th Infantry Division, an excellent force composed of men from Würtemberg-Baden. But, like all German infantry divisions, Von Senger thought the 305th suffered from a structural weakness; its reserves were not sufficiently mobile, the anti-tank defence was too weak and there was a lack of experience in cooperating with armour.

On the Adriatic front, Montgomery's lead divisions had crossed the River Trigno and, after very heavy fighting, had reached the River Sangro, their most formidable obstacle to date. The Sangro was 400 yards wide and in full flood; the approaches ran across a desolate flat plain a mile wide.

On 8 November Eisenhower endorsed the battle plan for Fifteenth Army Group. It took the form of a rather elaborate variation on the one – two approach, long favoured by Alexander. Montgomery was to strike first and break out across the Sangro by way of Pescara and Avezzano. This would place Eighth Army just 50 miles to the east of Rome. The Germans would be obliged, according to Alexander, to deploy troops to cover such a threat, thereby denuding the forces facing Clark. This, in theory, would be the time for Clark to begin an advance of 50 miles from the Bernhardt Line to Frosinone. The main weight of the offensive, aptly named Operation Raincoat, was to be at the centre of the Bernhardt Line, to break through the Mignano gap and thereafter storm Cassino. Once through, the road to the Liri Valley and Frosinone would be open. At that point Mark Clark could put one division behind the Germans in an amphibious hook onto the beaches at Anzio just 20 miles from Rome. An amphibious operation was only possible because Eisenhower had gone on bended knee to the Joint Chiefs for permission to keep a total of 68 landing ships in the Mediterranean rather than send them back to England. The Chiefs agreed but set a time limit, which ran out in mid-January.

For success, the plan hinged on getting Clark to Frosinone and Montgomery to Avezzano by Christmas at the latest. Anzio would get the green light if there were other Allied units within striking distance of the beachhead; there could be no thought of another Salerno. But if it worked, then the Germans would be forced to abandon Rome and Clark would be the first into the city. Clark was not aware that Alexander and Montgomery both believed that the Eighth Army advance up the Adriatic to Pescara before striking inland was the best chance of reaching Rome first. For Clark, the capture of Rome would establish the primacy of American force of arms, not just over the Germans but over the British, and that is what mattered.[2]

Before the onset of battle, Alexander visited Mark Clark at Fifth Army's tactical headquarters. He listened to the Fifth Army battle plan and then warned Clark that things would be different. Ever since Salerno the Germans had fought rearguard actions but they would defend the Winter Line hard. He questioned whether the Americans had taken sufficient account of this.

'Oh, don't worry. I'll get through the Winter Line all right and push the Germans out,' said Clark.[3]

It took both armies more than a fortnight to prepare for the battle. On 15 November Fifth Army was at the threshold of the Liri Valley. Truscott's exhausted 3rd Infantry handed over to the 36th Infantry Division, which had needed every day of the last six weeks to recover from its pasting at Salerno. When it returned to the front, the 36th Infantry was a Texan division in name only; replacements had watered down the unit's origins. Walker moved up his three regiments. They were to assault the centre of the Bernhardt Line. Their initial objective was the low-lying hill pass around Monte Lungo called the Mignano Gap. This was the obvious place to attack; Von Senger expected it and planned accordingly.

Conditions were appalling. The forward units occupied foxholes which were filled with water and it wasn't long before there were cases of trench foot. The positions were also under constant artillery fire which produced a mounting toll of casualties.[4] It took two men eight hours to carry a five-gallon can of water to the forward positions. The wounded could only be evacuated after dark when it would take four men another eight hours to take a stretcher back to the rear areas. The 36th Division were to be in action for an unbroken 50-day period, during which time most of the infantry companies had no hot food at all.

On 28 November Montgomery attacked first across the Sangro, according to plan. It was the only time the plan worked. His preparations had been heavily constrained by the build-up of the strategic bomber force while low mist, driving rain and sleet inland prevented the air assets that were allocated to him from lending their weight to the battle. Seas of mud and minefields made the going very tough. Makeshift tank roadways were created by throwing bundles of branches across the mud and spreading steel matting on top.

The Eighth Army attacked with Imperial and Commonwealth forces well to the fore. Fighting in the mountains inland, XIII Corps had the British 5th and Canadian 1st Infantry Divisions. A Canadian padre described infantry moving forward for the assault: 'We used to watch the infantry going up into the line. Single file they trudged along, guns carried anyhow, ammunition slung around them, trousers bagged and down at heels. No war posters at home would show them that way.'[5] In the foothills country and coastal sector, V Corps commanded the 8th Indian, 78th British and the 4th Armoured Brigade; commandos from the 2nd Special Service Brigade; and the 2nd New Zealand Division.

Behind a daunting artillery bombardment, the infantry attacked. Their momentum carried them across the river and into shallow bridgeheads on the opposite bank. Montgomery was jubilant. With his usual bombast he announced to all and sundry: 'My troops have won the battle as they always do. The road to Rome is open.'[6] The Eighth Army never forgave Montgomery for his false prophecy. Rome was seven months away and not to be their prize.

Attack after attack followed as the Eighth Army first attempted to consolidate its bridgeheads across the Sangro and then strike northwards for Pescara. It rained all day every day with snow falling in the mountains. An advance of a mile a day was considered laudable progress.

The Germans made the Eighth Army fight for every yard of ground as they fell back twelve miles to their main positions on the Moro river and the towns of Orsogna and Ortona which anchored the Gustav Line on the Adriatic Coast. Route 16 passed right through the middle of Ortona, and the town could not be by-passed. A battalion of the 1st Parachute Division made their stand in the town. It was a classic example of German defensive tactics at their very best, and the Canadians had little choice but to become experts in what was later to be known as FIBUA, fighting in built-up areas. Christmas came; there was no let-up in the battle. A radio correspondent described the Canadians' Christmas dinner at Ortona:

> Christmas dinner in the shelled, broken church at Ortona. Candles and white table cloths. . . not four hundred yards from the enemy, carol singers, the platoons coming in relays to eat a Christmas dinner – men who hadn't had their clothes off in thirty days coming in and eating their dinners, and carol singers singing 'Silent Night' . . . A carnival of fury.[7]

The German paras pulled back on 27 December, by which time the Canadian 1st Brigade had taken 650 casualties. The Canadian Division had suffered 1,300 battle casualties since it had crossed the Sangro.

It was much the same story throughout the Eighth Army. The New Zealanders had stalled in Orsogna in a battle in which some of the battalions had clearly shot their bolt. For one platoon the constant rain, the bitter cold and the casualties were too much. When their battalion was ordered to make a pre-dawn attack, of the 18 men left, 14 refused to go into action.[8] The platoon was placed under close arrest and sentenced to up to two years' imprisonment. The NCOs were reduced to the ranks.

Inland the 5th (Br) Infantry and the 8th Indian were having an equally bad time. Montgomery had no alternative but to call a halt. All thoughts of Pescara, let alone Rome, were forgotten. The Eighth Army commander was despondent, seeing his strategy in tatters.

Clark couldn't wait for Montgomery to reach Pescara. The deadline for the landing craft dictated his timetable. He ordered Fifth Army with the North Americans and the 1st Italian Motorized Group to open its offensive on 3 December. On Walker's left was the 56th British Infantry, the right-flank division of X Corps. Failure at the Volturno had been followed by the division's inability in November to take Monte Camino, a barren height some 3,000 feet above the Garigliano valley.

Monte Camino was now a threat to the Americans. Walker was dismissive of the British, writing of the 56th Division in his journal, 'I shall go on the assumption that I will receive no help from them.' Walker was also wrong in his assessment. The British had another crack at the mountain. They attacked in darkness on the night of 3 December; the battle see-sawed for three days and then the mountain was secured. It was a remarkable achievement by a very tired division.

Walker's mission was to kick down the door of the Winter Line. The task was daunting, even in perfect weather. This was the outer perimeter of the Gustav Line, used by the Italian Staff College for studies of defensive warfare. No-one had ever breached this ground from the south.

The town of San Pietro was the key to the approaches of the Liri Valley. The village itself was typical of dozens in Italy – a collection of stone houses built close together. With high walls it was a natural citadel. It nestled on the terraces of the steep western slopes of Monte Sammucro which towered some 4,000 feet to the north-east, while in front of San Pietro to the south-west was a narrow defile extending perhaps a mile until blocked by Monte Lungo which lay astride the entrance to the pass (ie the Mignano Gap). Beyond Monte Lungo on the west was Monte Maggiore and somewhat south and west of it the higher peaks of Monte La Difensa (Hill 960) and the adjoining Monte Camino (Hill 963). This area was known collectively as the Camino Hill Mass.[9]

Mark Clark wanted Walker to outflank San Pietro and approach the village from the east and along the terraces. This was easier said than done. The only way forward was to gouge out chunks of the flank defences and then go in through the front door by way of the Mignano Gap. The plan was to use the highly trained North Americans to scale the sheer rock faces of Monte Difensa as a preliminary to the main attack. Then the 142nd Infantry Regiment was to seize the area known as the Vallerona Plateau on top of Maggiore. Both hill masses were subjected to a preliminary bombardment by more than 900 guns, among them the new eight-inch howitzer used for the first time in sustained combat. The Americans called Difensa 'the million-dollar mountain', because they reckoned that was how much the artillery bombardment cost. But first the enemy was softened up by air attacks.

Major Luther Wolff MD, a surgeon with the Eleventh Field Hospital at Presenzano, five miles back, had a grandstand view.

I thought I had seen about as concentrated an artillery barrage and heavy air attacks as was possible, but today topped it by far. For a change the skies were perfectly cloudless and after the usual AM Spit patrol had come over, waves of medium bombers came from the east and unloaded. The Jerry AA was woefully weak, and we didn't see a single plane knocked down. This bombing continued all day with a lull at noon. There were still over 200 bombers and these in flights of twelve. The A-36 type bombed Jerry all day, must have been between 400 and 500 sorties. Don't see how anyone could stand it. Tonight at 6.10 pm the artillery really let go. . . . They all fired as fast and furiously as they could. This mountain was literally alive with shell bursts. I believe practically every inch of the mountain was hit. Nothing could live in it, I am sure, except Germans and they in their dugouts. The British on our left even had tracer Bofors anti-aircraft firing steady streams at the mountains. Well, this was the first time I had heard firing that was a continuous roar, and the flashing of the guns made it quite light outside. In fact I could have read a newspaper had I had one. Our four close batteries of Long Toms sounded like the Anvil Chorus, they were shooting so fast.[10]

After the bombardment the North Americans climbed Monte Difensa, caught the enemy by surprise, and secured the hilltop by dawn. Thereafter they were subjected to a series of probing counterattacks. In the hills, they had to endure biting wind, rock-hard ground and ice-cold sleet combined with a viciously accurate mortar bombardment.

The Germans pulled off the rear slopes of Monte Difensa once the British had secured Monte Camino. In the meantime the 142nd with its 3rd Battalion in the lead, had secured their objectives on the Vallerona Plateau and they experienced the same grim conditions punctuated by a series of counterattacks.

There was one incident which brought a typically Texan riposte from Walker. On 7 December, at the very height of the battle, the Army Public Relations at Headquarters Fifth Army summoned Lt Colonel Sam Graham who was commanding the 2nd Battalion/142nd to Caserta Palace. He was ordered to appear in dress uniform with his DSC (which had been awarded at Salerno) for a press interview!

The Americans and the British had made a dent in the left flank, but the centre held with the enemy on top of Monte Lungo, with the right flank at San Pietro as the key position before the road into the mile-wide valley that led to Cassino could be opened. Walker planned to attack Monte Lungo and Monte Sammucro, the hill mass above San Pietro, simultaneously. Their capture would make the German positions in San Pietro untenable, no matter the strength of the citadel.

The Italians attacked on 7 December. They were eager for the fray and determined to restore the honour of the Italian Army. Luther Wolff watched them pass the Eleventh Field Hospital on their way to the front.

Truck load after truck load went by, all the troops whooping and hollering, waving Italian flags and singing at the top of their lungs. One would think that they were bound for a glorious holiday rather than going to the front lines. The contrast with those troops and the Americans is startling. . . . Americans all sit quietly, grim-faced and serious.[11]

Their enthusiasm proved their undoing. The Italians were ordered to take Point 343 on Lungo, consolidate and dig in on the position. They were told to go no further since that would take them ahead of the forces on the lower slopes of Monte Maggiore on the left flank. Behind the new, highly orchestrated and devastatingly accurate American artillery bombardment, the Italians advanced and quickly secured their objective. It had all been very easy, deceptively so, and they were tempted into continuing the attack. But the Germans had suckered them in, and counterattacked with ruthlessly violent precision. The Italians held their ground for three hours. There were many individual acts of heroism, but the conditions, darkness and the weight of fire, broke their resolve and the survivors fled down the mountain.

At dawn the American artillery positions were filled with confused and demoralized Italian infantry. Out of an attacking force of 1,700 men there were less than 700 when it came to call the roll. But in the following hours, many more managed to make their way back to Allied lines. The Italians had done little to promote their cause. The ground would have to be taken all over again by American forces. And High Command was less than impressed when the following G2 report by 36th Division came to the attention of Army Group on 11 December: 'Engineers building a by-pass in our sector reported that an Italian Convoy was misdirected by an Italian Colonel past Mignano into the German lines and hasn't been heard from since.'[12]

Now came the moment for the assault on San Pietro. In the action report, the 36th Division Battle Diary described the awesome nature of the defences.

German defences, organized in depth, extended from the orchard-covered terraces east of San Pietro and across the mile-wide valley west to Monte Lungo. Two battalions of the 15 PG Regt held the main line of resistance behind an outpost line of mutually supporting pillboxes staggered in depth. These emplacements, nearly impervious to constant artillery fire and to attacks by fighter bombers, were deep pits covered by three layers of logs and further protected by earth and rocks. Each had only a single opening, just large enough for a man to crawl through. The T Patchers had first to penetrate a field of S mines, then barbed wire and still more S mines. If these earlier defences were pierced, the enemy could still rain down artillery, mortar and heavy machine gun fire without danger to his own troops, hidden in their shelters.[13]

The battle began with a predawn bombardment on 8 December and the struggle lasted for ten days.

While the 1st Battalion of the 143rd Infantry stormed the heights above the hamlet on Monte Sammucro, the 2nd and 3rd Battalions assaulted the village along the terraces. Walker failed to appreciate however, that the Germans, who were back on Monte Lungo, could direct mortar and artillery in support of San Pietro which was behind them on their left. The 1st/143rd fought their way to the top of Monte Sammucro, but could proceed no further. Intense Germans counterattacks prevented them from properly securing their position let alone attempting to push on and outflank San Pietro.

The familiar problem of re-supply became acute, as did the evacuation of the wounded and the dead. At the Eleventh Field Hospital Major Luther Wolff and his teams were operating on men who had been wounded for three or four days. Their mortality rate was appalling since they only dealt with the most desperate cases. In the mountains the dead were a low priority. They lay lashed to their litters outside the aid stations awaiting removal. The GIs built up an immunity to such grisly sights provided that a blanket or combat jacket hid the identity of the dead man and the evidence of his wound.

Mark Clark visited the Texas division and crawled up to talk with men in the very front line. Warren Thresher was with him. In one foxhole was a little man called Geb Hart. Clark noticed that he was wearing overshoes, or galoshes, but no boots. He asked him where his boots were and the boy replied that he had small feet and the quartermaster had run out of his size. Clark promised to have a pair the right size sent up. When he returned to headquarters Clark got a pair of boots and gave them to Thresher with precise instructions on which foxhole he would find Private Geb Hart. When Thresher handed over the boots, Hart put them on without a word.

'Aren't you surprised to see me here with these boots?' queried Thresher.

'Hell, no, Captain,' replied Hart. 'The General said he'd send them.'

The two battalions attacking San Pietro had barely made 400 yards from their start lines and could not penetrate the outer perimeter of the defences. After three days Walker paused to regroup and bring more units into the battle. He attacked again on 15 December, but he still had not appreciated the significance of Monte Lungo. The 2nd Battalion of the 141st Infantry joined the fray while Clark, fretting at the delay in reaching the Gustav Line, ordered Walker to use tanks to attack up the road from Venafro to San Pietro. Sixteen Shermans of Company A 753rd Tank Battalion attacked and twelve were destroyed. Enemy artillery and mortar fire directed from Monte Lungo did the damage. With the tanks knocked out the infantry failed to make any progress at all.

At last Walker got the message. On 16 December the 142nd Infantry sent a two-battalion attack on Monte Lungo. The attack caught the Germans unawares and the Americans quickly secured their positions only to find themselves subjected to intense and repeated counterattacks. The Germans knew the importance of the mountain.

In the meantime further efforts had taken battalions of the 141st and 143rd Regiments to the outer edges of the San Pietro defences, and a battle raged over the terraced vineyards and olive grove walls. The 2nd Battalion of 141st was down to 40 men after a week in battle.

Once Monte Lungo had been secured the Germans were forced to withdraw from San Pietro or risk being outflanked. To cover their retreat the Germans launched a series of counterattacks along the front, but it was now their turn to suffer. A withering wall of fire was put down 100 yards in front of the American positions on the terraced slopes of Monte Sammucro.

On 17 December American patrols entered San Pietro to find it deserted. The local people emerged from their caves to find their town in ruins.[14] In the 44 days the 36th Division had been in the front line it suffered 3,355 casualties. The 143rd Infantry had fared the best, since it was still up to 63% of its strength, whereas the 142nd Infantry was down to one-fifth of its normal size and the 141st had lost about half its effective fighting strength. The whole Mignano Gap area and the road to San Pietro was dubbed 'Purple Heart Valley' by the war correspondents. It is hard to avoid the conclusion that at San Pietro it was Walker, the master tactician, who got it wrong.

Mark Clark's attitude, his commitment to a hard-driving push, did not take account of the heavy losses suffered by American units. Alexander was deeply concerned about this extravagance with soldiers' lives and had every reason to be. The casualty statistics showed that for the month of December the attrition rate among lieutenants was 115% in US infantry units. But Alexander did not intercede. As for the Germans, they might have lost the ground, but they had won the battle.

Notes

1. Lamb, *Montgomery in Europe.*
2. This interpretation is also substantiated by Martin Blumenson in his biography of Clark. See Blumenson, *Mark Clark*, pp 149–57.
3. Matthews interview with Alexander, p 5.
4. The 141st Infantry for example had 200 casualties from shellfire in the two weeks before they attacked.
5. Ellis, John, *The Sharp End of War*, David and Charles, 1980, p 97.
6. Lamb, *Montgomery in Europe*, p 56.
7. Ellis, *The Sharp End*, p 311.
8. Kippenberger, H., *Infantry Brigadier*, OUP, 1949, pp 344–5.
9. I have based this description on Robert Wagner's account and my own observations from walking the ground. See Wagner, R., *The Texan Army: A History of the 36th Division in the Italian Campaign*, Austin, 1972.
10. Wolff, Luther, MD, *Forward Surgeon*, Vantage Press, New York, 1985, p 51.
11. Ibid., p 55.
12. Wagner, *The Texan Army*, p 74.
13. Ibid., p 71.
14. The town around the church has never been rebuilt.

30

All Change at the Top

Clark is evidently having trouble with the British who simply won't fight. Their men are braver than ours, but their officers have no push.[1]

General Patton's Diary

Ever since the breakout at Salerno Clark had never been at ease with British forces and would gladly have swopped them for an American corps. He complained to Alexander on a number of occasions that the American divisions in Fifth Army were carrying a disproportionately heavy burden of the fighting. On 16 November Alexander arranged for Clark to meet with General Sir Ronald Adam, the Adjutant General. Sir Ronald explained that the British were coming to the end of their manpower resources and if they expected to hold their own after the war, or even to last out this one, then a rigid policy of manpower conservation had to be enforced.

The Adjutant General showed Clark some top secret reports. The evidence was damning. In order to sustain the flow of battlefield replacements to Burma and the Mediterranean, one newly formed division in the UK was being dismembered every two months. Of course there were other options, although Sir Ronald did not elaborate. One was to break up the regiments of heavy AA batteries that stood guard along the Nile and elsewhere and turn them into infantry.

While the 36th Infantry were trying valiantly to break into San Pietro, Clark was ordered to report, in his best uniform, to Palermo, together with other officers who were recent recipients of the Distinguished Service Cross. Patton was on hand to greet Clark at the airport. Shortly afterwards another plane landed, carrying Roosevelt who was returning home from the Cairo and Tehran conferences.[2] The President briefed his generals.

It was widely believed at the time in American State and War Department circles that their British counterparts were haunted, as Secretary of War Stimpson put it, by the 'shadows of Passchendaele and Dunkirk'. The Americans were convinced that the British were fighting shy of Overlord and thus had raised the priorities and importance of the Mediterranean theatre and the Italian campaign. Cairo and Tehran were all about correcting the balance.

The Americans were also concerned about Stalin's position. Their Embassy in Moscow had reached an assessment which suggested that Stalin was more interested that Western Allies should draw German strength away from the Eastern Front.

At the Cairo Summit[3] the British came up with a firm list of proposals.

* To mount a cross-Channel operation at a time when German strength in France made it appropriate (the rider being that aggressive actions in the Mediterranean would advance not retard that date).
* To advance beyond Rome only as far as the Pisa–Rimini Line.
* To give more assistance to Tito's partisans with arms and commando raids.
* To bring Turkey into the war by 1 January 1944; and with Turkish consent open the Dardanelles as a strategic line of communication to Russia – this would require an attack on Rhodes, the largest of the Dodecanese islands which commanded access to the Dardanelles.

The British calculated that an active pursuit of Balkan strategy would not absorb more than one-tenth of the resources currently deployed in the Mediterranean. The exception would be the landing craft needed for Rhodes which were pencilled in for February. Their retention in the theatre would retard the planning date for Overlord from 1 May by about two months. An alternative was to denude the British amphibious operations in Mountbatten's South East Asia Command. The main operation there, code-named Buccaneer, was an amphibious assault planned for March/April 1944 on the Andaman Islands, south-west of Rangoon. Unbeknown to the British however, Roosevelt had given a private undertaking to Chiang Kai-shek that Buccaneer would go ahead, thereby diverting Japanese attention away from China. The British were unaware of this pledge.

The Americans were in broad agreement with the general aim of driving the Germans back in the Mediterranean, but the sticking point, inevitably, was the question of landing craft. They could see the virtues of a Turkish commitment, but doubted whether the Rhodes operation was feasible. The British had tried once, in the Aegean, and failed disastrously.[4]

For the Americans the choice was brutally simple; if they went along with the British proposals, they would have to accept a delay to Overlord. This of course was more than a tactical or even strategic consideration; the political ramifications had to be addressed.

There was no time left to discuss the issue in Cairo, so it was carried over to Tehran. There Stalin took everybody by surprise and gave a firm promise that the Soviet Union would intervene in the war against Japan. This concession was a cornerstone of the American war aims. Their fear was that if Chinese resistance collapsed, then the Japanese would be free to concentrate their strength upon the defence of the vital parts of their empire and the Home Islands. The scale of American casualties would be too awful to contemplate unless Russia could tie down Japanese strength.

When the question of Overlord was raised Stalin came down on the side of the Americans, again to everyone's surprise. He vehemently opposed any thought of postponement and dismissed the Italian campaign as of little consequence. The only value he could see in a Mediterranean strategy would be an invasion of the South of France. He even suggested that Italy could be the springboard for an early invasion to be followed by Overlord. It was the classic use of the pincers formula, a stratagem which the Russians had used to great effect at Stalingrad and elsewhere.

General Marshall and the American team were secretly delighted with Stalin. One of the reasons why they were content to leave the arbitration to Tehran was that Uncle Joe would simplify the problem and confound the British. They were under no illusions, however, that Stalin was wrong on two counts. Firstly, from a political and propaganda viewpoint, the Anglo-Americans were committed at least to the capture of Rome. Secondly, the shortage of Allied shipping in general and landing ships in particular meant that a fair proportion of the Allied troops were now condemned to fight, or at least remain, in Italy. The means did not exist to move them elsewhere.

Churchill and the British team were obviously taken aback by Stalin's views. This allowed the Americans to manipulate the various suggestions to their advantage and strike hard while they had the opportunity. Roosevelt outlined the options: agree to support Churchill's Aegean strategy and accept a delay in Overlord or attack the South of France one or two months before 1 May, and then conduct Overlord on the original date!

Stalin backed the Americans provided that Overlord took place on the date agreed, and he looked to the appointment of its commander as an indication of Anglo-American good faith. Churchill put up a spirited defence of his Mediterranean strategy, but despite his eloquence was able to wring very few concessions. The compromise at the end of the day allowed Eisenhower to retain 68 of the Overlord LSTs in the Mediterranean until mid-January to facilitate the capture of Rome. Thereafter sufficient landing craft should be available in the theatre to support a two-division assault on the South of France. The operation, now codenamed Anvil, would be launched three or four weeks before Overlord which in turn would be put back to about the middle of May. There was a broad consensus that it would be useful to have the Turks come off the fence and into the United Nations.

The final details were hammered out by the full planning teams back in Cairo. Operations Anvil and Overlord were now accepted by the Anglo-Americans as the major European undertakings in 1944. With Stalin's commitment on Japan, the Chinese were less important and Buccaneer was gently shunted off the planning board; Mountbatten was even required to transfer what amphibious assets he had (15 LSTs and six assault transports) back to European waters. The primacy of Overlord over the Mediterranean had been assured, and the Americans left Cairo convinced that they had scored a great political victory over the British. In this they were wrong. The British had never been opposed to Overlord in principle, but considered that timing and the relative military balance of power should dictate the moment, not a predetermined date.

Marshall was determined that the strategy agreed at Cairo/Tehran should be followed strictly, particularly with regard to the Mediterranean. Once Rome had fallen Fifteenth Army Group would be allowed to advance north to the Pisa–Rimini line, but with reduced forces. The main effort was be transferred to France.

At Palermo airport President Roosevelt briefed the senior American officers on the future Allied strategy. When he came to the landing in the South of France, the President turned to Clark and said, 'You, Mark, will command it.'[5]

The plan was for the Seventh Army headquarters, then currently unemployed, to take immediate responsibility for planning Operation Anvil. Mark Clark was to continue with Fifth Army a little while longer, before assuming command of Seventh Army. He would complete the planning and lead the landings into France. Clark had been recommended by Eisenhower. At the time it was widely believed that Marshall would become supreme commander in Europe for Overlord and that Patton would take command of a new army in Europe. Clark had every reason to be flattered and pleased. He had been singled out personally for yet more advancement by the President. Earlier, at the award ceremony, Roosevelt had, to Clark's surprise, not only presented him with a DSC for his actions at Salerno, but handed him a letter, written in case he had missed him in Sicily. The letter read:

> I am very sorry to miss seeing you, but much as I wanted to come to Italy and see you at the front and to greet your fighting army there, I was told I just could not go. You and your Fifth Army are doing a magnificent job under the most trying conditions imaginable. Eye witnesses have told me of your personal courage in leading your forces and especially of your gallantry. . . . Keep on giving it all you have, and Rome will be yours and more beyond. I am grateful to have such a staunch fighting general.[6]

There were other VIPs in Italy at about the same time, some no doubt talent-spotting for Overlord; Alan Brooke, the Chief of the Imperial General Staff was one. He spent time with Montgomery and was anything but impressed. He wrote in his diary:

> Frankly, I am rather depressed about what I have seen and heard today. Monty is tired out, and Alex fails to grasp the show. . . . Monty strikes me as looking tired and definitely in need of a rest. . . . I can see he feels Clark is not running the Fifth Army right; nor that Alex is grasping the show sufficiently. Monty saw little hope of capturing Rome before March . . . no longer any talk of turning left by his forces to capture Rome.[7]

Alan Brooke was also on the short list for the command of the Anglo-American forces but, in the event, Roosevelt chose Eisenhower. Montgomery was given command of the British forces in 21st Army Group and Bradley the Americans. When Clark learned the news he wrote to congratulate Eisenhower and at the same time raised questions about his own future. Who would succeed Eisenhower in Algiers? Clark was the senior American officer in the theatre. He was outranked in London by Lieutenant General Jacob Devers who was Commanding General European Theatre of Operations US Army (ETOUSA). If Devers came to the Mediterranean Clark told Eisenhower that he would prefer to take

Seventh Army into the South of France where he would come under the command of his old friend.

In the event, Clark got it wrong. The Mediterranean became a British theatre of operations. General Sir Henry Maitland Wilson, known as Jumbo because of his mighty girth, was currently Commander in Chief Middle East. A methodical, politician's general, with a reputation for having a safe pair of hands and a shrewd mind, Wilson was appointed to succeed Eisenhower as Supreme Allied Commander Mediterranean Theatre. Devers was slotted to come to the Mediterranean as Wilson's deputy and the senior American officer.

Shortly before Eisenhower left for London (his new appointment became effective on New Year's Eve), Clark met him in Naples. Clark was no advocate of Operation Anvil and believed it was a mistake to close down the Italian theatre; he was also reluctant to foreswear the Fifth Army. Clark angled to become Deputy Supreme Commander and the Commanding General of Seventh Army. Another option he raised was to take Fifth Army to the South of France and have Seventh Army Headquarters come to Italy to tidy up after Rome.

Eisenhower had no interest in either proposal. Clark was to capture Rome, hand over Fifth Army to Lucas and be in Sicily to complete the planning for Anvil by 1 February 1944 at the latest. Eisenhower did not, however, take Clark fully into his confidence. The Combined Chiefs had offered him the opportunity to stay in the Mediterranean until Rome fell, but with all the problems and obstacles which confronted Fifteen Army Group, Eisenhower did not envisage an early fall of Rome. He must have known that the timetable he had given Clark was a pipe-dream, but he had no intention of being around to pick up the pieces. For career-orientated generals, friendship had its place.

Montgomery too could not get out of Italy quickly enough. The Battle of Sangro was going badly and turning into a defeat for Eighth Army. His marching orders came on Christmas Eve and he left the country on New Year's Eve. Had Montgomery stayed around much longer the Sangro might have gone down on his record as a defeat. As things stood he could start the new job with a clean sheet.

The new Eighth Army commander was Oliver Leese. Ponderous and unimaginative, this Colonel Blimp look-alike was very typical of his generation. Methodical and very orthodox in his thinking, Leese was closely associated with Montgomery and as his disciple was the obvious choice of the military establishment to take over Eighth Army. After Sicily, Leese had taken Headquarters XXX Corps back to England to prepare for Overlord. The main headquarters was assembled in New-market with a Tac HQ located in a suite in the Dorchester Hotel, Park Lane, which made a pleasant change after some fly-blown Italian two-up-two-down.

On Christmas Eve Leese received a telegram from the Military Secretary instructing him to proceed to Italy as soon as possible and take over command of Eighth Army. There is no indication that Leese had received any prior warning. With a small staff, he left by air from RAF Lyneham on Boxing Day. The Military Secretary wanted Leese on his way quickly so that he could effect the handover with Montgomery in Italy. Had he waited for Montgomery to return to England he would have been kept in England and given command of the Second Army in the Twenty-first Army Group.

Even for an army commander, the flight to Italy was fraught with risk, and yet it was treated in a most casual manner. Their plane landed at an American airbase in Morocco where their hosts, mistaking the British red hats for military police, fed Leese breakfast in the GI cookhouse. They spent the night in Algiers and flew on to Palermo, arriving in Naples on 30 December. Leese thumbed a lift to Foggia from an RAF Wellington crew (the pilot had come south for a day to buy a hat). At Foggia, Eighth Army at last got their welcome act together and Leese was whisked away to see in the New Year with Montgomery in his Tac HQ at Paglieto. The next morning Leese saw Montgomery off in his personal Dakota, escorted by a full squadron of Spitfires.

That same evening Allied Forces Headquarters in Algiers relieved Patton of his command and appointed Mark Clark to assume command of Seventh Army. He lost no time in dispatching a liaison team to Sicily to start work on Anvil.

Notes

1. Patton had a shadow Seventh Army headquarters in Corsica and was being used in an attempt to dupe the Germans into thinking that he would invade either northern Italy or the South of France. They weren't fooled. In December he visited Clark in the field.
2. In Cairo Roosevelt and Churchill and their advisers met Chiang Kai-shek. The meetings lasted from 22 November to 7 December. In Tehran Roosevelt and Churchill, with their senior advisers, met Stalin between 28 November and 1 December. There was then a second

round in Cairo between 2 and 7 December, this time confined to the British and the Americans.

3. See note 2.

4. The capture and subsequent loss of Cos, Leros and Samos, Aegean islands in September/October 1943.

5. Blumenson, *Mark Clark*, p 154.

6. Ibid., p 157.

7. Lamb, *Montgomery in Europe*, pp 56–7.

31

Holding Court at Marrakesh

At a single blow Shingle will decide the battle of Rome and possibly achieve destruction of a substantial part of the enemy's army.

Churchill to Roosevelt, December 1943

When General Eisenhower moved to London in the New Year, Marshall passed over the executive control of the Mediterranean to Alan Brooke. From that time on Winston Churchill ran the war in the Mediterranean. It was no more and no less than Marshall expected,[1] but he was determined that, once Rome had fallen, Italy would become a sideshow.

After the Cairo and Tehran Summits, Churchill was laid low with pneumonia while visiting Eisenhower in his seaside villa at Carthage. By Christmas, however, he had recovered sufficiently to enjoy the festivities and his American hosts were more than generous in their provision of seasonal fare. In between banquets with the various Commanders in Chief, Churchill held court and reviewed the Italian campaign. He then flew on to complete his convalescence in Marrakesh.

On New Year's Day Montgomery and Eisenhower came to pay court en route to England. Churchill gave them copies of their sealed orders for Overlord; neither was impressed by what they read – it looked like Sicily all over again. Churchill was not in the least dismayed; with luck, their dissatisfaction could lead to a delay in Overlord and this would strengthen his hand to seek a decision in Italy.

Alexander was also in attendance. He got nothing out of the High Command reshuffle. Churchill did tell him, however, that Wilson was merely to handle the political and diplomatic aspects of the Mediterranean theatre so as to leave Alexander free to exert total tactical control.

Montgomery had now become not only Alexander's equal in terms of his appointment to an Army Group but also his superior, because Overlord was more important than Italy. Alexander entertained ambitions to succeed Eisenhower in the supreme command in the Mediterranean, and to be passed over in this fashion must have been a severe blow to his pride.

From the outset, Alexander had a very low opinion of Jackie Devers; he always reminded him of a boy who hadn't grown up. A large, shambling, untidy man, Devers was a contemporary of Patton's. He had taught mathematics at West Point and Clark was one of his students, who had not excelled at the subject. Clark also thought him a dope[2] and, when they met, made it clear to Jackie that he had too many bosses already.

Alexander was determined that Devers would never exert any influence on the conduct of the campaign. He even instructed his Chief of Staff to ensure that during his absence Devers was kept clear of the plans.

In Oliver Leese, Eighth Army had inherited a competent and popular commander. Alexander considered him to be very sound, trained in the Montgomery school, methodical as a fighter who wanted to get everything right just before an attack. Leese was as tall as Mark Clark but much broader, with great wide shoulders and a guffaw that came from the depths of his belly. He set a very high standard in everything except his own dress which was scruffy and unkempt. He would never read a brief if it could be avoided, and preferred to have ideas explained to him in as few words as possible by a member of his own tried and tested staff.

Leese quickly grew into the job, which was quite remarkable given that he had to build a new team and get to know his way around a polyglot army with distinct tribal characteristics. Fashioning a new team was not an easy task because Montgomery continued to pilfer the best and the brightest amongst staff and commanders to feed the needs of Twenty-first Army Group. Those who received no such summons felt they had been condemned to fight a secondary campaign in a second eleven.

Oliver Leese did his very best to overcome such doubts and to stamp his own personality on Montgomery's men. In one sense this was not as difficult as it might have been. The mood in Eighth Army was one of betrayal by Montgomery, who was seen to have left them in the lurch, in an awful country, while he went off to seek new glories and to go home. Leese liked to spend as much time as he could visiting his units in the field.

Whether in a staff car or jeep he carried cartons of cigarettes, largesse which he distributed to the troops at every opportunity.

He was able to establish a working relationship with Clark. This was all the more remarkable given that Oliver Leese, an Old Etonian and ex-Coldstream Guard, was the very epitome of the professional British officer. A bluff jovial man, quite without personal ambition and personal vanity, he represented no kind of threat to Clark which is perhaps why they got on – at least until Rome.

Leese could not have taken over Eighth Army at a more inauspicious time. After advancing 2,000 miles and winning countless battles in the 14 months since the odyssey had begun at El Alamein, the Germans were kicking the stuffing and the heart out of Eighth Army. Like the Americans on their left, the offensive spirit had deserted the fighting men; they were drained of strength, with morale at rock bottom. The feeling shared by generals and privates alike was that the 'soft underbelly' of Italy had become a tough old gut.

From the opulent comfort of the Flower Villa at Marrakesh, Churchill could not or would not appreciate the true nature of the battle conditions of the Fifteenth Army Group. So far as he was concerned, the fighting in Italy could not be allowed to stagnate, otherwise he would be forced to swap the Riviera for Rome. He enlisted the support of the British Chiefs in London and together they came up with a plan.

One glance at the map revealed the solution. An amphibious operation could outflank the Gustav Line and open up the way for a rapid advance on Rome. It was Anzio Mark II, albeit beefed up and under a new name. Eisenhower and Alexander had already outlined the plans and objectives behind Operation Raincoat. But before a landing could be mounted at Anzio, Fifth Army had to get within range. In this they had manifestly failed. If more landing craft could be made available however, then a much bigger force could be put ashore without having to wait for Fifth Army. Indeed, the roles would be reversed, and Anzio could be used to ease the pressure on the Gustav Line because the Germans would have to redeploy troops to counter the new threat.

There were 88 landing craft still available in the Mediterranean. The new plan was to land two divisions at Anzio which would require 104 ships, but 68 were to be withdrawn on 15 January for Overlord. That would leave 20 and the possibility of another 15 arriving in the Mediterranean en route home from the Indian Ocean. It would not be enough to do the job. Churchill and his Chiefs of Staff proposed keeping all the landing craft in the Mediterranean for an extra three weeks.

Landings at Anzio could be launched on 20 January and Rome captured thereafter.

Though now only a bystander, Eisenhower was not impressed when Churchill let him in on the discussions. He regarded the South of France landings – Operation Anvil – as essential, certainly more important than Anzio, code-named Shingle. Naval officers, however, wrote a stiff paper to show that such was the quality of the crews of the amphibious ships that they would need little retraining before Overlord/Anvil, which meant they could take Anzio without placing the major operations at risk. Eisenhower did not support Shingle, but he withdrew his objections. He had come a long way in the art of political gamesmanship.

All that remained was to secure Roosevelt's approval. In a personal telegram Churchill argued his case eloquently.

> What also could be more dangerous than to let the Italian battle stagnate and fester on for another three months thus certainly gnawing into all preparations for and this again affecting Overlord. . . . If this opportunity is not grasped we must expect the ruin of the Mediterranean campaign of 1944. I earnestly hope therefore that you may agree to the three weeks delay in the return of the 56 (*sic*) landing craft and that all the authorities should be instructed to make sure that the May Overlord is not prejudiced thereby.[3]

Eisenhower had already intimated to the Prime Minister that he favoured delaying Overlord from May until 4 June, when the moon and tides were right. This delay gave a week or two's grace before landing craft would need to leave the Mediterranean, which further strengthened the case for Shingle.

Marshall warned his president that this was another British plot to postpone Overlord, but reluctantly he gave his blessing provided that the dates and the status of the operation were guaranteed. On these conditions, Roosevelt gave his approval. Churchill was delighted and not a little surprised.

The case for Shingle rested on a single premise, namely that Kesselring would denude the Gustav Line to meet the threat. Nobody seems to have considered that he might deploy fresh divisions south of Rome, leaving the Gustav position intact. Yet Ultra reports in November revealed that Kesselring had assumed command of the whole of Italy as OB South-west and GOC Army Group C. Likewise, the existence of a new force under his command, Fourteenth Army, to control all the divisions which had previously been under Rommel in northern Italy, must have raised questions as to its purpose. One obvious answer was a

Every American's model of a proper British General. Alexander and an aide at Anzio.

Guardsmen tempt fate in Anzio.

Italians greet their Army. Bologna, June 1944. A Blackshirt Battalion marches through the streets, though the people seem less than enthusiastic.

A Roman triumph. Mark Clark enters Rome – preceded by his press corps.

Italians greet their liberators. One American makes the most of it. Rome, June 1944.

Old Scores.

Summary justice at the hands of the Carabinieri. The price of collaboration.

The Goumier. Preparing for war and its spoils.

"Stand still that Man!"

1st Battalion Duke of Wellington's Regiment, or rather its survivors, march past their Army Commander Mark Clark to take up their duty as the British contingent in the Rome Garrison. The American contingent was the whole of the 3rd Infantry Division.

One of those days when rain didn't stop play. British Gunners take a break on the road to the Gothic Line. Tuscany, August 1944.

The Italian Cabinet. Politicians love to pose. But this lot had no power.

Everything stops for tea.

Valet Parking, Indian Army style;
officer sahibs, of course, don't push –
at least this one didn't.

The Guards take a break in the
Apennines: ground which clearly
favoured the defence.

French Mountain troops and pack
transport.

Progress though the Apennines. The terrain was bad enough without the Germans, and, when the rain stopped, mud turned into a choking white powder.

Mud. The Gothic Line, September 1944.

strategic reserve and a contingency against further amphibious operations, but that consideration too seems to have been ignored.

Haste was the hallmark of the planning for Shingle. When Alexander came to brief Mark Clark (for it was to be a Fifth Army operation), there were 17 days to 20 January, the planned D-day. Was the intention to cut the German lines of communication to the southern front, forcing the enemy to abandon the Gustav Line and thereby take Rome by *coup de main* in the ensuing confusion? If so then the Allied forces would have to strike inland from their beachhead and sever the highways that ran through the Alban Hills and in particular the highest points around a feature called the Colli Lazialli.

Or was the intention to build a fortress behind the enemy lines which he would have to destroy, thereby allowing a breakthrough to be achieved on the Gustav Line? In this instance the mode was defensive. The need would be to take a secure and defensible beachhead and wait for the enemy to draw troops from the southern front and attack the threat to their rear.

Alexander issued his directive for Shingle on 12 January. The instructions from Caserta only served to muddy the waters further. On the one hand there was mention of a battle for Rome but without any emphasis on securing the high ground beyond the beachhead. The directive ordered an advance on Colli Lazialli. Alexander made his intentions clear long after the event, in his memoirs and in interviews with Dr Sidney Matthews. He expected Lucas, who was to command the operation, to push forward with a regimental combat team to the Alban Hills *once Anzio had been taken*.[4] The idea was that a threat to the German lines of communication, though largely a bluff, would have been sufficient to force a withdrawal from the southern front.

Clark did not question these orders or seek clarification. He had two concerns. The bruising experience of Salerno rang alarm bells, and he did issue a warning that two divisions were inadequate for the task. Alexander had insisted that one of the two divisions should be British. Shingle was likely to be a close-fought battle; there would be heavy casualties and, in the interests of Anglo-American relations, the agony had to be shared. Clark found this fatuous. In his view the British were planting a division on Anzio so that if there was a breakthrough to Rome they would be there to share the triumph.

But Shingle offered a way out of the stalemate and raised the tantalizing prospect of Rome. With the Eighth Army bogged down on the far side of the Apennines, the city could only fall to Mark Clark's Fifth Army.

Notes

1. Matthews interview with Marshall, p 9.
2. Matthews interview with Clark, p 65.
3. Gilbert, Martin, *Road to Victory*, p 622.
4. Matthews interview with Alexander.

32

Massacre at the Rapido

When I saw my Regimental Commander standing with tears in his eyes as we moved up to start the crossing, I knew something was wrong. I started out commanding a company of 184 men. Forty-eight hours later, 17 of us were left.[1]

Capt Z.O. Robertson
L Company 143rd Infantry

The Fifth Army at last made some ground along the VI Corps front. After the bloody battles for San Pietro, the Germans fell back across the Rapido/Garigliano rivers and it was seven miles before the 45th (US) Infantry and the French 2nd Moroccan Division regained contact. By this time the 45th (US) Infantry were exhausted. Clark pulled them out of the line and replaced them with the Algerian 3rd Division. Juin's French Expeditionary Corps (FEC) assumed responsibility for the sector and this released VI (US) Corps to plan the Anzio landings.

Keyes and II (US) Corps still battled to win the last few miles of high ground that dominated Route 6 below Cassino. The British X Corps had closed up to the Garigliano and McCreery pondered the best way to cross. He had no desire for a repetition of the Volturno nor to cross swords with Clark. But McCreery did have some reinforcements. The 5th (Br) Infantry Division came into the line from the Adriatic front where they had been neighbours of the New Zealanders who weren't too impressed with their new comrades. They found the division smart and disciplined, but too stiff and methodical in battle.

When the British reached the Garigliano, the men of the 7th (Br) Armoured Division, the Desert Rats, prepared to say goodbye to Italy. They returned to camps in the Naples area and there bequeathed their tanks and armoured vehicles to the 5th Canadian Armoured Division. The Canadians were none too impressed at their hand-me-downs. But then, the Desert Rats had inherited them in February 1943 from the 4th Indian Division who had fought and driven them across North Africa from Alamein. A large convoy took the division home. The desert veterans spent a wet and storm-tossed Christmas at sea, but none cared; at least they had kissed Italy goodbye.

In the meantime on that other flank, to the north of Cassino, the French were faced by trackless mountains. Fresh and anxious to make a name for himself, Juin believed that they were less of an obstacle than they appeared at first sight.

In the X (Br) Corps sector, a commando unit carried out an amphibious attack around the mouth of the Garigliano river which coincided with Scots and Coldstream Guards making a river crossing. The attack, conducted in the early hours of New Year's Eve, was brilliantly executed. The objective was to keep the Germans on their toes and take prisoners. The enemy was caught unawares, and the raid was a great success. In one sense however, it was counterproductive, for it showed Clark that the rivers might not be such formidable obstacles and it warned the Germans to watch out.

Alexander, as Army Group commander, supposedly, was the man possessed of a broad and detailed vision of what lay ahead before Rome. In his judgement the ground dictated the strategy.

I have already described the Liri valley as the gateway to Rome and alluded to the strength of the defences at the gate. A description of the terrain now facing us will make clear the reasons why this one sector was the only place where we could hope to develop an advance in strength and why I was obliged to transfer there ever increasing forces until by next May the bulk of my Armies was disposed in the Tyrrhenian sector. The Adriatic coastal plain in which the Eighth Army had been operating leads nowhere except eventually to Ancona. The centre of the peninsula is filled by the Apennines which here reach their greatest height: they are now under deep snow and even in summer are quite impracticable for the movement of large forces. The west coast rises steeply into the trackless Aurunci and Lepini mountains and the coastal road runs close to the seashore, except for a short stretch in the plains of Fondi until it debouches into the Pontine Marshes which the Germans had flooded. The Aurunci and Lepini mountains are separated from the main Apennine Ranges however, by the Valley of the Liri. The gap thereby formed through which runs Route 6, the Via Casilina, varies in width from four to seven miles.[2]

At Monte Cassino and the Liri Valley Alexander, Clark and Leese squandered fine divisions in isolated and inadequate frontal attacks against the strongest and least accessible portion of the Gustav Line. Ever since the Bernhardt Line had been breached, Fifth Army had had sight of Monte Cassino as they inched their way forward past the ruins of San Pietro to the line of the Rapido and Garigliano rivers.

The fortress monastery of Monte Cassino towered on a craggy promontory 1,693 feet high. From its foundation by St Benedict in AD 529 on the site of a Roman temple to Apollo, to 1799, the abbey was captured and destroyed four times by invading armies, only to be rebuilt.

Clark was at first depressed by an assessment from naval specialists. They calculated that with the shipping available, the landing and transit timetable would allow the two divisions to be landed and supported for eight days. Thereafter, according to the Overlord/Anvil timetable, they would be on their own. This meant that Fifth Army would have to be prepared to effect a relief, which meant divisions had to be poised to enter the Liri Valley before the Anzio landing.

Clark talked to Alexander who, in turn, put the problem to Churchill. The Prime Minister overrode the naval reports. Anzio was perfectly feasible he told his subordinate, if the landing was delayed to 22 January. Indifference to the evidence of experts and misplaced faith in Churchill's own judgement prodded the generals into taking foolish risks. It was Churchill's stubborn determination which drove the Italian campaign forward when sound military reasoning should have prevailed. Even in mid-January, it would have been more sensible to stop the offensive and wait for better weather. Instead the Allies hacked away without imagination and without success.

Clark had about a fortnight to get Fifth Army across the Garigliano and Rapido rivers. That battle was planned for 17 January. The day before he received the latest intelligence assessment from Fifth Army.

> It would appear doubtful if the enemy can hold the organized line through Cassino against a coordinated attack. Since this is to be launched before Shingle it is considered likely that this additional threat will cause him to withdraw from his defensive position once he has appreciated the magnitude of the operation.[3]

It is beyond comprehension how intelligence experts, with all the resources at their disposal – not least from Ultra – could arrive at a conclusion which owed more to wishful thinking than an objective assessment of the true situation.

The main battle, proclaimed by Fifth Army as the decisive battle for Rome, was timed for 20/21 January.

Let us look again at the master plan.

Phase One	All three Allied corps, X (Br), II (US) and FEC to attack the Gustav Line, draw German reserves south.
Phase Two	VI (US) Corps lands at Anzio 60 miles behind the German Lines. Germans denude Gustav Line to counter threat.
Phase Three	Second attack along the Gustav Line, punch holes in the enemy defence and release Allied armoured divisions into the Liri Valley, link up at Anzio and thence march on to Rome.

The three phases of the battle, what became the Stalingrad of the Italian campaign, were to last until the middle of March. Thereafter the Allies did what they should have done in mid-January, retired to winter quarters and waited for better weather.

Before the battle began, Clark had some mixed news. The opening artillery bombardment along the Gustav Line caused Kesselring to despatch two divisions (29th and 90th Panzer Grenadiers) to reinforce Von Vietinghoff's Tenth Army. Kesselring, who was looking to stabilize the Italian front at the Gustav Line, had no compunction about deploying those two excellent divisions southwards. But Mark Clark's interpretation was that the first part of the plan had succeeded, because Anzio was not covered by German troops.

There was a drastic shortage of DUKWs. Lucas was rehearsing the assault formations of his corps in the Bay of Naples when a fierce storm sank 40 of them. Lucas had to have DUKWs for Anzio and this meant taking away those which had been allocated to the divisions about to cross the Garigliano and Rapido rivers.

The French were the first away. Juin's 3rd Algerian and 2nd Moroccan Divisions swarmed across the upper Rapido with tremendous élan and moved quickly into the near trackless mountains north of Cassino. These mountain specialists overwhelmed the German defenders, the 44th Hoch and Deutschmeister Division, and were soon battling it out on Monte Croce and its adjoining peaks.

On the evening of 17 January the British corps in the coastal sector opened up with a tremendous artillery bombardment. Defences in the British sector were manned by a single German division, the 94th

Infantry. Two of the three British divisions attacked in the darkness of a fine night. The 56th (Br) Division attacked behind their bombardment and by daylight had shallow bridgeheads across the Garigliano. There was some further progress during the next day but the Germans still held the high ground and casualties were mounting.

The 5th (Br) Infantry attacked later the first night near to the sea without a preliminary bombardment, the hope being that the Germans would be fully occupied with the other assault. The plan worked after a fashion; bridgeheads were established, but in the face of fierce enemy resistance little progress was made. Both British divisions lacked sufficient engineers to exploit their success by clearing minefields and building bridges, while the loss of the DUKWs was clearly felt.

The 46th (Br) Infantry attacked on the right flank. Their task was to seize a bridgehead near St Angelo, to get onto the high ground above the village and cover the American operation on their right flank. The point chosen for the assault was just below the confluence where the Liri and the Rapido form the Garigliano. Not only was the enemy prepared, the majority of the assault boats were swept away in the fierce current, and the operation failed. Once again a British division had let down the Americans, at least that was how it was presented when it came to apportion the blame.

The American attack was to be undertaken on the night of Thursday 20 January by two RCTs from Walker's 36th (US) Infantry. The disaster on the Rapido – some have likened it to a massacre – was to stalk Mark Clark's military career for the rest of his service.

The Rapido, however formidable, did not approach the dimension of the Volturno. The river was 25–50 feet wide, and 9–12 feet deep. The approach to the river crossing, however, was over a wide flood plain which oozed mud, was still heavily mined and could be observed from the commanding heights on the opposite bank. With typical Teutonic thoroughness the Germans had zeroed their mortars and artillery onto the obvious assembly and crossing points, while the heavy Mg42 machine guns were sited to fire on fixed lines. The defenders, a regiment from 15th Panzer Grenadiers, occupied a main line of resistance which did not follow the river line, but was laid out behind it on high ground in a zig-zag fashion. This meant that those troops who made it to the opposite bank came under enfilading fire and suffered heavy losses.

Mark Clark[4] maintained that whereas Walker had his doubts, these were expressed mildly. In Walker's diary[5] the entry for 16 January (ie during the final planning and preparation stage) is quite unequivocal. He favoured an attack further north of Cassino where the Rapido was more fordable, and the enemy defences weaker, but: 'Clark and Keyes were not interested. They do not understand the problems and do not know what I am talking about.' Eye-witness accounts tend to support Walker's version of events. Brigadier Willie Wilbur, the Assistant Division Commander, was violently opposed to the operation. A couple of days before the battle, Clark and Keyes visited the division. There was apparently a fierce argument which took place on the side of the road. Walker protested the orders but, having made his point, walked away. Clark and Keyes remained in the jeep and were clearly anxious to leave. Wilbur, standing by the side, leaned across to Keyes and stabbed him hard in the chest with his finger. Those who watched could see that Keyes and Clark were both upset by the incident.

The failure by the 46th (Br) Infantry to secure a bridgehead meant that the high ground above Saint Angelo would be uncovered, adding measurably to the difficulties confronting Walker's troops. Major General Hawkesworth, the 46th Divisional Commander, at least had good grace to visit Walker's CP and to apologize for the failure of his men.

Walker timed the attacks to begin at 8.00 pm, three hours after sunset, and therefore with a long night of eleven hours in which to gain and consolidate a bridgehead. It had proved impossible to make adequate preparations for the operation beforehand, simply because the crossing sites were under enemy observation. This meant that the approach to the river bank had to be cleared of mines, and paths marked out with tape before the infantry moved forward. Neither was it possible to stockpile materials ahead of time, so the attacking forces had to carry the cumbersome rubber and wooden boats. There had been little time or opportunity to practise. And reconnaissance patrols had failed to penetrate the enemy defences on previous nights; all they had done was alert the Germans to the imminence of an attack.

Never in the campaign to date had the odds been so stacked against an attacking force as they were that night for the men of the 36th Division on the Rapido river. But that said, there are aspects in the preparation phase which stand out. Neither Walker nor his senior staff officers conducted a personal reconnaissance of the crossing sites. Everything was planned from maps at the command post. Secondly, Walker appears to have made no reference to the previous river crossing. He did not contact Truscott and no study of his operation was made by staff officers. This would surely have been time well spent. Lastly, the battle plan did not include any tactical air support, a remarkable oversight.

A cold, dense fog hung low over the river and in the confusion men wandered away from the taped paths and into the minefields. Others were killed on mines which the engineers had missed within the taped routes. The Germans, long since alerted, opened fire with deadly effect.

Walker used battalions from 143rd and 141st Infantry Regiments. Once the boats were in the water they were subject to heavy machine guns firing in enfilade. It was slaughter. The remarkable feature is, that despite these terrible conditions, isolated groups did make it to the far bank. Shallow bridgeheads were fiercely counterattacked. The 1st/143rd Infantry had a bridgehead for a while that night, but the Germans counterattacked in such strength that the survivors were forced to run the gauntlet of the river and the supposedly friendly bank. The 3rd battalion failed even to get across to the far bank. The leading companies were caught in the open approaches to the river. Minefields and enemy fire caused panic and confusion, and the officers lost control.

To the north of San Angelo a battalion of the 141st Infantry got two companies across, but their radios had been destroyed and nobody had the faintest idea of their predicament. In normal circumstances, the success or failure of a river crossing is heavily dependent upon the contribution made by the engineers. Lt Colonel Oran Stovall's divisional engineers were required to clear the mines from both river banks, run a ferry service across the Rapido, put up a footbridge and have the ground laid for a Bailey bridge, all in darkness. Such a herculean task would be impossible if the infantry could not clear the enemy from within small-arms' range of the crossing points.

Walker surveyed the damage from his CP at first light. He was still trying to form a clear picture when General Keyes telephoned. He ordered Walker to resume the offensive at once. Walker replied that he planned to do so at 9.00 pm that evening. Keyes repeated the order. Walker was to attack at once, preferably before noon; in Keyes' view the moment was opportune – the enemy would be tired and would have the sun in his eyes!

Keyes gave Walker until 2.00 pm to get moving. Amidst frantic preparations it was a little after 4.00 pm when the regiments made their second attempt. With a very heavy artillery bombardment in support, all three battalions of the 143rd Infantry attacked over the same ground. All got companies across the river. Once darkness fell, however, the close artillery support was lost. The Germans counterattacked and by daylight the bridgeheads had been eliminated. Men crossed to the east bank as best they could.

The 141st Infantry was still unnerved by the previous night's experience and their assault did not begin until after 10.00 pm that night. Both the 2nd and 3rd Battalions attacked and the experience was a bloody repeat of the previous evening. Remarkably however, both battalions had bridgeheads on the opposite shore, a maximum of some 600 yards from the river. By dawn further movement across the river was impossible. Smoke was put down on the crossing sites to conceal movement, but this drifted into the shallow bridgeheads which meant that close artillery support could no longer be effective.

While radio communication was possible, Walker ordered his men to hold tight. Frantic efforts were made to prepare the 142nd Infantry to cross into the bridgehead. Again Keyes demanded that the attack should be made as soon as possible, but Walker insisted that the attack could not be made before dark. By late afternoon the sound of firing from the opposite bank had all but stopped; there was just an occasional indication that the enemy were mopping up isolated pockets of resistance. Clark intervened and the third attempt was cancelled.

In the 48 hours of the battle the 36th Division had lost 2,000 men killed, wounded and, by far the greatest number, missing, presumably captured. This represents 60% of the attacking force, a staggeringly high casualty rate. 'My fine division is wrecked,' noted Walker in his diary.[6] Their sacrifice was made all the more poignant when it emerged that the Germans were unaware there had been a major attempt to cross the Rapido. Von Senger paid little heed to the action at the time because it caused no particular anxiety. The American assault was contained and the defenders did not even call for reserves from their own division. It was only after the war and the Congressional Committee of Enquiry that the Germans became aware of the extent of the attack, and the damage they had inflicted.

Who was to blame? On Sunday 23 January Clark and Keyes visited Walker; the latter clearly expected to be dismissed. Neither did he draw much comfort from Clark's opening remarks.

'Tell me what happened up here,' Clark asked.

The events were discussed in considerable detail. Afterwards Clark turned to Keyes and said, 'It was as much my fault as yours.'

Clark always maintained that Walker misunderstood the remark. The fault lay with Clark and Keyes in not supervising Walker more closely during the operation. One thing is clear. The battle was rigidly controlled by the corps and divisional commanders, yet neither Keyes nor Walker even conducted a personal reconnaissance of the ground. It was the

American way of doing things. The divisional commander did not stray beyond his regimental CPs and the regiment commanders did not go forward of the battalion CPs.

Clark criticized Walker because he had no faith in the second attack and failed to imbue his commanders with the necessary drive and conviction. Walker's doubts, genuine from the outset, were transmitted downwards at least to the regimental commanders who in turn passed it on to their battalions. Men of the 143rd Infantry recall Colonel Martin, their regimental commander, openly weeping as they walked past him on their way to the assault. This in turn raises the question of whether Walker should have resigned his command. After all, he protested his orders; but that is not the American way of doing things either. An officer can voice his objections to a superior and then has to obey. Perhaps in this instance Keyes should have relieved a commander in whom he could have no faith; but then Clark always maintained that Walker only protested mildly.

Perhaps the Rapido could have been crossed by another, maybe better, division than the 36th Infantry.

Other accounts have been critical of Walker and the 36th Division, rather than Clark or Keyes. One wrote: 'Clark had his faults, as most men have, but the 36th Division's difficulties in January 1944 were their own and could not rightfully be charged against him.'[7]

The respected Fred Majdalany wrote: 'It would appear that this operation was badly mishandled by the Command and Staff of 36th Division.'[8]. It is a valid judgement.

Just before the Rapido battle Walker wrote in his diary.

I talked with five Lieutenant Colonels of Infantry who arrived for duty with the Division. They are replacements for battalion commanders who have been killed, wounded or sick. All of them are over 35 years of age and one is close to 50. Some have never commanded an infantry battalion, even on manoeuvres. . . . With battalion commanders of this type casualties of the men will be greater . . . it is not a good thing to bring inexperienced battalion commanders in from the outside during combat.[9]

On 24 January Alexander sent General Jackie Devers, as his deputy, to see Walker and to report back. Keyes accompanied Devers on the visit. They asked a lot of searching questions. Devers asked Walker if he had given orders for his men to carry unloaded rifles when they crossed the Rapido. Walker told him 'No,' and asked why. Devers' reply made

Walker's blood boil: 'Some of your wounded back in the hospitals have said so to my interrogators.'

There was another confrontation, between Wilbur and Keyes, and again it was out on the roadside. Devers attempted to have his driver pull away, but Wilbur was determined to have his say. 'The whole trouble is that you people in the rear do not know what goes on up here.' Keyes was white with rage and Devers physically shaken by Wilbur's blistering attack.

On Saturday 29 January Clark arranged to meet Walker on the road near the little village of Mignano. Out of earshot of the others he told him that he was concerned about the division; morale was low and performance equally poor. It was time for change. Clark gave Walker a list of officers who were to be relieved. They included Wilbur, Colonel Kerr the Chief of Staff, Colonel Werner of the 141st Infantry and Walker's two sons. Two days previously Clark had ordered Walker to relieve Colonel Martin of the 143rd Infantry.

Clark also told Walker that he too was to be replaced but not yet.

'I will give you time to get one victory under your belt, Fred; I owe you that much,' Clark told him.

At the Rapido the Allies attacked the enemy at his strongest with too few troops. This mistake was to be repeated subsequently with the New Zealanders and the 4th Indian Divisions in what became known as the Second and Third Battles of Cassino. It was only in the Fourth Battle that the Allied generals had learned the obvious lesson that if you must attack the enemy where he is strongest, you do so with massive and overwhelming force. But it took them a long time to learn that lesson, and many men were to suffer as a consequence.

Notes

1. Quoted in *Daily Times Herald*, 20 January 1946, Dallas Texas; Wagner, *The Texan Army*, p 92.
2. This passage appeared in the *London Gazette*. It is quoted in Smith, E. D., *The Battles for Cassino*, David and Charles, 1989, pp 17–18.
3. Ibid., p 27.
4. In the form of his own book Clark, Mark, *Calculated Risk*, Harrap, 1951; see Blumenson, *Mark Clark*, p 167.
5. Walker, Fred, *From Texas to Rome*, p 300.
6. Ibid., p 311.

7. Sheehan, Fred, *Anzio: Epic of Bravery*, Oklahoma University Press, Norman, Okla., 1964.
8. Majdalany, Fred, *Cassino: Portrait of a Battle*, Longmans Green, 1957.
9. Walker, Fred, *From Texas to Rome*, pp 304–5.

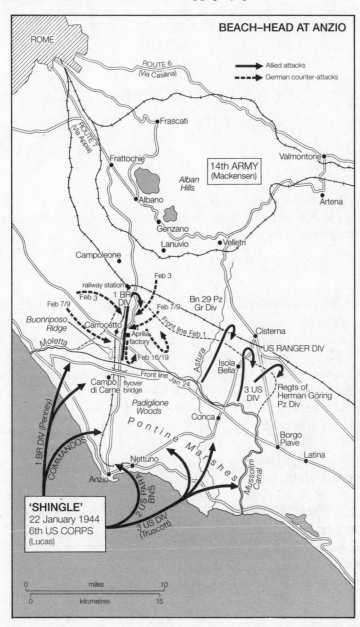

33

Operation Shingle: Somewhat in the Nature of a Bluff

We have launched the big attack against the German armies defending Rome which I told you about at Tehran. The weather conditions seem favourable. I hope to have good news for you before long.[1]

Churchill to Stalin, 21 January 1944

Churchill was right about the weather. When the Allied armada of 243 ships set sail from Naples Bay late on the afternoon of 21 January, the sea was calm. It must have appeared inconceivable that the Germans would not get wind of this great operation but apparently they did not. Allied aircraft made maximum use of the clear skies to attack every German air base the length and breadth of central Italy to ensure that reconnaissance planes were kept on the ground. There was a deception operation of sorts. Targets at Civitavecchia and Leghorn were bombarded by warships and medium bombers.

On that fateful January morning the military balance in Italy was as follows. Fifteenth Army Group had slightly over 20 divisions, but this figure included the Poles and more Canadians, neither of whom were ready for battle. The Germans had about 21 divisions. Thirteen of those were in Tenth Army facing ten Allied divisions on the Gustav Line. The remainder were north of Rome under Fourteenth Army, commanded by General von Mackensen; they comprised Kesselring's strategic reserve and guarded likely landing spots. In Kesselring's judgement the Allies were likely to attempt an operation which would seek to cut him off completely by landing well to the north of Rome. He thought the Tenth

Army was the target, and underestimated the importance of the Eternal City in Allied plans.

The Shingle armada[2] carried the assault elements of the VI (US) Corps commanded by Major General John W. Lucas. This consisted of Truscott's 3rd (US) Infantry Division and 1st (Br) Infantry Division under Major General W.R.C. Penny; the 1st, 2nd and 3rd Ranger Battalions under Darby; Colonel Reuben Tucker's 504th Parachute Infantry; the 83rd (US) Chemical Battalion; and No 9 Army and 43 Royal Marine Commando.

If necessary, one regimental combat team of the 45th (US) Infantry would join the beachhead in the first turnround of craft, within about three days, and would be followed by 1st (US) Armoured Division (less one combat command) as rapidly as the craft could be made available. The total force earmarked for Shingle numbered 110,000 men, configured in a defensive rather than offensive mode.

General Truscott described the beachhead:

Anzio, a small port, and Nettuno, about two miles to the east, are small resort towns on the coast about thirty miles south of Rome, once favoured, it was said, by the Roman emperors. A good road and railroad lead practically due north along a flat almost imperceptible ridge through Aprilia and Campoleone to Albano eighteen miles inland on the slopes of Colli Lazialli. There the road joins Highway 7, the coastal road from the south to Rome. Another road follows the coast northwest to Ostia and thence along the south bank of the Tiber to Rome. North of Anzio adjacent to the Albano road, the country is broken by numerous deep ravines – 'wadi country' our British comrades termed it. A few miles inland this area was covered with dense pine woods of a reforestation project. About eight miles north of Anzio, ravines or 'wadis' lead off westward to the sea and marking the Corps Beachhead Line in the sector of the British 1 Division.

Five miles east of Nettuno is a creek known as the Asturia River which had once drained from the southern slopes of Colli Lazialli to the sea. There were patches of woods along this stream near the coast, but for the most part the whole area to the north and east of Nettuno was farm land reclaimed from the Pontine Marshes in one of Mussolini's early reclamation projects. The main drainage canal began near Padiglione about six miles north of Nettuno and cut west between high dikes across the natural drainage lines to a point near the village of Sessano where it joined with an eastern tributary and flowed south to the sea nine miles east of Nettuno. This was the Mussolini Canal. The main canal and its western tributary marked the Corps Beachhead Line in the sector of the 3rd Infantry Division, with the boundary between divisions lying just east of the Albano Road. At the mouth of the Mussolini Canal, a pumping station emptied the waters into the sea.

This whole area of reclaimed marshland was passable enough in dry weather. The water line, however, was usually within two feet of the surface. When rains fell or the pumps stopped working, the area became so marshy that movement off roads was almost impossible, and fox holes filled with water. One road followed the coast eastward from Nettuno through Littoria and joined Highway 7 farther on down the coast. Still another road led north-east from Nettuno through Cisterna and Cori to Artena and Valmontone on Highway Six, the main road from Cassino to Rome. The whole area was dotted by two-storey farm houses or *poderi*, usually of plastered stone. The Beachhead area was an area roughly seven miles in depth and fifteen miles in width at its widest part.[3]

While the VI (US) Corps was landing in the beachhead, the Allied radio network broadcast to the resistance in Rome:

The hour has arrived for Rome and all Italians to fight in every possible way and with all force. Sabotage the enemy. . . block his roads or retreat, destroy his communications to the last wire, strike against him everywhere, continue the fight indefatigably, without thought of political questions until our troops have arrived. Notify all bands and parties.[4]

It was as well that few tried to translate these brave words unto deeds.

The landings were spectacularly successful. Complete and total surprise was achieved. The troops came ashore unopposed and un-hurried. The first solid news that Kesselring received was from a Luftwaffe pilot who, at 8.20 am, happened to fly over Anzio and looked down to see the invasion in full swing. That was nearly six hours after the first troops stepped ashore. Thereafter Operation Shingle degenerated into one of the most dismal chapters of the Second World War. The mystery at Anzio, from which all the subsequent agony and controversy flowed, was that there appeared to be a genuine confusion over aims and objectives. Once more the problem was one of communication between Churchill on the one hand and the three key commanders, Alexander, Mark Clark and Lucas, on the other.

Churchill was under no illusions. Anzio was about a drive on Rome. Indeed there had been a plan at one stage to form the Special Forces into a coherent group and land them at the coast nearest to Rome to seize the city. This plan was abandoned, however, because it was found they could not be put ashore nearer than 21 miles from Rome before 0200 hours and as no transport was available, dawn would break before they could reach the city.

Churchill sailed for England aboard the battleship *King George V* on 14 January. While at sea, his concern for Shingle centred upon the possibility that banner headlines might read: 'The Americans have taken Rome.'[5]

Before Anzio, Alexander expected[6] that VI (US) Corps' landing would be followed by the immediate thrust of small forces to the Alban Hills to get astride the enemy lines of communication and thereby cause the Germans on the southern front to pull back. He realized, however, this was 'somewhat in the nature of a bluff'.

The first objective was to secure the beachhead, a defensive position covering Anzio port. VI (US) Corps would then push patrols and light forces of, say, regimental strength – infantry, armoured cars and light tanks – to the Alban Hills. These hills were a formidable feature, a huge and towering volcanic formation overlooking the plain. The heights at Colli Lazialli dominated the two routes southwards which were the main line of communications to the Gustav Line.

Alexander knew that forces in the numbers landed could not hold the wide front based on the Alban Hills and the hills above Cori if the Germans counterattacked in strength, or brought in fresh forces from the north of Italy. Privately, he feared that the Germans might send down large reinforcements from the north and that they would withdraw nothing from the southern front to seal off the beachhead. He had every reason to fear what lay ahead. Major General Terence Airey, who headed the intelligence team at Army Group Headquarters, and who had access to Ultra, early in the New Year constructed a table that worked out the scale and movement of German reinforcements into the beachhead. The divisions which Hitler despatched from the Balkans, France and Germany itself were plotted exactly.

Alexander had not made his intentions clear, and Clark chose not to request clarification but to apply his own interpretation. With two divisions Lucas would not have the forces to secure the beachhead and extend it 20 miles into the Alban Hills. Clark expected the Germans to turn on Lucas with a powerful force, which would weaken the Gustav Line. Clark could then use this opportunity to punch through, unleash his armour, link up with the beachhead and take the Alban Hills. Thereafter the road to Rome would be open.

The instructions which Clark issued to Lucas further muddied the waters and were intended to do so. Since Clark had no idea what to expect at Anzio he determined to cover his backside. Lucas was ordered to 'seize and secure a beachhead' and then to advance on the Colli Lazialli.

Lucas understood Clark's intentions, as well as Alexander's. He knew it was his decision whether to advance on to the Alban Hills, when, and with what force. He was not a fit man, and was probably ill at the time (he died in 1949). He was popular enough with the men under his command, who nicknamed him 'Foxy Grandpa'. This intelligent, astute, corncob-pipe-smoker, who looked older than his 54 years, was sceptical from the outset. A diary entry revealed his feelings both about the operation and Churchill, who inspired the operation, when he wrote:[7] 'This whole affair has a strong odor of Gallipoli and apparently the same amateur is still on the coach's bench.' He complained whenever possible, to whomsoever would listen. It was a wonder that he was not relieved of his command. But perhaps his superiors wanted a fall guy. After meeting with Alexander on 9 January Lucas confided: 'I felt like a lamb being led to the slaughter.'[8]

Shortly after a briefing from Clark he wrote: 'They will end up by putting me ashore with inadequate force and get me in a serious jam. Then, who will take the blame?'[9] Shortly before he sailed, Clark warned Lucas enigmatically, 'Don't stick your neck out as I did at Salerno.'[10] The effect of the message on Lucas was to reinforce his caution and pessimism. He determined to secure his beachhead perimeter as a first priority, then advance inland as far as he thought it safe to do so.

The landings took the Allies as much by surprise as the Germans. Lucas was able to have more than 50,000 men ashore together with 5,000 vehicles in under 48 hours and with no interference of any consequence from the enemy. Rome was less than 30 miles to the north, and it was undefended.

If Rome had fallen in January rather than June, tens of thousands of Allied soldiers might have been spared the horrors of the Winter Battles. By late afternoon on D-day at the latest, Lucas could have had advance elements into the Eternal City. Lieutenant General Kurt Maelzer, the commandant of the city and a drunken sot, sobered up quickly on 21 January, and later declared: 'The first hours after the landing were decisive for Rome. If the enemy had taken full advantage of the situation then offering itself to him, Rome would have fallen as a ripe fruit into his lap without notable losses.' Colonel General Eugene Dallman, Himmler's representative in Rome was equally convinced that the Allies had made a blunder as was the astute General Westphal, Kesselring's Chief of Staff.

Lucas nevertheless did have his supporters. The aggressively minded Truscott was one. He was later to write:

'I suppose that armchair strategists will always labour under the delusion that there was a fleeting moment at Anzio during which some Napoleonic figure would have charged over the Colli Lazialli, played havoc with the German lines of communications and galloped on into Rome. Any such concept betrays lack of comprehension of the military problems involved. It was necessary to occupy the Corps beachhead line to prevent the enemy from interfering with the beaches. Otherwise every artillery and armoured detachment operating against the flanks could have cut us off from the beach and prevented the unloading of troops, supplies and equipment. As it was, the Corps beachhead line was barely distant enough to prevent direct artillery upon the beach.'[11]

The people of Rome could not have cared less about finely balanced military arguments. As far as they were concerned, Allied troops were less than 30 miles down the road and liberation surely was only a matter of hours away. They took to the streets in their thousands and jeered at the German soldiers, headquarters staff and supply echelons who fled the capital northwards, tails between their legs. Several dozen Allied flags were unfurled over balconies and every English dictionary in town was bought up; but the mood of optimism soon gave way to one of grim despair. Bands of armed partisans moved south of Rome and seized a number of road junctions leading to the beachhead, but when the Americans failed to put in an appearance, quickly dispersed.

Lucas was not the man for a bold enterprise. He did not plan to have the bulk of his armour move into the beachhead before D + 4 at the very earliest. But if a Patton-like figure had appeared at the gates of Rome with an armoured column, what would the Germans have done? Accept that they had been bettered by a *coup de main* and retreat northwards. Abandon the Gustav Line? Or would Hitler have ordered his divisions to recapture the city and hurl the Allies back into the sea? I believe that Hitler would have regarded Rome as no more of a constraint then he did Warsaw later that summer. The consequences for the people and their treasures could have been catastrophic. By the same token, had Lucas done what Alexander had intended, namely advance onto the Alban Hills, would the Germans have been bluffed into a premature abandonment of the Gustav Line? At this stage of the war the German generals were not panicked into hasty actions.

The window of opportunity for offensive action lasted for three days. At the end of that time Kesselring had ringed the beachhead. Having once again been caught strategically unawares, his tactical reaction to the situation was masterful. He moved mostly flak and anti-tank units from

Rome into the Alban Hills to bluff Lucas into believing there was strength in depth. The long-range bombardment did the trick and Lucas ordered the corps to dig its defences in readiness for a counterattack.

With the blessing of Berlin, Kesselring did what the Allied intelligence pundits predicted he would, and Alexander prayed that he wouldn't. He rushed reinforcements southwards. Fourteenth Army, under General Eberhard von Mackensen was brought south to cover the beachhead. Troops and tanks and guns came from Northern Italy, the South of France and the Balkans. By 25 January advance guards from eight divisions ringed the beachhead and within a week that number had reached 70,000 men and Rome was secured.

What must have been particularly galling for Lucas and his soldiers was that the Germans were able to complete these deployments almost without hindrance from Allied air forces. For some weeks, the latter had been concentrating on Operation Strangle, designed to isolate the Gustav Line by striking at road and rail communications. Once again the promises of the Air Staffs failed to live up to expectations.

Alexander and Clark visited the beachhead on D-day and both pronounced themselves satisfied with what had been achieved. Alexander fully expected Lucas to advance to the Alban Hills, but did not see fit to question Lucas on his intentions. Three days later Alexander returned to the beachhead, goaded by Churchill, who was angered at the inactivity of Lucas. Alexander was very disappointed[12] that Lucas had not pushed out and told him that Cisterna should be taken.

The beachhead appeared secure enough. It was seven miles deep and 16 miles wide but there was still little offensive activity. After that visit on 25 January, Alexander felt that Lucas was not measuring up and informed Clark.

Lucas devoted himself to the task in hand, to build up his forces and secure the beachhead. A few minor skirmishes were attempted but Lucas was determined to wait until the 1st (US) Armoured Division was ashore.

Clark returned to Anzio on 28 January and nearly lost his life. The PT boat in which he was travelling was fired upon by an American minesweeper. One round struck the wheelhouse and exploded less than six feet from Clark. Five of the crew were wounded and two later died.

At last Lucas was ready to launch an offensive. The main attack was to be made by an Anglo-American force comprising elements of 1st (Br) Infantry and 1st (US) Armoured Divisions to take Campoleone and attack Colli Lazialli from the west. The secondary objective was to capture Cisterna, cut Highway 7 and thereby block one of the Germans' main supply lines. This was the task for Truscott's 3rd (US) Infantry with Darby's Rangers and Reuben Tucker's paratroopers under command. But battlefield intelligence was faulty. Unbeknown to Truscott, who was told that the ground was lightly held, he was opposed by elements of the Herman Goering Division and 26th Panzers manning defences in depth.

Two Ranger battalions moved out at 0100 hours on the morning of 30 January. Their task was to infiltrate the German lines and seize key strongpoints in advance of the main attack. The Germans let the Rangers in and then shut the door, thereby isolating them from their infantry and armoured support. At daylight the Rangers were ambushed by German tanks and infantry. They fought as long as their ammunition lasted, but most of the 750 men in the two battalions were captured. Later the prisoners were marched through Rome. 'Here are the men you expected,' was the message. Their public humiliation was a clear demonstration of continued German military strength. The Romans returned to their everyday existence and all speculation over an imminent release ended.

General Clark visited Truscott the next day, criticized his use of the Rangers and told him that he had ordered an enquiry to attribute blame and responsibility. Truscott told him brusquely not to bother, it was his responsibility.

The offensive had got off to a bad start and matters didn't improve. The 3rd Infantry tried valiantly to break through the German defences but, in two days of fighting, failed to get within 1,000 yards of Cisterna. In that time Truscott's combined force had suffered 3,000 battle casualties and lost one-third of its armour.

The British fared little better. General Penny's attack into Campoleone was a disaster. With the flanks supposedly covered by the Guards Brigade, Penny ordered his 3rd Infantry Brigade (battalions of the Duke of Wellington's, Kings Shropshire Light Infantry and the Sherwood Foresters) to attack Campoleone. The German defences were formidable and the Scots and Irish Guards on the flanks suffered heavily and made no progress. This meant that the farther the 3rd Brigade advanced along the road into the town the more exposed they became to a murderous fire from front and flanks.

The Sherwood Foresters made a desperate attack to take Campoleone station, but the battalion was slaughtered. Every officer in the battalion at company commander level and above was either killed or wounded, and in the leading company every officer was a casualty. The battalion, with

260 men answering the roll call, was finished as a fighting unit. General Harmon of the 1st (US) Armoured Division visited the scene as the British brigade dug in on the ground they held, what was clearly a most dangerous salient. He reported: 'There were dead bodies everywhere. I have never seen so many dead men in one place. They lay so close that I had to step with care.'[13] For Mark Clark to continue carping about the lack of offensive spirit among the British troops was an outrage and a travesty of the truth. Perhaps if he had paid more attention to the reports of his own generals he would have been more rational in his judgements.

On the morning of 2 February Lucas called in both his divisional commanders. Fifth Army had just informed him of secret intelligence that the Germans were in far greater strength than had hitherto been appreciated, and were about to launch a major counter-offensive to drive the beachhead into the sea. Lucas ordered his forces to stop all attacks, dig in for defence and hold the corps beachhead line at all costs.

The only exception were the Rangers. Darby collected the remaining 4th Battalion and the six survivors from the attack on Cisterna and they were returned to the United States.

Notes

1. Churchill, Winston S., *The Second World War, Vol V, Closing the Ring*, Penguin Books, 1985, p 425.
2. The armada included 84 LSTs, 81 LSIs, 96 LCIs, 50 LCTs, four Liberty ships loaded with ten days' supplies and two command ships escorted by cruisers, destroyers, frigates and other warships.
3. Truscott, *Command Missions*, p 308.
4. Adleman and Walton, *Rome Fell Today*, p 183.
5. Gilbert, *Road to Victory 1941–45*, p 653.
6. Matthews interview with Alexander, p 7.
7. Adleman and Walton, *Rome Fell Today*, p 158.
8. Ibid.
9. Ibid.
10. Ibid., p 159.
11. Truscott, *Command Missions*, p 311.
12. Matthews interview, p 8.
13. Trevelyan, Raleigh, *History of the Second World War*, Vol 4, Purnell, p 1618.

34

The First Battle of Cassino, 25 January – 12 February 1944

Alexander and Clark conferred at Anzio on what to do next. Clark suggested another amphibious assault farther up the coast, possibly near the mouth of the Tiber or north of there at Civitavecchia. Alexander dismissed the proposal out of hand; there were too many administrative and logistical problems to overcome.

'Solving administrative and logistical problems is your job,' retorted Mark Clark;[1] but he didn't pursue the matter, it wasn't intended as a serious suggestion.

But Operation Shingle had both caught the Germans completely unawares and given them a nasty fright. Kesselring raised the question whether the Cassino front could really be held in the event of a major attack, or whether it would be better to cut their losses and withdraw the front to a position behind the beachhead at Anzio. The immediate advantage of such a move would be to allow the two German armies to collaborate very closely and economize their forces.

Kesselring visited Von Senger und Etterlin at the headquarters of his XIV Panzer Corps at Roccasecca where the issue was discussed at length. The balance of argument was in favour of XIV Panzer Corps holding the Cassino front because that line, running as it did across the waist of Italy, was short and geographically formidable. A line nearer to the gates of Rome would be longer and more difficult to defend. In any case, Kesselring confided that the Anzio beachhead, which Hitler had already dubbed 'the Abscess', would not be allowed to remain. Fourteenth Army were to be given the men and the means to hurl the VI Corps back into the sea, and teach them a lesson on the folly of amphibious warfare. However, such a strategy ran the risk that if the Allies attempted another amphibious operation there would be no reserve left to contain the threat. The Eighth Army appeared to have run out of steam on the Adriatic coast, but their limited offensives continued and the front had to be watched. Von Senger would have to handle the defence of the Gustav Line unaided.

Even though Kesselring had more divisions at his disposal than ever before in the campaign, they were all bespoken. He must have been mightily relieved that the Italians were not causing him any problems. Had the Allies and the Italian government been able to call to arms the Italian resistance in the countryside north of Rome, then Kesselring, faced by threats on three fronts, would have been severely overstretched. But the Italian resistance, as a national effort, was non-existent at this stage, and those who skulked in the hills were either fleeing the threat of forced labour or were brigands who preyed not on the enemy but on the local citizenry.

Although considerable efforts and resources were being channelled across the Adriatic to Tito and his partisans, nobody proposed a similar strategy for the Italian resistance. As for Badolglio and his Cabinet, they could only dream of restoring the good name to the Italian Army, even if the Allies had little interest.

Once the beachhead had been contained, the Germans turned their attention back to keeping the citizens of Rome in their place. Repression took all manner of forms, but a popular tactic was called the '*retata*'. A number of streets would be cordoned off and every room in every building searched. All the people were assembled and the men despatched as forced labour.

Sometimes the retata produced more valuable prizes such as Allied soldiers, downed airmen or POWs on the run. On one occasion Colonel Montezemelo, the 65-year-old head of the city's resistance was caught. He was taken to the jail on the Via Tasso and tortured to death. Gestapo thugs stuffed wads of cotton wool in his ears and set fire to them. They pulled out his nails and teeth, one by one. Montezemelo died cursing his tormentors, who had failed to make him talk.

On 24 January, Clark launched another attack across the Rapido. This time the offensive was undertaken by the 34th (US) Infantry and the French Expeditionary Corps. The Fifth Army attacked to the north of Cassino and, as the town was directly threatened, the Allies were later to designate the operation 'The First Battle of Cassino'. The battle was to last a month and leave the Allies exhausted, but they were to come within an ace of success.

It was to be a pincer movement. After dark on 24 January General Juin was to unleash his goumiers across the Rapido and attack Monte Cairo, then swing south towards the Liri Valley. Ryder's 34th Infantry were to mount a simultaneous attack at the heart of the German defences, into the 'Gustav Stellung' south of Monte Cairo, then swing south and conquer Monte Cassino from the north.

Mark Clark had his hands full with Anzio so he left Keyes to coordinate the battle. Keyes was a devout Roman Catholic who attended Mass every morning.

The soldiers liked that. It meant that their general would not be wasteful with human life. Eisenhower once described Keyes as a general who had everything but a sense of humour. He was a cavalryman with an instinctive touch for the use of armour in the offensive, but an infantry/artillery battle in a confined space against prepared defences was not to his liking.

The 34th (US) Infantry, the Red Bulls, was known as the hard luck outfit. It was the first American division to reach Europe, fought with distinction in Tunisia and showed dogged courage at the Volturno. It fought in every battle but never made the news, hence the nickname. Cassino tore the heart out of the Bulls, from which it took a year to recover and the division came close to disbandment.

Truscott knew Walker of the 36th and Ryder of the 34th, and viewed them as 'intelligent, well trained and professionally competent ... personable and well liked by their Divisions and by those with whom they came into contact. They were not however, outstanding battle leaders.'[2]

Their opponent in the high mountains was the 44th Hoch and Deutschmeisters under General Franck. The division had suffered heavily and was much reduced in numbers. As with most German infantry divisions at this time, its battalion commanders were young men, company commanders who became veterans before their time. They led their troops, amounting to no more than 100 men, in the forward front line as if they were mixed assault companies.

North of Cassino, the Rapido, though shallower, was still a formidable obstacle. The Germans had destroyed the flood dam below Sant Ella and the Rapido valley had flooded to a depth of about four feet. On the other side, the enemy waited behind minefields and belts of barbed wire.

On the 24th the 3rd Algerian Infantry Division poured over the Rapido, spearheaded by the 4th Tunisian Rifle Regiment who, heedless of casualties, negotiated the German minefields and swarmed all over their defences. These colonial troops – rugged, cruel men who neither gave nor sought quarter – were superbly led by their French officers. The division scaled Monte Belvedere, fought the Germans hand-to-hand, and by the afternoon of the second day had taken the peak.

On 26 January the Algerians took Monte Abate and had Cairo within their grasp. But the assault had lost momentum. A near-constant barrage of enemy mortar and artillery fire was coupled to a finely timed counterattack by a regiment of the newly arrived 71st Infantry Division. The Germans threw the French off Monte Abate but in turn could advance no further; lowland troops, unaccustomed to the hills and unsuitably clad in overcoats, were held in check by the exhausted French.

After laying down a heavy barrage, Ryder's 34th Infantry, with two regiments forward, attempted to seize bridgeheads across the Rapido. On the first night both operations were frustrated. But the Americans plugged away until, on the night of 30 January, the 168th Infantry Regiment succeeded in finding the way through. A bridgehead was secured as well as the critical Monte Cairo and the surrounding heights. While the 133rd Infantry advanced in the valley towards Cassino, the 135th and 168th attacked into the hills behind the town. Keyes now reinforced Ryder's command by giving him the 36th Division's 142nd Infantry Regiment, which had been uncommitted earlier.

The Texans swung into line on the right flank of Ryder's forces and linked up with the left flank of the French Corps. They pushed forward together and forced the Germans back. The Americans and the French were now up onto the high ground of which Monte Cassino was a part; beneath them the 133rd Infantry were into the outskirts of Cassino town. Behind them in the valley the Sherman tanks of Harmon's combat team from 1st (US) Armoured Division lent their fire support, champing at the bit to cross the Rapido and strike out on Route 6 up the Liri Valley and on to Rome.

The battle continued day after day. In mist and fog and driving rain company-sized rushes were made from one small hill-top to the next feature. Once a feature had been secured the men scraped a shallow hole and waited for the inevitable counterattack, preceded by the deadly barrage of German mortars. By 4 February Ryder's battalions were edging closer to the monastery itself. Vital features, Colle San Angelo and Point 593, were captured and lost again. It was a grim infantry encounter fought at close range where grenades were more important than artillery.

In masterly fashion Von Senger moved around the reserves immediately available to him. He had expected the British in the south to attack again but, by the beginning of February, it was clear that the battle to the north of Cassino was the main effort. Von Senger despatched regiments of 90th Panzer Grenadiers to that sector. The division was led by Generalmajor Ernst-Gunther Baade, a wealthy cavalry officer and renowned international horse rider of the inter-war years. Over his riding breeches this Afrika Korps veteran used to wear a Scottish khaki kilt. In place of the sporran he had a large pistol, suspended in a holster from his neck. Baade fought his battles from the forward CP, safe there from pestering staff and commanders.

The Germans suffered fearsome casualties. Divisions were losing fighting strength at the rate of a battalion a day. Kesselring had no choice but to accede to Von Senger's request for fresh troops and started to denude the Adriatic front.

Alexander broke his own rules and intervened directly in the battle. He despatched Lemnitzer, his Chief of Staff, to find out about morale. It emerged, hardly surprisingly, that the troops were 'almost mutinous'.[3] Alexander gave Clark until 12 February to keep the 34th in the Cassino battle. If by that time the division had not taken Cassino and the monastery, Alexander would order Clark to pull out the 34th and put fresh troops in, namely the New Zealanders and the Indian Division across from the Adriatic front. Clark worried that, with more foreigners coming in, Fifth Army would be even more diluted as an American force. He was also concerned that these two divisions, stalwarts of the Eighth Army, would enhance the British claim to a stake in the capture of Rome.

Clark turned on Keyes: 'If you don't make it this time, you're going to miss the boat because I'm going to bring the New Zealanders and Freyberg in – he'll do it.'[4] Before Cassino, Clark considered Keyes to be an outstanding commander, but now he was bitterly critical.

Ryder gathered his battalions for one last effort, and on 11 February, they stormed forward with that desperate, brittle energy that is displayed by men who have long since passed the limits of their endurance. But the Germans had strengthened their positions and outnumbered the attackers. In the driving rain the Americans could make no more the 300 yards up Monastery Hill before they were forced by weight of fire to go to ground, scraping what cover they could from the barren landscape. Clark ordered that the 34th Infantry should be relieved, but their agony was not yet over. The 4th Indian Division moved forward but could not effect a relief for two whole days. During that period the front battalions of the 34th Infantry were embroiled in pitched battles against wave after wave of German counterattacks.

The Germans fought themselves to a standstill. Ironically Von Senger advised Kesselring on 12 February that if the Allies should respond in strength to his counterattacks then the Gustav Line would not be tenable. Von Senger recommended a withdrawal to the Caesar Line, a German reserve position which ran through the Alban Hills and was anchored on its right flank behind Anzio. At last, on the evening of 13 February the lead brigade of the 4th Indian Division moved onto the hill, not to continue the attack but to take over the front. There would be a new offensive, but not yet. Von Senger changed his mind about withdrawing.

The 1st Battalion Royal Sussex Regiment moved into the positions occupied by the battalions of the 135th and 168th Infantry Regiments. There were just 840 left of the 3,200 Americans who had begun the battle. Many of them had to be carried down the mountain by British and Indian stretcher-bearers, who wept at the sight which greeted them on that rainswept lunar landscape. The dead and injured lay where they had fallen. In waterlogged foxholes and shell scrapes on the scree slopes many young soldiers were too weak to climb out unaided. Cramped and soaked through, any physical movement was agony.

The First Battle of Cassino was over. If we take the battle to have begun with the attack by the X Corps on 16 January, the Allied losses were very heavy. The British suffered 4,000 casualties. Although an important bridgehead had been secured across the lower Garigliano, two divisions, the 46th Infantry and the 56th Infantry, were totally played out.

The debacle on the Rapido for the 36th Infantry had achieved nothing in return for 1,700 casualties. Ryder's 34th Infantry had succeeded in driving a small breach in the Gustav Line just north of Cassino, but had suffered 2,200 casualties in the process. The French, on the far right flank, had advanced the farthest and driven a wedge deep into the mountains, but these two divisions had taken 2,500 casualties.

For what? General Von Senger offered his judgement:

> When I look at the Allied plan for a breakthrough, I cannot refrain from criticism. According to the original plan, which was tactically well thought out, there was to be an attack against the right wing of my corps, followed by a number of blows against the Cassino front. But after the first attack had failed, the original plan was followed too rigidly. This gave me the chance to draw reserves from the sectors where the attacks had failed, to constantly change the operational boundaries of the divisions, and to parry the blows one by one.
>
> Nor did I understand why the enemy attempted to break through at so many points of the front. It seemed to me that in doing so he was dissipating his forces.[5]

Kesselring had handled the two fronts at Anzio and Cassino with considerable aplomb. His task was made easier by the failure of Eighth Army on the Adriatic coast to distract him.

All that Alexander hoped that Eighth Army could do on the Adriatic coast was to hold Germans troops so that they could not be used to reinforce other sectors, either at Cassino or Anzio. He did not insist that Eighth Army make an attack to coincide with the Rapido and Anzio operations, because he believed that Fifth Army had sufficient troops to carry out its mission. There were enormous problems over loyalties. The lines of communication were at full stretch with two major operations, while the air forces at Foggia still had first call upon the supply chain. A third offensive would have placed additional burdens upon a system which could barely cope as it was. Even so, more could have been attempted. Leese's Eighth Army appeared a formidable force of four army corps. But much of this was on paper. Only V (Br) Corps and XIII (Br) Corps were operational. The Canadians had built up their forces into a corps of two divisions by a crash programme of expansion. The corps was imposed on Leese by Alan Brooke to be broken in for battle with the intention that it would be redeployed once it was trained. Leese did not consider that the corps commander, General Burns, was up to the job or that the bulk of his senior officers were capable of battle. The excellent Guy Simmonds had been posted back to the United Kingdom. The fourth corps was the Poles, but they had not arrived in strength and presented a number of problems, not least one of language.

On 17 January Leese organized a diversionary attack to help Mark Clark and entrusted it to the Canadians, albeit under the command of General Allfrey and the headquarters of his V Corps. The Canadian attack was not successful and a number of officers were sacked.

The fighting never stopped along the Gustav Line. Infantry battalions from the Indian division acclimatized through fighting patrols and reconnaissance of the enemy positions. Artillery and mortars from both sides continued the steady drip, drip, drip of casualties.

Notes

1. Clark to author.
2. Smith, *The Battles for Cassino*, p 41.
3. Alexander interview, p 37.
4. Adleman and Walton, *Rome Fell Today*, p 178.
5. Von Senger, *Neither Fear nor Hope*, p 196.

35

The Monastery

Once the enemy had decided to include Monte Cassino in his defensive system the building on its summit inevitably became a legitimate target; for though the mountain might have been defended, it could not had been captured without attention to the summit – it is the nature of war not to be played to the whistle between white lines.[1]

The Benedictine monastery atop Monte Cassino was bombed on 16 February 1944. To this day there are those who would maintain that the bombing was an act of barbarism. And there are those who believe that the preservation of masonry, no matter its antiquity or beauty, cannot be measured against a single human life.

Even though corps, army and Army Group commanders lived in the lap of luxury compared to the fighting soldier, these were not unfeeling men. Whatever their shortcomings they were not generals who modelled themselves on their predecessors in the First World War – men who lived lives remote from the reality of war. Yet that which they had most sought to avoid had come about. Conditions in Italy now mirrored those of the Western Front more than anywhere else in the Second World War.

One eye-witness account will help bring that experience home to whole generations who have been spared the misery of trench war in winter.

Our troops were living in almost inconceivable misery. The fertile black valleys were knee deep in mud. Thousands of the men had not been dry for weeks. Other thousands lay at night in the high mountains with the temperature below freezing and the thin snow sifting over them. They dug into the stones and slept in little chasms and behind rocks and in half caves. They lived like men of prehistoric times and a club would have become them more than a machine gun. How they survived the dreadful winter at all was beyond us who had the opportunity of drier beds in the warmer valley.

That the northward path was a tedious one was not the fault of our troops, nor of the direction either. It was the weather and the terrain and the weather again. If there had been no German fighting troops in Italy, if there had been merely German engineers to blow the bridges in the passes, if never a shot had been fired at all, our northward march would still have been slow. The country was so difficult that we formed a great deal of cavalry for use in the mountains. Each division had hundreds of horses and mules to carry supplies beyond the point where vehicles could go no further. On beyond the mules' ability were men . . . took it on their backs.

The front line soldier I know lived for months like an animal, and was a veteran in the cruel, fierce world of death. Everything was abnormal and unstable in his life. He was filthy dirty, ate if and when, slept on hard ground without cover.[2]

Now it was the turn of Commonwealth and Imperial troops to be tested at Cassino. The New Zealand Corps officially came into existence on 12 February. It immediately comprised the 2nd New Zealand Infantry and 4th Indian and later the 78th (Br) Infantry Divisions. The corps was led by Lieutenant General Sir Bernard Freyberg VC, one of the few senior commanders in the First World War to hold an active field command in the Second World War.

Freyberg was 55 at the time of the Second Battle of Cassino and in Mark Clark's eyes well past his 'sell-by date' for a battlefield commander. But there is little doubt that Clark held this great soldier in awe. Freyberg had won the Victoria Cross in December 1917 and, by the time his military career finally came to an end, was awarded four DSOs, countless foreign decorations and had been wounded twelve times. He was at his best commanding his superb New Zealand Division in fast-moving offences. At Crete and Cassino Freyberg moved into a higher command. Temperamental, headstrong and none too bright, on both occasions he was found wanting in his direction of the battle.

Freyberg had retired from the British Army in 1937, but he was recalled to the colours to lead the 2nd New Zealand Division into the Second World War. Under his inspired leadership the division became one of the elite units of the Eighth Army. The problem was they didn't like a slugging match which would result in heavy casualties. The New Zealanders were also renowned for their total disregard for officers who were not their own. When the Adjutant General visited the division he remarked to Freyberg:

'Your people don't salute very much, do they?'

Freyberg shrugged his bull-like shoulders and retorted:

'You should try waving to them. They always wave back.' Freyberg had an ability possessed by few generals. He could communicate with soldiers. Men will forgive an awful lot of such a man.

Patton was supposed to have that touch but he didn't. Despite the fact that the United States was the great classless society very few of their generals had an easy way with men. Bradley perhaps was the exception.

The trouble with Freyberg was that he was a law unto himself. Mindful of the dreadful slaughter of the Anzacs in Gallipoli and elsewhere in the First World War, he had been charged by the New Zealand government to preserve New Zealand manpower. Battle dead in 1943 in excessive numbers would have a profound effect on the New Zealand population for years to come.

Freyberg had a direct channel of communication to the New Zealand High Commissioner in London and, if necessary, to his Prime Minister in Wellington. As a recipient of the King's Commission and a serving officer Freyberg was under orders, but his diplomatic status took precedence. Freyberg enjoyed the position of an autonomous ally of whom things could only be asked; the fact that he was temperamental, headstrong, crusty and opinionated didn't help matters either. Freyberg laid down his conditions for exposing his New Zealanders to the monastery. These included the full weight of Allied air power and all the field and heavy artillery that could be mustered. Alexander accepted. He had little choice. The additional fire power was pillaged from Eighth Army. Leese had little choice either.

All of this was too much for Mark Clark. He left Freyberg and Alexander to get on with things at Cassino while he concentrated on the gathering crisis at Anzio. In the light of the attritional battles about to be fought at Cassino perhaps another division might have been better suited? But at the time the situation was read quite differently. While the New Zealanders took over from the 34th Division along the Rapido and in front of Cassino it was to be the task of the 4th Indian Division to take the high ground and clear the way for an advance into the Liri Valley.

The 4th Indian Division with its Red Eagle insignia was made up largely of volunteers. There were three brigades in the division, each comprising a British, an Indian and a Gurkha battalion. The three nationalities contributed a balanced fighting force; the British infanteer, dogged and unruffled in defence; the Indian *jawan* recruited from the martial castes, bold and dashing in attack; the Gurkha, loyal and steadfast, adept at patrolling, wicked in night operations and of course at home in the mountains. When they were well led by British and Indian officers, these troops were almost matchless in their military proficiency. Unlike the New Zealanders, especially when it came to military etiquette, spit and polish, these men were happier in the close infantry encounter rather than in exploitation, and had no problems with difficult terrain.

The German defenders had not been relieved though the 15th Panzer Grenadiers were now supported by the bulk of their corps artillery, some 180 guns, numbers of the terrifying Nebelwerfers and about 50 or 60 tanks. There were ample forces to hold that ground, given the geographical advantages.

The Indians were commanded by Major General 'Gertie' Tuker, a man with a brilliant military record, who had led his division through North Africa. Tuker was more akin to Von Senger, a man possessed of incisive intellect, prepared for the unconventional when it came to tactics, and always willing to try something new and different. It was Tuker who first called for the bombing of the monastery. That was directly after he learned that the 4th Indian Division were assigned to capture Monastery Hill. He was convinced that it was being used by the enemy for artillery observation. Mark Clark had placed the monastery out of bounds for Keyes in his attack and the Americans were bitterly resentful of such a limitation. Major Luther H. Wolff MD, still with the Eleventh Field Hospital on Monte Lungo, wrote:

> The infantry boys that come in wounded tell us they are taking a terrific beating trying to save the monastery at Cassino and it makes everybody angry that the big boys insist on saving this building. We simply have to get over this sentimental fair play, save-the-building-attitude ... the wounded GIs are universally in favour of knocking down the monastery.[3]

No one, either at Fifth Army or Army Group Headquarters, knew very much about the monastery. On 12 February Tuker wrote a paper to Freyberg which began: 'After considerable trouble and investigating many bookstalls in Naples I have at last found a book dated 1879 which gives certain details of the construction of the Monte Cassino Monastery.'[4] Tuker went on to describe the dimensions of this fortress-like structure which had walls which were 100 feet wide and 15 feet high, etc. In Tuker's judgement such a structure could only be reduced by blockbuster bombs. He went on to criticize the indolent staff at Caserta for not having such information to hand obliging the divisional commander 'to go to the bookstalls of Naples to find out what should have been fully considered many weeks before'.

Freyberg agreed with Tuker, and bluntly told Al Greunther, 'I want the convent attacked.'[5] Clark would have none of it. He did not consider the monastery a legitimate military target. Its destruction would be an act of historic vandalism. But, like Pontius Pilate, he passed the buck to Alexander. The Army Group Commander shouldered the responsibility and Jumbo Wilson, together with Devers, braved the elements and flew low over the monastery in a spotter aircraft. Both claimed to have seen radio aerials.

Freyberg repeated his demand that the monastery be bombed immediately, but was blocked by Mark Clark. At that time the II (US) Corps had a battalion on the hill awaiting relief from 4th Indian Division. These troops were too close to the monastery, inside the distance called the bomb safety line. Clark used this subterfuge to stall Freyberg until the New Zealand Corps assumed full responsibility for the front.

In his memoirs Alexander defended his decision to go ahead with the bombing.

> When soldiers are fighting for a just cause and are prepared to suffer death and mutilation in the process, bricks and mortar, no matter how venerable, cannot be allowed to wear against human lives. Every good commander must consider the morale and feelings of his fighting men and what is equally important, fighting men must know that their whole existence is in the hands of a man in whom they have complete confidence. How could such a structure which dominated the field of battle be allowed to stand? The Monastery had to be destroyed.[6]

Keen to examine all the options available, General Tuker spent time with General Juin who believed that the best avenue of attack still lay through the mountains, where his own people had failed. There was heavy snow, but the Indian Division had experienced mountain troops. Freyberg didn't agree.

On 12 February Tuker submitted another proposal. A wide swing through the mountains could deliver a sequence of fast, short-range jabs to the west and south-west of Monte Castellone and cut Highway 6 west of Monastery Hill. The fates conspired to rob the Allies of a victory. On the eve of the battle Tuker was taken seriously ill with a recurrence of a tropical disease and was evacuated to hospital. The division's CRA Brigadier Dimoline, assumed command of the division at a critical

THE STRUGGLE FOR CASSINO

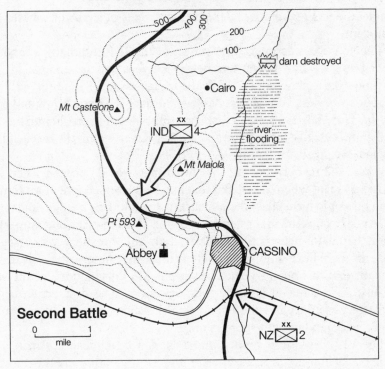

500
400
300
200
100

dam destroyed

•Cairo

Mt Castelone ▲

IND ⊠ 4

river flooding

▲Mt Maiola

Pt 593 ▲

Abbey ✝

CASSINO

Second Battle

0 _____ 1
mile

NZ ⊠ 2

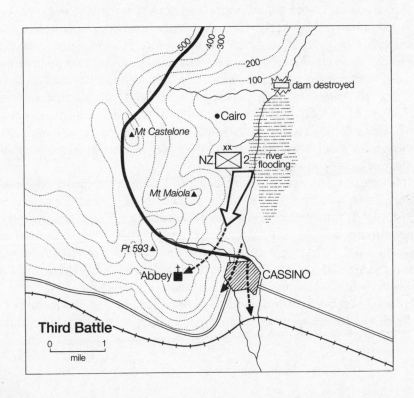

500
400
300
200
100

dam destroyed

•Cairo

▲ Mt Castelone

NZ ⊠ 2

river flooding

Mt Maiola ▲

Pt 593 ▲

Abbey ✝

CASSINO

Third Battle

0 _____ 1
mile

moment, and Freyberg was denied the services of a trusted adviser and confidant.

The solution was to go for a repeat of the II Corps battle – another frontal attack – only bigger and better. Freyberg planned to use his two divisions like a giant pincer. While the Indians scaled Monastery Hill and the monastery the New Zealanders would clear the town below and open the door for Harmon's armour, still waiting patiently to erupt into the Liri Valley and ride like the 7th Cavalry, not for Rome, but to the rescue of the Anzio beachhead.

Why did Freyberg believe that his troops would succeed where the Americans had failed? Clark felt that had he possessed one more combat team he would have taken the monastery. He told Freyberg as much, that with fresh troops the monastery should fall. The New Zealand Corps was fresh, battalions were up to full strength and Freyberg was arrogant enough to believe they were better than the Americans. Alexander thought that this plan, so singularly lacking in imagination, would work because of the magic ingredient of air power. The destruction of the monastery would blind the enemy and the shock bombardment would numb its defenders into submission.

The VI (US) Corps, pinned into a shallow beachhead at Anzio, with their backs literally to the sea, were under unrelenting pressure from a German counterattack. All things being equal Freyberg would probably have waited a few weeks for the promise of better weather before launching his assault, but now he was under real pressure from two sources. One was Churchill. A German victory at Anzio would have the most severe political repercussions for him at home, as well as with Roosevelt, who had been persuaded to delay Overlord in favour of Shingle. Mark Clark was none too happy either. A defeat at Anzio would be a terrible reverse for Fifth Army and bad for his reputation. Even though the Fifth Army strategy had been forced upon him by Churchill, this was of little comfort.

So great was the sense of urgency that Lemnitzer approached the air forces next morning, 13 February, to have them bomb the monastery. Fortunately the weather was not suitable for a heavy raid, and the delay permitted a little more time for the infantry divisions to get themselves sorted out. Leaflets were dropped on the monastery, warning the monks and refugees sheltering there to leave. Some of the refugees left and the 82-year-old abbot approached the Germans to arrange for an evacuation. General Von Senger was not only a devout Catholic but a lay member of the Benedictine Order. He knew the monastery was vulnerable and for some weeks had tried to persuade the abbot and his monks to leave. They had refused, but many of the monastery's art treasures had been removed to Rome for safe keeping. The Germans agreed to have transport available to evacuate all the remaining people in the monastery.

The sun shone on the morning of 15 February so the air forces decided to strike. There was no coordination between the various staffs to ensure that ground troops would be ready to follow up with an immediate attack, nor was any attempt made to ensure that the ground troops were a safe distance from the intended target.

Two hundred and twenty-five bombers took off. The first that the Indian Division knew about it was when the first stick of bombs fell amongst their forward troops. Some 142 B-17 Flying Fortresses dropped 350 tons of high explosives and incendiaries. They were followed by the medium bombers who were intended to complete the task. The magnificent basilica and the buildings within the monastery precincts were destroyed, but the outer walls remained intact. There were not many casualties because the abbot (who had not left) and his people took cover in the deepest cellars.

Luther Wolff had a grandstand view of the big event:

A sight to gladden the eye today. Seventy-two B-17s came over about 9.00 am, very high and knocked the monastery down. There were over 100 B-25s and B-26s which bombed the same areas while some A-36s finished it off. Boy! was that something to watch. It should have been done a month ago, though. It is said that 200 Germans ran out of the building after the first bombing run and our artillery really let them have it. Jerry is still throwing shells into the area just over the hill though. Another terrifically wounded case today, which I operated on, but I am afraid there is no chance for his survival. I am beginning to feel all is futile.[7]

After the bombers had finished, the artillery opened fire. A single company of the 4th Indian Division pushed forward to Calvary Hill. The New Zealanders had no intention of attacking, especially in broad daylight. Their avenue of advance lay west across the flood plain of the Rapido by way of the railway causeway and into the town. The ground was mined and had to be cleared and the causeway was breached in several places, which had to be bridged. The approach was wide enough to allow just one battalion to be deployed on a two-company frontage. In these confined conditions this was the total strength that the division could deploy, and even this advance would depend upon the speed and ability of the sappers to clear and bridge the causeway.

For the 7th Indian Brigade the task of supplying the forward battalions and securing ground could only be accomplished with heavy losses. The commanding officer of 1st Battalion Royal Sussex, Lt Colonel John Glennie, wrote in his diary:

> We were therefore in full view of the enemy from all sides – we had no reserve rations and barely one blanket per man . . . everybody behind worked hard to get us supplies, but the shortage of mules, the length of the daily march – seven miles each way after dark – and the heavy shelling and mortaring of mule tracks, all combined to keep the admin situation bad.[8]

The Germans were on Point 593 less than 70 yards away. Monte Calvaro (Calvary Mount) or Point 593 on military maps, overlooked the monastery. No assault on Cassino was possible as long as this shell-torn peak remained in German hands. It was destined to be captured and lost many times. When the 7th Infantry Brigade commander had reported to 34th (US) Division CP to liaise to hand over this part of the front he was assured, and the maps showed, that Point 593 was in American hands.

On the night of 15 February Glennie got one company of his Royal Sussex onto the lower slopes of Point 593. They hung on grimly until dark. The remainder of the battalion stormed forward with bayonet and grenade and reinforced their comrades. Fierce opposition from the enemy at last showed signs of weakening as the Royal Sussex reached the peak of the hill. A German fired three green flares. By a tragic coincidence this was the Royal Sussex withdrawal signal. Bewildered and confused, and out of radio contact, the leading company's commander ordered a withdrawal. The Royal Sussex fell back down the hill, taking scores of their wounded with them.

The battalion had lost 16 officers and 162 men to no good purpose – this was only meant to be a preliminary to the battle. The major offensive began when the two divisions launched their combined attack on 17 February, a bleak winter's night. The 28th Maori Battalion spearheaded the attack across the railway causeway. Under intense mortar and machine-gun fire they worked their way forward through the minefield. Behind them the sappers worked wonders to clear the way and bridge the gaps that would allow the tanks to roll forward. Daylight found the Maoris in the town's railway station and the sappers with all the gaps except the last bridged. There was no way they could work in the daylight. It would have been a massacre. The sappers retreated and the Maoris were cut off. The ruined station offered scant cover and from the mountainside looming over them the enemy could observe their every movement.

General Kippenberger, the division commander, was in a dilemma. He had to decide whether to have his artillery lay down smoke through the day to protect the Maoris, (which would allow the enemy to counterattack without being observed by the guns), or to leave them under observed enemy fire and hope the guns could beat off the counterattack.

Kippenberger chose the lesser of two evils and the guns kept up a bombardment of white smoke. In the mid-afternoon the Germans put in a counterattack spearheaded by tanks. The Maoris had little choice but to retire, which they did in good order, to their start lines. They suffered 130 casualties. In the meantime the Indian troops were having a bleak time on Monastery Hill. Point 593 could only be taken by infantry assault. With no-man's-land just 70 yards in width there was no way that artillery could be used.

It was now the turn of the three battalions of the 11th Indian Brigade. The plan was for the 4th/6th Rajputana Rifles to move through the 1st Royal Sussex positions and storm Point 593. Then two Gurkha battalions, 1st/2nd and 1st/9th Gurkha Rifles, were to assault the monastery. Once these positions were secure the battalions would move into the north of Cassino town and link up with the Maoris.

The 4th/6th Rajputana Rifles reached the top of Point 593 but were beaten back. The battalion suffered 196 casualties; only two of its British officers returned unscathed. The Gurkhas battled their way forward, but with Point 593 only partially covered, they were caught in a cross-fire and unable to make progress; by dawn they were back on their start line. There were rumours long after the battle that one platoon of Gurkhas reached the monastery, but there were no survivors and neither were any bodies found. Between them the two battalions of Gurkhas suffered 250 casualties and despite many acts of bravery and heroism not a yard of ground was gained.

With the Maoris beaten back out of the town, there seemed little point in prolonging the battle. The Germans were left in possession of the field and the well-oiled wheels of Dr Goebbels' propaganda machine made the most of the destruction of a holy shrine. Von Senger was now free to occupy the monastery and turn it into an impregnable fortress.

The Allied bombing was not wrong, though some regarded it as a sin. The great sin was the complete lack of coordination between the air and ground attacks.

And Anzio? The beleaguered beachhead would stand or fall through its own efforts.

Notes

1. Smith, *The Battles for Cassino*, p 86.
2. Ernie Pyle wrote about the experiences in his Scripps-Howard column. He covered the war from North Africa to the fall of Paris and then moved to the Far East. On 18 April 1945 he was killed by a Japanese sniper on a small island close to Okinawa.
3. Wolff, *Forward Surgeon*.
4. Smith, *The Battles for Cassino*, pp 86–7.
5. Ibid., p 87.
6. Ibid., p 89.
7. Wolff, *Forward Surgeon*, p 77.
8. Smith, *The Battles for Cassino*, p 89.

36

Lancing the Abscess

The German High Command viewed the Allied beachhead as a heaven-sent opportunity. Tenth Army was ordered to hold the Gustav Line at all costs. This explains the ferocity of some of the counterattacks in the closing stages of both the First and Second Battles of Cassino. The idea was that von Mackensen's Fourteenth Army should overwhelm the Allies at Anzio with the utmost ferocity and bring about the most monumental military disaster to complete the unfinished business at Salerno.

The German High Command intended to teach the Allies a lesson. If an amphibious operation failed in Italy what chance of success would there be for a landing on the French coast, which boasted the massive defences of the Western Wall and was masterminded by Rommel, the scourge of Allied generals? The long retreat which had begun at El Alamein would be halted.

The very best in men and weapons, top-grade units were despatched south. A total of 33 battalions of infantry, some of whom were elite *Lehr* (demonstration) units from the Infantry Battle Training School at Spandau; 250 guns and regiments of panzers, including the redoubtable Tigers and Panthers, massed for the counteroffensive. The beachhead was bombarded by the heaviest artillery, which included a mighty railway-mounted 28-cm gun dubbed 'Anzio Annie' or 'Anzio Express' by the Allies[1] (the Germans called it 'Leopold'). There was also a deluge of propaganda. The first batch (including surrender documents) was aimed at troops in the beachhead. Graphic cartoons spelled out the dire consequences that would shortly be visited upon the defenders. Cartoon drawings and lurid photographs also showed American GIs stationed in Britain with English women in postures which left little to the imagination. Amongst some units these leaflets became collectables, with the men swopping duplicates like the cigarette cards they had collected in their youth. The propaganda leaflets fulfilled another useful function; combat rations never had sufficient toilet paper.

Ultra proved invaluable in forecasting what Kesselring had in store. Hitler's flamboyant Order of the Day for 28 January, in which Anzio was described as an abscess, was being read at Caserta on 2 February. The Order gave the Allies chapter and verse on the planned offensive. Further decrypts revealed details of Kesselring's complete tank strengths and their deployment, along with a top-secret document which detailed the battle plan. Called *Fischtang* (Fishing), it revealed that von Mackensen had at least 25 Mark VIs, 20 Mark V (Tigers), 25 assault guns and 90 heavy anti-tank guns at his disposal.[2]

The plan was to strike down the main road, the Via Anziate, from Campoleone station to the beach at Anzio. Kesselring's orders also contained the complete order of battle for Fourteenth Army and named 1 February as the start of the battle provided that all the forces were assembled. If not, there would be a delay. Allied intelligence assessments were spot-on with their predictions.

The Allied commanders planned for the inevitable. Alexander withdrew Templer's 56th (Br) Infantry Division from the Cassino front and sent it up to the Anzio front as reinforcement. It was to take three weeks to complete the move. Frederick and his North Americans were also despatched to Anzio. There wasn't anything higher than a single-storey building in the beachhead for these lightly armed mountain specialists to defend, so their deployment can only be viewed as a terrible waste of expertise.

Alexander visited Anzio again before the big counterattack. He had, by this time, lost all confidence in Lucas. He voiced his fears to Penny and Truscott. Penny agreed, pointing out that the Corps Commander had never visited his front and didn't seem to have any ideas on what to do. Penny had been Alexander's signal officer in Fifteen Army Group and Alexander trusted him.

Truscott never uttered a word to Alexander about Lucas. But Alexander, convinced that Lucas never even ventured from the house which served as his CP, advised Clark that he should be replaced. At first Clark stood by Lucas, partly because he dismissed criticisms made by Penny. Indeed Clark sneeringly referred to Penny saying that as 'a division commander he made a good telephone operator'.[3]

The most obvious line of the German counterattack was against the British sector. Clark visited Penny and criticized his deployments. The

1st Infantry Division was badly strung out in an exposed salient manned by the 3rd Brigade which had been so savagely mauled. The salient, three miles in length, stuck out like a sore thumb and was asking to be amputated. Lucas had told Clark of his concern and that he had ordered Penny to pull his troops back, but he had refused. Clark advised Penny to pull out of the exposed salient but he dismissed such warnings and told the Army Commander that Alexander had been with him earlier in the day and told him he was doing fine.

Clark was right. Alexander and Penny were wrong. Lucas deployed the 3rd Battalion of the 504th (US) Parachute Infantry Regiment to reinforce the Irish Guards. They moved into a back-up position across the Albano–Anzio road in front of a village called Carroceto. National rivalries may have driven mighty wedges between commanders at the top but at this level there were no such problems. The American paras and Irish Guardsmen worked together with great rapport. Hitherto the Irish Guards had called the Germans 'Heimies', 'Boche' or 'Jerries'; from the Americans they learned a new word; they called them 'Krauts'.

The two commanding officers became close friends. They had a daily routine. Lt Colonel Andrew Scott, Eton, Sandhurst *et al.* would greet Lt Colonel Leslie Freeman of 3/504th with an exaggerated American accent. 'Hiya, Colonel Freeman, what d'ya know.'

The American would smile and respond every day with the same thing. 'Not a goddamned thing.'[4]

The Germans put in a limited attack. The key objective was Aprilia, known to the British as the Factory. It was important because it controlled the road network leading to Anzio and Nettuno. This collection of stone buildings had been constructed by Mussolini as a model farm community and the thick-walled structures and outbuildings were now pressed into service as a fort rather like Hougement at Waterloo.

The Germans attacked the thumb on the night of 3 February. They hit the British from three sides. The Germans broke through halfway down the thumb, from the west and east. The Irish Guards in the west and the Gordons in the east retreated in good order and fell back on a base line held steady by Freeman's paratroopers. The London Irish and the Royal Berkshires were cut off in the Factory. Clark was in the beachhead, extremely worried by the depleted strength of the British. By this stage Penny had used up all his reserves and had even taken the 168th Infantry Brigade of 56th Division as it stepped ashore. There was also a critical shortage of artillery shells. Clark ordered a last-ditch beach defence line to be constructed near a key feature called the Flyover.[5]

The battle for the Factory raged for 48 hours, while the Germans attacked elsewhere along the British front. In places the fighting was hand-to-hand. Buonriposo Ridge changed hands twice. On the morning of 9 February the Germans advanced behind an overwhelming barrage of shells and the Factory disappeared from sight. Some 40 men of the Royal Berkshires made it back to the Allied lines, but none from the London Irish. The German 735th Panzer Grenadier Regiment occupied the Factory and the thumb was amputated.

The losses on both sides were more appropriate to the first day on the Somme. The 1st British Infantry Division was down to less than half its fighting strength and there were no British reserves in the beachhead. The Allies estimated that, in the three days of the battle, the enemy had suffered 60% casualties.

Clark ordered the 45th (US) Infantry to take over a portion of the British line. The VI (US) Corps were now back on their last defence line anchored on the Flyover bridge; it was seven miles to the sea. An ominous calm fell across the front.

The Germans attacked again in strength on 16 February behind a 30-minute bombardment the like of which the Allies had never experienced. It was a wet, foggy day with a lot of low cloud, which grounded the Allied air force. Hitler insisted that the attack was to be led by the elite Berlin-Spandau Infantry Lehr Regiment. It was a mistake. The Lehr were drilled to perfection but they were not battle-hardened.

Along with the Lehr, von Mackensen had massed five divisions to strike at the Allied lines; these included 3rd Panzer Grenadiers and 114th and 715th Infantry Divisions. The 26th Panzers and 29th Panzer Grenadiers waited on the Albano–Anzio road ready to exploit the hole punched in the Allied defence by the Lehr and drive straight to the sea. The Germans also had a secret weapon. The Goliath was a robot mini-tank filled with high explosive. Thirteen were to be unleashed against the Allied frontlines – they proved quite ineffective.

The 45th (US) Infantry Division, defending a six-mile front, took the full force of the impact but along the perimeter the Germans mounted further attacks, masking their intentions and preventing Lucas from taking men from a quiet sector to reinforce that where the threat was greatest. In the east Truscott's 3rd Infantry held its own, but some British positions were overrun. The main blow struck the 45th (US) Infantry at the Flyover. The Germans attacked heedless of casualties. The Americans held firm and it was the Lehr, blasted by the tremendous weight of Allied fire power, who broke. With the majority of their officers dead the elite fled from the battlefield in disorder and panic. The rout of the infantry eased the pressure on the defenders and robbed the offensive of its momentum.

Alexander broached the matter of Lucas to Clark a third time. The Army Group Commander had already voiced his concern to Alan Brooke in London and asked him to consult with the Prime Minister and Eisenhower. Lucas, he said, was tired and depressed. He never strayed from his CP dug deep into a cellar in Nettuno and his depression had spread to his staff. What was needed at Anzio was a 'thruster like Georgie Patton'.[6] Brooke immediately got hold of Eisenhower, and he in turn contacted Patton who was in England preparing the Third Army for an as yet undefined role. Eisenhower told Patton to pack a bag and stand by for further instructions. Patton didn't know whether he would take over VI (US) Corps or Fifth Army, but it didn't matter, it was action.

Brooke was summoned to discuss the matter with Churchill. The Prime Minister proposed that Alexander should go to the beachhead and take over the battle. Uncharacteristically Alan Brooke turned on Churchill and snapped: 'Can't you, for once, trust your commanders to organize their command for themselves without interfering and upsetting all the chain and sequence of command?'[7]

Unusually Churchill did as he was told.

Alexander approached Clark again.

Wayne, I am very much dissatisfied with General Lucas. I have no confidence in him and his ability to control the situation. I very much fear that there might be a disaster at Anzio with Lucas in command and you know what will happen to you and me if there is a disaster at Anzio.[8]

It was as neat a piece of blackmail as one could imagine, but Clark still wriggled on the hook. That evening a signal was received at VI (US) Corps and at headquarters of the 3rd (US) Infantry Division.

ORDERS ISSUED THIS DATE AS FOLLOWS X MAJOR GENERAL TRUSCOTT RELIEVED FROM COMMAND OF THIRD DIVISION AND ASSIGNED AS DEPUTY COMMANDER SIXTH CORPS X BRIGADIER GENERAL O'DANIEL TO COMMAND THIRD DIVISION X COLONEL DARBY TRANSFERRED FROM RANGER FORCE TO THIRD DIVISION X ALL ASSIGNMENTS TO TAKE EFFECT SEVENTEEN FEBRUARY X I DESIRE THAT COLONEL SHERMAN BE DESIGNATED AS ACTING ASSISTANT DIVISION COMMANDER AND THAT DARBY BE PLACED IN COMMAND OF SHERMAN'S REGIMENT X ACKNOWLEDGE.[9]

Clark had reviewed his options. The solution was a compromise. He would leave Lucas where he was until the crisis at Anzio had been resolved. Then he would be replaced. The choice was Truscott or Harmon, who was his classmate at West Point and a close friend. Clark picked Truscott because though *'we had our little disagreements'*,[10] he had confidence in his tactical abilities and aggressiveness; he was a hard fighter. Truscott would be Assistant Corps Commander but in effect would take over the tactical direction of the battle and then, at the appropriate time, assume command. 'Iron' Mike O'Daniel was a close friend of Clark's who had been used hitherto as a sort of troubleshooter. Darby, of course, was without a command since the loss of his Rangers, and Clark was anxious to keep him in the theatre.[11] The compromise was accepted by everyone. The two disappointed men were Lucas, who was under no illusions about his position, and Patton who was told to unpack his bag.

The Germans tried again the next morning. Three regiments of panzer grenadiers and six battalions of infantry supported by 60 tanks advanced against the 179th Infantry Regiment. The Germans had been told that the 45th (US) Infantry was a National Guard outfit manned largely by Red Indians, racially inferior people who had no love of the white man and probably wouldn't fight. How wrong they were. But the sheer weight of the attack did force the American defenders to give ground. A wedge two and a half miles wide and a mile deep was punched in the line. But the Thunderbirds didn't flee, they packed the shoulders and the Germans were sucked into the killing ground.

As the Germans poured exultantly into the gap, the whole weight of Allied artillery (some 432 guns) and the broadsides from cruisers offshore opened fire. The situation was grave. As the day progressed the Germans, with elements of six divisions in the battle, had driven a salient nearly four miles deep in the centre of the Allied line. It was less than three miles to the sea.

British infantry on the western flank of the beachhead fought among the irrigation ditches that fed the Mussolini Canal. Though more akin to Passchendaele, the desert veterans among them called it 'wadi country'.

The Wadis – those muddy death traps into which complete subunits of men, tortured by lack of sleep, would vanish from the ken of commanding officers. . . . In the wadis there was a continuous draining of strength by casualties from mortaring and shelling and disappearances on reconnaissance and patrol. Another complete company disappeared, having stumbled by night into enemy-held territory, and was swallowed up. Unbeknown and heterogeneous reinforcements had to be absorbed in the heat of battle and there was constant reorganization and re-squadding. There had, by this time, been an 80% change-over in personnel since January.[12]

Truscott gathered what forces he could for a counterattack. There was the 6th (US) Armoured Infantry Regiment, 169th Infantry Brigade from 56th Division which had arrived that morning and the 30th Infantry Regiment from 3rd (US) Division where the front was secure.

On 18 February Clark was in the beachhead. He met with Lucas and Truscott in the corps CP and asked their intentions. Truscott proposed a counterattack against the flanks of the salient. Clark agreed with Truscott. The plans were drawn up, and Lucas' fate was sealed. It was simple enough. In a covering attack, General Harmon would lead Force H, which comprised his armoured infantry and 30th Infantry Regiment and push north-westwards into the salient. General Templer had Force T and would lead his 169th Brigade northwards from the Flyover. Clark promised to lay on maximum air support and the attack was to begin the following morning.

The timing was perfect. The Germans in the salient had suffered grievously and had lost their momentum when at 0600 hours on 19 February Allied artillery, some 400 guns joined by ships at sea, opened fire. The guns concentrated on the enemy front lines and assembly and artillery areas. Half an hour later both task groups began the advance and the artillery lifted in successive concentrations as the attack progressed. After first light more than 200 medium and fighter-bombers blasted enemy artillery and concentration areas and communications. But still the Germans resisted stubbornly. The battle continued without respite until 22 February. British and American troops fought side by side and in places used one another's weapons. Mutual exhaustion then set in and the battle died down.

Between 16 and 22 February the VI (US) Corps had suffered 5,000 casualties and since the start of Operation Shingle nearly 20,000 men in the beachhead were dead, wounded or missing. Long lines of Allied POWs being marched through Rome like a latter-day imperial triumph had become a common sight.

Clark relieved Lucas that same day. He tried to ease the blow by appointing him Deputy Commander Fifth Army, but the older man knew it was a sham and could not hide his bitter resentment. He believed that he had been the victim of a British conspiracy which Clark had been too weak to withstand. Clark maintained the façade for a month, then sent Lucas back to the United States.

Notes

1. Later captured at Civitavecchia and taken to the USA where it is now on show at the Artillery Museum of Aberdeen Proving Ground.
2. Bennet, Ralph, *Ultra and Mediterranean Strategy 1941–45*, Hamish Hamilton, 1989, p 267.
3. Matthews interview with Clark, p 76; Clark also said much the same thing to the author in 1980.
4. Breuer, W., *Agony at Anzio*, Robert Hale, 1985, p 86.
5. This was a bridge built over the Albano–Anzio road intended for a new east–west road, but the war came before the new road could be built.
6. Blumenson, *Mark Clark*, p 182.
7. Adleman and Walton, *Rome Fell Today*, p 164.
8. Matthews interview with Alexander, p 28.
9. Truscott, *Command Missions*, p 319.
10. Matthews interview with Clark, p 7.
11. In the event Darby actually replaced the Regimental CO of the 179th Infantry in the 45th Infantry Division.
12. Regimental History Royal Ulster Rifles (London Irish), quoted in Ellis, *The Sharp End*, p 72.

37

The Ides of March:
Third Cassino – The Unnecessary Battle

Amidst all the clamour and crisis the staff found time to play around with the titles of the forces in Italy. Between January and March 1944 it changed four times. Before 11 January it was Fifteen Army Group; from 11 to 18 January it became Allied Forces in Italy; on 18 January it became Allied Central Mediterranean Forces; and finally on 9 March Churchill suggested Allied Armies in Italy, AAI.

Another bone of contention was also resolved. Clark had been pestered by just about everybody from Marshall to Wilson, about his intentions with regard to the Seventh Army and Operation Anvil. Clark was under no illusions. Fame and fortune lay with the Seventh Army into France, but there was no way he could extricate himself from the current mess and retain any self-respect. Even though he knew that after Rome, Italy would be of marginal concern, he declined Seventh Army. Major General Alexander Patch, who had fought the Japanese in Guadalcanal in February 1943, had since been in North Africa where he served as commander of the Desert Training Centre. It was now considered unlikely that the Americans would be fighting in the desert, so Patch was promoted Lieutenant General and given command of Seventh Army.

In the meantime, Freyberg was determined to have another crack at Cassino. The Third Battle, in concept and execution, was probably the most controversial of the battles to break through the Gustav Line. It was also unnecessary.

The immediate need, when orders were first drafted, was to relieve VI (US) Corps at Anzio who at the time were experiencing the heaviest of the German counterattacks aimed to drive them into the sea. General Juin pleaded to be allowed another crack at the Germans north of Monte Caira but both Alexander and Clark turned this down. The weather in their view was just too awful in those high mountains, even for the hardy goumiers. It was up to the New Zealand Corps. However, Freyberg would not be rushed, and since he was a near co-equal rather than a subordinate, he got his way. By the time the battle began in mid-March the crisis had passed at Anzio and the front had stabilized, albeit precariously.

It was decided to apply air power on an unprecedented scale in an attempt to prove that strategic bombers could not only contribute tactically, but could win the land battle. Such was the confidence in this tactic of the very senior commanders that Major General Harding, Alexander's Chief of Staff at Fifteenth Army Group, started to plan the fourth battle before the third had even got underway.

The arrogance of the apostles of air power was staggering. A thousand tons of bombs dropped on Cassino town followed immediately by an artillery barrage of 200,000 shells, was reckoned to be enough to cause massive casualties. The assumption was that those who weren't dead or entombed would be too shell-shocked to offer any resistance. Alexander and Freyberg were sold on the idea, but in fairness Mark Clark remained more dubious.[1] Freyberg wanted a victory, but not at any price. He was mindful of the need to keep New Zealand casualties to a minimum and, if artillery could do the job for him, so much the better.

As far as the Third Battle was concerned, Mark Clark opted out of the chain of command. Freyberg worked out his own plans without much interference. Clark was more concerned with Anzio where he was to spend a lot of his time, and also wished to distance himself from this operation. Freyberg planned for the New Zealanders to advance on Cassino town after the bombardment, secure the town and take Castle Hill. The 5th Indian Brigade would then pass through the New Zealanders and attack the monastery from Castle Hill.

Kippenberger described the plan as follows:

> This time the two divisions would attack side by side from the north and roll up the defences one by one. New Zealand Division was to assault down the Rapido Valley, capture the town and castle and a bridgehead opening out into the Liri Valley through which the tanks could be poured. After we had gained the town, the Indians would move on our right flank, clear the hill-side by stages under full view and support of our guns and then turn uphill to storm the abbey, which meantime would be threatened from the opposite side, the line of the earlier attacks.

If all of this worked according to plan the New Zealanders would unlock the gate to Rome. Behind the New Zealanders the 78th (Br) Infantry Division together with Combat Command B of the 1st (US) Armoured Division would storm up the Liri Valley and link up with the embattled VI (US) Corps at Anzio before driving on to Rome.

Clark thought that the most that the New Zealand Corps could achieve was to take the town and establish a bridgehead across the Rapido – in other words to establish a jump-off position for a new attack. He did not expect that an attack on a limited front at that time would send the Germans reeling up the Liri Valley. The best that could be achieved was that the Germans would be forced to retreat to their next defensive position, still referred to as the Hitler Line and anchored in the beachhead at Anzio.

The enemy at Cassino had changed. General Heidrich's 1st Parachute Rifle Division had, since the end of February, taken over the critical eight miles of Cassino defences from Baade's 90th Panzer Grenadiers. The New Zealand Corps found themselves opposed by Germany's toughest fighting men. The paras were, however, much depleted in numbers; most battalions were down to 300 men and in many cases there were less than 40 to a company. The timing of the battle was also conditioned by the need for clear weather, otherwise the bombers would not be able to see the target. Rain and low cloud persisted throughout the first two weeks of March and then the forecasters predicted that from the 15th there would be three days of clear weather.

Enemy artillery and mortar fire continued to cause a steady drip of casualties and the paras suffered in equal measure. The front was littered with mines which even in the so-called rear areas were a threat to those who strayed from a well-trodden path.

On 2 March Major General Kippenberger was on Monte Trocchio viewing the enemy positions. On the way down he stepped on a mine. One foot was blown off and his other leg so badly mangled that it had to be amputated below the knee. This meant that both divisions were now in the hands of comparative newcomers. The 4th Indian Division's Dimoline had been replaced by Major General Galloway and the New Zealanders were led by Major General Parkinson. With both of these officers having their hands full fighting their first battles in command of divisions, it placed an even greater strain on Freyberg. Had Tuker and Kippenberger been with him things might have turned out differently.

In the night of 14, 15 March, Freyberg withdrew his forward units 2,000 yards behind the bomb line. Infantry hate to withdraw voluntarily across ground that has been hard-won, but on this occasion there was no alternative. The Germans failed to spot the move, so the air raids, when they started, took them completely by surprise. The first bombers attacked at 8.00 am that morning and most of the top brass were on hand to watch the show. Alexander arrived at nine o'clock. A special VIP observation post had been set up on the second floor of an old stone house at Cervaro, about three miles from the monastery. There Alexander was joined by Clark, Leese, Ira Eaker (who commanded the air forces) and lesser notables. The Generals stayed until after 2 pm, enjoying a picnic lunch while Cassino burned.

The target at Cassino was 400 yards wide by 1,400 yards long. Into that area 550 heavy and medium bombers aimed 1,250 tons of high explosive and incendiary bombs. Aimed of course is the operative word. It is conservatively estimated that about half of the bombs fell within the target area, but bombs fell liberally in the general area and some as much as ten miles to the south. Even the picnicking generals were at times a little concerned. A further 200 fighter-bombers and fighters strafed targets of opportunity. The town, which had been heavily damaged in the previous battles, was devastated. There was not a building left standing. Eyewitness accounts by paratroopers describe the terror of the attack.

Lt Schuster O/C 7 Coy wrote:

> We could no longer see each other, all we could do was to touch and feel the next man. The blackness of night enveloped us and on our tongues was the taste of burnt earth. I had to grope my way forwards and through a dense fog then down came the bombs again. Direct hits here, and here, and here – when I got back the men read in my face what I had seen. The same unspoken thoughts were in all our minds – when would it be our turn?[2]

The first wave of bombers hit the town and then there was a pause. Thereafter wave after wave of bombers passed over Cassino in a raid that lasted for four and a half hours. Once the last bomber had flown by it was the turn of the guns. The Staff Quartermaster of Fifth Army had assembled 600,000 shells for the third battle and they were all needed. There were 748 field and heavy pieces of artillery and for the rest of that day they expended 195,969 shells on Cassino – the town and the monastery. In mid-afternoon the guns fell silent, but the monastery was shelled through the rest of the day and into the early hours of the morning.

Beneath the town was an entire network of underground sewers and waterways. Most of the civilians had left Cassino, but some, those who couldn't or wouldn't, sought refuge in this subterranean labyrinth.

Barthel Kuckeritz was a paratrooper at Cassino:

Mostly it was old people, women and children, who were near starvation in the sewers. We didn't have orders to drive these people off, and were not able to care for them with the means we had available. It was sheer misery! There were corpses wrapped in sheets piled metre-high in individual niches. Most of the living were sick with rashes all over their bodies. Children with sunken eyes begged us for something to eat. We left bread and fruit in the entryways; we were afraid to go into these holes in the ground.[3]

The town of Cassino was garrisoned by the 2nd Battalion of the 3rd Parachute Regiment. The battalion started 15 March with 300 men, but after the bombing the battalion's commander Captain Foltin had lost at least 160 men dead, wounded or entombed beneath tons of masonry. The subsequent barrage took its toll. But, given the degree of collateral damage, German casualties were nothing like as heavy as they might have been. Captain Foltin seized the chance presented by the lull after the first bombing wave to put his reserve company into the cave where he had his command post. It was to prove a critical decision.

The New Zealanders attacked at 1530 hours. The 25th Battalion of the 5th Infantry Brigade led the assault. This was another flaw in the battle plan. Not only was the front too narrow and constricted, but the battalion had to advance along the same path as the Maoris had done previously. The New Zealanders moved slowly and methodically behind a lifting barrage, men confident that no one could have survived in the town. But the paras had survived, or at least enough of them with their wits about them to man positions and bring their weapons to bear. Machine guns and mortars began to tear great holes in the New Zealand ranks as they tried to cross the killing ground.

Alexander was genuinely amazed that there could be any resistance.[4] Loth to accept the fallibility of airpower, he maintained that only the Parachute Division had the discipline and training to survive and offer a coherent defence. In one sense he was correct. Parachute troops are trained to fight from the outset without the benefit of direction and coordination. At Cassino, the paras improvised strongpoints and cared not a jot whether their flanks were secure or they were in touch with the battalion. As the New Zealanders forced their way into the town isolated strongpoints held out with no thought of surrender simply because the battle had passed them by.

In such close-quarter fighting it was impossible for the New Zealanders to use their advantage in artillery. The paras also had another advantage. The ruined town was much easier to defend than one which was relatively intact. The streets had disappeared beneath mounds of rubble. The town had become featureless; there were no points of reference and the only identifiable features, other than the railway station, were the Hotel de Roses and the Continental Hotel, where the paras had their regimental headquarters. As they tried to level a route through for the tanks, the sapper bulldozers proved a most valuable armoured vehicle for the New Zealanders.

The weather forecasters got it wrong. By late afternoon of 15 March the heavens had opened. Craters filled with water, deep enough to drown a heavily laden man caught unawares, and the moonless night benefited the defenders.

At the end of the first day the New Zealanders had cleared about two-thirds of the town. It was not enough to secure the bridgehead. Parkinson fed in companies from the 24th and 26th Battalions of the brigade. The town had to be cleared street by street and the houses floor by floor and room by room. The sappers had thrown a bridge across the Rapido and a few tanks were in the town, but were heavily restricted by the rubble. The 25th Battalion captured Castle Hill, but in the confusion word did not get back and there was a delay before the lead battalion of the 5th Indian Brigade – 4th Essex – moved to take over.

There now began the epic struggle for the key features on a hill with a one-in-two gradient. The battles were for Hangman's Hill (also called Point 435), Points 165 and 236 (hairpin bends on the road to the monastery) and Castle Hill. Hangman's Hill was a jutting rock platform about 250 yards below the monastery wall. It was called Hangman's Hill because a broken pylon, once part of an aerial ropeway, looked like a gibbet. Castle Hill, with its ruined fort on top, was linked by a saddle of rock to the monastery. It was both the key feature and an insecure base from which companies of 1/6 Rajputana Rifles sallied forth to secure the hairpin bends only to be beaten back. In the meantime the 1/9 Gurkhas made Hangman's Hill their individual epitaph.

The Indian and Gurkha troops sustained casualties even before they could get to grips with the enemy. The Germans in the monastery had an unobscured view of their approach and made the most of such opportunities. The same applied at night for the other companies, who served as parties to bring supplies up and stretchers back. Manhandling a stretcher down a one-in-two gradient in the darkness, in the rain, under fire, was a nightmare.

The battle continued, day after day, in the most appalling conditions. Most of the engagements on those precipitous slopes above the town were of one or two companies at a time. Colonel Heydrich, the para division commander, threw his reserves into the battle whenever the need arose. The 2nd Battalion of the 155th Panzer Regiment was given to him by Von Senger. Unhesitatingly Heydrich deployed these troops in the less critical areas, and concentrated his paras for the decisive struggles.

Freyberg, in contrast, was hesitant in his decisions and parsimonious with reserves. Between 15 and 17 March he had only one chance to secure a victory and even that was a slim one. Up until this time the Germans were at their weakest, yet Freyberg had just two battalions committed to the fray, one in the hills and the other in Cassino. Had he used his reserves then it might just have worked. Thereafter there was no chance.

The battle became increasingly more difficult to direct, yet Freyberg resolutely refused to pass control to the officers on the spot. By the third day of the battle, the New Zealanders were attacking the railway station, the Continental Hotel and the Hotel de Roses, but the two battalions involved had too few tanks in support and at times their cooperation was ragged. The New Zealanders at last captured the station, but the attacks against the hotels failed, even though they came within yards of the final position. The paras punished every error unforgivingly. Above them the Gurkhas and the Rajputanas fought side by side. Indian porter companies, unnerved by the conditions, refused to carry supplies to Gurkha positions beyond Hangman's Hill so the Rajputanas took on the task. The Essex hung grimly on to Castle Hill.

On 18 March the Germans counterattacked the New Zealanders at the railway station. The attack failed, but it was a psychological blow; up to that moment the New Zealanders had been convinced the Germans were almost finished.

In the hills, the Indian Brigade regrouped and made a desperate attack on the monastery but some 300 men of the 1st Para Battalion charged out of the main gate down the hill and bottled up the surviving Essex and Rajputanas in the old fort on Castle Hill. That meant that the 1/9 Gurkha Rifles on Point 435, Hangman's Hill, were also isolated. Over the next week the paras kept up a constant pressure on the Gurkhas, but they refused to budge; supplied by air they clung on grimly to their positions. In the valley below, Freyberg sent in 28th Maori Battalion against the Continental Hotel but the attack failed.

However, during lulls in the bloody conflict, there were individual acts of decency. The Germans allowed the Medical Officer of 1/9 Gurkhas through their lines every night to reach his beleaguered companies on Hangman's Hill and bring out the wounded. An irate staff brigadier demanded the doctor reveal the German deployments, but the young officer refused.

On another occasion part of the outer wall on Castle Hill collapsed burying Essex and Rajputana Rifles in the debris. There were a number of para prisoners and wounded inside the castle. They helped pull the masonry off the defenders while their comrades obligingly held their fire.

By 20 March the battle had stalemated. Mark Clark, whose only interest to date was to criticize Freyberg's handling of the battle, now insisted that the New Zealand Corps should make one last effort. Why? Did he believe that Freyberg's troops were on the point of success? With the Germans counterattacking, the evidence pointed, if anything, in the other direction. Clark did, however, know that Allied Armies Italy (AAI) had a new plan in draft which envisaged bringing Eighth Army over from the Adriatic front and concentrating the combined weight of both armies in a massive offensive on the Cassino front. When this happened Cassino would no longer be a Fifth Army battle. Honours would have to be shared equally and maybe even extended to include an equitable division of the spoils of Rome.

The battle dragged on for two further days and then on 22 March Mark Clark gave Freyberg a deadline – 36 hours to get the job done. It is at this point that Alexander should have intervened but he did not.

Companies from the 2/7 Gurkha Rifles and 6th Battalion Royal West Kents attacked the hairpins and failed. The New Zealanders made a last attempt at the Continental Hotel and that failed too. Both divisions were literally at the end of their tether. Between them they had sustained over 2,000 casualties. Freyberg took the decision to wind up the battle and withdraw from the exposed positions such as the hairpin at Point 202, held by the New Zealanders, and Hangman's Hill. In the latter case there was no radio contact and the pigeons which had been tried at various times had proved very unreliable; disorientated by the smoke and noise of battle they frequently landed in German positions.

Three officer volunteers set out by different routes to Hangman's Hill to warn the beleaguered garrison of Gurkhas of the evacuation plan. One failed to get through, but two made it and on the night of 25 March the evacuation was successfully achieved. The Germans didn't bother to intervene but the withdrawal was hellish.

Those positions that were not abandoned were handed over to fresh battalions of the 78th (Br) Division. One young British officer described the march out for his Gurkha battalion.

The distance was probably less than about five miles, but for most of the battalion the men had hardly walked at all for six weeks. Men were cramped, unfit, mentally exhausted, without any will power. Even though the ordeal was nearly over the fact did not seem to be understood. . . . Never will I forget the nightmare of the march. Officers British and Gurkha, shouted at, scolded, cajoled and assisted men as they collapsed. At times we had no alternative but to strike the soldiers who just gave up interest in anything including the desire to live. By dint of all the measures we could think of, most of them reached their transport before daylight appeared.[5]

The Germans had won a victory, but with their battalions of paratroops down to anything from 40 to 120 men, they too had paid a fearsome price to keep the Allies out of Rome. The Allies had been found wanting in every department except the raw courage of the New Zealand, Indian, Gurkha and British infantry and their battalion officers. At the end of the day it was their generals who let them down.

General Tuker did not return to his beloved division, instead he was sent back to India and a new appointment. He later wrote:

An extraordinary obsession in British commanders' minds that they must challenge the enemy's strength rather than play on his weakness . . . the waste of hammering at the enemy's strongest point is seen at its most extreme form . . . at the battles of Cassino in the Spring of 1944, where men were hurled time and again against a mountain position which had for centuries defied attack from the south and which in 1944 was not only the strongest position in Italy, but was held by the pick of the German troops in that theatre of war. These battle in fact were military sins no less.[6]

Notes

1. Matthews interview, p 5.
2. Smith, *The Battles for Cassino*, p 119.
3. Steinhof, Johannes, Pechel, Peter and Showlter, Dennis, *Voices From the Third Reich: An Oral History*, Grafton Books, 1991.
4. Matthews interview, p 6.
5. Smith, *The Battles for Cassino*, p 158.
6. Tuker, F., *Approach to Battle*, Cassell, 1958.

38

Stalemate

Lucien Truscott was one of the very few generals in the regular US Army in the Second World War who had not been to West Point. A former Oklahoma school teacher he had received his commission in an officers' training camp in 1917. By the summer of 1941 he had reached the rank of Lieutenant Colonel which was exceptional for someone with his background. Eisenhower had marked him out as an officer of exceptional ability and a potential army commander and, now that he had a corps, Eisenhower slotted him into the short list of those who would be chosen to lead one of the American armies for Overlord, should there be a casualty among the trio of generals already selected.

Truscott cut a theatrical figure. He sported a riding crop, wore a burnished helmet, white silk scarf, faded cavalry breeches and highly polished boots. Yet he was no military peacock; he was tough, sharp of mind and tongue when necessary, but also shy and retiring.

Truscott breathed new life into VI (US) Corps headquarters, got them moved above ground and established an advanced CP nearer to the front. He visited every sector of the front and became a familiar enough figure. But there was little he could do to transform the situation militarily. In conditions which more closely resembled a medieval siege – though it begged the question of who was besieging whom – conditions in the beachhead remained fraught. The VI (US) Corps numbered about 100,000 men and women, three and a half divisions' worth of troops deployed in defensive positions which were thoroughly exposed to a superior enemy force numbering five divisions.

Truscott's command was hemmed into a narrow 21-mile arc of land along about 16 miles of shoreline, at its deepest nine miles from the sea. Much of the beachhead lay within three or four miles of German artillery.

From the hills to the front German artillery spotters with high definition binoculars and rangefinders could survey every inch of ground. There was nowhere to hide except by digging deep. The Allied position would have been even more perilous had it not been for the artillery support, augmented by ships at sea where cruisers and destroyers were moored like floating batteries. Air power also gave them a decisive edge.

At the front the conditions replicated the trench warfare of the Western Front more than anywhere else in the Second World War. Positions were secured and made fortress-like with sand-bagged emplacements and, where the water table allowed, dugouts and deep shelters. In conditions such as these soldiers, no matter what their nationality, adapt to circumstances. Parked vehicles left unattended lost alternators, dynamos, batteries and seats, looted in the greater cause of making dugouts a home-from-home. Petrol cans became stoves and brass artillery shell cases chimneys. Everything had a use. Gunners did a brisk trade in the heavy cardboard wrappings for shells, which made excellent insulation for dugout walls. Italian holiday villas along the seafront were raided for furnishings, drapes, crockery and cutlery; after all any fool can be uncomfortable. One artillery unit dug itself into a huge hole in which they had placed a grand piano liberated from a nearby villa. It didn't work but it looked great. All over the beachhead, home-made signs went up, like '42nd and Broadway' or the 'Good Eats Cafe'. Someone had calculated it was '4717¼ miles to the Golden Gate'. Reinforcements were greeted with 'The Beach Head Hotel, Special Rates to New Arrivals'.

There were rolls of concertina barbed wire and minefields to the front and in places the no-man's-land was measured in yards. Troops, British and American, rotated between the front-line trenches and the rear area, but nowhere was out of range, even of enemy field artillery.

Aware that they were constantly under observation, soldiers, whether at the front or further back, tried to make themselves as inconspicuous as possible whenever they moved about. Helmet on, head down between stooped shoulders was the normal posture; they called it the Anzio Crouch. Most of the soldiers wanted to establish a live-and-let-live relationship with the Germans, especially the British, who were by now desperately short of replacements. The number of platoons to a company and companies to a battalion was reduced to provide some semblance of fire power. Clark, though sympathetic to a degree, was dismissive of the British ability to mount offensive actions. He had become especially critical of the command and leadership, particularly at brigade level and upwards;[1] in his judgement the British were good for little more than the defence of a quiet sector.

Clark requested a specific report of shortages in infantry and artillery in the British division. Truscott replied on 27 February:[2]

> Deficiencies infantry and artillery British Division as of 26 February: 1st Division (less 18th Brigade) 2486; 56th Division 2520; Great bulk these deficiencies in fighting infantry soldiers. In the case of 56th Division, each battalion consists of not more than two weak companies, mostly replacements. Few have any experienced junior officers and NCOs remaining. Estimate present combat efficiency 56th Division at approximately 25 per cent.

The one 'light relief' in a generally dismal Anzio was the antics of Brigadier General Robert Frederick's First Special Service Forces, the North Americans. The Germans called them the Black Devils and with reason. Frederick had about 1,500 men, and none of them believed in a quiet life. Activity at the front came under two broad headings: raiding and killing the enemy. Raiding involved attacking the German positions for horses, cattle, pigs and chickens and looting anything they could find in the beachhead. When it came to killing the enemy the favoured method was a night raid in which enemy sentries had their throats slit. The Black Devils, so-called because they blacked out their faces, would invariably leave a calling card. Frederick had had some adhesive posters printed. One would be left stuck on the dead man's helmet; in German it said: 'You May be Next.'

There was no front line at Anzio, and the Allied garrison was composed of men and women. There were 200 US Army nurses working in the tented field hospitals, located in what was called 'Hell's Half Acre'.

There was a special affinity amongst the infantry, a unique sense of solidarity that characterized men at the front. A unit coming out of the line at the beachhead passed another who had just taken up their position:

> What's this mob by the side of the road clapping their hands for? . . . We should clap them poor bastards, they're staying. . . . Not decent this clapping. What's this? Thanks mate. That was a good swig of tea the bloke gave. . . . Right out of his own mug too. He didn't say a word but I saw it in his eyes. . . . No bullshit. They can't have much tea to throw away. Not much further to go now. Wonder why those blokes clapped us so much. Perhaps they thought we looked damned weary. We are.[3]

To feed, clothe, arm and equip this garrison was a formidable undertaking. It required a daily delivery of 2,700 tons of supplies simply to keep pace with immediate needs. To the men on the ground, the soldiers in the slit trenches and weapons pits, nationality mattered not a jot, but not so their seniors. Churchill had directed Alexander to rename the troops at Anzio and call them the Allied Bridgehead Forces.[4]

And what of the Italians? They endured. In the more isolated hill communities both those which war had passed by and those which still waited to be liberated, it was a matter of survival in a harsh climate, of subsistence farming with some surplus for markets, of shortages and deprivations and living from one season to the next.

In the towns and cities those who lived in the liberated south experienced harder times than those under German occupation. However, if a city or town was of commercial consequence it was bombed regularly and indiscriminately. The Germans also carried out periodic round-ups of the younger male population and sent them north as forced labourers in German industry and on the farms. By this stage of the war Germany was desperately short of manpower. Italian labour was used to release German men for military service.

In the south families would do anything to stay together. Women prostituted themselves to feed their families. Children and fathers would pimp for their womenfolk and it was a buyers' market. Sexual intercourse could be purchased for a packet of ten cigarettes or a tin of spam. The price was so low and the importuning so persistent that the Allied soldiers regarded the local people with contempt. The Italians were dirty and ragged too, and in their ignorance the soldiery thought they were always like that. Venereal disease afflicted soldier and civilian alike; cities like Naples experienced outbreaks of typhoid and TB, and malnourishment was commonplace. The Allied soldiers were struck by jaundice and a particularly virulent strain of hepatitis. Badoglio's government was totally ineffective, overwhelmed like the people by ruin and devastation.

Political parties did crop up, attracting the second-rate, the time-servers and the opportunists. In various places Committees of National Liberation (CLN) were set up, and were destined to prove a curse on Italian life for years to come. Socialists and Christian Democrats appeared on the scene but only the communists were actively interested in pursuing the war against Germany. But the mood amongst all politicians was increasingly anti-monarchy.

The Fascists had been hounded from office and upon liberation there had been the usual witch-hunts in towns and villages, providing an opportunity to settle old scores and pursue family feuds and vendettas.

There was an embryo Ministry of Foreign Affairs at Brindisi with a handful of secretaries and clerks; it received no diplomatic recognition.

The Roman Catholic Church remained a symbol for national unity for all Italians, with the exception of the diehard communists. But it was a target for Allied suspicion because of the Pope's perceived pro-Fascist policy of appeasement. Pius XII regarded communism as a greater evil than Fascism. He refused to sanction or bless partisan activities in the name of resistance because he believed the movement was communist-dominated; yet he blessed Mussolini's legions as they marched off to war. Pius XII won no friends among the Allies for his criticism of the bombing of the monastery at Monte Cassino, while never condemning the Germans for their atrocities, the execution of innocent civilians, the taking of hostages. There is no evidence to suggest that the Pope was pro-German, only that he saw Hitler to be the least of several evils. Apologists maintain that the Pius XII, a consummate diplomat versed in all the subtleties of international politics in the Curia, played the only hand he could, and ensured that the Vatican State survived.

On the evening of 5 November 1943 an unknown aircraft circled over the Vatican City for a long time and then, at 1910 hours, dropped four bombs. They fell in the vicinity of St Peter's Basilica. The Vatican blamed the Germans, the Americans and the British. A formal note was sent to the respective representatives to the Holy See in which the Curia demanded a speedy investigation and report of the results, as well as 'the adoption of measures which will make a repetition of the occurrence impossible'.[5] The note concluded by reminding the belligerents that by reason of the Lateran Treaties, flying over the Vatican City was forbidden.

On the plus side, hundreds of Allied soldiers and airmen, trapped behind German lines, found sanctuary in the Vatican. The Pope also sent his nuncio to Berlin to plead with Hitler for the Jews. The interview ended with Hitler smashing a glass at the nuncio's feet.[6]

When the Germans demanded a ransom in gold for Rome's Jews, the Pope ordered a number of priceless artifacts to be melted down. As a member of the wealthy Pacelli family he also spent a considerable amount from his personal fortune to help ransom Jews from Nazi persecution and certain death. Little of this was known at the time, and when the Allies came to liberate Rome the Pope was held in very low esteem by the High Command. These same generals, however, fell over themselves for an audience when the city was free.

By March 1944, resistance groups had begun to coordinate activities and, under Allied guidance, started to target German lines of communications leading to the fronts at Cassino and Anzio. Rome was supposed to be an open city and had been acknowledged as such by the Germans, the Allies and the Badoglio government. But there was ample evidence that the Germans used Rome as a hub on their line of communications to the battlefront. The Allies in return bombed what were considered to be legitimate military targets, such as railway marshalling yards and supply dumps, but with the same degree of accuracy as Cassino. The result was bitter anger from the civilian population. Major Peter Tompkins, an American secret intelligence agent (OSS) in Rome wrote in his diary:

> They miss the target so often, and sometimes by quite some distance, and the people of Rome are angry, and it creates a wave of hatred and bad feeling which isn't worth the candle – especially as I still don't believe that the railyards and stations of Rome are an effective target, when they could interrupt traffic more effectively and with no loss of civilian lives (and prestige) outside the city.[7]

German rule became even more repressive in Rome. The Gestapo requisitioned a five-storey apartment block in the Via Tosso as a detention centre. Few who entered saw the light of day again.

Mussolini sent down a man called Caruso, an ex-mobster, to act as chief of Italian police, but it was the duty of SS General Kurt Maelzer, Himmler's representative and governor of the Rome garrison, to ensure that the Romans complied with the edicts issued by the occupying force. Twenty years in prison was the sentence for failure to notify a change of address while death was automatic for anyone caught harbouring an Allied serviceman or possessing a radio transmitter. The Roman male, unless very young or very old, disappeared underground as the German round-ups increased in intensity. The city was run by women and Fascists.

And yet there were still incidents of resistance. On 23 March a partisan group ambushed a German military police patrol on the Via Rasella. They detonated a bomb as the troops passed by and 32 Germans were killed and many others wounded. As a reprisal, General Maelzer ordered the slaughter of every man, woman and child who lived in the Via Rasella.

Ettel F. Mollhausen, Head of Chancery at the German Embassy in Rome, interceded with the Führer. Hitler and Himmler rescinded the order and directed instead the deportation of every able-bodied male Roman to forced labour camps in Germany. Kesselring complained that this would severely overstrain his rail system and proposed that ten Romans should be executed for every German soldier killed. Obersturmbannführer Kapple, the SS Colonel in command of the execution squad, arbitrarily rounded up the shortfall from the prison in Via Tosso.[8] They were taken to one of the caves in the Fosse Ardeatine and gunned down. The bodies were covered with lime and the entrance to the cave sealed by dynamite.

Notes

1. Blumenson, *Mark Clark*, p 195.
2. Truscott, *Command Missions*, p 343.
3. Woodruff, W., *Vessel of Sadness*, Chatto and Windus, 1969; quoted in Ellis, *The Sharp End*, p 307.
4. Blumenson, *Mark Clark*, p 195.
5. CX/MSS/C215.
6. Adleman and Walton, *Rome Fell Today*, p 195.
7. Ibid., p 182.
8. In fact 315 men and women were executed.

39

Springtime

In April Mark Clark flew back to the United States in the greatest secrecy, which made a change. He was summoned home by Marshall on the pretext that the President wanted a personal briefing for the forthcoming offensive. The real reason was a growing concern about Clark's health and resilience. Always thin, he was by now positively gaunt in appearance. His face and eyes showed the strain of months of unremitting pressure. Clark found no relief from the strains of high command in female company, unlike Eisenhower and Patton. Instead he chose to bear the burden alone, and it showed. A string of failures through an Italian winter was not helped by a positively explosive relationship with his allies, contemporaries and subordinates.

It was arranged for Clark's wife, Renie, to meet him in Washington and the couple were housed in Marshall's home at Fort Meyer. Not even his mother knew he had been home. Clark and his wife then spent a few more days in seclusion at a guest house in the grounds of the Greenbrier Hotel in White Sulphur Springs, West Virginia, and then went on to Georgetown, South Carolina for a meeting with the President.

Clark was given the date for Operation Overlord. Could the Fifth Army be in Rome before 5 June? Its capture would provide a tremendous propaganda boost to the French Resistance. Clark was determined to be in Rome before that deadline, for another reason. Once the Allies landed in France, the Italian campaign would become a sideshow. The capture of Rome, if it occurred after the deadline, would be a postscript.

Two weeks to the day later, Clark returned to Italy. His visit had not been picked up by the newspapers and, remarkably, his absence appeared to have gone unnoticed in Italy by the press corps who attended on him. But Clark felt refreshed and ready once more for the fray.

Alexander flew home to London in April. He needed to get the War Office to increase the allocation of ammunition to the British forces in Italy. The Ministry of Supply had allocated 3.5 million rounds, but for the spring offensive Alexander's staff calculated they would need 10 million rounds to see him through the year. Alexander also used the opportunity to persuade the War Cabinet to oppose any landings in the South of France in favour of an all-out prosecution of the Italian campaign, not just for the junction of the two fronts and Rome, but up the Italian peninsula and beyond. The British Chiefs gave Alexander their full support and encouraged him in the belief that they would handle the Americans.[1] He returned to Italy reassured that there would be no landings in the South of France.

The British, in readiness for the planned and long-awaited breakout, received a mighty phalanx of armour. This included three armoured divisions (1st British, 6th British and 6th South African) and three separate armoured and tank brigades (21st and 25th Tank Brigades, 7th Armoured Brigade and 9th Armoured Brigade Group). In infantry there were the 4th British and 10th Indian Divisions, and brigades of Greeks and Jews from Palestine.

For the Americans two new divisions had arrived in the Mediterranean. The 85th and 88th (US) Infantry Divisions were the first major units to have been raised for war, according to the development programme which Clark himself had created in 1940 and 1941. They were later to be joined by the 91st Infantry Division which was deployed in full strength for the autumn battles. Predictably, all of these divisions were initially weak at battalion level, but their platoon leaders were, on the whole, good.

These draft divisions were made up of the sons of blue-collar workers in the ranks because that was the way the draft worked in the United States. There were very few college graduates in the ranks and even fewer Ivy League or West Point graduates in platoon commanders' positions. Both Eisenhower and Mark Clark had sons at West Point, but the course took four years, and there was no compromise for the war. In the United Kingdom, both the Royal Military Academy Woolwich and the Royal Military Academy Sandhurst closed their gates on the day war was declared, only to reopen the next week as Officer Cadet Training Units (OCTUs) producing a new batch of young officers every four months until the day the war ended.

In support of the 85th (US) Infantry, the Americans used two battalions of mule-pack artillery. Such units had long been a common feature of the

British Indian Army and had remained a part of the US military establishment.

Thanks to tradition, the United States Army had not abandoned all animal troops after World War I. A few mule-pack artillery battalions and some horse-drawn artillery along with several horse cavalry troops were maintained. But just prior to World War II the army replaced the horse-drawn artillery with trucks and the cavalry outfits found themselves in half-track personnel carriers. But the mules survived. There still seemed to be a place for them. . . .

But why keep the mules? What advantages did they have over horses as pack animals?

First of all, the mule is a strong, sturdy, intelligent animal that is easily trained to carry very awkward and heavy loads in narrow, rough and steep mountain trails. It can work in hot, humid conditions . . . Also, the mule is self disciplined so that it will not overeat or overdrink and make itself sick as a horse will do. It is sure-footed and will not venture into any place that may be dangerous. . . . It will not injure itself should it become entangled in barbed wire, briars or any other sharp obstacles. It can carry its own food on its back as well as graze in areas that seem almost barren. The mule does not panic readily under shell fire. It was the ideal pack animal for army mountain units. . . .

General Mark Clark requested two battalions of pack artillery to work with the Fifth Army in the Italian mountains. These were the 601st and 602nd Battalions. The Tenth Mountain Division had more pack battalions but it was still in training in Colorado to go to Italy at a later date.

These two battalions had just returned to the States from the Aleutian Islands campaign (sans mules). . . . They arrived in Naples, still without any animals, and discovered that their new mules would have to be conscripted from the Italian countryside.

Army procurement officers . . . scoured the farms of southern Italy and the islands of Sicily, Corsica and Sardinia to buy hundreds of animals of all sizes and description. In addition to the mules they also had to pick about eighty to one hundred riding horses, animals that could take the mountain trails. The animals were then parcelled out to the two units, now quartered on King Emmanuel's lush hunting grounds near Battipaglia, south of Salerno. Each battalion received about four hundred braying 'long ears' and forty to fifty horses. . . .

Time was of the essence. They were to be trained and ready to go into combat in just over a month and a half. The men were ready, but the animals were not. . . .

First, each mule driver had to become acquainted with his new animal. This relationship is very important in an animal outfit. Man and animal had to discover each other. The driver had to learn to share a new language – half

American and half Italian – with his charge. Each morning he would feed and curry his mule and then join in a three to five mile march just learning a mutual trust and respect. . . . Before long most of the drivers had added their own pet names to their mules. Every day each driver was taking a special pride in the fact that he had the best mule in his battery.

Next, the pack saddles, without loads, were added. The mules seemed to be elated. The drivers could almost feel their mules thought that this was all the load that they would have to carry. But finally, each mule was actually packed out with the specific load assigned to him. The gun mules had the greatest challenge. The army 75mm howitzer is broken down into several parts, or loads, for each of the mules . . . Most of the howitzer loads are top loads which means that the part is carried on a special adapter on the top of the saddle rather than being draped down the sides. Many of the more fortunate mules destined to carry ammunition, communications equipment or the kitchens had side loads.

Walking under a heavy top load became a new challenge to these mules. Most of the drivers had to encourage their animals by moving them along slowly until the mule got the feel of that high top load. They quickly learned that their steps had to become shorter. Fortunately they adapted rapidly to these new loads. The animals had been selected well for their jobs.[2]

A fourth American division appeared in the theatre. Unlike the British and Imperial and Commonwealth forces the US Army was still a racially segregated army. This did not mean that the combat troops were all white, because Red Indian and Mexican Americans were included. Neither were Negroes excluded from combat. The 332nd Fighter Group in Italy was an all-Black outfit. But at this stage there were no Negroes in combat units. All of that changed with the arrival of the 92nd Infantry Division, a Negro outfit with white officers.

While trench warfare was the order of the day at Anzio and Cassino the coming of spring allowed the Allies to concentrate on air power. On 19 March the combined air forces in the Mediterranean launched Operation Strangle. The objective was to strike at enemy lines of communications, road and rail bridges, tunnels and viaducts, transalpine routes and marshalling yards throughout the length and breadth of occupied Italy. Because the battle fronts were relatively quiet the air forces could concentrate on hitting communications. Newly introduced precision instruments, enhanced crew training and improving weather conditions were all cited in support of the promise that they could really deliver the goods.

Nardina Donatini was 21 years old. She lived with her parents in Marradi, a market town in the Apennines, north of Florence. Monday was market day in Marradi, when the town was always busy. Stalls were set up in the main square and peasants came from the surrounding villages to sell their produce, mostly livestock, clothes, linen and embroidery. Marradi was an important road junction which had two bridges over the River Lamone, one steel for the railway and the other stone for the road. For weeks trainloads of German troops and supplies had passed through Marradi on their way south to the front.

It was a time of sadness in my family, for just two months previously my sister, who was seventeen, had died of meningitis. We didn't know where the Allies were, but we all knew it wouldn't be long before Marradi too would be liberated. There was a small German garrison which came to our town when Mussolini fell from power. Their commandant was really very kind, he had lent his car to take my sister to the hospital in Florence. But many of our young men had been taken away to Germany to work; others had fled into the hills to hide or join the partisans.

We were always frightened of the SS because they would come into the town to look for our menfolk and take them away, some we never saw again. The SS wore the best uniforms and were handsome men, but very cruel and we always ran away and hid when the SS patrol came to Marradi.

The Americans bombed Marradi on this market day. I was on my way to the town from our house – we lived on the hillside across the river from Marradi – when I heard the sound of the planes. I immediately knew, something told me, the Americans were coming to bomb the bridges. I turned and ran back to the house to my mother and father; next door lived my aunt and my cousin.

'They're coming to bomb, run away, quick, quick,' I warned.

We ran up the hillside towards a cottage away from the town. My mother couldn't run fast enough and hid under a small shed which was built on stilts. My aunt and cousin hid in a tree.

I watched the planes fly up the valley; they had big white stars on the wings, the sky seemed to be full of planes. Some German guns, which guarded the bridges, opened fire, but they were few in number.

The bombs started to fall and I heard the scream as they fell. I threw myself flat on the ground and the bombs burst. I could feel the air beat over me and debris all over my head. I thought of my sister and I said, 'Oh, I'm coming to join you.'

When the bombers had finished, there wasn't much left of Marradi, the buildings in the square were flattened and there were fires everywhere. A terrible sound came from the town below, screams and moans of the injured and trapped; men's voices and animals in pain. Those sounds have stayed with me to this day. Many of the people were killed and injured, my aunt and my cousin were among the dead. The railway bridge and the road bridge were untouched, the bombers had missed their targets but had killed so many people and destroyed our town.

The bridges were still standing. We knew the Americans would come back and bomb Marradi again until the bridges were destroyed, so we decided to leave the town. We buried my aunt and my cousin and went to the little village high in the Apennines called Cignato; it is about five miles from Marradi.[3]

There were Marradis the length and breadth of Italy, bombed indiscriminately in the name of liberation.

Alexander was able, clinically, to measure the success of Strangle. Ultra reports gave him an often daily commentary on German ration strengths and supply returns. The results showed that there was a measure of 'success', but nowhere near the level of tactical damage which had been forecast. The Allies had spent three months and made as many attempts to break the Gustav Line. It had cost them about 5,200 casualties, it kept LSTs from Overlord, caused Anvil to be postponed and used up all the precious reserves of infantry earmarked for Europe.

And what had they achieved? Three shallow bridgeheads, one at Anzio, one across the lower Garigliano and the other across the upper Rapido. Even Marshall accepted that Rome had to be taken; too much blood had been spilled for the war in Italy to become a sideshow, not until Rome had fallen.

Notes

1. Matthews interview, p 8.
2. From a long essay written by Robert E. Reynolds, who served with the unit, entitled 'Long Ears . . . A Secret Weapon'. It cannot be bettered and I am honoured to include it in this account.
3. Author's interview.

40

Victory at Cassino

We Polish Soldiers
For our freedom and yours
Have given our souls to God
Our bodies to the soil of Italy
And our hearts to Poland
The Monument in the Polish Cemetery at Cassino

By making a virtue of necessity the Joint Chiefs were able to produce some sound strategic reasons for a fourth attempt at Cassino and by assigning the troops intended for the South of France to Italy first, to provide the wherewithal to do the job. But Marshall was adamant that, once Rome fell, the Italian campaign would, to all intents and purposes, be shut down and the main effort switched to France. It was therefore agreed that a spring offensive in Italy should take priority over Anvil, while the latter would become the means of transferring a strategic axis rather than part of the double-headed blow originally planned for the invasion of France. The idea was to draw German divisions into Italy and away from France and Hitler's strategic reserve. It was an argument that does not stand up to close scrutiny.

Major General John Harding, Alexander's Chief of Staff at Fifteenth Army Group, called his blueprint for the fourth attempt at Cassino, Operation Diadem. A decisive breakthrough was achieved and, for the first time since Allied troops had set foot on Italian soil, it was more like the good old days in the Western Desert. The Germans fell back from the Gustav Line in confusion and some disarray. The Allies were not to catch the enemy in such distress again until the Po Valley, the campaign in the

313

spring of 1945; by then Germany was already reeling on the verge of collapse and it no longer mattered.

Under a cloak of secrecy the whole of Eighth Army, bar one or two divisions, was moved across from the Adriatic. Alexander had Fifth and Eighth Army packed shoulder to shoulder on the southern front. Herein lay the greatest contribution made by the air forces. Allied air superiority (4,000 aircraft against 700) blinded the enemy and made it easier to deceive him.

Fifth Army included all the American and American-equipped divisions (ie the French) on a 20-mile front in the coastal sector and the VI (US) Corps at Anzio. The Eighth Army had all the British and British-equipped divisions (Indian, New Zealand, Canadian and Polish) with the bulk concentrated in front of Cassino and the Liri Valley. This meant that for the first time since it arrived in Italy McCreery and his war-weary X (Br) Corps reverted at last to British command. On the Gustav Line Alexander had 21 Allied divisions, rested, refitted and ready for the coming fray. He outnumbered the enemy three to one, that magic ratio demanded by military pundits as the optimum superiority for an offence.

Operation Diadem also involved a simple but effective deception. Besides masking the redeployment of Eighth Army and all that that entailed, the Allies made it appear that they were planning an amphibious landing near Rome, and also gave other indications that the reorganization of their forces would not be completed before mid-June at the earliest. Kesselring fell for the deception. He ordered his own forces to use the period until the end of May for rest and refitting. He pulled three of his panzer and panzer grenadier divisions out of the Gustav Line and dispersed them both to cover likely beaches for an amphibious operation, and to reinforce either Tenth or Fourteenth Armies as the need arose.

Kesselring was well aware that once the fine weather came he could no longer hold the Allies indefinitely at the Gustav Line, or bottle up their forces in Anzio. He planned instead a strategy of flexible defence along successive lines, ie the same approach as he had used from Salerno to the Gustav Line. By holding each defensive position until the last moment before German troops were cut off, Kesselring hoped to minimize superior Allied mobility, artillery and air power and to dissipate the momentum of an Allied push.

No new German divisions arrived in Italy after the winter offensive had come to an end; so if the Allies were trying to justify the Italian campaign as a magnet to draw German strength away from the east and the west, they had failed. And by careful husbandry, Kesselring was able to build up the strengths of his fighting units. There were numerous incidents of partisan activity, but Kesselring was able to cope. Mussolini's Blackshirt battalions and paramilitary formations were used with considerable effect in this role. In total, Kesselring had about 23 divisions with approximately 412,000 men. Of these, 19 divisions were considered capable of sustained defence of which 14 were in the line. Fourteenth Army had five divisions masking Anzio and Tenth Army had nine divisions garrisoning the Gustav Line. These divisions were the strongest in terms of manpower and included some of the very best soldiers in the Wehrmacht.

In April, for example, a report was sent to Berlin, decoded via Ultra, in which every division in Germany was graded on a 1–4 scale, ranging from 'capable of offensive action' to 'fit for static defence only'. Two divisions (29th Panzer Grenadiers and 1st Para) made the top category, eight the second, eight the third (for mobile defence) and four the bottom. All of this, together with deployment strengths, numbers of tanks in workshops and even what the commanding officers had for breakfast, was known by the Allies.

The primary purpose of Operation Diadem was not the capture of Rome. It was the defeat of the German Tenth Army stemming from which the fall of Rome would be an inevitable consequence. The Diadem plan called for Eighth Army to launch the main attack up the Liri Valley while Fifth Army conducted a supporting attack through the Aurunci Mountains west of the Liri Valley. At Anzio VI (US) Corps was not to be rescued or relieved. Indeed, heavily reinforced by both British and American divisions, and with more troops standing by, Truscott was to launch his own offensive, to attack on order (Alexander calculated on D + 4), advance and take the Alban Hills blocking the escape routes north and thereby trapping the Tenth Army.

Diadem was the classic one–two approach. A simultaneous attack was ruled out because Alexander felt that it would remove the element of surprise. Alexander was also influenced[1] by the fact that Allied intelligence told him that Kesselring expected an offensive in June, but to be launched first at Anzio. Clark did not read the battle or the objectives in the same way and, given Alexander's method of command, he had sufficient latitude at Fifth Army to run his own war. With Oliver Leese, however, Alexander kept a much tighter control over planning and execution. Indeed the development of the Fifth Army plan of attack was conditioned by two factors – Clark's obsession with Rome and a belief, that *his* army and not Leese's would make the decisive penetration.

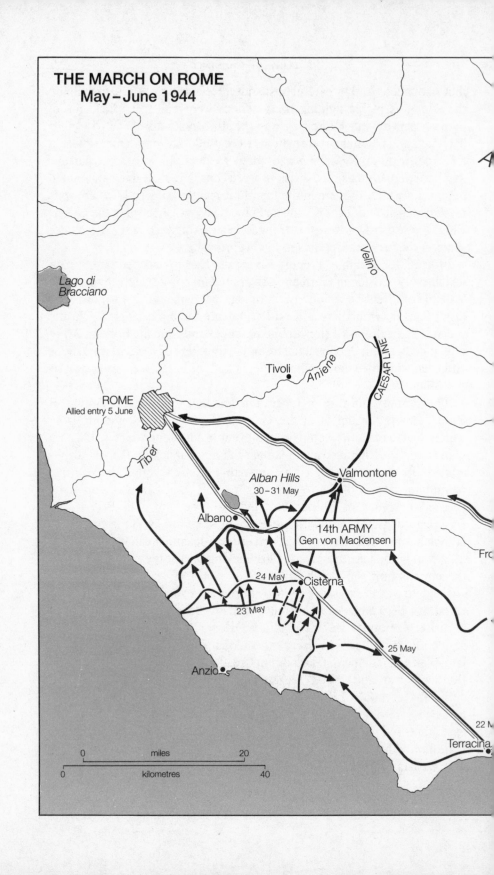

THE MARCH ON ROME
May–June 1944

Lago di
Bracciano

Velino

Tivoli

Aniene

CAESAR LINE

ROME
Allied entry 5 June

Tiber

Valmontone

Alban Hills
30–31 May

Albano

14th ARMY
Gen von Mackensen

Fr

24 May

Cisterna

23 May

25 May

Anzio

22 M

Terracina

| 0 | miles | 20 |
| 0 | kilometres | 40 |

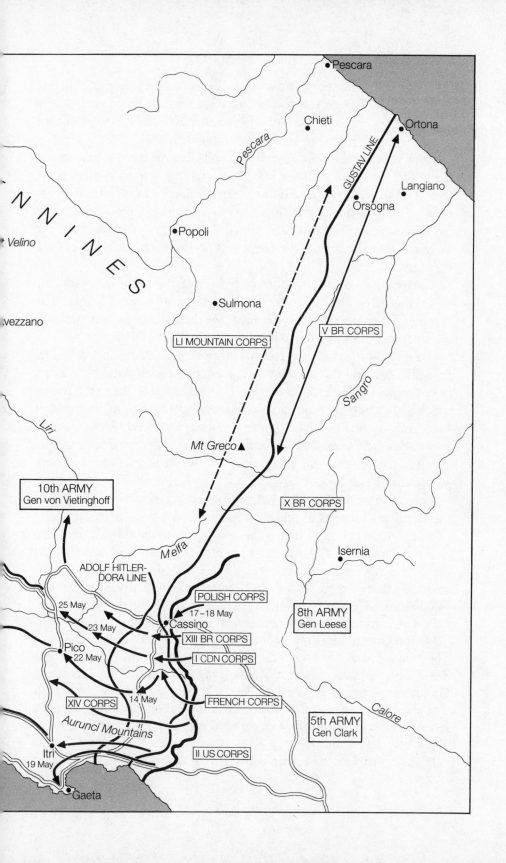

Pescara

Chieti

Ortona

Pescara

GUSTAV LINE

Langiano

Orsogna

Popoli

Velino

A N N I N E S

Sulmona

V BR CORPS

LI MOUNTAIN CORPS

vezzano

Sangro

Liri

Mt Greco ▲

10th ARMY
Gen von Vietinghoff

X BR CORPS

Melfa

ADOLF HITLER-
DORA LINE

Isernia

POLISH CORPS

25 May

17–18 May

8th ARMY
Gen Leese

23 May

Cassino

XIII BR CORPS

Pico

I CDN CORPS

22 May

14 May

XIV CORPS

FRENCH CORPS

Calore

Aurunci Mountains

5th ARMY
Gen Clark

Itri
19 May

II US CORPS

Gaeta

Numerically the odds were distinctly in Clark's favour. On the southern front he had 170,000 troops, seven-plus divisions in two corps with over 600 guns and 300 tanks. He was opposed by XIV Panzer Corps which totalled 27,000 men and about 200 guns.

Clark sensibly allowed General Juin considerable latitude in planning the battle. Where Alexander sought to create a war of movement by frontal assault followed by armoured exploitation, General Juin sought to create a war of movement by means of an envelopment through the mountains where his specially trained colonial troops might keep the Germans off balance until the operations opened up the Liri Valley from the rear.

The mountain barrier was formidable. Averaging 15 miles in width the mountains stretched some 60 miles north-west towards Rome. The Aurunci range where Juin planned the breakthrough was virtually trackless and extended for some 20 miles from the Garigliano.

General Juin had nearly 100,000 troops under command including four divisions and three groups of goumiers, numbering about 12,000 men. German defences in the Aurunci were manned by the 71st Division which had 12,000 men and about 100 guns of various types. The secret of success lay in the French being able to sustain a sufficient momentum to overwhelm the Germans, who would be unable to get word back to their headquarters in time for fresh troops to be deployed into defensive positions to block the advance.

The ration strength of Eighth Army stood at 300,000 men. There were some critical shortages. Worldwide the British Army was 42,000 infantry reinforcements short; 21,000 of this shortage were in Italy. At long last, after much haggling and shuffling of minutes, the Military Secretary and the Adjutant General had prevailed over the Master Gunner. Anti-aircraft artillery regiments were to be retrained as infantry, at least in the Middle East. They were still dithering in England when the V-1s arrived later that summer, which marked the end of that initiative.

On the Gustav Line, the right flank was held by McCreery's X Corps which included some of the more battle-weary British divisions, the New Zealanders and Italians. After Monte Lungo the 1st (Italian) Motorized Group was reformed and strengthened with a mixed infantry contingent. The group was redesignated 'Corpo Italiano d'Liberazione'. McCreery's forces were expected to tie down enemy forces and prevent their transfer to the key battle front.

In the centre Leese had two corps. The Poles were to attack Cassino itself and take the monastery. General Kirkman's XIII Corps with 4th British and 8th Indian Division in the line and 6th (Br) Armoured and 78th (Br) Infantry in reserve was to take a bridgehead over the Rapido, clear Cassino and sweep into the Liri Valley. Behind them were General Burns' 1st (Cdn) Corps who with the 1st (Cdn) Infantry and 5th (Cdn) Armoured stood ready to exploit the breakthrough as a *corps de chasse*.

The preparations proceeded apace throughout March and April. In May the war units started to move into the line. On the coastal sector the American 85th (or the Custer division as it was known) and 88th (US) Infantry divisions of Keyes' II (US) Corps, raw units, moved in behind the British who had been there all winter. Tom Holladay was a first lieutenant platoon leader, Company A, First Battalion 338th Infantry in the 85th Division. Everything had had an air of unreality about it until they reached the front line itself. They had landed in Naples some weeks before and started to work inland. Going up into the mountains he could see Vesuvius smoking away. He felt like a Roman soldier back in Biblical days, marching in columns by the volcano.

It all changed in the front line at Minturno. The Germans were across a valley, less than 600 yards away. The thing that impressed him most up there was the sickly sweet smell of death. In no-man's-land lay some dead soldiers; they had been there for months. Human flesh doesn't smell like horseflesh or dead meat. It had a sweet cloying smell that permeated clothes and seemed to taint everything they ate.

At first everything was done according to the book. All four battalions of the division's artillery were dug in at Minturno as if for exhibition purposes on how to construct a model gunpit. When it came to living accommodation it was a different matter. The Americans may have been green, but they took to heart the advice proferred to them by a 'fat limey general' when they landed at Naples. 'Remember men,' Wilson had said, 'any fool can be uncomfortable.' The gunners' dugouts resembled miniature pirates' dens for luxury and sumptuousness. The nearby towns of Minturno and Tufo had been ransacked for chairs, tables, beds – anything to improve a GI's foxhole. More things were done with empty shell cases and ammunition boxes than the Field Manuals ever dreamed of.

The grim reality of war also quickly made its presence known. From their all-seeing mountain peaks the Germans watched as a battery of 155-mm howitzers dug their still-shiny guns into position and then opened up when the work was about done. The second shell was a direct hit on one gunpit and ten men were killed.

The infantry acclimatized for battle and this involved night patrols. Holladay went out on each occasion, taking a different squad from his platoon. He was wounded by a German grenade and spent the next four days in a field hospital. This was the first of four Purple Hearts that Tom Holladay was to receive in Italy.

Polish General Anders had sought the honour of attacking the monastery. It was much harder for the Poles to get into position because their every movement was watched over by the Germans from the commanding height above. In places the dead still littered the battlefield. Captain Smerecznski entered a cellar of a ruined house on the lower slopes. He sat down and found he was next to a dead Indian:

> The corpse was buried under a few loose stones, as were dozens of other bodies we found scattered everywhere. . . . The place was alive with rats, big, bloated creatures that scurried about with impunity while we slept. The sweet sickly smell of decaying flesh was nauseating and we could do nothing to rid ourselves of it. We even sacrificed blankets, employing them as shrouds . . . but we could not eliminate the pestilential odours that clung to the whole area.[2]

Two or three days before the attack the artillery fired smoke into the valley to hide the final deployments of the Polish troops. Lance Bombardier Vladyslaw Karnicki was in the 4th Regiment Light Field Artillery, 5th Kresowa Infantry Division. He was 19 and had the misfortune to have been born on the right bank of the River Dvina in what used to be part of Tzarist Russia in pre-revolution days. In 1939 as a 15-year-old he was deported when the Russians occupied Eastern Poland and spent his 16th birthday in the Ljubyanka Prison.

Vladyslaw was a radio operator in the regimental headquarters. Beneath the black smoke cloud he worked with his comrades bringing their guns into position, camouflaging the gunpits and stacking row upon row of ammunition. There were heavy and light mortars to be deployed and all through the daylight hours they worked, handkerchiefs tied around their faces to keep out the worst of the smoke. There were also other signs of the imminence of battle. Behind the lines a bulldozer was excavating a long shallow trench and pioneers piled empty coffins in long tidy lines.

Operation Diadem began with a 2,000-gun bombardment at 11.00 pm that evening. It was the biggest artillery barrage since El Alamein. Major the Lord Tweedsmuir, who was on Oliver Leese's personal staff, remembers:

There was a silence before the barrage started at 11 o'clock and then we heard the most lovely nightingale song imaginable. Then the barrage started with heaven knows how many guns, then over the noise of the guns, the nightingale sang even louder so that you could hear their song above the barrage of the guns.[3]

The French moved confidently into the Aurunci Mountains preceded by a tremendous rolling barrage. Juin used his 2nd Moroccan Infantry Division (2DIM) to spearhead the attack. The Moroccans took heavy casualties but secured a bridgehead. On the right and left of the main effort the 1st Motorized Infantry Division (1 DMI) and 4th Moroccan Mountain Division (4 DMM) battled their way forward.

Kesselring believed that Fifth Army was making no more than a holding attack, so even though Eighth Army were at this stage making little progress he refused to reinforce the hard-pressed defenders in the Aurunci Mountains. On 13 May the French captured the critical Monte Magro. In two days they inflicted 5,000 casualties on the Germans. The 71st Infantry Division was split asunder and the French moved forward to exploit their success. Automatically the attack opened up the other fronts. On their right flank the Germans were forced to pull back the 94th Infantry Division which had hitherto done a good job stalling the two green divisions of the II (US) Corps.

On the night that the attack began Tom Holladay had called his platoon together and read the Twenty-Third Psalm – it seemed particularly appropriate – 'walking through the valley of the shadow of death'. The battalion was led by Willis Jackson, a 28-year-old lieutenant colonel who had yet to hear a shot fired in anger. That first night at Minturno was a night of hell. It turned him and his battalion of nice, clean-cut American boys into men who had to kill or be killed.

Jackson's companies moved out behind the guns. They crossed the front line and descended into the valley a little after midnight. The first thing Holladay had his men do was to dump their gas masks. These were bulky things 12 inches square and three or four inches thick which hung around the neck on a strap. They were an uncomfortable nuisance. Shells fell among the advancing lines before they had reached the bottom of the slope. Everything that could go wrong did go wrong. Enemy crossfire was heavy and machine guns herded the young Americans into killing zones, causing the battalion organization to fall apart. Officers were killed. Company C lost its captain and three young platoon commanders. The Executive Officer had taken over and cracked up. Jackson found him beating his head into the ground, eating grass like a cow and crying like a baby. Jackson took a young second lieutenant to one side and talked to him; he ran the show from then on.

Holladay had his Thompson sub-machine gun destroyed and went down with a shrapnel wound in the leg. The soldier behind him was killed outright. Bleeding profusely, Holladay tied a tourniquet on his leg, picked up the dead man's rifle and hobbled on into the battle. He led his platoon across the valley and up the slope on the other side. It was there that he killed his first German. At night the man, silhouetted against the sky looked ten feet tall, but unthinkingly he lunged forward and rammed the bayonet into his guts. The German went down without a sound. Holladay remembered his rifle drill, as if he was in a dream. He put his foot on the man's chest and pulled the rifle and bayonet clear.

There was confusion everywhere. Holladay had taken his objective but enemy artillery prevented the remaining companies from crossing the valley. The men occupied the German lines and the word was spread to hold on until another attack could be organized. After daylight Holladay made radio contact with his company commander. By this stage his leg had stiffened and he was in great pain. Holladay and his men awaited the counterattack, but none came. Later in the morning the battalion moved forward and Holladay was sent back to the casualty clearing station. From there he was sent to a field hospital. It was to take three operations and six weeks on crutches before he saw his outfit again; but he had won a Purple Heart, and a DSC for his gallantry at Minturno.

The French breakthrough at last offered an opportunity to exert pressure on the flanks of the German forces which were holding up the British in the Liri Valley. But the first Polish assault on the monastery ended in disaster. The Germans had laid new minefields and had stiffened the defences with additional troops. The Poles attacked with elan but the Germans inflicted terrible slaughter. As dawn broke the Poles were caught in exposed positions and Anders had no choice but to order a complete withdrawal. By the time they were back on the start lines they had suffered 4,000 casualties. Two young officer cadets had been captured; the Germans crucified them with barbed wire and rusty nails. After that there was no mercy shown by either side.

Major the Lord Tweedsmuir went to find Oliver Leese and reported on the situation.

When I saw Oliver he was in a field of cornflowers. He put out a hand to bring me to a halt and said, 'Stop!' before I had a chance to tell him anything. He said

'Let's pick some cornflowers.' Then he said, 'Right. Now tell me about the casualties.'[4]

Leese stopped to talk briefly with McCreery and then hurriedly drove across to a disconsolate Anders at his CP.

'*Ah, mon Général,*' wept Anders. '*Tout est perdu, tout est perdu.*'

'*Ah, mon Général,*' replied Leese. 'Nothing is fucking *perdu.*'[5]

Leese convinced him that the next time they would do it right. Anders immediately offered to attack again and General Rudnicki who led the Carpathians volunteered his forces. Leese ordered them to wait until he gave the word; in the event, that came five days later.

The infantry divisions under Kirkman, the 4th British and the Indians, plugged away in their slow methodical way. Behind pounding artillery, companies and platoons probed for weakness. If the resistance was too strong their battalions would pull them back and they would start again.

For the British, Cassino was not unlike Alamein – a steady disciplined firefight in which the bridgehead was gradually widened. By the morning of 14 May there were seven bridges across the Rapido and Leese warned the Canadians to be ready. Leese visited a battery of the Worcestershire Yeomanry, an anti-tank regiment. He wanted to look at a trout hatchery in their area. He chatted to the officers and added as he left: 'Last night the French unleashed the Goumiers.'[6]

The German battalions in the 71st and 94th Infantry Divisions fell back in total disarray. The goumiers moved with ease over razor-back ridges and across precipitous rock faces outflanking position after position. 'Those damned Frenchmen,' exclaimed Von Veitinghoff at his Tenth Army CP. 'We will exhaust them yet.'[7] But the Germans did not, and after eight days the French were up against the Hitler–Dora Line and Kesselring had no choice but to order a general retreat from the Gustav Line.

One of the soldiers that Leese encountered on 17 May was a West Indian REME mechanic, Derief Taylor, who was doing maintenance work on a 25-pounder gun. He was the only black man in the division and had been without sleep for several nights. Suddenly he felt a stick pushed against his back. He spun round: an officer, six feet four with a black moustache and brown twinkling eyes, was regarding him quizzically.

'Well, I hope you know what you're doing,' said Leese, 'because I don't. *Do* you know what you're doing?'

Derief Taylor, whose passion was cricket, decided to stonewall.

'Yes, sir.'

'Well, can I help?'

Derief Taylor's reply would not have won him a prize for diplomacy.

'No thank you, sir. This requires precision.'

'Well, at least I can get you a cup of tea.' Leese replied. 'Where's the cookhouse?'

Derief, speechless, pointed the way. Leese strode off, returning with two mugs.

'I hope we'll get this lot knocked off by tomorrow,' he said, and continued his tour of the battlefield. They were to meet again at Edgbaston in 1959; Leese as President of the Warwickshire Cricket Club, Derief Taylor as a famous cricket coach.

On 19 May the 4th British Infantry Division entered Cassino.

The previous day, the Poles had made another attempt on the monastery and were repulsed. On the morning of the 19th they noticed a deathly quiet had fallen over the monastery ruins. A scouting party of Polish Uhlans from the 12th Podolski Lancers, led by Lieutenant Casimir Gurbiel, found a huddle of abandoned German wounded – dying men who were too ill to be moved. The Lancers fashioned a makeshift regimental pennant from a Red Cross flag and planted it in the ruins. Then a bugler played the medieval Polish military signal, the Krakow 'Hejnal'. The haunting notes echoed across the valley from the ruined monastery, lifting above the sounds of the battle. In the town below, British infantry stopped and looked up at the monastery. Sappers paused in their bridging of the Rapido.

Vladyslaw Karnicki heard the 'Hejnal' in the 4th Regiment's command post. He looked up. His colonel, the other officers and the men were crying like children.

In the late afternoon General Anders walked up to Monastery Hill to pay his own tribute to the 3,784 men of the Polish Corps who died at Cassino.

The battlefield presented a dreary sight. There were enormous dumps of unused ammunition and here and there heaps of landmines. Corpses of Polish and German soldiers, sometimes entangled in a deadly embrace, lay everywhere, and the air was full of the stench of rotting bodies. There were overturned tanks with broken caterpillars and others standing as if ready for an attack, with their guns still pointing towards the monastery. The slopes of the hills, particularly where the fighting had been less intense were covered with poppies in incredible number, their red flowers weirdly appropriate to the scene. . . . Crater after crater pitted the sides of the hills, and scattered over them were fragments of uniforms and tin helmets, tommy guns, Spandaus, Schmeissers and hand grenades.

Of the monastery itself there remained only an enormous heap of ruins and rubble, with here and there some broken columns. Only the western wall . . . was still standing. A cracked church bell lay on the ground next to an unexploded shell of the heaviest calibre, and on shattered walls and ceilings fragments of paintings and frescoes lay in the dust and broken plaster.[8]

Notes

1. Matthews interview, Part II, p 1.
2. Whiting, Charles, *The Long March to Rome*, Guild Publishing, 1987, p 122.
3. Ryder, *Oliver Leese*, p 165.
4. Ibid., p 166.
5. Leese to author, November 1968, Attingham Park, Shrewsbury.
6. Ryder, *Oliver Leese*, p 167.
7. Adleman and Walton, *Rome Fell Today*, p 211.
8. Anders, W., *An Army in Exile*, Battery Press, Nashville, Tenn., 1987

41

All Roads Lead to Rome

You've got to remember that the longer troops fight, the more conservative they become – and the Eighth Army has been fighting for a hell of a long time.[1]

Mark Clark

As the advance gathered momentum beyond the ruptured Gustav Line it was not clear if the enemy would try to defend Rome and make the Allies fight for the city. Alexander had a very delicate task, and he was anxious not to offend the Catholic world by causing havoc and wholesale destruction. His plan was to encircle the city, cut it off and then lay siege until the Germans surrendered. If the enemy fought back with artillery and tanks, Alexander would be presented with an impossible option.[2] He conceded to his staff that the military situation and the Allied lives at stake would make necessary an attack against Rome.

The Eighth Army was making slow progress out of the Rapido bridgehead and Alexander found himself having to apologize for Leese to Mark Clark. It was now that the true irony of Cassino struck the Allies. The Liri Valley was not the highway to Rome that everyone expected. The plan was straightforward enough. After the bridgehead was secured, a spearhead of massed armour with immediate air support would penetrate first through the Hitler Line and then, when the infantry arrived with its armoured brigade, push forward at least as far as Frosinone, just 40 miles from Rome. But Eighth Army had difficulty in getting its armour forward because of the bottleneck caused by the bridges over the Rapido. And once across, the enemy's continued control of the heights along the Liri Valley meant that armour could not push up Highway 6, which was almost the only road in the area.

There were also traffic jams. An armoured division comprised 700 medium tanks, 300 armoured cars, 50 self-propelled guns, 2,000 half-tracks and 10,000 trucks and prime movers. Alexander had three armoured divisions jostling for space in the Liri Valley.

Then, surprise of surprises, it appeared that the Liri Valley was not ideal for the use of armour, even though an awful lot of men had died that winter because their generals thought it would be. The Liri Valley was flanked by mountains on either side, had a restricted road net and was cut by numerous streams. In places the road was blocked with trees, and the tanks couldn't advance across country. Most of this should have been evident from a cursory glance at a map and air photographs. In country such as this, enemy anti-tank guns (the 57-mm and the dreaded 88-mm), well-sited and camouflaged, caused fearful casualties among the Sherman tanks which lived up to their name of 'Ronsons', so easily did they burn. Lord Strathcona's Horse, British Columbian Dragoons and Princess Louise's Hussars, spearheaded the advance of the 5th (Cdn) Armoured Division and they were slaughtered. One squadron of Lord Strathcona's Horse lost 20 Shermans in as many minutes. Even so Leese became increasingly impatient with what he regarded as the over-cautious advance of the Canadians. General Burns, the Canadian Corps Commander was replaced after Rome.

By the time Eighth Army reached the Hitler–Dora Line the Germans were already well-entrenched. It would take a full-scale assault to dislodge them and, while Leese prepared his forces, heavy rain caused further delay.

Mark Clark was less than impressed with the arguments of the Britishers. Clark thought that Eighth Army was not only not 'pulling its load', but deliberately hanging back. These suspicions were given substance when he was told that for a coordinated mass attack on the Hitler Line, timed for 24 May, Leese planned to use just one division, the Canadians. Alexander even asked Clark if he could attack and outflank the Germans making it unnecessary for the Eighth Army to attack.

[Alexander] said he desired to conserve losses. I told him to conserve losses in one place we would have them in another, namely, the Fifth Army sector and that I strongly recommend that Leese speed up his attack and that both armies attack at the same time. . . . We agreed, although I am convinced that the Eighth Army will hold their attack and let the French carry the ball for them as they have done so far in this battle.[3]

Alexander confirmed Churchill's objective, 'our objective, namely the destruction of the enemy south of Rome'. And for once, Alexander made his views crystal clear. Truscott was to drive from the beachhead through the German stronghold of Cisterna to Valmontone. This would have the effect of appearing to block the Tenth Army's logical route of withdrawal. It could possibly trap the bulk of his forces, but would most likely undermine further enemy resistance on the front south of Rome.

Clark had doubts if VI (US) Corps was strong enough to perform this blocking move and also warned that the country around Valmontone offered the Germans a number of alternatives even if Route 6 was blocked. He argued the case with Alexander, insisting on the need for flexibility and deferring a final decision until enemy reactions were clear. Accordingly, Clark ordered Truscott to draw up plans to cover four different axes of advance, and to have his corps ready at 48 hours notice. This made Truscott piggy-in-the-middle. And it didn't help matters when Alexander, hitherto so scrupulous in his observance of military etiquette, by-passed Mark Clark and on 5 May visited Truscott at Anzio. Truscott recalled the occasion:[4]

> General Alexander, charming gentleman and magnificent soldier that he was, let me know very quietly and firmly that there was only one direction in which the attack should or would be launched and that was from Cisterna to cut Highway 6 in the vicinity of Valmontone in the rear of the German main forces. He, he said, reserved to himself the decision as to when he proposed to initiate it.

Truscott played it by the book and later that afternoon reported the conversation to Mark Clark. Clark was furious and objected formally that the Army Group Commander should give instructions to his subordinates.[5] Alexander explained that he hadn't given any instructions but had merely expressed his opinion when Truscott explained the plans he was preparing for the thrust out of the beachhead.

Clark came to the beachhead the following day. Again Truscott recalls the occasion:[6]

> [Mark Clark] was irked at General Alexander's 'interference' in his American chain of command. He remarked that 'the capture of Rome is the only important objective' and was fearful that the British were laying devious plans to be first in Rome. Clark agreed that the Cisterna–Valmontone assault would probably be the most decisive, he also thought that the quickest way into Rome might be via Carroceto–Campoleone passing west of the Colli Lazioli.

Clark was determined that the British were not going to be the first in Rome.

By 19 May the French troops, 20 miles beyond the Garigliano, had entered the Ausonia Mountains. In the valley of the Itri, as German resistance became more fragmented and uneven, the goumiers committed their atrocities. Women and young girls, youths and boys, were raped in the streets, many to death. Menfolk who tried to interfere were gunned down.

The Italian population blamed the goumiers (they called them *Marrochhi*) but such atrocities were also committed by French colonial forces. A well-oiled fighting machine they may have been, under inspirational leaders, but when it came to their treatment of civilians they behaved in a bestial fashion.[7] There was one rumour that they buggered their prisoners, another that they castrated captured officers. Occasionally if an officer witnessed a rape then he might horsewhip the miscreant but there was no other punishment. In Esperia the goumiers ran amok and their officers lost control. Women of all ages, children and young men were gang-raped and the village pillaged.

Where possible the Italians took what precautions they could. In the smaller communities women and young children took refuge in the mountains. Occasionally, in towns which the Germans had already evacuated, the women were collected into a church and guarded by Carabinieri. In one village near Pico, a battalion from the American 351st Infantry came upon a scene in the main square where women, young men and children were being violated. Roused to fury the American GIs moved forward to rescue the screaming victims. Their company commander reluctantly intervened and told his men they were there to fight Germans not goumiers. One American lieutenant who spoke some French found a French captain in the bar drinking wine. The French officer shrugged off the American's outraged reaction and asked whether he would like to hear of some of the atrocities committed by Italian troops against Arab women in Algeria?

The green American divisions in the II (US) Corps were making good progress along the coastal highway Route 7. The Germans put up a stubborn resistance for the small port at Formio. From sea and land the Americans poured in an overwhelming bombardment of artillery and mortar fire. They only stopped when night fell but opened up again the next morning. Francesco Bartolomeo was 13. He lived in a shack near the beach with his mother, but during the barrage they took cover in a culvert under Route 7 along with other terrified civilians. None dared leave the sanctuary of their shelter, not even to answer the call of nature. During the night, children whimpered, the adults prayed and most fell into a fitful sleep. After daylight the Germans retreated. To Francesco they were the enemy, but they also looked like a bunch of little children, scared of war and frightened of dying.[8]

When the Americans arrived, Francesco scampered among the ranks of dirty grim-faced soldiers, marching in columns down both sides of the road. He begged for candy and food and cigarettes and took what he had cadged back to his mother. Behind the leading echelons came more soldiers. These were armed with flamethrowers, which were used to burn the decaying bodies of German soldiers they were unable to move. Francesco watched as human remains, shattered by shellfire, were incinerated. The sweet smell of death was everywhere.

On 19 May as the Allied forces came within 40 miles of Anzio Alexander told Clark it was time to order Truscott to break out of the beachhead. Clark procrastinated. That afternoon General Lemnitzer delivered the following message to Clark's CP.[9]

1. The C in C directs the attack from the Anzio bridgehead on Cori and Valmontone is to be launched on the night of 21/22 May or on the morning of 22 May according to whether you have decided on a night or day attack.
2. Will you please report for the information of the C in C the how and date on which the attack will be launched, and at the same time inform Commander Eighth Army by letter. This Headquarters will inform CG M.A.T.A.F.
3. Please acknowledge receipt of this letter.

   I [Clark] was shocked when I received it to think that a decision of this importance would have been taken without reference to me. I sent that word back to General Alexander, who made the weak excuse that he felt that we had discussed it for the past three days.

The breakout began in the beachhead on the morning of 23 May. Alexander had specifically asked Clark not to include the two British divisions (1st and 5th Infantry) in his battle plans because of the difficulties of getting replacements from England. This suited Clark.[10] The 36th (US) Texas Division, which had been in reserve with II (US) Corps since the start of the battle, was hurriedly shipped from Naples to Anzio. Truscott demurred; he had little confidence in the division but was overruled by Clark. The British divisions made some diversionary operations, then Truscott struck with his three American divisions

(3rd, 36th and 45th) and the North Americans. Behind a rolling artillery bombardment there were immediate gains. The Germans had once again been caught by surprise. But Mackensen's Fourteenth Army resisted tenaciously and the Americans, though they battled into Cisterna, could not rupture the German lines.

The struggle continued throughout 24 May with the Americans now taking very heavy casualties. On the coastal highway II (US) Corps was at last making rapid progress. Willis Jackson and his battalion were in the lead for the 85th Division's advance. They had passed the beaches at Gaeta, once a candidate for the Avalanche landings along with Salerno, and moved out towards the port of Terracina, about 18 miles up the coast. Then the word came down from Regiment that the battalion was to halt and wait for orders which would be delivered the next morning. Willis lost no time; he ordered up the field kitchens and that night the men had a good hot meal followed by the luxury of a full and unbroken night's sleep. The next morning they had pancakes for breakfast. Willis turned and remarked to his Exec, 'Well, life is worth living after all, it's not going to be too bad, it's a nice sunny day.'

Willis was called to the phone, it was the Regimental S3 asking him to report back to Regiment and the Exec to march the battalion to Gaeta; it was ten miles back down the road. There is nothing guaranteed to put the infantry into a sweeter frame of mind than to have them march back down a road they have just marched up. At Regiment, Jackson met Colonel Safray, the Commanding Officer.

'Jack, I've selected your battalion to make an amphibious landing.'

'In what, Colonel?'

'DUKWs, Jack.'

'Where, Colonel?'

'At Terracina.'

'Hell, Colonel, we were halfway there in any case and now you brought us back?'

'Sorry, Jack, it's come down from Corps.'

Willis knew the Division G3 well. Colonel Ohme was a family friend, and he called him on the phone.

'Herman, what the hell's going on?'

'Jack, I don't know, but I'm on my way up.'

It transpired that Keyes, the Corps Commander, wanted to speed up the advance. The problem was that every bridge was destroyed and the advance was controlled by the speed set by marching infantry. Now if he could get ahead and seize Terracina then he could leapfrog his tanks and engineers forward and speed up the advance. Willis waited while 30 DUKWs were driven up from Naples and engineers, who should have been building bridges, cleared the mines off the beach at Gaeta so that the battalion could get aboard the DUKWs.

Willis gripped the S3 and said, 'This is a suicide job, here, take my watch and give it to Dot, my wife, will you?' He briefed the battalion. 'The boys didn't seem in the least concerned. All they picked up was they were about to take a ride. Any time you tell an infantryman he is going to ride he's like a collie dog.' The DUKWs were driven up by road and waited to be refuelled from a road tanker. Jackson's company commanders looked at these things and kidded their CO.

'Hey Colonel, you going in the lead DUKW?'

'Hell, you're going to be like Washington crossing the Delaware river.'

There was a carnival-like atmosphere but Jackson knew that it would only take one German 88 at Terracina to take the smile off their faces.

Mark Clark arrived on the scene. There was the usual cavalcade of wailing sirens, motorcade outriders, jeeps and photographers. Colonel Safray rode in the back of the General's jeep. The cavalcade stopped. Jackson saluted.

Clark stuck his big hand out and said, 'Hullo, Jackson. Clark's my name.'

'Yes, I know, how are you, Sir?'

Colonel Safray said, 'Jack, hop on and just ride up and show General Clark the mission.'

Jackson directed the jeep driver towards the beaches where there was a clear view out to sea. He pointed out Terracina which they could see in the mist; it was about 20 miles away.

'What are you going to do, Jackson?' asked Clark.

'We're going to take the DUKWs and my battalion's going to do a landing in the harbour.'

'Do you have artillery or naval support?'

'No, Sir.'

'Do you have air cover laid on?'

'No, Sir.'

'Who gave you this order?'

'I believe it came direct from the corps commander.'

'Well, that's the damn stupidest order I ever heard. The mission is cancelled,' said Clark.

'Thank you, Sir,' said Willis.

Back on the Hitler Line the Canadians launched a fierce assault taking

500 casualties in the process. The Germans were in an even worse plight. Some of their divisions had lost two-thirds of their fighting strengths and Kesselring, with all his reserves committed, was forced to acknowledge defeat. On 25 May, as the battle reached its climax, Hitler gave permission for Kesselring to pull back to the Caesar Line, the last prepared defensive position before Rome.

In Rome itself the local people watched as the Germans prepared to abandon the city. Ever since the Allies had begun the offensive, the Nazis had relaxed their repressive measures. The 'retata' all but ceased and the Gestapo were less in evidence. The Germans needed Rome not to fight in, but as an escape route. The last things they needed was a hostile populace making life even more difficult. Now the streets resounded to the boots of marching columns. German installations on both airfields were demolished, bonfires of documents burned in the courtyards of headquarters and a fleet of ambulances ferried the wounded to a hospital train. At the Pensione Jaccarino, the headquarters and prison of the Italian SS Battalion, shots and screams were heard from inside. When the last of the Italians left this torture house it was immediately torched.

Early that same morning Francis Buckley, a young engineer lieutenant attached to II (US) Corps headquarters was driving in his jeep along the coastal highway northward from Terracina; there was a soldier with him. They stopped by a blown bridge and the engineer surveyed the damage. Around a corner from behind a building emerged a patrol of soldiers, led by a captain called Ben Souza.

'Where the hell do ya think you're going?' said Souza.

'I'm trying to find the Anzio forces,' replied Buckley.

'Boy,' said Souza, 'you've made it.'

Notes

1. Adleman and Walton, *Rome Fell Today*, p 227.
2. Matthews interview, p 29.
3. Clark's Diary; Matthews Collection, 20 May 1944.
4. Truscott, *Command Missions*, p 369.
5. Matthews interview with Clark.
6. Truscott, *Command Decisions*, p 369.
7. These incidents occurred on such a wide scale that the Italians later investigated them and submitted a report to the Allied authorities. By

that time the French Corps had left Italy. The report has not been made available.

8. Correspondence with author.
9. Clark's Diary; Matthews Collection, p 93.
10. Clark's Diary for 23 May 1944 reads, 'Now is the time for Hawkesworth to go ... Gregson Ellis (GOC 5 Division) is not so good.' (Major General Penny had been wounded and Hawkesworth, who had previously commanded the 46th Infantry Division, replaced him.)

42

Rome

In Mark Clark's study, at his retirement home in the grounds of the Citadel in Charleston, South Carolina, there hangs a large battle-worn sign. The white-painted word against a blue background spells ROMA.[1]

To capture Rome before D-day (which only Clark knew as 5 June) Clark compromised. On the night of 15 May he decided to divide VI Corps and attack in both directions, north-east towards Valmontone and north-west towards the Alban Hills and Rome. The attack towards Valmontone was a secondary effort conducted by 3rd (US) Infantry Division, supported by an armoured task force and with Frederick's North Americans to cover the flanks. The 45th and 36th Infantry Divisions were to lead the main assault astride the line of the Naples–Rome railway. On the inland or right flank Walker's Texans and the bulk of the 1st (US) Armoured Division were to move towards Velletri. It was to be an all-American effort on Rome led by the two divisions, 36th and 45th, that had first landed at Salerno.

Clark sent General Brann his G3 to give Truscott his instructions. Contemporary evidence suggests that Truscott supported the decision. Yet years later Truscott was to write:[2]

Late that afternoon, I returned to the Command Post feeling rather jubilant – but not for long. Don Brann, the Army G-3, was waiting for me. Brann said: 'The Boss wants you to leave the 3rd Infantry Division and the Special Forces to block Highway 6 and mount that assault you discussed with him to the north-west as soon as you can.' I was dumbfounded. I protested that the conditions were not right. There was no evidence of any withdrawal from the western part of the beachhead, nor was there evidence of any concentration in the Valmontone area except light reconnaissance elements of the Herman Goering Division. This was no time to drive to the north-west where the enemy was still strong; we should put our maximum power into the Valmontone Gap to insure the destruction of the retreating German army.

I would not comply with the order without first talking to General Clark in person. Brann informed me that he was not on the beachhead and could not be reached even by radio, and that General Clark ordered the attack to the north-west. There was nothing to do except to begin preparations.

Such was the order that turned the main effort of the beachhead forces from the Valmontone Gap and prevented the destruction of the German X (*sic*) Army.

Clark briefed Gruenther, his Chief of Staff, so that he could break the news to Alexander next day. Clark could not have chosen a more able advocate to plead his case, or one of whom Alexander was more fond. Then, on the morning of the attack Clark called a press conference. Clark's diary reads:

General Clark returned to the command post at 1030 and had a press conference at which he oriented the press on the new attack to take place later this morning. He explained to them that this attack was a direct threat towards Rome and that it would be pushed vigorously – that it was an all-out attack and that he was shooting the works. General Clark brought out that the German was in a bad position and that this new attack was launched so that we do not lose any impetus to the gains already made by the bridgehead force. This attack pusing (*sic*) north-west can gain for us the high ground south of Velletri which would force the Germans to withdraw from the entire area to the north-west and by pushing vigorously northwards toward Rome we might crack a switch position which we know to be prepared between Lake Albano and the Tiber. The press asked several questions which General Clark answered frankly and to the point.[3]

The attack began at 1100 hours. Fifteen minutes later Alexander arrived at the main Fifth Army headquarters to be briefed by Gruenther. Alexander's orders had been disobeyed. He was informed of that fact 24 hours after the decision had been taken to disobey him and fifteen minutes after the battle started. It was a fait accompli which he accepted with aristocratic good grace and with his customary lack of resolve. But what else could he do? Fire Mark Clark after he had broken the Gustav Line, joined up with Anzio and restored mobility to a battlefield which had been stagnant for five months? Alexander saved face the only way he knew how.[4] 'I am sure the Army Commander will continue to push towards Valmontone, won't he? I know that he appreciates the importance of gaining the high ground.'[5]

336

Later, in his memoirs, Alexander was to write: 'I had always assured General Clark in conversation that Rome would be entered by his army; and I can only assume that the immediate lure of Rome for its publicity value persuaded him to switch the direction of his advance.'

Eighth Army was at last making good progress. The Canadians were moving; they had crossed the Melfa river and were about half-way to Frosinone. McCreery's X Corps had cleared Monte Cairo and the Poles had come out of the high ground behind Piedmonte. But the 3rd US Infantry Division, tired after heavy fighting and weakened by casualties, could not cut Highway 6 and, confronted by increasing resistance from regiments of the Herman Goering Division, assumed a primarily defensive role. The remnants of Tenth Army retired through the Valmontone Gap, threatened and savaged by American artillery, but never trapped. In the meantime the main attack along the railway line had hit the German Caesar Line at its strongest. The enemy stood rock solid as the right hinge while the remainder of Fourteenth Army retreated and Tenth Army struck north of Rome.

It is indeed ironic that after all the sins that had been visited upon them it was the Texans who gave Clark the key to Rome. Walker's regiments stood before Monte Artemiso, a hill mass which was considered too formidable to assault. The reconnaissance company (Reccon) found that there was a gap in the German defences. It might be possible to infiltrate the Texans in a night approach march across Artemiso and cut in behind Velletri, thereby outflanking the Caesar Line. Walker took his plan to Truscott, who was about to order another frontal assault on the Caesar Line. The American divisions, particularly the 34th Infantry, were showing distinct signs of battle fatigue. If the Reccon had made an error of judgement or if the Germans spotted the infiltration, the Texans would be finished.

Truscott talked with Clark who approved the change of plan. But no directive was given. 'And you had better get through,' were Truscott's parting words.[6] He assumed no responsibility. The failure would be Walker's. In the event the operation went smoothly. The Texans had sloughed off the grim memories of the Rapido, San Pietro and Salerno. It was a long time in coming, but at long last they had their victory.

The 142nd and 143rd Infantry Regiments caught the Germans completely unawares. Nevertheless the battle for Velletri on 2 June was a bloody affair with the Germans fighting for every yard of ground. Walker spent the afternoon with 1st Battalion 141st Infantry which spearheaded the attack. The Cannon Company moved down the road with infantry to either side. Walker was walking right up with the lead tanks, 'as if he was trying to get himself killed'.[7] Alongside him walked Lt Colonel Hal Reese, the division's Inspector General,[8] a First World War comrade and old friend. An anti-tank shell and a mortar shell simultaneously struck the side of the leading tank and a large shell fragment tore away Reese's left side. He died instantly.

The Texans had opened the road to Rome and Clark knew it would now only be a matter of time before he entered the city. The old suspicions and doubts resurfaced as his diary entry for 30 May quite clearly shows. The Army Commander dictated the following notes for inclusion in the diary:[9]

> Most of my worries have nothing to do with the immediate battle. They are political in nature. I will name them in order of the trouble they cause me.
>
> First the British have their eye on Rome, notwithstanding Alexander's constant assurance to me that Rome is in the sector of the Fifth Army. They have drawn the Army boundary south of Route No 6 just to the outskirts of Rome and then veered it to the north. The Eighth Army has done little fighting. It has lacked aggressiveness and failed in its part in this combined Allied effort. Yet, my effort to switch their boundary east met with a reply indicating that the Eighth Army must participate in the battle for Rome.
>
> I feel there is some indication on the part of Alexander to commence alibiing for his Eighth Army. I received indications that he is afraid I am attacking towards Rome instead of the high ground in the Colli Laziali area. He is wrong. I appreciate the importance of this high terrain and have directed all of my subordinates to take it. Alexander is worried that I have sabotaged his directive to attack Valmontone. I have not done so.

That day Eighth Army, its principal route of advance, namely Route 6, now pre-empted by the Americans, were moving slowly up the Liri Valley and entered Frosinone. There was now severe congestion and the Americans were ahead of the British on the road to Rome.

Alexander told Clark he wanted Eighth Army to participate in the capture of Rome. 'Clark got pretty sore. He told Alexander if he (Alexander) gave him (Clark) such an order he would refuse to obey it and if the Eighth Army tried to advance on Rome, Clark said he would have his troops fire on the Eighth Army.'[10] Alexander did not press the point any further.

On 3 June Hitler gave Kesselring permission to abandon Rome, but a general disengagement was underway. Rearguards from the 4th Parachute Division delayed the Allied advance. The last units of Tenth

Army skirted the capital to the north while the Fourteenth Army marched through Rome itself. There was little interference from the Italian population. German rearguards permitting, there was a race between Keyes' II Corps on Route 6 and Truscott's VI Corps on Route 7 to be the first into the city. At an intersection on the outskirts a column of tanks from Harmon's 1st Division, part of Truscott's command, met up with a regiment of the 85th Infantry which had come in from the south.

Frederick (now a brigadier) and his Devil's Brigade, riding tanks from 1st (US) Armoured Division, is generally regarded to have been the first force to reach the centre. They paused by the roadside and the blue and white sign which spelled ROMA. There was sniper activity ahead. Clark appeared and had his photograph taken under the sign, which Frederick then removed as a trophy for Clark. He then continued with the battle. By late evening on Sunday 4 June Frederick's battalions had secured the bridges over the Tiber. Frederick, as always, was at the forefront of the battle and was wounded twice that day. This brought his total of Purple Hearts to nine. He was without doubt the most shot-at general in the US Army.

The message was flashed to London and Washington: 'Rome fell today.' The irony is that if Clark had maintained the pressure at Valmontone after 26 May he would not only have reached Rome more quickly, but also would have destroyed a much greater proportion of Tenth Army in the process.

Clark thought he had beaten the Overlord deadline by 24 hours. In the event the weather, which had exerted such a profound influence on the Italian campaign, forced Eisenhower to delay by a day. Overlord began on 6 June. On that day Italy became a sideshow.

Notes

1. Author's visit and interview August 1980. The study is now part of a museum in the Citadel Military Institute in Charleston.
2. Truscott, *Command Missions*, p 376.
3. Clark's Diary for 26 May; Matthews Collection, p 105.
4. Matthews interview with Alexander.
5. Alexander, Harold (Earl Alexander of Tunis), *The Alexander Memoirs*, John North, 1962, p 127.
6. Walker, *From Texas to Rome*, p 375.

7. Author's interview with staff officer 36th Division who wished to remain anonymous.
8. Looked after personnel.
9. Clark's Diary for 30 May; Matthews Collection.
10. Matthews interview with Clark, p 60.

43

What Next?

Rome had been sacked by the Gauls and the Visigoths, the Vandals, Barbarians and Napoleon. Nero had burned it to the ground. It had taken the Fifth Army 275 days and 125,000 casualties since it landed at Salerno to get there. Twenty thousand men were killed, of whom 12,000 were Americans. Mark Clark was the first general since the Byzantine Belisarius, who entered Rome in AD 536, to capture the city from the south and he knew his history well.

In the days of self-indulgence that followed, Clark gave no sign that he was aware of the butcher's bill among the infantry for his Roman triumph. Since the start of Operation Diadem the British and Canadian rifle companies had suffered 30% casualties, dead and wounded. They had come off lightly compared to the Americans who had a casualty rate of 41%. The biggest price had been paid by the Poles. In Anders' II Corps there were 43% casualties among the infantry. Nearly every second Polish rifleman was either dead or wounded.[1]

Oliver Leese had already swung Eighth Army northwards. The troops continued to move at that same steady pace which had sustained the advance since the breakout. Von Senger und Etterlin, who was busy coordinating the German retreat north of Rome, found Eighth Army reluctant to force the issue and there was little attempt to harry the enemy rearguards unduly.

Apart from the Americans, all the other nationalities in Fifth Army were denied their moment of glory. The British 1st and 5th Infantry Divisions, who suffered such appalling casualties at Anzio, grounded arms at Ardrea on the coast west of the city. The French, who in May 1944 made their crucially important contribution, were halted east of Rome. The 3rd Algerian Division reached the blown bridges on the

Aniene river at Lunghizza on the afternoon of 4 June. To its right, below Tivoli, the 1st Motorized Division took up the advance and both divisions pushed on the Tiber. Given their behaviour in liberating smaller Italian towns and villages, it was probably a wise decision to prevent their participation in the triumph. Indeed, over the previous week, as enemy resistance had slackened, the French spearhead of armoured cars and reconnaissance troops was immediately followed by US army trucks whose task was to evacuate the women and children ahead of the goumiers. Clark did, however, invite Juin and his generals to the celebrations.

Fifth Army Operational Instruction No 27, dated 4 June, directed that the 3rd US Infantry Division would form a garrison under the Commanding General City Administrative Section, Fifth Army. The 10,000 men of the 3rd US Infantry were to be assisted in their duties by 1st Battalion Duke of Wellington's Regiment from the 1st British Infantry Division and one composite battalion from the French Expeditionary Corps. There were times when Mark Clark's largesse knew no bounds.

The reception given to the American troops was hysterical. The roads leading into the city from the east and south were filled by cheering people. There were casualties, inflicted by snipers, the occasional Italian Fascist fanatic and by other American troops. The rivalry over boundaries became intense as elements from six American divisions moved into the city. Across the Tiber, on the north and north-western sides of the city, the Germans were still fleeing. An eye-witness described the scene.

> The Germans went on, wild-eyed, unshaven, unkempt, on foot, in stolen cars, in horse-drawn vehicles, even in carts belonging to the street cleaning department. There was no attempt at military formation. Some of them dragged small ambulances with wounded in them. They went, some with revolvers in hands, some with rifles cocked.
>
> On Corso Umberto, when one of them stumbled, his rifle went off and caused a panic among the crowd; for a moment there was indiscriminate shooting. Whereas last September they had come with machine guns trained on the Romans, it was a different matter now. They were frightened. . . . Most of the Republicans had fled the day before, but in the German rout were to be seen handsome motor cars with Fascist dignitaries looking anything but dignified in their anxiety to get away.

'Doc' Waters (his real name was Claude which is why he preferred to be called Doc) was a radio operator with an infantry squad in Company A 1st Battalion 349th Infantry 88 US Infantry Division. His company was tasked to set up a series of road blocks along the roads leading north-west towards Tivoli.

The German rear-echelon troops were surrendering in droves. Doc's squad occupied a road block on an intersection with Route 5, near to the ruins of Hadrian's Palace. One night they bagged a German paymaster. He was in a truck which pulled a trailer, a sort of mobile office. The inside of the trailer was crammed with money. The paymaster told them it was genuine Italian currency worth about 10 million dollars. Doc and the boys didn't believe him. They thought it was counterfeit, but it came in handy for lighting fires. When they were down to the last few lire they found out it was real!

The young American soldiers were overwhelmed by the welcome. A column of infantry wound its way past the Coliseum. 'Gee,' remarked one young wide-eyed GI, 'I didn't know our bombers had done that much damage.' Hollow-eyed from lack of sleep, bone weary from the long march, the mud of the mountains still on their stained uniforms, these soldiers, used only to the sight of ruined towns and haggard refugees, were traumatised by the sights and sounds that greeted them. Tall, beautiful buildings undamaged by the bombing, the dome of St Peter's basilica shimmering in the sun; for many it was their first experience of a big city. There were attractive women in fashionable clothes and wearing make-up. To the sex-starved GIs they looked like Hollywood film stars. Cheering, clapping, happy people swarmed all over the vehicles and the foot-slogging infantry. That night there wasn't a brothel in Rome which didn't have a line of soldiers waiting their turn. Wine was five cents a bottle and the services of a prostitute could be purchased for twelve cents or a dollar for the night. But many GIs were not required to pay for the privilege of being a liberator. Others that night were lucky enough to be invited into a home, to eat at a table spread with fresh linen and then to sleep between clean sheets on a soft mattress.

The Excelsior Hotel was requisitioned as a sort of officers' club. Women were freely available and went with the room, bed and board. Then somebody complained to the Military Authorities and MPs started to patrol the corridors. No women were allowed beyond the lobby and the public rooms (officially, that is).

Arthur B. Dodge, a sergeant in 350th Infantry, entered Rome on 4 June. He led his platoon through the Borghese Gardens and over the Tiber, securing the bridge at the Forum Mussolini. He was tasked to take the escarpment on the high ground to the north of the city to make sure that no one could fire upon Mark Clark and his men as they came riding into Rome. Finding himself in the smarter end of town, Dodge knocked at the door of a large villa with an ornate tower. It had a commanding view and would be ideal for a radio man. The door was opened by a little old lady who promptly slammed the door in Dodge's face when he tried to explain his mission. After continued knocking, the door was opened by an immaculately dressed woman who spoke to Dodge in impeccable English:

'Sergeant, what do you wish?'

Her perfume wafted over him. Restraining the temptation to answer truthfully, Dodge told her that he wished to use the tower as an observation post. She explained that this would be difficult. The residence was a convent for young girls. Dodge persuaded her to compromise, one man with a radio in return for some coffee and other basic rations.

His meeting at the convent with this beautiful woman, who turned out to be the Countess Juliana de Compagna, was not Dodge's only contact with the Catholic Church in Italy. On a subsequent visit to the eternal city the Countess arranged for the sergeant to have a private audience with the Pope!

On 4 June Rome was put out of bounds to the Eighth Army. American military police established road blocks on every road at the city limits. A major on the staff of General Kirkman's XIII (Br) Corps was arrested at gun-point by a white-helmeted policeman. Major Philip Sidney VC, Grenadier Guards (later Lord de Lisle and Dudley) had a similar experience. Actions such as these did little to cement the special relationship.

Truscott was summoned by Mark Clark to join him on the Capitoline Hill. Neither Truscott nor his Italian-speaking aide had ever been in Rome before and hadn't the slightest idea where the Capitoline Hill might be. Even with the sirens blaring Truscott's jeep was forced by the press of the crowd to move at a snail's pace. The aide grabbed hold of a young boy and sat him on the bonnet with instructions to guide them to the Capitoline. Halfway there they met the official party forcing its way through the swelling crowds. There was jeep after jeep – Clark, Keyes, Juin, dozens of staff officers, who believed their pen-pushing had earned them a place in the entourage and hundreds of reporters and photographers. One 'photo-opportunity' turned out to be a very embarrassing non-event for Clark's PR team. The convoy stopped at the Town Hall and cameras flashed as Clark hammered on the great wooden doors beneath the balcony where Mussolini had once strutted and postured to his crowds. The door remained locked.

Truscott eventually arrived at the Capitoline Hill and joined Clark and his staff. Bulbs flashed, correspondents pushed and jostled one another in their eagerness to put questions to the new conqueror of Rome. 'This is a great day for the Fifth Army,' Clark began. Truscott quickly tired of the pomp and posturing, and beat a retreat.

For a while even Clark lost interest in the Italian campaign. With the news of Overlord, every newspaper reporter and photographer in the theatre clamoured for reassignment. So Clark played the tourist, visited the ancient sites and met the Pope. It was hardly surprising that the pursuit of the Germans north of Rome lacked drive and coordination. And, arguably, Alexander lost a marvellous opportunity to inflict a crushing defeat on the retreating Germans. The gently rolling country-side north of Rome, stretching into Tuscany, was more open. Under a hot summer sun the ground was firm and the terrain more suited to armoured warfare. Alexander had four divisions' worth of armour, command of the air and ample stocks of fuel and ammunition. Kesselring's forces were disorganized, outnumbered and lacked mobility. They had never been in worse shape.

Could Alexander have brought them to book and finished the campaign once and for all? The generals were not totally diverted by the attractions of Rome. Logistically the city was a choke point which played havoc with the Allied lines of communication. With too few routes supporting too many troops there was confusion and chaos at times. And there were still ample opportunities for the German rearguard to delay and to obstruct, especially when confronted by a cautious foe.

The French halted and Oliver Leese fed the 6th (South African) Armoured Division into line for the pursuit. As the Eighth Army fumbled out, the divisions spread across the peninsula to the Adriatic coast and continued a broad advance towards the Pisa–Rimini Line and the next major obstacle along the River Arno. On the left flank, Truscott's VI (US) Corps advanced on a two-division front with regiments from the 34th (US) Infantry and 1st (US) Armoured Division taking it in turns to lead. At Civitavecchia the Americans captured the Anzio Express and learned for the first time that there were two guns not one. Allied aircraft had destroyed the bridges and prevented the Germans from taking the guns with them. Nobody's heart was in the advance. Regiments were rotated back to Rome for rest and recuperation, although after the first week the cynical citizenry were no longer so free with their favours. The Americans were to find that Rome was no different from anywhere else. Everything had its price.

There were parades and yet more parades. Awards and honours were distributed. Clark reviewed the 350th Infantry on the racecourse outside Rome. After the march-past the general addressed the soldiers. Clark spoke first followed by Major General Twain who commanded the Twelfth Air Force. Twain had a novel approach.

'Men,' said the General, 'why don't you yell at us what you need?'

There was silence. Then from deep in the ranks a voice yelled back.

'Hell, General. You can keep your god-damned air force. You bombed us more than the Germans did.'

Clark didn't ask Twain again.

On 11 June Truscott handed over to General Willis D. Crittenberger and his staff. The IV US Corps were now responsible for the advance to the Arno. The Americans were 85 miles north of Rome. An advance which averages just eleven miles a day against a supposedly beaten foe speaks for itself. Truscott and VI (US) Corps fell back to prepare for the invasion of Southern France. Clark was not consulted over which of the divisions were to be used. It so happened they were the 3rd, Walker's 36th and the 45th Infantry. This left Ryder's 34th Infantry as the longest-serving in the Italian campaign and they were none too happy at the prospect.

Walker was not to lead his beloved division to France. Clark had been true to his word after the disaster at the Rapido. He had allowed Walker to remain until he had secured a victory. On 23 June Clark told him that he was to be relieved of his command and sent back to the United States as Commandant of the Infantry Training School at Fort Benning, an appointment which did not carry a promotion. Frederick, who had been a brigadier for less than a month, was to take over command of the division as Major General. Brigadier Robert Stack, who had been Assistant Division Commander since the Rapido, and the three regimental commanders – all of whom were senior to Frederick – were passed over for command. Clark took the opportunity to spring-clean. Walker was not the only one to get his marching orders. The entire G staff in the division's headquarters were replaced or reassigned.[3] Clark also gave a direct order that both of Walker's sons were to be relieved and sent back to the United States.

Ironically the 36th (US) Infantry Division moved back to Paestum in preparation for the South of France and it was there that Walker took his farewell of his beloved Texans. On the very same ground where they had stormed ashore on 9 September 1943, the division marched past their general in review order. The place was appropriate.

Earlier that morning Walker had received a personal letter from Clark.

Dear General Walker:

My heartiest congratulations for your new appointment. I am delighted that The Infantry School will have such a skilled and experienced commandant.

I know how much the 36th Division will miss you after all you have done for it. Few Divisions have had the good fortune to be guided continuously through as many different and important campaign phases by the same able hand. The long period of thorough training in French Morocco and Algeria, the initial landing at Salerno, and the bitter fighting which ensued; then the long gruelling winter campaign on the main Italian front, particularly hard on the Division commander because of unavoidable, slow progress in comparison to the splendid effort put forth; finally, leading your Division into the fight at the crucial moment of the beachhead break-out and the brilliant operations which resulted in the capture of Rome, all have associated you indissolubly with the 36th Division and the Fifth Army.

The Fifth Army regrets the loss of one of its veteran commanders, but realizes the great role you are to play in the training of infantry for future battles.

At this time, I wish to express my very best wishes for every success as Commandant of The Infantry School, as well as to extend my congratulations for the superior job which you performed as Commander of the 36th Division. With my sincere thanks for your constant and loyal cooperation, I am,

Sincerely yours,
/s/ Mark W. Clark
Lieutenant General, USA, Commanding[4]

General Marshall was in Italy at this time. Alexander and Clark argued determinedly against the South of France operation but Marshall was adamant.

The result was that on 15 August 1944 VI (US) Corps and French Expeditionary Corps, a total of seven divisions in the Seventh Army, (under General Patch) landed on the French coast east of Marseille. It was called the champagne landing because Patch's forces punched empty air. Within a month they had swept up the Rhone Valley and linked up with General George Patton's Third US Army.

The landings, code-named Dragoon (the name was changed from Anvil), took place nine weeks after the invasion in Normandy and to this day have remained one of the most controversial operations of the Second World War. The Americans, with the exception of Mark Clark, saw Dragoon as the logical outcome of the decision on grand strategy taken by the Big Three in Tehran; namely that the Italian campaign should be closed down and the bulk of the Mediterranean war effort transferred to France to support the decisive effort against the Wehrmacht which, in turn, could only occur in Germany. Thereafter the war was to be fought against the Japanese.

Winston Churchill, and most of the British staff who were also in Italy that summer, considered Dragoon to be strategically flawed and unnecessary. Eisenhower's forces were firmly ashore in Normandy and the landing in the South of France, in their judgement, made no strategic contribution. Moreover the withdrawal of the troops, including the French with their specialist mountain warfare skills, denied Alexander the opportunity not just to drive the Germans out of Italy, but to advance south-east of the Alps by way of the Ljublijana Gap and beat the Russians to Vienna. In the light of subsequent events and the onset of the Cold War a whole generation of historians regarded the American decision to insist on Dragoon as a fateful error.

Back in April, the only way in which the necessary superiority in men and fire power could be devoted to the Fourth Battle of Cassino was to abandon Anvil as a simultaneous operation with Overlord. Anvil was deferred indefinitely. As the Allied Armies swept into Rome and ashore in Normandy the debate between the British and the Americans reopened. Marshall could see every virtue in liberating Rome and no compelling strategic reason for pushing the Germans beyond the Pisa–Rimini Line.

Early in June 1944 shortly after D-day, the US Chief flew to London for an informal conference with the British. Together they explored a number of options. Jumbo Wilson was asked to put the cases for landings for Anvil, an advance through the Pisa–Rimini Line into Austria, and a third option, landing at Sete 90 miles west of the Rhone Valley. Eisenhower was asked to present the case for a landing in the Bay of Biscay. Each amphibious operation was to be considered as a three-division lift to be launched about 25 July.

The debate developed across the agreed lines. Wilson ended up presenting the case for an advance via the Ljublijana Gap into Austria and southern Hungary. In this he was clearly prompted by Winston Churchill, who was increasingly concerned about the postwar European balance of power and the need to counter the Russians.

Eisenhower was backed both by the President and Marshall. They were in favour of Dragoon. The American position was clear. The need was to capture a major port like Marseille (there was no equivalent on the northern coast of France except Cherbourg and that was too far from the battle front) with excellent communications that could bring American divisions into Europe for the decisive battle. There were 40 divisions waiting in the United States. The Americans were not interested in the postwar picture, for the simple reason that the President had to win the war in Europe as quickly as possible and bring the boys home.

The Americans also feared a Balkan adventure. In fairness to Churchill, he never considered the support of Tito's partisans, even with the occasional deployment of Special Forces and artillery back-up, as the preliminary to a major new initiative. Churchill argued his case with his customary style, but people like Marshall were not particularly impressed. While the Allies were locked into the beachhead in Normandy the arguments for a South of France operation were persuasive, if not compelling. On 2 July President Roosevelt asked the Prime Minister to direct General Wilson to set the wheels in motion. In the last week of July, the British made one last effort to have Dragoon cancelled, but to no avail. Alexander was mortified.

Operation Dragoon might be viewed as the last gasp of the peripheral strategy, the indirect approach so long favoured by the British. But it is important to note that the failure of the British to get their way highlights the changing nature of the Anglo-American relationship. The United States had the military power but chose not to use it; the British had the political will but lacked the wherewithal to pursue it. The decline of Britain from the ranks of the great powers had begun.

Was Churchill right? If the Allies had entered south-eastern Europe in military strength would the Soviets have been deterred from making their play for Berlin? Churchill was accurate in predicting some postwar concerns, but a Western military presence stuck down in south-eastern Europe would have had little influence on Stalin, neither would it have affected events as they unfolded in postwar Berlin. Given the rapid demobilization of Anglo-American forces in the immediate postwar period there would probably have been little more than a token presence in the region. And even if there had been a sizeable contingent it was too far removed from the focus of attention at Berlin.

The British also accused the Americans of political naivety. But Roosevelt and Marshall had a clear grasp of what the American electorate was prepared to sacrifice. In this they showed great political awareness: Churchill completely misread his own domestic scene.

There was another consideration to take into account over Operation Dragoon. The French Expeditionary Corps would not have taken kindly to being confined to the Italian theatre, and denied the opportunity to liberate their own country. In July 1944 Marshal Juin had 100,000 men in

Italy and more on the way. The Americans fed, clothed, armed and paid them.

Under Allied Military Authorities' investigation, it emerged that the French plundered Italy, not on a personal but on an official basis.

The first hint of the irregularities committed by the French reached the Allied Information Services during the summer of 1944, a little after the occupation of Rome. It seems, however, that the plundering had started in Southern Italy, when the frontline was stationary at Cassino. It appeared strange that the French Government in exile (which possessed so little money that it was forced to depend upon the Americans if it wanted to pay its soldiers) could organize this large-scale purchasing, and at first it was thought that this affair was carried out by a large organization of private speculators.

This first interpretation appeared to be supported by the fact that the purchases were initially limited to vehicles: trucks, luxury motor cars and spare parts. But suspicions hardened when it was discovered that the mysterious organization was purchasing any kind of goods. The first information picked up by the American Civilian Administration signalled intensive purchases of ink, clothes, hemp, ropes, precious metals for industry, nails, lathes, electrical equipment, various machinery, skins. This great variety was contrary to the habit of ordinary speculators and of the gangs of black-marketeers who generally specialized in a well determined traffic only.

It was enough to follow a few and relatively easy clues to understand that the enormous purchasing organization was headed by the French Military Command in Italy. The Quarter Masters Corps of the French Army, Air Force and Navy, and especially the Headquarters of Palazzo Vidoni in Rome, not only participated, but directed, the scam. French Officers, whose sole military purpose was to act as buyers, were lodged at the Plaza Hotel not to raise too much suspicion. But this precaution was soon abandoned and Palazzo Vidoni became a sort of large procurement executive or agency. Several Italian civilians, who had gone there for other reasons, reported their surprise at being asked by the Moroccan guards, 'What have you got to sell?' instead of the usual, 'What do you want?' The actual seller was sent to the proper *rayon*, where an office adorned with military nomenclature was actually dealing with the purchase of olive oil or of vehicles.[5]

The French officers used an outside network of traffickers or agents, mostly Levantine with French citizenship.

The French did not care about the source of the purchased goods or question the authenticity of ownership. It is hardly surprising that in a country where the black market was so prominent some gangs of thieves worked exclusively for the French officers. They paid far better than the normal receivers and, what was more important, were untouchable by the Italian police. The case of the Roman lawyer who, 24 hours after his automobile had been stolen, recognised it in Via Condotti with a French officer at the wheel, became notorious. The evidence showed that the French, in the Rome area alone, from 4 June to 1 December 1944, procured over 800 cars, most of which were luxury models; they were marked with military numbers.

The French used three main warehouses: the former Mussolini barracks of the *milizia* in Viale Mazzini, a store in Viale Manzoni and another store behind Palazzo Venezia. From these places everything was despatched to Bagnoli by means of French military motor vehicles. From this little port the goods were shipped to North Africa.

In September American investigators submitted their findings to Fifteenth Army Group headquarters at Caserta. In early November reports were sent to the appropriate officers in London and Washington. The latter replied in December suggesting that the matter be handed over to the Criminal Investigation Division (the military version of the FBI). The officers on the case quickly came up with some damning evidence. The French were quietly approached and, realizing the game was up, they undertook to cease such activities forthwith. Nothing more was said of the matter.

Notes

1. The official casualty figures for the three and a half weeks of Diadem are:

United States forces	18,000
British/Commonwealth/Poles	15,000
French	11,000

2. Adleman and Walton, *Rome Fell Today*, p 256.
3. Colonel Carl Ives, G1; Colonel Walter Crowther, G2; Colonel Fred Walker Jnr, G3; and Colonel Carl Finney, G4.
4. Walker, *From Texas to Rome*, p 406.
5. *Risorgimento Liberale*, 5 July 1946. Carried in WO 204/10915.

44

The D-Day Dodgers

Lady Nancy Astor could see no virtue in the Italian campaign and said as much. When she called the troops in Italy suntanned malingerers or the 'D-day Dodgers', news of the insult spread like wildfire. There was even one story that an American master sergeant of Italian extraction from the Lower East Side of New York, had placed a 'contract' on the lady.

Soldiers gave vent to their bitterness at this unwarranted slur with their own campaign lament, sung to the tune of Lili Marlene.

> We're the D-day Dodgers out in Italy
> Always drinking vino, always on the spree,
> Eighth Army skivers and the Yanks,
> We live in Rome and dodge the tanks
> For we're in the D-day Dodgers
> The boys whom D-day dodged.
>
> Look around the mountains in the mud and rain,
> There's lots of little crosses, some which bear no name,
> Blood, sweat and toil are all gone
> The boys beneath them slumber on.
> These are your D-day Dodgers,
> And they're still in Italy.

The German Army under Kesselring was to exhibit quite remarkable powers of recovery. Initially, as the Fourteenth on the German right flank and the Tenth on the left – or Adriatic side – retreated they were in a very shaky condition. When Rome fell, three good formations, the 65th, 362nd and 715th Infantry Divisions had been practically annihilated. Most of the others had a deployable infantry strength of about two battalions. There were heavy losses in transport and material and on congested narrow roads, through villages, they suffered constantly from Allied air strikes.

Fifth Army bulldozers made their appearance with the spearhead units. In bottlenecks, where the air force had left its calling card, white-eyed young GIs, wearing goggles and dirty handkerchiefs around mouth and nose to stop them gagging on the stench, cleared a path. Twisted, burnt-out vehicles and impediments, animal and human remains, were shoved aside.

While Alexander lost the divisions earmarked for Dragoon, together with more than one-third of his heavy artillery and air assets, Kesselring received fresh reinforcements. But Germany was beginning to scrape the bottom of the manpower barrel. The 20th Luftwaffe Field Division, aircraft mechanics and the like, no longer had aeroplanes to service and maintain, and they made reluctant infanteers. Within a month and after heavy losses, they were fit only to be attached to 26th Panzers as a rear-echelon formation. The 356th Infantry Division had been in the theatre since May, performing coastal defence and anti-partisan duties in the Genoa area. The division had previously been a training unit but it was now pressed into battle. The 162nd Turkeman Infantry division had three-quarters of its fighting strength recruited from ex-POWs drawn from the Soviet Asian Republics. They were poor value.

Three days after Rome fell, Alexander issued his directives. Eighth Army was to advance in the Adriatic sector to seize Arezzo and Florence. Fifth Army on the left was to move on Pisa, Lucca and Pistoia. The war would not be won in Italy but in Germany. So what contribution could be made by a continued Allied offensive in northern and mountainous regions of Italy? Other than the vague notion of tying down German divisions which might otherwise be deployed elsewhere, there was a need, for political reasons, to complete the task of liberating Italy, and to deny the enemy the industrial resources of the Po Basin. These were at best secondary objectives and second-best reasons for asking men to go through a second winter in this bleak and unforgiving country. Marshall was right in advocating an advance to the Pisa–Rimini Line and no further.

But there were other considerations. Publicity-hungry as he was, would Clark have been content to see out the rest of the war in a sideshow? What might the fate of the Italian campaign have been if Clark's earlier proposals to Eisenhower, for the Seventh Army to be brought in to run Italy after Rome while Clark took the Fifth to France, had been put into practice? Equally, could the British government have left the much-vaunted and nationally popular Eighth Army to wither on the vine? Too much blood had been spilled in Italy for the campaign to be discarded. But a lack of purpose, coupled to the appalling winter conditions in the high Apennines, was to prove a major contributory factor to all sorts of disciplinary problems later.

Even though the Fifth Army had lost a quarter of a million men to Dragoon, Clark could still have inflicted a major reverse on the enemy had he pursued them relentlessly on a narrow front. Instead, Fifth Army rested on its laurels and advanced at width. The Germans made a stand at Orvieto, where the bridge was particularly important. The 6th (South African) Armoured Division inflicted heavy casualties on the Turkestans. Hitler despatched the 16th Panzer Grenadier Division Reichsführer SS from OKW Reserve; it went straight into battle and it soon made its presence felt. Kesselring had sacrificed the weaker formations against a cautious advance, and in two weeks his better units began to recover their strength and resilience.

On the Adriatic sector the Eighth Army's advance was uneven. The left flank moved quickly but the centre and right were held up in the difficult Abruzzo country. The 8th Indian Division made a splendid advance which took them from Spoleto to Perugia by the 20 June, a distance of 20 miles on the Adriatic front. Alongside the Indians in V (Br) Corps, were the 1st (Cdn) Infantry and the Italian Utili Division which had just entered the line for the first time. There were now two divisions in the Italian Liberation Corps which numbered about 22,000 men. The Nembo Division was structured around a parachute division. The Utili, which was derived from the Motorized Group which had fought so disastrously at Monte Lungo, did not have a name, so they called it after the Corps Commander, General Umberto Utili.

The Polish Corps spent the early days of August in anguish. News of the Warsaw uprising by the underground army filtered through. Russian intransigence and Western procrastination could have produced a very ugly situation had not Anders and his officers kept a tight rein over the flow of information. Thus broadcasts told of mercy flights by Eighth Air Force Liberators and their heavy losses, while the Russian attitude to overflying and other obstacles were played down. It helped, in a perverse fashion, that the Poles were in action at the time and had other things on their minds.

Kesselring defined clear strategic aims to his troops. The rearguards were to delay the Allies to allow the main defence positions known as the Gothic Line to be prepared. They held the Allies on the Albert Line astride Lake Trasimene, south of Arezzo, and Siena, where tentacles from the Apennine spine filled more of the peninsula. The Albert position was no more than a temporary obstacle, but the Allies were forced to pause, regroup and mount a set-piece attack, which took time and lost men. It took three weeks to advance 45 miles.

Domenick Consalvo was a GI in C Company 361st Infantry, 91st Division. He was wounded when his unit attacked in the advance to the Arno river.

> We started to crawl up the hill. I didn't know who was in front of me but as we were going he got hit on the foot with one of the shells exploding near us. His foot was in bad shape. My head was not far from his foot. We were near a tree, I told him to move behind the tree and he did, but as he was doing that I was in a prone position and was just about to raise myself up on my arms to crawl some more. I did not hear anything for a moment, my body was being crushed. I felt like a truck was running over me and trying to push me into the ground. The pressure was so great on my body and in a minute it released me. And the next thing I remembered I was thrown into the air and going around and around. It was a long way up to me with my arms and legs flying around and yelling and screaming while this was going on. I came down and bounced a couple of times and started to slide down the side of the mountain. I then came to a sudden stop and more pain. It was not until I stopped falling that I realised that a shell exploded near me and that I had been hit. I really did not know if I was dead or alive. It is just a feeling you have when something like that happens. I lay there with my legs dangling over the edge in so much pain. It was so hard to describe the pain. I was crying, it hurt so bad. I must have lain there for what seemed eternity with the fear of moving the wrong way and falling off the side of the mountain which was certain death, not that I did not feel like I wasn't dead already.
>
> An officer who was also wounded asked me how bad I was hurt and where did I get hit. I told him I really did not know. But I soon found out as I was feeling my back, because that is where most of the pain was coming from and the blood. I reached around with my right hand and all I felt was a big hole in my back and blood was coming out. My fingers went inside the hole. I knew then how bad I was hit. In fact, whenever I was breathing in, I could feel air coming through the hole in my back. I asked the officer if there was anything I could do for him. I did have my sulfa kit on my belt yet. That is all I had on me. When I got hit with the shell, the shrapnel came across my back and took my pack and canteen clean off. All I had left was the two front straps on to my cartridge belt.

Consalvo was captured by the Germans and eventually taken to a field hospital:

It was my turn to be carried in. They were carrying them in pretty fast. When they carried me in, I seen why. There were about ten or more tables lined up and each one had a soldier on it and the doctors had rubber aprons on and they were full of blood. It was so horrible and the smell, I cannot put the smell on paper. I wish I could. Just picture, say a dog, that just got hit by a car, and it is just lying there with its guts half out and it is 98 degrees out and the flies all over its guts. Can you imagine the smell with one? Well, that would be just a sample of what it would be like, only ten times greater with a human being, and closed in a room with about twenty soldiers being cut up at the same time, and the temperature in the nineties.

As they put me on the table the doctor said to me in very good English, 'Son, you have been hit pretty bad. I will see what I can do.' He knew I was an American because first of all, he could tell by my uniform, at least what was left of it. He finished tearing the rest of my shirt off. I was lying on my stomach, looking at the table next to me. And they were operating on that, and they were cutting his arm off near the shoulder. I was horrified. I tried to turn my head the other way and when I looked the other way the other side was not any better. I saw all kinds of blood coming from there, too. About that time my doctor started to put something on my back which made it feel cool. I think it was what they called liquid ether. It felt numb and cold. I felt no pain for a little while anyway.

He was talking to me and said that most of them spoke English, as doctors. As he put that stuff on me he reached out and got what looked like a knife and I turned my head and looked up into what looked like a mirror and I could see what he was doing. You know all the time this was going on, and I was seeing all this. Every once in a while I was getting sicker by the minute. He started to cut into my back. I could not feel anything because it was dead back there. After he cut something out. He took what looked like a fork and stuck it in my back and pulled out a piece of meat and metal and bloody all over and put it in front of my face and said do you want this as a souvenir. About that time I heaved, but nothing was in my stomach to come out, except some wine they gave me. So I spilled my guts out all over the place. But I guess they were not surprised. I guess that was the straw that broke the camel's back.

As he was putting the dressing on he was talking to me and said that he could not get all of the shrapnel out, but got all of the big pieces out, and said that I was very lucky. The way it hit me it went right between my lungs and my kidneys, but it did cut a lot of my muscles in my back on my right side. I could have imagined how open it was because now after 40 years, the scar after it closed up is still about two inches wide and about six inches long. He must have been able to see my lungs and my kidney. That is probably why when I was breathing, I felt air coming in the back. They finished bandaging me. Of course, I still had all the blood on me. The part they cleaned up was the part they were working on.

They put me on a stretcher and carried me out and put me in the other big tent and waited for transportation to a hospital in Florence.

In the summer the Americans introduced the Combat Infantry Badge. Nobody wanted to serve in the infantry and the badge was the equivalent of a pilot's wings. It was intended to be won worn with pride. Infanteers wore it with distinction; staff officers and rear-echelon stallions hankered to find ways around the tight rules and conditions that controlled qualifications and eligibility. There was also combat pay too, $10 a month irrespective of rank.

Relations between the British and the Americans were still very strained. On 14 July Oliver Leese was invited by Juin to the *Quatorze Juillet* ceremony in Siena. At the appointed time, and accompanied by a couple of aides, Leese was escorted to a makeshift stand at the bottom of the main square. He described events later in a letter home.

Everyone waited – and about half an hour late two motorcyclists drove into the square at a terrific rate, followed by a jeep, and then a vast limousine with an enormous American flag on one side and a great huge red flag with 3 stars on the other. Out stepped Mark Clark, very like Mistinguett. Meanwhile General Alex, who had been waiting till this eccentricity occurred, came in next, and was welcomed by Clark and Juin. The three then went to the centre of the Parade, and then they played the national anthems. They then inspected the Parade. No one took the slightest notice of me, except photographers, who quite obviously came and photographed me . . . in the crowd standing at the salute during the national anthems. This behaviour on the top of their insolence in Rome, which they put out of bounds to me and the 8th Army, and the fact that they never asked us to a single ceremony in Rome, or ever mentioned the 8th Army in any speech – was over the odds. It is bad for the 8th Army repute. So I walked out on them in the middle – I sent a telegram to Juin saying I was sorry I had to leave for operational reasons. But I trust the Americans noticed something."

Italian popular resistance began to gather momentum. The German High Command ordered that for every German soldier killed, ten Italians were to be executed. Today, driving through the pretty hill-top towns in Tuscany and the Chianti country, you may find the names of those who paid that price preserved in the names of streets and on other war memorials. Men and women were rounded up and deported as slave labour to the Reich. More fled into the hills. There were few refugees in the sense of the Eastern Front or North West Europe. As war

357

approached, the local population would simply take to the hills and await the arrival of the Allies. In the summer and early autumn of 1944 this was no great hardship; the weather was fine and the advance predictable and fairly fast. Later, in the Apennine winter, it was a different story.

At the end of July the Eighth Army had a VIP visit. Accompanied by the Prime Minister, George VI travelled to Italy under the pseudonym of General Lyon. In a letter home Oliver Leese described the occasion at Alexander's forward CP at Viterbo.

I have not written for two days as we have had the King with us. He thoroughly enjoyed himself – was the most cheerful – and the visit was the greatest success. He loved his caravans with their glorious view, and was most comfortable.

We were lucky, as the Indians fought a good little battle about six miles away. He had a wonderful view, first from an OP (observation post) in Arezzo and then from his bath, while the Grenadier band played just behind his caravan. He was thrilled. Few Kings these days can have watched a battle from his bath to the strains of martial music by his own guards. . . . We went to Perugia and met Dick McCreery and motored through large numbers of cheering British and Indian Troops. He stopped several times and talked so nicely to officers and men.

He knighted Dick (McCreery) after tea. We then went to the OP and then here. . . . Alex came to dinner and Dick.

Next day was a long one. We started at 8.30 am with Kirkie, and drove through many British, Indian, Canadian, NZ and SA troops, to say nothing of our Basuto boys who greeted him with loud 'WHOOS'. . . . He had two parades. At the first he gave two VCs to Capt Wakeford and to our friend Fusilier Jefferson. At the second he presented the VC to the Indian (Sepoy Kamal Ram) who won it on the Rapido. . . . We then flew to Castiglione, on Lake Trasimene, where I presented my Army HQ's brigadiers, and then we had a great parade of the Poles. 1,000 of them. . . . In the morning the King knighted me at TAC. I knelt bareheaded with my right knee on a small stool. He touched me on both shoulders with his sword and then shook me by the hand. I put my hat on and saluted. It was wonderful to be knighted in the field, and I was very proud. A wonderful week for me.

When we came back in the evening it was nice and early, and he came and had a quiet tea under the trees in the cool. . . . Then some Brigade officers came in to meet him. Charles Haydon – Andrew Scott – Erich Gooch – George Burns. Bob Coats – Jocelyn Gurney – (Derek) Cardiff – John Nelson – who was Lascelles's Coy Commander when he was captured – Leveson, whom the King specially asked to see. Sosnowski and Anders came to dinner. We had the Polish orchestra play and also the Pipes of the Scots Guards. We made the band play 'Lili Marlene' – three times. It is now well known as my favourite tune. We also made Anders sing his folksong of Lwow – and the King and I sang the chorus in what we called Polish.[2]

Shortly before the royal visit there were some changes in the higher command at Eighth Army. General Allfrey left V Corps for an appointment in the United States and was succeeded by General Keightley. Gerald Templer, who must have been in line for a corps command, was moved from 56th Infantry to command 6th Armoured Division. Oliver Leese had tremendous confidence in Templer and saw him as a corps commander but felt he needed the experience of a term with an armoured division. Templer assumed command the day the King arrived at Army Group headquarters. It was a pleasant interlude and then back to business – clearing the Germans out of the hills above Arezzo.

On 5 August the forward units of 6th Armoured were just twelve miles south-east of Florence. On the same day the vanguard of the South African Division, on their left, entered the city. Templer set out for the front, accompanied by his ADC and a driver, who sat in the back. The General invariably drove himself. The road up the Arno Valley was narrow and twisting. On the verges white tapes indicated the presence of uncleared mines. A 15-cwt Bedford utility rumbled towards them down the single-track road. It was returning to the rear echelon with a grand piano which had been used by the Guards Brigade officers' mess while they had been out of the line. The driver, spotting the jeep with the general at the wheel, painstakingly pulled over onto the verge and onto a mine as the jeep drew level. The rear wheel of the Bedford sailed up into the air and hit Templer a shattering blow that crushed him against the steering wheel.

The ADC and the driver lifted Templer onto a front door torn from a deserted cottage and tied him down with piano wire. His backbone was broken. The division lost a very fine commander but, in a perverse fashion, the tragedy was a morale booster to the Eighth Army. The word spread like wildfire that the General had been hit by a grand piano. It appealed to a soldier's sense of humour.[3]

On 18 August Leese enjoyed a few days in Rome. The Americans by this time had got over their silliness and the city was open to all Allied personnel. Leese stayed in the Grand Hotel where he was given the VIP treatment. As usual he kept his wife well informed.

[writing] in a vast sitting room – the Royal suite with pile carpets, tapestry,

painted furniture and vast mirrors. A great contrast to the caravans. Goering and Hitler were in this room. It is said to have microphones concealed all over it! When Hitler was here he had 700 police guards in the hotel. At a black market restaurant signed the visitor's book: it was very interesting – Goering, Goebbels, Ciano, Kesselring, Funck and all their wives, headed by Frau Goering. It must have been an extraordinary racket.[4]

Tom Holladay, by now a first lieutenant and with a DSC for his gallantry at Minturno, also enjoyed a break from the line and instead found himself serving on another front.

Fifth Army Public Relations, aware of the discord that existed between the air forces and the fighting units on the ground, arranged an exchange. An officer and a sergeant from the infantry, both decorated for valour, were to change places with a similar pair from a bomber squadron. Tom Holladay was chosen to represent the infantry. In Rome they put him in a plane for the first time in his life. The aircraft, an L5 or Cub observation aircraft (the air forces called them grasshoppers), had no passenger seats so Holladay sat on his duffel bag in the back. When the plane took off he went head over heels and ended up wedged against the rear fuselage. By the time he had extricated himself and scrambled back to a window they were over the sea and en route to Corsica. There Holladay joined a medium bomber Air Group flying B-25 Mitchells.

The second time Holladay flew, was in a Mitchell on an operation to bomb bridges in the Po Valley. He sat right up in the Plexiglass nose with the bombardier. When they came over the target, puffs of white smoke appeared in the sky around them.

'There's flak out there,' said the bombardier into his radio mike. Holladay could see that it scared the hell out of him. But Holladay just laughed; to him it looked like firecrackers. When they landed, a tight-lipped bombardier showed him the holes caused by flak in the aircraft's fabric.

'Hell, man,' Holladay said, 'if I'd been on the ground with that ordnance around I'd have dirtied my pants.'

He spent two weeks with the Group and flew on five missions. There were good rations, he slept in a cot with a hair mattress and clean sheets in a centrally heated room with hot showers. And in the morning if it was foggy, they didn't go to war, but went back to bed. The PR men had a field day taking photographs and arranging press interviews. Then came the moment when they brought the four men together for a radio broadcast. Each was supposed to praise the other's efforts. The air force Captain who never went further forward than the battalion headquarters told the interviewer. 'Man, that infantry thing is hairy.' Holladay let the side down. When asked for his view of air force life he said he'd join tomorrow. 'They had it real easy compared to us dogfaces.'

Tom Holladay was sent back to the battalion. He didn't know it then but the air force had given him the only glimpse he was going to have of the Po Valley.

Notes

1. Ryder, *Oliver Leese*, p 178.
2. Ibid., pp 181–2.
3. Templer recovered from his injuries, though he did not return to a combat command in the war. He later became the Governor General in Malaya during the Emergency, and a field marshal.
4. Ryder, *Oliver Leese*, p 186.

45

Florence

Kesselring decreed there should be no sustained defence of precious Florence. Even so all the bridges across the Arno at Florence were blown with the exception of the Ponte Vecchio, which was blocked by craters and demolished buildings and not strong enough for heavy traffic anyway.

These instructions were 'interpreted' by the soldiers on the ground with typical Teutonic thoroughness. Daniel Lang, a correspondent with *New Yorker* Magazine later described the scene:

> The German treatment of Florence amounts to an atrocity story. Most of the city is still standing, but thanks to the enemy's well-placed demolitions, many of the most beloved parts are gone. According to Lt Frederick Hartt, a former Yale art instructor, now serving as the A.M.G's Fine Arts and Monuments Officer for this region, about a third of medieval Florence has been destroyed or damaged beyond repair. Much of the section that was always considered most characteristic of old Florence – the walk along the Arno, where the thirteenth- and fourteenth-century houses, with their bell towers and enclosed balconies, lined the river's bank – is now rubble. After the war, there may be an attempt to put up facsimiles of these houses, but there is certainly reason to doubt that it will be possible to recapture the atmosphere of these buildings that Dante and Petrarch and other immortals once knew. With these buildings disappeared their contents, irreplaceable furnishings, invaluable libraries and collections, among them the books and photographs assembled by the late Raimond van Marle, the noted Dutch art historian.
>
> All this destruction can be ascribed to what appears to have been one of the rare attempts of the Germans to preserve *Kultur* outside their own country. As the Allies moved towards the city, the Nazis, using understandable military tactics, decided to destroy the bridges across the Arno to delay our advance. Although they had no hesitation about blowing up the Ponte Santa Trinita,

one of the finest of all Renaissance bridges (it resisted three charges of explosives before it fell), they felt the shop-encrusted Ponte Vecchio, which is somewhat reminiscent of Nuremburg architecture, ought to be spared. They were not, however, prepared to cede any military advantages to the Allies. They therefore set demolition charges in the houses at both ends of the bridge, to block it with huge mounds of rubble. To keep the partisans from learning of their plans and possibly deactivating the mines, the Germans gave the occupants of the houses no warning. After the explosions, an uncounted number of corpses lay buried under the ruins, and part of the Via de'Bardi, the Via de'Guicciardini, the Borgo San Jacopo, the Via Por Santa Maria, and several other streets – the heart of Giotto's Florence – were wrecked. Among the more heavily damaged buildings were the Churches of Santo Stefano and Santa Trinita and the Palazzo di Parte Guelfa, all particularly fine structures. Several of the Uffizi Gallery's sixteenth-century frescoed ceilings fell and the north end of the Pitti Palace is scarred and windowless. Now that the Nazis have begun shelling the city, there will be further destruction. So far, the Strozzi Palace has been struck thirty-nine times. Brunelleschi's Church of San Lorenzo has suffered seven hits and the churches of the Santo Spirito and Santa Croce have gaping holes in their roofs. Just the other day the Germans damaged a new military objective, the Duomo's Baptistry.[1]

Ever since Franco Magrini had discharged himself from the Italian Army at the time of the capitulation he had lived in Florence. Franco had been a lieutenant in the Italian Army serving with a unit on the Yugoslav border at the time of the armistice. In the confusion at the time he had discharged himself and headed for home in Florence. His father and mother lived in retirement in their villa on the outskirts of the city. There were communist partisans operating in the area and, because his father was a count, they didn't trust him, so he formed his own underground group from among his friends. His contact man was the bartender at the Hotel Excelsior. The hotel had been requisitioned by the Germans for their senior officers, but was still managed by the Swiss family who were the owners. They would let Franco use their private apartment in the hotel and he went there every Friday to collect information. He was protected by the fact that his father knew General Dollmann, the SS Commander in Florence. Dollmann loved Italy and also believed that the war was lost unless the Americans and the British joined with the Germans to fight the Russians; so he tolerated his activities.

Franco's father told him he had been given the German plans for destroying the bridges in Florence although they had decided not to make a fight for the city. By the middle of July 1944, the Germans were falling back. But every day German tanks would rumble through the old city to

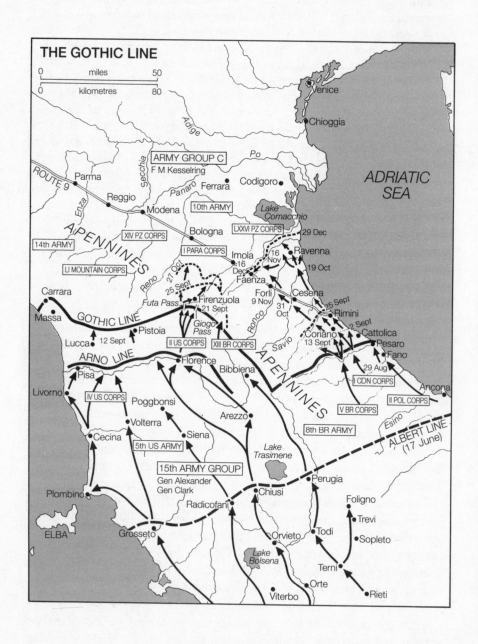

THE GOTHIC LINE

0 miles 50
0 kilometres 80

ROUTE 9

Parma

Reggio

Modena

A P E N N I N E S

XIV PZ CORPS

14th ARMY

LI MOUNTAIN CORPS

Secchia

Enza

Panaro

Adige

Po

ARMY GROUP C
F M Kesselring

10th ARMY

Ferrara

Codigoro

Lake
Comacchio

LXXVI PZ CORPS

29 Dec

ADRIATIC
SEA

Venice

Chioggia

Bologna

I PARA CORPS

Imola

16
Dec

16 Oct

Ravenna

19 Oct

27 Oct

Reno

25 Sept

Faenza

16
Nov

Carrara

GOTHIC LINE

Futa Pass

Firenzuola
21 Sept

Forli
9 Nov

Cesena

31
Oct

25 Sept

Massa

Pistoia

Giogo
Pass

Ronco

Rimini

Coriano
13 Sept

2 Sept

Cattolica

Lucca

12 Sept

II US CORPS

XIII BR CORPS

Savio

Pesaro

ARNO LINE

Florence

Bibbiena

A P E N N I N E S

Fano

29 Aug

Pisa

Livorno

IV US CORPS

Poggbonsi

Arezzo

I CDN CORPS

Ancona

II POL CORPS

Volterra

Siena

V BR CORPS

Cecina

5th US ARMY

Lake
Trasimene

8th BR ARMY

Esino

ALBERT LINE
(17 June)

15th ARMY GROUP
Gen Alexander
Gen Clark

Perugia

Foligno

Trevi

Plombino

Grosseto

Radicofani

Chiusi

Orvieto

Todi

Sopleto

ELBA

Lake
Bolsena

Terni

Orte

Viterbo

Rieti

cow the people and prevent rioting and opposition. There were also Fascist snipers who fired indiscriminately into the street, especially if a crowd gathered.

Franco wanted to inform the Americans about the German plans to destroy the bridges. He crossed the German lines very easily and came upon the American 1st Armoured Division, where he was screened by G2 officers, the American intelligence, and denounced by the communist partisans 'who had come over like heroes'.

'You cannot take him,' the partisans declared. 'His father was a big Fascist.'

'Are you a Fascist?' they asked.

'Of course I was,' he replied. 'Everybody was a Fascist under Mussolini.'

'You're the first Fascist we've met,' the American declared.

Franco knew everything would be all right especially when he explained that his mother was English and Jewish. The Americans offered him a choice, to serve either with the Eighth Army or to stay with them. Franco became a liaison officer in Fifth Army.

In late July the Allies closed up to the south bank of the River Arno, and by 21 August, the last of the German rearguards had retreated to the Gothic Line.

Earlier in the month the Fifth Army received some much-needed reinforcements; but it was a question of quantity rather than quality. The 92nd (US) Infantry Division, an all-Black infantry division led by white officers, arrived from the United States. They were joined by the Brazilian Expeditionary Corps, a force of 25,000 men under the command of Major General Jono Batista Mascarenhes de Moraes. The Brazilians had no combat experience at all and lacked the necessary training to handle the rigours of campaigning in Italy. All that they represented for Mark Clark was a long-term investment of dubious value and an immediate logistical headache.

Florence marked the Allies' army boundary. Beyond the city it was planned to feed the 88th (US) Infantry into the line and to attack northwards from positions currently held by the New Zealanders. In order to implement the plan the 88th sent twelve junior officers, platoon leaders, to the New Zealanders. Each was to be attached to a particular infantry company, monitor progress and then guide their own companies into the position ready take over the offensive. The plan was to complete the change-over secretly, preserve surprise and sustain the momentum of the attack.

Second Lieutenant John Campbell, a platoon leader in the 88th (US) Infantry, was given orders to liaise with B Company 23rd New Zealand Infantry Battalion. A truck took him to a road junction in the extreme southern outskirts of Florence where a patrol from B Company was to guide him forward to company headquarters. He waited all afternoon at the road junction. About 11.00 pm a six-man patrol arrived. Veterans of Tobruk and El Alamein, these men wore no helmets and sneakers instead of shoes. They moved swiftly and silently, rifles at the ready. Campbell was told to follow the last man, a muscular Mickey Rooney type whom he nick-named 'Mushroom'. As they moved out on a zig-zag course into the city proper on this pitch-black moonless night, Mushroom quickly became the most important factor in Campbell's young life.

They zigged and zagged for several miles, working their way closer to the Arno river and to the familiar sound of battle. When they reached Via Maggiore, the wide boulevard that runs straight through the business and commercial district of central Florence, they hugged the right-hand side and dashed quickly across each side street. Blue and white tracer bullets, in one- and two-second bursts, swept Via Maggiore. The patrol could no longer function as a unit. They moved forward from doorway to doorway and across each intersection one man at a time, darting forwards between bursts of tracer fire without loss. Each time Campbell moved forwards he was reassured to find Mushroom awaiting his arrival. As they worked their way forward, Campbell could see a German machine-gun crew firing from a second-storey window on the opposite side of Via Maggiore. Every minute or so they would fire a burst in their direction, fanning the fire to secure unpredictable ricochet tracers from which there was no true defilade protection. Clearly the sooner they reached B Company the better. Cordite smoke gave them some cover, and, from experience, they knew that a machine-gun crew is briefly blinded and deafened by the noise and flash of their own fire.

With instinctive infantryman timing, Mushroom waited for the end of a long burst of fire then, at a crouch, moved out into an extremely wide intersection through dense smoke. Campbell found himself totally alone. He had no idea where the New Zealand patrol had gone. He crouched low and prepared to make a dash for it. Just then Jerry opened up with sustained machine-gun fire, from the second-floor gun across the street about 85 yards ahead, and from both right and left, sweeping the wide cross street. Campbell made it unharmed to the side of a dark stone structure perhaps four stories tall. There was another burst from the second floor, but it seemed to be aimed far behind him down the Via

Maggiore. He crept forward and found cover in a doorway. No Mushroom. The heavy door was shut and locked. Jerry ripped off a few more rounds. Campbell felt his way forward some 20 yards to the next door. Still no Mushroom!

The next few minutes seemed like eternity itself. Campbell tiptoed to a doorway directly across the street from the German gun crew. He had his little carbine ready in case he was spotted. He had no idea if he had passed beyond New Zealand lines into no-man's-land or German territory. He was stuck, and couldn't help thinking what the hell he was doing in this predicament 3,500 miles from home. Should he go forward? Should he go back? Should he stay here until dawn's early light? 'Where are you Mushroom . . . where the hell are you?'

Without the slightest warning his arms were pinned. His head was turned sharply to the right, mouth firmly covered and carbine twisted away. There was the unmistakable chill of cold steel pressed on his throat. Campbell didn't attempt to struggle. The knife at his throat never moved while his bayonet and grenades were removed. Deft fingers explored across his crossed rifle insignia and along his uniform. Campbell was in total blackness, unable to see the street or the Jerries. Then he was spun through a burlap curtain into a dimly lit room full of soldiers.

Mushroom introduced Campbell to the company commander, Major Brown, who explained he was on the verge of sending his men to find him. Campbell breathed a sigh of relief.

Tossing grenades ahead as they 'cleaned and tidied up the block', the men of B company seemed unconcerned with the machine gun chattering away every few minutes not 20 yards away. The Major's personal bodyguard was an enormous Maori, powerful, broad-shouldered and as graceful as a cat. He was the man who had held that knife to Campbell's throat and afterwards gave him the warmest handshake of his life.

On the Adriatic front, the 91st (US) Infantry Division was tasked with the capture of Pisa. Roy Livengood, a PFC with E Company 363rd Infantry was with the lead unit for the attack:

The jump-off for Pisa was set at 0300 hours.

In 1944, the Arno River Valley above Leghorn was a flat, canal checkered plain; two miles north of Leghorn was a series of five large canals and several smaller ones. The plan was to cross the canals and move straight up the highway in a column of platoons to the river. We got as far as the very outskirts of the city before we were fired on from enemy guns located in a cemetery and in part of the factory district to the north. One of our squads reached the airport east of the highway where it met a small force of machine gunners who were on a railroad overpass.

In spite of the occasional gunfire it was a quiet night and very dark and over the noise of the burst we could hear the throaty cries of the Germans as they yelled commands to their men. We kept moving forward.

Then a lone sentry near the highway squeezed off a single round: seconds later, the entire enemy final protective line opened fire on us. Our platoon quickly moved into some tall grass near the cemetery to the right of the highway and we began firing with everything we had.

We hauled up a couple of air-cooled '30s and put them into action and the weapons platoon mortars squad dug in nearby and began lobbing rounds at targets along the river.

By dawn we had advanced about 50 yards, then were pinned down by the tremendous fire of the Germans.

With the first light we could see the Arno ahead of us and the curve of the river and the electric lamp-posts that followed the curve and the riverside buildings, most still undamaged, though with the increasing artillery barrage, the shells smashed into the sides in quick, sudden puffs of grey and the stones and concrete rolled into the streets, some splashing into the water.

From dawn until nearly noon we lay and listened to the bullets rasp over us. The tall grass bent in the breeze, helped along by the force of the German fire. To raise one's head meant instant death, so we hugged the earth and cursed the war and the exploding shells and tried to work our way out of our ordeal. Even in the early morning the July sun was hot and heat waves hung over the grass and the machine gun fire seemed to rip open the waves and burn its way over us.

To our left some members of the First Platoon had occupied a large stone building in the railroad yards. Shortly after nine o'clock an 88 came crashing into the building toppling a wall and crushing the life out of three men, one of whom was an elderly private named John Bolman. I remembered Bolman as a gentle man with a smirk for a smile who had pulled guard duty with me in Naples and who said as he ate the cheese from a C ration can, 'I could eat this stuff every day of the week.' I don't know why this trivial remark stayed in my mind, but it did.

By one o'clock we had made our way almost to the river's edge. A final, ferocious barrage of artillery fire forced the Germans from the southern bank and we moved up and began digging in along the concrete wall by the water. We were at the far end of the railroad yards. The ground was dry and sandy and our shovels sank easily into the dirt.

Lieutenant Knowland came up from the rear. His face was streaked with sweat and grime. He wore his usual scowl, though it was more severe than normal.

'Dig in deep,' said Knowland. 'I mean deep. We'll be here for a while.'

So I joined forces with Birdy and the Scholar and we took to our task with a will. When we had dug nearly four feet into the grainy soil we spotted a large wooden door to our right and we fitted it over the hole and tossed dirt on the top; soon, we had us a fine little bunker and we took a break and broke out our rations. Gunfire still came from across the river but the enemy artillery had slackened.

As we munched our canned eggs and ham, meat and beans, and the assorted morsels, the Scholar suddenly said: 'I don't believe it!'

'What?'

'That's Shelley's house over there,' said the Scholar.

'Shelley?'

'Yeah, Shelley. The English poet,' said the Scholar.

'How in the hell would you know that?' I asked him.

'I got a book. *The Homes of Shelley*. By God! That's one of them.' He pointed to a three-storey building on the far side of the north river bank.

'That's it!' said the Scholar. 'Just as sure as I'm sitting here in Pisa, Italy, that's it.'

'Why did he need so many homes?' asked Birdy.

'He lived in a lot of places,' said the Scholar.

'He had a lot of homes in Italy?'

'Yeah, I guess so.'

'Why?'

'Hell, I don't know why,' said the Scholar, 'but he did.'

As we watched the house, a German ambulance pulled in front and two medics carrying a stretcher, got hurriedly out of the cab and went inside. They came out struggling with the stretcher and loaded a body into the open back doors, then the ambulance started, pulled away from the house and disappeared around the curve of the river.

'You don't suppose that was Shelley?' said Birdy.

Notes

1. *The New Yorker Book of War Pieces*, Bloomsbury, 1989, pp 385 – 6.

46

The Gothic Line

Gentlemen, we march on Vienna.[1]

Oliver Leese

The battle for the Gothic Line began on 25 August. By the time that Alexander called a halt to the offensive on 25 October the Allied armies had broken the line, but not the Germans, in the Apennines. The Fifth Army suffered 17,388 American casualties, most of them in the US infantry divisions. British units in the Fifth and the Eighth Army divisions suffered similar losses. Throughout October, Eighth Army was losing 300 men a day and there were no fresh replacements. The Germans were as resilient as ever, with shorter lines of communication and a holding position which was a more formidable obstacle than Cassino.

The Gothic Line ran slightly south of La Spezia, in the Gulf of Genoa, 200 miles right across Italy west to east, crossing the Apennines near Florence and continuing to Pesaro on the Adriatic. The defences, all but the last 50 miles on the Adriatic flank, were sited on difficult mountainous terrain where the peaks were twice the height of those on the Gustav Line. Each main route through the mountains was covered by strongpoints, dug by forced labour of the Todt Organization, and sited with all the tactical ingenuity which had by this time become the hallmark of the German engineers.

There were 500 pieces of artillery to cover the defences, including 30 Panzer Mark VI (Panthers) tank turrets mounted on steel-reinforced concrete bases. Interlocking defence lines extended to a depth of ten

The Unholy Trinity. Generals Juin, Alexander and Mark Clark at the Bastille Day parade, Siena, 14 July 1944.

Kesselring decreed that the architectural glories of Florence would not be destroyed. The Ponte Vecchio in August 1944 after the German Retreat.

Eyes Right. The New Zealanders in Florence, August 1944.

The advantages of air superiority. Vehicles and men can rest safely at the side of the road without fear of German attack. Adriatic Front, 1944.

The results of air superiority. Enemy lines of communication were attacked without mercy. Adriatic Front, August 1944.

Ingenuity of the Engineers. An improvisation in the High Apennines.

The weather was the greater enemy on occasion. Eighth Army in the Adriatic Front.

Shades of the Great War of 1914–18. The Infantry invariably marched. Footsore and weary, a platoon of Royal Fusiliers take a welcome break.

Breaching the Gothic Line.

Resupply in winter in the high Apennines.

When the snow plough gets stuck then there is real trouble.

The Sorrow and the Pity. Italian peasants mourn a loved one killed in reprisal.

Breakout into the Po Valley. A tremendous feat of military engineering.

Frank Battye and Nardina. Her two-piece costume was fashioned out of a British Army blanket.

PHOTOS OF MUSSOLINI
AND OF HIS MISTRESS
EXECUTED BY PARTISANS

MILAN - APRIL 28TH 1945

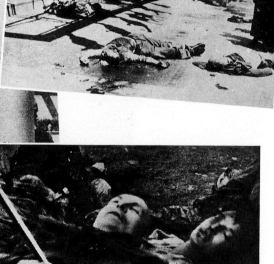

Sold to the victors as souvenirs.

Circles of Hell.

miles and included 2,500 machine-gun emplacements, many of which were sited on mountain peaks and crest lines.

The Adriatic flank was no soft option. The Lombardy Plain, crossed by a dozen rivers and low foothills, was nothing more than reclaimed swampland and prone to flooding in the autumn rains.

The defenders had one further advantage. On the northern side of the Apennines Route 9, the Via Emilia, passed close below the mountains from Rimini right through Modena to Parma giving the Germans an excellent lateral line of communication.

Kesselring was ordered to hold the Gothic Line at all costs. His objective was to inflict such damage on the attacking forces that they would not only be unable to penetrate the line before winter, but would have neither the strength nor the resilience to contemplate further offensives into the southern Reich or Austria. Early in August Kesselring lost two of his best divisions. The 3rd and 15th Panzer Grenadiers were withdrawn to France. Allied objectives, which had previously defined a minimum requirement of tying down German divisions and possibly even encouraging more to be deployed into the theatre, were conspicuously unachieved.

The Tenth Army was deployed on the Adriatic front opposite Eighth Army. Fourteenth Army was on their right flank. The figures supplied by Ultra showed that Eighth Army had a superiority of 3.5:1 in infantry strength and the American Fifth Army 5:1. The Germans had lost a great deal of their mobility, thanks to Allied air attacks. There was a shortage of fuel, spare parts, and a desperate lack of tyres. The enemy defences extended more than 20 miles deep in places, although they lacked the strength in depth of the Gustav Line. However the Allies were presented with an even bigger problem. Once they had broken through they had to advance with infantry through the high Apennines, unable to deploy the massive superiority the Fifth enjoyed in armour. In the mountain sector, the enemy could delay the advance indefinitely.

Nevertheless, Alexander's generals displayed a confidence that bordered on fantasy. They believed the Gothic Line could be assaulted on the run, so to speak. There was still a fair momentum to their advance and the weather was dry. Secondly, they had a surprise up their sleeve which might catch Kesselring unawares. It was called 'Plan Olive', and its author was Oliver Leese.

In July 1944, when the plans of attack for the Gothic Line were being considered, Alexander favoured a push[2] by both armies on the Florence–Bologna axis, expecting to break through by sheer weight of attack on the most direct line to Bologna. There were drawbacks to such an approach. One was that the element of surprise was sacrificed; the enemy could concentrate his strengths on the obvious avenue of attack. And if there was only one main attack the enemy was free to deploy even more forces in the battle. When one considers how close Fifth Army came to attacking along this axis, at half strength, Alexander would have been well-advised to stick to the original plan. It was Oliver Leese who tempted him into other avenues.

Leese argued that the Eighth Army had never been trained for mountain warfare; its experience lay in the desert and armoured war in flat country. Leese chose to ignore the mountain warfare experience of his two Indian Army divisions, indeed of all those formations who had struggled through the previous winter. But this was because neither Leese nor his senior commanders had any confidence in the Army Group plan, which required a very close cooperation between British and American forces.

Alexander conceded. He was also not unaware of the tensions between Leese and Clark.

Leese proposed an alternative that gave Alexander the opportunity to carry out the type of tactical manoeuvre he liked – the 'one–two punch'. The concept called for one army to strike first, drawing off German reserves, while the second army struck on another part of the front after the enemy had been weakened. Even at this late stage of the war British generals, hankering back to the desert, were seduced by the thoughts of a swift assault on a fortified line followed by an armoured breakthrough.

Eighth Army's objectives now were to break through to the Po Valley and seize Bologna and Ferrara. The Fifth was to attack along the central axis up the main road to Bologna. Alexander agreed to shift the axis of the Eighth Army attack to the Adriatic flank – to the Rimini sector. But what Alexander failed to appreciate was that the axis of advance proposed by Leese would take Eighth Army through the Romagna, the south-east corner of the Lombardy Plain. This was reclaimed swampland which, in the autumn rains, was guaranteed to produce the most glutinous mud in Italy. However, the Army Commander made it very clear that the change of plan was on Leese's head.

Plan Olive called for the redeployment of two Eighth Army corps, the Canadian and 5th British, some eight divisions, secretly crossing the Apennines and concentrating their strength behind the front-line units of the II Polish Corps. Poor old Dick McCreery and his orphaned X (Br) Corps found themselves once again under the dubious patronage of Mark

Clark. McCreery had the 10th Indian Division and 9th (Br) Armoured Brigade acting as a light screening force linking the two armies. But at least this time he wouldn't be the only British force west of the Apennines. On 7 August Leese and Clark met to sort out the command arrangements for XIII (Br) Corps.

There were no official records kept of what must have been a stormy meeting between Alexander, Harding, Clark and Leese. Clark wanted to keep things simple and proposed that XIII Corps which contained 1st, 6th Armoured and 8th Indian Divisions should pass into Fifth Army command. Leese, anxious to keep Eighth Army intact, suggested that, as a temporary measure, McCreery should become Clark's British deputy commander to look after XIII Corps at Fifth Army headquarters, while Kirkman (the corps commander) would be responsible for operations. Clark refused and Alexander ruled in his favour. Leese lost XIII (Br) Corps to the Americans.

The battle began in the style to which the Eighth Army had grown accustomed; a mighty barrage. The Prime Minister, who had dined well that night with Leese at army headquarters, stayed to watch the show. With champagne and a large cigar to hand, he sat thrilled by the spectacle.[3]

The guns opened fire at midnight on 25/26 August and, an hour later, the 1st (Cdn) and 46th (Br) Infantry crossed the start lines in utter silence and were quickly into the forward enemy positions. The Germans, caught completely by surprise, fell back in disarray as the rolling bombardment rippled across the front. The River Metauro was crossed and bridged. Other Eighth Army units joined the fray; the Canadians used their 5th Armoured Division and Keightley's V Corps had the 4th and 56th British and 4th Indian Divisions, plus brigades of tanks ready for battle.

In the German Tenth Army, regiments of the 1st Parachute Division and the 26th Panzers, now dismounted and largely tankless, suffered heavy casualties as they fell back on their main line of resistance.

The British had to clear twelve miles of country between the Metauro and Foglio rivers where the Gothic Line proper began. Leese's forces reached the Foglio more or less on schedule after four days and prepared to make yet another river crossing against formidable defences. Memories of the Volturno, Garigliano and Rapido loomed large in the minds of the seasoned veterans as they prepared for battle.

Kesselring had been caught wrong-footed yet again and Von Vietinghoff, the Tenth Army's commander, was away on leave when the offensive began. The Germans believed that this was the main Allied effort. After all, Mark Clark's army had been milked of its best for the South of France and the paras had captured an Eighth Army order-of-the-day which revealed this push to be the big one. Kesselring had ten infantry divisions in the Tenth Army while against the Americans the Fourteenth Army numbered eight divisions. There was one German division in reserve at Bologna.

An artillery barrage from 1,000 guns signalled the start of the real battle. Attacking forces crossed the river and secured their bridgeheads, but the Germans fell back behind the concrete bunkers and strongpoints in the Gothic Line proper and the Eighth Army lost momentum. Alexander and Harding became tetchy with Leese. The advance through the Gothic positions had proved uneven, with the result that Leese had what amounted to a salient on his hands. He elected to pause and regroup, and put in a typical Eighth Army meat-grinder attack. It took a week to prepare. Ahead lay the Corriano Ridge. Once over the ridge they would be into the plain and Rimini; from there to Bologna it would be easier going, provided the weather held.

A gunner serving with the heavy artillery watched a British infantry battalion moving up to the front:

> I stood watching the infantry. Without any show of emotion they got up, picked up their PIAT mortars, their rifles and ammunition, and walked slowly up the road towards the enemy with the same bored indifference of a man who goes to work he does not love. . . . No hesitation, no rush on the part of anybody. Men moved slowly against death, and although the shaft of every stomach was a vacuum of bile and lead, no sign was given and I tried to cover my fear.[4]

The Eighth attacked on the night of 12 September. Again, it was the set-piece battle with an overture from 1,000 guns, scores of bombers and broadsides from warships in the Adriatic Sea. It was the hardest battle since Cassino, and it had started to rain.

The plan was for the infantry and artillery to blast a way through and then release the armoured divisions to swan around the plains of Lombardy and drive the Germans back across the Po. The tactics were simple, even crude, and quite lacking in any imagination. None of the past lessons on the need to have tanks and infantry working closely together, with the foot soldiers controlling events, had been learned.

At the Gothic Line, Leese's tactics were not a whole lot different from those of the Western Front where the cavalry divisions were massed behind the lines waiting for the infantry to effect the breach. In Italy the infantry, working largely without armour in support, failed to achieve the breakthrough and, with the timetable falling further and further behind, Leese, on a number of occasions, hurled masses of tanks at the enemy guns. These 'Armoured Balaclavas' resulted in needlessly heavy casualties for no gains whatsoever.

One incident involved the 1st British Armoured Division. The division, which had been out of the line since the fall of Tunis in May 1943, was commanded by 37-year-old Major General Richard Hull. They took the Corriano Ridge, but casualties were high. The town of Corriano was the scene of some of the bitterest fighting of the whole campaign. Rain fell incessantly and the advancing Allied tanks, guns and vehicles were soon bogged down. Under overcast skies the degree of air support dropped drastically. Desperate to break through and with the infantry stalled, the Second Armoured Brigade attempted to charge the German positions.

When the Shermans hove into sight the German gunners at their 88-mm guns were presented with targets which were sitting ducks. An anonymous officer of the Queen's Bays has left an account of what followed:

> We were ordered to make an attack in the face of an anti-tank screen firing down the line of the advance. We knew that we should not get far even if we could spot the guns that had already fired. . . . While we waited for the word to go, we looked at the ground we had to advance over. There wasn't a stitch of cover anywhere that a tank could get hull-down behind and fire. . . . [We topped the crest and] armour-piercing shot seemed to come from all directions. . . . As they halted to fire, to locate the opposition, the tanks were knocked out one by one.
>
> Most of them burst into flames immediately. A few were disabled, the turrets jammed or the tank made immobile. As the survivors jumped out, some of them made a dash across the open to get back over the crest . . . but they were almost all mown down by German machine gun fire. . . . All but three tanks (i.e. twenty-four) of the two squadrons that took part in the attack were destroyed, and many gallant officers and men were killed in action that morning.[5]

The response from brigade headquarters was to order the 9th Royal Lancers to drive through the wreckage and continue the attack. The Brigadier only relented when the two regimental commanders threatened to disobey any further orders.

The brigade's three regiments began the attack on 3 September with 141 Shermans; at the end of that day they had lost 55 tanks. Tank losses were so formidable elsewhere that, even before it could reach the open country, 1st British Armoured ceased to be a viable division.

Eighth Army continued its attack. Rimini was finally taken on 20 September by the Canadians and a Greek mountain brigade with British armour in support. Inland, V Corps pressed ahead, crossing one river barrier after another; but the losses could not be sustained indefinitely.

In Marradi the news spread like wildfire. The Allies were near, just down the valley, liberation would only be a matter of hours. There was fear, not joy at the news. The townspeople heard from partisans that their town was in the path of Indian troops. Everybody knew about the Indians. All had relatives who lived further south. The Indian liberators were just like the French native troops, they raped and they killed and looted. The village priest advised that everyone should flee to the hills. The partisans would protect them until they could contact English or American troops. But the Germans took the decision for them. That evening soldiers rounded up everyone they could find and marched them away. They took Nardina, her sister, her mother and father. There was no time to gather any belongings. The Germans retreated from Marradi and headed on up the valley towards Foiano. The people were told they were to be taken to Germany to work in the factories. Most of the women and many of the men walked barefoot in the rain. Two days later they reached Foiano. The Germans herded everybody into the town square, formed them into groups of 100 and marched away.

The people argued about what to do. Nardina's father was an important man, he had been to Rome, and people listened to him. They could not return home because the Indians would be in Marradi and would be looking for women. Neither could they stay in Foiano. Anyone from Marradi would tell you that anyone from Foiano was not to be trusted, they stole sheep and cattle. Apart from that, if the Indians were in Marradi they would come next to Foiano. The answer, her father reasoned, was to go into the mountains and head west to find the Americans. He had a nephew who had gone to live in America and perhaps somebody would know him.

Nardina's father was a much-travelled man in those parts and knew the mountains. He suggested they go into the hills and cross down into Firenzuola by the Il Goigo Pass. There they would be safe. The 100 people agreed to follow the lead of Nardina's father. They went up into the mountains and came to a small hamlet, a dozen ramshackle single-storey cottages at the end of a track called San Martino. Unwittingly Nardina's father had led the group into the middle of a battle.

The German paras held this sector of the line. They were kind enough but had little food to spare for the Italians. Nardina remembers the noise of battle, the shells falling and people crying. They were all packed tight into a two-roomed cottage, 100 people – Nardina remembers the lice.

Then the shelling stopped. It must have been two or three days that they had been confined to the cottage and the Germans were nowhere to be seen. A couple of the men went to take a look. The Germans had gone. Only the dead remained.

Three British soldiers appeared. They were scouts and told Nardina's father to take the people back down the hill before the battle started again. It was raining hard. The townspeople huddled together, helping the old and the very young. Nardina's mother was terrified. When they hurried across no-man's-land the guns on both sides fell silent. The three scouts led them to the safety of the British lines where they were ushered quickly through the forward units. Nardina remembers seeing young men waiting to go to war, their faces white and tense. They walked down a track which led off the hillside and into the safety of the tree-line.

The track rounded a bend and led out into a broader valley. There were soldiers there who had just come out of battle. Some were wounded. They stood in a line being counted. They were Indians. The Italians stopped and the groups stared at one another. Some of the women began to weep, the men muttered, but Nardina could see there was nothing her father or the others could do. A number of Indian soldiers started to break ranks, but a big bearded soldier in a turban shouted out loud, and the men stood still. A young British officer stepped forward, looked at the Italians and pointed down the track.

'Go,' he ordered. 'Go quickly.'

Notes

1. Ryder, *Oliver Leese*, p 187.
2. Matthews interview, p 32.
3. Ryder, *Oliver Leese*, p 187.
4. Ellis, *The Sharp End*, p 98.
5. Ibid., p 142.

47

Monte Altuzzo

I'm going to throw you fellas a long forward pass into the Po Valley. And I want you to get it.

> Lt General Mark Clark to
> Lt Colonel Willis Jackson,
> 11 September 1944

The Fifth Army plan for breaking the Gothic Line called for a coordinated attack in which IV and II US Corps and X (Br) Corps were involved. The British XIII Corps, about which there had been so much fuss, remained in a lodgement area near Lake Trasimene. The critical zone of operations, however, was that of II (US) Corps which had three divisions in the line and one in reserve.

Mark Clark had intended to make his main push straight up Route 65 via the Futa Pass to Bologna where the gradient was relatively easy but the enemy defences formidable. Intelligence reports and Ultra intercepts showed that the Il Giogo Pass to the east on the road to Firenzuola, although more difficult, was less well defended. The pass also lay on the Germans' inter-army boundary and therefore might fracture more easily. So Keyes was ordered to attack up Route 65 with 34th and 91st US Divisions west and east of the road and apparently heading for the Futa Pass. Then, at the given moment, he was to unleash the 85th into the Il Giogo Pass. In reserve was the 88th Infantry Division, ready to exploit whichever of the two attacks proved to be successful.

The day before the offensive Lt Colonel Willis Jackson was at the 338th Infantry CP awaiting the regimental commander to give his final briefing. He was a little early and chatted with the only other officer around, Bob

378

Cole, who had the 2nd Battalion. It was about 7.30 on the morning and they heard some jeeps coming up the track. Willis stepped outside the derelict farmhouse which served as the CP to see what the fuss was all about. There was by now quite a commotion as Mark Clark and his entourage of photographers, aides and bodyguards, followed by Geoffrey Keyes and Willis' own division commander Major General Coulter, gathered in the yard.

The officers saluted and Willis Jackson said, 'Yes, Sir, General, can we help you?'

'Where's Mikkelson?'

At that moment the Regiment S3, Major Jack Heliker put in an appearance. 'The Colonel is asleep right now, Sir; he was up all night. Shall I wake him?'

'No,' said Clark, 'I'll talk to Cole and Jackson.'

Clark stood between Cole and Jackson, put an arm around each and led them out into the light, so that the photographers could get some good shots of the General briefing his young battalion commanders. Despite the charade Clark's words were none the less genuine. 'Jackson, Cole, I'm depending on you fellas. Tomorrow you're making the main attack on the Gothic Line, the Il Giogo Pass. You guys are leading the main effort of the whole army.'

Then lapsing unto the football idiom, Clark said, 'I'm going to throw you fellas a long forward pass into the Po Valley. Into the Po Valley. And I want you to get it.'

'Yes, Sir,' said Jackson, 'We'll do our best.'

The Po Valley was 50 miles away. Between them and their objective lay the 4th Parachute Division. Although over 600 replacements arrived shortly before the Fifth Army offensive, the division was spread thin and with no available reserves. The enemy defences protecting Il Giogo Pass were designed to take full advantage of an interlocking series of mountain peaks, Monticelli, Calvi, and Altuzzo, all over 3,000 feet high. Each peak was the responsibility of one of the three parachute regiments and the battalions deployed along the lesser peaks which festooned this inhospitable landscape. The ground is vividly described in the historical journal of the 91st Division Association:

The 85th Division, attacking on the east side of the pass, was faced with four prominent peaks: Mount Altuzzo, Mount Verruca, Hill 918 and Signorini Hill, arrayed shoulder to shoulder from west to east. Due to the eroding effect of mountain streams draining south to the Sieve Valley the southern slopes of these hills have been broken up into a series of roughly parallel ridges and deep gullies. The narrow, knife-edged ridges are covered with stunted brush and scattered patches of pines except where bare rock out-croppings and sheer cliffs furnish no foothold for vegetation. There are few trees on the forward slopes of Mount Altuzzo, but parts of Mount Verruca are heavily wooded with pines and chestnuts. North of the crests there had been thick stands of pines before the Germans began cutting them to build defenses; many more on the south slopes were felled to provide barriers as well as to clear fields of fire; and artillery shells tore away most of the remaining trees during the course of the action.

The portion of the Gothic Line just west of Il Giogo Pass where the 91st Division was to make its main effort is shaped like a huge amphitheater with two wings extending south from the main east–west divide. Mount Calvi, a smooth, dome-shaped hill, forms the end of the west wing and Mount Monticelli, the key objective west of the pass, forms the tip of the east wing. The rough floor of the amphitheater is divided by a secondary ascending ridge running north from the village of Sant' Agata to the main divide. The same confusion of brush-clad ridges and gullies which characterizes the approaches to the heights east of the pass is true of those on the west, although the upper slopes of Mount Monticelli are more even and are almost devoid of cover. Other than Highway 6524, no road crosses the divide and only narrow trails penetrate beyond the lower slopes of the mountains. To open the highway it would first be necessary to capture Mount Altuzzo and Mount Monticelli, the two heights dominating Il Giogo Pass. These two objectives were in turn subject to observation and crossfire from the adjoining heights. If the enemy made good use of the mountains and his prepared defenses which in fact proved to be much more extensive than preliminary air photos had indicated, only a coordinated attack against the heights on both sides of the road could achieve success.[1]

The American attempts to break through at Il Giogo and Futa were the scenes of a dozen or more battalion-sized engagements. Willis Jackson's experience with his 1st battalion was typical of many:

We moved up on the night of 12 September. I went up before dark in my jeep with my S3 and the company commanders behind me in another jeep and tried to reconnoitre the land as best we could. All we knew was what the maps had told us. It was about twelve miles from Baglia to the jumping off point at Altuzzo. A winding road, not easy walking but easy for vehicles.

I left word with my executive officer to start the Battalion marching at dark to an assembly area which I'd have to pick out. I'd get word back to him where the assembly area was, but to start marching. . . .

We got there, best I can remember, about five or six o'clock in the evening, just before dark, an hour or so before dark. . . . we had to select an assembly area first where we were going to assemble our battalion. This we did near the little farm house on the map. It was called Il Paretaro. . . . I circled the map and sent it back to the rear with a note to the Exec: 'This is where I want the battalion assembly area to be.' I indicated on the map where I wanted each company to deploy.

We looked at the ground ahead and decided what we thought was the best line of approach. The last point we could be unobserved by the Germans in the high points of the Altuzzo mountain chain, was the Il Paretaro farm house. Anywhere to the south of that was hidden because it was on the reverse slope. Anything north of that farm house was wide open to observation.

I had been told that the 363rd Infantry 91st Division was on the hill, but I didn't know how far they were. I didn't know where they were. . . .

I couldn't use fire artillery to support my attack because the regimental commander of 363rd would not let any artillery be fired till he knew where his troops were. So we changed our plans because of the fact that we would be firing possibly on our own troops. The 363rd thought they were on Altuzzo, but it later transpired they were not even close.

We jumped off at 6 am the next morning. My men had moved up during the night. We'd received some shelling in our bivouac area and there were some casualties. The Germans must have guessed that the farm would be used for such a purpose and I should have thought about it too, but there wasn't much choice.

I decided the battalion would attack with A Company on the left and C Company on the right, two companies abreast with B Company in reserve. We changed that at the last minute. . . . There was no way we could have gone up there with two companies abreast unless they were in single file. So we chose to go one company at a time, but with the squads abreast so they could deploy quickly if they were fired on.

There was an early morning fog from first light – which I guess was about a few minutes before 6 o'clock. The haze allowed Lt Graysham, an A Company platoon leader and his platoon and the rest of A Company to move up onto the nose, almost, of the German main line of resistance without being observed. I thought, 'This is going to be a piece of cake, we haven't received any direct fire. We're going to take this damn thing before noon the way it's going, even if there is some artillery fire coming in back of us!'

Then we got the sun; it burned right through the fog. A Company began to get fire from what we later called Peabody Peak, or Peabody Ridge.

With the sun up we were suckered. The battalion went to ground. We knew we were under observation from the enemy OP. They were looking right down our throat. We couldn't move anything in the day time without them seeing it. The rest of the day passed in a sort of haze. A Company – I knew where they were – but they weren't moving, they weren't communicating. I kept trying to call them, but I couldn't. Pete King, the Company Commander, didn't have a spare battery for some reason, so it was several hours later before he was able to get a battery in his radio so we could talk.

The next night it was Captain Peabody and B Company's turn. Peabody had been with me at the CP because his was to be the company to move up. We kept him waiting because we didn't want to get him up there and get him trapped. I said, 'Move your company out at last light and move up to the right of Pete King of A Company; if you want you can get Pete to send a guy back to lead you up to their right flank where you won't get twisted up.'

Maurice Peabody was a pretty good company commander, in fact very competent. He was sometimes a little bit obstinate, but he was a good man – a very good man. He told me he didn't need a guide because he was an old Georgia coon hound who could find his way anywhere. So he moved out at last light to the right of A Company. Old coon hound he might have been in Georgia but in Italy that night Peabody got the company lost. What he thought was the Altuzzo was the west ridge of the mountain. He ended up, very much to his surprise and my surprise and everybody's surprise, on the left of A Company instead of being on their right.

At the time, however, he didn't know this and neither did anybody else. Peabody was right in the saddle, right in the middle of the Germans' main line of resistance and defence. He was in a hornets' nest. As soon as first light the next day, 14 September, he began to receive sporadic fire from all sides, from the front and flanks.

I was in contact with Peabody. He insisted he was on Altuzzo. I kept looking through the field glasses everywhere trying to locate him. The Germans finally found him first and launched the first of three counterattacks. B Company suffered very heavy casualties. In desperation, we'd been firing artillery on what we thought was north of him, but all the while he was a couple of hundred yards to the left, on the other ridge. Finally I radioed, 'Hell, Pete, we're going to fire a smoke round to the left of Altuzzo on the ridge and you tell us where you are in relationship to that smoke round.' That's how hard it was to tell where you were in those woods and mountains. Farber, my artillery officer, pinpointed and put a smoke round on the top of what we later called Peabody Peak. It happened to be right smack dead in front of Peabody, like when the Germans were launching the fourth attack. Pete said, 'That's where I want it, Colonel, right there, fire, fire, fire!' It was only about 50 yards ahead of him, where he was. And we fired right in the middle of the Germans, they were exposed and lots of Germans were killed. Our artillery, by the way, was extremely good, extremely accurate. I can't say that much for all the artillery, but I know that ours was.

Peabody's company suffered heavy casualties. Heroes. Every man was a hero that came off that hill. I had to evacuate them that night because they were spent. They had nothing left. Sergeant Keithly was recommended for, and received posthumously, a medal of honour. They fought gallantly and bravely and Peabody didn't know what fear was. I kidded him later that he didn't have enough sense to be scared, but they did a great job and I was proud of them, every one, but they suffered a lot. They had many casualties – I could count them up and tell you because I know every man's name. But we had to pull them back.

So that was the 14th. That was a bad day. The 15th I pulled them back behind, in the assembly area and tried to get some replacements up there. We couldn't evacuate the dead – the Germans were all around them. We had to leave them there. The German dead and our dead, they were all there, it was a terrible sight.[2]

Jackson's battalion had just received a swift but deadly demonstration of the Germans' determination to hold their position.

On the night of 12/13 September the 91st (US) Infantry Division sent two battalions to seize the summits of both Mount Monticelli and Mount Altuzzo. Twenty-four hours later, with all three of its battalions committed against Mount Monticelli, the 363rd Infantry had succeeded only in making contact with the enemy's prepared defences. Those defences had not been dented at any point and casualties in the assault units had begun to mount. The enemy were fighting a very skilful defensive action, spraying mortar rounds in every gully where American soldiers sought cover, and sweeping the open slopes with automatic fire.

Roy Livengood was on Monticelli with the 363rd Infantry:

We moved out again and dug in on the rim of a barren hill. Around noon a shell came screaming in and exploded amidst the 1st Platoon killing a boy in the 2nd Squad. A piece of shrapnel the size of a man's fist hit him in the stomach and he died very quickly; so quickly his comrades did not even have time to pull him from the foxhole.

Soon, after the first shell landed, the Germans opened up on us with a thunderous barrage. The first man I saw killed in this section was a medic who left the safety of his slit-trench to go to the aid of a wounded man. He was running in a crouch when a shell came in and lifted him violently up into the air, blowing his kit from his hand and throwing him against the ground; after the rocks and clods stopped falling I saw him lying on his back and he was nothing more than a bundle of blackened clothing. In the same barrage another medic took off to give a buddy a helping hand and another shell came in and burst several feet from him. A piece of the red hot metal clipped his arm at the shoulder as one would lop off the small branch of a tree with a single blow of an axe. The medic struggled to his feet, his entire side a mass of blood, took a few steps forward, then fell again; once more he got to his feet only to fall again, then once more he struggled upright only to fall again, this time for good.

It is impossible to define the term 'in combat'. When an infantryman first enters 'combat' he is likely to be hit with an artillery or mortar barrage. There is no defense against shelling except a very deep foxhole and then one had to hope whoever pulled the lanyard, miles away, miscalculated and the shell will fall on someone else's hole: one simply has to suffer through it – and suffering it is! There is always the shriek, wham and crash of artillery; it's another story being under mortar fire. A mortar round whispers; unlike an artillery shell, it doesn't seem to be in any hurry to kill you. Mortar rounds are fired in a high arc over the battlefield and take their time coming down to earth.

The Todt Organization had their defence positions so skilfully sited that their location was exposed only as the forward troops came within range of the hidden machine-gun emplacements or when artillery fire ploughed up the earth and tore away the protective camouflage. The attacks on 13 September, although they failed to attain their objectives, served to locate many of these positions, but the work of reducing them had hardly begun.

Jackson's battered but indomitable battalion returned to the assault, determined upon revenge:

A Company was still in position around La Rocca on the west side of the Altuzzo ridge.

Next day was the 15th, nothing was done during the day. It was limited action. Pete King moved up his A Company. That night I sent C Company out; I couldn't move anyone back there in the daytime, it would have been murder. On the night of 15th Captain L.C. Souder's C Company moved up – an excellent company with excellent non-commissioned officers. Captain Souder a school teacher type, very calm, collected and conservative but not very aggressive. He moved up and took good positions on the Altuzzo Ridge ridge where he was supposed to. He kept in contact with A Company.

On the 16th we hoped that somebody else would do what we were trying to do. The 2nd Battalion was bogged down, they weren't moving. The units on our right were bogged down, the 91st Division on our division's left were not moving. It was frightening. I said, 'God damn it, won't we ever take these hills? Won't somebody get through?' I could not believe that everybody was having the same tough time as we were, but apparently they did. Finally on the afternoon of 16th at about three o'clock, Brigadier General Lee Geroe (the Assistant Divisional Commander) came up to my CP and we were out in the yard talking. He had taken over the regiment because Colonel Mikkelson had apparently become ill with a fever and from exhaustion, but General Geroe asked the Divisional Commander to allow him to take over the regiment because he had previously commanded it in training. He came up to me and said, 'Jack, it's up to you. You've got to do it, there's no such thing as saying you can't.' He kicked me hard in the butt and I said, 'OK, we'll do it one more time.' We'd made about five different efforts and each time we'd suffered heavy casualties.

So I got word to R.C. Souder and Pete King of what we were up to. Peabody's company, in effect, were out of the game. Right at that moment they were still bloody. Very calmly Pete and RC – they weren't excited about it – said, 'Sure, we'll do it, we can do it.' They encouraged me.

It was three o'clock and the General wanted them to jump off at four, but you just can't communicate that fast. I told the General that it was impossible to do it that quickly but we'd do it if we could. He asked how quickly it could be done and I told him to make it five o'clock. He said, 'How about 4.30?' and I told him we'd do our best. We quickly got the artillery lined up to fire on the top of the hill which was our objective. RC was as calm and collected as if he was playing golf, so was Pete King. 'OK, we're going to take it this time, damn it!'

Sure enough, with some damn good leadership by Lt Al Crashman and Walter Strausmather our staff sergeant, our platoon sergeant and the whole darn bunch of C Company and A Company, they did it like it was supposed to be done. The school solution.

The next morning Souder called me on the radio telephone, 'Colonel, I got a birthday present for you.' (My birthday was on the 16th.) 'We've got Altuzzo.' I told him he was a day late. I hadn't slept, neither had anyone else since the battle had first started – not an hour, not a minute. This was about five days and nights with no sleep; we were exhausted. We were living on coffee and cigarettes.

The 3rd Battalion was ordered to pass through us and mop up north to the top of the Il Giogo Pass. They did.

We were allowed about one day of rest and we were ordered to proceed on, to continue the chase towards Firenzuola. A couple of days later we moved into Firenzuola. Knocking out an outpost, they were going out on one little ledge there and I was using an OP looking right down on Firenzuola. General Geroe came up to look over the situation, to see what was going on. I took him out on the ledge to show him. While we were out there the Germans saw us, I guess, because mortar rounds started popping in all around us and we decided we'd better get back under cover. We started crawling back on the reverse slope of the hill and got back in the little house where one of my companies had a CP.

General Geroe said, 'Christ, Jack, you trying to kill me?'

Notes

1. *Powder River Journal*, 91st Infantry Division Association.
2. Interview with the author.

48

The Road to Bologna

Oliver Leese left Eighth Army at the end of September, promoted to assume command of the land forces in South-east Asia. Eighth Army had advanced 250 miles in the nine months that Leese had been with them. This hardly compares with the 1,500 miles that XXX Corps covered when he commanded them in the Western Desert, but Italy was a land with a climate and terrain which favoured the defender. Richard McCreery took over Eighth Army and John Harding, Alexander's Chief of Staff, exchanged the comforts of Army Group headquarters in the palace at Caserta for the more primitive conditions of a CP when he assumed command of X (Br) Corps. It was Leese's turn to milk Eighth Army of the talent he wanted to take with him, and McCreery's turn to complain.

Even before Leese left it was obvious that Plan Olive had failed. Nothing much had gone right for Eighth Army since the capture of Rimini on 21 September. Leese unleashed the New Zealanders to break into the flat country of the Romagna. The doughty New Zealanders crossed the Marecchia river on 22 September. The stream was ankle-deep and presented no problem. Hitler's 'Islamic' 162nd Turkeman legions offered no real resistance and spirits soared as the New Zealanders' advance gathered momentum.

The River Uso was something else. The line here was manned by their old foes, the 1st Parachute Division, and the New Zealanders were repulsed. The paras clung grimly to their position. The rain fell in torrents and Eighth Army ground to a halt. The Marecchia became a raging torrent 14 feet deep and all its crossing points impassable. The only hope for a breakthrough rested with Clark's Fifth Army high in the Apennines, to prevent Kesselring from withdrawing units from the coastal sector and reinforcing in the mountains.

Meanwhile, the Eighth Army was bogged down in the plains. Alexander described the conditions: 'The whole is nothing but a reclaimed swamp – and not wholly reclaimed in some parts . . . even in the best drained areas the soil remembers its marshy origins and when it rains forms the richest mud known to the Italian theatre.'[1]

When it came to mud Captain John Guest, a British gunner, was something of an expert. He described it graphically.

The ground for fifty yards outside is mud – six inches deep, glistening, sticky, holding pools of water. Great excavations in the mud, leaving miniature alps of mud, show where other tents had been pitched in the mud and moved on account of the mud to other places in the mud. The cumulative psychological effect of mud is an experience which cannot be described. . . . My men stand in the gunpits stamping their feet in the mud, heads sunk in the collars of their greatcoats. When they speak to you they roll their eyes up because it makes their necks cold to raise their heads. Everyone walks with their arms out to help them keep their balance.[2]

However, the 1st (Br) Infantry Division, part of XIII Corps, managed to advance astride the road to the Casaglia Pass and by 15 September had pushed the Germans off Mount Prefetto. On their right the 8th Indian Division advanced through a region devoid of roads. Attacking by night, and with nothing more than three-foot-wide mule tracks to support them, the Indians hustled the 725th Grenadier Regiment out of their prepared positions on the peaks leading to the Appennine watershed.

Clark's method of widening the base of II (US) Corps' offensive was to order the 85th Infantry to commit its reserve regiments through the 1st (Br) Infantry Division. The 337th Infantry moved through the position of the 2nd Battalion Royal Scots, and they took Mount Pratone, the main watershed feature to the east of Altuzzo. Fifth Army was deep in the Gothic Line. But apart from these successes, the odds were already heavily stacked against the Americans. Their losses were heavy and steadily mounting.[3] Almost continuously under fire, the forward troops received only a minimum of supplies. What the Americans did not know was that the battered parachute battalions were also close to a state of exhaustion. Reinforcements despatched by Kesselring, line infantry units as battle replacements and a Lithuanian labour battalion, either failed to arrive or were too demoralized to offer substantial support, such was the harassing fire laid down by II (US) Corps artillery.

The capture of Altuzzo, Montecelli and Pratone took the attackers through and over the watershed and gave II (US) Corps control of a seven-mile stretch of the Gothic Line on each side of the Il Giogo Pass. All along the II (US) Corps front, German resistance began to falter. Kesselring had no choice but to extricate what he could of his shattered units and withdraw to positions north of the Santerno river. In the meantime the 362nd Infantry of the 91st Infantry Division had attacked and cleared the Futa Pass, a symbol of the Gothic Line. Once the positions along the Il Giogo Pass had been taken Futa was outflanked and untenable. The German defenders put up a stout resistance until they were in danger of being cut off. Then, in accordance with Kesselring's doctrines, they retreated in their own time.

While the 85th and 91st Division were making the main Corps effort, the 34th (US) Infantry delivered a two-regiment containing attack to the left of the Futa Pass. It was a battle in keeping with the traditions of the hard-luck outfit – going largely unnoticed and unsung. Nevertheless it played a vital part in the offensive protecting the corps' left flank and pinning down enemy forces which might otherwise have been shifted east to the Il Giogo Pass sector.

Air bombardment played an important part in breaching the Gothic Line. Preliminary strikes were limited by the necessity of concealing the point of main attack. Once the offensive was underway, there was about a week when the air forces were able to give full support. But bad weather from 20 September onwards severely reduced effectiveness.

The capture of the Futa Pass on 22 September, after two weeks of fighting, brought to an end the Gothic Line phase of the Fifth Army's drive to the Po Valley. But the price paid by the three assault divisions, a total of 2,731 casualties, was excessively high.[4]

Keyes pushed steadily down Route 65 in the Santerno Valley in the most appalling weather. Bologna lay just 24 miles away but 15 of these miles were through extremely rugged terrain. The advance was led by the 88th (US) Infantry Division, freshly committed to the battle, but, for the drive towards Bologna, Keyes planned to employ all four of his infantry divisions attacking simultaneously on a broad front. This left the corps without a reserve, except for two combat teams of the 1st (US) Armoured Division which was of little offensive value in the mountains. So Keyes ordered the infantry divisions each to hold back one regiment and to rotate regiments into the line approximately every five days. The offensives were to be timed as a sequence of hammer blows to coincide with the appearance of fresh units in the line.

The plan looked good on paper and Clark was already planning ahead to the moment when his army would debouch into the Po Valley. But first there were those mountains.

The 2nd Battalion 351st Infantry in the 88th Division fought on Mount Capello. Sgt Leonard Dziabis was a squad leader and machine gunner in Company H, the support company. The battle started in the rain:

My god, how it did rain. It rained so hard it was solid water. If a body stretched out his arms and waved them he would have been swimming.

We went down the north slope of the last mountain before Mount Capello on what appeared to be a cow path. The mud was thick and juicy, the soldiers were sliding, slipping and falling into it.

We proceeded to descend in a gully filled with water, mud and brush. As the man in front moved through the brush the limbs would snap back and give you a nasty smack across the face, causing even greater discomfort and misery than before.

Two-thirds of the way down the mountain we approached a clearing. About a hundred yards across the clearing was a farmhouse. Jerry had a machine gun fixed on this clearing, it was firing at a steady rate and each man would have to take his turn at running this gauntlet to the farmhouse.

As I took off to cross the clearing I noticed the rounds were hitting around my feet. If the dumb gunner would elevate his piece one notch he would be cutting us in half.

John Simons made it through with no problem. It was Thesolin's turn next; he fell to the ground. Mitchell and Tex, waiting to make the dash, took off, grabbed Thesolin and the radio receiver and dragged him to the lee of the building where Simons and I were waiting. Thesolin said, 'My carbine went off while I was running and I'm hit in the leg.' He was carrying the muzzle of the carbine down because of the rain. . . .

John Simons and the rest of the squad began cleaning the gun; it looked like a club of mud. Sgt McCormick came over to me and said, 'I'm breaking up one squad and dividing the remaining men with the other squads.' Simons heard this and asked if he could grab the other squad's gun, because it was already clean, and leave ours in its place. I didn't like the idea, but just then McCormick yelled, 'Dzab, you're attached to F Company, hurry, they are leaving now.' I told Simons to grab the other squad's gun and go.

The rain was still as fierce as ever, in two seconds we were drenched. On each side of the cart track the wounded were lying. The water running down the track was pouring over them. Some were crying in pain, others moaning and some were dead. The column stopped and Captain Radosevich came charging back, waving his arms and swearing, 'I've had it, I can't take it any more, I'm through.' He had completely lost his cool.

As we waited for our next order, our platoon runner found us and told us to rejoin the platoon; our instructions were to find G Company.

After joining the platoon we proceeded straight down the mountain. We reached the valley and started to cross. Jerry spotted us and laid a carpet barrage on us. We dashed back to the protection of the mountain. As we were getting our wits together again, A Company runner informed us that Lt Birch had been killed . . . in the farmhouse we had just left. The Germans had shelled it, killing him. Lt Birch had told McCormick and the others that if anything should happen to him to see that his watch would get back to his family, it was a family heirloom. McCormick detailed two men to go back to the farmhouse and get the watch.

Just then a miracle happened, the rain stopped and within a couple of minutes the moon came out. While we awaited the return of the watch detail, Mac ordered James Besse and Joe Johnson to go ahead and see if they could contact G Company.

The men returning from the farmhouse reported that the watch was gone. We moved along the edge of the valley in the direction Besse and Johnson had gone. After a short time we could see them coming at a run.

Out of breath, Besse told us they had come to a trail coming down off the mountain when they heard troops approaching. Ducking into a small depression at the side of the trail with the troops almost upon them they realized that they were German. Besse said, 'I've never seen so many Germans at one time, if I had stuck out my foot I would have tripped them. I was so scared I almost loaded my pants.'

We hurried over to that trail. Mac told me to take the squad up the trail, find a good spot to cover it but not to shoot until he had opened up down there. About 300 yards up I found a beauty spot where I could see the whole trail. The timing was excellent, for we had no more than gotten in position when we heard the troops coming. As they passed us and headed down the trail I figured it was at least a battalion in strength, by jove we had them good. When the column reached Mac I heard a challenge to halt. The column stopped, and in stopping I could see they were American troops. It turned out that they were our 1st Battalion!

. . . Crossing the valley we came to a base of a rather steep mountain. Colonel Boyd stopped and one of the officers with him handed him a map board. The other officer flipped on a flashlight and held it over the map. Seeing that light go on in the middle of no-man's-land caused me to panic. I wanted to get away from it, fearing every Jerry for miles around was zeroing in on me. However, I managed to hold my ground.

The Colonel pointed up and said, 'This is it. Let's go.' Now I had always considered him an old man, but he took off at a crouch with his two feet and I had a devil of a time trying to keep up on all fours.

Near the peak the ground levelled a bit. The Colonel gestured to the right so I moved my squad along a cart track on the right of the flank. After a short distance I made for the peak. We came upon a sunken cart track, cut across the peak and about ten feet deep. Looking down the track I had found G Company. In the moonlight they lay in grotesque positions. One soldier in particular caught my eye. His helmet had fallen off. He had long blond hair and the wind blowing down the track was blowing his hair. This was all that was moving.

As I paused a platoon runner found us and said, 'Mac wants you to come back with the rest of the platoon.' . . .

Colonel Boyd ordered me to get my gun on the ridge and lay down fire so he could get the riflemen up there. I froze. My mind wanted to go but my body was paralysed. The Colonel became furious; if I didn't get up and move right away he said he'd have me court-martialled.

Just then something landed by my head. Thinking it was a Jerry grenade I grabbed it with the intention of throwing it away from us. As I grabbed it I realized it was a rock, the size of a baseball. The sons-of-a-bitch were throwing rocks at me. I got mad, I got up, I got ready to charge the ridge, my squad behind me every step of the way. Just then everything went silent, it became so still that a body could hear the gunsmoke swirling around. We were moving towards the ridge when the Colonel yelled, 'Get your gun on the right. Quick. They are going to hit us on the right flank.'

All remained quiet so I set up a watch for the rest of the night. Besse and Tex took the first watch. Simons and I found a well-concealed foxhole and bedded down for the next two hours.

I had just dozed off when a voice in very precise English and right above our foxhole began pleading, 'Please, someone, help me, it hurts so bad. Please help me, please.'

The pleading kept up for a number of minutes. John finally nudged me and whispered, 'Do you think we should go help him? He sounds like he's in bad shape.'

'No John,' I said. 'I think that it's a German trying to get us to reveal our position. I just hope no one falls for it.' The pleading stopped and all was quiet once again.

Morning found me at the edge of our foxhole eating a breakfast of K ration ham, eggs and crackers. Coming down the cart track was Sgt Joe Turk from F Company. He was prodding two Jerry prisoners in front of him. He had a great limp and I noticed his pants leg cut along the side and his leg was wrapped with a bloody bandage.

'Joe,' I called to him. 'It looks like you got a million-dollar wound.'

He waved with his rifle and said, 'Hi Leonard, glad to see you made it. I got hit with a bullet in my leg, but it don't seem too bad. Heading for the aid station. Good Luck.' Down the mountain he went.

A platoon runner informed me that McCormick wanted my squad back with the platoon. We joined them and I was instructed to set up the left flank. McCormick crawled up beside me and said, 'I want you to start firing on that ridge over there, right now.'

'Mac,' I said, 'I heard Colonel Boyd say that E Company was working its way along that ridge.'

McCormick became angry and replied, 'I said I want fire on that ridge, that is an order. I saw Germans there.'

I gave Simons orders to fire on the ridge. Nothing happened, the gun had a stoppage. John went through the ritual of correcting a stoppage, still no fire. I laid the spare parts from my knapsack alongside him. John put them in, still no fire. McCormick went into a rage. Pointing his finger at Simons he yelled at us and told us that as soon as we got back he would have us court-martialled. I told him that he would have to come down on me because I had given them permission to exchange guns at the farmhouse. He immediately replied, 'No way. The gunners are responsible for their own weapons at all times.' With this he got to his feet and began walking to the peak of Mount Capello, muttering words that were not very clear.

Hiffner came over from the 2nd squad and he tried with his spare parts to get the gun firing, but to no avail.

A short time passed when Sgt Skite came over to our position and informed us that Sgt McCormick was dead. He said that Mac had ordered the gunners on the gun near the peak to get out and as he got behind the gun a sniper shot him in the head. . . .

As the day was nearing its end I wondered about our predicament. Here I sat in the midst of a great battle with only three men left in my squad and a machine gun that would not fire. McCormick and Lt Birch were dead. Our platoon was down to about a dozen men. The high explosive shells that were meant for us, due to the sheer slope of the mountain skimmed by us and landed at the base. Our mortar platoon was dug in at the base; many were wounded and many were killed. F Company was now a skeleton of its former self. G Company was completely wiped out. If Jerry had a go at us tonight I didn't know what we would do.

That night we were relieved by elements of the 1st Armoured Division acting as infantry.[5]

Fifth Army were just 15 miles from Bologna and Clark was desperate to achieve success before the full onset of winter thwarted his efforts. Increasingly he blamed the British. Meeting with his corps commanders in mid-October, he displayed a chart which showed that since 12 September the Americans had lost six times the number of men and captured 14 times as many of the enemy as the British. He pilloried Alexander because of what he saw as a lack of effort by Eighth Army, yet failed to appreciate that the British were close to exhaustion. If Clark had taken the time to visit the Adriatic sector and see things for himself or if Alexander had argued more forcefully, perhaps the problem would not have arisen with such ferocity.

Willis Jackson was relieved of command of his battalion. They were north of Firenzuola and it had rained every day. His men were at the end of endurance, and Willis was suffering from dysentery. Every day it was another attack, and every attack was uphill. There was one hill, called Point 141 on the maps, which they had failed to take. At the top was a small stone cottage with clear ground all around. It was the killing ground. The 1st Battalion had two companies in the line on a front of about 1,000 yards. One platoon from A Company had been repulsed suffering some 30% casualties. Willis decided to pull back and try again the next day, but this time with additional artillery in support. He took bitter comfort from the fact that over on his left flank the 337th Infantry, under Colonel Hughes, was also stalled: that was until the call came through from Colonel Mikkelson, his regimental commander.

'Jack, Colonel Hughes says you're holding up the advance,' Mikkelson said.

'Colonel,' replied Jackson, 'he's wrong, he's not where he says he is and we're being used to cover his own failures.'

'Jack, attack immediately. I've told division we will have 141 today.'

'OK, Colonel, but not in daylight.'

'Jack, this is a direct order.'

'I can't do it.' Jackson was not prepared to sacrifice his men for another's reputation.

'You're relieved of command. I'll send down Colonel Boulden [regimental executive officer] and Major Rice [2nd Battalion executive officer]. Rice will take over the battalion. You are to report to regimental headquarters.'

Jackson's company commanders, King, Souter and Peabody, had all heard the conversation over the field telephones. All three went to the battalion CP and told Jackson they were coming with him. Willis Jackson was touched by their loyalty, but talked them into staying with their companies. One officer from the battalion in trouble was bad enough. More would be like mutiny.

Later that afternoon Boulden appeared, followed shortly by Rice. Both men were polite and clearly embarrassed.

'Rice, I'm turning over a damned fine battalion – look after them.' With that, Jackson walked out of the CP and down the track. It was a few miles to the regiment CP; he went alone.

Jackson had time to dwell upon the possible repercussions of his refusal to obey a command. When he reached the CP he was greeted as if nothing had happened. There was no sign of Mikkelson. Brigadier General

Geroe, the division's second-in-command took him on one side, out of earshot of anyone else.

'General Keyes and Coulter are good officers,' said Geroe, after he'd heard Jackson's explanation, 'but they are both cavalrymen – don't know a damn thing about infantry war. Get a good meal and have a good night's sleep. Tomorrow, get back up there and take that battalion of yours.'

Nothing more was said about the matter.

Fifth Army suffered 17,388 American battle casualties from 10 September to 28 October, most of them in its four US infantry divisions. British units in Fifth Army and Eighth Army suffered similar casualties, causing McCreery to convert his 1st Armoured Division to infantry, disband two infantry brigades and reduce each British infantry battalion from four to three rifle companies.

The fighting also took its toll on the Germans. On 25 September Von Vietinghoff reported to Kesselring that of his 92 infantry battalions, ten were 'strong' (i.e. more than 400 men); 18 were 'fairly strong' (300–400 men); 26 were 'average' (200–300 men) and 38 were weak (less than 200 men). The Germans, however, were not attacking.

Eighth Army was stranded before the Plain of Lombardy. Roads were washed out. All bridges over the Foglia river, including the steel-built Baileys on the Allied lines of communication, were washed downstream. Artillery could be towed only by bulldozers and there was no air support. The physical and psychological condition of the troops began to deteriorate. Desertion reached serious proportions.

American infantry from the 34th and 88th Divisions continued to engage in small-scale actions with German paratroopers and SS grenadiers; losses were heavy on both sides. In the high passes the driving rain turned to sleet and snow. There was no way forward.

Late in October the Allies had used up their available artillery ammunition. On 25 October, General Keyes, in command of II (US) Corps, called a halt. His men alone had suffered 15,700 casualties since the start of the main battle in September. In this desperate war of attrition, in which neither side could hope for reinforcements, it was the Allies who had run out of infantrymen first. Army Group ordered its divisions to go on the defensive.

Ultra revealed that the Germans were in equally dire straits. Had the Allies maintained their momentum for just another day the Germans would have been forced to retreat from the Apennines. When the Americans came to a halt they were only four miles short of their final hill objectives. Bologna was tantalizingly close.

Notes

1. Orgill, Douglas, *The Gothic Line*, Heinemann, 1967, pp 184–5.
2. Ellis, *The Sharp End of War*, p 25
3. Jackson's rifle companies had attacked with 400 men of whom 252 were casualties after five days of fighting.

4.

	Killed	Wounded	Missing	Total
34th Division	118	465	28	611
85th Division	171	642	60	873
91st Division	235	987	25	1247
Total	524	2094	113	2731

5. This account was sent to the author by Leonard Dziabas for inclusion in this book.

49

Uncertain Allies

Marshall had introduced a replacement system for the army which aimed to ensure that battalions were up to strength every night. He wanted trained replacements ready to take the place of losses. The British could not do this because of the territorially-based regimental system. But Marshall ensured that the infantry depots to the rear of the battle area were able to top up battalions after a day's fighting.

The Replacements Depot for US troops joining Fifth Army was at Caserta; it was located at Count Ciano's[1] dairy farm. The replacements received 13 weeks' basic infantry training and little else. It was a crude system; the men were sent to battalion rear areas, there to await a guide to take them to specific companies. Many died before they even had time to get to know another man in their unit. The veterans clung together, survivors who looked down upon the new arrivals until they had time to prove their worth.

Willis Jackson would not permit fresh troops to come forward to any of his companies until the battalion was out of the line, and he had the opportunity to meet and talk with the men; otherwise they were worthless. But even Jackson's scrupulousness didn't always bring results. One replacement into A Company went absent as the battalion moved back into the line. He was caught by the MPs and brought back. He took off for a second time and again was caught by the military police, who returned him under armed guard. Jackson was furious, and wanted the man shot. He spoke to the S1 at regiment and asked for the man to be tried as a deserter, but was told that this was not possible. The quota of deserters for the corps had been filled for the month!

The soldier was returned to the battalion. Willis met him, along with his company commander. The man was truculent and unrepentant.

396

'I'm trained as a truck driver, not a rifleman,' he said. Jackson explained as patiently as he could that service troops and AA gunners were being converted to infantry because of the casualty situation.

'I can have you shot as a deserter,' Willis told him.

The man's face fell, and he begged for another chance.

'OK,' said Willis, 'I'll give you a break. Your squad leader will treat you like any other rifleman, but if you disobey a single order I will order the squad leader to shoot you.'

Two weeks later he deserted to the enemy.

The oldest man in 1/338th was Thomas H. Quisinberry, the battalion S3. He was 33, and came from Kentucky Blue Grass country where he was a successful cattle and horse breeder. Everybody called him 'Uncle Tom' and he was particularly close to Willis Jackson.

After Altuzzo, the battalion was in a very bad state, not just from casualties but disease. The battalion medical officer, Jesse Lawrence, was a red-haired Jewish doctor who had qualified in Hamburg; he spoke fluent German and so doubled as the POW interrogator.

Uncle Tom had pneumonia, so Jackson called up Lawrence to the command post which was in a partially ruined cottage. The Doc told Uncle Tom to lie on the dilapidated bed, took his temperature and told him to move over. Willis looked up five minutes later; they were both asleep.

When a battalion was under such constant stress and pressure a good doctor was an invaluable asset. Doc's sick calls were famous.

'What's your trouble?'

'Spots in front of my eyes.'

'What colour?'

'Black.'

'Sergeant, paint this SOB's spots white and kick his arse out of here.'

Doc always knew when they were 'gold-bricking'.

But there was little that Doc, or indeed any other medical officer, could do for an epidemic of hepatitis which spread through Fifth Army that winter. In a two-month period some 40% of Jackson's battalion alone were laid low, and other units suffered similarly. Symptoms were easy to recognize and diagnose. Soldiers became listless, their skin and eyes turned yellow. The cause was never isolated, although the doctors blamed the water, which, with the incessant rain, was fertilized by both human and animal remains and excreta. The only remedy was a period out of the line, a diet of fruit and eggs and a convalescence of five weeks or more.

Once out of the line, convalescing soldiers were prey to all sorts of temptations. Venereal disease was a major problem, though less so for the Germans, because brothels were licensed and supervised. Every six months the battalion had a 'Morality Lecture' on venereal disease from the chaplain – who described it as immoral; the MO – who advised them to take precautions; and the CO – who warned them not to 'catch a dose'. But it was a waste of time. According to Captain Peabody the men 'screwed everything in sight'. Patton perhaps had set the standard in Sicily when he was widely reported as saying: 'Soldiers who don't fuck don't fight.'[2]

Desertion was another problem, as it had been throughout the North African campaign. The situation in the Middle East in 1942, before Alamein, was sufficiently serious for the then C-in-C, Auchinleck, to cable London suggesting the immediate reintroduction of the death penalty. The Americans retained the death penalty, although only one soldier, Private Slovak, was executed as a deterrent to others at a time in France when desertion figures reached alarming proportions.

When Oliver Leese assumed command of Eighth Army at the Sangro, he wrote in a despatch home: '78 Div was very tired and depleted of men after the Sangro battle, when they had 350 desertions in a fortnight.'[3]

In July 1944 Lt Colonel John Sparrow (who later became Warden of All Souls, Oxford) was despatched by the War Office to investigate the problem of desertion. He came to the conclusion that the chief cause was prolonged action which was greatly increased by close contact with the enemy. He also classified deserters and absentees into two broad categories: the 'deliberate', who preferred disgrace and imprisonment to the continued dangers of battle, and the 'involuntary', men with nervous breakdowns who would often welcome a second chance to prove themselves. Most deserters belonged to the second group.

Regardless of motive, however, it wasn't easy to desert. Soldiers had to get back from the line and beyond the immediate rear area, avoid military police patrols, and find somewhere to hide. One American officer[4] during the Third Battle of Cassino recalled meeting a British lieutenant patrolling the area immediately behind the 8th Indian Division. The young officer had a drawn pistol and told the American he had orders to prevent men leaving the front and to shoot them if necessary. Desertion was not a problem in the Burma campaign nor in the Western Desert. It was when Eighth Army was in Egypt, and Cairo beckoningly close, and it was in Italy. Most men who deserted were fighting soldiers, particularly infantry, so their absence was all the more keenly felt and represented a more serious loss than when presented as an overall percentage of the army's ration strength.

In Italy British and American soldiers were pushed beyond the limits of endurance in a campaign which they now recognized had lost its purpose. Soldiers tended not to go AWOL in the midst of battle, but found reasons for not returning to their units after being sent to the rear. And in cities like Rome, Florence and Naples, a man could effectively lose himself for a week or more. There were rumours of multinational gangs of men who took to the hills and lived as brigands. A group known as the Free English were supposed to have deserted shortly after Salerno.[5] But these hard-core opportunists did not survive the onset of winter, nor the establishment of government which brought some order out of chaos after the front line had moved northwards.

In North West Europe there was the allure of Paris. When American First and Third Armies by-passed Paris in their pursuit of the Germans, 10,000 GIs 'went over the hill' to enjoy the fleshpots of the liberated capital. Most returned after a week or so, but Eisenhower declared Paris off-limits to US troops. Deserters and absentees needed an accomplice and money. The accomplice tended to be a female who lost interest once the money had run out.

After July 1943 the British suffered some 40,000 recorded cases of desertion.[6] Of these, 80% were from infantry companies and 70% were in Italy in the last winter of the war. Eighth Army experienced the highest recorded percentages of desertion amongst the Western armies in the Second World War. The losses were felt all the more keenly because they occurred in infantry companies already depleted of manpower. The recorded figures are misleading. Such were the numbers involved, that battalions frequently chose to deal with the problem in-house rather than through official channels. However, the vast majority of soldiers did not desert. They chose to grin and bear it and for a host of reasons which included personal and regimental pride, but more especially because they didn't want to let their mates down. And many of those who did desert reappeared in time for the spring offensive.

In the autumn of 1944 General Marshall offered a new light division, the 10th Mountain, to General Eisenhower, but he refused it unless it was reorganized as a standard infantry division. Marshall then offered the division to Clark who didn't hesitate. The 10th Mountain was a 'middle-class' division; it contained a high percentage of expert skiers, mountaineers and sportsmen. College graduates abounded as well as woodsmen and forest rangers. The 10th Mountain came to Italy confident that it was something special.

In the autumn of 1944, and in what represented nothing less than a complete volte-face on the part of the Allied High Command, the Italians were grudgingly invited to participate more fully in the liberation of their country. But on Allied terms. There was still a marked reluctance by the British to accept Italian troops and official documents show a deep-rooted prejudice against the project. Earlier in the spring Oliver Leese wrote an official despatch to London:

I visited Utili and his Italians today. He is a good man and respected by his men. They have carried out some quite good operations around Monte Marrone and are proud of their exploits. I inspected two Bersaglieri and Alpini Coys which had been in action on the mountain; they had done very well and were proud of their work. They look a good class of men; they were friendly and keen. I had the usual enormous continental lunch with them; and I came away – quite apart from the lunch – with a good general impression! I am willing to accept the other Italian Bde from Sardinia, but I am not sure yet how many battalions of Italians it is wise to fight in one place. I remember so often how we in North Africa used to concentrate our attacks on the sectors held by the Italians. It is important in this respect to ensure that they do not have a setback; and to keep them on the crest of a wave.[7]

On another occasion, prior to the fall of Rome, Leese wrote:

The French have found the Goums invaluable as recce elements in front of their formations across the mountains and as sweeps well around the enemy flanks. They are adept at dealing with small enemy positions. They are, of course, useless against organized resistance. I am investigating the possibilities of using Italians in this way. The difficulty is that one of the chief merits of the Goums is that they have got guts. This, as you know, is not a characteristic of the Italian race. I talked to George Walsh today on the telephone and asked him if he thought he could accumulate some 2,000 Italians with guts. After some discussion we came to the conclusion that there were probably not that number of Italians with the necessary characteristics south of ROME![8]

In August, the British authorities sent to the Italian Chief of the General Staff a directive which spelled out the Italian order of battle.[9]

It was important to conceal, at least from the British public, the true picture of the Italian war effort and since the new units were to be uniformed and equipped by Eighth Army, it was the British who dictated the conditions.

The Italians were invited to raise Combat Groups, 'Gruppo di Combattimento'. Each Combat Group comprised 10,000 men (432 officers and 9,568 soldiers) equipped with 116 pieces of artillery, 170 mortars, 500 light machine guns and about 1,300 vehicles. These new units could not be called battalions or brigades. Neither could they be described as regiments or divisions. The Italian press could give them full publicity, but they were to receive scant coverage in Britain. Nevertheless, by the time that the final spring offensive began, five such Combat Groups were deployed in Army Group's order of battle, and a sixth as a training unit was stationed at Cesano near Rome.[10]

There were also plans afoot to re-equip the Italian Air Force with British or American aircraft. Once again the terms were specifically spelt out by the Chiefs of Staff. The Italians could only be re-equipped with superseded, but battleworthy aircraft. There were about 250 Italian fighter pilots who were operationally trained and about 50 bomber crews. Some of the latter were the first to return to combat. Two squadrons were equipped with ex-RAF Baltimores and the crews were in service before the year's end. But inevitably there was a marked reluctance by these crews to bomb targets close to populated areas. And in some cases, crews refused to fly.

In December a US Army surgeon went to inspect a Veterinary Hospital and reported as follows:

At the time of my visit the Commanding Officer informed me that his unit of four Officers, seven Non-commissioned Officers and 97 lower ranks, were not equipped with sufficient clothing to protect them during the cold weather, the total stock of two overcoats were being used by the four officers. Many men were reported as without serviceable underwear, outer garments and blankets. Time did not permit, neither was it deemed necessary to make a close inspection of the unit to determine its deplorable condition. In addition to the conditions reported by the Commanding Officer I observed many men wearing all types of uniform and civilian clothing, all of which were dirty and in worn condition. Furthermore, I doubt if sufficient cleaning material has been furnished the unit to adequately provide for personal hygiene. This opinion is based on the fact that during my interview with the Commanding Officer several men in the room were observed to be constantly scratching the pubic region of their body.

The Commanding Officer informed me that he called on Colonel Cocco of the Italian Army stationed in Naples with a request for clothing and transportation and all he received was a wave of the hand with instructions to see American officials.[11]

Logistics presented the Italians with near-insurmountable problems. In

August 1944 five out of the nine divisions under arms were still in Sardinia.

The Combat Groups were quite distinct from the Pack and Mechanical Transport Companies. The Cyprus Regiment, first formed in April 1940 had long since provided companies for the Eighth Army. The Italian units comprised Italian soldiers and volunteers, mostly men skilled in dealing with mules. They wore British battledress, dyed dark green, and their own original headdress; often Alpini.

Not all Italians welcomed the call to arms from a discredited government. Neither did they wish to fight on behalf of the Allies whose occupation of their country was the cause of so much frustration and anger. In Sicily the response to a call to arms in December 1944 was widespread disorder and riots. Pamphlets and posters were widely distributed, of which the following is a translation:

TO THE YOUTH OF SICILY

Once again after many long years at war, after disappointments (sic) and misery, we are asked contrary to the wishes of the people to spill our blood.

In the past the vile monarch obligated us to die for the conquest of other empires, today with the same vileness, he burdens us to save for him without sacrifices that crown which he has not the right to hold because of his treachery to the whole people.

We will not take up arms.

'Youth of Sicily' – remain united in expressing your determination not to enlist – peace, bread and work – that is what we want.[12]

Separatists and communists made common cause and trouble flared across the island through to mid-January. In most instances the Carabinieri and local police were able to contain the demonstrations, though on both sides people got hurt.

Absenteeism in the Gruppos, prompted not simply by political criticism but by boredom and inactivity caused by the failure of the Allies to deliver the promised clothing and equipment, was a constant problem.[13]

In October, General Alexander wrote a personal despatch to the Prime Minister in which he outlined the then state of the Italian forces and their prospects:

... of the six combat groups for which equipment has been authorised one had been equipped and is now training (.) it should be ready to undertake a defensive role at the end of this month (.) the second group will I hope be ready for operations in the second half of November (.) as regards the remaining four groups I am told that as none of the equipment promised for these Italian troops had yet arrived from the U.K. they can NOT be provided with more than training scales before 1 Jan 45 (,) and that even then the prospects of completing their equipment are doubtful (,) but I can NOT be sure of that as responsibility for the provision of equipment and vehicles for these troops rests with AFHQ (.) in any case unless something drastic is done to accelerate deliveries of vehicles and equipment it seems that the last two groups will NOT be fully equipped before March (.) that means they will NOT be fit for operations till April which will be ten months from the time I asked for them[14]

TOP SECRET

Lt. Col.
MA to C-in-C

One Italian memorandum complained that their labour units operating in rear areas such as Naples were required to take orders from Allied coloured troops. But a letter of complaint written by the Minister for War, received short shift from the Allied headquarters.[15]

The Allied High Command was not without fault when it came to questions of race. Almost without exception Indian troops were treated with some respect, a lot of condescension, and even affection, tinged with a healthy respect by white soldiers – American, British and Commonwealth – who also gave the French Colonial forces a very wide berth while they were in country.

Black American troops had a difficult time of it. The southern states still practised a form of apartheid, and racial segregation was the order of the day in the US armed forces.[16] Service Force branches – labourers, drivers, cooks, etc – accounted for about 40% of the total strength, but they contained 75% of the Black troops.[17] There were two American Black combat outfits. The all-Black 366th Infantry had been in the theatre since May; the unit had been used for menial tasks such as guarding air bases against a non-existent threat of enemy saboteurs and parachutists.

The 92nd Infantry Division were called the Buffalo soldiers. The division had an honourable lineage back to the days of the 9th US Cavalry, an all-Black regiment which fought the Apache Indians in Arizona territory in the third quarter of the nineteenth century and received their nickname from the Apache. Contrary to Western mythology not all US Cavalry were white troops in blue uniforms and yellow bandannas.

The Buffalo soldiers were also called 'Eleanor's Own Royal Rifles' by the white officer establishment. It was widely believed the Black outfits had been raised only because of pressure on Marshall by Mrs Roosevelt. The Black troops were also given the best of everything; at least that is what the white troops believed. They were given more uniforms and clothing, and some went to tailors in Italy and had 'zoot suits' made out of their uniforms. A zoot suit had peg bottoms and a jacket down to the knees with heavily padded shoulders; the outfit was completed with a waistcoat, a heavy gold chain and a wide-brimmed fedora hat.

Clark's finely tuned political antennae warned him to tread carefully in his treatment of these Black soldiers. Further personal advancement depended upon the white senior officer establishment, and a mistake could have been very costly, particularly as Clark had made enough enemies already. He knew that the attempts to deploy Black troops in a combat role was likely to fail,[18] but it was important to be seen to have made every effort to stave off a disaster; the British would call it 'covering your backside'. So Clark introduced the 92nd Division gradually into war through a programme of battle familiarization, but there was nothing he could do to remove prejudice. Racial tensions persisted and these soldiers were made to feel inferior.

Black battalions were fed into the line alongside white troops. With some exceptions, junior officers and senior NCOs lacked leadership qualities under fire, while their soldiers were below average in almost every respect. In November Clark sent a confidential despatch to Washington advising Marshall that the 92nd was not ready for combat, but he was overruled. The problem was that by this time the Fifth Army was desperate for manpower. Clark had a choice: move the 92nd into the line or use the Brazilians. The latter had been in Italy since the early summer and had yet to earn their keep. The soldiers were poorly trained and the officers behaved like military peacocks, even though they had no idea of command and were totally ignorant of the profession of arms. Neither officers nor soldiers had the slightest desire or indeed intention of closing with the enemy.

It was Hobson's choice. Clark moved the 92nd into the line. He beefed them up with the hitherto separate Black 366th Infantry. The division was deployed to a supposedly quiet sector in the Serchio Valley north of Leghorn, and it was there the enemy struck on the day after Christmas. Fortunately Ultra and other sources of battlefield intelligence gave the Allies warning of an impending attack, identifying elements from two Mussolini Fascist divisions and one German division in the line. The

92nd's commander, Major General Almond,[19] aware that his troops were still unsteady, requested support. The Eighth Indian Division and two regiments of the 85th US Infantry were moved into position behind the 92nd as a backstop.

Mussolini wanted to launch a spectacular offensive using the Monte Rosa and Italia Divisions. The Serchio Valley came under the operational control of the German LI Mountain Corps whose commander, General Feuerstein, doubted the quality of the Monte Rosa and reserved judgements on the Italia, which had just arrived in the line. However, raids against an all-Black American outfit had an obvious appeal, especially if it resulted in that force's humiliation.

In the event the Italians made some demonstrations but the attack on Boxing Day was an all-German affair and faultlessly executed. They attacked with just two battalions (fourth Alpine and the Mittenwold Alpine Training Battalion) drawn from the 286th Grenadiers of the 148th Infantry Division, supported by artillery. The attackers were outnumbered, but behind a lethally accurate artillery bombardment, the two battalions launched their assault down the sides of the valley. The 366th Infantry gave way under the artillery fire before the attacking infantry had closed, and fell back in disarray. Panic spread to other units and the 92nd streamed back in disorder through the stop-line established by the 8th Indian Division. Some battalions of the 92nd were able to reorganize behind the Indian front, but most kept on going until they ran out of steam.

Having achieved their objective the Germans turned back before they reached the forward positions of the Indian troops. The latter advanced up the valley the following day hindered by nothing more than mines and booby traps; there was no contact with the enemy. By 30 December all the ground lost had been retaken.

So ended a raid which the press and other publications subsequently have called the 'Serchio Offensive'. It is widely accepted in Italy to this day that the attack was conducted by Italian troops, but the records show that they were not involved. The political fallout was as the Germans had anticipated. The public outcry began immediately.

As *Time* magazine wrote after the war:

It was the hottest potato in the USA. . . . The 92nd was mostly a Negro outfit and the cynosure of the sensitive liberal press. Its rank and file had the handicap of less-than-average literacy and more than average superstition. The 92nd didn't learn combat discipline easily.

Newsweek was even more precise:

> Given the racial climate of the time the key question was: would the Negro make the grade as a fighting soldier.

The War Department proposed that the solution lay in racially integrated military units. Clark and most of his contemporaries rigorously opposed the suggestion. Integrating Blacks and whites in the same outfit would merely lead to 'our biggest defeat'.[20] But the generals were overruled and a programme was introduced into the European theatre whereby Black platoons were included in white battalions. All rear area facilities, clubs and rest centres were to be desegregated.

By this time, there were further changes in the Allied High Command of the Italian campaign. At the end of November, Field Marshal Sir John Dill, the British Chief of Staff in Washington, died. Field Marshal Jumbo Wilson was selected by Churchill to go to Washington. The President and the Prime Minister then set about playing musical chairs with the upper echelons in Italy. Alexander moved up to become Supreme Commander in the Mediterranean. He was promoted Field Marshal but the appointment was back-dated to June and the fall of Rome. The British requested that Clark should become the Army Group Commander.

Clark's biographer is absolutely correct in his analysis of the significance of this promotion.[21] Italy and the Mediterranean were, after all, a British theatre of operations; the only other was South-East Asia. A British general could have expected the critical appointment over the land forces in Italy. In that sense Clark was fortunate in that McCreery was relatively new to Eighth Army. Some have argued that had Leese still been there things might have been different, but this would be to ignore the fact that, in every major battle and every single controversy from Salerno to the Volturno, Cassino, Anzio, Rome and northwards through the Gothic Line, Clark's influence, for good or for ill, was predominant.

Churchill asked for Lucien Truscott, at the time leading VI (US) Corps in Alsace-Lorraine, to take command of Fifth Army. Truscott had shown tact and common sense with British troops in the Anzio beachhead.

The 92nd were given one more opportunity to prove their worth. In February the Buffalo soldiers launched an offensive in the Serchio Valley. The Italian Monte Rosa Division melted away, but in the face of a fierce counterattack from the German 148th Infantry, the Americans fell apart once more. Truscott took the best that remained of the Black battalions and created a single regiment. To these he added the 473rd Infantry, which had been created out of dismounted anti-aircraft battalions, and the renowned 442nd Infantry which comprised battalions of Japanese Americans (Nisei), who had been brought across from France in March.

Clark still had to tread very carefully with regard to the 92nd because of the political lobbies in the United States. The remaining Black troops were used to guard prisoners of war. It later transpired that when the Nisei troops captured Germans they were passed back to the Black troops where publicity photographs were taken.[22] Nobody in the United States was interested in the exploits of the Japanese Americans, whereas the liberal lobby of the Democratic party had become a major force.

Notes

1. Mussolini's son-in-law and one time Foreign Minister; Ciano sided with the conspirators in the Fascist Grand Council in 1943; Mussolini later, in the Salo Republic, had him shot.
2. Tables 6 and 7 illustrate the extent of the problem.
3. WO 216/168 180559.
4. Interview with author: interviewee wished to remain anonymous.
5. Watts, J., *Surgeon at War*, Allen & Unwin, 1955, p 63.
6. See Tables 3–5.
7. WO 216/168, p 3.
8. Ibid., p 5.
9. See Appendix 5.
10. There was also a Special Force, raised from units of Italian 185th Parachute Regiment. Eventually it became 'Squadrone da Ricognizione F' and operated behind the lines for the last twelve months of the war.
11. WO 204/988 18094
12. WO 204/2/81 XCI 70802. A further example is in Appendix 7.
13. In December 1944 the Fruili Gruppo had 1,489 absentees and Cremona, 1,262 (WO 204/10176 180550).
14. WO 214/53 180559.
15. WO 204/9888 /80094. See Appendix 6.
16. The US Army was not effectively desegregated until 1950.
17. Ellis, *The Sharp End of War*, p 328.
18. Interviews with the author.
19. Who later commanded a corps in Korea.
20. Blumenson, *Mark Clark*, p 237.
21. Ibid., p 235.
22. Author interview with a Fifth Army staff officer who wishes to remain anonymous.

50

The Million-Dollar Wound

Lucien Truscott assumed command of Fifth Army on 16 December 1944; Mark Clark had given him a week to settle into the job, which was longer than Montgomery ever allowed Oliver Leese. The ceremony, such as it was, occurred in the forward CP set amongst the ice, snow and the fog of the Futa Pass. At that time the balance of forces in Italy was as follows. Kesselring had a paper strength of some 33 divisions (27 German and six Italian Fascist). The Allies also had 27 divisions.

The Germans were depleted in strength, especially in infantry battalions, as were the British. British brigades had been despatched by Churchill to intervene in the Greek civil war. The American generals smiled because Churchill appeared to have got his Balkan deployments after all. The American divisions remained the strongest of the forces in Italy.

Truscott inherited an army and an offensive. The purpose of the offensive was to tie down German units to prevent them from leaving for other theatres, and to break through to the Po Valley. Both ideas were a nonsense. The Germans by this time lacked the logistical means to move large numbers of troops from one theatre to another. Hitler launched his Ardennes offensive at the same time as the 92nd was being ousted from the Serchio Valley. No troops were withdrawn from Italy to serve in that operation.

Clark had planned a 15-day winter offensive; it was called Operation Pianoro and envisaged the Fifth Army breaking through to the Po Valley. On the Adriatic plain, flood conditions had brought Eighth Army to a complete standstill. The Apennines lay under a blanket of ice and snow which made any movement along the precipitous mountain roads highly dangerous and unthinkable for a general offensive.

Truscott spoke his mind and Clark took offence. But, backed up by McCreery and with Alexander also opposed, the Army Group Commander reluctantly decided to halt any large-scale offensive until the weather and the supply position improved. Both armies instituted a series of limited offensives which involved attacks at regimental and, occasionally, divisional strength. For everybody else it was a question of winter quarters.

The Allies were at the end of an extended line of communication. The main ports of entry were Naples, Bari and Leghorn, from where everything was moved to forward army bases near Florence, Pisa and Rimini. The Fifth Army was obliged to truck goods forward as far as possible along inadequate and grossly congested roads. Thereafter it was a case of jeep and trailer or mule train. Fifth Army used 15 Italian pack trains which had a total strength of over 4,000 mules. Without these units the campaign in the Apennines would have been impossible. Even so, there were never enough mules, and in the last resort supplies had to be manhandled to the front.

Walter D. Pearson, then a PFC in the 88th Division, described one detail:

In August my sergeant told me I was going to flame-thrower school. That was when I considered myself a dead man, as the three lines we were planning to break through were all defended and crossed by pill boxes, and even though I had not done this assignment before, I knew that the first bullet of the enemy would be reserved for the man with the match. Imagine my relief when we found, on returning to the front, that the Arno had been crossed, the three lines had been breached and we were again keeping the Germans on the run.

One morning, when we had spent the night on a mountain top, I woke just before daybreak, and watched the sun rising, bouncing from one mountain top to another. I remarked to some of the fellows who were standing there that I thought it was a beautiful sight, and that they might look back in later years and recall the beauty of that morning. (I recall that they all looked at me as if I had holes running directly through my head.)

From time to time the Germans would stop and fight to hold their ground. But it was when we got to Monte Grande that I ran into trouble. At about 4 pm one evening, we were told to fall out and dig in. I found a niche in the mountainside, just big enough for one man and I grabbed it gladly because as usual it was raining and I would be out of the weather. At just about that time the sergeant from the second squad came over and said, 'Pearson, you have been assigned to our carrying party.' I was angry because I had not slept rain-free for many nights. He told me to check with my own sergeant, which I did, only to learn that I had indeed been assigned to his carrying detail.

We had gone without food for three days, and the infantry had to go back to get rations, because the men in the Service units, who were supposed to bring it to us, did not make it. Back we went over the mountains to a house where the rations were supposed to be. There was nothing there and our only choice was to return to our troops empty-handed. The captain informed us that we had indeed been at the right house, but that the others had not been able to get the food there by that time. Back we went again, up and down the mountains. During both trips the enemy was throwing mortar shells at us, but luckily no one was hit. When this time we did find the rations, all of the carrying party men grabbed a 'dinner' box and began ravenously to munch on the cheese. I did the same, but although I put it into my mouth I was unable to chew it. My mouth just would not operate. (I didn't know it then but I had come down with battle fatigue.) After everyone had eaten and rested a bit we began our return journey. Each man carried a carton of K rations, about four feet by two feet square, and weighing about 40 pounds. The ascent we had to make was so steep in places that we were forced to dig hand and footholds in the mountain and force the cartons up the hill in front of us. As we reached the halfway point we were shelled again. I was about twenty-five feet behind the others and when the shelling stopped I was too weak to get up so they took my box and left without me. After I had rested a while, I climbed to the top of the hill and dropped into a foxhole that had been dug previously. It began to pour and the rain did not stop for three long days and nights. When it finally ceased, I got out of the hole only to discover that my rifle had rusted shut and was of no use at all. I gladly threw it away. As time passed I finally located the aid station and told the doctor my problem. He told his assistant I had battle fatigue and that he should ticket me and send me back to hospital. 'I can't send him back, sir,' the assistant replied, 'We're all out of tickets.'

So for two more days I just wandered around. The first night I slept in an abandoned Italian house. During the night two GIs came in and took up quarters in the front room. One said to the other, 'I'm going to shoot my finger off.' The other replied, 'You'll be court-martialled if you do that. But I'm going to lay my leg over a trench and break it with my rifle butt.' They had evidently had more than enough of the war. But then, every GI at the front was looking for the million-dollar-wound. The next morning they were gone and I still did not know what to do.

I was quite weak at this point and not of much use to anyone. As I moved out of the house I ran into a few other fellows, one of whom was barely able to walk because he had acquired trench foot. He asked where the battalion aid station was and I had to admit that I did not know as they constantly moved it. One of the others overheard our conversation and informed us that it was down the road some distance. 'But,' he said, 'the Germans have been knocking out everything that moves in that area.' I looked at the injured soldier's feet and he looked at me. 'I'm willing to go if you are.' I said. 'Let's go,' he replied and the two of us staggered down the road each holding the other up as we went.

Not a shot was fired. I think the Germans could see that neither of us was of any use and were better kept alive to require the attention of a few others.

When the doctor examined me and found that I did have battle fatigue he asked me if I thought I could possibly return to the front as they needed men desperately. I thought about it and hated to say no, but it had now been five days since I had eaten anything and I just didn't have the strength to return and fight.

While I was in hospital I met a GI from my platoon and he told me that on the night that we were carrying rations our squad had led the attack and, except for the sergeant they were all killed or severely maimed. I had been spared because of that carrying detail.

Kesselring had also been injured. On the road from Forli to Bologna, his staff car drove full tilt into the armour-plated flank of a self-propelled gun as it emerged from a side turning. Kesselring suffered severe concussion and was unconscious for over twelve hours. He was invalided home to Germany and did not return to the Italian front until mid-January.

In the British corps' area, it was a constant struggle to keep the roads open throughout the winter. Corporal Frank Battye, Royal Engineers, had swopped the crane on Bari docks for a bulldozer and was based at Chignato, just below Marradi. He was with a group of ten men who manned what was called a 'road post'; the team included a couple of Royal Signals operators, an ambulance with some medics, two bulldozers and their drivers and a fitter to carry out emergency repairs. Battye's beat was from Marradi to Palazzuola. The bulldozers were used as snow ploughs and for recovery. They were given a wooden hut, but the road team preferred to live with the locals. Shortly after they arrived, Battye recovered a supply truck which had skidded off the road. As a reward for a quick response the driver gave Battye a large piece of beef.

There was no cook in the road team. Sergeant Jack Rosser, who was in charge, said, 'There's some birds living across the road.' Frank Battye took the meat across and knocked on the door. Nardina Donatini came to the door.

'Cook this,' said Frank.

'No,' she said and shut the door.

Frank went back to the sergeant. 'Bloody Eyeties are too lazy to cook a bit of meat.' From what he had seen, however, Battye thought the girl very attractive, so he knocked again. Nardina's sister answered on this occasion and nervously asked him inside. Frank quickly saw why Nardina had refused to cook the meat; the house had no fireplace and the stove had been 'liberated'. Battye and Sergeant Rosser liberated another stove and installed it in the Donatini household. The sisters lived with their mother and father but there was a spare room. The two soldiers moved in and shared their rations with the family.[1]

Lt John Campbell was made Executive Officer when he returned to I Company 351st Regiment 88th Infantry. The battalion was bivouacked about eight miles back from the front line. The division had taken over this part of the front from the 91st Infantry who had originally captured the ridge and suffered heavily in the process. The forward positions, now snow-covered, were a series of deep bunkers connected by a shallow trench system on the crest of a ridge. Platoons took it in turns to occupy the front line. They were supposed to be rotated every ten days but this proved too difficult. They stayed for two weeks or longer before being relieved. In the sector Campbell had drawn, the enemy (in this case a rifle battalion from the 16 SS Panzers) was in a ruined church just 80 yards away.

The Americans had dug a series of tunnels from the reverse slope into the covered positions. The enemy was so close that any movement during the daylight hours immediately drew fire. Campbell had some periscopes which the guard detail used to watch the front. The time that a platoon spent in this forward position was always fraught with danger. Not only were the Germans too close, but the SS were mean bastards who kept up harassing fire which denied the young Americans any chance of rest.

But the SS did have a weakness; they were creatures of habit. Every night at eleven a train of 15 to 20 mules brought supplies to the church. Campbell used to watch as the mule train crossed the snowfield, casting ghostly shadows in the moonlight. He had considered hitting them with small-arms and machine-gun fire, but the promise of retribution SS-style was more than a deterrent. Instead he discussed it with battalion who in turn passed it up the line to regiment and division. One morning a call came through on the field telephone. It was G2 intelligence from division.

'Lieutenant. Can you see the church and the snowfield from your position?'

'Yes, Sir.'

'Okay son, tonight we are going to have a barrage at 2300 hours. I want you to make sure all your men are down in their bunkers and I want you up there where you can see. You will call the barrage on that mule train and we'll give them hell. But make sure your boys are under cover. There's always the chance of a round falling short.'

The mules arrived on time.

The minute I called it the world came to an end. I could hear the shaking, the noise, the flashing. How many guns they fired. . . Somebody ordered a Corps artillery TOT[2] barrage on that thing. How many rounds, only God knew. And they wanted me to observe it while it was going on. And I did. I got in my helmet as far as I could, and I looked at that thing and I had never seen a barrage like that before in my life. Ever. They were all in the air and they followed the curve of the field. Just magnificent. And when it was over, which was eight seconds or something like that, there were no mules left, there were no men left; there was nothing.

Tom Holladay had come down out of the line from Monte Grande and stopped at a semi-derelict farm cottage which served as the battalion CP. He was cold and miserable after five days in the trenches and it was a six-mile trek down the valley before transport could meet the platoon and lift them back to what was laughingly described as the regimental rest area. But at least there was the promise of ten days of warm feet and a dry place to sleep, so Tom chatted away to Willis Jackson and censored some of his platoon's mail before moving on down the line. He sent his platoon on ahead.

A single mortar shell burst in the deserted courtyard and a single piece of shrapnel tore through a shattered window, across the room where the radio operator worked and into another where it struck Holladay in the right arm and penetrated through into his chest. He had a hole the size of a silver dollar; the medic who patched him up could see through the blood that muscles were damaged in the arm.

The men in the CP gathered round Holladay to share in his good fortune.

'Tom,' Willis Jackson said, 'even if that wasn't a million-dollar wound I'm still going to send you stateside. God, man, that shrapnel came looking for you. That's got to be a message not to be ignored.'

Holladay's war was over.

Notes

1. Frank Battye was posted home shortly after – he was time-expired on overseas service. By this time he had fallen in love with Nardina and must have been one of the very few British soldiers to go AWOL from England to return to Italy. They married in 1947.
2. TOT – Time on Target.

51

Partisans

Positional warfare raised the question of using the partisans in a more active role. Precise figures are elusive, but it is estimated by the Italian military[1] that there were, in December 1944, perhaps 100,000 partisans behind enemy lines of whom no more than 10,000 carried the war to the enemy as true guerrillas. The remainder were refugees or fugitives from the threat of German forced labour.

In the Wehrmacht anti-partisan army tactics were not primarily designed to kill partisans,[2] but to simulate organized action, to scare them back into the hills where they could do little damage. In this they were extremely successful, even when the guerrillas had superior numbers and firepower. Another German device was known as the *rastrellamento*, literally meaning a raking or dragnet. In this instance a large number of troops would be deployed to sweep through a valley or mountain area. Wherever possible hostages were taken. The Wehrmacht maintained that it always treated these hostages humanely, but this was not the case with SS units.

Civilians were a constant source of information, and the Germans quickly tumbled to the fact that churches were frequently the centre of partisan activity, for meetings, as observation points and for the bells which were used to relay messages from one valley to the next.

Double agents were frequently used. Erstwhile Fascists joined partisan bands to gather information. English-speaking Germans posing as escaped Allied prisoners of war were another method of infiltration. Captured Wehrmacht personnel tried to give the impression to their captors that they operated a benign policy when it came to dealing with captured partisans. This impression is not borne out by reports from British liaison officers. One wrote in his debrief after crossing back into Allied lines:

The Germans, as often before, have bungled things and have played straight into our hands. Their terrorist policy of killing men, women and children without distinction and of stealing anything they can lay their hands on has shocked and enraged the population but has not cowed it into submission.

There are many German soldiers who would like to go over to the Partisans but cannot do so as they don't know how to get in touch. Many ask the civilians, but these are frightened of a trap and pretend they don't know. A few have gone over. I spoke to a Captain who had joined one of the Bands, and he told me that many more would come if they were given an assurance that they would not be interned when the Allies arrived. Obviously, this is not possible, but perhaps one could say that preferential treatment would be granted. That would not bind one to any specific promise.

While in German-occupied Italy I did not think that such subterfuges would be necessary but now I am inclined to think that any small suggestion to shorten the war should be investigated.

I often tried to impress upon the Partisans that the Germans, when they came up to attack them in the mountains, were probably more scared than the Partisans themselves. In fact, whenever the Germans were badly punished, they never returned to the particular area where they got beaten up.

I am not in a position to express an opinion as to the morale of the German troops in Italy.[3]

The presence of a BLO made the partisans and local population alike feel that they were not forgotten. The officer, who would often be accompanied by a small team including a radio operator and some weapon specialists, would frequently come from Special Forces. These teams were ambassadors and coordinators. But their effectiveness depended on the relationships they were able to establish.

The debrief report of one British officer makes interesting reading on popular attitudes:

The feelings and support of the civilian population vary greatly. In the towns the great majority of the population are only concerned about their own skins. Many inveigh against the Germans and some against the Partisans, but this is only because the Germans and Partisans are a cause of danger to their well-being and possibly to their lives. In the industrial towns there is, of course, a large Communist element, such as in Turin and Milan and they are all pro-Partisan. Then there are, of course, a few Fascists. The non-Partisan country areas are half-way between the two extremes of stupid, short-sighted selfishness and open support. The Partisan areas are almost entirely pro-Partisan with very few exceptions and the exceptions are generally very careful to hide their feelings. Generally speaking, the poorer the people are, the stronger is their support. This 'class-scale' applies on the whole to the entire country. The richest men in my area, which was a very poor one, were the least helpful to the Partisan cause – in fact, they did the least they could without getting into trouble. First, because being the richest men they had been connected with the Fascist administration and, secondly, because being rich they wanted to be quite sure that neither Germans nor Partisans would cause them to lose their fortunes.

In my area the population were first class. They were only too willing to give us a bed to sleep in and whatever food they had. I generally had my meals with some peasants who had their house and all their belongings burnt by the Germans, all their food reserves too. They lived in a barn where they previously kept their sheep, sleeping in their clothes on the straw. They had practically no blankets or change of clothing. They lost most of their cash, as when the Germans arrived they had but little warning and had to flee for their lives without having time to save their belongings. All they had left were a couple of barns, their land, a cow and the clothes they stood in. They knew that what they had lost was due to their having identified themselves so openly with the Partisans and with British officers and yet never did they utter a word of complaint or reproach. They were always willing to give us food; in fact were almost hurt when occasionally we ate elsewhere, and the same applied to any Partisan friend of theirs who happened to pass by. Naturally, we did all we could for them, such as giving them a parachute on the rare occasions when we had a drop. When the Germans came in their last 'rastrellamento' prior to my departure, on October 8th/10th, every civilian fled, of course, but the old lady who befriended us remained by her barn. 'If the Germans come here, they might kill me, but if I'm not here they are sure to burn my barn and, in that case, it's just as well to die now,' she said. Luckily the Germans did not go there.

Most of the villagers considered it an honour if any of us, officers or O/Rs invited ourselves to a meal. Yet they knew what the penalty for helping either escaped P.O.W.'s or Partisans was. All the streets of non-Partisan towns and villages are plastered with notices of the dreadful consequences which will be the lot of anybody assisting Partisans and P.O.W.'s. Hundreds of British ex-P.O.W.'s have now regained their freedom or are still at large owing to the hospitality they received from peasants and country people, hospitality given at very great risk to themselves. Many have been guests (not paying guests) of families for over a year, and they were complete strangers.

There are many just accusations which can be levelled at the Italian people, but their behaviour to escaped British P.O.W.'s must not be forgotten.

Morale and Allied Prestige

The morale of the Partisans varies greatly from area to area. This is natural – some areas are rich, others poor; some Bands are continually harassed, others live in comparative peace in their little kingdoms.[4]

The Allies also conducted a number of psychological-warfare operations against the Germans. The first were introduced after the fall of Rome and were applied and extended throughout the last winter of the war. A particularly imaginative scheme, code-named Operation Benedict, was copied from the Russians who had used it with considerable success on the Eastern Front.[5] The scheme involved segregating a batch of prisoners immediately after capture, and making sure they had plenty of cigarettes and hot food. After a day or so they would be informed that there were so many prisoners in Allied hands it would be a nuisance to send them back to cages. They could find their own way back to the enemy lines. The Russian experience was that the prisoners who returned immediately spread the story of their good treatment, and the number of desertions increased immediately. This scheme led to more ambitious operations which involved selecting suitable candidates from amongst POWs and infiltrating them behind enemy lines.

The tasks which could be carried out by such persons may be divided into three main categories:
(a) Propaganda aimed at creating general confusion, distrust of the German High Command and a realization of the uselessness of further fighting.
(b) The organization of groups within enemy units, particularly groups of non-Germans, with a view to bringing about the desertion en masse of such groups, desertion to be preceded by such acts of resistance and destruction as are possible.
(c) Contacting certain senior and influential officers in the German Army of definite anti-Party conviction and persuading them to act more readily and drastically than they would act if left entirely to their own initiative.[6]

Eighth Army Intelligence considered the most suitable candidates were the Poles, Slovaks and Russians. These agents were expected to cross the front line, get back into their old units with some plausible explanation for their absence, and then set about recruiting fellow countrymen on the 'cell principle'.

The misbegotten agents were also required to instil the view that:

... desertion in itself is not enough and that it should be immediately preceded by one or all of the following exploits according to circumstances:

(i)   Liquidation of Germans officers or NCOs;
(ii) Simple sabotage such as that of petrol supplies;
(iii) Failure to carry out demolitions.

In addition it should be stressed that deserters should bring with them arms and any documents to which they may have access.

Inducements would be offered – £25 per head on the completion of a mission, or £100 to dependents in the event of the agent becoming a casualty. Of course the only way in which an agent could claim their bounty was to desert for a second time! The official documents do not reveal how many men were persuaded to embark upon such an enterprise.

In February 1945 the Allied High Command believed that there was every possibility that the Committee of National Liberation for Northern Italy could cause trouble after that area was liberated.[7] It was proposed that a liaison team be despatched to keep an eye on the situation.

Another suggestion involved making the partisans less warlike. The issue of British army battledress, for example, 'would not necessarily provide an inducement to them to return peacefully to civil life. Civilian clothing would appear to be more suitable for this purpose.'

These bureaucratic absurdities could not obscure the fact the Allies would not entertain the possibility that the Committee of National Liberation in Northern Italy would be allowed to set itself up in opposition to Rome. Imperfect as the Allied creation might be, Alexander was ordered if necessary to denounce all agreements with the partisans and to support Rome, with military force if necessary.

Notes

1. Interview with author.
2. WO/208/4554 165475.
3. WO/208/4554/165475.
4. WO/208/4554 165475.
5. WO 204/10299 179874.
6. WO 204/10299 179874.
7. WO/106 3964 X 0170802.

52

The Last Great Offensive

Thank you for liberating us. We have been waiting for so long.
Street Poster

By the end of January 1945 SS General Karl Wolff, who commanded the SS and the police in Mussolini's Salo Republic, had come to the conclusion – as had Himmler, his master – that the war was lost. Nevertheless, both men believed it might still be possible to negotiate with the Allies. It was clear to them that Russia was the real enemy, and that it was logical that the Western Allies would welcome the opportunity to join with Germany in making common cause against the Bolshevik menace. Secret approaches were made by way of Swiss intelligence to the American Office of Strategic Services (OSS), the forerunner of the CIA. The head of station in Berne was Allen Dulles (later head of the CIA), a personal friend of Roosevelt. The Germans were rapidly disabused of any thought of a Grand Alliance.

Earlier in February the Big Three had met for the last time at Yalta. The outcome was not good, especially for the Poles. Churchill had played his best cards in a losing hand to secure a reasonable deal for a new and democratic Poland. Stalin had no intention of permitting a Western-style democracy taking root on his front door. And Roosevelt, desperate to get the Soviets into the Far Eastern war at the earliest possible moment, was not about to offend Stalin. There wasn't much that the Anglo-Americans could have done. Possession, after all, is nine points of the law and the Soviet Red Army occupied all of Poland.

General Anders approached Alexander. 'How can I ask my men to go on fighting? It's a lie to make them die for a free and independent Poland. Field Marshall, I must withdraw my forces from the line.'' Alexander explained that to do so would leave a terrible gap and place an intolerable strain upon the rest of Eighth Army. Anders agreed that they would defeat the Germans first and worry about their future after. They were told that Churchill was to speak to the Polish troops on radio. Vladyslaw Karnicki rigged up his 22 radio set with loudspeakers which were fixed to telegraph poles outside the CP. The men gathered around and Churchill spoke. Most did not understand what he said, but it was explained to them afterwards.

Karnicki remembered that Churchill had said he had to give up part of Poland because of something called the Curzon Line. When they looked at a map the meaning became clear. The Anglo-Americans had given Stalin that part of Poland which was the homeland of the II Polish Corps.

Churchill concluded. 'After the war, if you wish you can go back home, but if you don't want to, we will welcome you into England, we will give you homes and employment.' The men were immediately very bitter and angry. One of the gun sergeants spoke out. 'Why the hell are we fighting now? We've got no country to go to.' The Colonel stepped in and calmed things down. He and some of the battery commanders had been to London. They showed the men photographs of double-decker buses, and told them how good the country was.

'That's for me,' said Karnicki. 'I'm not going to the Russians.'

Even so, the Polish division, though they saw the campaign through to the end, did not show quite the same dash in battle as before.

Washington made one last attempt to close down the campaign and reduce the forces in Italy to a purely defensive role. The Ardennes offensive had shaken the Anglo-American High Command to its very foundations. It gave them a clearer appreciation of what still lay ahead before the final victory could assured. A further cause for concern was that the Russian advance from the east had lost momentum and was stalled on the Polish–German borders. The answer was to concentrate the Anglo-American effort on one front and that could only be in the west. Italy was seen to be of marginal significance unless Alexander could bring the combined forces of Army Group C to battle and destroy them in the Po Valley. There was one last great conference held in the Mediterranean. In January, Roosevelt, Churchill and their military chiefs and advisors gathered in Malta en route to Yalta.

It was agreed that Alexander could retain sufficient troops and resources provided that he launched an offensive no later than the beginning of April and succeeded in defeating the Germans in the Po Valley. If the enemy eluded him once again and made it in strength across the River Adige to the mountains beyond, then the whole of the Fifth

Army and a substantial part of the air forces would be withdrawn. In any case the Canadian Corps and two British divisions were to be moved to the Western Front.

Alexander fought his own corner well during the winter interlude, with the result that reinforcements and supplies flooded into the theatre. By April, Fifteenth Army Group had 600,000 troops and a further 100,000 Italian partisans who supposedly operated behind the German lines and confused enemy intelligence. Welcome quantities of ammunition were delivered together with new specialized vehicles, bridging equipment and armoured amphibious tanks specifically designed to cope with the sort of marshy areas that had proved so frustrating to the advance of Eighth Army. They were called fantails. Developed originally to cross the swamps of Florida, the fantail was a large, tracked, amphibious, thinly armoured personnel carrier which could carry about a dozen men. The fantails had proved successful in the Pacific on atolls and coral reefs and were introduced into Italy in limited numbers alongside other 'funnies'. There were flame-throwing Churchill tanks called 'Crocodiles' and turret-less Sherman tanks called 'Kangaroos' to carry assault infantry. As the weather improved, morale lifted and the Allied air forces enjoyed complete superiority over the Luftwaffe.

Rigorous new training schedules and new weapons honed the Eighth Army's fighting edge. Men reappeared from their private winter quarters and many were despatched to detention centres. But the vast majority soon found themselves back in the line rather than facing a court martial. In some units the malcontents were distributed amongst the platoons. Other battalions concentrated them in a single platoon, gave them the best NCOs and a top-rate platoon commander; this worked wonders.

The Fifteenth Army Group's front in March 1945 ran from just below Massa on the Ligurian Sea to the Comacchio lagoon on the Adriatic. The Fifth Army held the mountainous zig-zag line from Monte Grande, less than ten miles south-east of Bologna. The Fifth Army comprised the IV and II Corps. On the left flank IV Corps had the 92nd Infantry on the Ligurian coast together with the Brazilians. In the mountainous interior were the 10th Mountain and 1st (US) Armoured. Still astride the main route to Bologna, II Corps had the 88th, 91st and 34th Infantry Divisions in the line, along with the Combat Group Legnani with the 6th South African Armoured ready to exploit the breakthrough into the Po. Held in Army Reserve were 85th Infantry Division and Combat Group Mantova.

The Eighth Army line stretched south-east from Monte Grande, astride the Sillaro and Santero rivers and then north-east along the

Senio's south bank to Lake Comacchio's southern lagoon-like shore and the Adriatic. For this, the last offensive, some of the Eighth Army's long-serving corps had taken on a very strange complexion. In XIII Corps were the 10th Indian Division and Combat Group Folgore. The X Corps had the Jewish Brigade Group and the Combat Group Fruili. In the II Polish Corps the two infantry divisions had been joined by 2nd (Polish) Armoured Brigade and the 7th Armoured Brigade.

Only V Corps had a traditional Eighth Army feel with 2nd New Zealand, 8th Indian, 56th and 78th British, 2nd British and 9th Armoured Brigades, 21st Tank Brigade, No 2 Commando and the Combat Group Cremona. 6th Armoured Division was in Army Reserve. Besides the mule trains there were five Italian combat groups in Fifteenth Army Group, each of which contributed about two battalions to the order of battle.

The Germans were in dire straits even before the Allies unleashed their offensive. In March, Hitler ordered Kesselring to assume overall command in the West (which included Italy and the Rhine) and promoted Von Vietinghoff to command Army Group C. Some of the better divisions, like the Herman Goering, had been withdrawn to other fronts and there were few replacements. Veteran formations, such as the 29th and 90th Panzer Grenadier Divisions, were much reduced in strength. The average German infantry battalion at this time was considered fortunate if it could count 200 men on its ration strength. In contrast both the parachute divisions remained in the theatre and each, the 1st and 4th, were up to strength with 15,000 men each and morale remained good.

In the mountainous west, pillboxes and machine-gun nests had been improved. And in the east the Germans were dug in along the raised embankments of fortified river lines. Behind the front, Von Vietinghoff had prepared a number of rudimentary defence positions which stretched across the Po Valley all the way to the Alps. The only suitable course of action would have been to continue the Kesselring policy of a fighting retreat. But Hitler would have none of it and Von Vietinghoff did not have the access to his master that Kesselring had enjoyed.

The spring proved both exceptionally mild and dry. The result was that the snow melted early and the rivers, which ran north from the Apennines into the Po, became narrow, shallow, streams at the bottom of high flood banks. This meant they were relatively easy to bridge and the high banks would protect the engineers while they worked.

Mark Clark planned the offensive in three continuous phases.

Phase One was a bludgeon; a massive blunt instrument of air power and artillery with infantry behind to force a way through the German defences out of the Apennines and into the Po Valley. There was also a deception plan to convince Von Vietinghoff that the Allies were planning another amphibious operation in the Adriatic aimed at outflanking his mountain positions.

The offensive was to begin with a commando assault, riding the fantails across Lake Comacchio. This was to be followed by Eighth Army attacking on a broad front across the Senio river. Once German reserves had been drawn into the Adriatic sector, Truscott's Fifth Army would fight its way out of the Apennines.

Phase Two provided for an encircling breakthrough by either or both armies to bring the enemy to battle south of the River Po. The plains of Lombardy were to provide the venue for the killing ground of Army Group C. Here it was envisaged that the Allies' enormous superiority in armour and air power, some 3,000 tanks and 2,000 aircraft, properly coordinated, would be the ruination of Von Vietinghoff's forces.

Phase Three was a pursuit across the Po which would take the Allies at least as far as Verona.

Three nights before the battle, a cinema at Cesna showed the latest British release – Laurence Olivier in *Henry V*. It was a clear and inspiring message on the eve of a great battle.

In the event, Phase One proved to be another mighty attritional struggle which the Allies won, but at heavy cost. Phase Two was an exhilarating pursuit in which the 3,000 tanks massed in the *corps de chasse* at last came into their own; the divisions in Army Group C were decimated. Phase Three proved to be something of a walkover.

The battle got under way on 1 April, but it was the Germans who were caught napping on this April Fool's Day. Mounted in fantails, commandos and companies from 24th Guards Brigade moved through the front held by 56th Infantry Division and seized the northern spit and islands on Lake Comacchio. With the forecasters predicting three or four days of good weather Clark fixed 9 April for the start of the main attack by Eighth Army across the Senio river. It began with a massive air attack. The only people who arrogantly spurned the need for a rehearsal were the strategic air forces. All along the front the Eighth Army assault units withdrew 400 yards. One group of 20 US Army Air Force bombers released their bombs several thousand yards short and caught a Polish brigade out in the open and formed up for the assault. 160 men were killed and wounded.

The strategic air forces tried what had become known as carpet bombing. The theory was that a concentration of 25-pound bombs would inflict maximum casualties on the enemy without causing heavy structural damage, thereby impeding the advance. This was another promise from the pundits which failed to live up to expectations. The German troops were well dug in to heavily protected emplacements and there were few casualties.

The Eighth Army had always been well served by its Desert Air Force. These squadrons were probably the finest exponents of tactical air support and enjoyed a reputation not dissimilar to that of the fighter-bombers flown by the US Marine Corps in the Pacific. Throughout the Italian campaign (and in France too) the US Army Air Force had failed dismally to give the sort of support which the ground forces had every right to expect. But there had been changes. In the autumn battles, when weather permitted, the tactical air wings provided a solid service to the ground troops. Now, at last, in the spring offensive, air power contributed significantly in the campaign.

At 1345 hours the distant roar of heavy bombers seemed the signal for the first guns to speak. These were the 3.7s firing a line of airbursts as markers to guide the heavies on to their targets.

And then it was the turn of all the guns. The 2nd New Zealand Division on the Senio used as many guns as the entire Eighth Army at El Alamein.

The whole eastern horizon was solid with sound. Overhead shells raced with all their multitudinous sounds: 25-pdrs slithering or tearing past like a long curtain being ripped in two, the 4.5 and 5.5 churning their way through the air, as if they were whole trains behind driven at speed, invisibly over our heads, and hurtling down the bank. Sometimes the noise would seem to get harsher, as if the sky were a vast steel shutter, being hauled down on the enemy. . . . It seemed impossible that all this noise could come from something invisible and you looked as if expecting to see the hazed sky streaked and torn by passing shells, as artists show them in comic cartoons. But there was nothing there but the haze and the circling planes.[2]

Shells tore into the flood banks of the Senio from all angles, some from artillery which had been carefully sited to enfilade the river, while others crashed headlong into the wire entanglements, mines and pillboxes that guarded the far bank.

Then the guns fell silent and the fighter-bombers took over. Thunderbolts and Kittyhawks unleashed their bombs and rockets, Spitfires zoomed low to lace the German positions with cannon fire. Back came the guns with another programmed bombardment once again to give way to the aircraft. Five times the process was repeated until H-hour at 1920. The battlefield fell silent only to be broken by the aircraft returning low over the front to keep the German heads down and to mask the sound of the crocodiles as they clambered up the near bank ready to set torch to the enemy side.

At 1930 the artillery opened up once more. A curtain of steel fell on positions a quarter of a mile from the river. This isolated the enemy from their support and allowed the attacking infantry to secure the forward positions. At H + 40 the barrage began to creep forward and the assault companies kept pace. Apart from short spells to cool the guns, the battle continued to midnight. It was still a hard slog. The 8th Indian Division, the New Zealanders and the Italians of the Cremona Gruppo, seized a bridgehead across the Senio and moved against heavy resistance to attack the main line of defence on the far bank of the Santerno river. Meanwhile the 3rd Carpathian Division from the Polish Corps pushed up Route 6 towards Bologna.

It was at this stage of the war that Vladyslaw Karnicki was wounded. He was ambushed riding a despatch motor bike from the regiment's CP to division. A single bullet, fired by he knew not who, went through his leg and punctured the petrol tank. The heavy BSA went into a skid and somersaulted him over the handlebars. Karnicki landed up in a ditch. He grabbed his revolver and loosed off two shots in the general direction of where he thought his attacker might be before he realised that was all he had. The other four bullets had been expended earlier that day killing two chickens. They were in the saddlebags. There was no further firing. Karnicki waited a while and then climbed out of the ditch and limped over to the bike. There was petrol everywhere. The road ahead was a gentle decline and so he climbed aboard and painfully scooted his way back to the regiment. An ambulance took him to the Polish hospital at Forli.

The hospital was a terrible place. Large tents had been joined together and the stretchers rested on empty tea chests. Karnicki was undressed by an orderly, a fresh bandage was applied to his wound and his clothes were placed underneath the stretcher. He lay there with others, maybe a hundred or more, waiting to be attended to by the surgeons. Karnicki looked around him. There were men with no legs, soldiers with their stomachs open. 'Bugger this,' he said to the man on the next stretcher. 'I'm not staying here.' He reached down for his clothes and tried to dress quietly but he was spotted. A sister noticed his antics and summoned a couple of orderlies who carried his stretcher into another tent. The sister inspected his wound, cleansed it and left the orderlies to encase his leg in plaster. After they had finished they took him to another tent, still on the same stretcher, rested it on tea chests, and took away his clothes. Karnicki couldn't run away without his trousers.

In five days of bitter fighting the Eighth Army breached three river lines and in doing so overcame stubborn defenders. The Eighth Army advanced inland along the Via Adriatica, which ran through a narrow gap in the German-induced floods around the village of Argenta and thence to the Po at Ferrara. The problem lay at the Argenta gap, a bottleneck just two miles wide and eight miles deep, and easy to defend in depth. If the Eighth Army divisions could force the gap quickly, their line of advance would bring them into the German rear. The Poles and Combat Group Fruili found it equally hard going but were closing on Imola, just north of the Santerno and 15 miles from Bologna.

On 14 April Fifth Army joined in the fray; their attack had been postponed for two days because of bad weather; the forecasters had promised three days and no more. Amongst the line companies of the 85th, 88th and 91st Infantry Divisions, only about 30% of the men had been with their outfit when it landed in Italy. All the rest were replacements.

Truscott had the 34th and 91st Infantry Divisions astride Route 65 on the main road to Bologna; on their right was the 88th Division. These three divisions had to force their way through the last nine miles of mountain barriers. The right flank rested on Route 64 through the Reno Valley where the 6th South African and the 1st US Armoured Divisions waited to exploit the situation. On the left, Truscott deployed the 10th Mountain Division to take the 3,000-foot Rocca di Roffeso and the Brazilians to clear Montese. Truscott left the beefed-up 92nd Infantry on the Adriatic front in the full knowledge that the Japanese-Americans would do a superb job.

It took the Americans 48 hours to overcome tenacious resistance, before the Germans were forced off the heights and into the foothills. The 88th and 91st Infantry Divisions had a hard tussle for Livignano and when Monte Adone fell Von Vietinghoff was staring defeat in the face. The assault by 10th Mountain on Rocca di Roffeso was a splendid achievement and, in the short period of combat, the division proved to be one of the best in the theatre.[3] Earlier in February, when it cleared the high ground from Monte Belvedere to Monte Torraccia, the division secured its objectives, scaled precipitous rock faces and withstood counterattacks from elements drawn from four German divisions.[4] But the British Official History describes these actions as 'relatively minor operations'.[5]

The 10th Mountain would have us believe that they opened the door which made the Germans fall back in retreat. On 20 April the Americans broke through in the Apennines and cut the Via Emilia, Route 9, in two places. By then, however, Eighth Army were through the Argenta Gap and 6th British Armoured Division, the Eighth Army's 'old racehorses', after a doubtful start, was enjoying a blitzkrieg. The Poles had outfought their old enemies from Cassino, captured the 1st Para Division's battle flag and beaten the 34th (US) Infantry into Bologna. Von Vietinghoff's position was untenable and he knew it; it was only his master who wouldn't see reason.

Von Vietinghoff delayed another day before defying his Führer and ordering a general withdrawal. By then it was too late. The capture of Bologna and the Argenta Gap laid open the whole plain of the Po, and outflanked the Germans in the Apennines. With their line of retreat exposed, German divisions, which by then had no fuel and were practically immobile, disintegrated. In the first 14 days of the battle the Germans suffered some 70,000 casualties, half of whom were prisoners. Allied aircraft had bombed the bridges across the Po. The river, instead of becoming another line of resistance, became a trap. The Germans were forced to abandon much of their equipment, and, with the Allies striking them in the flank as they debouched from Argenta and Bologna, it was as complete a defeat as could be imagined.

In the last phase of the war the Allies were to experience once again the exhilaration of the chase. Disorganized and demoralized German units were out-pursued by the dash and elan of the Allied 'cavalry' – armoured cars, tanks and jeeps with lorried infantry in support – who ranged far ahead of the main advance. For many it must have brought back memories of the heady chase in the Western Desert or Patton's 'end runs' in Sicily.

And where had the mud gone? A New Zealand veteran of the desert campaign wrote, 'It turned overnight to a white powder which is the dust of Italy, fine and more irritating than any dust the desert ever saw.'[6]

In wooded country the armoured spearhead shot up every likely ambush site ahead of the advance, or called for air support. Villages, small towns, even isolated cottages which might harbour an enemy rearguard were blasted to rubble. Despite these awesome displays of firepower and the destruction brought down on their heads, the Italian people greeted the Allies as liberators, writing messages on sheets or daubing walls with slogans.

> Thank you for liberating us. We have been waiting for so long.

Every river previously had proved a barrier to the Allies. When they came to the Po it was the Germans' turn to suffer. They left their guns, tanks and trucks south of the river.

> On the night of April 22nd I had to decide whether to be taken prisoner with my Corps HQ staff while still south of the Po, or whether to cross the river. I decided to attempt the crossing. My HQ staff were dissolved into separate groups. At dawn on the 23rd we found a ferry at Bergantino. Of the thirty-six ferries in the zone of Fourteenth Army, four only were still serviceable. Because of the incessant fighter-bomber attacks it was useless to cross in daylight. As the level of the water in the Po was low, many officers and men were able to swim across. The access road at Revere was blocked by many columns of burning vehicles. I had to leave my cars behind. In the morning twilight we crossed the river and together with my operations staff I marched the 25 kilometres to Legnano.[7]

The Allied spearheads were already across. The 10th Mountain reached the Po at San Benedetto on Sunday evening, 22 April, and immediately crossed in assault boats, under fire, and secured a beachhead. On the following day, 23 April, the 85th, 88th and 91st Divisions and the 6th South Africans reached the river and crossed over. The Germans by now had fled, with the exception of an occasional rearguard. The 10th Mountain, which had covered 55 miles in ten days, was first into Verona. The Red Bulls captured Parma on 25 April. While the New Zealanders and 56th British Infantry raced each other to the Adige, the 6th (Br) Armoured headed for the Austrian border.

Even in this desperate retreat the German soldier was still to prove a formidable opponent. Determined rearguards stood their ground and in these, the closing days of the war, many a soldier, even the combat-wise and experienced, was to die. These included Colonel Bill Darby of Ranger fame who had returned to Italy in command of one of the regiments in 10th Mountain Division. The total Allied casualties from 9 April to 2 May were 16,747 men.

While the battle raged a number of different agencies and organizations were out seeking the whereabouts of Il Duce including the American OSS, British Special Forces and numerous secret agents. Was it a coordinated search and if so, ordered by whom? Mussolini was known to have had some papers with him which would have proved extremely embarrassing had they ever seen the light of day.[8] He was carrying two briefcases of papers, believed to include evidence that would help him in the event of a trial.

The Italian Committee of National Liberation ordered a general insurrection in northern Italy. Italian partisans and British paratroopers fell upon Milan and Genoa; partisans seized control in Venice; while another happy band of brigands (in this instance a communist partisan group) came upon Mussolini and his mistress near Lake Como.

Mussolini had spent six days in the Milan Prefectura. Surrounded by a hard core of maybe 20 Fascists, he planned to open negotiations with the Allies. Then the Archbishop of Milan told him the Germans had beaten him to it, so on the 25 April he and his party left for Como. There he waited for some of his subordinates to arrive with 3,000 Blackshirts to make a last stand at Valtellina. A truck was also supposedly en route carrying several million lire in gold bars, Swiss francs, US dollars and French francs. The vehicle never arrived. It is generally supposed that it was captured by the partisans and the funds 'donated' to the Italian Communist Party.

Il Duce and his entourage, including a close escort of SS, joined a Luftwaffe communications convoy which was retreating northwards alongside Lake Como to Innsbruck. The convoy was waylaid by the partisans who allowed the Germans to pass unmolested provided they handed over any Italian Fascists. Mussolini was arrested. He was wearing the overcoat of a Luftwaffe corporal, a poor attempt at disguise. Clara Petacci was also recognized and apprehended along with 15 other leading Fascists. The partisans reported their find to the CLNAI headquarters in Milan. The original armistice terms had required that Mussolini should be handed over to the Allies, but the terms did not state in what condition. Palmino Togliatti, the head of the Communist Party in Italy, had already ordered the execution of Mussolini and his mistress as soon as they had been captured and positively identified. The Americans were known to be looking for Mussolini, and the forward units of the 1st (US) Armoured Division had reached Como on 27 April.

Walter Andisco, a Communist Party member and partisan liaison officer who was also known as Colonel Valerio, was sent by the Committee in Milan to bring back Mussolini, dead.

Mussolini had been held at a farm on the outskirts of Mazzegra. On Saturday 28 April in the late afternoon, Colonel Valerio and two

accomplices arrived at the farm. Masquerading as Fascists, they persuaded Mussolini and Clara Petacci they had come to rescue them. The
pair left with the three men in a waiting car. Three hundred yards down
the road, outside the gates of the Villa Belmonte, Mussolini and his
mistress were summarily despatched and their bodies taken for public
exhibition to the Piazzale Loreto in Milan. They were left to hang by their
ankles from girders of the roof of a half-built garage, where a crowd
abused the remains and themselves in the process.

Most of Italy's major cities in the north had already fallen. The
remaining enemy forces were split and fragmented. German formations
began to surrender independently. Advancing Allied forces moved
wherever they wished and the partisans were ever more active. In those
last heady days of April, Fifth Army had fast, mobile columns fanning out
along all the highways in its area of operations. Genoa fell to the 442nd
and 473rd Regiments. To the north-east, the 34th – the old Red Bulls –
were spread out from Cremona to Piacenza.

Beyond the Po, columns from 1st (US) Armoured reached the Swiss
frontier and sealed the border. Another team headed towards Trento and
the Brenner Pass where they joined hands with Patton's forces advancing
south through Bavaria. The 85th Infantry was west of Vicenza. The 88th,
still hitting pockets of fanatical resistance and taking casualties in the
process, had pushed north of Padua. The 6th South African Armoured
met up with the New Zealanders at Legnano, west of the Venetian lagoon.

The Eighth Army's 8th Indian and 56th Divisions were converging on
Rovigo. The 91st was to their north-east at Treviso. Together these
divisions of Fifth and Eighth Armies formed a near-solid line and there
was no way out of Italy for the Germans. Generals Von Vietinghoff and
Wolff (the latter representing SS forces) sent emissaries in secret to
negotiate a surrender. Terms were agreed at Mark Clark's headquarters
on 29 April; a million Germans in Austria and northern Italy laid down
their arms. Von Vietinghoff as an Army Group commander was the first
theatre commander to capitulate in what proved to be the only negotiated
surrender of the war in Europe. The surrender became effective on 2
May, a full week before the total capitulation of the Germans at Rheims
and Berlin.

Earlier, on 29 April, as the battle beyond the Po drew to its close,
Churchill cabled Alexander. The telegram has since become enshrined
as a fitting epitaph for the Italian campaign.[9]

I rejoice in the magnificently planned and executed operations of 15th Groups of Armies which are resulting in the complete destruction or capture of all enemy forces south of the Alps.

That you and General Mark Clark should have been able to accomplish these tremendous and decisive results against a superior number of enemy divisions, after you have made great sacrifices of whole armies for the Western Front, is indeed another proof of your genius for war and of intimate brotherhood-in-arms between British Commonwealth and Imperial Forces and those of the United States.

Never, I suppose, have so many nations advanced and manoeuvred in one line victoriously. The British, Americans, New Zealanders, South Africans, British Indians, Poles, Jews, Brazilians and strong forces of liberated Italians have all marched together in that high comradeship and unity of men fighting for freedom and the deliverance of mankind. This great final battle in Italy will long stand out in history as one of the most famous episodes of the Second World War.

Pray give my heartfelt congratulations to all your commanders and principal officers of all Services and above all to the valiant and ardent troops whom they have led with such skill.

Notes

1. Matthews interview.
2. Ellis, *The Sharp End of War*.
3. It is perhaps of interest to note that the 10th Mountain, which was in action from February to May 1943 and wrote up its own citation for the Bronze Star, made 7,729 such awards. We may compare this figure with the 34th Infantry who fought in Italy from beginning to end (2,535), or the 88th Division which had twelve months of war (3,784), or the 91st with eight months of war – as a complete division – (4,154).
4. The whole operation had cost 1,450 casualties and all three regiments were deployed.
5. Jackson, Gen. Sir William, *The Mediterranean and Middle East, Vol VI, Part III*, HMSO, 1988, p 161.
6. Orgill, Douglas, *The Gothic Line, The Autumn Campaign in Italy, 1944*, Heinemann, London and Norton, New York, 1967, quoted in pp 184–5.
7. Von Senger, *Neither Fear Nor Hope*, pp 300–1.
8. There are rumours that Mussolini was in contact with the British in about September 1944 in an attempt to negotiate a surrender. If that is the case, and assuming the relevant official papers are ever released, they will not see the light of day in London before 1 January 1995.
9. Jackson, *The Mediterranean and Middle East*, pp 335–6.

Postscript

Warriors for the Working Day

Shakespeare

The Allied armies continued with their advance, to the French, Austrian and Yugoslav frontiers. There were complications on two borders. French troops had crossed into the Val d'Aosta on the Italian Riviera where the sovereignty of a large strip of territory had long been in dispute. There were rival factions and well-armed Italian partisans but the French were prevailed upon by Fifth Army to withdraw.

The Yugoslavs were an entirely different matter. The territory in dispute covered much of the Province of Venezia Giulia, namely the Gulf of Trieste and the Istrian peninsula.[1] This was once Imperial Austria's outlet to the sea but the port of Trieste and the surrounding territory became Italian in 1918. The Germans, in the name of the Third Reich (which then included Austria), annexed the province in 1943, at the time of the Italian armistice.

An agreement was reached at the Yalta conference. The Anglo-Americans, who would need a line of communications from the sea to their occupation forces in Austria, were given the largely Italian-speaking port of Trieste and the Slovene-populated hinterland. This was called Zone A. Tito, who claimed all the territory, was given Zone B, the Croatian coastal strip to the south of Trieste. Tito's partisans and Freyberg's New Zealanders arrived in Trieste at the same time. At first neither side wanted to risk a confrontation and so each occupied a part of the city and port area while they waited for their political masters to sort things out. There were, however, frequent incidents between the Italian

432

and Yugoslav elements of the population and then Tito moved large contingents of partisans into the area. Mark Clark responded by re-deploying the 91st (US) Infantry and the 56th (Br) Infantry Divisions into Trieste and Zone A. The quarrel escalated into a full-blown crisis in mid-May when divisions in both Eighth and Fifth Armies were put onto alert. The Trieste crisis threatened to become the last battle of the Italian campaign, or, as some feared, the opening shots of the Third World War.

Alexander, who at last came into his own as a soldier/diplomat, bluntly warned Churchill that if the Allies had to occupy the whole of Venezia Giulia then there would be a fight with the Yugoslavs who, in turn, might well be supported by the Soviets. Clark ordered his divisions to advance several miles along the front facing Yugoslavia in order to protect the railway line from Trieste to the Tarvisio Pass on the Austrian border. It was all done very carefully, nobody wanted the distinction of being the last casualty of the Second World War in Europe. In the meantime Alexander despatched his Chief of Staff, Lieutenant General Sir William Morgan, to Belgrade, there to meet with Tito and hammer out a solution. The Yugoslavs, in the face of an overwhelming show of force, withdrew behind the agreed lines.[2]

There were further problems with Tito's forces in south-eastern parts of Austria where military units attempted to occupy territory which had been demarcated within the Anglo-American sphere of responsibility. In this confusing and complex situation there were further casualties, not least those minorities who, having backed the wrong side, ended up as the flotsam of war. Cossacks and Croatians were handed back by the British to the tender mercies of their Soviet and Yugoslav overlords.

Allied soldiers were not unaffected by such tragedies, but neither did they wish to become involved. All they wanted was to go home. The demobilization programmes quickly gathered momentum with the Americans far outstripping the British in speed and efficiency. Indeed one of the most remarkably successful military operations of the Second World War was the movement of American troops home from Europe and their demobilization. Most of the American and all the Imperial and Commonwealth troops simply left. The British replaced those who were needed with national service conscripts.

Some became impatient and took the law into their own hands. One Australian medium-bomber squadron just packed their ground crews and personal kit into planes and took off from Foggia without telling a soul. They flew in formation and bluffed their way across the Middle East and Persian Gulf whenever they landed for fuel and rest. It wasn't until

Bombay that the system caught up with them. They were persuaded to hand over the aircraft and continued home by the next available troopship.

There were other losers, besides the Germans, Cossacks and Croatians. The Poles had no home to go to. Very few took up the offer to return to a Poland under Russian domination and the vast majority languished, an army in exile, in Italy. Various rehabilitation programmes were established, a technical college, courses to learn civilian trades and language schools. But the treatment of the Poles by the British in the immediate postwar years was shoddy. There were no Polish contingents in the Victory Parade through London and the trade union movement effectively blocked their absorption into the labour force for some time. There were still Poles in uniform in Italy as late as 1947 waiting for resettlement. Eventually they were offered jobs as coalminers, farm labourers or fishermen.

Vladyslaw Karnicki came to South Wales to work as a coalminer. At first he and his colleagues spent months living in a hostel while the local unions haggled over terms and conditions. Not unnaturally, demobilized Welsh miners were given preference. At last he was employed as an apprentice and spent the next three years working at the hardest and most menial tasks before eventually being accepted into the community.

Winston Churchill, the architect of the Italian campaign and, at times, its *de facto* commander, also lost. The result of Britain's general election, the first for ten years, was declared on 26 July, three weeks after polling day. For the first time in the history of the country, the Socialist Party was returned to power with a landslide victory, gaining nearly 400 seats in the House of Commons. Sergeants in the Army Education Corps taught civic affairs to disgruntled soldiers waiting to go home. It is not difficult to imagine which party the bulk of Eighth Army voted for. In 1947 the Army Education Corps received its Royal accolade to much barbed humour of some in the British Army who subsequently referred to the 1945 General Election as the RAEC's battle honour.

The ultimate military accolade eluded Mark Clark, so arguably he lost too. At the war's end he went on to command the US troops in Austria and was the American representative on the Four Power Control Council in Vienna. Bradley had become Army Chief of Staff (Truman had selected Marshall to be Secretary of State) and Clark must have entertained hopes that in time he would occupy this position. The 36th Texas Division's Veterans Association forced a Congressional Committee Enquiry on the crossing of the Rapido and though Clark was cleared, some believe it finished his chances for the top job. Clark's last combat command was C-in-C UN Forces in Korea (where he succeeded Ridgway, who had been his subordinate in Italy) but he returned home a rabid and vocal anti-communist in the style of Senator Joseph McCarthy. Such intemperate behaviour probably did him even greater harm.

The verdicts on the war in Italy point conclusively to the tactical excellence of the Germans. They fought a defensive campaign against which the Allies, with the single exception of the final offensive across the Po, can lay claim to no more than modest successes. A defensive campaign is a stronger form of strategy than an offensive, and more economical on lives and resources. Even so, the war in Italy must rank as one of the greatest defensive campaigns in the annals of military history. This does not detract from the fighting qualities of the Allied soldiers, but is an indictment of the generalship and leadership qualities displayed by the High Command.

The Germans did enjoy very important advantages. The weather and the terrain were decidedly in their favour for much of the time. Their military formations and the chain of command were so much more flexible than those of the Allies – British or American. The ability to form ad hoc battlegroups, the speed at which a division shattered in battle could quickly be restored and reformed, both were quite beyond the Allies to emulate.

'Mystify, mislead and surprise' had been Stonewall Jackson's motto in the American Civil War. In Italy the best the Allied generals could manage was brute force. Even when an element of surprise had been achieved and Kesselring wrong-footed, subsequent events degenerated into a battle of attrition where the only solution was simply to overwhelm the enemy by weight of fire power and sheer material superiority. Now there is nothing wrong with such tactics if it saves Allied lives, but neither should we pretend that the Allied generals were masters of their art. This was a war in which infantry, artillery and engineers were pitted in offensives along lines of greatest expectation, against fortified positions, often of great depth. Yet the Allies persisted in keeping armoured divisions and tank brigades poised, like the cavalry in the First World War, for a breakthrough. And this in a land which was only rarely suited to the deployment of a *corps de chasse*. This again, is not to decry the value of tanks, but in a campaign which cried out for the closest cooperation between infantry and armour, it was the cavalry who called the tune and set the rules of engagement, and that was plain nonsense.

How can we account for such sterility in Allied tactics? Not one Allied general who fought in Italy was outstanding.[3] Truscott was probably top of a class where the best of the rest were barely adequate. On the British side Templer showed the greatest potential. All had risen through the ranks of their profession in the inter-war period, years in which there was little to encourage innovation. The British belonged to an Imperial gendarmerie and the Americans moved from one dusty post to the next. Both armies were starved of resources. Nobody gave much thought to fighting the next war with means and methods other than those which had been used in the last war. Against such complacency the Germans created a climate which was far more conducive to original thought.

In 1935 the British Army contained 20 horsed cavalry regiments and the following year the Army Estimates for 1937 showed expenditure on hay to be four times as much as petrol. These were the years when many of the generals who commanded in Italy were lieutenant colonels and earmarked for high command. But even for these fliers, the writings of such brilliant outsiders as the British strategist Basil Liddell Hart largely went unread. His analysis of 20 centuries of warfare allowed him to formulate definite conclusions. Victors in decisive battles from Hannibal to Sherman, always put their opponent at a psychological disadvantage first. No general was justified in attacking an enemy in position and on guard. Never should an attack be renewed on the same line if it had once failed. Had the generals in Italy been more mindful of these basic principles in war, the human cost and suffering would have been vastly reduced in scale.

In the Western Desert, Eighth Army had evolved a very high level of cooperation with the Desert Air Force, but all these lessons seemed to largely disappear in Italy and the Americans did not get the message until the Gothic Line. Instead, air power was applied in its crudest form as a great, blunt, highly inaccurate and invariably counter-productive instrument of war largely waged against civilians. Over 865,000 operational sorties were flown but the price was heavy. More than 8,000 aircraft were lost between September 1943 and May 1945, some carrying as many as eight crew. The official histories show that 64,000 Italians were killed by Allied air raids (compared to 56,000 British civilians by the Luftwaffe). A further 10,000 Italians were killed by the Germans, some as reprisals. Figures are hard to come by, but about 9,000 Italians were deported to Germany as forced labour and few returned home. So the figures suggest that the Allies, in the name of liberation, killed more Italians than the Germans.

Statistics on the partisans make little sense. If we assume there were

150,000 partisans in the field by the time of the final offensive, the Italian authorities claim that 50,000 Germans were killed as a result of guerrilla warfare. In return 35,000 partisans were killed and 20,000 injured. One statistic which does appear reliable is that 410,000 Italians were killed in the war, which is considerably less than the Italian dead of the First World War.

And what of the main combatants? Strangely the butcher's bill puts the honours about even. The Germans suffered an estimated 336,650 casualties to tie the Allies down in Italy (a further 200,000 prisoners were taken before the final capitulation, but this has little meaning as they became part of the general collapse of Hitler's Germany). The Allied casualties were slightly lower at 313,495 men. One could argue that since the Allies were on the offensive their casualty figures ought to have been much higher.

Did the Allied armies in Italy contribute to the defeat of Nazi Germany? It was Hitler's indecision in the autumn of 1943 that suckered the Allies into an offensive in this most unsuitable of countries. The traditional arguments are that the Allies tied down German divisions which might have otherwise been deployed in France or on the Eastern Front. But the same is true of the Allies. So who ended up containing whom? There is only one occasion when the Germans outnumbered the Allies and that was in February 1944 during the counterattack at Anzio.

The final word belongs to the Italians. A plebiscite, held in June 1946, resulted in the abolition of the monarchy and the election of a constituent assembly which drew up a new republican constitution. This came into force in January 1948.

Earlier, the Allies had heaped the final indignity on the Italians. Even though Italy had been accepted as a co-belligerent, in 1947 the country was lumped along with the other minor belligerents – Hungary, Bulgaria, Romania and Finland.

A peace treaty was imposed upon them by the four great powers.

Notes

1. The term Venezia Giulia embraced the provinces of Gorizia, Trieste, Istria (Pola), Carnaro (Fiume) and Zadar (Zara) on the Dalmatian Coast.
2. It was left to the United Nations to resolve, but the dispute became an early casualty of the Cold War. In 1954 the Italian and Yugoslav

governments hammered out an agreement of sorts. The Italians got
Trieste and freedom of access and the Yugoslavs the rest, with both
sides agreeing to respect the rights of minorities.

3. There was some exceptional talent on the staff, notably Greunther
and Harding.

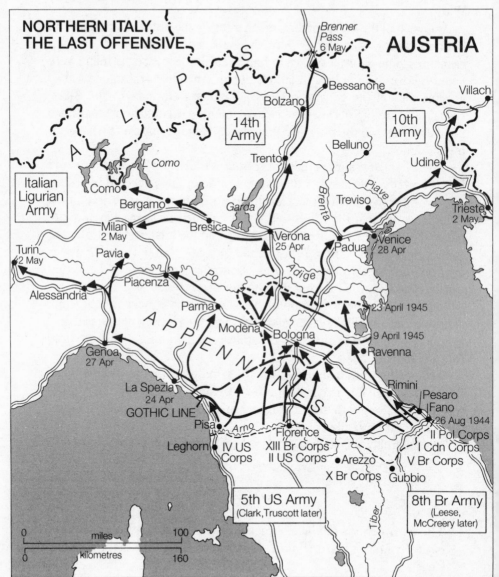

NORTHERN ITALY,
THE LAST OFFENSIVE

AUSTRIA

Brenner Pass 6 May

Bessanone

Villach

Bolzano

14th Army

10th Army

Belluno

Trento

Udine

L. Como

Italian Ligurian Army

Como

Bergamo

Treviso

Trieste 2 May

Milan 2 May

Bresica

L. Garda

Verona 25 Apr

Padua

Venice 28 Apr

Turin 2 May

Pavia

Piacenza

Parma

Modena

Bologna

23 April 1945

9 April 1945

Ravenna

Alessandria

Genoa 27 Apr

La Spezia 24 Apr

GOTHIC LINE

Rimini

Pesaro Fano

26 Aug 1944

Pisa

Arno

Florence

II Pol Corps

I Cdn Corps

Leghorn

IV US Corps

XIII Br Corps

II US Corps

Arezzo

V Br Corps

X Br Corps

Gubbio

5th US Army
(Clark, Truscott later)

8th Br Army
(Leese, McCreery later)

Tiber

0 — miles — 100
0 — kilometres — 160

APPENDICES

"Beautiful view. Is there one for the enlisted men?"

Appendices

Appendix 1

**Remarks made at Conference
at
ALGIERS on 2 May 43
by
General Montgomery, Eighth Army**

1. I know well that I am regarded by many people as being a tiresome person. I think this is very probably true. I try hard not to be tiresome; but I have seen so many mistakes made in this war, and so many disasters happen, that I am desperately anxious to try and see that we have no more; and this often means being very tiresome. If we have a disaster in HUSKY, it would be dreadful.
2. We have now reached a very critical stage in the planning for HUSKY.

    Unless some final decision is reached within the next few days it is very doubtful if we will be able to launch the operation in July.

    I would like to put before you the problem as it appears to me, the commander of the Army which has got to be landed in Horrified, and there fight a hard battle.
3. Three outstanding factors are as follows:

    (a) The capture of HORRIFIED will depend ultimately on the effective operations of the land army.

    (b) The army has to be got there by the Navy, and the Navy has to be able to maintain the army once it is ashore.

    (c) The above two things cannot possibly happen unless the RAF can operate effectively, and it cannot do so unless suitable airfields are acquired quickly so that fighter squadrons can be stepped forward, and the enemy air is pushed well back and is generally dominated.

4. We next want to be clear that enemy resistance will be very great; it will be a hard and bitter fight; we must go prepared for a real killing match. That is nothing new, and we have had many parties of that sort; but there are certain rules in that sort of game or killing match, which have to be observed; if you do not observe them, then you lose the match.

   The outstanding and great rule is that dispersion of effort by the land army leads to disaster. The army must keep collected with Corps and Divisions within supporting distance of each other.

5. We next have to consider in what way the Army must be put on shore by the Navy so that it is then well placed to develop its operations and to maintain itself.

   The area selected must be inside fighter cover; a good port must be seized quickly; good airfields must be secured quickly for the RAF.

   The size of the initial bridgehead you can establish is limited by your resources.

   With limited resources you will be very lucky if this bridgehead includes a good port and *all* the airfields you want; some may have to come later as operations are developed. Therefore it is very important that with limited resources, and against strong resistance you act as follows *in the first instance*:

   (a)   Keep concentrated.
   (b)   Secure a suitable area as a firm base from which to develop your operations.
   (c)   Keep the initial operations within good fighter cover of your own airfields.

7. I have made it clear in para 6 that the extent of the bridgehead is limited by your resources.

   What we must now be clear about is that the initial bridgehead must include the *immediate essentials*, without which the whole combined operation would merely collapse.

8. Let us now apply the above principles to HUSKY – the S.E. portion.

   The best place for the Eighth Army to put ashore is in the ACID and BARK areas.

This would meet every requirement that I have brought out in the preceding paragraphs, except one.

And *that one is very important*; it does not secure sufficient airfields for the RAF, or deny to the enemy the use of airfields from which he could interfere with our seaborne traffic and operations generally. The airfields in question are those in the general area COMISO–GELA.

These airfields must, according to the air, be included in the initial bridgehead. In the words of para 7 they are 'immediate essentials, without which the whole combined operation would merely collapse'.

9. I must here state very clearly, and beyond any possibility of doubt, that I will never operate my Army 'dispersed' in this operation. I consider that to do so would mean failure and HUSKY, instead of being a success, would involve the Allied Nations in a first class disaster; this is exactly what the Germans would like, and would be a shattering blow to Allied morale all over the world.

It is not merely a matter of capturing some beaches, or some airfields, or some ports. It is a matter of the conduct of offensive operations in an enemy country; the objectives include airfields, ports and so on, and finally we require the whole island. See para 4.

10. Are there are alternatives?

   (a) You could shift the whole bridgehead layout northwards to include the CATANIA area and the airfields there.
      This can be discarded *at once*, if only for the reason that it is outside fighter cover of our own bases.
   (b) You could shift the whole layout westwards to the area of CENT and DIME.
      This gets the airfields we require. But you have no port, and the force could not be maintained for long through the beaches.

11. The whole point turns on the size of the initial bridgehead we can secure. The factors are as follows:

   (a) The Army won't have dispersion, and must have a port.
   (b) A bridgehead to satisfy the Army can NOT include, with the resources available, certain airfields to the west which are essential for the RAF.

443

(c)   I understand the RAF point of view to be that these airfields must be denied to the enemy at once, and then quickly secured for our own use. Unless this is done the RAF cannot guarantee air protection beyond the initial stage, i.e. for say the first 48 hours.

12.   It is therefore quite obvious that these airfields must be taken.

But we have not any troops for the purpose.

Two Divisions, assault loaded, would be necessary, and they would carry out the CENT and DIME landings.

13.   We have now reached the stage when we can say quite definitely that we require *two more* Divisions, assault loaded and to be landed on D-day at CENT and DIME, if HUSKY is to be a success.

Given these two Divisions, then all the requirements of the Army, Air and Navy are met and this very difficult and tricky operation will be a complete success.

Without these two Divisions, it would seem – in view of what the air say – that we may well have a disaster.

[The final note (14) is handwritten – by Montgomery?]

14.   I consider that the answer to the problem is to shift the US effort from the Palermo area and to use it on CENT and DIME. Husky would then be a complete success.

signed B. L. Montgomery
General, Eighth Army
2.5.43.

Appendix 2

CAB 101/144
165363

The Prime Minister had already hastened to put on paper what he described as 'Thoughts on the Fall of Mussolini'.

1. It seems highly probably that the fall of Mussolini will involve the overthrow of the Fascist regime, and that the new Government of the King and Badoglio will seek to negotiate a separate peace with the Allies. Should this prove to be the case, it will be necessary for us to make up our minds first of all upon what we want, and secondly upon the measures and conditions required to gain it for us.

2. At this moment above all others, our thoughts must be concentrated upon the supreme aim, namely, the destruction of Hitler, Hitlerism and Nazi Germany. Every military advantage arising out of the surrender of Italy (should that occur) must be sought for this purpose.

3. The first of these is, in the President's words, 'the control of all Italian territory and transportation against the Germans in the north and against the whole Balkan Peninsula, as well as the use of airfields of all kinds'. This must include the surrender to our garrisons of Sardinia, the Dodecanese and Corfu as well as all the naval and air bases in the Italian mainland as soon as they can be taken over.

4. Secondly, and of equal importance, the immediate surrender to the Allies of the Italian Fleet or at least its effective demobilization and

paralysis and the disarmament of the Italian Air and ground forces to whatever extent we find needful and useful. The surrender of the Fleet will liberate powerful British naval forces for service in the Indian Ocean against Japan, and will be most agreeable to the United States.

5. Also, of equal consequence, the immediate withdrawal from or surrender of all Italian forces in Corsica, the Riviera including Toulon, and the Balkan Peninsula, together with Yugoslavia, Albania and Greece.

6. Another objective of the highest importance, about which there will be passionate feeling in this country, is the immediate liberation of all British prisoners of war in Italian hands and the prevention, which can in the first instance only be by the Italians, of their being transported northwards to Germany. I regard it as a matter of honour and humanity to get our own flesh and blood back as soon as possible and spare them the measureless horrors of incarceration in Germany during the final stages of the war.

7. The fate of the German troops in Italy, and particularly those south of Rome, will probably lead to fighting between the Germans and the Italian army and population. We should demand their surrender and that any Italian Government with whom we can reach a settlement shall do their utmost to procure this. It may be however that the German divisions will cut their way northwards in spite of anything that the Italian armed forces are capable of doing. We should provoke this conflict as much as possible, and should not hesitate to send troops and air support to assist the Italians in procuring the surrender of the Germans south of Rome.

8. When we see how this process goes, we can take a further view about action to be taken north of Rome. We should, however, try to get possession of points on both the west coast and east coast railways of Italy as far north as we dare. And this is a time to dare.

9. In our struggle with Hitler and the German army, we cannot afford to deny ourselves any assistance that will kill Germans. The fury of the Italian population will now be turned against the German intruders who have, as they will feel, brought all these miseries upon Italy and then come so scantily and grudgingly to her aid. We should stimulate this process in order that the new liberated anti-Fascist Italy shall afford us at the earliest moment a safe and friendly area on which we can base a whole forward air attack on South and Central Germany.

10. This air attack is a new advantage of the first order, as it brings the whole of the Mediterranean Air Forces into action from a direction which turns the entire line of Air defences in the West and which furthermore exposes all those centres of war production which have been increasingly developed to escape Air attack from Great Britain. It will become urgent in the highest degree to get agents, Commandos and supplies by sea across the Adriatic into Greece, Albania and Yugoslavia. It must be remembered that there are 15 German divisions in the Balkan Peninsula of which 10 are mobile. Nevertheless once we have control of the Italian Peninsula and of the Adriatic, and the Italian armies in the Balkans withdraw or lay down their arms, it is by no means unlikely that the Hun will be forced to withdraw northwards to the line of the Soave and Danube, thus liberating Greece and other tortured countries.

11. We cannot yet measure the effects of Mussolini's fall and of an Italian capitulation, upon Bulgaria, Rumania and Hungary. They may be profound. In connection with this situation the collapse of Italy should fix the moment for putting the strongest pressure on Turkey to act in accordance with the spirit of the Alliance, and in this Britain and the United States, acting jointly or severally, should if possible be joined or at least supported by Russia.

12. The surrender, to quote the President, of 'the head devil together with his partners in crime' must be considered an eminent object and one for which we should strive by all means in our power short of wrecking the immense prospects which have been outlined in earlier paragraphs. It may be however that these criminals will flee into Germany or escape into Switzerland. On the other hand, they may surrender themselves or be surrendered by the Italian Government. Should they fall into our hands, we ought now to decide in consultation with the United States and after agreement with them and the USSR what treatment should be meted out to them. Some may prefer prompt execution without trial except for identification purposes. Others may prefer that they be kept in confinement till the end of the war in Europe, and their fate decided together with that of other war criminals. Personally I am fairly indifferent on this matter, provided always that no solid military advantages are sacrificed for the sake of immediate vengeance.

Appendix 3

MOST SECRET   *IMMEDIATE*

BIGOT AVALANCHE   CIPHER MESSAGE   FOLIO NO. 0994 8
                            IN   1 SEPT 43.

FROM:–   AFHQ   TOO: 011311B
TO:–   GOC 15 ARMY GP   THI:
                                            TOR: 012255B

ORIG. NO. 8843

PERSONAL FROM EISENHOWER TO ALEXANDER

MESSAGES SENT YOU YESTERDAY BY CLARK ON REVISED USE OF AIRBORNE TROOPS IN AVALANCHE WERE BASED ON PURELY MILITARY GROUND ESPECIALLY MAINTENANCE. HIS REVISED PLAN WAS DEEMED MAXIMUM THAT AIR FORCE COULD SUPPORT AND MAINTAIN AND WAS CONCURRED IN BY MCCREERY, TEKER (*sic*) AND OTHERS CONCERNED.

MESSAGES RECEIVED HERE THIS MORNING FROM SMITH INDICATE PROJECTED USE OF ALL AIR TROOPS POSSIBLE ON NIGHT D MINUS ONE TO STIFFEN ITALIAN FORMATIONS THAT PROMISE COLLABORATION IN ROME AREA.

PROVIDED ALL REQUISITE CONDITIONS LAID DOWN BY SMITH ARE MET BY ITALIANS, I APPROVE THIS VENTURE. GENERAL C IS BEING NOTIFIED OF APPROVAL IN PRINCIPLE, SUBJECT TO MEETING OF CONDITIONS. MAC IS STUDYING MAXIMUM LIFT POSSIBLE WHILE C IN C MED IS EXAMINING POSSIBILITY OF TAKING IN AMMUNITION BY BOAT. I BELIEVE THAT IF POSSIBLE

COMPLETE COMBAT ELEMENTS OF ONE DIVISION SHOULD BE
USED. THIS PROJECT WOULD OF COURSE PRECLUDE AIRBORNE
OPERATION IN AVALANCHE ON NIGHT D MINUS ONE BUT ONE
ATF DIVISION WOULD STILL BE AVAILABLE FOR REINFORCING
AVALANCHE. IN VIEW OF FACT 82ND DIVISION HAS BEEN
INTEGRATED WITH AVALANCHE FROM BEGINNING, BELIEVE IT
BETTER TO COUNT ON 82ND SUPPORTING TENTH CORPS
WHILE BRITISH DIVISION DOES ROME JOB BUT I AM HAVING
THE IMPLICATIONS EXAMINED.

DISTRIBUTION: – MA TO GOC IN C (PERSONAL)   SMC 0020/2

T.T. 0057/2 AF.

Appendix 4

MOST SECRET *IMMEDIATE*

BIGOT AVALANCHE   CIPHER MESSAGE   FOLIO NO. 00181.
                          IN   1 SEPT 43.

FROM:–   5 ARMY.   SIGNED CLARK   TOO.
TO:–   CG 15 ARMY GROUP
            CG 15 MAIN ARMY GROUP.
NO:–   6046 (6036)

AFTER CONFERENCE TODAY WITH COMMANDER IN CHIEF AND AIR COMMANDER IN CHIEF, MEDITERRANEAN IT WAS MANDATORY THAT THE AIRBORNE TASK FORCE OF THE 82ND AIRBORNE DIV FOR OPERATION AVALANCHE BE REDUCED FROM A STRONGLY REINFORCED RCT TO AN RCT LESS ONE BATTALION. THIS CHANGE NECESSARY BECAUSE IT IS DEEMED IMPOSSIBLE TO *RESUPPLY* THE FORCE ORIGINALLY PLANNED FOR THIS TASK. WITH REDUCED FORCE IT WILL BE POSSIBLE TO CARRY GREATER QUANTITY OF SUPPLIES EXACT AMOUNT TO BE GIVEN YOU LATER.

GENERAL LEMNITZER . . .
. . . ON THIS MISSION. REQUEST APPROVAL

MA TO GOC IN C   S.M.C. 0415B/3
                             T.T. 043B/3. HW.

MOST SECRET
AVALANCHE

Appendix 5

WO204/9886   180094

Secret
Army Sub Commission MMIA
H.Q.A.C.C.
ROME
TS/G/29
28 Aug. 44.

To:–   H.E. General OXILIA Under-Secretary of State for War.
H.E. General BERARDI Chief of the General Staff – Italian
Army

Reorganization Italian Combat Force

Your Excellency

1. I am directed to inform you that is has been decided that as and when equipment can be provided certain units of the Italian Army will be re-equipped from Allied sources on a combat basis.

2. These units are to be organized by you into standard Gruppi di Combattimento in accordance with approved outline war establishments which will be given you. You will be notified from time to time of units selected, as equipment becomes available.

3. The first two units selected are the FRIULI and CREMONA Divisions, which will at once be concentrated by you in the area allotted you east (*sic*) of BENEVENTO for re-organization and training.

4. The reorganization required to bring the units of these divisions

451

into conformity with the outline war establishments will be completed as quickly as possible and in any case before 17th September. Particular care and firmness will be exercised by you in the deletion of all officers, NCOs and men who are for any reason unsuitable for combat duties. This process will be supervised and assisted by British Liaison Officers who are being sent at once the S. GIORGIO for that purpose.

5. The training of Italian personnel in the operation and maintenance of British weapons, transport and equipment will include the following:–

(a) The technical training of Italian regimental instructors at British schools in accordance with arrangements already made.

(b) The instruction of Italian personnel in units by Italian instructors (see above) supervised and assisted by British Training Teams which will remain with Italian units during this phase.

(c) Tactical exercises for officers and NCOs (without and with troops) demonstrating the employment of British weapons by Italian sub-units; these will be arranged by British Staffs in collaboration with Italian commanders.

(d) Specialist and administrative training in supply, replacement and other technical details which will be undertaken by British technical units.

Speed and energy are essential during this period which, it is considered, should (for the first two groups) be completed by the end of October provided essential equipment arrives in time.

6. The issue of equipment will be made as quickly as possible under arrangements which will be notified separately. In the meantime you are to ensure that all the necessary administrative arrangements are ready for its receipt, distribution and safe custody.

7. The method of employment of these divisions in the line will be notified later when their potentiality can be more definitely assessed in relation to future needs. Meanwhile you may work on the following promises.

(a) Gruppi will be employed independently under Allied Formation Commanders.

(b) Necessary Italian supporting arms and maintenance services will be provided under arrangements to be notified separately.

(c) Gruppi will be capable of moving in it's (sic) own Motor Transport with the exception of Infantry Rifle Coys.

(d) Extra transport or special equipment (such as for mountain warfare) will be provided from Allied sources when required subject to operational availability.

(e) It is not intended that Gruppi will be called on to undertake major offensive operations unaided.

(f) Gruppi may be required to undertake Internal Security or Garrison duties if the need arises.

8. The selection and preparation of further units for training is now being studied and you will be informed of any decisions reached.

Major General
Army Sub Comm. A.C.C.
M.M.I.A.

Appendix 6

WO204/9888   180094

Subject: *Auxiliary Troops supervised by Colored Allied Troops*

Land Forces
Sub Commission, AC (MMIA)
Rome
AQ/S
10 December 1944

To:–   *Minister for War*

Reference your 306150/1/CA of 6 December

1.   The Allied Armies consist of the troops of a large number of nations, who are fighting the common enemy without regard to race, creed or color.

2.   There can be no question regarding the color of Allied troops. It must be insisted that soldiers, Italian or Allied, do what they are told to do without question.

/s/   Clayton P. Kerr
CLAYTON P. KERR, Colonel
for Major General
Land Forces
Sub Commission, AC (MMIA)

CPK/1sk
cc: AFHQ for G-3 Org

Copy Translation

MINISTER FOR WAR

Ref 307342/1/C.A.   21 December 1944

Subject: Auxiliary Troops Supervised by Allied Colored Troops
To: Land Forces Commission – A.C. (M.M.I.A.)

This Ministry is fully in agreement with MMIA as regards the setting aside of all prejudice of race, color, and religion insofar as it affects every Armed Force which today fights to attain common victory. This Ministry is also fully aware of the honours and consideration won specially by those coloured soldiers who, arriving from the most distant continents, have contributed so many sacrifices and so much courage to the common cause just for the sake of the universal principles of liberty, human dignity and equality.

The report contained in our previous letter dated the 6th inst was not meant to be a departure from the above policy but was only meant to submit to your consideration a situation which, exclusively from a *military and disciplinary* point of view, was certainly not such as to maintain among the Italian soldiers that level of morale and spiritual contentment which is a basic requirements of every military formation and which is the best means of insuring a maximum capacity and output.

Today the chief aim of the Italian Army is to contribute, with all its energy and in every way, to the war effort of the United Nations and, with this aim in view, in fact, Italian units glory in any duties entrusted to them, be they amid the thunder and flash of battle or in dark and hard labour in the rear.

Allied reports and commendations have often given proof of the contribution made by these soldiers who deserve all the more consideration because they work humbly and in silence. It is therefore to safeguard their morale that once again I appeal to you, encouraged in my appeal by the fact that already the advisability of not putting Italian soldiers under the supervision and control of colored military has been admitted for the ports of Southern Italy since it often the case that these colored military, possible in good faith, and without realizing the lowering of morale which they cause, carry out their duties without any consideration to what is an insuppressible their own of sensitiveness and dignity (sic).

It is therefore not a matter of prejudice, which I, myself, would condemn in honour of the right principles of democracy in which Italy herself, is today being reborn, but it is simply a matter of morale, which I have the honor to submit to your consideration, fully confident that your usual benevolent understanding will not fail me even on this occasion.

THE MINISTER
/s/ A. Casati

Appendix 7

WO/204/2/81XC/70802
Appendix 'A'

Translation of leaflet found at NARO

SICILIANS, ex-service men of all ranks DO NOT REGISTER FOR MILITARY SERVICE!

Do not allow the name of MERCENARY to be added to those of TRAITOR and VANQUISHED.

Do not leave your work.

Remember the humiliations and sufferings you have undergone in vain. Think of our dead and of our brothers who are still in prisoner-of-war camps.

For what object? For whom? For what ideal?

If the English minister EDEN announced that Italy must resign herself to the loss of her colonies, if they talk of giving TRIESTE and the whole of ISTRIA to YUGO-SLAVIA, and the Dodecanese to GREECE, perhaps you must fight so as not to be deprived of these things?

Or maybe as a reward for your sacrificings (*sic*), you are told of the foul terms of an Armistice which they have dared to sign in the name of the People?

SICILIANS, now is the time to demonstrate that you are no longer sheep.

DO NOT REGISTER FOR MILITARY SERVICE!

A man of honour should not put on a uniform which reeks of shame, dishonour and defeat, nor, what is worse, still wear a mercenary one.

Are you not aware that the MONARCHY and the GOVERNMENT

457

are both subordinated to others, and are looking after their own interests?

Do you not see that the people are being betrayed?

Peasants, workers, brain-workers, do not allow your blood to be bartered for a few sacks of flour or for a dozen or so flannel pyjamas!

Do not make your mothers weep any more!

DO NOT REGISTER FOR MILITARY SERVICE!

The military authorities have no expectations of successful results from the call-up. They are trying out the ground. And, when a people says 'NO', it means NO!

(Copy of a leaflet in circulation in Sicily).

Appendix 'B'

Translation of pamphlets stuck on walls at ALESSANDRIA della ROCCA.

(1) *NOTICE.*

Citizens, do not report to the Distretto Militare. The time's come to put an end to it. Any Carabiniere who tries to root us out will die quickly. Anyone who does report is to be pitied. We have no Country. We're nobody's tool. And we won't let anyone trouble us. We brothers in arms must see eye to eye: we've pulled ourselves out of the frying-pan and now they want to chuck us in the fire. Let's all rebel! Long live Giuliani! We're your friends.

(Anyone who tears this down will be torn apart.)

---

(2)   Alessandrian youth, join Giuliani's band! Down with the Army!

ANNEXES

Annexes

Annex A: The US Infantry Division

The organization of the wartime US infantry division was the brainchild of the commander of army ground forces, General Lesley J. McNair. He cut the cumbersome '*square*' division, with four regiments in two brigades, which had survived from the First World War, to a '*triangular*' organization, with three regiments, which was more suited to open warfare. This organization was adopted in June 1941 and modified in 1942 and 1943.

At every level the new division was based on a triangular structure. The three regiments each controlled three battalions, each with three companies of three platoons each, and three squads to a platoon. Each headquarters also controlled additional support weapons, ranging from the company's 60-mm mortars and .3-inch machine guns to the regimental cannon company with 75-mm or 105-mm howitzers.

The numbers of the regiments within the divisions (excluding the old regular army divisions, namely 1st–5th, and the 34th Infantry) followed the square formation minus the fourth regiment. Thus for example, the three infantry regiments in the 36th were $36 \times 4 - 1 = 143$rd, 142nd, 141st; or in the 85th Division: $85 \times 4 - 1 = 339$th, 338th, 337th etc.

In support of the infantry were two light artillery battalions, each with eighteen 105-mm howitzers and a medium artillery battalion with twelve 155-mm howitzers. Each division also possessed a reconnaissance squadron of mechanized cavalry and an engineer battalion with construction plant and light bridging equipment. There was a large medical battalion. American divisions were not responsible for supplying their battalions; this was done from army-dumps. Each division, therefore, had only one quartermaster company, with trucks to carry reserve supplies or one infantry battalion. The ordnance company was responsible for some vehicle repairs, although as much work as possible was done by units themselves, and really serious repairs by army workshops. The signal company was responsible for divisional headquarters' communications, and the division was completed by the military police platoon and the headquarters company.

The total manpower of the division varied between 14,000 and 15,000. Just over 5,000 of these were front-line infantrymen. In battle, divisions were reinforced by other units, such as tank battalions and engineers, and commanded three regimental combat teams – all-arms groupings based on infantry regimental headquarters.

Annex B: The British Infantry Division

The infantry division was the largest permanent tactical unit, with a paper strength that varied from 15,000 to 18,000 men. Above the division (as with the US Army) were the higher formations of corps, army and Army Group.

The infantry division was organized into three brigades (roughly the equivalent of a US Army regiment). Each brigade contained three battalions of four rifle companies, and the rifle company was subdivided into platoons and sections (the latter the equivalent of a squad in the US Army).

In the battalion there was a headquarters company with six platoons, separately responsible for anti-aircraft defence, mortars, signals, pioneers, administration and intelligence.

The artillery component of a division comprised three regiments totalling 72 guns. There were, in addition, an anti-tank regiment with the 17-pounder anti-tank guns and an anti-aircraft regiment with Bofors 40-mm and 20-mm quick-firing guns.

Annex C: The British Regiments Explained

The modern British Army can trace its origins back to the mid- seventeenth century and the restoration of the monarchy in 1660 after the death of Oliver Cromwell and the Republic. Except for a period during the First World War, the Second World War, and a decade or so after 1945, the British Army has always been an all-volunteer regular force organized on the regimental system. A soldier who served in the infantry or the cavalry joined a regiment and stayed there throughout his military service. He lived in a closely knit 'family' group, which was the regiment.

The regiment promotes tremendous pride and *esprit de corps* that has been the envy of many other armies. The soldier knows the history of his regiment and can recite its battle honours and the great moments from its past.

The fighting regiments of the British Army, the infantry and the cavalry have a long and glorious history. The first regiments were raised after the restoration of the monarchy and were named after the colonel who was appointed by the King to recruit and command them. This system caused administrative problems because sometimes there would be more than one colonel with the same name. Another problem was that the colonel might be killed during a battle and a new officer appointed to command; thus could happen perhaps two or three times in a single day, and it caused considerable confusion. Nevertheless, by the beginning of the eighteenth century, when the Duke of Marlborough commanded a British army in Europe, there were some 39 regiments of infantry (or foot, as they were then called).

In 1751 the Duke of Cumberland, the Commander in Chief, changed the system. He dropped the colonels' names and instead gave each regiment a number that roughly corresponded to their 'seniority'.

Cumberland's system survived for 130 years until 1881, when a further reform was introduced. The army was reorganized with regiments that were really about a battalion in strength, being paired into a single new regiment and then associated with a particular county or part of Britain. A new regiment, with its 1st and 2nd battalions, was also associated with the militia and volunteers of its local area. Since the army was still a volunteer force, this allowed the regiments to recruit in the local district. The cavalry regiments were later reorganized in a similar fashion.

In 1908 the volunteer battalions were reorganized into a new force called the Territorial Army (roughly similar to the National Guard in the United States).

After the First World War, the army was reduced in size and as a consequence a number of regiments, both infantry and cavalry, were amalgamated. Those regiments that came from the South of Ireland were disbanded upon the emergence of the Republic of Eire. During the interwar years, the cavalry regiments gave up their horses and were mechanized and re-equipped either with armoured cars or, later, tanks. Even so, they retained their original 'horse organization' of troops and squadrons.

The various battalions of infantry and the regiments of cavalry were organized into the higher formations of brigades (which roughly correspond to the US Army's regiment) and then placed into divisions. Sometimes the division would draw all its component units from the same geographical area of Britain. Others would contain a mixture of British and Indian Army battalions and brigades.

Annex D: The Special Forces

The British Commandos

The British Army and Royal Marine Commandos in 1943 together with the battalions of US Rangers were all of broadly similar structure and organization.

The Commando Idea
The first British special forces were formed into independent companies and first used as raiding forces in German-occupied Norway in May 1940. After the fall of France the idea of raiding groups took shape in the minds of the High Command. The troops were organized into commandos in memory of the Boer farmers in the South African War who, through their skill and mobility, defeated ten times their number of British troops in the war between 1899 and 1902.

No. 2 Army Commando
First raised in 1940 as a parachute unit, it was later retrained for amphibious warfare. The commandos took part in a raid on Vaagso in Norway and then in August 1942 formed the principal fighting forces on the famous raid at St Nazaire, where it was, to all intents and purposes, destroyed.

This commando unit was re-formed under Lt Colonel Jack Churchill, MC, and in 1943 arrived in the Mediterranean.

41st (Royal Marine) Commando
This commando unit was raised in the autumn of 1942 and landed in

Sicily. In structure and organization it was broadly similar to an army commando unit.

The Special Boat Section (SBS)

The Special Boat Section was composed of special teams of highly trained troops charged with general reconnaissance and sabotage raids. They used the two-man Folbot canoe. The unit was first created in the summer of 1940.

A section comprised 47 men and contained four operating groups each of seven canoeists.

US Rangers

1st Ranger Battalion and Darby's Rangers

When the United States entered the Second World War in 1941, President Roosevelt was determined to have commando-like formations in the United States Army and Marine Corps. In this he was undoubtedly influenced by Prime Minister Winston Churchill. The Rangers took their name from the force of the same name raised by Major Robert Rogers to fight the American Indians in the mid-eighteenth century.

In May 1942 an order was posted throughout the US forces then stationed in Northern Ireland 'for volunteers not averse to dangerous action'. Two thousand men answered that call, and from them 500 were selected to join the first Ranger Course at the Commando School in Scotland. The 1st Ranger Battalion was formed on 19 June 1942.

The battalion, under Colonel Bill Darby, fought in North Africa, where it was split in April 1943 to provide the cadres for the 3rd and 4th Battalions. Other volunteers were recruited from US forces in North Africa and all three battalions landed in Sicily as special forces for Operation Husky.

These three battalions were roughly similar. Each had a complement of 419 (all ranks). A battalion was divided into six companies. A company had two platoons each of about 30 riflemen and a support section.

The US 82nd Airborne Division

The 82nd was raised in March 1942 as the initial airborne division in the United States Army. The success of German parachute troops in the early campaigns of the Second World War proved a major incentive and stimulant for the Americans to create their own forces. In June 1941 the United States Army created the 501st Parachute Battalion as an experimental force. By the time the Allies landed in Normandy three years later, the US Army had five divisions of airborne troops.

The airborne division was an infantry division in miniature. It had a total strength of 8,505 men divided into three regiments. The 82nd Airborne had two regiments of parachute infantry and one glider infantry regiment. There were 1,985 men in a parachute infantry regiment (compared to 3,333 in a regiment of an infantry division), while the glider-borne infantry had 1,605 men to a regiment.

Annex E: German Divisions

In 1943 the Wehrmacht possessed there categories of divisions: panzer, panzer grenadier and infantry. That said, the German divisions varied considerably throughout the war, and particularly after 1943, with regard to their size, composition, organization and weaponry. But they all had one thing in common; they were very flexible and adaptable. Their ability to create all-arms fighting groups was an asset which neither the British nor the American division was able to replicate.

Even though the German divisions were such a mismatch of size and numbers, the staff structures of a combat division, in contrast, were very similar. There were three functional sub-divisions:

Führungsabteilung, the tactical group, comprised Chief of Operations (Ia) and Chief of Intelligence (Ic) and their staffs who, together with liaison officers, made up the tactical headquarters or CP.

Quartermaster or supply group, who usually lived apart from the tactical headquarters and included the chiefs of supply, administration, medical, veterinary, transport.

Adjutantur or personnel team, which included the Chief of Personnel, Judge Advocate, chaplains and who were responsible for manning, discipline, promotions, decorations and replacements.

In addition various specialists were attached to a division as specialist staff officers. These included artillery and military police, etc.

The Infantry Division

After 1942 infantry divisions comprised (on paper) two infantry (grenadier) regiments, each of three battalions, an artillery regiment, a signal company, an anti-tank battalion, an engineer battalion, a reconnaissance battalion (though by 1944 these battalions were generally down-graded to company size) and supply/transport battalions.

An infantry battalion had three rifle companies and a heavy weapons or support company. The artillery regiment comprised three battalions of towed/horse-drawn 105-mm howitzers and a fourth with 155-mm howitzers.

The equipment and weaponry of an anti-tank battalion came in all shapes and sizes from SP guns to 88-mm and infantry-held panzerfausts, their equivalent of the bazooka.

The engineer battalions comprised some of the most skilled and versatile of troops. The German pioneers were expert practitioners in penetrating and laying minefields, breaching fortifications and constructing obstacles, in booby traps and delayed action devices.

Most infantry divisions had a veterinary company because they relied so heavily upon the horse. Again numbers varied; an infantry division had anything from 3,000 to 6,000 horses on its ration strength.

The Panzer Division

By 1943 the average panzer division considered itself fortunate if it had 164 tanks, and by the time the Germans stood on the Gothic Line this was down to 54 tanks. The division typically had a panzer regiment of two tank battalions; usually one regiment of panzer grenadiers, probably consisting of three battalions of motorized infantry and a reconnaissance battalion. The remainder, artillery, engineers and anti-tank battalions, signals and support, were similar to the infantry division, albeit motorized rather than horse-drawn.

The Panzer Grenadier Division

These were motorized infantry redesignated in 1943 as panzer grenadier divisions. The division comprised two regiments each of three battalions of motorized infantry, if they were lucky, mounted in armoured half-tracks and a panzer assault gun battalion of 30 to 50 AFVs or tanks.

The support units were similar to the panzer divisions.

The Mountain Division

Mountain divisions were similar to the infantry except in training, the use of lighter equipment, light/pack artillery and mules rather than horses.

The Waffen–SS Division

The 16th SS Panzer Grenadier Division 'Reichsführer SS' fought in the Italian campaign from the Anzio beachhead in January 1944 to December of that year when it was withdrawn to the Hungarian sector of the Eastern Front.

Equipment and composition varied enormously. The 16th SS had two regiments of panzer grenadiers, a panzer battalion with artillery, anti-tank, engineers and reconnaissance similar to panzer grenadiers.

Generally the Waffen–SS, particularly ethnic German units, received the best equipment and on a priority basis. The men tended to fight with a fanaticism not associated with the average line infantry unit. Their officers were highly motivated but they were invariably younger, less experienced and not as competent as their army counterparts.

Annex F: Landing Craft

The Royal Navy

Landing Ship Tank (LST) Boxer Class
These were specially built British ships with a displacement of nearly 6,000 tons. Their funnel was built on the starboard side, which gave them a very distinct and odd shape, but it allowed them to have a clear tank deck through to the stern. There were two decks, providing space for 25 tanks on the lower deck and 30 trucks on the top. A couple of hundred troops could also be carried. Despite their capacity, they were not a success. The complicated design did not lend itself to mass production, while their deeper draft meant that they could not beach in shallow water.

Landing Craft Tank (LCT)
The Landing Craft Tank Mark II displaced 460 tons fully laden and could carry seven tanks. The Mark II craft displaced 640 tons and could take eleven tanks, but it was slower. Both versions carried a crew of twelve and had a defensive armament of two two-pounder guns.

Landing Craft Infantry (Small) (LCI(S))
These were much smaller craft, 105 feet in length and with a 22-foot beam; they could carry up to 100 fully armed troops.

Landing Craft Vehicle (Personnel) (LCV(P))
A high-sided craft measuring 36.5 feet by 11 feet, built to carry vehicles or troops from a mothership to shore. The craft had a square bow that lowered onto a beach to form a ramp.

Landing Craft Gun (Large) (LCG(L))

These were converted LCTs, 192 feet long and 31 feet in beam. They were armed with two 4-inch or 4.7-inch guns of ancient vintage, together with some lighter weapons for anti-aircraft defence. The crew comprised two officers and ten ratings, together with one officer and 22 Royal Marines to man the guns.

Landing Craft Tank (Rocket)

This was an LCT converted to carry up to 1,000 five-inch rockets. These were fitted in launch tubes on a superimposed deck. They were introduced to meet the requirement for devastating fire to hit the beach in the path of the first wave of assaulting infantry to demoralize the enemy, or at least to make them keep their heads down while the troops landed. Conventional gunfire from supporting warships had to be stopped before the assault waves hit the beach to avoid causing casualties among the assault troops. The rocket craft were developed to fill this gap.

US Navy

Many of the British craft were built in American yards to British Admiralty requirements, so the US Navy in some instances by 1942 had broadly similar amphibious warfare craft to those used by the Royal Navy. The US Navy, in turn, gave its requirements to the shipyards and many of these designs were also adopted by the Royal Navy. As the war progressed there was a considerable proliferation of design and adaptation to even more functions, too numerous to mention here. The following, however, were at Salerno and Anzio.

Landing Ships Tank (LST)

By the war's end a total of 1,152 ships of this class had been constructed in American yards. They were built originally to a British specification for a craft capable of carrying tanks across the Atlantic from the United States to the beaches. In both navies they were more popularly known as Large Slow Targets; herein lay their weakness, for at a top speed of 9 knots they were dreadfully slow. For amphibious – that is beaching – operations, they displaced 2,366 tons fully loaded and could carry 20 tanks on the main deck. Lighter vehicles such as trucks and towed guns were stored on the weather deck. The early ships had an elevator to the tank deck, but later ships had a ramp which allowed for a much faster rate of unloading via the bow doors and ramp.

Landing Craft Infantry (Large) (LCI(L))

The Landing Craft Infantry (Large) also started life as a British Admiralty requirement. Like the craft discussed above, it became the basis for numerous specialized amphibious warfare craft. The craft had a capacity of 300 troops, who disembarked from gangways rather than elaborate bow doors. The craft displaced 385 tons with a full load, carried a crew of 24 men and had a top speed of 15 knots.

Landing Craft Personnel (Ramped) (LCP(R));
Landing Craft Vehicle/Personnel (LCVP)

These were shipborne landing craft designed to operate from a mothership and negotiate surf and beach. Again, there were numerous versions. The earlier versions were made of wood and could carry only troops. After 1942 a more sophisticated craft appeared with an armoured ramp and the capability to carry vehicles up to a light tank. So the standard landing craft (LCVP) appeared. The early work and designs were carried out by the Eureka (Higgins) Company of New Orleans, hence their nickname 'Higgins boats'. By the end of the war more than 22,000 of these craft were built. They could carry three tons of vehicles or 36 fully armed troops and had a three-man crew.

Annex G: Equivalent Military Ranks

Flag Ranks

United States Army	British Army	German Army
None	None	Reichsmarschall
General of the Army (Five Star)	Field Marshal	Generalfeldmarschall
General (Four Star)	General	Generaloberst
Lieutenant General (Three Star)	Lieutenant General	General der Infanterie General der Artillerie General der Panzertruppen General der Kavallerie General der Luftwaffe etc
Major General (Two Star)	Major General	Generalleutnant
Brigadier General (One Star)	Brigadier	Generalmajor
Colonel	Colonel	Oberst
Lieutenant Colonel	Lieutenant Colonel	Oberstleutnant
Major	Major	Major
Captain	Captain	Hauptmann
First Lieutenant	Lieutenant	Oberleutnant
Second Lieutenant	Second Lieutenant	Leutnant

TABLES

Tables

TABLE 1
Total Allied Battle Casualties

	Killed in Action	Wounded in Action	Missing in Action	Total
9 September 1943–15 August 1944				
US	13,225	53,896	8,012	75,133
UK	5,017	23,070	9,736	37,823
French	5,246	20,852	1,943	28,041
Italian	179	378	442	999
	23,667	98,196	20,133	141,996
16 August–15 December 1944				
US	3,585	16,130	1,738	21,453
UK	1,373	5,875	873	8,121
Brazilian	103	551	230	884
	5,061	22,556	2,841	30,458

Source: Jackson, Sir William, *History of the Second World War: The Mediterranean and Middle East, Volume VI*, HMSO Books, 1987.

TABLE 2
Total German Casualties on Mainland Italy

1 Sept 1943–10 May 1944	
Tenth Army	54,690
Fourteenth Army	32,889
11 May 1944–31 January 1945	
Army Group C	194,330
1 February 1945–31 March 1945	
Army Group C	13,741
1–22 April 1945	
Army Group C (estimate)	41,000
Total	336,650

Source: As Table 1.

TABLE 3
Desertions and Absence without Leave:
British Forces in Italy, January 1944–May 1945

1944					
Jan.	349 ⎫		Oct.	905 ⎫	
Feb.	207 ⎬ Cassino and		Nov.	1200 ⎬ Battles of	
Mar.	521 ⎭ Anzio		Dec.	1211 ⎭ Romagna rivers	
Apr.	583	Regrouping	1945		
			Jan.	1127 ⎫	
May	495 ⎫		Feb.	616 ⎬ Retraining	
Jun.	994 ⎭ ‘Diadem’				
			Mar.	404 ⎫	
July	779 ⎫	Advance to	Apr.	153 ⎬ Final	
Aug.	628 ⎭	Gothic Line	May	242 ⎭ offensive	
Sept.	944	‘Olive’			

Source: As Table 1, pp 376–7.

TABLE 4
Desertions and Absence without Leave:
by Formations, August–December 1944

Units	Deserters/Absentees	
British Infantry Formations		
1st Division	626	
4th Division	664	
46th Division	1059	
56th Division	990	
78th Division	927	(Oct., Nov. and Dec. only)
1st Guards Brigade	81	
24th Guards Brigade	102	
British Armoured Formations		
1st Armoured Division	95	
6th Armoured Division	220	
2nd Armoured Division	220	
7th Armoured Brigade	4	
9th Armoured Brigade	13	
25th Tank Brigade	3	

Source: As Table 3.

Three things stand out from Table 4: the bulk of the 'runners' came from the infantry divisions as expected. Even the resting of divisions in the Middle East did not reduce the problem, since 78th Division had the highest monthly figures of all divisions when it returned to the front in October. The armoured formations were scarcely affected. Sixth Armoured Division's 220 (judging by comparative figures produced by Colonel Sparrow) probably came mostly from the infantry for which there are no separate figures.

Set in the context of other crimes, desertion and absence were by far the most prevalent, as is shown by Table 5.

TABLE 5
Court-Martial Convictions, Eighth Army, 1 January–3 September 1944

Charge	Number
Desertion	878 ⎫ 1,289
Absence without leave	411 ⎭
Cowardice	3 ⎫
Sentry offences	54
Mutiny	7
Striking or threatening a superior officer	131 ⎬ 368
Disobedience	147
Insubordination	15
Neglect of orders	12 ⎭

Source: As Table 3.

TABLE 6
Incidence of Venereal Disease:
US Combined White and Coloured Rates

Month	Per annum per thousand
1944	
October	64.6
November	64.8
December	70.1
1945	
January	49.5
February	45.4
March	43.3

Preventive measures were aimed at arresting and treating prostitutes. In a sample of 532 prostitutes:

152 (29%) were diagnosed as having gonorrhoea;
62 (12%) were diagnosed as having syphilis;
122 (23%) were diagnosed as having both gonorrhoea and syphilis.

On these figures only one in three prostitutes was likely to be free from venereal disease.

Source: WO 204/10571 180200.

TABLE 7

Incidence of Venereal Disease: British Army, 1941–45: Cases per Annum per Thousand Ration Strength

Year	Middle East			Italy			NW Europe			Burma		
	VD[2]	BC[3]	Rating[4]	VD	BC	Rating	VD	BC	Rating	VD	BC	Rating
1941	41.2	35.5	3	—	—	—	—	—	—	—	—	—
1942	31.4	31.1	4	—	—	—	—	—	—	2.2	4.5	3
1943	21.8	22.5	5	31.3	63.9	6	—	—	—	157.9	13.9	2
1944	—	—	—	49.9	89.6	4	5.9	61.3	7	69.2	101.9	5
1945	—	—	—	68.8	9.8	1	19.3	33.7	5	72.2	73.2	2

[1]British ORs only.
[2]VD Venereal Disease.
[3]BC Battle Casualties.
[4]Indicates nth most frequent disease.

Source: Ellis, *The Sharp End of War*.

Bibliography

Adleman, Robert and Walton, George (Col), *Rome Fell Today*, Little, Brown and Company, Boston, 1968.

Alexander, Harold (Earl Alexander of Tunis), *The Alexander Memoirs*, John North, 1961.

Anders, W., *An Army in Exile*, Battery Press, Nashville, Tenn., 1987.

Barnett, Corelli, *Engage the Enemy More Closely*, Hodder and Stoughton, 1991.

Barzini, Luigi, *The Europeans*, Simon and Schuster, New York, 1983.

Bennet, Ralph, *Ultra and Mediterranean Strategy, 1941–45*, Hamish Hamilton, 1989.

Blumenson, Martin, *Mark Clark*, Jonathan Cape, 1985.

Breuer, W., *Agony at Anzio*, Robert Hale, 1985.

Butcher, H.C., *Three Years With Eisenhower*, Heinemann, 1944.

Churchill, Winston S., *The Second World War: The Hinge of Fate, Vol IV*, Cassell, 1951.

Churchill, Winston S., *The Second World War: The Closing Ring, Vol V*, Cassell, 1952.

Clark, Mark, *Calculated Risk*, Harrap, 1951.

Deakin, F.W., *The Brutal Friendship, Mussolini, Hitler and the Fall of Italian Fascism*, Penguin, 1966.

De Guingand, Sir Frances, *Operation Victory*, Hodder & Stoughton, 1947.

D'Este, Carlo, *Bitter Victory: The Battle for Sicily 1943*, Collins, 1988.

Ellis, John, *The Sharp End of War*, David and Charles, 1980.

Gayne, G.R., *Italy in Transition*, London, 1946.

Gilbert, Martin, *Road to Victory 1941–45*, Guild Publishing, 1986.

Howard, Michael, *Grand Strategy, Vol IV*, Weidenfeld and Nicolson, 1968.

Hunt, Sir David, *A Don At War*, Frank Cass, 1990.

Jackson, Nigel, *Alex*, Weidenfeld and Nicolson, 1973.

Jackson, Gen. Sir William, *The Mediterranean and Middle East, Vol VI, Part III*, HMSO, 1988.

Jackson, W.G., *Alexander of Tunis*, Batsford, 1971.

Kippenberger, H., *Infantry Brigadier*, OUP, 1949.

Ladd, James, *Commandos and Rangers of World War II*, MacDonald and Jane's Ltd, 1987.

Lamb, Richard, *Montgomery in Europe*, Buchan and Enright, 1987.

Lochner, Louis P. (ed.) *The Goebbels Diaries, 1941–43*, Garden City, NY, 1948.

Majdalany, Fred, *Cassino: Portrait of A Battle*, Longmans Green, 1957.

Moorehead, Alan, *Eclipse*, Hamish Hamilton, 1947.

Morison, Samuel (ed.), *Sicily–Salerno–Anzio*, Little, Brown and Company, Boston, 1975.

Morris, Eric, *Salerno*, Hutchinson, 1983.

Orgill, Douglas, *The Gothic Line*, Heinemann, 1967.

Patton, George S. Jnr, *War as I Knew It*, Bantam, 1980.

Rosignoli, Guido, *The Allied Forces in Italy 1943–45*, David and Charles, 1981.

Ryder, Rowland, *Oliver Leese*, Hamish Hamilton, 1987.

Sheehan, Fred, *Anzio: Epic of Bravery*, Oklahoma University Press, Okla., 1964.

Sheppard, David, *The Italian Campaign 1954–45*, Morrison and Gibb, 1968.

Smith, E.D., *The Battles for Cassino*, David and Charles, 1989.

Steinberg, Jonathan, *All or Nothing*, Routledge, 1990.

Steinhof, Johannes, Pechel, Peter and Showlter, Dennis, *Voices From the Third Reich: An Oral History*, Grafton Books, 1991.

Sterling, Claire, *The Mafia*, Hamish Hamilton, 1990.

Strawson, John, *The Italian Campaign*, Secker and Warburg, 1987.

Trevelyan, Raleigh, *History of the Second World War*, Vol 4, Purnell, Partwork.

Truscott, Lucien, *Command Missions*, Arno Press, New York, 1979.

Tuker, F., *Approach to Battle*, Cassell, 1963.

Villari, Luigi, *The Liberation of Italy*, C.C. Nelson Publishing Company, Appleton, Wisc., 1959.

Von Senger und Etterlin, General, *Neither Fear Nor Hope*, MacDonald, 1963.

Wagner, R., *The Texan Army: A History of the 36th Division in the Italian Campaign*, Austin, Texas, 1972.

Walker, Fred L., *From Texas to Rome*, Taylor Publishing Company, Dallas, Texas, 1969.

Watts, J., *Surgeon At War*, Allen and Unwin, 1955.

Whiting, Charles, *The Long March to Rome*, Guild Publishing, 1987.

Wolff, Luther H., MD, *Forward Surgeon*, Vantage Press, New York, 1985.

Index

486

British Corps
  V Corps, 150, 223, 271,
    354, 359, 372, 373,
    376, 422
  X Corps, 120, 122, 123,
    125, 146, 148, 152,
    159, 178, 187, 191,
    202, 209, 224, 245,
    246, 248, 270, 314,
    337, 372–3, 378, 422
  XIII Corps, 223, 271, 373,
    378, 387, 422
  XXX Corps, 46, 48, 63, 86,
    89, 386
  Royal Army Education, 434
British Divisions
  1st Airborne (Red Devils),
    56, 57, 58, 64, 86–8,
    116, 150
  1st Armoured, 308, 375–6,
    394
  6th Armoured, 308, 319,
    359, 422, 427, 428
  7th Armoured (Desert
    Rats), 125, 184, 209,
    245–6
  51st Highland, 48, 63, 82,
    180, 191
  1st Infantry, 257, 262,
    284–5, 286, 302, 330,
    341, 342, 382
  4th Infantry, 308, 319, 323,
    324, 373
  5th Infantry, 63, 89, 120,
    126, 163, 190, 223,
    224, 245, 249, 330,
    341
  46th Infantry, 122, 123–4,
    125, 127, 147, 191,
    192, 249, 250, 270,
    373
  50th Infantry, 48, 63, 88,
    89, 180
  56th City of London, 122,
    127, 190, 191, 192,
    209–10, 224–5, 249,
    270, 284, 285, 289,
    302, 373, 422, 423,
    428, 430
  78th Infantry (Battleaxe),
    89, 206–7, 223, 273,
    293, 298, 319, 398,
    422, 481
  organisation of infantry
    division, 463
British Brigades
  Air Landing, 57–8
  2nd Armoured, 375, 422
  4th Armoured, 223
  7th Armoured, 308
  9th Armoured, 308, 373,
    422
  22nd Armoured, 125, 127
  Guards, Brigade of, 263,
    359

24th Guards, 423
201st Guards, 122
3rd Infantry, 263–4, 285
38th Infantry (Irish), 207
169th Infantry, 209, 289
231st Infantry, 126, 163
21st Tank, 308, 422
25th Tank, 308
British Regiments
  8th Argyll and Sutherland
    Highlanders, 207
  Border, 57
  Coldstream Guards, 246
  Duke of Wellington's, 48,
    263, 342
  Durham Light Infantry, 48,
    88
  Essex, 296, 297, 298
  Glider Pilot, 57
  Gordon Highlanders, 285
  Grenadier Guards, 132,
    156, 358
  Irish Guards, 263, 285
  The Kensington (London),
    207
  King's Shropshire Light
    Infantry, 263
  London Irish, 285, 286
  Northamptonshire, 64
  Northumberland Fusiliers,
    48
  Queen's Bays, 375
  56th Reconaissance, 206–7
  Royal Berkshires, 285, 286
  Royal Engineers, 57, 63
  Royal Fusiliers, 147, 156
  Royal Hampshires, 147
  Royal Irish Fusiliers, 207
  9th Royal Lancers, 375
  Royal Scots Fusiliers, 64,
    387
  Royal Sussex, 270, 280
  44th Royal Tank, 88
  Royal Scots Greys, 156,
    195
  Royal West Kents, 298
  Scots Guards, 158, 246,
    263, 358
  Sherwood Foresters,
    slaughtered at
    Campoleone, 263–4
  South Staffordshire, 57
  Worcester Yeomanry, 323
  explanation of regiments,
    464–5
British Special Boat Section
  (SBS), 467
Brooke, Field Marshal Sir Alan
  (later 1st Viscount
  Alanbrooke), 206, 210,
  235, 287
  executive control of the
    Mediterranean, 239,
    271
  supports Sicilian invasion, 9

  unimpressed by
    Montgomery and
    Alexander, 235
Brown, Major, 367
Buckley, Francis, 333
Bucknell, General, 190
Burns, General (Canadian
  Corps commander),
  271, 319, 327

Caesar Line, 270, 333, 337
Cairo, 24, 25, 32, 398
  conference, 232, 233, 234,
    237, 238
Cairo, Monte (Italy), 267, 268,
  337
Calabria (Operation Baytown),
  action by Eighth Army,
  118, 120–1, 126, 150,
  151–2, 153, 163–4, 167
Calboli, Marquis Paolucci de',
  201
Caldonazzo, Lake, 1
Caltagirone, 65
Calvaro, Monte, 280, 281
Campbell, Lieutenant John,
  366–7, 412
Camino, Monte, fall of, 224–5,
  226
Campoleone, 262, 284, 328
  slaughter of Sherwood
    Foresters, 263–4
Canadian units in Italy, 48, 63,
  75, 81, 86, 107, 126,
  153, 256, 271, 323,
  332–3, 337
  1st Corps, 319, 372, 421
  5th Armoured Division,
    246, 319, 327, 373
  1st Infantry Division, 109,
    120, 223, 224, 319,
    354, 373
  casualties, 341
Cancello, 153
Capello, Mount, 389–92
Capri, 132
Capua, 153, 215, 219
Carboni, General, 129, 137
Carroceto, 285, 328
Caruso (chief of Italian police in
  Rome), 305
Caruso, Mount, 208
Casablanca summit conference,
  7, 9, 10, 17, 18, 39
Caserta, 35, 151, 226, 243, 275,
  284, 351, 396
Cassibile, 89, 113
Cassino, 8, 27, 197, 203, 219,
  221, 222, 245, 246,
  274, 278
  Allied casualties, 270
  battles: (1) 266–70, (2)
    273–81, (3) 291–9, (4)
    Operation Diadem,
    313–25